University Textbook Series

October, 1982

Especially Designed for Collateral Reading

HARRY W. JONES
Directing Editor
Professor of Law, Columbia University

ADMIRALTY, Second Edition (1975)
Grant Gilmore, Professor of Law, Yale University.
Charles L. Black, Jr., Professor of Law, Yale University.

ADMIRALTY AND FEDERALISM (1970)
David W. Robertson, Professor of Law, University of Texas.

AGENCY (1975)
W. Edward Sell, Dean of the School of Law, University of Pittsburgh.

BUSINESS ORGANIZATION AND FINANCE (1980)
William A. Klein, Professor of Law, University of California, Los Angeles.

CIVIL PROCEDURE, BASIC, Second Edition (1979)
Milton D. Green, Professor of Law Emeritus, University of California, Hastings College of the Law.

COMMERCIAL TRANSACTIONS, INTRODUCTION TO (1977)
Hon. Robert Braucher, Associate Justice, Supreme Judicial Court of Massachusetts.
Robert A. Riegert, Professor of Law, Cumberland School of Law.

CONFLICT OF LAWS, COMMENTARY ON THE, Second Edition (1980)
Russell J. Weintraub, Professor of Law, University of Texas.

CONSTITUTIONAL LAW, AMERICAN (A TREATISE ON) (1978) with 1979 Supplement
Laurence H. Tribe, Professor of Law, Harvard University.

CONTRACT LAW, THE CAPABILITY PROBLEM IN (1978)
Richard Danzig.

CORPORATIONS, Second Edition (1971)
Norman D. Lattin, Professor of Law, University of California, Hastings College of the Law.

CORPORATIONS IN PERSPECTIVE (1976)
Alfred F. Conard, Professor of Law, University of Michigan.

CRIMINAL LAW, Third Edition (1982)
Rollin M. Perkins, Professor of Law, University of California, Hastings College of the Law.
Ronald N. Boyce, Professor of Law, University of Utah College of Law.

UNIVERSITY TEXTBOOK SERIES—Continued

CRIMINAL PROCEDURE (1980) with 1982 Supplement

Charles H. Whitebread, II, Professor of Law, University of Virginia.

ESTATES IN LAND & FUTURE INTERESTS, PREFACE TO (1966)

Thomas F. Bergin, Professor of Law, University of Virginia.

Paul G. Haskell, Professor of Law, University of North Carolina.

EVIDENCE: COMMON SENSE AND COMMON LAW (1947)

John M. Maguire, Professor of Law, Harvard University.

EVIDENCE, STUDENTS' TEXT ON THE LAW OF (1935)

The late John Henry Wigmore, Northwestern University.

JURISPRUDENCE: MEN AND IDEAS OF THE LAW (1953)

The late Edwin W. Patterson, Cardozo Professor of Jurisprudence, Columbia University.

LEGAL CAPITAL, Second Edition (1981)

Bayless Manning.

LEGAL RESEARCH ILLUSTRATED, Second Edition (1981) with 1982 Assignments Pamphlet

J. Myron Jacobstein, Professor of Law, Law Librarian, Stanford University.

Roy M. Mersky, Professor of Law, Director of Research, University of Texas.

LEGAL RESEARCH, FUNDAMENTALS OF, Second Edition (1981) with 1982 Assignments Pamphlet

J. Myron Jacobstein, Professor of Law, Law Librarian, Stanford University.

Roy M. Mersky, Professor of Law, Director of Research, University of Texas.

PROCEDURE, THE STRUCTURE OF (1979)

Robert M. Cover, Professor of Law, Yale University.

Owen M. Fiss, Professor of Law, Yale University.

THE PROFESSION OF LAW (1971)

L. Ray Patterson, Professor of Law, Emory University.

Elliott E. Cheatham, Professor of Law, Vanderbilt University.

PROPERTY, Second Edition (1975)

John E. Cribbet, Dean of the Law School, University of Illinois.

TAXATION, FEDERAL INCOME, Third Edition (1982)

Marvin A. Chirelstein, Professor of Law, Yale University.

TORTS, Second Edition (1980)

Clarence Morris, Professor of Law, University of Pennsylvania.

C. Robert Morris, Professor of Law, University of Minnesota.

TRUSTS, PREFACE TO THE LAW OF (1975)

Paul G. Haskell, Professor of Law, University of North Carolina.

WILLS AND TRUSTS, THE PLANNING AND DRAFTING OF, Second Edition (1979) with 1982 Supplement

Thomas L. Shaffer, Professor of Law, University of Notre Dame.

FUNDAMENTALS
OF
LEGAL RESEARCH

By

J. MYRON JACOBSTEIN
Professor of Law and Law Librarian
Stanford University

and

ROY M. MERSKY
Professor of Law and Director of Research
University of Texas, Austin

SECOND EDITION

Mineola, New York
The Foundation Press, Inc.
1981

Printed in the United States of America

Library of Congress Cataloging in Publication Data

Jacobstein, J, Myron
Fundamentals of legal research.
(University textbook series)
Includes bibliographical references and index.
1. Legal research—United States. I. Mersky, Roy M.
II. Title. III. Series.
KF240.J3 1981 340'.07'2073 81-5589
AACR2

ISBN 0-88277-034-9

J. & M.Fund.Legal Research 2d Ed. UTB

3rd Reprint—1984

To our Families

Bennett, Ellen, and Belle
Lisa, Deborah, Ruth and Deena

He Who Cites His Source, Brings Deliverance to the World.

Mishnah, Avot. VI

PREFACE

Perhaps nothing reflects the ever-changing patterns and growth of law better than the changes required in preparing a new edition of a text on legal research. The preparation of this second edition of *Fundamentals of Legal Research* required substantial changes in nearly every chapter—brought about by the publication of works in new fields of law, new editions of older titles, new titles for established fields of law, and the elimination of titles that have ceased publication. Included in this edition are a completely revised chapter on Canadian law (Chapter 22), and a new chapter on federal tax research (Chapter 24).

In this edition, we have again resisted the temptation of making this work the definitive source for legal bibliography. Rather, it has been designed primarily as a basic text for students who are learning to do legal research. A careful study of the text should enable law students, lawyers, and others to locate and use the legal resources necessary to solve their research problems. For those instances when it may be necessary to consult sources beyond those covered in this text, we have provided references in the footnotes where legal research may be pursued in greater depth.

Since most law students begin the study of law with the finding and reading of cases, it has been our experience that it is easier to begin by studying the method of publishing and of locating court decisions. We have followed these primary sources with detailed descriptions of secondary sources for legal research. The organization of the chapters, however, is such that instructors may conveniently begin with any part of the book.

Supplement and Assignments, a separate pamphlet containing research problems and exercises in memorandum writing and case citing, is available to students for use with this book. In addition, an *Instructor's Manual* (for instructors only) contains assignments and answers.

Twice a year, a *Noter Up* supplement will be published which will update changes made in the publications discussed, as well as call attention to new publications for use in legal research. Issues of the *Noter Up* will be cumulated periodically.

J. MYRON JACOBSTEIN
ROY M. MERSKY

June, 1981

ACKNOWLEDGMENTS

We are happy for this opportunity to express our gratitude to the many people who have helped in the preparation of this new and completely revised edition of *Fundamentals of Legal Research.*

Foremost among those to whom we are indebted are three members of the Tarlton Library Staff. Stanley Ferguson, Publications Coordinator, contributed invaluable editing and proofreading experience to the entire project, from manuscript to final page proof. He was ably assisted throughout by James M. Murray, Reserve Librarian, who generously offered much-appreciated expertise and advice on substantive and stylistic matters, as well as many hours of proofreading. Long and wearisome days were spent by Monty Waters, Research Assistant, in the meticulous task of checking details. Only a bravura performance by these three enabled us to meet our deadlines without sacrificing the quality and integrity of this new edition of the book.

Other Tarlton Library Staff members who read parts of the manuscript and offered helpful suggestions are: Carole Knobil, Associate Law Librarian; Anne Rimmer, Assistant Librarian for Technical Services; Jim Hambleton, Assistant Librarian for Public Services; Jeanette Yackle, Reference Librarian; Daniel Martin, Librarian for Management and Physical Operations; and Patricia Harris, Research Assistant.

Our grateful thanks are also due the following persons from the Robert Crown Law Library, Stanford University:

Rosalee Long, Associate Law Librarian; Iris J. Wildman, Public Service Librarian; and Joan Howland, Reference Librarian, for their constructive criticism which has been reflected throughout this work.

Kathy Shimpock, Assistant Reference Librarian, for her most admirable and valuable research assistance.

To the entire Library Staff, who have all helped in so many different ways.

A special note of appreciation is due our secretaries, Gwyn Anderson and Susan Coto of the Tarlton Law Library, and Ann Vogel of the Robert Crown Law Library, for their continuing assistance, dedication and perseverance.

We must pay particular tribute to Gail Richmond, Associate Professor of Law, Nova University Center for the Study of Law, who not only contributed an exhaustive and scholarly chapter on federal tax law (Chapter 24), but who heroically read both the manuscript and the galleys throughout the final stages of pregnancy and following the birth of her daughter.

Thanks also to Douglass T. MacEllven, Director of Libraries, Law Society of Saskatchewan Libraries, for the preparation of Chapter 22, Canadian Law; and to Jenni Parrish, Assistant Professor and Director of the Law Library, University of Pittsburgh, for her contributions to Chapter 25.

Finally, we again wish to express our deep appreciation to the many instructors who have adopted *Fundamentals of Legal Research* for classroom use. Their suggestions concerning possible additions to the text, and their thoughts on revision of it, have been most useful to us in the preparation of this edition.

SUMMARY OF CONTENTS

APPENDICES

*

TABLE OF CONTENTS

APPENDICES

*

GLOSSARY OF TERMS USED IN LEGAL RESEARCH

This glossary of terms is limited in scope and the definitions of words are restricted in meaning to their legal or legal research context. Words whose meanings conform to general usage and are obvious are omitted from the list, e. g., Index.

ACQUITTAL—
the verdict in a criminal trial in which the defendant is found not guilty.

ACT—
an alternative name for statutory law. When introduced into the first house of the legislature, a piece of proposed legislation is known as a bill. When passed to the next house, it may then be referred to as an act. After enactment the terms "law" and "act" may be used interchangeably. An act has the same legislative force as a joint resolution but is technically distinguishable, being of a different form and introduced with the words "Be it enacted" instead of "Be it resolved."

ACTION—
the formal legal demand of one's rights from another person brought in court.

ADJUDICATION—
the formal pronouncing or recording of a judgment or decree by a court.

ADMINISTRATIVE LAW—
law which affects private parties, promulgated by governmental agencies other than courts or legislative bodies. These administrative agencies derive their power from legislative enactments and are subject to judicial review.

ADVANCE SHEETS—
current pamphlets containing the most recently reported opinions of a court or the courts of several jurisdictions. The volume and page numbers usually are the same as in the subsequently bound volumes of the series, which cover several numbers of the advance sheets.

ADVISORY OPINION—
may be rendered by a court at the request of the government or an interested party indicating how the court would rule on a matter should adversary litigation develop. An advisory opinion is thus an interpretation of the law without binding effect. The International Court of Justice and some state courts will render advisory opinions; the Supreme Court of the United States will not.

AFFIDAVIT—

a written statement or declaration of facts sworn to by the maker, taken before a person officially permitted by law to administer oaths.

AMICUS CURIAE—

means, literally, friend of the court. A party with strong interest in or views on the subject matter of the dispute will petition the court for permission to file a brief, ostensibly on behalf of a party but actually to suggest a rationale consistent with its own views.

ANALYSIS—

generally follows the scopenote in an ALR Annotation, giving a conceptual breakdown of the topic into main and subordinate categories.

ANNOTATIONS—

(1) Statutory: brief summaries of the law and facts of cases interpreting statutes passed by Congress or state legislatures which are included in codes, or (2) Textual: expository essays of varying length on significant legal topics chosen from selected cases published with the essays.

ANSWER—

the pleading filed by the defendant in response to plaintiff's complaint.

APPEAL PAPERS—

the briefs and transcripts of records on appeal filed by attorneys with courts in connection with litigation. A brief consists of a summary of the facts and circumstances or legal propositions as presented by a party to a pending action.

APPELLANT—

the party who requests that a higher court review the actions of a lower court. Compare with APPELLEE.

APPELLEE—

the party against whom an appeal is taken (usually, but not always the winner in the lower court). It should be noted that a party's status as appellant or appellee bears no relation to his status as plaintiff or defendant in the lower court.

ARBITRATION—

the hearing and settlement of a dispute between opposing parties by a third party. This decision is often binding by prior agreement of the parties.

ASSAULT—

an unlawful, intentional show of force or an attempt to do physical harm to another person. Assault can constitute the basis of a civil or criminal action. See also BATTERY.

ASSAULT AND BATTERY—

See BATTERY.

ATTORNEY GENERAL OPINIONS—

are issued by the government's chief counsel at the request of some governmental body and interpret the law for the requesting agency in the same manner as a private attorney would for his client. The opinions are not binding on the courts but are usually accorded some degree of persuasive authority.

AUTHORITY—

refers to the precedential value to be accorded an opinion of a judicial or administrative body. A court's opinion is binding authority on other courts directly below it in the judicial hierarchy. Opinions of lower courts or of courts outside the hierarchy are governed by the degree to which it adheres to the doctrine of stare decisis. **STARE DECISIS.**

Authority may also be either primary or secondary. Statute law, administrative regulations issued pursuant to enabling legislation, and case law are primary authority and if applicable will usually determine the outcome of a case. Other statements of or about law are considered secondary authority, and thus not binding.

BAIL—

security given, in the form of a bail bond or cash as a guarantee that released prisoners will present themselves for trial. This security may be lost if the released person does not appear in court at the appointed time.

BATTERY—

an unlawful use of force against another person resulting in physical contact (a tort); it is commonly used in the phrase "assault and battery," assault being the threat of force, and battery the actual use of force. See also ASSAULT.

BILL—

refers to a legislative proposal introduced in the legislature. The term distinguishes unfinished legislation from directly enacted law.

BLACK LETTER LAW—

an informal term indicating the basic principles of law generally accepted by the courts and/or embodied in the statutes of a particular jurisdiction.

BLUE BOOK—

a popular name for *A Uniform System of Citation,* which is published and distributed by the Harvard Law Review Association et al., and which is bound in a blue cover.

BREACH OF CONTRACT—

the failure to perform any of the terms of an agreement.

BRIEF—

(1) in American law practice, a written statement prepared by the counsel arguing a case in court. It contains a summary of the facts of the case, the pertinent laws, and an argument of how the law applies to the facts supporting counsel's position; or (2) a summary of a published opinion of a case prepared for studying the opinion in law school.

BRIEFS AND RECORDS—

See APPEAL PAPERS.

CALENDAR—

can mean the order in which cases are to be heard during a term of court. *Martindale-Hubbell Law Directory* contains calendars for state and federal courts, and includes the name of the court, the name of the judge, and the date of the term's beginning.

CASE IN POINT—

a judicial opinion which deals with a fact situation similar to the one being researched and substantiates a point of law to be asserted. (Also called Case on All Fours)

CASE LAW—

the law of reported appellate judicial opinions as distinguished from statutes or administrative law.

CASEBOOK—

a textbook used to instruct law students in a particular area of substantive law. The text consists of a collection of court opinions, usually from appellate courts, and notes by the author(s).

CAUSE OF ACTION—

a claim in law and in fact sufficient to bring the case to court; the grounds of an action. (Example: breach of contract.)

CERTIORARI—

a writ issued by a superior to an inferior court requiring the latter to produce the records of a particular case tried therein. It is most commonly used to refer to the Supreme Court of the United States, which uses the writ of certiorari as a discretionary device to choose the cases it wishes to hear. The term's origin is Latin, meaning "to be informed of."

CHARTER—

a document issued by a governmental entity which gives a corporation legal existence.

CHATTEL—

any article of personal property, as opposed to real property. It may refer to animate as well as inanimate property.

CHOSE—

any article of personal property. See PROPERTY.

CITATION—

the reference to authority necessary to substantiate the validity of one's argument or position. Citation to authority and supporting references is both important and extensive in any form of legal writing. Citation form is also given emphasis in legal writing, and early familiarity with *A Uniform System of Citation* will stand the law student in good stead.

CITATORS—

a set of books which provide, through letter-form abbreviations or words, the subsequent judicial history and interpretation of reported decisions, and lists of cases and legislative enactments construing, applying or affecting statutes. In America, the most widely used set of citators is *Shepard's Citations.*

CITED CASE—

a case which is treated by other cases.

CITING CASE—

the case which operates on the cited case.

CIVIL LAW—

(1) Roman law embodied in the Code of Justinian which presently prevails in most countries of Western Europe other than Great Britain and which is the foundation of Louisiana law; (2) the law concerning noncriminal matters in a common law jurisdiction.

CLAIM—

(1) the assertion of a right, as to money or property; (2) the accumulation of facts which give rise to a right enforceable in court.

CLASS ACTION—

a lawsuit brought by a representative party on behalf of a group, all of whose members have the same or a similar grievance against the defendant.

CODE—

by popular usage a compilation or a revised statute. Technically the laws in force are rewritten and arranged in classified order, with the addition of material having the force of law taken from judicial decrees. The repealed and temporary acts are eliminated and the revision is re-enacted.

CODIFICATION—

the process of collecting and arranging systematically, usually by subject, the laws of a state or country. The end product may be called a code, revised code or revised statutes.

COMMON LAW—

is the origin of the Anglo-American legal systems. English common law was largely customary law and unwritten, until discovered, applied, and reported by the courts of law. In theory, the common law courts did not create law but rather discovered it in the customs and habits of the English people. The strength of the judicial system in pre-parliamentary days is one reason for the continued emphasis in common law systems on case law. In a narrow sense, common law is the phrase still used to distinguish case law from statutory law.

COMPILED STATUTES—

by popular usage means a code. Technically, however, it prints acts verbatim as originally enacted but in a new classified order. The text is not modified; however, the repealed and temporary acts are omitted.

COMPLAINT—

the plaintiff's initial pleading and according to the Federal Rules of Civil Procedure, no longer full of the technicalities demanded by the common law. A complaint need only contain a short and plain statement of the claim upon which relief is sought, an indication of the type of relief requested, and an indication that the court has jurisdiction to hear the case.

CONGRESSIONAL DOCUMENTS—

are important sources for legislative histories, which are often necessary for proper interpretation of statute law. Congressional documents are most accessible through specialized indexes and include hearings before Congressional committees, reports by or to House or Senate committees, and special studies conducted under Congressional authority.

CONSIDERATION—

something to be done or abstained from, by one party to a contract in order to induce another party to enter into a contract.

CONSOLIDATED STATUTES—

by popular usage means a code. Technically, however, in it the text of the acts are rewritten, arranged in classified order and re-enacted. The repealed and temporary acts are eliminated.

CONSTITUTION—

contains the fundamental law of any organization possessing one. Most national constitutions are written; the English and Israeli constitutions are unwritten.

CONVERSION—

the wrongful appropriation to oneself of the personal property of another.

CONVEYANCE—

the transfer of title to property from one person to another.

COUNT—

a separate and independent claim. A civil petition or a criminal indictment may contain several counts.

COUNTERCLAIM—

a claim made by the defendant against the plaintiff in a civil lawsuit; it constitutes a separate cause of action.

COURT DECISION—

the disposition of the case by the court. See OPINION.

COURT RULES—

rules of procedure promulgated to govern civil and criminal practice before the courts.

DAMAGES—

monetary compensation awarded by a court for an injury caused by the act of another. Damages may be *actual* or *compensatory* (equal to the amount of loss shown), *exemplary* or *punitive* (in excess of the actual loss and which are given to punish the person for the malicious conduct which caused the injury), or *nominal* (less than the actual loss—often a trivial amount) which are given because the injury is slight or because the exact amount of injury has not been determined satisfactorily.

DATA BASE—

the accumulation of textual or other material available to the user of an on-line information service.

DECISION—

See COURT DECISION.

DECREE—

a determination by a court of the rights and duties of the parties before it. Formerly, decrees were issued by courts of equity and distinguished from judgments which were issued by courts of law. See EQUITY.

DEFENDANT—

the person against whom a civil or criminal action is brought.

DEMURRER—

a means of objecting to the sufficiency in law of a pleading by admitting the actual allegations made, but disputing that they frame an adequate legal claim.

DICTUM—

See OBITER DICTUM.

DIGEST—

is an index to reported cases, providing brief, unconnected statements of court holdings on points of law, which are arranged by subject and subdivided by jurisdiction and courts.

DOCKET NUMBER—

a number, sequentially assigned by the clerk at the outset to a lawsuit brought to a court for adjudication.

DUE CARE—

the legal duty one owes to another according to the circumstances of a particular case.

DUE PROCESS OF LAW—

a term found in the Fifth and Fourteenth Amendments of the Constitution and also in the constitutions of many states. Its exact meaning varies from one situation to another and from one era to the next, but basically it is concerned with the guarantee of every person's enjoyment of his rights (e.g., the right to a fair hearing in any legal dispute).

EN BANC—

refers to a session where the entire bench of the court will participate in the decision rather than the regular quorum. In other countries, it is common for a court to have more members than are usually necessary to hear an appeal. In the United States, the Circuit Courts of Appeal usually sit in groups of three judges but for important cases may expand the bench to nine members, when they are said to be sitting *en banc.*

ENCYCLOPEDIA—

contains expository statements on principles of law, topically arranged, with supporting footnote references to cases in point.

EQUITY—

justice administered according to fairness as contrasted with the strictly formulated rules of common law. It is based on a system of rules and principles which originated in England as an alternative to the harsh rules of common law and which were based on what was fair in a particular situation. One sought relief under this system in courts of equity rather than in courts of law.

ESTATE—

(1) the interest or right one has in real or personal property;
(2) the property itself in which one has an interest or right.

EXECUTIVE AGREEMENT—

is an international agreement, not a treaty, concluded by the President without senatorial consent on his authority as Commander-in-Chief and director of foreign relations. The distinction between treaty and executive agreement is complicated and often of questionable constitutionality, but the import of such agreements as that of Yalta or Potsdam is unquestionably great.

EXECUTIVE ORDERS—

are issued by the President under specific authority granted to him by Congress. There is no precise distinction between presidential proclamations and executive orders; however, proclamations generally cover matters of widespread interest, and executive orders often relate to the conduct of government business or to organization of the executive departments. Every act of the President authorizing or directing the performance of an act, in its general context, is an executive order. See PRESIDENTIAL PROCLAMATIONS.

FORM BOOKS—

include sample instruments which are helpful in drafting legal documents.

FORMS OF ACTION—

governed common law pleading and were the procedural devices used to give expression to the theories of liability recognized by the common law. Failure to analyze the cause of the action properly, to select the proper theory of liability and to choose the appropriate procedural mechanism or forms of action could easily result in being thrown out of court. A plaintiff had to elect his remedy in advance and could not subsequently amend his pleadings to conform to his proof or to the court's choice of another theory of liability. According to the relief sought, actions have been divided into three categories: real actions were brought for the recovery of real property; mixed actions were brought to recover real property and damages for injury to it; personal actions were brought to recover debts or personal property, or for injuries to personal, property, or contractual rights. The common law actions are usually considered to be eleven in number: trespass, trespass on the case, trover, ejectment, detinue, replevin, debt, covenant, account, special assumpsit, and general assumpsit.

FRAUD—

a deception which causes a person to part with his property or a legal right.

GRAND JURY—
a jury of six to twenty-three persons that hears criminal accusations and evidence, and then determines whether indictments should be made. Compare with PETIT JURY.

HEADNOTE—
is a brief summary of a legal rule or significant facts in a case, which, among other headnotes applicable to the case, precedes the printed opinion in reports.

HEARINGS—
are extensively employed by both legislative and administrative agencies and can be adjudicative or merely investigatory. Adjudicative hearings can be appealed in a court of law. Congressional committees often hold hearings prior to enactment of legislation; these hearings are then important sources of legislative history.

HOLDING—
is the declaration of the conclusion of law reached by the court as to the legal effect of the facts of the case.

HOLOGRAPH (olograph)—
a will, deed, or other legal document that is entirely in the handwriting of the signer.

HORNBOOK—
is the popular reference to a series of treatises published by West Publishing Company which reviews a certain field of law in summary, textual form, as opposed to a casebook which is designed as a teaching tool and includes many reprints of court opinions.

INDEMNITY—
a contractual arrangement whereby one party agrees to reimburse another for losses of a particular type.

INDICTMENT—
a formal accusation of a crime made by a grand jury at the request of a prosecuting attorney.

INFORMATION—
an accusation based not on the action of a grand jury but rather on the affirmation of a public official.

INJUNCTION—
a judge's order that a person do or, more commonly, refrain from doing a certain act. An injunction may be preliminary or temporary pending trial of the issue presented, or it may be final if the issue has already been decided in court.

INTESTATE—
not having made a valid will.

JURISDICTION—
the power given to a court by a constitution or a legislative body to make legally binding decisions over certain persons or property, or the geographical area in which a court's decisions or legislative enactments are binding.

JURISPRUDENCE—
(1) the science or philosophy of law;
(2) a collective term for case law as opposed to legislation.

KEY NUMBER—
a building block of the major indexing system devised for American case law, developed by West Publishing Company. The key number is a permanent number given to a specific point of this case law. (For examples, see page 68.

LEGISLATIVE HISTORY—
provides the meanings and interpretations (intent) of a statute as embodied in legislative documents. Also, citations and dates to legislative enactments, amendments and repeals of statutes are sometimes imprecisely identified as legislative histories. More accurate designations of these citations of legislative changes, as included in codes, are historical notes or amendatory histories.

LEXIS—
the pioneering computerized full text legal research system of Mead Data Central. The data base organizes documents into "libraries" and "files." Documents may be court decisions, statutory, or administrative provisions.

LEXISIZE—
search for references or citations to a specific authority in the Lexis files by entering the citation to the authority.

LIABILITY—
the condition of being responsible either for damages resulting from an injurious act or for discharging an obligation or debt.

LIBEL—
(1) written defamation of a person's character. Compare with SLANDER.
(2) in an admiralty court, the plaintiff's statement of his cause of action and the relief sought.

LIEN—
a claim against property as security for a debt, under which the property may be seized and sold to satisfy the debt.

LITIGATE—

to bring a civil action in court.

LOOSELEAF SERVICES AND REPORTERS—

contain federal and state administrative regulations and decisions or subject treatment of a legal topic. They consist of separate, perforated leaves in special binders, simplifying frequent substitution and insertion of new leaves.

MALPRACTICE—

professional misconduct or unreasonable lack of skill. This term is usually applied to such conduct by doctors and lawyers.

MEMORANDUM—

(1) an informal record.

(2) a written document which may be used to prove that a contract exists.

(3) (referred to as a MEMORANDUM OF LAW) an exposition of all the points of law pertaining to a particular case.

(4) an informal written discussion of the merits of a matter pending in a lawyer's office, usually written by a law clerk or junior associate for a senior associate or partner. (Referred to as an OFFICE MEMORANDUM).

MODEL CODES—

are formulated by various groups or institutions to serve as model laws for legislatures, and may be intended as improvements over existing laws or as sources of unification of diverse state legislation.

MOOT—

points are no longer subjects of contention and are raised only for purposes of discussion or hypothesis. Many law schools have moot courts where students gain practice by arguing hypothetical or moot cases.

MOTION—

a formal request made to a judge pertaining to any issue arising during the pendency of a lawsuit.

NATIONAL REPORTER SYSTEM—

the network of reporters published by West Publishing Company, which attempt to publish and digest all cases of precedential value from all state and federal courts.

NEGLIGENCE—

the failure to exercise due care.

NISI PRIUS—

generally refers to a court where a case is first tried, as distinguished from an appellate court.

NOTER-UP—

is the term used in the British Commonwealth countries for a citator.

OBITER DICTUM—

is an official, incidental comment, not necessary to the formulation of the decision, made by the judge in his opinion which is not binding as precedent.

OFFICIAL REPORTS—

are court reports directed by statute.

OPINION—

an expression of the reasons why a certain decision (the judgment) was reached in a case. A *majority* opinion is usually written by one judge and represents the principles of law which a majority of his colleagues on the court deem operative in a given decision; it has more precedential value than any of the following. A *separate opinion* may be written by one or more judges in which he or they concur in or dissent from the majority opinion. A *concurring opinion* agrees with the result reached by the majority, but disagrees with the precise reasoning leading to that result. A *dissenting opinion* disagrees with the result reached by the majority and thus disagrees with the reasoning and/or the principles of law used by the majority in deciding the case. A *plurality opinion* (called a "judgment" by the Supreme Court) is agreed to by less than a majority as to the reasoning of the decision, but is agreed to by a majority as to the result. A *per curiam opinion* is an opinion "by the court" which expresses its decision in the case but whose author is not identified. A *memorandum opinion* is a holding of the whole court in which the opinion is very concise.

ORDINANCE—

is the equivalent of a municipal statute, passed by the city council and governing matters not already covered by federal or state law.

PAMPHLET SUPPLEMENT—

a paperbound supplement to a larger bound volume usually intended to be discarded eventually.

PARALLEL CITATION—

is a citation reference to the same case printed in two or more different reports.

PER CURIAM—

literally, by the court. Usually a short opinion written on behalf of the majority of the court. It may be accompanied by concurring or dissenting opinions.

PERMANENT LAW—

is an act which continues in force for an indefinite time.

PERSONAL PROPERTY—

See PROPERTY.

PERSUASIVE AUTHORITY—

that law or reasoning from another or lower jurisdiction which a given court is likely but not bound to follow.

PETIT JURY—

a group of six, nine, or twelve persons that decides questions of fact in civil and criminal trials. Compare with GRAND JURY.

PETITION—

a formal, written application to a court requesting judicial action on a certain matter.

PETITIONER—

the person presenting a petition to a court, officer, or legislative body; the one who starts an equity proceeding or the one who takes an appeal from a judgment.

PLAINTIFF—

the person who brings a lawsuit against another.

PLEA BARGAINING—

the process whereby the accused and the prosecutor in a criminal case work out a mutually satisfactory disposition of the case. It usually involves the defendant's pleading guilty to a lesser offense or to only one or some of the counts of a multi-count indictment in return for a lighter sentence than that possible for the graver charge.

PLEADINGS—

are the technical means by which parties to a dispute frame the issue for the court. The plaintiff's complaint or declaration is followed by the defendant's answer; subsequent papers may be filed as needed.

POCKET SUPPLEMENT—

is a paper-back supplement to a book, inserted in the book through a slit in its back cover. Depending on the type of publication, it may have textual, case or statutory references keyed to the original publication.

POWER OF ATTORNEY—

a document authorizing a person to act as another's agent.

PRECEDENT—

See STARE DECISIS.

PRESENTMENT—

in criminal law, a written accusation made by the grand jury without the consent or participation of a prosecutor.

PRESIDENTIAL PROCLAMATIONS—

are issued under specific authority granted to the President by Congress. Generally, they relate to matters of widespread interest. Some proclamations have no legal effect but merely are appeals to the public, e. g., the observance of American Education Week. See EXECUTIVE ORDERS.

PRIMARY AUTHORITY—

judicial precedent or legislative enactment which is cited as first or mandatory authority.

PRIVATE LAW—

is an act which relates to a specific person.

PROCEDURAL LAW—

that law which governs the operation of the legal system, including court rules and rules of procedure, as distinguished from substantive law.

PROPERTY—

ownership or that which is owned. Real property refers to land; personal property refers to moveable things or chattel; chose in action refers to a right to personal property of which the owner does not presently have possession but instead has a right to sue to gain possession (e.g., a right to recover a debt, demand, or damages in a contractual action or for a tort or omission of a duty).

PUBLIC LAW—

is an act which relates to the public as a whole. It may be (1) general (applies to all persons within the jurisdiction), (2) local (applies to a geographical area), or (3) special (relates to an organization which is charged with a public interest).

RATIO DECIDENDI—

is the point in a case which determines the result—the basis of the decision.

REAL PROPERTY—

See PROPERTY.

RECORDS AND BRIEFS—

See APPEAL PAPERS.

REGIONAL REPORTER—

a unit of the National Reporter System which reports state court decisions of a defined geographical area.

REGULATIONS—

are issued by various governmental departments to carry out the intent of the law. Agencies issue regulations to guide the activity of their employees and to ensure uniform application of the law. Regulations are not the work of the legislature and do not have the effect of law in theory. In practice, however, because of the intricacies of judicial review of administrative action, regulations can have an important effect in determining the outcome of cases involving regulatory activity. United States Government regulations appear first in the *Federal Register*, published five days a week, and are subsequently arranged by subject in the *Code of Federal Regulations*.

REMAND—

to send back for further proceedings, as when a higher court sends back to a lower court.

REPORTS—

are (1) (court reports) published judicial cases arranged according to some grouping, such as jurisdiction, court, period of time, subject matter or case significance, (2) (administrative reports or decisions) published decisions of an administrative agency, (3) annual statements of progress, activities or policy issued by an administrative agency or an association.

RESOLUTION—

a formal expression of the opinion of a rule-making body adopted by the vote of that body.

RESPONDENT—

the party who makes an answer to a bill in an equity proceeding or who contends against an appeal.

RESTATEMENTS OF THE LAW—

an attempt to restate in systematic form the existing common law in certain areas as developed by the courts. This project, directed by the American Law Institute since 1923, provides a valuable secondary research source, but lacks the legislative sanction to make it binding.

REVISED STATUTES—

by popular usage means a code. Technically, however, it identifies a compilation of statutes in the identical order as originally passed by the legislature with the temporary and repealed acts eliminated.

RULES OF COURT—

regulate practice and procedure before the various courts. In most jurisdictions, these rules are issued by the court itself, or by the highest court in that jurisdiction.

SANCTION—

(1) to assent to another's actions;
(2) a penalty for violating a law.

SCOPE NOTE—

delimits and identifies the content of a topic and appears below the topic's heading in a publication.

SECONDARY AUTHORITY—

source of the law which has only persuasive and no mandatory authority, e. g., encyclopedia.

SECTION LINE—

in West's key number digests, the section line is preceded by the key number, indicating the subject of the key number.

SESSION LAWS—

are published laws of a state enacted by each assembly and separately bound for the session and for extra sessions. The session laws are published in bound or pamphlet volumes after adjournment of the legislatures for the regular or special sessions.

SHEPARDIZING—

is a term which is the trade-mark property of Shepard's Citations, Inc. and is descriptive of the general use of its publications.

SLANDER—

oral defamation of a person's character. Compare with LIBEL.

"SLIP" LAW—

is a legislative enactment which is separately and promptly published in pamphlet or in single sheet format after its passage.

"SLIP" OPINION—

is an individual court decision published separately soon after it is rendered.

SQUIB—

a very brief rendition of a single case or a single point of law from a case. Compare with HEADNOTE.

STAR PAGINATION—

is a scheme in reprint editions of Court reports, showing on its pages where the text of the pages of the official edition begins and ends.

STARE DECISIS—

is the doctrine of English and American law which states that when a court has formulated a principle of law as applicable to a given set of facts, it will follow that principle and apply it in future cases where the facts are substantially the same. It connotes the decision of present cases on the basis of past precedent.

STATUS TABLE—

gives the current status of a bill or court decision.

STATUTES—

are acts of a legislature. Depending upon its context in usage, a statute may mean a single act of a legislature or a body of acts which are collected and arranged according to a scheme or for a session of a legislature or parliament.

STATUTES AT LARGE—

the official compilation of acts passed by the Congress. The arrangement is currently by Public Law number, and by chapter number in pre-1951 volumes. This is the official print of the law for citation purposes where titles of the United States Code have not been enacted into positive law.

STATUTES OF LIMITATIONS—

laws setting time periods during which disputes may be taken to court.

STATUTORY INSTRUMENTS—

are English administrative regulations and orders. The term applies especially to the administrative rules published since 1939, supplementing the English administrative code, Statutory Rules and Orders . . ..

STATUTORY RULES AND ORDERS—

are English administrative regulations and orders.

STYLE OF A CASE—

the parties to a lawsuit as they are written in the heading at the beginning of a written case.

SUBPOENA—

a court order compelling a witness to appear and testify in a certain proceeding.

SUBSTANTIVE LAW—

that law which establishes rights and obligations as distinguished from procedural law, which is concerned with rules for establishing their judicial enforcement.

SUMMONS—

a notice delivered by a sheriff or other authorized person informing a person that he/she is the defendant in a civil action and telling him/her when and where to appear in court to present his/her side.

SUPERSEDE—

to displace or to supplant one publication or its segment with another.

SUPREME COURT—

(1) the court of last resort in the federal judicial system. (It also has original jurisdiction in some cases.)
(2) in most states, the highest appellate court or court of last resort (but not in New York or Massachusetts).

SYLLABUS—

See HEADNOTE.

TABLE OF CASES—

is a list of cases, arranged alphabetically by cases names, with citations and references to the body of the publication where the cases are treated.

TEMPORARY LAW—

an act which continues in force for a specific period of time.

TERM OF COURT—

signifies the space of time prescribed by law during which a court holds session. The court's session may actually extend beyond the term. The October Term of the Supreme Court of the United States is now the only term during which the Court sits, and lasts from October to June or July.

TORT—

a civil wrong which does not involve a contractual relationship. The elements of a tort are a duty owed, a breach of that duty, and the resultant harm to the one to whom the duty was owed.

TRANSCRIPT OF RECORD—

refers to the printed record as made up in each case of the proceedings and pleadings necessary for the appellate court to review the history of the case.

TREATISE—

is an exposition, which may be critical, evaluative, interpretative, or informative, on case law or legislation. Usually it is more exhaustive than an encyclopedia article, but less detailed or critical than a periodical article.

TREATY—

is an agreement between two or more sovereign nations.

TRESPASS—

an unlawful interference with one's person, property, or rights. At common law, trespass was a form of action brought to recover damages for any injury to one's person or property or relationship with another.

UNIFORM LAWS—

on various subjects have been drafted. A considerable number have been approved by the National Conference of Commissioners on Uniform State Laws, and may have been adopted in one or more jurisdictions in the United States and its possessions. The Uniform Commercial Code is now the law in forty-nine states.

UNIFORM SYSTEM OF CITATION—

See BLUE BOOK.

UNOFFICIAL REPORTS—

are court reports published without statutory direction. They are not distinguished from official reports on grounds of varying quality or accuracy of reporting.

VENUE—

the particular geographical area where a court with jurisdiction may try a case.

WAIVER—

the voluntary relinquishment of a known right.

WESTLAW—

a computer data base and legal research system available through West Publishing Company. The data base contains statutory material and cases from components of the National Reporter System. They may be searched using any word or combination of words or West key-numbers.

WRIT—

of which there are many types, is a written order, issued by a court and directed to an official or party, commanding the performance of some act.

WRONGFUL DEATH—

a type of lawsuit brought on behalf of a deceased person's beneficiaries that alleges that death was attributable to the willful or negligent act of another.

*

FUNDAMENTALS OF LEGAL RESEARCH

Chapter 1

THE LEGAL PROCESS

SECTION A. SOURCES OF THE LAW

1. Introduction

The American legal system, as that of most English-speaking countries, is part of the common law tradition. The term "common law" is used here in the sense that distinguishes it from Roman law, modern civil law, canon law, and other systems of law.

The common law has been defined as that body of law which originated and developed in England and is in effect among those states which were originally settled by and controlled by England. It consists of those principles and rules of action applicable to the government and security of persons and property which do not rest for their authority upon the positive declarations of the will of the legislature.[1]

In the early history of English law, the custom developed of considering the decision of the courts as precedents. This was interpreted as "furnishing an example or authority for an identical or similar case afterwards arising or for a similar question of law."[2] This, in turn, led to the development of the doctrine of *stare decisis* which has been defined as:

> * * * [T]hat when [a] court has once laid down a principle of law as applicable to a certain state of facts, it

[1] BLACK'S LAW DICTIONARY 250–51 (5th ed. 1979). [Hereinafter cited as BLACK'S.]

[2] *Id.* at 1059. For a succinct and scholarly treatment of the development of case law, *see* J. DAWSON, THE ORACLES OF THE LAW 1–80 (1968).

will adhere to that principle, and apply it to all future cases where facts are substantially the same.[3]

Under the doctrine of *stare decisis* the law became embodied in the written decisions of the English courts and was to be found in the decisions of the courts rather than in a codified body of law as in other countries of Europe with legal systems based on the Roman law. It is in this sense that the common law became known as the "unwritten" law. The doctrines of *precedent* and *stare decisis* necessarily require access to the decisions of the courts and resulted in their publication under the generic term of *law reports.* To "find the law," then, a lawyer has to search the law reports for opinions of the courts that arose from a similar fact situation to the one at hand and then determine if the cases located can serve as a precedent for the present case.

While the development of case law was predominant, the role of statutes cannot be ignored. The earliest statutes were enacted by the King with the concurrence of his Council, and then gradually the role of statute-making was assumed by Parliament. It was not until after the passage of the *Reform Act of 1832* that statutes played a significant role in the English legal system. The real growth of statutory law reflected the impact of the industrial revolution on society as it became apparent that a jurisprudence based only on judicial decisions could not meet the needs of a growing dynamic society. Situations soon developed where answers were needed that were not found in the court reports, or the answers found no longer met current needs, or resulted in actions that were felt to be unjust. To remedy this, Parliament began to pass statutes which changed the prior rules for circumstances not found in any decisions of the court. A statute has been defined as:

> "An act of the legislature declaring, commanding, or prohibiting something; a particular law established by the will of the legislative department of government * * * according to the forms necessary to constitute it the law of the state." [4]
>
> "The word is used to designate the written law in contradistinction to the unwritten law."[5]

Therefore, the sources of law in common law jurisdictions originate from the enactments of their legislative bodies and from the de-

[3] Moore v. City of Albany, 98 N.Y. 396, 410 (1885). *See also* West, *The Doctrine of Stare Decisis*, 21 WAYNE L.REV. 1043 (1975).

[4] BLACK'S, *supra*, note 1, at 1264.

[5] *Id.*

cisions of their courts.[6] The authorities of law in all common law jurisdictions[7] are separated into two divisions—primary and secondary. Primary law is found in: (1) written constitutions and the enactments of legislatures (and in those adopted in some jurisdictions through the vote of their electorate); and (2) the body of law found in the written opinions of the courts.

Primary laws or sources are also designated as either mandatory or persuasive. The former are either constitutions, statutes, or decisions of the highest court of a jurisdiction and must be followed by all lower courts within the jurisdiction. The latter consist of appellate court opinions of other jurisdictions. Constitutions and statutes are published in statute books, and court opinions are published in sets of court reports. All other written expressions of the law are known as secondary sources.

The term "sources of the law" has been variously defined. In relation to legal research, the phrase is employed to denote the literature of the law, the authoritative organ of the state which formulates the legal rules, or the derivation of the concepts or ideas expressed in the body of the law. These meanings do not exhaust the definitions of the term; however, the present discussion will be limited to the concepts they impart.

2. The Literature of the Law

It is axiomatic to describe law libraries as containing the literature of the law.[8] This material includes statutes, administrative rules, judicial decisions, digests of case law, treatises, encyclopedias and other publications.

American law libraries contain large, diffuse collections since, pursuant to the common law, much of our law is "found" or "made" by judicial decisions. Determining the decisions of present cases on the basis of precedents results in legal literature accumulating and assuming large proportions. Another factor resulting in the growth of American legal collections is the multiple system of state and federal laws which makes necessary the acquisition and maintenance of primary sources for fifty states as well as those of the federal government. Moreover, American law school libraries should also con-

[6] For a more detailed discussion of the common law, *see* R. JACKSON, THE MACHINERY OF JUSTICE IN ENGLAND 9–17 (7th ed. 1977). *See also* L. FRIEDMAN, A HISTORY OF AMERICAN LAW 17–25 (1975).

[7] "Jurisdiction" in this sense is used to describe the territory over which a government or subdivision thereof has control.

[8] For a collection of essays examining the role of law libraries in the legal profession and in legal education, *see* READER IN LAW LIBRARIANSHIP (B. Reams ed. 1976).

tain at least the court decisions of England; and many contain the decisions of Canada, Australia, New Zealand and other common law jurisdictions.

3. The Authoritative Organ of the State

The officials or bodies of officials whose acts give validity to the law are descriptive of another meaning of its source. In the democratic countries, there are two types of officials with such authority. They are legislators and judges. The former include legislators and administrative rule-makers. These officials produce two authoritative forms of law: legislation and case law. The latter group includes ordinary judges and administrative hearing officials.

4. The Derivation of Legal Concepts

The third meaning given to the sources of the law relates to the derivation of the concepts contained in the body of law. This meaning indicates intellectual sources for the legal concepts which are ultimately reflected in statutes or court decisions. For example, the source of the modern law of vicarious liability is considered by some as having its origin in the slave law of the Romans.[9] The source of the doctrine in American law of the right to privacy is attributed to an article first published in *Harvard Law Review*.[10] The ideas as expressed in the writings of Chancellor Kent and Justice Story also contributed significantly to the early development of American law.

However, we use the term "source of law" throughout this book to mean source as contained in the literature of the law.

SECTION B. THE LEGAL SYSTEM OF THE UNITED STATES: SOURCES

As a result of our federal system, any particular legal transaction may be governed solely by state law, or solely by federal law, or perhaps both. Although the question of determination of jurisdiction is beyond the scope of this book, its significance cannot be overlooked in determining the answer to a legal question and knowledge is needed of both federal and state law.

As previously indicated, the United States is a common law jurisdiction. The federal system of government in this country, however, has made its legal system extremely complex. Under our federal constitution, each state, except for those powers delegated to the federal government, is a sovereign state. This means, in effect, there

[9] O. HOLMES, COMMON LAW 16–17 (1881).

[10] Warren & Brandeis, *The Right to Privacy*, 4 HARV.L.REV. 193 (1890).

is not one legal system in this country, but there are fifty-one, including the federal system.

1. Federal Government

The primary sources of the United States Government are found in its Constitution,[11] the Acts of Congress, and in the decisions of the Supreme Court of the United States and other lower federal courts.

2. States

In addition to the above, the primary sources for each of the fifty states are found in each state's constitution as adopted by the people, the enactments of the legislature (and those initiated and enacted directly by the electorate) and the written decisions of its highest court of appeal, and in the law of England as delineated in its reception statute.[12]

SECTION C. THE LEGAL SYSTEMS OF OTHER COUNTRIES

The doctrine of judicial precedent is not recognized by the European countries,[13] whose legal systems are derived from the Roman law, to the degree followed by common-law countries. Justinian, in codifying the law for the Roman state, declared that his code was to be the exclusive source of the law "on penalty of forgery," [14] thus attempting to discourage reference to earlier sources. Codification as a

[11] To date, there have been 26 amendments proposed, ratified, and incorporated into the Constitution. Seven amendments proposed by Congress have not been ratified by the states, and only two of these are still pending before it. For more detailed information on proposed and unratified amendments, *see*: U. S. CONGRESS. HOUSE, THE CONSTITUTION OF THE UNITED STATES OF AMERICA: AS AMENDED THROUGH JULY 1971; ANALYTICAL INDEX: UNRATIFIED AMENDMENT, H.DOC.NO. 93–215, 93rd Cong., 2d Sess. (1974); U. S. CONGRESS. SENATE LIBRARY, PROPOSED AMENDMENTS TO THE CONSTITUTION, 69th Congress – 87th Congress, S.DOC.NO. 163, 87th Cong., 2d Sess. (1963), and 88th Congress – 90th Congress, S.DOC.NO. 91–38, 91st Cong., 1st Sess. (1939); U. S. CONGRESS. SENATE, COMMITTEE ON THE JUDICIARY, SUB-COMMITTEE ON CONSTITUTIONAL AMENDMENTS, ANNUAL REPORTS *e. g.*, S.REP.NO.94–1373, 95th Cong., 2d Sess. (1976).

[12] All states except Louisiana (whose legal system is based on the civil law) have adopted the English common law as the basis of their jurisprudence. *See* 1 POWELL ON REAL PROPERTY § 45 (1969). For representative statutes adopting the English common law as part of their law, *see* SMITH-HURD, ILL.ANN.STAT. Ch. 28, § 1 (1969); TEX.REV.CIV.STAT. Art. 1 (1969).

[13] For articles on judicial precedent in Europe, *see* Von Mehren, *Judicial Process: A Comparative Analysis*, 5 AM.J.COMP.L. 197 (1956); Dietze, *Judicial Review in Europe*, 55 MICH.L.REV. 539 (1957).

[14] A. KOCUREK, AN INTRODUCTION TO THE SCIENCE OF LAW 162 (1930).

legal instrument was later adopted by the countries which followed the Roman law. However, in recent years, on the continent of Europe, judicial decisions are assuming a more significant authoritative role, claiming recognition with commentaries in interpreting the civil law. Modern European codes also recognize that no codification scheme can be all-inclusive and complete; thus, courts may be required to go outside the code, when its text is silent, obscure or deficient, for the solution to controversies.

The Latin American courts have followed a modified procedure. If a rule has been applied several times in different cases by the highest court, it is considered as binding. The French practice is also a compromise between the rule of *stare decisis* and the civil-law concept. A single decision by a court is not binding on it or on subordinate courts. While another lower court in a comparable case is not bound to follow the highest court's twice-told precedent, in practice the lower courts are prone to follow the precedent. Further, a uniform pattern of decisions is considered as binding in all courts in a manner similar to that of the highest courts in the United States.[15]

Other legal systems or conceptions that should be mentioned here are: Socialist law, based on the theories and writings of Marx, Engels and Lenin, adopting and building upon the civil law systems; Muslim, Hindu and Hebrew conceptions of law, with strong religious principles; and African law, which, although based upon local customs, has been influenced by the laws of colonial powers.[16]

SECTION D. LEGAL RESEARCH

The short summary so far presented on the structure of the legal system must be understood before one can approach the methods of doing legal research. What is involved in this process is a search for authorities. When engaged in legal research (more properly, legal search), lawyers are seeking to find those authorities in the primary sources of the law that are applicable to a particular legal situation. In short, they are seeking to find applicable statutes or court decisions (or both) [17] from the particular jurisdiction wherein the legal

[15] Goodhart, *Precedents in English and Continental Law*, 50 LAW Q.REV. 40 (1934). *See also* J. DAWSON, *supra* note 2 at 100; J. MERRYMAN, THE CIVIL LAW TRADITION: AN INTRODUCTION TO THE LEGAL SYSTEMS OF WESTERN EUROPE AND LATIN AMERICA (1969).

[16] For an excellent work on the subject of this section, *see* THE LEGAL SYSTEMS OF THE WORLD: THEIR COMPARISON AND UNIFICATION (R. David ed. 1975).

[17] The place of administrative regulations and rulings will be covered in Chapter 13.

situation has occurred or will occur. The search is always first for mandatory primary sources, that is, constitutional or statutory provisions of the legislature, and court decisions of the jurisdiction involved. If these cannot be located, then the search focuses on locating persuasive primary authorities, that is, decisions from courts of other common law jurisdictions. Statutes of other jurisdictions are never considered persuasive authority. When in the legal search process primary authorities cannot be located, the searcher will seek for secondary authorities. These usually are considered to be the writings of lawyers as found in treatises or law reviews, or the publications of law reform organizations such as the American Law Institute and the law revision commissions of the various states.

1. Professional Responsibility

The *Code of Professional Responsibility* of the American Bar Association states that a lawyer must maintain high standards of professional conduct, and Canon 6 of this Code requires a lawyer to represent a client competently. For such representation, it is clear that a lawyer must be able to research the law, and all lawyers are expected to know "those plain and elementary principles of law which are commonly known by well-informed attorneys, *and to discover the additional rules which, although not commonly known, may readily be found by standard research techniques*"[18] (emphasis ours). The ability to find the law, to locate the applicable ruling authorities, and to ascertain their current status must become part and parcel of every lawyer's training if he is to uphold the standards of the legal profession.

2. Legal Book Publishing

To engage in legal research, one must have an understanding not only of the organization of the legal system, but also of how law books are published and organized. In the American colonial period law books were extremely scarce, and consisted mostly of English law reports. The most extensive law collections of attorneys numbered from fifty to one hundred volumes.[19]

[18] Smith v. Lewis, 13 Cal.3d 349, 118 Cal.Rptr. 621, 530 P.2d 589 (1975). In this case the plaintiff received a judgment of $100,000 in a malpractice action based on the negligence of the defendant lawyer in researching the applicable law. *See also* 1:4 LEGAL RESEARCH JOURNAL (1976). This is a symposium issue on legal malpractice based on the *Lewis* decision.

[19] A. HARNO, LEGAL EDUCATION IN THE UNITED STATES 19 (1953); L. FRIEDMAN, *supra* note 6, at 538–46. The first law book written by an American was printed in Virginia in 1736. This was W. PARK, THE OFFICE AND AUTHORITY OF A JUSTICE OF PEACE, AND THE DUTY OF SHERIFFS, CONSTABLES, CORONERS, CHURCH WARDENS, SURVEYORS OF HIGHWAYS, CONSTABLES AND OFFICERS OF THE MILITIA. For a thorough discussion of

The situation did not prevail for long. As the economy of the country changed from agrarian to industrial, and greater demands were made upon the courts and the legislatures, the repositories of the law grew proportionately.

Over the years, there have been various statistics used by legal authorities on quoting the tremendous volume of reported decisons in the American legal system. The preface to the Century Edition of the American Digest System states that the courts made 500,000 decisions during the period 1658–1896.[20]

In trying to determine the number of cases reported since the Century Edition, the authors of this book in cooperation with the editors of West Publishing Company determined that up to 1980 there were over three million reported decisions in the United States.

In 1979 the National Reporter System, including State and Federal volumes, reported 47,000 cases. In 1950 there were 21,000 cases. Thus, in a 30-year period the number of cases more than doubled. Congress and state legislatures produce about 50,000 pages of statutory law per year, and the *Federal Register* annually publishes about 75,000 pages of federal administrative regulations.[21]

This flood of court decisions has from early times caused concern to the legal profession.[22] But despite all efforts to control the ever-increasing number of court opinions, they continue to proliferate. Moreover, all fifty states as well as the federal government publish their own statutes and administrative regulations. To help lawyers cope with this multitude of primary sources, private publishers publish numerous types of secondary sources, such as treatises, periodicals, citators, digests, and annotations to assist lawyers in finding and understanding the law. A short discussion of the law book publishing industry will be helpful in understanding the use of law books, the subject of remaining chapters.

The largest law book publisher is the West Publishing Company of St. Paul, Minnesota. This company primarily publishes court reports and statutes but also offers many secondary sources. The next largest law book publishing company is the Lawyers Co-operative Publishing Company of Rochester, New York and its affiliate, the Bancroft-Whitney Company of San Francisco, California. Both em-

early law book publishing, see Parrish, *Law Books and Legal Publishing in America, 1760–1840,* 72 LAW LIB.J. 355 (1979).

20 1 *Century Digest* iii (1897).

21 The *Federal Register* for 1980 contained 87,012 pages, an increase of over 10% in the number of pages over the preceding year. In 1981 the number of pages was 63,553, or a decrease of nearly 27%.

22 For a discussion of the problem of excessive court reporting, *see* Jacobstein, *Some Reflections on the Control of the Publication of Appellate Court Opinions,* 27 STAN.L.REV. 791 (1975).

phasize the publications of primary sources. The Commerce Clearing House Company, the Bureau of National Affairs, and the Prentice-Hall Company are publishers of looseleaf publications which emphasize areas of law requiring frequent updating. The Matthew Bender Company and Callaghan Law Book Publishing Company specialize in publishing treatises for practicing lawyers. Many other smaller companies also publish legal materials most useful in legal research.[23]

When engaged in legal research, searching for the law may involve statutes and court reports of many states as well as countless numbers of secondary sources. The important point to remember, however, is that both legal finding aids and primary repositories of the law are predominantly products of the private law book publishing industry.[24]

SECTION E. SUMMARY

The sources of American law for the purpose of legal research are found in the United States Constitution, the constitutions of the fifty states, the statutes of the United States Congress and of the fifty state legislatures, and in the appellate court decisions of the vari-federal and state courts.

Constitutions, statutes, and court decisions are primary sources of the law. Other law books are secondary sources of the law.

[23] A thorough discussion of the law book publishing industry may be found in M. MAYER, THE LAWYERS 417–50 (1966). *See also Lamson, For Lawyers, West Isn't a Direction—It's a Way of Life,* 4 JURIS DOCTOR 28 (1974); *Sandza, Lawbook Publishing: A $145 Million-a-Year Business,* 4 JURIS DOCTOR 31 (1974).

[24] The reliance of lawyers on private law book publishers led the Federal Trade Commission to promulgate standards for the law book trade. *See* 16 C.F.R. § 256 (1980).

Chapter 2

PRELIMINARY PROCEDURE IN LEGAL RESEARCH

Let us begin our study by surveying the procedure which is preliminary to the actual use of research publications. This entails three steps: (1) the determination and integration of facts; (2) the determination of the legal issues; and (3) the procedure to be applied in searching for the law.

To understand a legal problem clearly, carefully screen and ascertain the relevant facts. Though the legal principle may be constant, its application to different facts may result in different conclusions. Thus, incisive interrogation of the parties and resourceful investigation to derive the facts frequently determine the results of a problem.

SECTION A. DETERMINATION AND INTEGRATION OF FACTS

After assembling the facts, screen, integrate, and evaluate the information. Though these are not distinct processes, each possesses distinguishing characteristics. Screening entails the eliminating of nonessential facts; integration is the process of assembling the pertinent data; and evaluation gives direction to the research.

To appraise the relevant issues factually, recognize and weigh the following factors:

T—*Thing* or subject matter

A—Cause of *Action* or ground of defense

R—*Relief* sought

P—*Persons* or parties involved

1. *Thing or subject matter.* The place or property involved in a problem or controversy may be a significant element. Thus, where a passenger is injured in a skidding automobile, the personal property, the automobile, becomes an essential factor in the dispute.

2. *Cause of action or ground of defense.* A claim is asserted or a defense is made. The action centers around a point of controversy or a circumstance relating to the problem. The cause of action may be a breach of contract, negligence, or some other claim.

3. *Relief sought.* This relates to the purpose of the lawsuit or the claim. It may be a civil suit for damages, an equity matter seek-

ing affirmative or injunctive relief, or a criminal action being brought by the state.

4. *Persons or parties involved in the problem; their factual and legal status and relationship to each other.* The parties or persons may fit within a group or class which is significant to the solution of the problem or the outcome of the lawsuit. Thus, infancy or insanity may have an important bearing on a result.

The commercial or professional activities of the parties or persons may be pertinent, for example, banking or medicine.

The relationships between the parties or persons may be of special importance, such as exist between husband and wife or employer and employee.

Factual analysis using the TARP rule should suggest headings to be examined during the research.

SECTION B. DETERMINATION OF THE LEGAL ISSUES

When the facts are ascertained and integrated, determine the legal issues. Legal controversies frequently involve more than one point of law. In such cases, the issues should be interrelated, not merged, and should be given separate treatment.

Some secondary sources are useful to orient the researcher if general, introductory information is required. They include treatises, periodical articles, and general and local encyclopedias.

As the methods of research vary greatly with the problems and the subject matter, no single example can illustrate adequately all phases of research methodology. However, to facilitate the present study, an example case is analyzed below.

Example Case

The XYZ Auto Sales Company placed an advertisement in a local newspaper advertising a sports model Studecar ZZ–88 for $4,988.00. Through an inadvertent error, the advertisement listed the price as $4,088.00. A customer entered the salesroom and told a salesperson that she wanted to purchase a Studecar ZZ–88 for $4,088.00 as advertised. After checking with the Sales Manager, the salesperson told the customer that the advertisement was a mistake and that the car could not be sold for less than $4,988.00. The customer consults a lawyer.

Let us analyze this case.

(1) *Thing or subject matter.* Here the subject matter is an automobile, but this is not the essential matter. The same rules of law would apply for an erroneous advertisement in a newspaper for near-

ly any type of consumer goods. The matter in question here is whether the advertisement was a valid offer which upon acceptance created an enforceable contract.

(2) *Cause of action or ground of defense.* The cause of action is an alleged breach of contract; the defense being the lack of a binding contract.

(3) *Relief sought.* Customer seeks delivery of auto at advertised price, or difference between this price and price customer actually paid for similar model.

(4) *Persons or parties involved.* The parties include customer and Auto Sales Co., and perhaps all others who want to purchase a Studecar ZZ–88 at the advertised price.

This problem now has to be researched to find the law on the following issues and perhaps others that will become apparent during the research.

Does an advertisement in a newspaper constitute a valid offer?

Can an action be maintained against the XYZ Company for specific performance? That is, can it be made to deliver a ZZ–88 to the customer at the advertised price? If not, what other remedies does customer have? Is it possible to make this into a "class action" suit?

Do the facts of this case apply only to state law, or are there elements which could bring this case under the jurisdiction of a federal court?

During the research for the law, the researcher will first determine whether state or federal law is applicable. Under the facts presented, state law will apply as there are no federal issues present. Next, the researcher should ascertain if the state where this transaction occurred has a statute controlling this type of newspaper advertising. If it does, the next step is to determine if there are any court decisions which interpret the statute. If there is no statute, the researcher will search first for appellate court decisions in the state where the transaction occurred, then for appellate court decisions in other states. The search will be for cases with fact situations as similar as possible to the one being researched.

The remaining chapters of this book will be devoted to demonstrating how this research is accomplished and the different methods which may be used in finding the law.

Chapter 3

COURT REPORTS

SECTION A. THE REPORTING OF COURT DECISIONS

1. Introduction

The editing and publishing of court decisions have assumed special characteristics in American law. These manifestations were influenced significantly by the doctrine of judicial precedent or *stare decisis*. Since past decisions play such an important role in our law, the tremendous growth and inclusiveness of court reports are quite understandable. However, this extensive development in turn has created problems for the legal profession—problems relating to the informational content of case law, publication costs, absorption of office space and related issues.

As indicated previously, there are over three million reported judicial opinions in the United States, and over 47,000 American cases are published each year. These mostly include decisions of federal and state appellate courts. As a general rule, decisions of trial courts are not reported. A few states, such as New York, Ohio and Pennsylvania, do publish some trial court opinions but those so selected are few in number and represent only a very small proportion of the total cases heard by the trial courts. Moreover, opinions of trial courts do not serve as mandatory precedents and they do not play an important role in legal research.

Not all appellate court opinions, however, are necessarily published and the publication procedures differ in the various appellate courts.[1] Many judges and lawyers believe that far too many opinions are written and reported which do not merit the treatment of permanent publication. It is claimed that a significant number of reported decisions relate merely to prosaic problems and make no doctrinal advancements. Although of value to the parties involved in the litigation, these cases add little or nothing to the existing law.

Despite Justice Holmes' observation that, "It is a great mistake to be frightened by the ever-increasing number of reports. The reports of a given jurisdiction in the course of a generation take up

[1] Chanin, *A Survey of the Writing and Publication of Opinions in Federal and State Appellate Courts*, 67 LAW LIB.J. 362 (1974); *Unreported Decisions in the United States Courts of Appeal*, 63 CORNELL L.REV. 128 (1977). See also: Reynolds and Richman, *An Evaluation of Limited Publication in the United States Courts of Appeals: The Price of Reform.* 48 U.Chi.L.Rev. 573 (1981).

pretty much the whole body of the law, and restate it from the present point of view. We could reconstruct the corpus from them if all that went before were burned," [2] the tremendous growth of recent decisions has increased the attempts to restrict the number of reported court decisions.[3]

2. Court Organization

Each jurisdiction has its own system of court organization, and although there may be differences in detail, the general structure is the same. In general, there are trial courts and appellate courts. The former are the courts where the trial is first held (courts of the first instance). It is here the parties appear, witnesses testify, and the evidence is presented. The trial court usually determines any questions of fact that may be in dispute and then applies the applicable rules of law.

Once the trial court reaches its decision, the losing party has a right of appeal to an appellate court. Generally, the appellate court can only decide questions of law and its decision in each case is based on the record made below. Appellate courts do not receive new testimony or decide questions of fact, and in most jurisdictions only the appellate courts issue written opinions.

Each state has a final court of appeal (usually called the Supreme Court). Additionally, thirty-two states have intermediate courts of appeal.[4] [See Illustration 1]

3. Methods of Court Reporting

When a case has been appealed to an appellate court, both parties submit written briefs which contain a summary of the facts and arguments on the points of law involved, and the court may hear oral arguments by the attorneys. The court then writes an opinion in which it states the reasons for its decision. Technically speaking, the decision of a court only indicates the action of the court and is indicated by the words *Affirmed,* or *Reversed,* or *Remanded,* or similar

[2] Holmes, *The Path of the Law,* in COLLECTED LEGAL PAPERS 167, 169 (1975).

[3] A full discussion of this may be found in Jacobstein, *Some Reflections on the Control of the Publication of Appellate Court Opinions,* 27 STAN.L.REV. 791 (1975). *See also* Landes and Posner, *Legal Precedent: A Theoretical and Empirical Analysis,* 19 J. LAW & ECON. 249–307 (1976); Merryman, *Toward a Theory of Citations: An Empirical Study of the Citation Practice of the California Supreme Court in 1950, 1960, and 1970,* 50 SO.CALIF.L.REV. 381–428 (1977); Reynolds and Richman, *The Non-Precedential Precedent—Limited Publication and No-Citation Rules in the United States Courts of Appeals,* 78 COLUMBIA L.REV. 1167 (1978).

[4] Marvell and Kuykendall, *Appellate Courts—Facts and Figures,* STATE COURT JOURNAL, Spring 1980, at 9.

words and phrases. The reasons for this action are then stated in the opinion of the court. However, in actual practice, the terms *opinion* and *decision* have become interchangeable, and the word *decision* herein will be used to describe both.[5]

SECTION B. THE SEGMENTS OF COURT DECISIONS

The segments of an American court decision are as follows:

1. Name or Title of the Case

Cases generally are identified by the names of the parties to a lawsuit:

Payne v. *Green*—in table of cases as *Payne* v. *Green*.

In re Payne—in table of cases as *Payne, In re*. Judicial proceedings in which there are no adversary parties. Such designations usually denote a bankruptcy case, a probate case, a guardianship matter, a contempt case, a disbarment, or a habeas corpus case.

Ex parte Payne—in tables of cases as *Payne, Ex parte*. This is a special proceeding.

State on the relation of Payne v. *Green*—in tables of cases as *State ex rel. Payne* v. *Green*. These cases involve the extraordinary legal remedies, viz.: Mandamus, prohibition, certiorari, quo warranto, or habeas corpus.

State v. *Payne*—in tables of cases as *State* v. *Payne*. Suit by the state in its collective capacity as the party wronged by a criminal deed. In some sets the criminal cases are arranged in alphabetical order under the names of the respective states. "People" or "Commonwealth" are used in some states instead of "State."

In maritime law, a suit may be brought against the ship, e. g., The Caledonia.

Cases involving the seizure of commodities are brought in their names, e. g., *United States* v. *45 Barrels of Whisky*.

Usually, the plaintiff-defendant names remain in that order when cases are appealed by a defendant; however, in some states, they are reversed and the defendant on appeal becomes the plaintiff in error.

2. Docket Number

A docket number is the numerical designation assigned to each case by a court. It is the means of identifying the case as the suit

[5] For a discussion of the difference between "decision of the court" and "opinion of the court," *see* Rogers v. Hill, 289 U.S. 582, 587 (1933).

progresses. Also, it is a convenient method for filing briefs in cases in libraries.

3. Date of Decision

This is the date on which the decision was rendered, and generally it appears after the docket number in the reported case.

4. Prefatory Statement

The prefatory statement explains the nature of the case, its disposition in the lower court, the name of the lower court and sometimes its judge, and the disposition of the case in the appellate court as being affirmed or reversed.

5. Syllabus or Headnote

Headnotes, or syllabi, are brief summaries of the rules of law or significant facts in a case. They are usually drafted by editors, although in a few states they are prepared by the judges who rendered the decisions. Each headnote represents a point of law extracted from the decision and the number of headnotes will vary from case to case.

The syllabi or headnotes are useful in allowing the reader to grasp quickly the legal issues discussed in the case. They also serve a very useful function in the process of locating cases on the same or similar points of law. This feature will be discussed in more detail in Chapter 5. [See Illustrations 3 and 4 for examples of headnotes.]

6. Names of Counsel

The names of counsel for both parties to a suit precede the opinion of the court.

7. Statement of Facts

A statement of the facts in the case usually follows the names of counsel.

8. Opinion of the Court

Although, as previously mentioned, a few trial court decisions are reported, most court opinions that are published are those of appellate courts. Every appellate court has at least three judges and in some jurisdictions the courts may have five, seven, or nine judges. The opinion of the court is the explanation of the court's decision, the latter being the conclusion or result in a controversy. The opinion is written by one member of the court after the majority has agreed to a decision. A member of the majority, while agreeing with a decision, may disagree with its reasoning; he then may write a concurring opinion which gives his reasons for the decision. The views of the minority generally are expressed by a dissenting opinion which is written by one of the dissenting judges. An opinion, in accord with the dissent, may be written by a dissenting judge when he agrees with the conclusions and result of the dissent but disagrees with its reasoning. Or several dissenting opinions may be rendered independently by the judges, each expressing different views. A *per curiam* opinion is an opinion of the entire majority as distinguished from an opinion written by a specific judge. It may present a lengthy or a brief discussion of the issues in the case, *e.g.*, New York Court of Appeals. In some courts, it may only give the conclusion without any reasoning, *e.g.*, United States Supreme Court. A memorandum opinion is a brief holding of the whole court in which the opinion is limited or omitted.

Dissenting opinions are not the law in a case; nor are they binding as precedent. They assume the characteristics of *dicta* and serve merely as secondary authority. However, not infrequently the controlling opinion may later be overruled and the dissenting opinion is then accepted as the correct statement of the law.

There are two additional elements of a case which merit brief attention. The first is the *ratio decidendi*, or the point in a case which determines the result. In other words, it is the basis of the decision, explicitly or implicitly, stated in the opinion. The second is *obiter dictum.* The latter is a collateral statement contained in the opinion which does not relate directly to the issues raised in the case. *Dictum,* therefore, is an official, incidental comment, not necessary to the formulation of the decision, made by the judge in his opinion which is not binding as precedent.

9. Decision, with Judgment or Decree

This refers to the actual disposition of the case by the court. Thus, a decision is noted by such terms as "affirmed," "reversed," "modified," etc. Often the words "decision" and "judgment" are synonymously used. However, a judgment upon the verdict of a jury is the most common of the judgments upon facts found, and is for the party, *i.e.*, plaintiff or defendant, obtaining the verdict.

SECTION C. OFFICIAL AND UNOFFICIAL REPORTS

If the publication of the court reports is sanctioned by statute, they are called "official reports." [See Illustration 2.] Those published without such authority are referred to as "unofficial reports," *i.e.*, commercial or private publications. Neither term reflects quality or accuracy, for both originate from the clerks and the judges.

See Illustrations 3 and 4 for an example of the same case as reported in an official and unofficial set of reports. Very few cases are reported in official reports only, though many are published in both editions. The success of unofficial reports in the United States is due materially to the frequency and speed of those publications.

1. Unofficially Reported Cases as Authority

Since decisions of courts are not copyrighted,[6] numerous sets of court reports have been published by private firms which either duplicate the official reports or include decisions not officially published. Since the early nineteenth century legal scholars have warned against such uncontrolled proliferation of court reports.[7] In the past, courts and legislatures have attempted to control the publication of court opinions by limiting the publication of opinions in the official reports to those decisions which (1) lay down a new rule of law or alter or modify an existing rule; (2) involve a legal issue of continuing public interest; (3) criticize existing law; or (4) resolve an apparent conflict of authority.[8] But, inevitably, each such attempt has resulted in those opinions not appearing in the official reports being published in unofficial sets of reports. Only recently have some courts attempted to control this by prohibiting the citing of opinions not specifically marked "For Publication."[9] This practice in turn has been severely criticized by some members of the bar.[10] The final solution to the proliferation of court opinions has still not been found. It is reasonable to conclude that so long as precedent plays a dominant role in American law, the number of published court decisions will continue to grow. Care should be taken, however, to check the authority of unofficially reported decisions before citing them as authority.

SECTION D. THE ELEMENTS OF JUDICIAL REPORTING

Several techniques are used in publishing court cases. Generally, the order of their release is determined by their decision dates and not by a logical arrangement, such as subject. Some decisions are published individually, when rendered by a court, and are called "slip" opinions. Usually, the "slip" opinions do not contain syllabi, nor are they indexed.

[6] Wheaton v. Peters, 33 U.S. 591 (1834). *See also* Annotation, Law Reports as Subject of Copyright, 8 L.Ed. 1055 (1883); Banks v. Manchester, 128 U.S. 244 (1888).

[7] Jacobstein, *supra* note 3.

[8] *Id.* at 794.

[9] Id. at 796; CAL.SUP.CT. (Civ.) R. 977 (West Supp.Pam.1980).

[10] Jacobstein, *supra* note 3 at 798–99.

"Advance sheets" contain decisions of a court or the courts of several jurisdictions. They typically are published as quickly as they can be assembled after the decisions are rendered. Their format is that of a periodical pamphlet, and the emphasis is on speed of publication. The paging of the "advance sheets" ordinarily is the same as the bound volumes which the latter eventually cumulate. This permits quick, permanent citations to cases. The features of the cases in the "advance sheets" are identical with those included in the bound volumes. Some jurisdictions do not publish "advance sheets."

1. Features of Bound Volumes of Reports

As indicated above, the cases are finally cumulated in bound volumes. The bound volumes include most of the following significant features:

a. A table of cases contained in the volume.

b. A table of statutes interpreted by the decisions reported.

c. The opinions are cumulated from advance sheets and have the same volume and page numbers as the advance sheets.

d. The types of opinions are (1) written by a judge (majority, dissenting or concurring), (2) *per curiam* and (3) memorandum.

e. Subject index or digest of the cases reported.

f. Judicial definition of words and phrases used in the cases reported.

g. Court rules.

h. The various volumes of unofficial reports generally contain cross reference tables to the official reports.

SECTION E. ORGANIZATION OF COURT REPORTS

Court reports are organized (1) jurisdictionally, (2) geographically and (3) by subject. They are published in series and the bound volumes and advance sheets are consecutively numbered.

1. Jurisdictional Reports

The decisions of a specific court or several courts within a system may be published in a set of volumes and kept current by advance sheets and new bound volumes.

Examples:

United States Supreme Court Reports
Minnesota Reports (reports cases of the Minnesota Supreme Court)
California Appellate Reports (reports cases of the District Courts of Appeal of California)

2. Geographical Reports

Cases covering several courts of a state may be published in a reporter.

Examples:

New York Miscellaneous Reports
Ohio Opinions

Also, the decisions of small numbers of states, divided into geographical regions, are grouped together and published as units. This grouping is called the National Reporter System and will be discussed in Chapter 5.

Examples:

North Western Reporter (includes cases from Iowa, Michigan, Minnesota, Nebraska, North Dakota, South Dakota and Wisconsin)
South Western Reporter (includes cases from Arkansas, Kentucky, Missouri, Tennessee and Texas)

3. Subject Reports

Another category of reports is that of subject reports, which are collections of decisions on specific legal subjects such as taxation, labor law and criminal law. Since the standard sets of court reports include cases on all subjects, these special reports have found a ready market in lawyers who specialize in a particular area of the law. For the most part, cases in these reports are reprints but some are not reported in the jurisdictional or geographical reports.

This feature has also been adopted by a number of the looseleaf services. A few examples of current special reports are:

a. Commerce Clearing House, Trade Regulation Reporter (Trade Cases).

b. Negligence and Compensation Cases, Annotated.

c. Prentice-Hall, Tax Court Memorandum Decisions.

d. Public Utilities Reports.

e. U.S. Patents Quarterly.

SECTION F. ILLUSTRATIONS

[Illustration 1]

COURT ORGANIZATION CHART

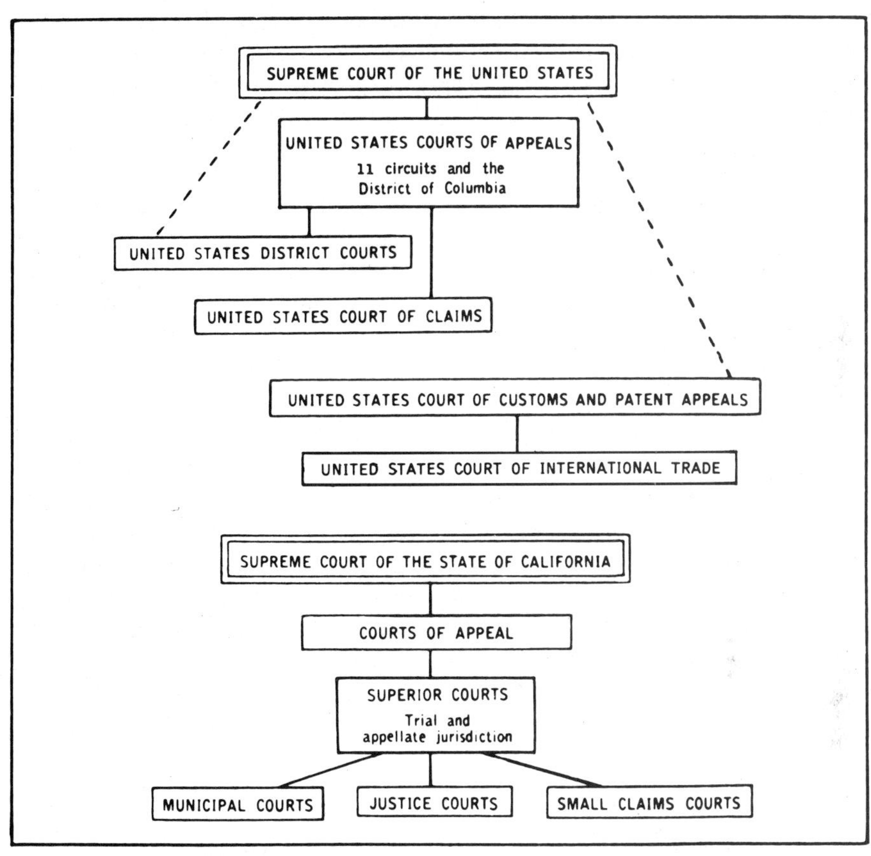

[Illustration 2]

TYPICAL STATUTORY PROVISIONS FOR PUBLICATION OF COURT REPORTS

Excerpt from West's Ann.Calif. Gov't Code

§ 68902. Publication of reports: Supervision by Supreme Court.

Such opinions of the Supreme Court, of the courts of appeal, and of the appellate departments of the superior courts as the Supreme Court may deem expedient shall be published in the official reports. The reports shall be published under the general supervision of the Supreme Court.

Excerpts from McKinney Consol.Laws of N.Y. Judiciary Law

§ 430. Law reporting bureau; state reporter

There is hereby created and established the law reporting bureau of the state of New York. The bureau shall be under the direction and control of a state reporter, who shall be appointed and be removable by the court of appeals by an order entered in its minutes. The state reporter shall be assisted by a first deputy state reporter and such other deputy state reporters and such staff as may be necessary, all of whom shall be appointed and be removable by the court of appeals.

§ 431. Causes to be reported

The law reporting bureau shall report every cause determined in the court of appeals and every cause determined in the appellate divisions of the supreme court, unless otherwise directed by the court deciding the cause; and, in addition, any cause determined in any other court which the state reporter, with the approval of the court of appeals, considers worthy of being reported because of its usefulness as a precedent or its importance as a matter of public interest.

Each reported decision shall be published as soon as practicable after it is rendered. Added L.1938, c. 494, § 1, eff. July 1, 1938.

Excerpt from Vernon's Ann.Mo.Stat.

§ 477.231. Designation of private publication as official reports

The supreme court may declare the published volumes of the decisions of the supreme court as the same are published by any person, firm or corporation, to be official reports of the decisions of the supreme court, and the courts of appeals may jointly make a similar declaration with respect to published volumes of the opinions of the courts of appeals. Any publication so designated as the official reports may include both the opinions of the supreme court and the courts of appeals in the same volume.

[Illustration 3]

A TYPICAL CASE AS REPORTED IN AN OFFICIAL SET OF COURT REPORTS

(128 Ill.App.2d)

O'KEEFE v. LEE CALAN IMPORTS, INC.
128 Ill App2d 410

James L. O'Keefe, Public Administrator of the Estate of Christopher D. O'Brien, Plaintiff-Appellant, v. Lee Calan Imports, Inc., an Illinois Corporation, Defendant-Appellee, Third-Party Plaintiff, v. Field Enterprises, Inc., Third-Party Defendant.

Gen. No. 54,102.

First District, Third Division.

September 3, 1970.

1. **Contracts, § 31 *—offer and acceptance.**
In order to form a contract, there must be an offer and acceptance.

2. **Contracts, § 23 *—mutual assent.**
Contract requires mutual assent of parties.

3. **Contracts, § 31 *—newspaper advertisement containing erroneous price.**
Newspaper advertisement which contains erroneous purchase price through no fault of advertiser and which contains no other terms amounts only to invitation to make an offer and is not offer which can be accepted so as to form contract.

4. **Contracts, § 31 *—price misstatement in newspaper advertisement.**
Newspaper advertisement which, through error of newspaper and without fault of advertiser, stated price for certain motor vehicle less than price newspaper was instructed to advertise, and which did not call for any performance by plaintiff reader of advertisement who stated desire to buy at advertised price, and which did not refer to several matters relating to buying of automobile, such as equipment to be furnished or warranties to be offered, did not amount to offer which could be accepted so as to form contract.

Appeal from the Circuit Court of Cook County; the Hon. WAYNE OLSON, Judge, presiding. Judgment affirmed.

John D. Vosnos, of Chicago, for appellant.

Zenoff, Westler, Jones & Kamm, of Chicago, for appellee.

*** See Callaghan's Illinois Digest, same topic and section number.**

[Illustration 3–a]

SAMPLE PAGE FROM 128 Ill.App.2d 410

O'KEEFE v. LEE CALAN IMPORTS, INC.
128 Ill App2d 410

MR. JUSTICE McNAMARA delivered the opinion of the court.

Christopher D. O'Brien brought suit against defendant

Published opinions of the Illinois Appellate Courts are printed in the official Illinois Appellate Reports.

The name of the judge writing the opinion is always given. All matter preceding this is editorial and usually consists of (1) headnotes, (2) summary of facts, (3) judgment of the court, (4) names of attorneys.

facts as set forth in the pleadings and cross-motions for summary judgment are not in dispute.

On July 31, 1966, defendant advertised a 1964 Volvo Station Wagon for sale in the Chicago Sun-Times. Defendant had instructed the newspaper to advertise the price of the automobile at $1,795. However, through an error of the newspaper and without fault on part of defendant, the newspaper inserted a price of $1,095 for said automobile in the advertisement. O'Brien visited defendant's place of business, examined the automobile and stated that he wished to purchase it for $1,095. One of defendant's salesmen at first agreed, but then refused to sell the car for the erroneous price listed in the advertisement.

Plaintiff appeals, contending that the advertisement constituted an offer on the part of defendant, which O'Brien duly accepted and thus the parties formed a binding contract. Plaintiff further contends that the advertisement constituted a memorandum in writing which satisfied the requirements of the Statute of Frauds.

[1, 2] It is elementary that in order to form a contract there must be an offer and an acceptance. A contract requires the mutual assent of the parties. Calo, Inc. v. AMF Pinspotters, Inc., 31 Ill App2d 2, 176 NE2d 1 (1961).

[Illustration 3–b]

CONCLUDING PAGE FROM 128 Ill.App.2d 410

PEOPLE v. CHILIKAS
128 Ill App2d 414

model at no additional cost. Plaintiff purchased a 1954 automobile and subsequently attempted to exchange it for a 1955 model, but was refused by defendant. The court held that the advertisement was an offer, the acceptance of which created a contract. However, in that case, the advertisement required the performance of an act by plaintiff, and in purchasing the 1954 automobile, plaintiff performed that act. In the case at bar, the advertisement did not call for any performance by plaintiff, and we conclude that it did not amount to an offer.

Because of our view of these proceedings, it is unnecessary to consider the issue of whether the newspaper advertisement constituted a memorandum in writing satisfying the requirements of the Statute of Frauds.

The judgment of the Circuit Court is affirmed.

Judgment affirmed.

DEMPSEY, P. J. and SCHWARTZ, J., concur.

An opinion always ends with the statement of the court's judgment and an indication whether the other members of the court concur or dissent from the opinion as written. Frequently, there are also written concurring or dissenting opinions.

[Illustration 4]

A TYPICAL CASE AS REPORTED IN A SET OF UNOFFICIAL REPORTS

758 Ill. 262 NORTH EASTERN REPORTER, 2d SERIES

128 Ill.App.2d 410

James L. O'KEEFE, Public Administrator of the Estate of Christopher D. O'Brien, Plaintiff-Appellant,

v.

LEE CALAN IMPORTS, INC., an Illinois Corporation, Defendant-Appellee, Third-Party Plaintiff,

v.

FIELD ENTERPRISES, INC., Third-Party Defendant.

Gen. No. 54102.

Appellate Court of Illinois, First District, Third Division.

Sept. 3, 1970.

Action to recover for alleged breach of contract for refusal to sell automobile at price quoted in newspaper advertisement. The Circuit Court, Cook County, Wayne Olson, J., granted advertiser's motion for summary judgment, and plaintiff appealed. The Appellate Court, McNamara, J., held that advertisement, which, through no fault of advertiser, contained erroneous purchase price for automobile, did not constitute offer but only invitation to make offer, and thus prospective buyer, who unsuccessfully attempted to buy such vehicle at price given in advertisement, was not entitled to recover for breach of contract.

Judgment affirmed.

1. Contracts ⚷16

To form contract there must be offer and acceptance.

2. Contracts ⚷15

Contract requires mutual assent of parties.

3. Sales ⚷22(1)

Newspaper advertisement, which, through no fault of advertiser, contained erroneous purchase price for automobile,

This is the same case as shown in Illus. 3 as it appears in the North Eastern Reporter, an unofficial set of court reports. The headnotes are prepared by the publisher's editorial staff. Note how they differ from the headnotes for this case in the Illinois Appellate Reports (Illus. 3).

Although the material preceding the opinion of the court varies in the unofficial reports from the official reports, the text of the opinion is exactly the same.

The difference between the official and unofficial reports and other features of court reports will be discussed in Chapters 4, 5, and 6.

[Illustration 4–a]

CONCLUDING PAGE FROM 262 N.E.2d 758

sewing machine was for sale at a stated price. Plaintiff visited the store, attempted to purchase the sewing machine at that price, but defendant refused. In holding that the newspaper advertisement did not constitute a binding offer, the court held that an ordinary newspaper advertisement was merely an offer to negotiate. In Ehrlich v. Willis Music Co., 93 Ohio App. 246, 113 N.E.2d 252 (1952), defendant advertised in a newspaper that a television set was for sale at a mistaken price. The actual price was ten times the advertised price. The court found that no offer had been made, but rather an invitation to patronize defendant's store. The court also held that defendant should have known that the price was a mistake. In Lovett v. Frederick Loeser & Co., 124 Misc. 81, 207 N.Y.S. 753 (1924), a newspaper advertisement offering radios for sale at 25% to 50% reductions was held to be an invitation to make an offer. Accord, People v. Gimbel Bros., 202 Misc. 229, 115 N.Y.S.2d 857 (1952).

We find that in the absence of special circumstances, a newspaper advertisement which contains an erroneous purchase price through no fault of the defendant advertiser and which contains no other terms, is not an offer which can be accepted so as to form a contract. We hold that such an advertisement amounts only to an invitation to make an offer. It seems apparent to us in the instant case, that there was no meeting of the minds nor the required mutual assent by the two parties to a precise proposition. There was no reference to several material matters relating to the purchase of an automobile, such as equipment to be furnished or warranties to be offered by defendant. Indeed the terms were so incomplete and so indefinite that they could not be regarded as a valid offer.

In Lefkowitz v. Great Minneapolis Surplus Store, 251 Minn. 188, 86 N.W.2d 689 (1957) defendant advertised a fur stole worth $139.50 for sale at a price of $1.00, but refused to sell it to plaintiff. In affirming the judgment for plaintiff, the court found that the advertisement constituted a valid offer and, upon acceptance by plaintiff, a binding contract. However in that case, unlike the instant case, there was no error in the advertisement, but rather, defendant deliberately used misleading advertising. And in *Lefkowitz,* the court held that whether an advertisement was an offer or an invitation to make an offer depended upon the intention of the parties and the surrounding circumstances.

In Johnson v. Capital City Ford Company, 85 So.2d 75 (La.App.1955), defendant advertised that anyone who purchased a 1954 automobile could exchange it for a 1955 model at no additional cost. Plaintiff purchased a 1954 automobile and subsequently attempted to exchange it for a 1955 model, but was refused by defendant. The court held that the advertisement was an offer, the acceptance of which created a contract. However, in that case, the advertisement required the performance of an act by plaintiff, and in purchasing the 1954 automobile, plaintiff performed that act. In the case at bar, the advertisement did not call for any performance by plaintiff, and we conclude that it did not amount to an offer.

Because of our view of these proceedings, it is unnecessary to consider the issue of whether the newspaper advertisement constituted a memorandum in writing satisfying the requirements of the Statute of Frauds.

The judgment of the Circuit Court is affirmed.

Judgment affirmed.

DEMPSEY, P. J., and SCHWARTZ, J., concur.

SECTION G. ABBREVIATIONS AND CITATIONS OF COURT REPORTS

Court reports are published in numbered sets [11] with the name of the set reflected in its title; for example, the *Illinois Reports* (the opinions of the Illinois Supreme Court) or the *Supreme Court Reporter* (the opinions of the Supreme Court of the United States) or the *Oil and Gas Reporter* (opinions from all U.S. jurisdictions dealing with the law of oil and gas). In all legal writing it is customary when referring to a court decision to give the name of the case and its citation in the appropriate court reports. But rather than citing to, for example, "Volume 132 of the Michigan Reports for the case starting at page 235," a citation is given using a standard format and a standard abbreviation for the name of the set of reports, e.g., 132 Mich. 235, or 41 S.Ct. 191, or 18 Oil & Gas Rptr. 1289.

It is extremely important in any legal writing to give a complete citation to the source or sources relied on in reaching one's conclusions. Tables of abbreviations should be consulted for the proper method of abbreviation, and citation manuals for proper form of citation.[12]

A Table of Abbreviations with reference to the full name of court reports is set forth in Appendix A.

SECTION H. SUMMARY

To facilitate learning the essential features of the significant publications described in the following chapters, a summary of them is provided towards the end of the various chapters. The summaries are generally arranged with the following points in mind: (1) scope —indicating coverage by subject matter and chronology, if any; (2) arrangements—for example, alphabetically by subject, by names or titles, or by chronology (following a time sequence); (3) index; and (4) supplementation.

[11] The first American decisions were reported by private reporters and were cited to the name of the reporter. In Masschusetts, for example, the first volume of court reports was reported by Williams and is cited as 1 Will.Mass.; the next sixteen volumes were reported by Tyng and are cited as 1–16 Tyng. The practice of citing to named reporters ceased in most jurisdictions during the middle of the nineteenth century.

[12] There is no universally accepted table of abbreviations or manual of citations. In addition to those in Appendix A, tables of abbreviations may be located in law dictionaries and in other books on legal bibliography. A commonly used citation manual is the *Uniform System of Citation*, published by the Harvard Law Review, Columbia Law Review, University of Pennsylvania Law Review and the Yale Law Journal.

1. Segments of a Court Decision

a. Name of the case.

b. Docket number.

c. Date of decision.

d. Synopsis, or Summary, of case.

e. Syllabus or headnote—brief summary of the legal rule or significant facts in a case.

f. Names of counsel.

g. Statement of facts.

h. Opinion of the court—explanation of the court's decision.

Concurring opinion—opinion of a judge which agrees with the decision of the majority but disagrees with the reasoning.

Dissenting opinion—expressed disagreement of one or more judges of a court with the decision reached by the majority in a case before them.

Per curiam opinion—opinion of the majority of the court as distinguished from an opinion written by a specific judge.

Memorandum opinion—a brief holding of the whole court in which the opinion (explanation) is very concise or totally absent.

Ratio decidendi—the point in a case which determines the result.

Obiter dictum—official, incidental comment, not necessary to the formulation of the decision, made by the judge in his opinion which is not binding as precedent.

i. Decision of the court—disposition of the case by the court.

2. Official and Unofficial Reports

a. Official reports—court reports directed by statute.

b. Unofficial reports—court reports published without statutory direction.

3. Elements of Judicial Reporting

a. "Slip" opinion—an individual court decision published separately soon after it is rendered.

b. Advance sheets—contain the decisions of a court or the courts of several jurisdictions decided just prior to publication and are in pamphlet format.

c. Order of release of cases is determined by their decision dates and not by a logical arrangement, such as subject.

d. A bound volume includes:

(1) Table of cases contained in the volume.

(2) Table of statutes interpreted by the decisions reported.

(3) Opinions (comprised of cases from preceding advance sheets)—written, *per curiam* or memorandum.

(4) Subject index or digest of the cases reported.

(5) Judicial definitions of words and phrases used in the cases reported.

(6) Court rules.

(7) Unofficial reports generally contain cross reference tables to the official reports.

4. Organization of Court Reports

a. Jurisdictional reports—decisions of a specific court or several courts within a system.

b. Geographical reports:

(1) Cases from several courts of a state.

(2) Regional reporters.

c. Subject reports—collections of cases on a specific subject.

Chapter 4

FEDERAL COURT DECISIONS

For present purposes, the federal court system can be described as consisting of three main divisions: The Supreme Court of the United States (the highest court), the courts of appeals (intermediate appellate courts), and the district courts (courts of original jurisdiction.)[1]

All written opinions of the Supreme Court of the United States are published in the official and unofficial reports. Most *per curiam* decisions also are reported. All written opinions designated "For publication" by the courts of appeals are unofficially published. Memorandum opinions are not published. As for the district court decisions, only selected opinions of those courts are unofficially reported. Typewritten unreported cases of the district courts generally are available through the court clerks.

SECTION A. UNITED STATES SUPREME COURT REPORTS

The decisions of the United States Supreme Court are published in five current reports:

1. United States Reports (official edition), cited "U. S."

2. United States Supreme Court Reports (Lawyers Co-operative Pub. Co.), cited "L.Ed." and "L.Ed.2d."

3. Supreme Court Reporter (West Publishing Co.), cited "Sup. Ct." or "S.Ct."

4. United States Law Week (Bureau of National Affairs), cited "U.S.L.W." or "U.S.L. Week."

5. Commerce Clearing House, United States Supreme Court Bulletin.

1. **United States Reports** (Official Edition)

Prior to 1817, the United States Reports were published by private reporters. Since that date they have been published by official reporters. The reports were cited by the name of the reporters from

[1] For a more detailed description of the federal court system, *see* HOUSE COMM. ON THE JUDICIARY, 92d CONG., 1st SESS., THE UNITED STATES COURTS: THEIR JURISDICTION AND WORK, by J. Spaniol. (Comm. Print, 1975).

Dallas through Wallace. The seven early reporters, with their abbreviations, are as follows:

Dallas (Dall.)	4 v.	v. 1– 4	U.S.	(1789–1800)
Cranch (Cranch)	9 v.	v. 5–13	U.S.	(1801–1815)
Wheaton (Wheat.)	12 v.	v. 14–25	U.S.	(1816–1827)
Peters (Peters)	16 v.	v. 26–41	U.S.	(1828–1842)
Howard (How.)	24 v.	v. 42–65	U.S.	(1843–1860)
Black (Black)	2 v.	v. 66–67	U.S.	(1861–1862)
Wallace (Wall.)	23 v.	v. 68–90	U.S.	(1863–1874)

The first ninety volumes, from Dallas through Wallace, were later numbered consecutively and beginning with volume 91 (1875) this method of numbering was adopted. 1 Dallas, although a volume of the U. S. Reports, contains only Pennsylvania decisions. The other volumes of Dallas contain U. S. Supreme Court and Pennsylvania decisions.[2]

It is the custom of the Supreme Court of the United States to have one term of court each year. The term starts in October and ordinarily adjourns in June or July. This is known as the October Term. The opinions of the Supreme Court are printed and sold by the United States Government Printing Office. They are initially issued separately as "slip" opinions and then subsequently published in advance sheets (called preliminary prints). The Reporter of Decisions of the Supreme Court prepares a summary of facts, syllabi and an index. After the end of the October Term each year, the advance sheets are replaced by bound volumes. There are usually three or four volumes per term.

Sample pages of an opinion are shown in Illustration 5.

2. United States Supreme Court Reports (Lawyers' Edition)

This set of the reports of the Supreme Court of the United States is privately published by the Lawyers Co-operative Publishing Co. and the Bancroft-Whitney Co. It is presently in two series. The first series contains all of the opinions that appear in 1 U.S. through 349 U.S. The second series commences with 350 U.S. As this set uses smaller type than do the official reports, the opinions for each term are in fewer volumes. For example, the 1976 term required five volumes for the *United States Reports,* but only two for the *Lawyers' Edition.* The opinions in it are exactly the same as the opinions that appear in the official edition. The difference lies in the editorial treatment given to the opinions by the publishers, who prepare their own summary of cases and headnotes which precede the

[2] Keefe, *More Than You Want to Know About Supreme Court Reports,* 62 A.B.A.J. 1057 (1976).

opinions. Additionally, an appendix to each volume contains, for selected important cases only, summaries of attorneys' briefs submitted to the Court and annotations written by the editorial staff of the publishers. Annotations are articles or essays on significant legal issues discussed in the reported cases. These are very useful in gaining an understanding of the impact and meaning of the decisions. Annotations will be discussed in more detail in Chapter Seven. A separate volume supplements the annotations in Volumes 1–31 of the *Lawyers' Edition*, Second Series. Starting with Volume 32 of the Second Series, each volume is provided with pocket supplementation in the back of the volume. Pocket supplementation is in three parts: (1) *Citator Service*, consisting of brief summaries of the pertinent holdings from Supreme Court opinions subsequent to those reported in the volume, (2) *Later Case Service*, supplementing the annotations in the volume, and (3) *Court Corrections*, consisting of any corrections made by Justices of the Supreme Court after the volume was printed.

In 1978, a *Desk-Book to the United States Supreme Court Reports, Lawyers' Edition*, was published. This volume contains (1) a Table of Cases for all full decisions found in volumes 1–49 of L.Ed. 2d, (2) a Table of Justices of the Supreme Court of the United States since 1789, and (3) an index to all annotations in L.Ed.2d or in ALR Federal. An annual supplement is issued.

Current decisions are issued biweekly in advance sheets during the course of each term. The pagination of the advance sheets is the same as in subsequent bound volumes, but they do not contain annotations.

3. **Supreme Court Reporter** (West Edition)

This set is published by the West Publishing Co. and contains many of the editorial features common to their other sets of law reports. These will be discussed in detail in Chapter Five. This edition begins with volume 106 (1882) of the official set; therefore, it does not contain the cases reported in volumes 1–105 of the official reports. The full text of the opinions is reported with the publisher adding its own editorial features and headnotes. Decisions are first issued in advance sheets biweekly during the term of Court, and after the adjournment of the Court the advance sheets are replaced by two or more bound volumes containing all of the decisions of the term. Sample pages from the *Supreme Court Reporter* are shown in Illustration Six.

4. **Other Publications**

As the decisions of the Supreme Court of the United States become the "law of the land" and must be followed as precedent by all other American courts, both federal and state, it is rather obvious that lawyers as well as lay persons have a need for immediate access to the current decisions of the Supreme Court of the United States. Before opinions can be published in the advance sheets of the sets mentioned above, they must receive editorial treatment such as preparing the summary and the headnotes, resulting in a delay of several weeks from the date a decision is rendered and its appearance in advance sheets.

More rapid access to current U. S. Supreme Court decisions is available through one of the two following publications. Each receives the slip decisions on the day they are handed down, photocopies them, and mails them weekly to its subscribers. These sets of Supreme Court opinions have few editorial features added to them, but they do allow opinions to become available within a week after they have been released by the Supreme Court.

a. *United States Law Week*

This is published in two or more looseleaf volumes by the Bureau of National Affairs, Inc. in Washington, D. C. Volume One contains the Supreme Court of the United States opinions in complete text and is in looseleaf form. In addition to the current opinions, this volume contains the following features:

(1) Summary of Orders: This is a summary of cases finally acted upon as well as the lower court holdings that the Supreme Court consented to review with the questions presented for review.

(2) Journal of Proceedings: This contains the minutes of all sessions of the Court held during the week.

(3) Cases Docketed: This includes citations to opinions in the lower court, and the general subject matter of the case.

(4) Summary of Cases Recently Filed.

(5) Arguments Before the Court: A summary of the oral arguments of the more important cases argued each week.

(6) Table of Cases and the Case Status Report: Issued every three to four weeks. For most cases the user can determine the current status of a case by consulting this table.

(7) Topical Index: Issued seven times annually.

Volume Two deals with other matters not connected with the Supreme Court of the United States.

b. *Commerce Clearing House Supreme Court Bulletin*

This set is also in looseleaf format. In addition to photocopies of the current opinions, it includes an index to opinions, an index to docket numbers and a status table of cases pending before the Court.

5. Chamber Opinions of Supreme Court Justices

Each Supreme Court Justice is assigned at the beginning of each term the supervision of one or more federal judicial circuits. Frequently, when the Supreme Court is not in session, a petition may be directed to a Justice in his capacity as Circuit Justice. When an opinion is written on this, it is known as a "Chamber Opinion." Before the 1970 Term, these chamber opinions appeared only in *Lawyers' Edition* and the *Supreme Court Reporter.* Starting with the 1970 Term, they also appear in the official *United States Reports.*[3]

6. Summary of United States Supreme Court Reports

The opinions of the Supreme Court of the United States are published in three sets: the official *United States Reports,* the *United States Supreme Court Reports, Lawyers' Edition,* and the *Supreme Court Reporter.* Each set first publishes the opinions in advance sheets. As proper citation practice calls for only citing to *United States Reports,* the two unofficial sets which have their own distinct pagination also show the pagination of the official reports so that the proper citation can be made to the *United States Reports.* This is sometimes denoted as "star-pagination." [See Illustration 7–c] Both the *Lawyers' Edition* and the *Supreme Court Reporter* have in each volume a cross reference table listing the cases in the *United States Reports* and showing where they are reported in their volumes.

As the United States Government Printing Office is much slower in publishing its advance sheets, and as the two unofficial sets have editorial features facilitating their use, most lawyers and researchers prefer using them to the *United States Reports.*

United States Law Week and the *Commerce Clearing House Supreme Court Bulletin* are most useful for use during the current term of the Court. For older decisions it is preferable to use one of the three other sets.

SECTION B. LOWER FEDERAL COURT REPORTS

Although the Supreme Court of the United States is the highest court in the country, it actively deals with a small fraction of the total litigation within the Federal court system. With certain exceptions, the Supreme Court selects only the cases it wishes to hear on

[3] R. STERN AND E. GRESSMAN, SUPREME COURT PRACTICE 811–913 (5th ed. 1978); Wiener, *Opinions of Justices Sitting in Chambers,* 49 LAW LIB.J. 2 (1956); Boner, *Index to Chambers Opinions of Supreme Court Justices,* 65 LAW LIB.J. 213 (1972).

appeal[4] and they are relatively few in number. The bulk of the work of the Federal courts occurs in its trial courts—the federal district courts and in the appeals from them to the United States courts of appeals. These are divided geographically into twelve circuits.

In addition to the above-discussed courts, there exist federal courts with limited or specialized jurisdiction. The more important ones are the Court of Claims, the Court of Customs and Patent Appeals, and the Tax Court.[5]

1. Privately Published Editions of Lower Federal Court Reports

a. *Federal Cases*

Prior to 1880, the decisions of the district courts and the circuit courts of appeals were published in many different sets of law reports. In 1880, the West Publishing Company reprinted all of the previously reported lower federal court decisions in one set of 31 volumes called *Federal Cases*. This set contains 18,000 cases reported between 1789 and 1879. Unlike most sets of court reports where the cases are arranged chronologically, the decisions in this set are arranged alphabetically by name of case and are numbered consecutively. Volume 31 is the Digest volume, and includes Blue Tables which cross reference from the citations of the original volumes of reports to *Federal Cases*.

b. *Federal Reporter*

This set is published by the West Publishing Company and started in 1880. Until 1932 it included opinions from the court of appeals and the federal district courts. The *Federal Reporter* consists of two series. The First Series stopped with Volume 300 and the Second Series started numbering anew from Volume 1. This scheme of starting a new series for the numbering of court reports is a common one, as it serves to avoid long and unmanageable numbers.

Until recently, nearly all written opinions of the courts of appeals were published in the *Federal Reporter*. The increasing caseload placed on the courts, however, has caused reconsideration of this practice[6] and all circuits have now adopted rules restricting the number of published opinions.[7]

[4] Technically, cases reach the Supreme Court either by Writ of Certiorari or by Appeal. *See* R. STERN AND E. GRESSMAN, *supra* fn. 3 at Chapters 2 and 3.

[5] For a history of the development of the Federal Judicial System, *see* C. WRIGHT, HANDBOOK ON THE LAW OF FEDERAL COURTS 1–5 (3d ed. 1976).

[6] NLRB v. Amalgamated Clothing Workers, 430 F.2d 966, 971 (5th Cir. 1970).

[7] Jacobstein, *Some Reflections on the Control of the Publication of Appellate Court Opinions*, 27 STAN.L.REV. 791, 796 (1975).

Since Volume 34 of the Second Series (1929), the *Federal Reporter* includes the reports of the United States Court of Customs and Patent Appeals and in Volume 276 it began to include the decisions of the United States Court of Claims. The *Federal Reporter* also reports the decisions of the Temporary Emergency Court of Appeals.

c. *Federal Supplement*

This set started publication in 1933 and is also published by the West Publishing Co. It contains selected opinions of the federal district courts. As these courts are the trial courts within the Federal court system, they are exceptions to the general rule that only appellate court opinions are reported. It must, however, be emphasized that only a very small percentage of the cases heard in the federal district courts are ever reported in the *Federal Supplement.* From Volume 1 to Volume 181 it also contained the decisions of the United States Court of Claims and in Volume 135, it began to include the decisions of the United States Customs Court (now the Court of International Trade). The *Federal Supplement* also includes decisions of the Special Court of the Regional Rail Reorganization Act and rulings of the Judicial Panel on Multidistrict Litigation. Since 1880 there have not been any officially published sets of reports for the federal courts of appeals and the federal district courts. The *Federal Reporter* and the *Federal Supplement* are relied on for these reports. Both of these sets are first issued in advance sheets and subsequently replaced by bound volumes.

Many federal district court decisions can be located only by consulting a looseleaf service (discussed in Chapter 14) covering a narrow subject area. These services make a special effort to make such decisions available to subscribers though the case may not be important enough for a general reporter like the *Federal Supplement.*

d. *Federal Rules Decisions*

This set will be discussed in Chapter Twelve.

2. Officially Published Reports of Special Federal Courts

Cases decided in the Court of Claims. Washington, Government Printing Office, 1863 to date. v. 1 et seq.

U. S. Court of Customs Appeals and U. S. Court of Customs and Patent Appeals. Reports. Washington, Government Printing Office, 1911 to date. v. 1 et seq. (Customs). 1929 to date. v. 1 et seq. (Patents).

U. S. Customs Court. Reports. Washington, Government Printing Office, July 1938 to date. v. 1 et seq. (now the Court of International Trade).

Tax Court of the United States. Reports. Washington, Government Printing Office, Oct. 1942 to date. v. 1 et seq. (now the United States Tax Court).

SECTION C. ILLUSTRATIONS

The opinion of TVA v. Hill [437 U.S. 153, 98 S.Ct. 2279, 57 L.Ed. 2d 117] as it is published in:

5. Advance Sheets (Preliminary Print) to the U.S. Reports (Official)

6. Bound Volume to the Supreme Court Reporter (West Publishing Co.)

7. Bound Volume 57 of the Lawyers' Edition of the United States Supreme Court Reports (Lawyers Co-operative Publishing Co.)

[Illustration 5]

TVA v. HILL AS REPORTED IN THE ADVANCE SHEETS OF THE UNITED STATES REPORTS

TVA *v.* HILL 153

Syllabus

TENNESSEE VALLEY AUTHORITY *v.* HILL ET AL.

CERTIORARI TO THE UNITED STATES COURT OF APPEALS FOR THE SIXTH CIRCUIT

No. 76-1701. Argued April 18, 1978—Decided June 15, 1978

The Endangered Species Act of 1973 (Act) authorizes the Secretary of the Interior (Secretary) in § 4 to declare a species of life "endangered." Section 7 specifies that all "Federal departments and agencies shall, . . . with the assistance of the Secretary, utilize their authorities in furtherance of the purposes of [the] Act by carrying out programs for the conservation of endangered species . . . and by taking such action necessary to insure that actions authorized, funded, or carried out by them do not jeopardize the continued existence of such endangered species and threatened species or result in the destruction or modification of habitat of such species which is determined by the Secretary . . . to be critical." Shortly after the Act's passage the Secretary was petitioned to list a small fish popularly known as the snail darter as an endangered species under the Act. Thereafter the Secretary made the designation. Having determined that the snail darter apparently lives only in that portion of the Little Tennessee River that would be completely inundated by the impoundment of the reservoir created as a consequence of the completion of the Tellico Dam, he declared that area as the snail darter's "critical habitat." Notwithstanding the near completion of the multimillion-dollar dam, the Secretary issued a regulation in which it was declared that, pursuant to § 7, "all Federal agencies must take such action as is necessary to ensure that actions authorized, funded, or carried out by them do not result in the destruction or modification of this critical habitat area." Respondents brought this

This page is taken from the Advance Sheets to the U.S. Reports. As customary, indication is given to the court from which the case is being appealed.

Note that docket number, date of argument, and date of decision are also given.

[Illustration 5–a]

SAMPLE PAGE FROM 437 U.S.

154 OCTOBER TERM, 1977

Syllabus 437 U. S.

judgment of the District Court and ordered that court permanently to enjoin completion of the project "until Congress by appropriate legis-

Each opinion is preceded by a summary and the syllabus, prepared by the Reporter of Decisions.

Congress to encompass the terminal phases of ongoing projects. At various times before, during, and after the foregoing judicial proceedings, TVA represented to congressional Appropriations Committees that the Act did not prohibit completion of the Tellico Project and described its efforts to transplant the snail darter. The Committees consistently recommended appropriations for the dam, sometimes stating their views that the Act did not prohibit completion of the dam at its advanced stage, and Congress each time approved TVA's general budget, which contained funds for the dam's continued construction. *Held:*

1. The Endangered Species Act prohibits impoundment of the Little Tennessee River by the Tellico Dam. Pp. 172–193.

(a) The language of § 7 is plain and makes no exception such as that urged by petitioner whereby the Act would not apply to a project like Tellico that was well under way when Congress passed the Act. Pp. 172–174.

(b) It is clear from the Act's legislative history that Congress intended to halt and reverse the trend toward species extinction—whatever the cost. The pointed omission of the type of qualified language previously included in endangered species legislation reveals a conscious congressional design to give endangered species priority over the "primary missions" of federal agencies. Congress, moreover, foresaw that § 7 would on occasion require agencies to alter ongoing projects in order to fulfill the Act's goals. Pp. 174–187.

(c) None of the limited "hardship exemptions" provided in the Act would even remotely apply to the Tellico Project. P. 188.

(d) Though statements in Appropriations Committee Reports reflected the view of the Committees either that the Act did not apply to Tellico or that the dam should be completed regardless of the Act's provisions, nothing in the TVA appropriations measures passed by Congress stated that the Tellico Project was to be completed regardless of the Act's requirements. To find a repeal under these circumstances, as petitioner has urged, would violate the " 'cardinal rule . . . that repeals by implication are not favored.' " *Morton* v. *Mancari,* 417 U. S. 535, 549. The

[Illustration 5–b]

SAMPLE PAGE FROM 437 U.S.

doctrine disfavoring repeals by implication applies with full vigor when the subsequent legislation is an appropriations measure. When voting on appropriations measures, legislators are entitled to assume that the funds will be devoted to purposes that are lawful and not for any purpose forbidden. A contrary policy would violate the express rules of both Houses of Congress, which provide that appropriations measures may not change existing substantive law. An appropriations committee's expression does not operate to repeal or modify substantive legislation. Pp. 189–193.

2. The Court of Appeals did not err in ordering that completion of the Tellico Dam, which would have violated the Act, be enjoined. Congress has spoken in the plainest words, making it clear that endangered species are to be accorded the highest priorities. Since that legislative power has been exercised, it is up to the Executive Branch to administer the law and for the Judiciary to enforce it when, as here, enforcement has been sought. Pp. 193–194.

549 F. 2d 1064, affirmed.

BURGER, C. J., delivered the opinion of the Court, in which BRENNAN, STEWART, WHITE, MARSHALL, and STEVENS, JJ., joined. POWELL, J., filed a dissenting opinion, in which BLACKMUN, J., joined, *post*, p. 195. REHNQUIST, J., filed a dissenting opinion, *post*, p. 211.

Attorney General Bell argued the cause for petitioner. On the briefs were *Acting Solicitor General Friedman, Deputy Solicitor General Barnett, Herbert S. Sanger, Jr., Richard A. Allen, Charles A. Wagner III, Thomas A. Pedersen,* and *Nicholas A. Della Volpe.*

Zygmunt J. B. Plater argued the cause for respondents. With him on the brief was *W. P. Boone Dougherty.**

The third page of the TVA opinion. Note the indication as to which Justice wrote the opinion, which Justices agreed with the opinion, and which dissented.

Note also how the names of the attorneys who were involved in the case before the Supreme Court are given.

[Illustration 5–c]

SAMPLE PAGE FROM 437 U.S.

156 OCTOBER TERM, 1977

Opinion of the Court 437 U.S.

MR. CHIEF JUSTICE BURGER delivered the opinion of the Court.

The questions presented in this case are (a) whether the Endangered Species Act of 1973 requires a court to enjoin the operation of a virtually completed federal dam—which had been authorized prior to 1973—when, pursuant to authority vested in him by Congress, the Secretary of the Interior has determined that operation of the dam would eradicate an endangered species; and (b) whether continued congressional appropriations for the dam after 1973 constituted an implied repeal of the Endangered Species Act, at least as to the particular dam.

I

The Little Tennessee River originates in the mountains of northern Georgia and flows through the national forest lands of North Carolina into Tennessee, where it converges with the Big Tennessee River near Knoxville. The lower 33 miles of the Little Tennessee takes the river's clear, free-flowing waters through an area of great natural beauty. Among other environmental amenities, this stretch of river is said to contain abundant trout. Considerable historical importance attaches

The first page of the actual opinion. All material preceding the name of the Justice writing the opinion is editorial and not considered part of the opinion.

---

[1] This description is taken from the opinion of the District Judge in the first litigation involving the Tellico Dam and Reservoir Project. *Environmental Defense Fund* v. *TVA,* 339 F. Supp. 806, 808 (ED Tenn. 1972). In his opinion, "all of these benefits of the present Little Tennessee River Valley will be destroyed by impoundment of the river . . . ." *Ibid.* The District Judge noted that "[t]he free-flowing river is the likely habitat of one or more of seven rare or endangered fish species." *Ibid.*

[Illustration 5–d]

SAMPLE PAGE FROM 437 U.S.

TVA *v.* HILL 195

153 POWELL, J., dissenting

sit as a committee of review, nor are we vested with the power of veto. The lines ascribed to Sir Thomas More by Robert Bolt are not without relevance here:

> "The law, Roper, the law. I know what's legal, not what's right. And I'll stick to what's legal. . . . I'm *not* God. The currents and eddies of right and wrong, which you find such plain-sailing, I can't navigate, I'm no voyager. But in the thickets of the law, oh there I'm a forester. . . . What would you do? Cut a great road through the law to get after the Devil? . . . And when the last law was down, and the Devil turned round on you—where would

Last page of majority opinion and the judgment of the Court.
Beginning of the first dissenting opinion.

> Seasons, Act I, p. 147 (Three Plays, Heinemann ed. 1967).

We agree with the Court of Appeals that in our constitutional system the commitment to the separation of powers is too fundamental for us to pre-empt congressional action by judicially decreeing what accords with "common sense and the public weal." Our Constitution vests such responsibilities in the political branches.

Affirmed.

MR. JUSTICE POWELL, with whom MR. JUSTICE BLACKMUN joins, dissenting.

The Court today holds that § 7 of the Endangered Species Act requires a federal court, for the purpose of protecting an endangered species or its habitat, to enjoin permanently the operation of any federal project, whether completed or substantially completed. This decision casts a long shadow over the operation of even the most important projects, serving

[Illustration 5–e]

SAMPLE PAGE FROM 437 U.S.

unnecessary action by interpreting a statute to produce a result no one intended.

MR. JUSTICE REHNQUIST, dissenting.

In the light of my Brother POWELL's dissenting opinion, I am far less convinced than is the Court that the Endangered Species Act of 1973, 16 U. S. C. § 1531 *et seq.* (1976 ed.), was intended to prohibit the completion of the Tellico Dam. But the very difficulty and doubtfulness of the correct answer to this legal question convinces me that the Act did *not* prohibit the District Court from refusing, in the exercise of its traditional equitable powers, to enjoin petitioner from completing the Dam. Section 11 (g)(1) of the Act, 16 U. S. C. § 1540 (g)(1) (1976 ed.), merely provides that "any person may commence a civil suit on his own behalf . . . to enjoin any person,

First page of second dissenting opinion.

Not all opinions have dissenting opinions. Some cases will also have written concurring opinions.

This Court had occasion in *Hecht Co.* v. *Bowles,* 321 U. S. 321 (1944), to construe language in an Act of Congress that lent far greater support to a conclusion that Congress intended an injunction to issue as a matter of right than does the language just quoted. There the Emergency Price Control Act of 1942 provided that

> "[u]pon a showing by the Administrator that [a] person has engaged or is about to engage in any [acts or practices violative of this Act] a permanent or temporary injunction, restraining order, or other order *shall be granted* without bond." 56 Stat. 33 (emphasis added).

But in *Hecht* this Court refused to find even in such language an intent on the part of Congress to require that a

[Illustration 6]
SAMPLE PAGE FROM 98 S.Ct.

437 U.S. 153, 57 L.Ed.2d 117

TENNESSEE VALLEY AUTHORITY, Petitioner,

v.

Hiram G. HILL, Jr., et al.

No. 76-1701.

Argued April 18, 1978.

Decided June 15, 1978.

Environmental groups and others brought action under Endangered Species Act of 1973 to enjoin Tennessee Valley Authority from completing dam and impounding section of Little Tennessee River. The United States District Court for the Eastern District of Tennessee, 419 F.Supp. 753, refused a permanent injunction, and plaintiffs appealed. The Court of Appeals, 549 F.2d 1064, reversed and remanded, and certiorari was granted. The Supreme Court, Mr. Chief Justice Burger, held that Endangered Species Act of 1973 prohibited completion of dam, where operation of dam would either eradicate known population of the snail darter, an endangered species, or destroy its critical habitat, even though dam was virtually completed and even though Congress continued to appropriate large sums of public money on project even after congressional appropriations committees were apprised of project's apparent impact upon survival of snail darter.

Affirmed.

Mr. Justice Powell, with whom Mr. Justice Blackmun joined, filed dissenting opinion.

Mr. Justice Rehnquist filed a dissenting opinion.

1. Fish ⚩12

Where completion and operation of dam by Tennessee Valley Authority would either eradicate known population of the snail darter, an endangered species, or destroy its critical habitat, completion and operation of dam were prohibited by explicit provisions of Endangered Species Act, even though dam was virtually completed and even though Congress continued to appropriate large sums of public money for project after congressional appropriations committees were advised of project's apparent impact upon survival of snail darter. Endangered Species Act of 1973, § 7, 16 U.S.C.A. § 1536.

2. Fish ⚩12
Game ⚩3½

The first page of the TVA opinion as it appears in the bound volume of the Supreme Court Reporter, an unofficial set published by West Publishing Co. The summary is prepared by its editors.

Under Endangered Species Act of 1973, Congress intended protection of endangered species to be afforded highest of priorities. Endangered Species Act of 1973, § 7, 16 U.S.C.A. § 1536.

4. Statutes ⚩190

When confronted with statute which is plain and unambiguous on its face, courts ordinarily do not look to legislative history as guide to its meaning.

5. Fish ⚩9

Plain intent of Congress in enacting Endangered Species Act of 1973 was to halt and reverse trend towards species extinction, whatever the cost. Endangered Species Act of 1973, § 7, 16 U.S.C.A. § 1536.

6. Fish ⚩12
Game ⚩3½

Pointed omission, in Endangered Species Act of 1973, of type of qualifying language previously included in endangered species legislation revealed conscious decision by Congress to give endangered species priority over the "primary missions" of federal agencies. Public Works Appropriations

[Illustration 6–a]
SAMPLE PAGE FROM 98 S.Ct.

437 U.S. 154 TENNESSEE VALLEY AUTHORITY v. HILL 2281

Cite as 98 S.Ct. 2279 (1978)

15. Injunction ⇐1

Since equitable remedies are usually discretionary, balancing of equities and hardships is generally appropriate as guide to chancellor's discretion.

16. Constitutional Law ⇐50

While it is province and duty of judicial department to say what the law is, it is equally the exclusive province of Congress not only to formulate legislative policies, mandate programs and projects, but also to establish their relative priority for the Nation, and, once Congress, exercising its delegated powers, has decided the order of priorities in a given area, it is for the executive to administer the laws and for the courts to enforce them when enforcement is sought.

17. Constitutional Law ⇐70.3(4)

Court's appraisal of wisdom or unwisdom of particular course consciously selected by Congress is to be put aside in process of interpreting a statute, and once meaning of enactment is discerned and its constitutionality determined, judicial process comes to an end; a court does not sit as a committee of review, nor is a court vested with power of veto.

Syllabus *

The Endangered Species Act of 1973 (Act) authorizes the Secretary of the Interior (Secretary) in § 4 to declare a species of life "endangered." Section 7 specifies that all "federal departments and agencies shall, . . . with the assistance of the Secretary, utilize their authorities in furtherance of the purposes of [the] Act by carrying out programs for the conservation of endangered species . . . and by taking such action necessary to insure that actions authorized, funded, or carried out by them do not jeopardize the continued existence of such endangered species and threatened species or result in the destruction or modification of habitat of such species which is determined by the Secretary . . . to be critical." Shortly after the Act's passage the Secretary was petitioned to list a small fish popularly known as the snail darter as an endangered species under the Act. Thereafter the Secretary made the designation. Having determined that the snail darter apparently lives only in that portion of the Little Tennessee River that would be completely inundated by the impoundment of the reservoir created as a consequence of the completion of the Tellico Dam, he declared that area as the snail

Note how 17 headnotes have been assigned to this case. The significance of headnotes will be discussed in Chapter 6.

While the summary as shown in Illustration 6 and the headnotes are prepared by the editorial staff of the publisher, note how the syllabus is reproduced in its entirety from the official U.S. Reports.

"[a]t some point in time a federal project becomes so near completion and so incapable of modification that a court of equity should not apply a statute enacted long after inception of the project produce an unreasonable result. . . ." The Court of Appeals reversed and ⊥ordered the District Court permanently to enjoin completion of the project "until Congress, by appropriate legislation, exempts Tellico from compliance with the Act or the snail darter has been deleted from the list of endangered species or its critical habitat materially redefined." The court held that the rec- ⊥154

* The syllabus constitutes no part of the opinion of the Court but has been prepared by the Reporter of Decisions for the convenience of the reader. See *United States v. Detroit Timber & Lumber Co.*, 200 U.S. 321, 337, 26 S.Ct. 282, 287, 50 L.Ed. 499.

[Illustration 6–b]

SAMPLE PAGE FROM 98 S.Ct.

2302 98 SUPREME COURT REPORTER 437 U.S. 194

cally—the exclusive province of the Congress not only to formulate legislative policies and mandate programs and projects, but also to establish their relative priority for the Nation. Once Congress, exercising its delegated powers, has decided the order of priorities in a given area, it is for the Executive to administer the laws and for the courts to enforce them when enforcement is sought.

Here we are urged to view the Endangered Species Act "reasonably," and hence shape a remedy "that accords with some modicum of common sense and the public weal." *Post,* at 2302. But is that our function? We have no expert knowledge on the subject of endangered species, much less do we have a mandate from the people to strike a balance of equities on the side of the Tellico Dam. Congress has spoken in the plainest of words, making it abundantly clear that the balance has been struck in favor of affording endangered species the highest of priorities, thereby adopting a policy which it described as "institutionalized caution." . .

[17] Our individual appraisal of the wisdom or unwisdom of a particular course consciously selected by the Congress is to be put aside in the process of interpreting a statute. Once the meaning of an enactment is discerned and its constitutionality determined, the judicial process comes to an
195 end. We do not ⌊sit as a committee of review, nor are we vested with the power of veto. The lines ascribed to Sir Thomas More by Robert Bolt are not without relevance here:

> "The law, Roper, the law. I know what's legal, not what's right. And I'll stick to what's legal. . . . I'm *not* God. The currents and eddies of right and wrong, which you find such plain-sailing, I can't navigate, I'm no voyager. But in the thickets of the law, oh there I'm a forester. . . . What would you do? Cut a great road through the law to get after the Devil? . . . And when the last law was down, and the Devil turned round on you—where would you hide, Roper, the laws all being flat? . . . This country's planted thick with laws from coast to coast—Man's laws, not God's—and if you cut them down . . . d'you really think you could stand upright in the winds that would blow then? . . . Yes, I'd give the Devil benefit of law, for my own safety's sake." R. Bolt, A Man for All Seasons, Act I, p. 147 (Three Plays, Heinemann ed. 1967).

We agree with the Court of Appeals that in our constitutional system the commitment to the separation of powers is too fundamental for us to pre-empt congressional action by judicially decreeing what accords with "common sense and the public weal." Our Constitution vests such responsibilities in the political branches.

Affirmed.

Mr. Justice POWELL, with whom Mr.

This is the last page of the majority opinion. All cases in the S.Ct. Reporter are exactly the same as in the official U.S. Reports. Only the editorial material preceding the majority opinion differs.

Note, however, the smaller typeface. This allows the unofficial reports to reproduce cases of each term in fewer volumes.

discovered. Nor can I believe that Con-

1. Attorney General Bell advised us at oral argument that the dam had been completed, that all that remains is to "[c]lose the gate," and to complete the construction of "some roads and bridges." The "dam itself is finished. All the landscaping has been done . . . [I]t is completed." Tr. of Oral Arg. 18.

[Illustration 7]

TVA v. HILL AS REPORTED IN 57 L.Ed.2d

[437 US 153]

TENNESSEE VALLEY AUTHORITY, Petitioner,

v

HIRAM G. HILL, Jr., et al.

437 US 153, 57 L Ed 2d 117, 98 S Ct 2279

[No. 76–1701]

Argued April 18, 1978. Decided June 15, 1978.

SUMMARY

The Tennessee Valley Authority began constructing the Tellico Dam and Reservoir Project on a stretch of the Little Tennessee River in 1967, shortly after Congress appropriated initial funds for development. Subsequently, after passage of the Endangered Species Act of 1973 (16 USCS §§ 1531 et seq.), the Secretary of the Interior, acting pursuant to § 4 of the Act (16 USCS § 1533), declared that a species of small fish popularly known as the "snail darter" was an "endangered species" under the Act. Having determined that the snail darter apparently lived only in that portion of the

First page of the <u>TVA</u> decision as it appears in the bound volume of L.Ed.2d.

Summary is prepared by the publisher's editorial staff.

Note the citations to the other two sets of reports of opinions of the U.S. Supreme Court.

reservoir on the ground that such would violate the Act by causing the snail darter's extinction. Despite finding that creation of the reservoir would possibly completely destroy the snail darter's critical habitat, making it highly probable that the darter's continued existence would be jeopardized, the District Court refused an injunction and dismissed the complaint (419 F Supp 753). On appeal, the United States Court of Appeals for the Sixth Circuit, having determined that closure of the nearly-completed, multimil-

Briefs of Counsel, p 1173, infra.

117

[Illustration 7–a]

SAMPLE PAGE FROM 57 L.Ed.2d

lion dollar Tellico Dam would violate the Act, reversed and remanded with instructions that a permanent injunction issue so as to halt all activities incident to the Tellico Project which would destroy or modify the snail darter's critical habitat (549 F2d 1064).

On certiorari, the United States Supreme Court affirmed. In an opinion by Burger, Ch. J., joined by Brennan, Stewart, White, Marshall, and Stevens, JJ., it was held that (1) the Endangered Species Act prohibited the TVA from impounding the river, notwithstanding that the Tellico Dam had been well under construction when the Act was passed and when the snail darter had been declared an endangered species, and notwithstanding that Congress, in every year since the starting of the dam (even after the

Note references to other related publications of the publisher. These will be discussed in later chapters.

discovered.

Rehnquist, J., dissented on the ground that the Endangered Species Act did not prohibit the District Court from refusing, in the exercise of its traditional equitable powers, to enjoin completion of the dam.

TOTAL CLIENT-SERVICE LIBRARY® REFERENCES

35 Am Jur 2d, Fish and Game § 50
16 USCS §§ 1531 et seq.
US L Ed Digest, Fish and Fisheries § 4; Injunction § 72
ALR Digests, Fish and Fisheries §§ 9, 16
L Ed Index to Annos, Conservation; Fish
ALR Quick Index, Conservation; Fish and Fisheries
Federal Quick Index, Conservation; Endangered Species Act; Environment and Environmental Law; Fish and Game

ANNOTATION REFERENCE

Validity, construction, and application of Endangered Species Act of 1973 (16 USCS §§ 1531–1543). 32 ALR Fed 332.

[Illustration 7–b]

SAMPLE PAGE FROM 57 L.Ed.2d

TVA v HILL

437 US 153, 57 L Ed 2d 117, 98 S Ct 2279

the Act reasonably and to shape a remedy that will accord with some modicum of commonsense and the public weal.

Statutes § 80 — interpretation — wisdom

16. In the process of interpreting a statute, the United States Supreme Court's individual appraisal of the wisdom or unwisdom of a particular course consciously selected by Congress is to be put aside.

Supreme Court of the United States § 3 — power

17. The United States Supreme Court does not sit as a committee of review, nor is it vested with the power of veto.

SYLLABUS BY REPORTER OF DECISIONS

The Endangered Species Act of 1973 (Act) authorizes the Secretary of the Interior (Secretary) in § 4 to declare a species of life "endangered." Section 7 specifies that all "Federal departments and agencies shall, . . . with the assistance of the Secretary, utilize their authorities in furtherance of the purposes

The headnotes in the Lawyers' Edition of the U.S. Supreme Court Reports are prepared by the publisher's editorial staff and differ from those in the U.S. Reports and the Supreme Court Reporter.

. . . to be critical. Shortly after the Act's passage the Secretary was petitioned to list a small fish popularly known as the snail darter as an endangered species under the Act. Thereafter the Secretary made the designation. Having determined that the snail darter apparently lives only in that portion of the Little Tennessee River that would be completely inundated by the impoundment of the reservoir created as a consequence of the completion of the Tellico Dam, he declared that area as the snail darter's "critical habitat." Notwithstanding the near completion of the multimillion-dollar dam, the Secretary issued a regulation, in which it was declared that, pursuant to § 7, "all Federal agencies must take such action as is necessary to ensure that actions authorized, funded, or carried out by them do not result in the destruction or modification of this critical habitat area." Respondents brought this suit to enjoin completion of the dam and impoundment of the reservoir, claiming that those actions would violate the Act by causing the snail darter's extinction. The District Court after trial denied relief and dismissed the complaint. Though finding that the impoundment of the reservoir would probably jeopardize the snail darter's continued existence, the court noted

ment of the District Court and ordered that court permanently to enjoin completion of the project "until Congress, by appropriate legislation, exempts Tellico from compliance with the Act or the snail darter has been deleted from the list of endangered species or its critical habitat materially redefined." The court held that the record revealed a prima facie violation of § 7 in that Tennessee Valley Authority had failed to take necessary action to avoid jeopardizing the snail darter's critical habitat by its "actions." The court thus rejected the contention that the word "actions" as used in § 7 was not intended by Congress to encompass the terminal phases of ongoing projects. At various times before, during, and after the foregoing judicial proceedings, TVA represented to congressional Appropriations Committees that the Act did not prohibit completion of the Tellico Project and described its efforts to transplant the snail darter.

121

[Illustration 7-c]

SAMPLE PAGE FROM 57 L.Ed.2d

prior statute has been superseded. See United States v Langston, 118 US 389, 393, 30 L Ed 164, 6 S Ct 1185 (1886). But these precedents are inapposite. There was no effort here to "bootstrap" a post-enactment view of prior legislation by isolated statements of individual Congressmen. Nor is this a case where Congress, without explanation or comment upon the statute in question, merely has voted apparently inconsistent financial

[437 US 210]

support in subsequent appropriations Acts. Testimony on this precise issue was presented before congressional committees, and the committee reports for three consecutive years addressed the problem and affirmed their understanding of the original congressional intent. We cannot assume—as the Court suggests—that Congress, when it continued each year to approve the recommended appropriations, was unaware of the contents of the supporting committee reports. All this amounts to strong corroborative evidence that the interpretation of § 7 as not applying to completed or substantially completed

interpretation of the Act that requires the waste of at least $53 million, see n 6, supra, and denies the people of the Tennessee Valley area the benefits of the reservoir that Congress intended to confer.[19] There will be little sentiment to leave this dam standing before an empty reservoir, serving no purpose other than a conversation piece for incredulous tourists.

But more far reaching than the adverse effect on the people of this economically depressed area is the continuing threat to the operation of every federal project, no matter how important to the Nation. If Congress acts expeditiously, as may be anticipated, the Court's decision probably will have no lasting adverse consequences. But I had not thought it to be the province of this Court to force Congress into otherwise

[437 US 211]

unnecessary action by interpreting a statute to produce a result no one intended.

Mr. Justice **Rehnquist,** dissenting.

In the light of my Brother Pow-

Last page of the first dissenting opinion.

The opinions as they appear in each of the three sets of the reports of the U.S. Supreme Court are the same. Only the editorial treatment of the summary, the headnotes, and other materials differ in each set.

Note the references to the pages of this case in the U.S. Reports. These cross-references are also given in the bound volumes of the Supreme Court Reports.

that body will wish to defend an

of the Act, 16 USC § 1540(g)(1)

19. The Court acknowledges, as it must, that the permanent injunction it grants today will require "the sacrifice of the anticipated benefits of the project and of many millions of dollars in public funds." Ante, at 174, 57 L Ed 2d, at 134.

SECTION D. SUMMARY

1. United States Supreme Court Reports

a. *United States Reports* (Official Edition)

(1) Text of all cases of the Supreme Court of the United States.

(2) First ninety volumes are cited frequently by reporter, for, originally, they were not consecutively numbered.

(3) Bound volumes and advance sheets have same volume and page numbers.

(4) "Slip" opinions are initially printed.

(5) No summaries of briefs of counsel; other standard reporting features are included.

b. *United States Supreme Court Reports* (Lawyers' Edition)

(1) Includes all Supreme Court cases—two series.

(2) Bound volume combines several volumes of official edition.

(3) Advance sheets and bound volumes have same volume and page numbers.

(4) Reference table appears at the beginning of each volume unit which cross references from the official citations to Lawyers' Edition pages.

(5) Briefs of counsel are summarized.

(6) Annotations in increasing number since volume 92, 1st Series.

(7) Index to Annotations—subject index to annotations in *Lawyers' Edition* through 31 L.Ed.2d. Starting with Volume 32 L.Ed.2d, pocket supplements keep annotations up to date.

(8) Star-pagination.

(9) Standard reporting features are included.

c. *Supreme Court Reporter* (West Edition)

(1) Part of the National Reporter System; key-numbered sections of headnotes.

(2) Begins with volume 106 of the official set.

(3) Each volume contains several volumes of the official reports.

(4) Advance sheets and bound volumes have same volume and page numbers.

(5) Cross reference table from the official citations to the *Supreme Court Reporter* volume and pages.

(6) Star-pagination.

(7) No summaries of briefs of counsel; other standard reporting features are included.

d. *United States Law Week*

(1) Supreme Court Sections—speedy publication of Supreme Court decisions and journal of cases.

(2) General Law Sections—include more important current federal statutes, summary of federal legal trends, some federal agency rulings and the texts of significant new court decisions; general topical index.

e. *Commerce Clearing House, U. S. Supreme Court Bulletin*

(1) Looseleaf reporter of current Supreme Court decisions; provides fast service.

(2) Docket of Supreme Court cases.

f. *Chamber Opinions of the Justices*

Until 1969, published only in *Lawyers' Edition* and *Supreme Court Reporter*; starting in 1970 are also published in the *United States Reports*.

2. Federal Cases

a. Reprinted reports of all available U. S. circuit and district court decisions, 1789–1879.

b. Cases are arranged alphabetically by case names and consecutively numbered.

c. Cases are cited by number.

d. Annotations are brief notes to the cases.

e. Digest volume, volume 31, includes Blue Tables which cross-reference from the original reporter citations to the *Federal Cases* Numbers.

3. Federal Reporter

a. Part of *National Reporter System*; key-numbered sections of headnotes.

b. Only current reporter for federal appellate cases.

c. Reports cases from 1879 to date.

d. Prior to 1932 included District Court decisions.

e. Now reports cases of the courts of appeals, the U. S. Court of Customs and Patent Appeals and the Court of Claims (Court of Claims since 1960).

f. Advance sheets and bound volumes have same volume and page numbers.

g. No summaries of briefs of counsel; other standard reporting features are included.

4. Federal Supplement

a. Part of *National Reporter System*; key-numbered sections of headnotes.

b. Only current reporter of lower federal court cases.

c. Reports cases since 1932.

d. Now includes cases of the district courts and the U. S. Customs Court (U. S. Customs Court since 1949).

e. From 1932 to 1960, included the Court of Claims cases.

f. Includes *selected* district court cases.

g. Advance sheets and bound volumes have same volume and page numbers.

h. No summaries of briefs of counsel; other standard reporting features are included.

Chapter 5

STATE COURT DECISIONS AND THE NATIONAL REPORTER SYSTEM

SECTION A. STATE COURT REPORTS

As has been indicated previously, the laws of the several states generally provide for the method of publishing state court decisions. Opinions published in accordance with such legislation are called "official" reports. [See Illustration 2] Private companies also publish judicial decisions, with or without legislative directives. The private publications that are not legislatively endorsed are called "unofficial" reports, although they are no less accurate than the official reports. The unofficial reports may duplicate official reports or may be the only source of publication. The unofficial reports fall into three categories. The first consists of those sets that were or are published to compete directly with the officially published state reports. These reports are published chronologically as issued and usually have more useful editorial features and faster publication than the official reports. In most states the unofficial sets are units of the *National Reporter System,* which is discussed later in this chapter. The other two categories are annotated reports and special or subject reports. These will be discussed in subsequent chapters.

At one time, all states published their judicial decisions in bound volumes of reports such as the *Michigan Reports.*[1] Those states having intermediate courts of appeal[2] may also have separately bound

[1] While printing began in the Colonies in 1638, the first case reported appears to be the *Trial of Thomas Sutherland* for murder, printed in 1692. About 30 of the 150 English reports were being used in this country prior to the American Revolution as the written case law, because only about 35 to 40 legal books or pamphlets had been printed here.

Connecticut was the first state to publish an official law report after a 1784 statute entitled "An Act Establishing the Wages of the Judges of the Superior Court" was passed which required judges of the supreme and superior courts to file written opinions. The first volume, known as *Kirby's Reports,* was published in 1789 by Ephraim Kirby in Litchfield, Connecticut. In 1790 came Dallas' *Pennsylvania Cases*; in 1792 followed Hopkinson's *Admiralty Reports*; and Chipman's *Vermont Reports* in 1793. Through the early 1800's reports followed in North Carolina, Virginia, Kentucky, New Jersey, Maryland, Louisiana, New York, and Tennessee.

[2] As of 1980, 32 states have intermediate courts of appeal. *See* AMERICAN JUDICATURE SOCIETY, STATE INTERMEDIATE APPELLATE COURTS (1980).

sets of reports, such as the *Illinois Appellate Reports*. The decisions are published chronologically by terms of court. An increasing number of states, however, have discontinued publishing their official reports and are relying solely on the *National Reporter System*.[3] Below is a list giving the year of the first case decided in all of the states' or territories' highest appellate courts.

YEAR OF THE FIRST REPORTED CASE DECIDED IN THE STATES'[4] APPELLATE COURTS

State	Year
Alabama	1820
Alaska	1869
Arizona	1866
Arkansas	1820
California	1850
Colorado	1864
Connecticut	1764
Delaware	1814
District of Columbia	1801
Florida	1846
Georgia	1805
Hawaii	1847
Idaho	1866
Illinois	1819
Indiana	1817
Iowa	1839
Kansas	1858

For additional references to early law reporting in America *see*:

1. C. EVANS, AMERICAN BIBLIOGRAPHY vols. I, II, III (1893).
2. I. THOMAS, HISTORY OF PRINTING IN AMERICA vol. VI.
3. AMERICAN ANTIQUARIAN SOCIETY, PROCEEDINGS (1874).
4. C. WARREN, HISTORY OF THE HARVARD LAW SCHOOL AND OF EARLY LEGAL CONDITIONS IN AMERICA vol. I. ch. X (1908).
5. CONNECTICUT ACTS AND LAWS 1784, at 267.
6. M. CHAPMAN, BIBLIOGRAPHICAL INDEX TO THE STATE REPORTS PRIOR TO THE NATIONAL REPORTER SYSTEM (Transmedia 1977).

---

[3] The following states no longer publish their own official reports and either have officially adopted or rely on the decisions as reported in the regional reporters of the *National Reporter System*. These states are: Alabama, Alaska, Arizona, Delaware, Florida, Iowa, Kentucky, Louisiana, Maine, Mississippi, Missouri, North Dakota, Oklahoma, Tennessee, Texas, Utah and Wyoming. *See* 73 LAW LIB.J. 247 (1980).

[4] Many of the states were territories or colonies at the time of their first appellate decision. Pennsylvania was a commonwealth. In 1840, what is now the State of Texas was an independent republic.

Kentucky	1785
Louisiana	1809
Maine	1820
Maryland	1658
Massachusetts	1786
Michigan	1836
Minnesota	1851
Mississippi	1818
Missouri	1821
Montana	1868
Nebraska	1860
Nevada	1865
New Hampshire	1796
New Jersey	1789
New Mexico	1852
New York	1791
North Carolina	1778
North Dakota	1867
Ohio	1816
Oklahoma	1890
Oregon	1853
Pennsylvania	1754
Philippine Islands	1901
Puerto Rico	1899
Rhode Island	1828
South Carolina	1783
South Dakota	1867
Tennessee	1791
Texas	1840
Utah	1855
Vermont	1789
Virginia	1729
Washington	1854
West Virginia	1864
Wisconsin	1839
Wyoming	1870

Advance sheets or slip opinions precede the publication of the official reports in several states. The unofficial publications generally include advance sheets for the state cases.

A court or its reporter may have the power to select the decisions for publication in the official state reports. In the exercise of that power some less important cases may be eliminated from the official reports.[5]

[5] Chanin, *A Survey of the Writing and Publication of Opinions in Federal and State Appellate Courts*, 67 LAW LIB.J. 362 (1974).

In a general survey, such as this, it would be inappropriate to present a detailed study of the reporting systems of each state.[6]

SECTION B. NATIONAL REPORTER SYSTEM

The *National Reporter System,* published by the West Publishing Company, consists of three main divisions: (1) opinions of state courts, (2) opinions of federal courts, and (3) opinions of two special courts. This system of court reporting was initiated in 1879 with the *North Western Reporter.* The state reporting units consist of seven regional reporters each containing the opinions of several adjacent states. Additionally, there are two units which only contain the opinions of single states, namely, the *California Reporter* and the *New York Supplement.* There are four units which cover the various federal courts and two that report the opinions of special federal courts: *Bankruptcy Reporter* and the *Military Justice Reporter.* The entire system, with its coverage, is outlined below:

	Began in	Coverage
Atlantic Reporter	1885	Conn., Dela., Maine, Maryland, N. H., N. J., Penna., R. I., Vermont, and District of Columbia Municipal Court of Appeals.
North Eastern Reporter	1885	Ill., Ind., Mass., N. Y., and Ohio
North Western Reporter	1879	Ia., Mich., Minn., Nebr., N.D., S. D., and Wis.
Pacific Reporter	1883	Alaska, Ariz., Calif. to 1960, Calif. S.Ct. since 1960, Colo., Hawaii, Idaho, Kan., Mont., Nev., N. M., Okla., Ore., Utah, Wash., and Wyo.
South Eastern Reporter	1887	Ga., N. C., S. C., Va., and W. Va.
South Western Reporter	1886	Ark., Ky., Mo., Tenn., and Tex.
Southern Reporter	1887	Ala., Fla., La., and Miss.
Supreme Court Reporter	1882	Supreme Court of the United States.
Federal Reporter	1880	From 1880 to 1932: Circuit Courts of Appeals and District Courts of the U. S., U. S. Court of Cus-

[6] For a list of state guides to legal research, see Appendix B.

	Began in	Coverage
		toms and Patent Appeals, Court of Claims of the U. S., and Court of Appeals of the District of Columbia. From 1932 to date: U. S. Courts of Appeals, and U. S. Court of Customs and Patent Appeals. From 1942 to 1961: U. S. Emergency Court of Appeals. Since 1960: U. S. Court of Claims. Temporary Emergency Court of of Appeals since 1972.
Federal Supplement	1932	U. S. District Courts, Court of Claims to 1960, U. S. Customs Court since Vol. 135 (1949). Special Court, Regional Rail Reorganization Act since 1974. Judicial Panel on Multidistrict Litigation since 1969.
Federal Rules Decisions	1940	District Courts of the U. S.
New York Supplement	1888	N. Y. (all state courts). Since 1932, the N. Y. Court of Appeals opinions are published here as well as in the North Eastern Reporter.
California Reporter	1959	Calif.S.Ct., District Courts of Appeal and Appellate Dept. Superior Court.
Military Justice Reporter [7]	1975	U. S. Court of Military Appeals and the Courts of Military Review for the Army, Air Force, Navy, and Coast Guard.
West's Bankruptcy Reporter	1979	Bankruptcy decisions from the U. S. Bankruptcy Courts, U. S. District Courts, U. S. Courts of Appeals, and the U. S. Supreme Court.

[7] This set replaces the U.S. Court of Military Appeals, *Decisions*, and *Court-Martial Reports*, which have ceased publication.

The full texts of the decisions of the courts are provided by this service. The editors prepare headnotes which then are Key-Numbered to the *American Digest* classification system. This is a very significant and helpful feature, the nature of which is described in Chapter 6. However, because it was not developed until the turn of the century, cases in the early volumes of the units of the *National Reporter System,* although headnoted, are not integrated into the Key-Number system.

The development of the *National Reporter System* had a profound impact on the method of finding court opinions and indeed on the development of American law. By 1887, nearly all federal and state court opinions were being reported by the West Publishing Company with each opinion receiving similar editorial treatment. As will be described in the next chapter, this made possible a relatively simple method for researchers to find cases on the same points of law for all of the states as well as those decided in the federal courts. The development of the various regional reporters of the *National Reporter System* also provided a much faster method of making available the opinions of the state courts. The opinions of several adjacent states could be published quickly in the advance sheets which usually contained the same pagination as in the subsequent bound volumes.[8]

In addition to the opinions and the headnotes, the volumes of the *National Reporter System* contain many other useful editorial features. These include tables of cases reported in the volumes and a list of words and phrases as defined in the opinions. Each advance sheet and bound volume also includes a digest section containing the Key-Numbered headnotes of the cases covered.[9] The sole exception is the Bankruptcy Reporter bound volumes, which do not have digest sections.

The publishers note that the *National Reporter System* contains over 90,000 cases which are not in the official state reports.

The decisions of all state intermediate appellate courts are now included in the *National Reporter System.* For each intermediate court, the inclusion of its cases in the *Reporter System* began at dif-

[8] Occasionally after an opinion has been published in an advance sheet, the judge who wrote the opinion may, for one reason or another, recall the opinion and not publish it. In such instances, another opinion is published in the appendix of a subsequent advance sheet with the same pagination as the withdrawn case. By this means, the original pagination is preserved in the bound volume.

[9] In volumes which it reprints, West Publishing Company may not include all of the tables mentioned in this section. Since tools such as the digest section are primarily current awareness devices, and are repeated in the cumulations of digests on the state, regional, and national levels, West has elected not to reproduce them when reprinting older volumes.

ferent times. For example, Missouri appellate cases are included in the *South Western Reporter,* beginning with 93 Mo.App. (1902); Illinois appellate decisions are contained in the *North Eastern Reporter,* beginning with 284 Ill.App. (1936). Variations also exist between the *Reporters* as to general inclusion of state trial court cases, and the trial courts which are covered have different starting dates in each set.

See Illustration 8 for a map of the *National Reporter System.*

[Illustration 8]

MAP OF THE NATIONAL REPORTER SYSTEM

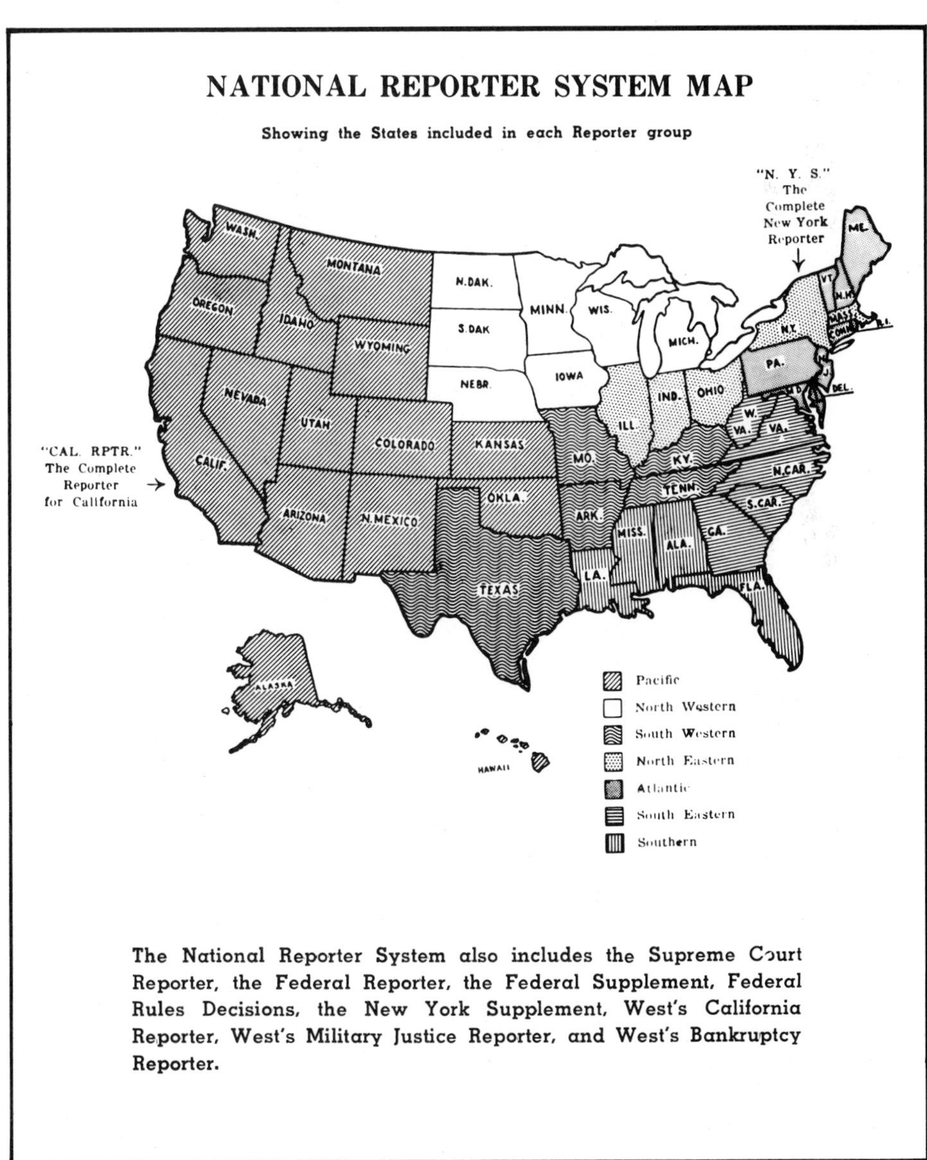

The National Reporter System also includes the Supreme Court Reporter, the Federal Reporter, the Federal Supplement, Federal Rules Decisions, the New York Supplement, West's California Reporter, West's Military Justice Reporter, and West's Bankruptcy Reporter.

SECTION C. METHODS OF CITATION

1. State Opinions

a. *Name of Case*

When an opinion is cited, it should contain the name of the case and the citation to the case in the official reports, if available, and in the corresponding unit or units of the *National Reporter System*. The full name of the case appears at the beginning of each opinion, and then there is usually a short form used as a "running" title at the top of each subsequent page of the opinion. It is the short form which is used in the citation, e. g.:

Harvey HERMAN, Plaintiff-Appellant,

v.

Michael J. HAMBLET; Herrick, McNeill, McElroy & Peregrine; Thomas H. Miner; AMH Industries, Inc., an Illinois Corporation; AMH Industries of Nevada, Inc., a Nevada Corporation, Defendants-Appellees.

Its short title is Herman v. Hamblet.

v.

b. *Parallel Citations*

When a case has been reported in an official state reporter, the citation to the state report is given first, followed by the citation to the appropriate regional reporters, and, when available, its citation in the *American Law Reports.*[10] The year of the decision is then given in parentheses, e. g.:

Wenish v. Polinger Co., 277 Md. 553, 356 A.2d 74, 95 A.L.R. 3d 1 (1976)

Barber v. Municipal Court, 24 Cal.3d 742, 598 P.2d 818, 157 Cal.Rptr. 658 (1979)

City of New York v. Baker, 46 N.Y.2d 790, 386 N.E.2d 825, 413 N.Y.S.2d 913 (1979)

When a case is not in the official state reports, citation is given first to where it is reported within the *National Reporter System* and then, if available, to the *American Law Reports,* with an indication of the court and year of decision in parentheses.

Fuss v. Comm., 589 S.W.2d 215 (Ky.1979)

Thompson v. State, 318 So.2d 549, 90 A.L.R.3d 641 (Fla. App.Dist. 4, 1975)

[10] The *American Law Reports* will be discussed in Chapter 7.

c. *Early State Reporters*

Where the name of a reporter is used in citing an early state report, the favored practice is to indicate the state and the date.

Day v. Sweetser, 2 Tyl. 283 (Vt.1803)

2. Federal Court Opinions

a. *Supreme Court of the United States*

Since both the *Supreme Court Reporter* and the *United States Supreme Court Reports, Lawyers' Edition* give cross references to the pages of the official *United States Reports,* it is customary to cite only to that set, e. g.:

University of California Regents v. Bakke, 438 U.S. 265 (1978)

b. *Courts of Appeals and District Courts*

As there are no official reports for the opinions of these courts, citations are given to the appropriate unit of the *National Reporter System,* e. g.:

United States v. Five (5) Coin-Operated Gambling Devices, 248 F.Supp. 115 (W.D.Va.1965)

In re Irving, 600 F.2d 1027 (2d Cir. 1979)

SECTION D. CROSS REFERENCE TABLES

1. State Court Citations

Frequently, a researcher has only the citation to the official state reports or to the regional unit of the *National Reporter System* and will need to find the parallel citation.

a. *State Citation to* National Reporter *Citation*

When only the state citation is available, refer to one of the following:

(1) *National Reporter Blue Book.* This set is presently in six bound volumes and is kept current by an annual cumulative pamphlet. It lists all state citations, alphabetically by state, and gives for each state citation its parallel citation in the appropriate unit or units of the *National Reporter System.* [See Illustration 9]

(2) *Shepard's Citations* for the state.

(3) The Table of Cases in the appropriate state or regional digest.

2. National Reporter Citation to State Citation

When only the *National Reporter* citation is available, refer to one of the following:

a. [State] *Blue and White Book.* This volume is provided to subscribers by the West Publishing Company. It is only sent to subscribers for the state in which the subscriber is located. The blue pages repeat for the state the information available in the *National Reporter Blue Book* described *supra.* The white pages give the citations from the regional reporter or reporters to the official state reports. [See Illustration 9] It is only useful in locating state citations for the state where the research is taking place.

b. *Shepard's Citations* for the appropriate regional reporter.

c. Table of Cases in the appropriate state or regional digest, or Table of Cases volumes in the appropriate unit of the *American Digest System.*

3. Federal Citations

a. United States Supreme Court. As the two unofficial sets of the U.S. Reports give citations to the official U.S. Reports [see Illustration 7–c], it is the general practice to cite only to the official reports. When, however, the only citation available is the *Supreme Court Reporter* or the *United States Supreme Court Reports, Lawyers' Edition,* the citation to the other two sets may be obtained by referring to:

(1) *United States Shepard's Citations: Case Volumes.*

(2) Table of Cases in one of the digests for federal cases.

Table of Cases and the *American Digest System* are discussed in Chapter 6. *Shepard's Citations* are discussed in Chapter 15.

[Illustration 9]

AN EXCERPT FROM THE NATIONAL REPORTER BLUE BOOK

20 CALIFORNIA REPORTS, THIRD SERIES

Cal.3d Page	Parallel Citation Vol.		Page
1	141	CalRptr	28
	569	P2d	133
10	141	CalRptr	20
	569	P2d	125
25	141	CalRptr	315
	569	P2d	1303
55	141	CalRptr	146
	569	P2d	740
73	141	CalRptr	169
	569	P2d	763
90	141	CalRptr	157
	569	P2d	751
109	141	CalRptr	177
	569	P2d	771
130	141	CalRptr	447[2]
	570	P2d	463[2]
142	141	CalRptr	542
	570	P2d	723
150	141	CalRptr	698
	570	P2d	1050

Cal.3d Page	Parallel Citation Vol.		Page
232	142	CalRptr	171
	571	P2d	628
238	142	CalRptr	279
	571	P2d	990
251	142	CalRptr	414
	572	P2d	28
260	142	CalRptr	411
	572	P2d	25
267	142	CalRptr	418
	572	P2d	32
285	142	CalRptr	429
	572	P2d	43
300	142	CalRptr	286
	571	P2d	997
309	142	CalRptr	439
	572	P2d	53
317	142	CalRptr	443
	572	P2d	57
327	142	CalRptr	904
	572	P2d	1128

Cal.3d Page	Parallel Citation Vol.		Page
457	143	CalRptr	215
	573	P2d	433
476	143	CalRptr	205
	573	P2d	423
489	143	CalRptr	212
	573	P2d	430
500	143	CalRptr	240
	573	P2d	458
512	143	CalRptr	247
	573	P2d	465
523	143	CalRptr	609
	574	P2d	425
550	143	CalRptr	253
	573	P2d	472
552	143	CalRptr	408
	573	P2d	852
560	143	CalRptr	625
	574	P2d	441
567	143	CalRptr	542
	573	P2d	1360

Cal.3d Page	Parallel Citation Vol.		Page
679	143	CalRptr	885
	574	P2d	1237
→ 694	144	Cal.Rptr.	751
	576	P.2d	466
708	144	CalRptr	133
	575	P2d	285
717	144	CalRptr	214
	575	P2d	757
725	144	CalRptr	380
	575	P2d	1162
765	144	CalRptr	758
	576	P2d	473
788	144	CalRptr	404
	575	P2d	1186
798	144	CalRptr	408
	575	P2d	1190
813	144	CalRptr	905
	576	P2d	945
844	143	CalRptr	695
	574	P2d	[illegible]

The National Reporter Blue Book consists of a main bound volume, bound volume supplements, and an annual cumulative pamphlet. This Blue Book contains tables showing volume and page of the National Reporter volume for every case found in the corresponding state reports.

In this example, if one had only the citation to 20 Cal.3d 694, the table may be used to locate the citation of this case in the California Reporter and the Pacific Reporter.

AN EXCERPT FROM THE WHITE TABLES IN CALIFORNIA BLUE AND WHITE BOOK

Page	Parallel Citation
1190	20 Cal.3d 798
	144 Cal.Rptr. 408

576 P.2d

Page	Parallel Citation
92 [1]	Not officially published
92 [2]	20 Cal.3d 878
	144 Cal.Rptr. 609 [2]
93	20 Cal.3d 888
	144 Cal.Rptr. 610
→ 466	20 Cal.3d 694
	144 Cal.Rptr. 751
473	20 Cal.3d 765
	144 Cal.Rptr. 758
945	20 Cal.3d 813
	144 Cal.Rptr. 905
963	20 Cal.3d 893
	145 Cal.Rptr. 1
971	20 Cal.3d 906
	145 Cal.Rptr. 9
1342	21 Cal.3d 1
	145 Cal.Rptr. 176

579 P.2d

Page	Parallel Citation
1	21 Cal.3d 337
	146 Cal.Rptr. 352
7	21 Cal.3d 471
	146 Cal.Rptr. 358
441	21 Cal.3d 322
	146 Cal.Rptr. 550
449	21 Cal.3d 386
	146 Cal.Rptr. 558
476	21 Cal.3d 431
	146 Cal.Rptr. 585
495	21 Cal.3d 349
	146 Cal.Rptr. 604
505	21 Cal.3d 497
	146 Cal.Rptr. 614
514	21 Cal.3d 482
	146 Cal.Rptr. 623
1043	21 Cal.3d 513
	146 Cal.Rptr. 727
1048	21 Cal.3d 542
	146 Cal.Rptr. 732
1053	21 Cal.3d 523
	146 Cal.Rptr. 737

SECTION E. SUMMARY

1. State Court Reports

a. Official reports are court reports published by statutory authority.

b. Unofficial reports are court reports published without statutory authority.

c. Advance sheets and slip opinions are published in several states—most states rely on unofficial advance sheets, e.g., *National Reporter System* or other private publication.

2. National Reporter System

a. Opinions of state appellate courts, arranged geographically into seven regional reporters and two state reporters.

b. Opinions of the federal courts in four reporters plus two special subject reporters.

3. Cross Reference Tables

a. *National Reporter Blue Book* refers the user from the official citation to the unofficial *National Reporter* citation.

b. White Tables in [*State*] *Blue and White Book* refer the user from the unofficial *National Reporter* citation to the official citation.

Chapter 6

DIGESTS FOR COURT REPORTS

SECTION A. DIGESTS: IN GENERAL

As our system of law follows the doctrine of *stare decisis,* the location of past cases in the various sets of court reports described in the previous chapters is an essential requirement to legal research. It has been noted that cases are published in the law reports in chronological order rather than by subject. Each volume of reports may contain cases dealing with diverse subjects ranging from *Abatement* to *Zoning.* It is evident that there must be a method of searching for cases by subject or else locating cases with the same or similar points of law would become unwieldy and unmanageable. For example, assume the following problem:

> A child is standing with her step-grandmother on a street corner when an automobile jumps the curb and severely injures the grandmother. The observation of this accident causes severe mental suffering to the child. The child's parents wish to know if they may recover damages from the driver of the automobile for the child's emotional distress.

Before being able to answer this inquiry, the researcher must first determine the important issues involved in this fact situation. One of these is whether damages may be allowed for mental anguish caused to one person by an injury to another. In order to find the law applicable to this situation, the researcher must search for appellate court decisions with the same or similar facts. From these cases, the rules of law should be determined. If this accident had happened, for example, in Ohio, and all that were available to the researcher were the volumes containing the opinions of the Ohio appellate courts, it would be necessary to examine the individual indexes to hundreds of volumes of the Ohio reports in order to determine if there were any cases on point. To alleviate this laborious task, sets of law books known as "digests" have been developed which rearrange cases by subject. Instead, however, of reprinting the entire opinions, only abstracts or digests are given. Digests are one method by which cases may be located by subject.

There are various kinds of digests available, each with different coverage. Some include only cases for a single state, court or system of courts; others include cases from a group of neighboring states; some, only federal cases; and one includes cases from all appellate courts, federal and state.

In this chapter we shall describe primarily digests published by the West Publishing Company. Other digests as well as different techniques for locating cases will be discussed in subsequent chapters.

SECTION B. THE AMERICAN DIGEST SYSTEM

1. Key Number System

The *American Digest System* is a subject classification scheme whereby decisions that were reported chronologically in the various units of the *National Reporter System* are rearranged by subject, bringing together all cases on a similar point of law. Instead, however, of rearranging complete decisions, it rearranges digests (abstracts) of decisions. The West Publishing Co. has developed its own classification of law and classifies the digests of all cases to its system of classification. The system divides the subject of law into seven main classes. Each class is then divided into sub-classes and then each sub-class into topics. There are over 435 topics, each of which corresponds to a legal concept. [See Illustration 10] The topics are then divided into subdivisions of the topic and each subdivision is given a paragraph number called a "Key Number." The Key Numbers vary from topic to topic from a few to many hundred.

With this outline in mind, it is necessary to examine the actual steps involved in the making of the *American Digest System.* Basically, it all starts with a slip decision. After a decision is written, a copy of it goes to the West Publishing Company and is assigned to an editor. Keep in mind that all the editor has is the decision with no other information than the name of the case, the name of the judge who wrote it, and the name of the court. The editor reads the case and determines the headnotes. In theory, each headnote represents a particular point of law. The editor takes each point of law which is about to be made into a headnote and assigns to it a Topic and Key Number. The editor decides that a particular paragraph deals with, for example, damages, and then turning to the *Table of Key Numbers* [Illustration 11–11a] under *Damages,* further decides that it specifically is involved with Mental Suffering—Injury to the Person of Another and thus gives it the Topic and Key Number *Damages* 51. Frequently a paragraph will deal with two points of law and will then get two Topics and Key Numbers.

2. Units of the American Digest System

The next step is found in a publication called the *General Digest*. The *General Digest* is no longer issued in pamphlet form; the monthly issues are hard-backed. The Descriptive-Word Index and Table of Cases affirmed is still issued in pamphlet form, then cumulated into bound volumes. The January issue, for example, will consist of *all* the headnotes taken from *all* of the units of the *National Reporter System*. These again are arranged alphabetically by Topic and then numerically by Key Number under Topic. Thus, in the January issue of the *General Digest*, by looking under a particular Topic and Key Number, digests of all cases that dealt with that particular point of law reported in the January issue can be located.

From this point on, the digest building becomes mechanical. The monthly issues of the *General Digest* are cumulated periodically into bound volumes. This process has now been going on since 1896. If no further cumulation had taken place, digests of all the cases, arranged topically, would be in all of the bound volumes of the *General Digest*. In order to find all the cases dealing with a particular topic, it would be necessary to examine each one of hundreds of bound volumes. As this was not practical, the publishers in 1906 cumulated all the topics from all of the volumes from 1897 to 1906 into one alphabet. This is called the *First Decennial*. Now, by examining the volume containing a particular Topic and Key Number, all of the cases decided on that point during the years 1897–1906 may be located. This process has taken place since 1896 with a new *Decennial* every ten years. The latest one is the Eighth, covering the years 1966–76. All of the cases since 1976 are in the *General Digest*, 5th Series. Thus, given a Topic and Key Number, one can start with the *First Decennial* and then proceed through the *Eighth Decennial* and then examine the individual bound volumes of the *General Digest*, and then the monthly issues and thereby locate all cases on a point of law under a particular Key Number from 1897 to approximately six weeks ago.

It is actually possible to find all cases from 1658, as cases from 1658 to 1896 are in the *Century Digest*. However, the *Century Digest* did not use Key Numbers. This means that the numbering in the *Century* is different from that of the *Decennials*. For example, the Topic *Damages* Key Number 51 in the *Decennials* stands for "Mental Suffering Caused by Injury to the Person of Another," whereas in the *Century*, Damages 51 stands for "Damages Flowing Directly From Intervening Agency of Third Person" and cases dealing with mental suffering caused by injury to a third person are digested under Paragraph Numbers 103, 255 and 256. [See Illustration 15]

Should the search be started in the *Century Digest,* a means of transfer from the *Century* paragraph number to the equivalent Key Number is needed. This is accomplished by using the *Table of Key Numbers Section for Century Digest,* located in the Table of Cases volume to the *First* and *Second Decennials.*

The *American Digest System* consists of the following sets:

	Chronological Coverage	No. of Vols.
Century Digest	1658–1896	50 vols.
First Decennial	1897–1906	25 vols.
Second Decennial	1907–1916	24 vols.
Third Decennial	1916–1926	29 vols.
Fourth Decennial	1926–1936	34 vols.
Fifth Decennial	1936–1946	49 vols.
Sixth Decennial	1946–1956	36 vols.
Seventh Decennial	1956–1966	38 vols.
Eighth Decennial	1966–1976	42 vols.
General Digest (5th Series)	1976 to date	

Several bound volumes of the *General Digest* are published each year. They are preceded by unbound monthly supplements. A new *Decennial* appears each ten years and supersedes the *General Digest* for that period. Thus, the *Eighth Decennial* takes the place of the *General Digest,* 4th Series, and covers the period 1966–1976. The *General Digest,* 5th Series, will span the ten-year period, 1976–1986, and eventually will be superseded by the *Ninth Decennial.*

3. Keeping Key Number System Current

Law, of course, is constantly expanding or changing. It is obvious that when the original Key Number classification was prepared in 1896 no provisions were made for cases dealing with damages resulting from a jet plane breaking the sound barrier or for the control and regulation of nuclear energy. Consequently, in order to keep abreast of the law, new topics have to be added and at times older ones expanded. Thus, in the *Eighth Decennial Digest* the following titles were added or expanded: *Arbitration, Civil Rights, Drugs and Druggists, Federal Courts, Pretrial Procedure, Products Liability, Public Contracts, Securities Regulation, Social Security, Public Welfare,* and *Taxation.* As additional new titles are required, or revisions to older titles needed, they will be incorporated into the volumes of the *General Digest,* 5th, and then eventually in the *Ninth Decennial.*

4. Table of Key Numbers

After one has searched through the *Eighth Decennial Digest,* it is necessary to start examining the digest paragraphs under the same

Topics and Key Numbers in the individual volumes of the *General Digest,* 5th Series. This series will contain digests of cases decided between 1976 and 1986. As each volume contains cases only for a two-to-four-month period, there may be as many as sixty individual volumes to search before the publication of the *Ninth Decennial.* To avoid the necessity of examining a volume of the *General Digest* which may not include any cases for a particular Key Number, the publisher includes a *Table of Key Numbers* in the volumes of the *Descriptive-Word Index* to the *General Digest.* This table indicates in which volumes of the *General Digest* there are cases digested for a particular Key Number. [See Illustration 17]

Illustrations in Section C show the development of headnotes from reported cases, the assignment of Topics and Key Numbers to headnotes, and how the headnotes become part of the various units of the *American Digest System.*

The methods of finding what Topics and Key Numbers to search under are described in Sections D & E *infra.*

SECTION C. ILLUSTRATIONS: KEY NUMBER CLASSIFICATION AND UNITS OF THE AMERICAN DIGEST SYSTEM

10. Sample page from List of Digest Topics

11. Sample pages of Topic: Damages, from Eighth Decennial Digest

12. Sample pages from Pacific Reporter

13–15. Sample pages from units of the American Digest System

16. Page from Table of Key Numbers in Descriptive-Word Index to the General Digest, 5th Series, Volumes 1–10

17. Example of Key Number Translation Table

[Illustration 10]

SAMPLE PAGE FROM ALPHABETICAL LIST OF DIGEST TOPICS USED IN KEY NUMBER SYSTEM

DIGEST TOPICS

See, also, Outline of the Law by Seven Main Division of Law, Page VII

Abandoned and Lost Property
Abatement and Revival
Abduction
Abortion and Birth Control
Absentees
Abstracts of Title
Accession
Accord and Satisfaction
Account
Account, Action on
Account Stated
Accountants
Acknowledgment
Action
Action on the Case
Adjoining Landowners
Administrative Law and Procedure
Admiralty
Ambassadors and Consuls
Amicus Curiae
Animals
Annuities
Appeal and Error
Appearance
Apprentices
Arbitration
Armed Services
Arrest
Arson
Assault and Battery
Assignments
Assignments for Benefit of Creditors
Assistance, Writ of
Associations
Assumpsit, Action of
Asylums

Attachment
Attorney and Client
Attorney General
Auctions and Auctioneers
Audita Querela
Automobiles
Aviation
Bail
Bailment
Bankruptcy
Banks and Banking
Bastards
Beneficial Associations
Bigamy
Bills and Notes
Blasphemy
Bonds
Boundaries
Bounties
Cancellation of Instruments
Carriers
Cemeteries
Census
Certiorari
Champerty and Maintenance
Charities
Chattel Mortgages
Chemical Dependents
Citizens
Civil Rights
Clerks of Courts
Clubs
Colleges and Universities
Collision
Commerce
Common Lands
Common Law
Common Scold

Compositions with Creditors
Compounding Offenses
Compromise and Settlement
Condominium
Confusion of Goods
Conspiracy
Constitutional Law
Consumer Credit
Contempt
Continuance
Contracts
Contribution
Conversion
Convicts
Copyrights and Intellectual Property
Coroners
Corporations
Costs
...sioners
...ion of
...ng Agencies
Crops
Curtesy
Customs and Usages
Customs Duties
Damages
Dead Bodies
Death
Debt, Action of
Debtor and Creditor
Declaratory Judgment
Dedication
Deeds
Depositaries
Depositions
Deposits and Escrows
Deposits in Court
Descent and Distribution
Detectives

There are over 435 Topics in the American Digest System. Each Topic is subdivided into "Key Numbers." See next Illustration.

[Illustration 11]

FIRST PAGE OF TOPIC: DAMAGES, FROM EIGHTH DECENNIAL DIGEST

DAMAGES

SUBJECTS INCLUDED

Pecuniary compensation, indemnity or satisfaction allowed by law for injuries by the unlawful act or default of another

Nature and grounds of recovery thereof in general

Rights to substantial or nominal damages, to immediate, consequential, remote or prospective damages, and to compensatory or exemplary damages

Penalties and liquidated damages and measure of damages for breach of contract in general

Measure of damages for torts in general

Interest as an element of damages

What amounts are inadequate or excessive as awards of damages

Proceedings relating to recovery and assessment of damages in general

SUBJECTS EXCLUDED AND COVERED BY OTHER TOPICS

Correction of errors in and review of awards of damages, see NEW TRIAL, APPEAL AND ERROR

Death, damages for, see DEATH

Exemplary damages for particular torts, see AUTOMOBILES and other specific topics

In each unit of the Decennial Digests and in the special Key Number digests, each Topic has a list of subjects excluded and an analysis of the Key Number classification for the Topic.

For detailed references to other topics, see Descriptive-Word Index

Analysis

I. NATURE AND GROUNDS IN GENERAL, ⚷1–7.

II. NOMINAL DAMAGES, ⚷8–14.

III. GROUNDS AND SUBJECTS OF COMPENSATORY DAMAGES, ⚷15–73.

(A) DIRECT OR REMOTE, CONTINGENT, OR PROSPECTIVE CONSEQUENCES OR LOSSES, ⚷15–57.

(B) AGGRAVATION, MITIGATION, AND REDUCTION OF LOSS, ⚷58–65.

(C) INTEREST, COSTS, AND EXPENSES OF LITIGATION, ⚷66–73.

IV. LIQUIDATED DAMAGES AND PENALTIES, ⚷74–86.

V. EXEMPLARY DAMAGES, ⚷87–94.

[Illustration 11-a]

SAMPLE PAGE OF TOPIC DAMAGES—Cont'd

16-8th D—1167 **DAMAGES**

VI. MEASURE OF DAMAGES, 🔑95–126.

(A) INJURIES TO THE PERSON, 🔑95–102.
(B) INJURIES TO PROPERTY, 🔑103–116.
(C) BREACH OF CONTRACT, 🔑117–126.

VII. INADEQUATE AND EXCESSIVE DAMAGES, 🔑127–140.

VIII. PLEADING, EVIDENCE, AND ASSESSMENT, 🔑141–228.

(A) PLEADING, 🔑141–162.
(B) EVIDENCE, 🔑163–192.
(C) PROCEEDINGS FOR ASSESSMENT, 🔑193–224.
(D) COMPUTATION AND AMOUNT, DOUBLE AND TREBLE DAMAGES, AND REMISSION, 🔑225–228.

I. NATURE AND GROUNDS IN GENERAL.

🔑1. Nature and theory of pecuniary reparation.
2. What law governs.
3. Injuries for which pecuniary reparation may be made.
4. Presumptions as to damage from injury.
5. General and special damage.
6. Certainty as to amount or extent of damage.
7. Right to damages as right of property.

II. NOMINAL DAMAGES.

🔑8. Nature and theory of award.
9. Award irrespective of actual damage.
10. Nominal or substantial damages.
11. —— In general.
12. —— Extent of damage not shown.
13. —— Damage not pecuniary.
14. Amount of nominal damages.

III. GROUNDS AND SUBJECTS OF COMPENSATORY DAMAGES.

(A) DIRECT OR REMOTE, CONTINGENT, OR PROSPECTIVE CONSEQUENCES OR LOSSES.

🔑15. Nature and theory of compensation.
16. Direct or indirect consequences.

Immediately following the analysis there appears a detailed listing of the Key Numbers, each representing a minute point of law. Each time a headnote deals with anxiety or mental distress as caused by an injury to the person of another as it relates to the law of damages, it will receive the Topic Damages and the Key Number 51.

37. —— Loss of earnings or services.
38. —— Impairment of earning capacity.
39. —— Loss of or injury to property.
40. —— Loss of profits.
(1). In general.
(2). Breach of contract.
(3). Interruption or destruction of business.
(4). Preventing or delaying performance of contract with third person.
41. Expenses incurred.
42. —— In general.
43. —— Medical treatment and care of person injured.
44. —— Injury to property.
45. —— Breach of contract.
46. —— Necessity of actual payment or legal liability.
47. Mental suffering.
48. —— In general.
49. —— As distinct cause of action or element of damage.
50. —— Physical injury to the person.
→51. —— Injury to the person of another.
52. —— Fright or apprehension of personal injury.
53. —— Anxiety or mental distress.
54. —— Humiliation, insult, or other indignity.
55. —— Injury to property.
56. —— Breach of contract.
57. Motive or intent of wrongdoer as affecting award of compensation.

(B) AGGRAVATION, MITIGATION, AND REDUCTION OF LOSS.

🔑58. Matter of aggravation.
59. Matter of mitigation.
60. Benefits incident to injury.
61. Expenses incurred by wrongdoer.

[Illustration 12]

SAMPLE PAGE FROM THE PACIFIC REPORTER

766 Hawaii 520 PACIFIC REPORTER, 2d SERIES

plaintiff-witness to the accident, the manner in which he witnessed it or learned of it, his relationship to the victim and the foreseeability of his and the victim's pres-

parents, while an adult would be adopted as a form of showing affection or respect. On the other hand, a *keiki hanai* is a child given to another to raise, as a foster child.

This is a typical page from a case reported in a unit of the National Reporter System. It illustrates how headnotes are developed. The bracketed numbers are inserted by the editors. Each paragraph so bracketed has been rewritten into a headnote. See next Illustration.

presence. Like the court in Dillon v. Legg, *supra,* we cannot doubt that the plaintiff would suffer some degree of shock when he witnessed his foster grandmother being killed as he stood several feet away. Whether the degree of stress engendered by the circumstances of this case is beyond the amount of stress with which a reasonable man can be expected to cope is a question for the trial court.

[10] Neither should the absence of a blood relationship between victim and plaintiff-witness foreclose recovery. Hawaiian and Asian families of this state have long maintained strong ties among members of the same extended family group. The Hawaiian word *ohana* has been used to express this concept. It is not uncommon in Hawaii to find several parent-children family units, with members of three and even four generations, living under one roof as a single family.

[11] The Hawaiian concept of adoption also differs from that in other common law jurisdictions.[2] The ancient Hawaiians cherished the principle of adoption, which took two forms: A child or adult one loves, but for whom one might not have exclusive care, might be adopted as a *keiki ho'okama* (child), or *kaikua'ano ho'okama, kaikaina ho'okama, kaikuahine ho'okama, kaikunane ho'okama* (adult). A child so adopted would be adopted as a child of the family, and entitled to inherit through his

custom of giving children to grandparents, near relatives, and friends to raise whether legally or informally remains a strong one. Hence the plaintiff should be permitted to prove the nature of his relationship to the victim and the extent of damages he has suffered because of this relationship.

V

The final question we face is the standard of objective proof of the nature and severity of mental distress necessary to properly assess damages in this case. A cogent analysis of this problem may be found in Comment, "Negligently Inflicted Mental Distress: The Case for an Independent Tort" 59 Geo.L.J. 1237, 1248–1263 (1971). From a medical perspective, negligently-inflicted mental distress may be characterized as a reaction to a traumatic stimulus, which may be physical or purely psychic. Traumatic stimulus may cause two types of mental reaction, primary and secondary. The primary response, and immediate, automatic and instinctive response designed to protect an individual from harm, unpleasantness and stress aroused by witnessing the painful death of a loved one, is exemplified by emotional responses such as fear, anger, grief, and shock. This initial response, which is short in duration and subjective in nature, will vary in seriousness according to the individual and the particular traumatic stimulus.

2. In Hawaii, unlike in the majority of mainland states and England, adopted children are considered issue of their adopting parents, and may inherit through them. HRS § 578–16; O'Brien v. Walker, 35 Haw. 104 (1939).

[Illustration 12–a]

SAMPLE PAGE FROM THE PACIFIC REPORTER

defendant for any damages arising from consequences of his negligent act.

8. Damages ⟹53

The granting of damages for mental distress at witnessing accident caused by defendant's negligent act should not be contingent upon defendant's actual knowledge of plaintiff's presence.

9. Damages ⟹208(6)

Whether degree of mental stress engendered in ten-year-old boy who witnessed stepgrandmother being killed when struck by defendant's automobile was beyond amount of stress which a reasonable man could be expected to cope with was a question for trial court in action on behalf of such boy to recover damages for mental distress.

10. Damages ⟹51

Absence of a blood relationship between accident victim and plaintiff witness thereof did not foreclose recovery from defendant for mental distress.

11. Adoption ⟹21

Adopted children in Hawaii are considered issue of their adopting parents and may inherit through them. HRS § 578–16.

12. Damages ⟹53

In assessing degree of mental distress caused by the witnessing of consequences of negligent act by defendant, the severity of mental distress may be approached in terms of amount of pain and disability caused by witnessing consequences of defendant's negligent act.

13. Evidence ⟹528

In assessing the degree of mental distress allegedly caused by defendant's negligence, psychiatrist may not be able to establish negligent act as sole cause of plaintiff's neurosis but he can give a fairly accurate estimate of probable effects act will have upon plaintiff and whether the trauma induced was a precipitating cause of neurosis and whether the neurosis is beyond level of pain with which reasonable man may be expected to cope.

14. Damages ⟹192

The absence of a secondary response and its resulting physical injury should not foreclose relief for mental distress caused by the witnessing of consequences of defendant's negligent act, and plaintiff should be permitted to prove medically damage occasioned by his mental responses to defendant's negligent act.

Syllabus by the Court

1. Where the defendant is the moving party, there is no genuine issue as to any material fact and the defendant is entitled to a judgment as a matter of law if, upon viewing the record in the light most favorable to the plaintiff, it is clear that the plaintiff would not be entitled to re-

Note how the wording of Headnotes 10 and 11 are paraphrased from the opinion. See previous Illustration.

Also note how separate headnotes of a case may be assigned several different Topics and Key Numbers.

would not be able to cope with the mental distress engendered by such circumstances, the trial court should conclude that defendant's conduct is the proximate cause of plaintiff's injury and impose liability on the defendant for any damages arising from the consequences of his negligent act.

5. The absence of a blood relationship between accident victim and plaintiff-witness should not foreclose plaintiff's recovery of damages for emotional distress occasioned by the accident.

6. The physician or psychiatrist must rely on the plaintiff's testimony, the context in which the trauma occurred, medical testing of any physical ramifications, the psychiatrist's knowledge of pain and disability likely to result from such trauma, and even the framework of human experi-

[Illustration 13]

SAMPLE PAGE FROM THE EIGHTH DECENNIAL DIGEST

16–8th D—1239 **DAMAGES** ⚷51

injuries of the child.—City Stores Co. v. Langer, 308 So.2d 621.

Ga.App. 1976. Except under circumstances in which defendant's willful act has been directed against plaintiff, recovery cannot be had for emotional distress and mental suffering flowing from injuries to another unless defendant's conduct has resulted in actual bodily contact to plaintiff.—Howard v. Bloodworth, 224 S.E.2d 122.

Ga.App. 1975. Parents of 11-year-old girl injured in automobile collision were not entitled to recover damages for their emotional distress and mental suffering on learning of such collision where parents were not present at collision scene and where other driver's actions, although they might have constituted gross neglige... —Strickland ... Ga.App. 909

Hawaii 19... allegedly cau... Hawaii did n... from negliger... tress upon r... killed in tha... resided in C... and Supply,...

Defendant... ly caused au... not reasona... their neglige... jured and k... where such...

A person l... heart attac... deaths of hi... an automobi... sonable dist... mobile accid... did not have a cause of action for negligent infliction of severe mental distress.—Id.

When the Topic and Key Number are known, the digest paragraphs are consulted to select cases in point with the problem under research. For those so selected, the full cases should be read. Note how citation is given to where the case is reported.

Note also how the digest paragraphs are reprinted as they originally appeared as headnotes in the reported decisions.

Hawaii 1974. Since other standards existed to test authenticity of plaintiff's claim for damages because of emotional distress in witnessing death of his stepgrandmother, requirement of physical impact should not stand as an artificial bar to recovery, but merely be admissible as evidence of the degree of mental or emotional distress suffered.—Leong v. Takasaki, 520 P.2d 758.

Absence of a blood relationship between accident victim and plaintiff witness thereof did not foreclose recovery from defendant for mental distress.—Id.

Ind.App. 1976. In actions by tenant against apartment landlord for injuries, property damage and wrongful death of his two minor children in apartment fire, jury could consider mental suffering accompanying tenant's injuries as well as physical pain and suffering in making award of damages.—Old Town Development Co. v. Langford, 349 N.E.2d 744.

La.App. 1976. A cause of action does not lie for emotional distress or resulting physical injury caused by injury to or death of another person.—Bertrand v. State Farm Fire & Cas. Co., 333 So.2d 322.

La.App. 1975. No person may recover damages for mental anguish in an action in tort resulting from injury to another person.—Hickman v. East Baton Rouge Parish, 314 So.2d 486, writ denied 318 So.2d 59.

La.App. 1974. Parent could not recover for his own mental pain and anguish over injury to minor child.—Reid v. Clearfield Cheese Co., Inc., 307 So.2d 115.

La.App. 1974. Granddaughter who was passenger on motorcycle operated by her grandfather at time of accident was not entitled to recover damages for mental anguish which she might have sustained as result of seeing her grandfather gravely injured.—Smith v. Manchester Ins. & Indem. Co., 299 So.2d 517, writ denied 302 So.2d 617 and 302 So.2d 618.

La.App. 1974. Reasons why, except in death cases, Louisiana jurisprudence has denied recovery for mental pain and anguish sustained by one person because of injuries to another are to protect a tort-feasor from unreasonable demands of myriads of claimants who sustain no personal injury as result of the tort; also, under such circumstances, there is no breach of a legal duty toward the party claiming damages.—McKey v. Dow Chemical Co., Inc., 295 So.2d 516.

La.App. 1973. ...

learning of their brother's injury, loss of possible future financial assistance, and loss of pride and hope for his future career.—Robertson v. Aetna Cas. & Sur. Co., 232 So.2d 829.

One person cannot recover damages for mental anguish as a result of injuries to another where there is no breach of an independent ex contractu or ex delicto duty owed directly to the claimant.—Id.

Mich.App. 1976. Recovery for emotional suffering and resulting physical injury to person who was not involved in accident causing injury to third person and who did not witness accident may be allowed; however, injuries threatened or inflicted upon third person should be of nature to cause severe mental disturbance to plaintiff, plaintiff should be member of immediate family of deceased, plaintiff should suffer actual physical harm, and injury to plaintiff should be fairly contemporaneous with accident.—Gustafson v. Faris, 241 N.W.2d 208, 67 Mich.App. 363.

Mich.App. 1975. Parents did not have an independent cause of action for emotional injury resulting from concern for their injured child when they were neither witnesses to accident causing their child's injuries nor present near scene of accident at time of its occurrence.—Perlmutter v. Whitney, 230 N.W.2d 390, 60 Mich.App. 268.

Mich.App. 1973. Plaintiff need not have been within "zone of danger" as condition precedent to maintaining action for mental suffering generated by witnessing negligent infliction of tortious injury upon immediate family member.—Toms v. McConnell, 207 N.W.2d 140, 45 Mich.App. 647.

Problem of limiting bystander recovery in mental suffering cases is best surmounted and justly resolved by treating each case on its own individual facts.—Id.

When child is in danger of negligent injury by third parties, it is foreseeable that mother may be somewhere in vicinity and will suffer serious shock.—Id.

Where mother as result of seeing her daughter killed withdrew from normal forms of socialization, was for period of nine months following accident unable to function as she had previously and continued in state of depression, her inability to function and continued state of depression were "physical injury" for purposes of recovery for mental suffering.—Id.

Parent may maintain cause of action for mental anguish resulting in definite and objective physical injury generated by witnessing negligent infliction of injuries upon parent's ...

must be proved, and the parent may not recover for injury to his feelings or mental distress.—Brennan v. Biber, 225 A.2d 742, 93 N.J.Super. 351, affirmed 239 A.2d 261, 99 N.J.Super. 247.

N.M.App. 1971. Mother's allegations of fright, shock and emotional distress upon witnessing death of her son as a bystander failed to state claim upon which recovery could be permitted.—Aragon v. Speelman, 491 P.2d 173, 83 N.M. 285.

N.Y. 1969. No cause of action lies for unintended harm sustained by one, solely as a result of injuries inflicted directly on another, regardless of the relationship and whether the one was an eyewitness to the incident which resulted in the direct injuries.—Tobin v. Grossman, 301 N.Y.S.2d 554, 24 N.Y.2d 609, 249 N.E.2d 419.

Mother, who was nearby and heard the screech of automobile brakes and who immediately went to the scene, a few feet away, and saw her injured two-year-old child lying on the ground, could not recover against person whose automobile hit child for her own mental and physical injuries caused by shock and fear for child.—Id.

N.Y.A.D. 1976. In action brought by husband and wife premised on alleged malpractice of defendants resulting in amputation of husband's right leg, defendants owed no duty directly to wife in regard to alleged injury to husband's leg, thus precluding wife's recovery under portion of complaint seeking recovery for mental and emotional anguish she was allegedly caused to suffer by witnessing her husband's suffering and eventual amputation.—Bessette v. St. Peter's Hospital, 381 N.Y.S.2d 339, 51 A.D.2d 286.

Generally, no action lies for unintended harm sustained solely as the result of injuries in-

For references to other topics, see Descriptive-Word Index

[Illustration 14]

SAMPLE PAGE FROM THE SEVENTH DECENNIAL DIGEST

11–7th D—1117

DAMAGES ⚷51

⚷51. —— Injury to the person of another

D.C.Ark. Under Arkansas law, plaintiff's emotional distress, and effect thereof upon her physical and mental condition, could not be considered as an appropriate element of damage in her action for injuries sustained in automobile collision, where such emotional distress resulted not from accident upon which she based her suit, but from seeing her father injured and killed in second accident which, although following the first very closely, was nevertheless entirely separate and distinct from it.—Beaty v. Buckeye Fabric Finishing Co., 179 F.Supp. 688.

D.C.Ark. 1961. Court in awarding damages to serviceman, whose wife was permanently injured by negligence of army officers at Oklahoma army base, could not consider mental anguish, if any, that husband had or would endure, but he was entitled to be compensated for loss of services, society and companionship of his wife. 28 U.S.C.A. § 1346(b).—Redding v. U. S., 196 F.Supp. 871.

D.C.Cal. Under California law, as generally, recovery may not be had for mental distress

This illustrates how a search may be continued from one Decennial to another. While not illustrated, a researcher, after examining the Eighth Decennial will normally next examine the individual volumes of the General Digest, 5th ser. and then may examine the earlier Decennials.

In all of the Decennial Digests, cases under a Key Number are arranged alphabetically by jurisdiction with those from the federal courts given first.

physical repercussions allegedly proximately resulting from witnessing killing of her sister by motor vehicle driven by post office employee, only if plaintiff was exposed to hazard of physical harm. 28 U.S.C.A. § 1346(b).—Id.

D.C.La. 1962. Under Louisiana law, parent may not recover for his own mental anguish and anxiety resulting from tort committed against his child. LSA–C.C. art. 2315.—Mahaffey v. Official Detective Stories, Inc., 210 F.Supp. 251.

D.C.Or. 1962. Mother's emotional anguish resulting from child's injury due to drinking of poison would be reasonably foreseeable result to any reasonably prudent manufacturing and dispensing pharmacist who failed to label, as required by law, the poisonous substance drunk by the child.—Rogers v. Hexol, Inc., 218 F.Supp. 453.

Recovery can be had for one's emotional distress incidental to and directly resulting from a violation of one's right to be free from personal hurt and right of privacy or property, and probably from fear for one's safety, but not as incident to and result of a violation of same rights of a third person.—Id.

Under Oregon law, manufacturer-wholesaler of liquid disinfectant-cosmetic, which allegedly contained a poisonous substance, but which was not labeled as poisonous, was not liable to mother for her foreseeable emotional distress and resulting minor physical injury flowing from knowledge that her young son had been injured as a result of manufacturer-wholesaler's failure to properly label disinfectant-cosmetic. Federal Food, Drug and Cosmetic Act, § 1 et seq., 21 U.S.C.A. § 301 et seq.; ORS 453.210.—Id.

D.C.Puerto Rico. Under Puerto Rican law, man who allegedly lived continuously in concubinage with a child's maternal grandmother and claimed to be foster father of the child, could not recover damages for mental and moral anguish from contemplating the child's condition and sufferings resulting from injuries caused by negligence of defendant. Rules of Civil Procedure Puerto Rico, rule 17(k); 31 L.P.R.A. §§ 561, 562, 568, 5141, 5142; 32 L.P.R.A. §§ 310, 311.—Gonzalez v. U. S., 140 F.Supp. 102.

Cal. 1963. Generally, recovery is not permitted for mental or emotional disturbance, or for bodily illness resulting therefrom, in absence of contemporaneous bodily contact or independent cause of action, or an element of wilfulness, wantonness, or maliciousness, where there is no injury other than one to a third person, even though recovery would have been permitted had wrong been directed

promptly advise parents as to nature of poison used on parents' premises and eaten by their minor child constituted sufficient ground on which to base an action against exterminator.—Holland v. St. Paul Mercury Ins. Co., 135 So.2d 145.

La.App. Father could not recover for mental anguish he allegedly suffered as result of injury negligently caused by another to daughter.—Vinet v. Checker Cab Co., 140 So.2d 252.

One person cannot recover damages for worry and mental suffering as result of injuries to another; right to damages is personal to that other.—Id.

La.App. 1963. Husband could not recover for mental agony suffered as result of his wife's injuries, since mental sufferings of one person as result of physical injuries received by another are not recoverable under Louisiana law.—Johnston v. Fidelity Nat. Bank of Baton Rouge, 152 So.2d 327.

La.App. 1965. Parents cannot recover for shock and mental suffering to themselves which results from physical injuries of their child.—Laplace v. Minks, 174 So.2d 895, writ refused 176 So.2d 452.

Law has not permitted recovery to one for his own physical disability, loss of earning capacity, or pain and suffering sustained by him as result of either seeing personal injuries of another, or learning of death of another, against tort-feasors, who are responsible for personal injury or death of other.—Id.

La.App. 1965. Plaintiff who suffered no physical injury when his automobile collided with defendant's oncoming vehicle could not recover for his mental anxiety and suffering and medical expenses caused by his emotional upset, subsequent nausea and stomach ailment arising out of his getting out of his automobile after accident and going to defendant's vehicle and seeing defendant's small daughter with a bloody forehead.—Duet v. Cheramie, 176 So. 2d 667.

One person cannot recover damages for worry, anxiety, depression, mental anguish, or other mental suffering as result of injuries to person of another.—Id.

La.App. 1966. Daughter's apprehension about father's condition following automobile accident in which they were both involved formed no basis for judgment in her favor.—Sabatier v. Travelers Ins. Co., 184 So.2d 594.

One person cannot recover damages for worry and mental suffering as result of injuries to another.—Id.

Miss. 1965. Jury should have been permitted to consider effects upon mother involved in collision of resulting death of her unborn child,

Sup. A parent's rights in an action for injuries to his child are restricted to an action for loss of the child's services and for medical expenses, and damages for mental suffering caused by the child's injuries are not recoverable.—Kalina v. General Hospital of City of Syracuse, 220 N.Y.S.2d 733.

Sup. No recovery could be had for fright and ensuing mental and physical suffering of bystander allegedly occasioned by negligence of motorist whose vehicle struck bystander's child. Rules of Civil Practice, rules 113, 114.—Berg v. Baum, 224 N.Y.S.2d 974.

Sup. Mother of child, killed allegedly through negligence of another, was not entitled to recover for severe emotional and neurological disturbances with resulting physical manifestations, where there was no physical contact or impact with mother, and defendant from whom recovery is sought did not owe duty to mother.—Lahann v. Cravotta, 228 N.Y.S.2d 371.

Sup. 1962. Parents' complaint to the effect that the negligent killing of their son in a hunting accident caused personal injuries to plaintiffs without otherwise showing how injuries were sustained and without alleging physical contact or even actual observation of killing failed to state a cause of action.—Robbins v. Castellani, 239 N.Y.S.2d 53.

Pa.Com.Pl. 1965. Where the plaintiffs instituted action to recover damages for grief and mental anguish and the physical conse-

For subsequent case history information, see Table of Cases

[Illustration 15]

SAMPLE PAGE FROM THE SECOND DECENNIAL DIGEST

[8—2d Dec.Dig.,Page 857] DAMAGES 🔑51

III. Grounds and Subjects of Compensatory Damages. (A) Direct or Remote, Contingent, or Prospective Consequences or Losses.

ments entering into the computation of pecuniary damages for personal injuries.—Souleyret v. O'Gara Coal Co., 161 Ill. App. 60.

(**Ill.App.**1911) In an action for personal injuries, it was not error to authorize the jury in estimating damages to consider the mental suffering of plaintiff, if any such suffering resulted from the injury.—Haywood v. Dering Coal Co., 161 Ill. App. 544.

(**Ind.**1906) In an action for personal injuries, plaintiff is not entitled to recover for unhappiness resulting from impaired freedom of action and from being deprived of social intercourse with friends.—Indianapolis St. Ry. Co. v. Ray, 78 N. E. 978, 167 Ind. 236.

(**Ind.**1910) Damages for mental anguish arising from apprehensions merely of a person injured are not recoverable.—Vandalia Coal Co. v. Yemm, 92 N. E. 49, 175 Ind. 524, rehearing denied (1911) 94 N. E. 881, 175 Ind. 524.

(**Ind.App.**1911) Worry and mental pain resulting from the contemplation of a deformity caused by a negligent injury, or the humiliation of going through life in that condition, are too remote to be considered as damages, but personal disfigurement resulting from a negligent

(**N.D.**1915) That a woman's fright from a prairie fire induced her to overwork herself in attempting to stop it *held* not to preclude her from recovering for injuries sustained by thus overworking.—Wilson v. Northern Pac. Ry. Co., 153 N. W. 429, 30 N. D. 456, L. R. A. 1915E, 991.

(**Or.**1914) Mental suffering accompanying personal injury is the subject of compensation, but should be connected with the injury, and its natural consequence and damages for prospective mental anguish are too speculative.—Adams v. Brosius, 139 P. 729, 69 Or. 513, 51 L. R. A. (N. S.) 36.

(**Pa.**1913) There may be recovery for shock caused by physical injury.—Samarra v. Allegheny Valley St. Ry. Co., 86 A. 287, 238 Pa. 469.

(**S.C.**1914) In an action for personal injuries the jury may consider in fixing damages plaintiff's mental anguish and worry, but only in connection with her physical injury and the injury to her nervous system.—Folk v. Seaboard Air Line Ry., 83 S. E. 452, 99 S. C. 284.

(**Tex.Civ.App.**1907) A child four years old

This is an illustration from the Second Decennial Digest. Under the same Topic and Key Number cases can be located that were decided between 1907 and 1916. If desired, the First Decennial can also be examined, and then the Century Digest under Damages, Paragraph Numbers 103, 255, and 256 to locate cases decided before 1897.

(**Mo.App.**1909) An instruction that if plaintiff suffered no physical injury, or injuries, in alighting from defendant's train at an improper place, she could not recover damages from fright or mental anguish, if any she suffered, but that bodily suffering from cold, or from being wet, if any, would be a physical injury within such instruction, was proper.—Dye v. Chicago & A. R. Co., 115 S. W. 497, 135 Mo. App. 254.

(**Mont.**1909) Where a woman suffers a miscarriage as a result of physical injury, she may recover for any mental or physical suffering attending the miscarriage as a part thereof, but cannot recover for injured feelings or lamented loss of her offspring.—Hosty v. Moulton Water Co., 102 P. 568, 39 Mont. 310.

(**N.J.**1908) In an action for personal injuries from an assault committed by defendant, mental suffering resulting from the injuries is a proper element of damage.—Bernadsky v. Erie R. Co., 70 A. 189, 76 N. J. Law, 580.

(**N.C.**1908) Mental suffering accompanying physical injury is a proper element of damages to be considered by the jury.—Britt v. Carolina Northern R. Co., 61 S. E. 601, 148 N. C. 37, motion for rehearing dismissed Britt v Carolina & N. R. Co., 64 S. E. 1135, 149 N. C. 581.

🔑51. —— Injury to the person of another.

See 15 Cent. Dig. Damag. §§ 103, 255, 256.

(**Ala.**1908) In an action by a parent for negligent injury to a minor, he may recover only compensatory damages, not including recovery for mental suffering by himself.—Reaves v. Anniston Knitting Mills, 45 So. 702, 154 Ala. 565.

(**Ala.App.**1911) One suffering physical injury from a nuisance may not recover for any mental suffering due to sickness of members of his family, caused by the nuisance.—Birmingham Waterworks Co. v. Martini, 56 So. 830, 2 Ala. App. 652.

(**Ky.**1913) A woman, traveling with her father, *held* not entitled to recover from the carrier for mere fright resulting from a wrongful assault upon him by the company's employés in her presence, nor for mere fright resulting from his wrongful ejection, nor from being left alone on the train during the rest of her journey.—Chesapeake & O. Ry. Co. v. Robinett, 152 S. W. 976, 151 Ky. 778, 45 L. R. A. (N. S.) 433.

(**La.**1907) A father is entitled to be paid for his loss of time resulting from the negligent injury of his minor son and for his expenditures for his son made necessary by the ac-

For earlier cases in First Decennial or cases in later Digests, see same topic and Key-Number.

[Illustration 16]

TABLE OF KEY NUMBERS FROM THE DESCRIPTIVE-WORD INDEX TO THE GENERAL DIGEST, 5th SERIES, VOLUMES 1–10

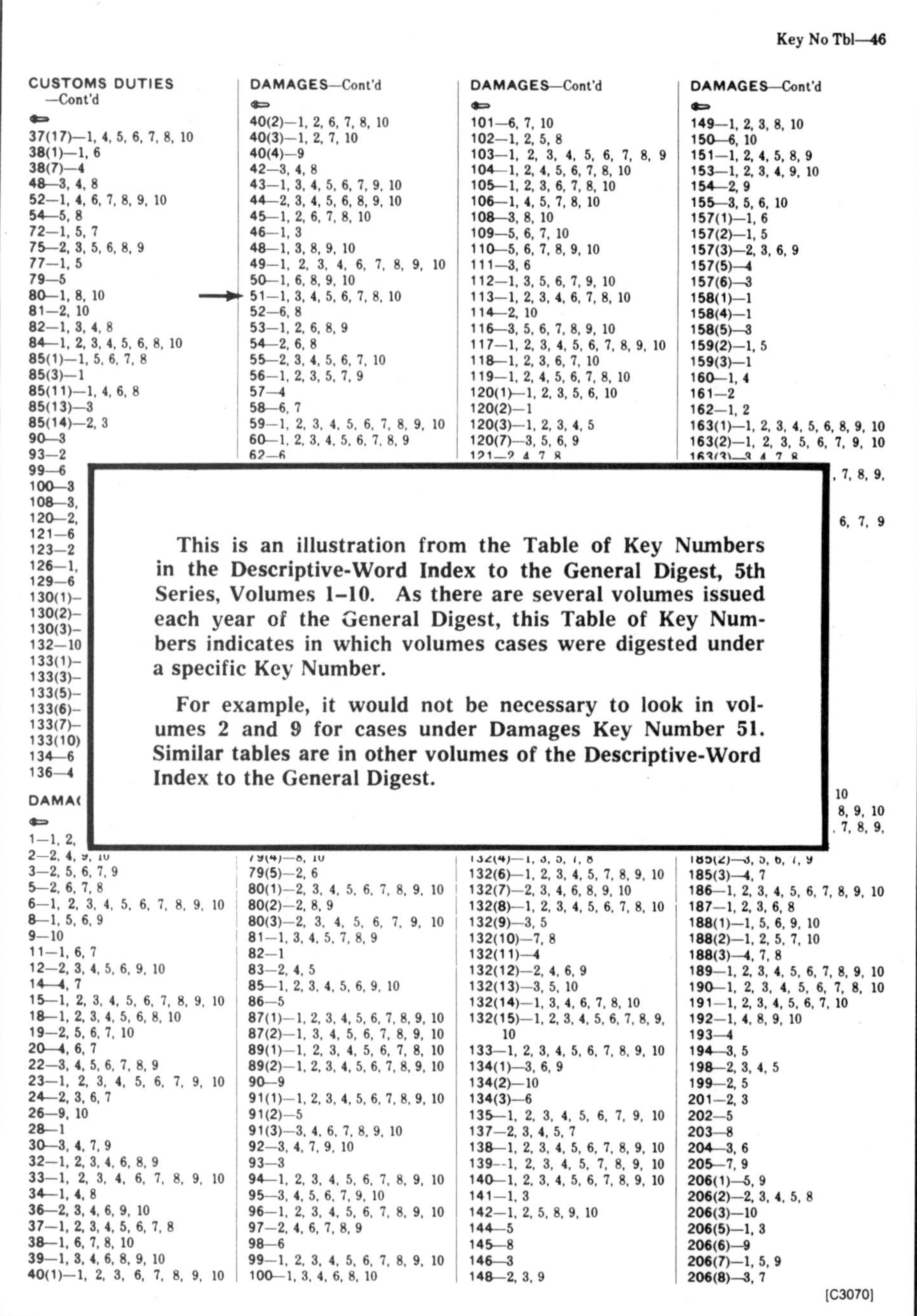

Key No Tbl—**46**

CUSTOMS DUTIES —Cont'd

37(17)—1, 4, 5, 6, 7, 8, 10
38(1)—1, 6
38(7)—4
48—3, 4, 8
52—1, 4, 6, 7, 8, 9, 10
54—5, 8
72—1, 5, 7
75—2, 3, 5, 6, 8, 9
77—1, 5
79—5
80—1, 8, 10
81—2, 10
82—1, 3, 4, 8
84—1, 2, 3, 4, 5, 6, 8, 10
85(1)—1, 5, 6, 7, 8
85(3)—1
85(11)—1, 4, 6, 8
85(13)—3
85(14)—2, 3
90—3
93—2
99—6
100—3
108—3,
120—2,
121—6
123—2
126—1,
129—6
130(1)–
130(2)–
130(3)–
132—10
133(1)–
133(3)–
133(5)–
133(6)–
133(7)–
133(10)
134—6
136—4

DAMA(

1—1, 2,
2—2, 4, 9, 10
3—2, 5, 6, 7, 9
5—2, 6, 7, 8
6—1, 2, 3, 4, 5, 6, 7, 8, 9, 10
8—1, 5, 6, 9
9—10
11—1, 6, 7
12—2, 3, 4, 5, 6, 9, 10
14—4, 7
15—1, 2, 3, 4, 5, 6, 7, 8, 9, 10
18—1, 2, 3, 4, 5, 6, 8, 10
19—2, 5, 6, 7, 10
20—4, 6, 7
22—3, 4, 5, 6, 7, 8, 9
23—1, 2, 3, 4, 5, 6, 7, 9, 10
24—2, 3, 6, 7
26—9, 10
28—1
30—3, 4, 7, 9
32—1, 2, 3, 4, 6, 8, 9
33—1, 2, 3, 4, 6, 7, 8, 9, 10
34—1, 4, 8
36—2, 3, 4, 6, 9, 10
37—1, 2, 3, 4, 5, 6, 7, 8
38—1, 6, 7, 8, 10
39—1, 3, 4, 6, 8, 9, 10
40(1)—1, 2, 3, 6, 7, 8, 9, 10

DAMAGES—Cont'd

40(2)—1, 2, 6, 7, 8, 10
40(3)—1, 2, 7, 10
40(4)—9
42—3, 4, 8
43—1, 3, 4, 5, 6, 7, 9, 10
44—2, 3, 4, 5, 6, 8, 9, 10
45—1, 2, 6, 7, 8, 10
46—1, 3
48—1, 3, 8, 9, 10
49—1, 2, 3, 4, 6, 7, 8, 9, 10
50—1, 6, 8, 9, 10
→ **51**—1, 3, 4, 5, 6, 7, 8, 10
52—6, 8
53—1, 2, 6, 8, 9
54—2, 6, 8
55—2, 3, 4, 5, 6, 7, 10
56—1, 2, 3, 5, 7, 9
57—4
58—6, 7
59—1, 2, 3, 4, 5, 6, 7, 8, 9, 10
60—1, 2, 3, 4, 5, 6, 7, 8, 9
62—6

79(4)—8, 10
79(5)—2, 6
80(1)—2, 3, 4, 5, 6, 7, 8, 9, 10
80(2)—2, 8, 9
80(3)—2, 3, 4, 5, 6, 7, 9, 10
81—1, 3, 4, 5, 7, 8, 9
82—1
83—2, 4, 5
85—1, 2, 3, 4, 5, 6, 9, 10
86—5
87(1)—1, 2, 3, 4, 5, 6, 7, 8, 9, 10
87(2)—1, 3, 4, 5, 6, 7, 8, 9, 10
89(1)—1, 2, 3, 4, 5, 6, 7, 8, 10
89(2)—1, 2, 3, 4, 5, 6, 7, 8, 9, 10
90—9
91(1)—1, 2, 3, 4, 5, 6, 7, 8, 9, 10
91(2)—5
91(3)—3, 4, 6, 7, 8, 9, 10
92—3, 4, 7, 9, 10
93—3
94—1, 2, 3, 4, 5, 6, 7, 8, 9, 10
95—3, 4, 5, 6, 7, 9, 10
96—1, 2, 3, 4, 5, 6, 7, 8, 9, 10
97—2, 4, 6, 7, 8, 9
98—6
99—1, 2, 3, 4, 5, 6, 7, 8, 9, 10
100—1, 3, 4, 6, 8, 10

DAMAGES—Cont'd

101—6, 7, 10
102—1, 2, 5, 8
103—1, 2, 3, 4, 5, 6, 7, 8, 9
104—1, 2, 4, 5, 6, 7, 8, 10
105—1, 2, 3, 6, 7, 8, 10
106—1, 4, 5, 7, 8, 10
108—3, 8, 10
109—5, 6, 7, 10
110—5, 6, 7, 8, 9, 10
111—3, 6
112—1, 3, 5, 6, 7, 9, 10
113—1, 2, 3, 4, 6, 7, 8, 10
114—2, 10
116—3, 5, 6, 7, 8, 9, 10
117—1, 2, 3, 4, 5, 6, 7, 8, 9, 10
118—1, 2, 3, 6, 7, 10
119—1, 2, 4, 5, 6, 7, 8, 10
120(1)—1, 2, 3, 5, 6, 10
120(2)—1
120(3)—1, 2, 3, 4, 5
120(7)—3, 5, 6, 9
121—2, 4, 7, 8

132(4)—1, 3, 5, 7, 8
132(6)—1, 2, 3, 4, 5, 7, 8, 9, 10
132(7)—2, 3, 4, 6, 8, 9, 10
132(8)—1, 2, 3, 4, 5, 6, 7, 8, 10
132(9)—3, 5
132(10)—7, 8
132(11)—4
132(12)—2, 4, 6, 9
132(13)—3, 5, 10
132(14)—1, 3, 4, 6, 7, 8, 10
132(15)—1, 2, 3, 4, 5, 6, 7, 8, 9, 10
133—1, 2, 3, 4, 5, 6, 7, 8, 9, 10
134(1)—3, 6, 9
134(2)—10
134(3)—6
135—1, 2, 3, 4, 5, 6, 7, 9, 10
137—2, 3, 4, 5, 7
138—1, 2, 3, 4, 5, 6, 7, 8, 9, 10
139—1, 2, 3, 4, 5, 7, 8, 9, 10
140—1, 2, 3, 4, 5, 6, 7, 8, 9, 10
141—1, 3
142—1, 2, 5, 8, 9, 10
144—5
145—8
146—3
148—2, 3, 9

DAMAGES—Cont'd

149—1, 2, 3, 8, 10
150—6, 10
151—1, 2, 4, 5, 8, 9
153—1, 2, 3, 4, 9, 10
154—2, 9
155—3, 5, 6, 10
157(1)—1, 6
157(2)—1, 5
157(3)—2, 3, 6, 9
157(5)—4
157(6)—3
158(1)—1
158(4)—1
158(5)—3
159(2)—1, 5
159(3)—1
160—1, 4
161—2
162—1, 2
163(1)—1, 2, 3, 4, 5, 6, 8, 9, 10
163(2)—1, 2, 3, 5, 6, 7, 9, 10
163(3)—3, 4, 7, 8
, 7, 8, 9,
6, 7, 9

10
8, 9, 10
, 7, 8, 9,
185(2)—3, 5, 6, 7, 9
185(3)—4, 7
186—1, 2, 3, 4, 5, 6, 7, 8, 9, 10
187—1, 2, 3, 6, 8
188(1)—1, 5, 6, 9, 10
188(2)—1, 2, 5, 7, 10
188(3)—4, 7, 8
189—1, 2, 3, 4, 5, 6, 7, 8, 9, 10
190—1, 2, 3, 4, 5, 6, 7, 8, 10
191—1, 2, 3, 4, 5, 6, 7, 10
192—1, 4, 8, 9, 10
193—4
194—3, 5
198—2, 3, 4, 5
199—2, 5
201—2, 3
202—5
203—8
204—3, 6
205—7, 9
206(1)—5, 9
206(2)—2, 3, 4, 5, 8
206(3)—10
206(5)—1, 3
206(6)—9
206(7)—1, 5, 9
206(8)—3, 7

This is an illustration from the Table of Key Numbers in the Descriptive-Word Index to the General Digest, 5th Series, Volumes 1–10. As there are several volumes issued each year of the General Digest, this Table of Key Numbers indicates in which volumes cases were digested under a specific Key Number.

For example, it would not be necessary to look in volumes 2 and 9 for cases under Damages Key Number 51. Similar tables are in other volumes of the Descriptive-Word Index to the General Digest.

[C3070]

[Illustration 17]

KEY NUMBER TRANSLATION TABLE FROM THE EIGHTH DECENNIAL DIGEST

FEDERAL COURTS

TABLE 1

KEY NUMBER TRANSLATION TABLE

COURTS AND APPEAL AND ERROR TO FEDERAL COURTS

The topic FEDERAL COURTS was formerly part of the topic COURTS. This table lists key numbers in the topic COURTS together with the corresponding key number(s) in the topic FEDERAL COURTS (or reference to another topic) where cases are now digested.

Federal cases formerly under certain key numbers of the topic APPEAL AND ERROR are also included in the topic FEDERAL COURTS. This table also lists key numbers of the topic APPEAL AND ERROR involved, with the key number(s) under FEDERAL COURTS where federal cases are now digested.

For present classification of a particular case, see the Table of Cases.

Courts Key Number	Federal Courts Key Number	Courts Key Number	Federal Courts Key Number
23 (selected pars.)	31	263(5)	15
101	742	263(6)	17
101.5(1)	991, 1008–1010	263(7)	16
101.5(2)	992, 998, 1002, 1008–1010	264(1)	20, 23, 24
101.5(3)	997	264(2)	21, 23, 24
101.5(4)	993–996, 998–1002, 1008–1010	264(3)	22
101.5(5)	1003–1006, 1008–1010	264(4)	21
101.5(6)	1007	264(5)	25
101.5(7)	1011	264.1	8

This illustrates how the Key Number classification is kept current. In the Eighth Decennial Digest, Federal Courts was made a separate Topic. This Table, which precedes the Topic, allows one who has been searching in earlier Decennials under a Courts Key Number to translate into the new Federal Courts Key Number. While not shown, Table 2 translates Federal Court Key Numbers to Court Key Numbers.

Courts Key Number	Federal Courts Key Number	Courts Key Number	Federal Courts Key Number
262.3	(specific topics)	274.4	91
262.4	6 (and specific topics)	274.5	86
262.5	(Injunction)	274.6	78
262.6	(Injunction)	274.7	77, 89
262.8	27 (and specific topics)	274.8–10	88
262.9	28 (and specific topics)	274.11	90
263(1, 2)	14	274.12	77, 92
263(3)	18	274.13	80
263(4)	19	274.14(1, 2)	79, 82, 87, 92

SECTION D. FINDING TOPICS AND KEY NUMBERS

The *American Digest System* as classified to the *Key Number System* provides a means to locate all decisions on the same point of law. Once it is determined to what Topic and Key Number a particular point of law has been classified, searching for cases can commence in the various units of the *American Digest System.*

The important matter is to learn how to find the Topic and Key Number. There are three common methods provided for within the *American Digest System.*

1. The Descriptive-Word Index

The *Descriptive-Word Index* is arranged alphabetically and includes: (1) all topics of the digest classification; (2) all Key Number section lines and editorial reference lines in the *Decennial Digests;* (3) "catch" words or descriptive words relating to parties to the suits who are members of a class, occupation, or legal relation; (4) place names and physical objects; (5) questions of law; (6) constitutional and legislative provisions; and (7) legal principles which relate to the subject matter of the suit.

There is a separate *Descriptive-Word Index* to each of the *Decennial* units as well as to the *General Digest.*

Let us examine the problem described in Section A to see how the *Descriptive-Word Index* to the *Decennial* units of the *American Digest System* is used to locate Topics and Key Numbers for locating cases dealing with damages to a child who has suffered emotional or mental distress by observing an accident to a close relative.

In starting the search, it is best to start with the *Descriptive-Word Index* to the latest *Decennial* or to the *General Digest.* When using an index, the first entry looked under should be the *least common denominator* to the problem researched. In this instance, it may be *Step-Grandmother* or *Grandmother* or *Grandparent.* If no suitable index entry is found, then try *Shock.* If still no entry is located, then broaden the search, and if necessary use legal concepts such as *Emotional Distress,* or *Mental Anguish,* or *Damages.* At times, it may be necessary to consult the *Descriptive-Word Indexes* to earlier *Decennials.* After a Topic and Key Number have been identified from the Index volume, the volume containing the digests for this Topic should be consulted to locate cases analogous to the problem being researched.

Illustrations 18–18a-b demonstrate in detail the use of the *Descriptive-Word Index* as a means of locating Topics and Key Numbers.

2. Analysis or Topic Method

As the *American Digest System* is based on a classification system, it is possible to analyze a fact situation and to determine from this analysis which Topics and Key Numbers will be applicable to the problem being researched. In the problem used to illustrate the *Descriptive-Word Index* approach, *supra*, one could determine that the topic of law involved is *Damages* and then check the *Analysis and Outline* that appears immediately after the Topic *Damages* in the *Eighth Decennial* and then locate the appropriate Key Numbers. [See Illustrations 11–11-a]

The method requires a certain amount of legal sophistication and should not be used without having a fairly good knowledge of law. Moreover, there is always the danger inherent in this approach that the researcher may arrive at one analysis which leads to a specific Topic and Key Number, whereas the editors in their analysis assigned a different Topic and Key Number. Hence, it is recommended that this method be used with care and only after one has had considerable experience in legal research.

3. Table of Cases Method

Each *Decennial* unit and each volume of the *General Digest* has an alphabetical table of cases by plaintiff. Each case listed gives its citation and what Topics and Key Numbers the case has been digested under. Thus, if one knew, for example, that *Leong v. Takasaki* dealt with the question of damages as related to mental suffering, by consulting the Table of Cases volumes of the *Eighth Decennial* the citation and Topics and Key Numbers can easily be located. [See Illustration 19]

This method is most useful when one knows the name of a case and wishes to find additional cases on the same points of law.

SECTION E. ILLUSTRATIONS: FINDING THE TOPICS AND KEY NUMBERS

18. Sample pages from the Descriptive-Word Index to the Eighth Decennial Digest

19. Sample page from Table of Cases Volumes of the Eighth Decennial Digest

[Illustration 18]

SAMPLE PAGE FROM DESCRIPTIVE-WORD INDEX TO THE EIGHTH DECENNIAL DIGEST

DAMAGES

DAMAGES—Cont'd
Roof repair work, limitation to contract price. **Damag 189**
Rubella, doctor not informing pregnant woman of effects on a fetus, measure of damages. **Phys 15(8), 18.110**
Rule to show cause, damages not recoverable on. **Motions 24**
Running at large, automobile collision. **Damag 132(2)**
Sales, appeal causing delay in sales of property. **Decl Judgm 392**
Scars, elements considered. **Damag 98**
Scope of project—
  Eminent domain, lands within project when announced, compensating condemnees for enhanced value. **Em Dom 131**
  Enhanced value attributable to, compensation. **Em Dom 124**
Scars on face. **Damag 132(7)**
Scars on woman's face. **Damag 132(1)**
School board's failure to act on claim within 45 days, rejection by operation of law. **Schools 112**
Scuba diver, oxygen poisoning. **New Tr 140(3)**
Seamen, life expectancy, measure of damages. **Damag 99, 100**
Seamen, nervous condition precipitated by sinking of ship, compensable cause of separation and divorce. **Damag 53**
Seamen injured in automobile rear-end collision. **Damag 132(3)**
Search, compensible injury from unreasonable search not shown, damages reduced from $500 to $1. **Civil R 13.17**
Searches and seizures, unreasonable, civil action. **Searches 8**
Seatbelts—
  Failure to use, mitigation. **Damag 62(2)**
  Injured party not wearing, evidence for reduction of damages.

DAMAGES—Cont'd
Shoe machinery manufacturer, monopolistic leasing practices. **Monop 28 (7.7)**
Sick leave pay, loss of earnings, deductions—
  App & E 1067
  Damag 214
Simultaneous collisions, full amount from each tort-feasor. **Autos 200**
Slander of title. **Libel 135**
Small property damage claims, penalty, failure to pay. **Damag 71½, 227**
Spastic torticollis, not excessive. **Damag 132(3)**
Special damages, excessiveness. **Damag 135**
Special damages—
  Not pleaded, amendment of complaint—
    Damag 157(6)
    Plead 236(5)
Specification, items of damages. **Damag 141**
Sprains. **Damag 130(1)**
Sterility caused by injury. **Damag 132(4)**
State, liability for sweet potato crop damaged by wild deer. **States 112.2 (3)**
Sterilization, malpractice. **Trial 114**
Sterilization operation, pregnancy occurring after. **Phys 18(11)**
Stock and stockholders—
  Breach of sale contract. **Corp 121(7)**
Strikes, unlawful strike. **Labor 768**
Strip search, pupils, school officials present while police conducted search. **Civil R 13.7**
Subjective opinion, pain and suffering. **Evid 496**
Subjective symptoms. **Damag 130(4)**
Subsequent accident, aggravation, instructions to jury—

DAMAGES—Cont'd
Time—
  Disability at time of trial, elapsed time after accident. **Damag 185 (2)**
  Loss from work, compensable notwithstanding sick leave or vacation taken. **Damag 37**
Tips, proof of average earnings. **Damag 172(1)**
Tire blowout resulting in destruction of truck, damages for truck loss and use. **Sales 442(1)**
Trade secret appropriation, burden of proof. **Torts 27**
Traumatic neurosis, amount of award. **Damag 130(3, 4)**
Trespassing livestock, grazing district. **Anim 51, 57**
Truth in lending, rescission of interest paid and award of double same amount. **Pawnb 6.9**
Uninsured motorist, judgment against, reduction on appeal due to assets possessed. **Damag 128**
Uninsured motorist insurers, recovery against, split of tortfeasor's insurance causing recovery lower than statutory minimum. **Insurance 531.3**
Uninsured motorists coverage, cervical strain and arthritis aggravation, award of $3,500. **Insurance 531.3**
United States contracts, breach by government, forfeiture of damages. **U S 74(13)**
Union members, no-strike clause violation by refusing to cross picket line. **Labor 752**
United States, unauthorized use of rust removal invention, measure of damages. **U S 97**
Unliquidated tort claims, medical malpractice. **Execution 47**
Vacation, loss of vacation time due to rear end collision. **Damag 37**

We can now start to illustrate how Topics and Key Numbers can be located using the Descriptive-Word Index for the fact situation set forth in Section A. The first step is to choose a word or concept.

If the search is started under Damages, this is such a broad topic that it may be difficult to find an entry leading to cases exactly on point.

Although the two entries outlined below are very close, it is usually better to enter an index under a more specific entry as shown by Illustrations 18, 18–a, 18–b.

damages. **Fed Civ Proc 1954**
Severance damages—
  Condemned land within scope of project when announced, compensating condemnee for enhanced value. **Em Dom 137**
  Expropriation of land for public use, offset by increase in highway frontage. **Em Dom 145(4)**
  Landlocked land parcel. **Em Dom 124**
  Loss of access as element. **Em Dom 106**
Ships, canal operation. **Canals 30**
Shock, nervous, recovery by husband who saw accident in which wife was injured. **Damag 51**
→ Shock, parents seeing child killed in vehicle accident. **Damag 51**
→ Shock and fear, mother suffering mental and physical injuries, automobile striking child. **Damag 51**

  Discriminatory refusal to rehire, declining to move out of state to reduce damages. **Damag 62(1)**
  Insubordination, termination of contract without notice. **Civil R 13.16, 13.17**
  Wrongful discharge. **Schools 142**
Teeth, loss of. **Damag 130(1), 132(7)**
Telephone company's underground cables and conduit, recovery of nominal damages. **Tel 127**
Telephone yellow pages, omission of professional listing. **Tel 277**
Television film, cutting to accommodate commercials. **Tel 442**
Temporary easements, measure. **Em Dom 147**
Testicles, shrinkage. **Damag 208(3)**
Therapy sessions, painful, interference with possible dancing career. **Damag 134(3)**

Whiplash injury. **Damag 132(3)**
  Damag 185(1), 208(1)
  Automobile accident. **Damag 130 (3, 4), 134(1)**
  Excessiveness. **Damag 132(3)**
  Excessiveness of award five months' loss of work and medical expenses. **Damag 130(3)**
  Pain and suffering, change of work required. **Damag 130(3)**
  Prior arthritic condition aggravated. **Damag 130(3)**
Wills—
  Negligence of attorney in drafting—
    Loss to estate—
      Atty & C 109
      Ex & Ad 426
Women, employment discrimination, class action. **Fed Civ Proc 184**
Work record of manual laborer, loss of future earnings. **Damag 133**

[Illustration 18–a]

EXCERPTS FROM THE DESCRIPTIVE-WORD INDEX TO THE EIGHTH DECENNIAL DIGEST

46–8th D—1082

EMOTIONAL DISTRESS—Cont'd
Death, collision in territorial waters, damages for distress of survivors. **Death 89**
Drowning, oxidation pond attractive nuisance, grandfather's fatal heart attack at child's funeral. **Death 15**
Extreme conduct toward immediate member of plaintiff's family. **Torts 7**
Foreseeable and proximate result of intentional, wanton, or wilful wrongful conduct. **Damag 49**
Heart attack emotionally initiated, accidental injury. **Work Comp 571**
Impact or injury rule, less strict application, sufficient guarantees of genuineness found in facts of case. **Damag 53**
Insurer's liability, evidence. **Insurance 602.9**
Intentional infliction, elements of prima facie case. **Torts 27**
Intentional infliction of severe emotional distress, extreme and outrageous conduct. **Torts 7**
Internal revenue investigation, threats, damages. **Damag 53**
Maritime law, compensable damages. **Damag 48**
→ Mother seeing negligently caused death of nonnegligent minor son. **Damag 51**
Outrageous conduct toward immediate member of plaintiff's family. **Torts 7**
→ Parents, mental suffering on learning of collision injuring minor daughter. **Damag 51**
Physical injury, emotional distress causing, damages. **Damag 50**
Premature infant, dead body exhibited in formaldehyde jar to mother, outrageous conduct. **Dead Bodies 9**
Relative, witnessing employee's fatal injury. **Work Comp 2145**
Securities, violations of statutes causing emotional distress, damages.

Tort liability. **Torts 24**
Unaccompanied by physical harm. **Damag 49**

47–8th D—266

MENTAL SUFFERING—Cont'd
Damages in general—Cont'd
→ Mother viewing son's injuries, shortly after explosion, institutionalization. **Damag 51**
Physical injuries, allegation required. **Damag 149**
Whiplash injuries, mortality tables as evidence. **Damag 167, 185(2), 216(5)**
Dead bodies, intentional and wanton mishandling, liability to parents, applicability of impact rule. **Dead Bodies 9**
Death—
Adult child, validity of statutes denying parents damages. **Death 9**
Amount. **Death 95(1)**
Beneficiaries of death action, recovery. **Death 78**
Deceased's suffering. **Damag 82**
Disposition of body by funeral home, appeal. **Courts 100(1)**
Heart attack, workmen's compensation. **Work Comp 1536**
Hospital inaccurately informing daughter of mother's death. **Hosp 8**
State hospital misinforming patient's daughter of. **Damag 53**
Minor child, damages to parents living apart—
Death 21(7)
Parent & C 7(6)
Railroad crossing accident, mental anguish, grandparents' right to recovery. **Death 103(4)**
Deformed infant, medicine taken during gestation. **Parent & C 7(1)**
Discriminatory discharge from employment, unsupported testimony insufficient to sustain damages award. **Civil R 64**
Distinct cause of action or element of damages—
Daughters, father's injuries causing. **Damag 51**

Damag 167, 185(2), 216(5)
Executions—
Dissolution of wrongful seizure.

This illustrates how by looking under the main entries of Emotional Distress or Mental Suffering, the researcher would be led to Damages Key Number 51.

[Illustration 18-b]

SAMPLE PAGE FROM THE DESCRIPTIVE-WORD INDEX TO THE EIGHTH DECENNIAL DIGEST

STEPCHILDREN AND STEPPARENTS—Cont'd
Wrongful death of unadopted stepdaughter, stepfather's action rights. **Death 31(7)**

STEPFATHER
Duty to support children. **Parent & C 14**
Support of stepdaughter. **Parent & C 14**

STEPGRANDCHILDREN
Inheritance tax, validity of different tax for grandchildren. **Tax 859(4)**

STEPGRANDCHILDREN AND STEPGRANDPARENTS
Mental suffering, ten-year old child seeing stepgrandmother killed. **Damag 51, 178**

STEP-IN-THE-DARK RULE
Contributory negligence, ballroom patron, entering storage room, opening door inside, taking step and falling

STERILIZATION—Cont'd
Action for refusal, hospital's later performance of operation not making moot. **Actions 6**
Bilateral tubal legation, computation of malpractice limitation. **Lim of Act 55(3)**
Billboard, telephone numbers concerning sterilization information, clear and present danger of evils not presented—
Abort 1
Health & E 33.5
Birth of mentally and physically retarded child, wife's breach of contract action against physician. **Lim of Act 21(3)**
Child born after procedure performed on wife, suit for cost of rearing and educating, public policy regarding procreation. **Phys 18(11)**
Child custody, award to father because he had vasectomy. **Parent & C 2 (3.1)**
Constitutional and statutory provisions,

STERILIZATION—Cont'd
Sickness or injury policy, insurer denying coverage for elective operation. **Insurance 467.5**
State physician, refusal to operate for lack of consent by patient's husband, sufficiency of complaint. **Civil R 13.12(8)**
Wife, right to obtain operation without husband's consent. **Const Law 82**
Wrongful life, unsuccessful operation—
Hosp 8
Phys 18.12

STERILIZATION OPERATION
Malpractice action, statute of limitations, running from date of pregnancy discovery. **Lim of Act 55(3)**

STETSON PLAYBOY
Trade marks, proposed clothing sale mark Playboy of Miami, likelihood of confusion. **Trade Reg 196**

STEVEDORES
"Accident free" ship, shipper's duty to

This illustrates how by looking in the Index under the most specific word in the fact situation, in this instance "Step-grandmother," one is led quickly and directly to a Topic and Key Number directly on point.

After locating the Topic and Key Number, it is now necessary to examine the digest paragraphs under the Key Number in the Eighth Decennial Digest and then in other units as shown in Illustrations 18—18-b.

STEPS
Elevated floor levels, public places, constituting negligence per se. **Neglig 44**
Fall, deterioration of nonslip material on steps. **Neglig 31**
Negligence, presumptions and burden of proof. **Neglig 121.1(8)**
Real estate agent, fall, owner's liability. **Neglig 121(5)**
Sidewalk, negligence of lowering street level, leaving step between. **Mun Corp 768(3)**
Wet steps, invitee slipping, corporate owner liability. **Neglig 44**

STEREO CABINETS
Customs, radio-phonograph combinations and parts, or furniture. **Cust Dut 26(2)**

STEREO DEVICE
Automobile insurance—
Defrauding insurer—
Theft. **Crim Law 406(1)**

STEREO EFFECT
Overdubbed songs monaurally recorded, stereo label on album cover. **Trade Reg 422, 628**

STEREO PHONOGRAPH
Sales on chain referral system, mail fraud. **Crim Law 676**

STERILITY
Childhood disease causing, paternity disavowal forbidden. **Bast 7**
Divorce, independent ground. **Divorce 16**
Paternity proceedings, subsequent discovery, reopening proceedings. **Bast 73, 75**

STERILIZATION
Generally, see this index **Social Security 13, 241.95**

Mentally retarded child, juvenile court, jurisdiction. **Mental H 57**
Negligence action against surgeon—
Pregnancy after sterilizing wife—
Breach of warranty. **Phys 14 (3)**
Caesarean section resulting, wife's mental and physical suffering issues precluding summary judgment. **Fed Civ Proc 2515**
Husband's part creating condition, intervening cause relieving surgeon's liability. **Phys 15(4)**
Limitation of action. **Lim of Act 95(1)**
Negligent surgeon, recovery of damages imposing financial responsibility for raising and educating subsequently born child violating public policy and provable damages law. **Phys 18.110**
Nontherapeutic, legality, competent consent. **Phys 10**
Operation on husband, subsequent conception by wife, physician liability. **Phys 15(12)**
Paternity, default judgment, voluntary vasectomy not warranting setting aside. **Bast 75**
Physicians and surgeons—
Damages for ineffective sterilization. **Phys 18(9, 11)**
Liability, pregnancy following operation on woman. **Phys 15(12)**
Pregnancy after operation, damages. **Phys 18(11)**
Private nonprofit hospital rule prohibiting sterilization, statute violations. **Hosp 6**
Probate judge, immunity, issuance of order for girl to submit to operation. **Civil R 13.8(5)**
Public welfare. **Social S 241**
Right of individuals to have sterilization operation. **Mental H 57**

(6)
Charter party terms, failure to investigate. **Mar Liens 28, 30**
Contractor, limited sales, excise and use tax liabilities. **Licens 15.1(5)**
Cotton bales, loading, injuries, fall. **Ship 84(3¼)**
Custody and control of goods, workmanlike performance, contractual duty. **Ship 110**
Dangerous or defective condition of vessel, appliances or places for work—
Fumes in hold, failure to stop work or turn on blowers. **Ship 84(6)**
Death—
Measure of damages. **Death 95(2, 3)**
Michigan territorial waters, state wrongful death act applicable. **Death 14(1)**
Discarded plastic bags, failure to remove from dock areas, tripping injuries. **Wharves 21**
Employees, injury 200 yards from ship, applicability, seaworthiness warranty. **Ship 84(1)**
Equipment, latent defect constituting unseaworthy condition. **Ship 84(6)**
Fall, employee, proximate cause, oil, grease, and water on deck, seaworthiness. **Ship 84(3¼)**
Fall, longshoreman on oil patch from shipboard winch, indemnification of shipowner. **Ship 84(6)**
Fellow servant doctrines—
Negligence rendering vessel unseaworthy. **Ship 86(2¾)**
Fraud, employees handling and watching cargo. **Ship 110**
Guaranteed annual wage of employees, charterer paying fixed charge per ton unloaded. **Mar Liens 25½**

[Illustration 19]

SAMPLE PAGE FROM THE TABLE OF CASES VOLUMES OF THE EIGHTH DECENNIAL DIGEST

LEONARDIS

References are to Digest Topics and Key Numbers

Leonardis v. Local 282 Pension Trust Fund, DCNY, 391 FSupp 554—Courts 489(9); Fed Cts 201, 205; Labor 759, 777; Mast & S 78.1(8); Rem of C 11, 19(1).
Leonardo v. Civil Service Commission, NYAD4th, 337 NYS2d 613, aff 358 NYS2d 136, 314 NE2d 876—Mun Corp 191.
Leonardson v. Country Mut Ins Co, IllApp, 239 NE2d 498. See Country Mut Ins Co v. Murray.
Leonardson v. Moon 92 Idaho 796, 451 P2d 542—App & E 883, 969, 977(5), 1010.1(6); Const Law 26, 48(1, 3), 229(2); Counties 2; Licens 5, 7(1); States 130, 131; Tax 38, 191, 194, 1217, 1219.
Leonardt Imp Co v. Southdown, Inc, DCCal, 313 FSupp 1146. See C Leonardt Imp Co v. Southdown, Inc.
Leonardziak Liquor License Case 210 PaSuper 511, 233 A2d 606. See Pennsylvania Liquor Control Bd v. Leonardziak.
Leonas v. Johnson, GaApp, 176 SE2d 506—Courts 217(3); Ex & Ad 85 (5); Joint Ten 3, 8; Plead 354(17).
Leone, In re, NYAD1st, 359 NYS2d 293—Atty & C 58.
Leone v. American Can Co, MoApp, 413 SW2d 558—Work Comp 630, 1348, 1358, 1583, 1966, 1969.
Sun Leong v. Honolulu Rapid Transit Co.
Leong v. O'Shea, CAHawaii, 363 F2d 426. See Kee Yiu Leong v. O'Shea.
Leong v. Takasaki, Hawaii, 520 P2d 758—Adop 21; Damag 51, 53, 178, 192, 208(6); Evid 528; Judgm 181(2, 33), 185.3(21).
Leong v. Wright, TexCivApp, 478 SW2d 839, ref n r e—Damag 63; Phys 18.80(2); Plead 236(3); Release 27; Stip 14(7).
Leong Chong Wing v. U S, CCAWash, 95 F2d 903—Drugs & N 128, 191.
Leon Grande, Tug El, DCLa, 396 F Supp 1020. See Seley Barges, Inc v. Tug El Leon Grande.
Leonhard v. Mitchell, CANY, 473 F2d 709, cert den 93 SCt 3011—Fed Cts 11, 243; Mand 140; Parent & C 1; U S 125(24).
Leonhard and Askew v. Joachim Memorial Home, ND, 234 NW2d 226. See Askew v. Joachim Memorial Home.
Leonhardt, M/V Bernd, CAMd, 393 F2d 756. See Partenreederei M S Bernd Leonhardt v. U S.
Leonhardt v. Cammack, FlaApp, 327 So2d 848—Cert 5(2); Discov 93.
Leonhardt v. Harimon, Neb, 174 NW 2d 926—App & E 1064.1(1), 1064.4; Trial 228(3), 296(1).
Leonhart v. Atkinson, Md, 289 A2d (1), 698(1); Homic 257(1); Infants 68.
Leo Wallace Ins Agency v. Hatem, MdApp, 348 A2d 879. See Wallace v. Hatem.
LePage v. City of Oakland, CalApp, 91 CalRptr 806—Decl Judgm 5, 62, 68, 207, 319, 385; Mand 66, 75; Mun Corp 187(5), 200(5); Pensions 1.
LePage v. Picard, CAMass, 495 F2d 26, cert den 95 SCt 144—Courts 100 (1); Crim Law 414; Hab Corp 85.5 (14), 90.
L E Pauling Decorating Co v. Rountree, MoApp, 412 SW2d 545. See Pauling v. Rountree.
Lepel v. Hitch, CAColo, 468 F2d 149—Anim 22.
Lepel v. Lepel, Idaho, 456 P2d 219—App & E 878(1); Const Law 84; Divorce 25, 27(1), 130, 223, 286(1), 296, 309; Hus & W 249(2, 6), 250, 255, 264(1); Joint Adv 8.
Lepera v. Lepera, NYSup, 290 NYS 2d 268—Divorce 216, 243.
LePera v. Snider, ND, 240 NW2d 862—Const Law 273; Contempt 52, 53, 60(1), 61(4), 70; Hab Corp 113 (3).
LePere v. Obernuefemann, IllApp, 328 NE2d 583—Zoning 743.
Le Pes v. State Farm Mut Auto Ins Co, IllApp, 279 NE2d 184. See

A page from the Table of Cases volume of the Eighth Decennial Digest.

When a case is known to deal with a topic of law, Key Numbers can be located by the use of the Table of Cases.

Note also how a Table of Cases may be used to determine if a particular case has been appealed to a higher court and the results of the appeal. See Leonescu v. Star Liquor Dealers, Inc.

Leone v. Putnam, CAFla, 466 F2d 512—Hus & W 14.2(7), 14.10; Spec Perf 33.
Leone v. Smith, NYAD4th, 370 NYS 2d 760. See Klinger v. Dudley.
Leone v. State, FlaApp, 233 So2d 404 supplemented 238 So2d 433—Crim Law 1077.3.
Leone v. State, FlaApp, 238 So2d 433—Crim Law 1077.3.
Leone v. U S 204 CtCl 334—Fed Cts 1102; U S 36.
Leone v. Valiant Ins Co, TexCivApp, 461 SW2d 426—Judgm 185(2, 6); Mtg 395, 415(1).
Leone Management Corp v. Board of Com'rs of North Bergen Tp, NJ SuperL, 328 A2d 26. See Leone Management Corp v. Board of Com'rs of Town of West New York.
Leone Management Corp v. Board of Com'rs of Town of West New York, NJSuperL, 328 A2d 26—Land & Ten 200.10, 200.11; Mun Corp 62, 111(4), 122(2), 592(1), 619.
Leonescu v. Star Liquor Dealers, Inc, AD3d, 270 NYS2d 480, aff 286 NY S2d 849, 233 NE2d 853—Work Comp 2064.
Leong v. Flynn-Learner, Hawaii, 472 P2d 505. See Mew Sun Leong v. Honolulu Rapid Transit Co.
Leong v. Honolulu Rapid Transit Co, Hawaii, 472 P2d 505. See Mew
Leopold v. Fitzgerald, CANY, 421 F2d 838—Fed Cts 595.
Leopold v. Leopold, NYAD2d, 269 N YS2d 167—Divorce 302, 308.
Leopold v. Levin, Ill, 259 NE2d 250—Const Law 90.1(8); Judgm 297, 340, 345, 354; Torts 8.5(1, 4, 5).
Leopold v. Richard Bertram & Co, FlaApp, 265 So2d 710—App & E 1157.
Leopold v. Richard Bertram & Co, FlaApp, 276 So2d 225—Jury 28 (17).
Leopard v. State, TexCrApp, 429 SW 2d 150—Crim Law 1131(5).
Leopold v. Tofany, NYSuper, 325 NYS 2d 24, aff 327 NYS2d 999—Autos 144.1(1); Courts 485; Crim Law 388.
Leopold v. U S, CACal, 510 F2d 617—App & E 170(1); Fed Cts 612; Int Rev 1001, 1010, 2164.
Leopold v. Young, DCVt, 340 FSupp 1014—Fed Cts 61, 222, 1002; Schools 53(1).
Leopold Morse Tailoring Co v. U S, CtCl, 408 F2d 739—Fed Cts 1111; U S 64, 73(9, 15, 20, 21), 74(8, 11).
Leopoldo Z, In re, NYFamCt, 358 N YS2d 811—Infants 16.11.
Leo Realty Co v. Redevelopment Authority of City of Wilkes-Barre, Pa Cmwlth, 320 A2d 149—Em Dom 45, 171, 181.
Leos v. State, TexCrApp, 410 SW2d 445—Crim Law 165, 517(1, 5), 517.3
after remand 210 NW2d 517—Licens 16(11); Mand 164(1), 174.
Lepofsky v. City of Lincoln Park, MichApp, 210 NW2d 517—App & E 1177(9); Cert 1, 14, 68; Const Law 72, 73; Courts 204; Mand 11, 70, 172.
LePore, In re, NYAD4th, 334 NYS2d 102—Atty & C 58.
Lepore v. New York News Inc, DC NY, 346 FSupp 755—Inj 136(3); Monop 17(1.3), 24(7, 9), 28(1.6).
Lepore v. New York News, DC NY, 365 FSupp 1387—Inj 157; Monop 24(7).
LePore v. State, NYCtCl, 339 NYS 2d 259—Colleges 5; Mun Corp 768 (1), 851; States 112.2(1).
Leppala v. Sawbill Canoe Outfitters, Inc, DCMinn, 361 FSupp 409—Const Law 307; Fed Cts 421; Work Comp 19, 2142.
Lepper v. Langlois, RI, 222 A2d 678—Courts 100(1); Crim Law 517.1(1), 532.
Leppig v. Green, FlaApp, 201 So2d 803—Hab Corp 113(12).
Leppig v. Martin, CAFla, 386 F2d 190—Hab Corp 113(10).
Leppo, Petition of, CAFla, 497 F2d 954—Tel 491.
Leppo v. City of Petaluma, CalApp, 97 CalRptr 840—Const Law 278(4); Health 32; Mun Corp 628, 742(4, 5), 751(1).

SECTION F. SPECIAL DIGESTS

As the *American Digest System* with its *Key Number* classification is made up from the headnotes from all of the units of the *National Reporter System*, it is all-inclusive and most useful when one is interested in locating decisions from all American jurisdictions. More typically, however, when engaged in legal research, one is primarily interested in locating opinions from a particular state or group of states, or in only those opinions decided in the federal courts. In such instances, it is better and easier to use a digest less comprehensive than that of the *American Digest System.*

1. State Digests

The West Publishing Company publishes for nearly every state a *Key Number* digest.[1] A typical state Key Number digest consists of digest paragraphs for all the cases of the particular state, including those that originated in the federal courts of the state. It is kept current through the issuing of annual cumulative pocket supplements for the set and each state digest has its own *Descriptive-Word Index* and table of cases volumes.

2. Regional Digests

There are regional digests corresponding to most of the regional reporters of the *National Reporter System.* These digests are arranged under the Key Number classification and include digests of cases for each of the states within the particular region. The digest paragraphs under each Key Number are arranged alphabetically by the states included within the digest. Each regional digest has its own volumes of the Descriptive-Word Index and its own volumes of Tables of Cases. They are kept current by the issuing of annual cumulative pocket supplements and interim pamphlet supplements. The regional digests are:

Atlantic Digest, First and Second Series
North Western Digest, First and Second Series
Pacific Digest, First, Second and Third Series
South Eastern Digest, First and Second Series
Southern Digest

See Illustration 20 for an example of a regional digest.

[1] The West Publishing Company publishes Key Number digests for every state except Delaware, Nevada, and Utah. Additionally, a few states have digests available from other publishers.

3. Digests for Federal Court Opinions [2]

a. *Federal Practice Digest, 2d*

This set is another Key Number digest and contains digests of opinions from 1961 to date for all of the federal courts. It is kept up to date by annual cumulative pocket supplements and interim pamphlet supplements. Other features are:

(1) Under each Key Number, cases are arranged first for the Supreme Court, then the courts of appeals, and then the district courts arranged alphabetically by jurisdiction.

(2) The digest paragraphs include information as to whether a case has been affirmed, reversed, or modified.

(3) Table of Cases volumes including a Defendant-Plaintiff table.

(4) Words and Phrases volumes

(5) A complete numerical listing of all patents adjudicated is included under the Topic, "Patents", Key Number 328.

(6) An alphabetical table of all *Trade-Marks and Trade-Names Adjudicated* is included in the *Trade Regulations* volume at Key Number 736.

b. *Earlier Federal Digests*

Cases prior to 1961 are available in earlier Key Number digests. These are (1) *Modern Federal Practice Digest* which includes all federal cases from 1939 through 1960, and (2) the *Federal Digest* which digests all federal cases prior to 1939. Both of these sets have most of the features described for the *Federal Practice Digest, 2d.* The *Descriptive-Word Index* to the *Modern Federal Practice Digest* also indexes cases included in the *Federal Digest.*

Whenever a researcher is aware that the problem under research is one under the jurisdiction of a federal court, it will be quicker and more accurate to confine the research to a federal digest.[3]

c. *Digests for the Supreme Court of the United States*

As the Supreme Court of the United States plays such a significant role within the American legal system, it is extremely useful to have digests that only contain its opinions. There are currently two

[2] Because West Publishing Company publishes the slip opinions for the Fifth and Ninth Circuit Courts of Appeals, they are able to prepare monthly cumulative digests to their opinions. These circuit digests are prepared for the Courts and their personnel and have limited distribution to others.

[3] Jurisdiction for some areas of law are restricted by the Constitution to the federal courts e. g., U. S. CONST. art. 1, sec. 8, cl. 8 (Copyright) or U. S. CONST. art. 1, sec. 8, cl. 4 (Bankruptcy). For further information on the relationship between state courts and federal courts, *see* 1 MOORE'S FEDERAL PRACTICE ¶ 0.6 (2d ed. 1948).

such digests. One is published by Lawyers Co-operative Publishing Company, whose publications are described in more detail in Chapter 7. The other is a Key Number digest of the West Publishing Company.

(1) U.S. Supreme Court Reports Digest (Lawyers Co-operative Publishing Co.)

This is a 20-volume digest, with cumulative annual pocket supplements, to all U.S. Supreme Court decisions. Since this set is not published by the West Publishing Co., it does not employ the *Key Number System* and follows the publisher's own distinct classification.

(2) U.S. Supreme Court Digest (West Publishing Co.)

This 17-volume digest of all decisions of the Supreme Court of the United States is classified under the *Key Number System,* and duplicates the Supreme Court cases in the *American Digest System.* It is kept up to date by cumulative annual pocket supplements.

d. *Digests for Other Federal Courts*

(1) West's Bankruptcy Digest

This Key Number digest includes cases from *West's Bankruptcy Reporter* and selected Bankruptcy cases from the *Federal Reporter* and the *Supreme Court Reporter.*

(2) Military Justice Digest

This digests cases from the *Military Reporter* and is a Key Number digest.

(3) U.S. Court of Claims Digest

This digests all cases from the Court of Claims from 1855 to date, and decisions of other federal courts in cases appealed from the Court of Claims. This Key Number digest is updated by cumulative annual pocket parts.

(4) West's Federal Case News

This is a weekly pamphlet which provides a summary of cases decided in all federal courts. It is arranged by court, and then the summaries are printed under topics arranged alphabetically. As this pamphlet does not cumulate, it is only useful as a current awareness service.

(5) Tax Cases (See Chapter 24)

SECTION G. USING THE DIGEST SYSTEM

1. Flow Chart

Special digests which cover cases dealing with federal taxes are covered in Chapter 24.

The chart below illustrates how the digest system should be used. The segment to the right is most inclusive, the segment to the left is most specific. The *General Digest* includes all American appellate courts, the regional digests include the courts of groups of contiguous states and the state digests include only the courts of individual states. The federal courts are a separate digest subsystem which operate on the same principle. The *Supreme Court Digest* is subsumed in the *Federal Digest 2d* which is in turn subsumed in the all-inclusive *General Digest.*

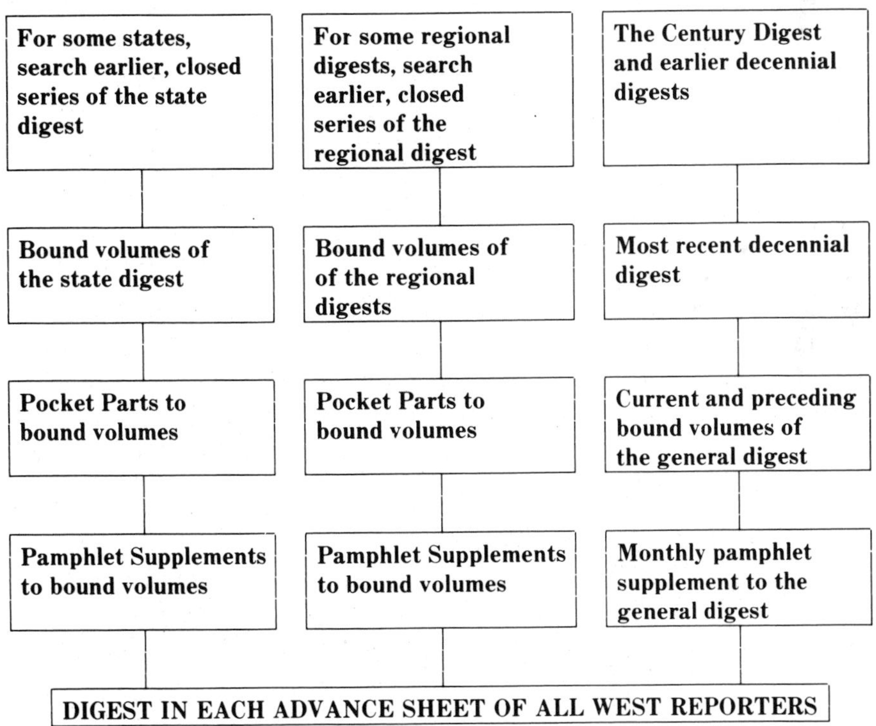

Once a particular digest is selected, it is important to completely update the search. Or, in terms of the chart above, cover each updating publication by following the vertical line down. Note that the upper items of the chart will generally be useful only for historical purposes. Each pocket part and pamphlet supplement will indicate which volumes of the component reporter are digested within. The digests at the front of the recent advance sheets are the only place where very recent cases are digested. For federal cases, summaries of cases not yet published can be found in *West's Federal Case News.*

2. Special Digests: Summary

Nearly all of the special digests previously described are those published by the West Publishing Company and use the Key Number System. This is most significant as it allows a researcher to broaden or narrow the search to accommodate the needs of a particular research problem. For example, a researcher may start in the state digest, and if not satisfied with cases located, switch by using the same Topic and Key Number to a regional digest, and then perhaps to the all-inclusive *American Digest System.* In fact, all of the special digests published by the West Publishing Company are segments of the *American Digest System.* This can be illustrated by the following chart.

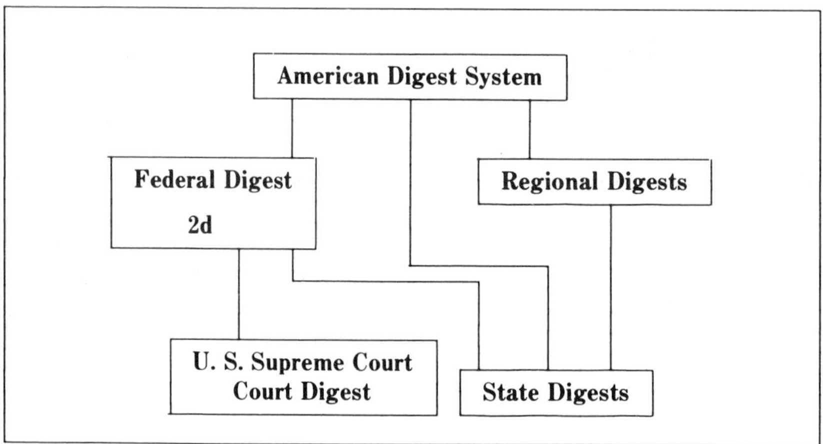

There are some state digests published by other companies; and some of the West state digests have special features unique to a particular state. Researchers should examine carefully the state and regional digests that are available for their state or region and familiarize themselves with their special features.

[Illustration 20]

SAMPLE PAGE FROM PACIFIC DIGEST

DAMAGES ⚷52

For references to other topics, see Descriptive-Word Index

Actor who is merely negligent is not liable to one who claims injury through fright or shock induced by conduct directed not to allegedly injured person but to a third person.

Amaya v. Home Ice, Fuel & Supply Co., 379 P.2d 513, 29 Cal.Rptr. 33, 59 C.2d 295.

Colo.App. 1977. Notwithstanding fact that 11-year-old boy suffered mental and psychological injuries which manifested themselves in physical problems such as night-

did not foreclose recovery from defendant for mental distress.

Leong v. Takasaki, 520 P.2d 758, 55 Haw. 398.

N.M.App. 1971. Mother's allegations of fright, shock and emotional distress upon witnessing death of her son as a bystander failed to state claim upon which recovery could be permitted.

Aragon v. Speelman, 491 P.2d 173, 83 N.M. 285.

When doing research for cases, it is frequently better to start the search in a special digest. This illustrates the search for cases under the Topic, Damages, Key Number 51 in the Pacific Digest. While not illustrated, the search can be made current by examining the pocket supplement to the volume.

The search may be narrowed or broadened by switching to other Key Number digests.

resided in California.

Kelley v. Kokua Sales and Supply, Ltd., 532 P.2d 673, 56 Haw. 204.

Defendants whose negligent actions allegedly caused automobile accident in Hawaii could not reasonably foresee the consequences of their negligent act to relative of persons injured and killed in the automobile accident where such relative resided in California.

Kelley v. Kokua Sales and Supply, Ltd., 532 P.2d 673, 56 Haw. 204.

A person located in California who died of a heart attack after being informed of the deaths of his daughter and granddaughter in an automobile accident was not within a reasonable distance from the scene of the automobile accident which occurred in Hawaii and did not have a cause of action for negligent infliction of severe mental distress.

Kelley v. Kokua Sales and Supply, Ltd., 532 P.2d 673, 56 Haw. 204.

Hawaii 1974. Since other standards existed to test authenticity of plaintiff's claim for damages because of emotional distress in witnessing death of his stepgrandmother, requirement of physical impact should not stand as an artificial bar to recovery, but merely be admissible as evidence of the degree of mental or emotional distress suffered.

Leong v. Takasaki, 520 P.2d 758, 55 Haw. 398.

Absence of a blood relationship between accident victim and plaintiff witness thereof

daughter, and other expenses, stated a cause of action.

Schurk v. Christensen, 497 P.2d 937, 80 Wash.2d 652.

Wash. 1971. In enacting 1967 amendment providing that damages may be recovered for loss of love and companionship of child and for injury to or destruction of parent-child relationship, the legislature authorized recovery of damages for parental mental anguish in cases involving wrongful death of or injury to a child. RCWA 4.24.010.

Wilson v. Lund, 491 P.2d 1287, 80 Wash.2d 91.

Wash.App. 1974. Grief and mental anguish suffered by parents as result of injuries to their child are consequential rather than direct damages because their recovery is necessarily dependent upon injury to another person. RCWA 4.24.010.

West Am. Ins. Co. v. Buchanan, 525 P.2d 831, 11 Wash.App. 823.

⚷52. —— Fright or apprehension of personal injury.

Cal. 1968. Plaintiff claiming fear for his own safety resulted in physical injury is a well recognized case for recovery of damages.

Dillon v. Legg, 441 P.2d 912, 69 Cal.Rptr. 72, 68 C.2d 728, 29 A.L.R.3d 1316.

Cal. 1963. Liability could not be predicated upon fright or nervous shock, with consequent bodily injury, induced in pregnant mother by her apprehension of negligently caused danger or injury to her 17-month-old child

SECTION H. POPULAR NAME TABLES AND WORDS AND PHRASES

1. Popular Name Tables

Frequently a case becomes known by a popular name rather than by its actual name. Examples of such cases are *Brown v. Board of Education* or *United States v. Nixon.* They are frequently cited by their popular names as the *School Desegregation Case* or the *Nixon Tapes Case.* When only the citation of the popular name of a case is at hand, it is necessary to consult a table of cases by popular name in order to obtain the actual name of the case. These tables may be located as follows:

a. *Sixth Decennial* of the *American Digest System.* The Table of Cases volume contain a cumulative *List of Popular Name Titles* in the *American Digest System.* This feature has been discontinued in the subsequent *Decennials.*

b. Tables of Cases by Popular Names in the various special digests.

c. *Shepard's Acts and Cases by Popular Names.* [See Illustration 21]

2. Words and Phrases

Sometimes a problem in legal research involves the definition of certain words or phrases as, for example, "good faith" or "reasonable market value." Courts constantly must define the meaning of such words and phrases. In cases reported in the units of the *National Reporter System,* such definitions are usually included as headnotes, as in the following example from 606 P.2d 1314 (1980).

2. Divorce 🔑252.3(1)

In division of marital property, value of goodwill incident to husband's dental practice acquired during his marriage must be considered as "marital property." C.R.S. '73, 14-10-113(2).

See publication Words and Phrases for other judicial constructions and definitions.

All such headnotes are subsequently reprinted in a publication called *Words and Phrases.* This set contains 46 volumes and includes over 350,000 court definitions of legal and non-legal terms. They are arranged alphabetically under a word or phrase. *Words and Phrases* is kept up to date by annual cumulative pocket supplements which are further supplemented by *Words and Phrases Tables* in the current volumes and advance sheets of the various units of the *National Reporter System.* Many of the special digests discussed in Section F also contain such tables. [See Illustration 22 for an example of a page from *Words and Phrases*]

SECTION I. ILLUSTRATIONS

21. Sample page from Shepard's Federal and State Cases Cited by Popular Names

22. Sample page from Words and Phrases

[Illustration 21]

AN EXCERPT FROM A PAGE OF SHEPARD'S FEDERAL AND STATE CASES CITED BY POPULAR NAMES

FEDERAL AND STATE CASES CITED BY POPULAR NAMES Sch

Schenectady Six Tickets for a Quarter Case
2 DeptR 284

Schenk Case
253 Fed 212; 249 US 47, 63 LE 470, 39 SC 247

Schiedam Schnapps Cases
18 HowPr 64
15 AbbPr 336

Schlesinger Cases
14 Fed 682; 120 US 109, 30 LE 607, 7 SC 442
14 Fed 687; 120 US 264, 30 LE 656, 7 SC 546
153 Minn 88, 189 NW 415
153 Minn 136, 189 NW 714

Schoharie Valley Railroad Case
12 AbbPr (NS) 394

School Board Cases
213 Ala 106, 104 So 273
221 Ala 217, 128 So 435

School Bus Case
132 NJL 98, 39 A2d 75; 133 NJL 350, 44 A2d 333; 330 US 1, 91 LE 711, 67 SC 504; 330 US 855, 91 LE 1297, 67 SC 962

School Cases
296 Fed 928; 268 US 510, 69 LE 1070, 45 SC 571
281 F2d 452
284 F2d 377; 163 FS 637
361 F2d 250
127 FS 591
141 FS 777
142 FS 916
152 FS 84
161 FS 409

372 US 901, 83 SC 715; 83 SC 869; 232 Md 368, 193 A2d 554
18 Misc2d 659, 191 NYSupp2d 453; 11 AppDiv2d 340, 206 NYSupp2d 183; 10 NY2d 174, 218 NYSupp2d 659, 176 NE2d 579; 370 US 421, 8 LE2d 601, 82 SC 1261; 12 NY2d 712, 233 NYSupp2d 766, 186 NE2d 124; 368 US 982, 82 SC 597; 369 US 809, 82 SC 686

School Segregation Cases
344 US 873, 97 LE 676, 73 SC 173; 345 US 972, 97 LE 1388, 73 SC 886; 347 US 497, 98 LE 884, 74 SC 693; 348 US 886, 75 SC 210; 349 US 294, 99 LE 1083, 75 SC 753
270 F2d 209
369 F2d 55
373 F2d 75
380 F2d 955
98 FS 529; 342 US 350, 96 LE 342, 72 SC 327; 345 US 972, 97 LE 1388, 73 SC 1118; 347 US 483, 98 LE 873, 74 SC 686; 348 US 886, 75 SC 210; 349 US 294, 99 LE 1083, 75 SC 753; 349 US 914, 75 SC 602
98 FS 797; 344 US 1, 97 LE 3, 73 SC 1; 344 US 141, 97 LE 152, 73 SC 124; 345 US 972, 97 LE 1388, 73 SC 1118; 347 US 483, 98 LE 873, 74 SC 686; 348 US 886, 75 SC 210; 349 US 294, 99 LE 1083, 75 SC 753
103 FS 337; 344 US 1, 97 LE 3, 73 SC 1; 345 US 972, 97 LE 1388, 73 SC 1118; 347 US 483, 98 LE 873, 74 SC 686; 348 US 886, 75 SC 210; 349 US 294, 99 LE 1083, 75 SC 753
32 DelCh 343, 87 A2d 862; 33 DelCh 144, 91 A2d 137; 344 US 891, 97 LE 689, 73 SC 213; 345 US 972, 97 LE 1388, 73 SC 1118; 347 US 483, 98 LE 873, 74 SC 686; 348 US 886, 75 SC 210; 349 US 294, 99 LE 1083.

A typical page of Cases Cited by Popular Names. This set is kept current by publication of a periodic pamphlet supplement.

Other Tables of Popular Names appear in many of the state, regional, and other special digests.

371 US 807, 9 LE2d 52, 83 SC 25; 371 US 907, 83 SC 251; 371 US 944, 83 SC 499; 372 US 901, 83 SC 715; 374 US 203, 10 LE2d 844, 83 SC 1560; 83 SC 870
228 MD 239, 179 A2d 698; 374 US 203, 10 LE2d 844, 83 SC 1560; 371 US 809, 9 LE2d 52, 82 SC 21; 371 US 907, 83 SC 251; 371 US 944, 83 SC 498; 372 US 901, 83 SC 714;

Schwegmann Case
184 F2d 11; 340 US 928, 95 LE 669, 71 SC 491; 341 US 384, 95 LE 1035, 71 SC 745; 341 US 956, 95 LE 1377, 71 SC 1011

Schwimmer Case
27 F2d 742; 278 US 595, 73 LE 526, 49 SC 80; 279 US 644, 73 LE 889, 49 SC 448

[Illustration 22]

SAMPLE PAGE FROM VOLUME OF WORDS AND PHRASES

MARINE CAUSE

26 W & P—120

MARINE CAUSE

Action by seaman for wages and an additional sum for withholding of wages constituted a "marine cause" within New York City Court Act. Dooley v. Moore-McCormick Lines, Inc., 183 N.Y.S.2d 43, 44, 16 Misc.2d 534.

MARINE INSURANCE

The characterization of all-risk "Jewelers' Block Policy" as "marine insurance" by virtue of statutory definition is a mere label and has no effect on substantive rights. Woods Patchogue Corp. v. Franklin Nat. Ins. Co., of N. Y., 173 N.Y.S.2d 859, 864, 5 A.D.2d 577.

MARINE INSURANCE COMPANY

Company which issued public liability and propr... lege cense insur tion again count Pan 321 S

MAR

"M storn Treas and F.2d Dar auton yacht any "marine peril" within yacht policy. Hanover Ins. Co. v. Sonfield, Tex.Civ.App., 386 S.W. 2d 160, 162.

The test of "marine peril" as basis for recovery for salvage is not whether the peril is imminent, but whether it is reasonably to be apprehended, and vessel stranded so that it is subject to potential danger of damage or destruction may be a subject of salvage services. Fort Myers Shell & Dredging Co. v. Barge NBC 512, C.A.Fla., 404 F.2d 137, 139.

MARINER

See, Also, Negligence of a Mariner.
Negligence of Masters, Mariners or Pilots.

MARINE RAILWAY

"Marine railway" is a permanently fixed system of tracks or rails which extends from point on shore well above waterline to point offshore well below waterline, along which tracks a cradle can move docked ship into or out of water; marine railway is to be distinguished from building way, for purposes of determining coverage under Longshoremen's and Harbor Workers' Compensation Act. St. Louis Shipbuilding Co. v. Director of the Office of Workers' Compensation Programs, U. S. Dept. of Labor, C.A.8, 551 F.2d 1119, 1123.

A permanent shipyard structure located entirely on land, designed and used exclusively for new ship construction did not constitute a "drydock" or "marine railway" within the act, and therefore the act did not apply to injuries sustained by a shipyard employee working on construction of a new ship on such structure, even though a portion of the structure extended into the water on an incline to facilitate launching of completed vessels. Puget Sound Bridge & Dry Dock Co. v. O'Leary, D.C.Wash., 224 F.Supp. 557, 559.

MARINE RULE

The so-called "marine rule" provides that if cost of restoration of leased premises is more than one-half of value of building just before fire, then there is total destruction. Old Line Co. v. Getty Square Dept. Store, Inc., 322 N.Y.S.2d 149, 151, 66 Misc.2d 825.

MARITAL

See, Living in Marital Union.

MARITAL AGREEMENT

"Marital agreement", as term is used in statute pertaining to deportation of immigrants who used marital agreement to procure entry, means more than mere indulgement in marriage ceremony, and means that contracting parties at least begin in good faith to live together as husband and wife. Giannoulias v. Landon, C.A.Cal., 226 F.2d 356, 359.

MARITAL ASSETS

... the of a sent Ind.

dis- lia- hich and hich clud- as- hich con- tem-

A page from Words & Phrases. The paragraphs are essentially the same as they appeared as head-notes in the volumes of the National Reporter System. The pocket supplement of the volumes of Words & Phrases should always be checked.

MARITAL COMMUNICATIONS

"Marital communications", within statute providing privilege with respect to the same, connote confidential communications. State v. Benner, Me., 284 A.2d 91, 108.

MARITAL DEDUCTION BEQUEST

"Marital deduction bequest" defined. In re Rogers' Estate, Fla.App., 180 So.2d 167, 171.

Testamentary provision expressly recognizing specific bequest to daughter and bequeathing to widow full undivided one-half of residuary estate to be so computed as to entitle estate to full "marital deduction" used quoted phrase as referring to marital deduction for federal estate tax purposes and disclosed testamentary purpose to minimize estate taxes. Id.

Will, construed as a whole, bequeathing to testator's widow a full undivided one-half of residuary estate to be so computed as to entitle estate to full marital deduction disclosed testamentary intent and purpose to make a "marital deduction bequest" to widow. Id.

MARITAL DEDUCTION TRUST

See, Pecuniary Formula Marital Deduction Trust.
Percentage or Fraction Marital Deduction Trust.

MARITAL, FILIAL AND DOMESTIC CIRCUMSTANCES AND OBLIGATIONS

Employee who left work in order to care for her mother who was suffering from cancer had left for a "marital, filial or domestic circumstance or obligation" and not for "good cause" within Employment Security Law and was not entitled to unemployment benefits. Mississippi Employment Sec. Commission v. Stafford, 158 So.2d 55, 56, 248 Miss. 95.

For purposes of statutory provision stating that marital, filial and domestic circumstances and obligations shall not be deemed good cause for leaving work within meaning of statutory provisions conditioning right to receive unemployment compensation benefits upon having

SECTION J. CITING DIGESTS

Digests serve as a means of locating cases by subject. As they are merely finding aids with no legal authority, they are seldom, if ever, cited.

In connection with the use of digests, a further caveat is appropriate. Do not rely on the text of the digest-paragraphs for the essence of theory of a case. They merely serve as a means of obtaining citations to the cases. Digest-paragraphs are necessarily brief and can be misleading, or can fail to suggest a nuance or shading of a case or may omit an element which may have a specific bearing on the problem being researched.

In all instances the actual opinion from which the digest was obtained should be read.

SECTION K. SUMMARY

1. Digests

Digests give brief, unconnected statements of court holdings or facts of cases, and are classified by subject.

2. Types of Digests

a. All courts, federal and state.

b. Regional digests for a group of adjacent states.

c. State.

d. Specific court or court system.

3. American Digest System

a. *Scope*

(1) Digest which purports to cover every reported case, federal, state or local, from 1658 to date.

(2) Consists of a *Century Digest* (1658–1896), eight *Decennial Digests* (1897–1906, 1907–1916, 1916–1926, 1926–1936, 1936–1946, 1946–1956, 1956–1966, and 1966–1976), and the *General Digest, 5th Series* (1976 to date).

b. *Arrangement*

(1) All cases are assigned headnotes which are then classified to the Key Number classification system. These headnotes then become the digest paragraphs.

(2) Corresponding Key Numbers used in all *Decennial Digests, General Digest* and other West digests.

(3) Scope-note (delimits and identifies the content of a topic).

(4) Analysis (conceptual breakdown of a topic).

(5) Section lines, preceded by the Key Numbers, indicate the content of each Key Number under a topic.

(6) Digest-paragraphs arranged under Key Numbers by: Supreme Court of the United States, other federal courts, and state cases listed alphabetically by names of states. The name and citation of each case follows the digest-paragraph.

(7) Expanded or new topics are periodically added.

c. *Century Digest (1658–1896)*

(1) Not classified by Key Number System.

(2) To refer from *Century Edition* to the *Decennials,* use the pink reference table in volume 21 of the *First Decennial.*

(3) When a Key Number is known and one wishes to locate the corresponding section in the *Century Edition,* refer to the cross reference included in the *First* or *Second Decennials* under the appropriate Key Number. The references in the *Second Decennial* are more complete.

d. *Use of Indexes with the* American Digest System

(1) Each *Decennial* and the *General Digest* have a *Descriptive-Word Index.*

(2) Since recent cases are preferred, begin research with the latest *Decennial's Descriptive-Word Index.* After locating a Key Number, check it in all *Decennials* and the *General Digest* for cases in point. Then consult the cross reference under the Key Number to the *Second Decennial* to identify the corresponding section in the *Century Edition.* Examine the *Century Edition,* under that section number, for early cases. This research will disclose cases in point from 1658 to date.

e. *Using the Topic Method with the* American Digest System

(1) Avoids use of the *Descriptive-Word Index.*

(2) Examine the scope-note and analysis under the appropriate title. Select the Key Number and proceed as above.

(3) Requires careful analysis and should be used with care.

4. U. S. Supreme Court Reports Digests

5. Federal Practice Digest, 2d

a. *Scope*

(1) Digests federal cases since 1961.

(2) Covers decisions of the Supreme Court of the United States, and *Federal Reporter, 2d Series,* the *Federal Supplement,* and the *Federal Rules Decisions.*

(3) Kept up to date with cumulative pocket supplements.

6. Modern Federal Practice Digest

a. *Scope*

(1) Index to federal cases between 1939 and 1960.

(2) Covers decision of the Supreme Court of the United States, the *Federal Reporter, 2d Series*, the *Federal Supplement* and the *Federal Rules Decisions.*

b. *Arrangement*

(1) Under the Key Number System.

(2) Descriptive-Word Index to *Federal Digest* and to *Modern Federal Practice Digest.*

7. Federal Digest

a. *Scope*

(1) Indexes federal case law of historical significance, some of which is no longer controlling, from the foundation of the government to 1939.

(2) Covers *Federal Cases*, the U.S. Supreme Court Decisions, the *Federal Reporter* and the *Federal Supplement.*

8. Regional Digests

a. Segments of the *American Digest System*, arranged by states which form the units of the *National Reporter System.*

b. Some *Regional Digests* do not include cases prior to the unit of the *National Reporter.*

c. Classified under the Key Number System.

d. Contain standard digest features, e.g., Descriptive-Word Index, Table of Cases, etc.

9. State Digests

a. West state digests follow the Key Number System and are fragments of the *American Digest System.*

b. Standard features common to many state digests:

(1) Cover all reported state decisions and federal cases arising in each state or applying state law from the earliest period to date.

(2) Classified by subject, with titles, sections, scope-notes and analysis.

(3) Descriptive-Word Index.

(4) Table of Cases.

(5) Words and phrases judicially defined by the digested cases.

(6) Kept up to date by replacement volumes and cumulative pocket and pamphlet supplements.

c. Some states have digests which are not Key Number Digests.

Chapter 7

ANNOTATED LAW REPORTS

The *National Reporter System* with its *Key Number Digest System* provides for the comprehensive reporting of all reported decisions. Another private publishing company, the Lawyers Co-operative Publishing Co. (and its related company, the Bancroft-Whitney Co.) publish court reports on a selective basis. Their theory is that only a small portion of the total number of cases handed down each year is of interest to most lawyers, as most cases deal with either strictly local matters, or cover an area of law so well settled that they add very little to an understanding of the law. What would serve lawyers better, they claim, is reporting only significant court decisions, those that deal with points of law not previously decided, or that indicate a change in the law, or indicate a new trend in legal thinking. By this manner of selective reporting lawyers could have all important decisions and not have to burden their bookshelves with thousands of cases that really add nothing to the corpus of the law.

Although selective law reporting was the basis for their first venture in publishing court reports, they realized that lawyers would also have to be able to locate other decisions not reported in their publication and have a method of locating current decisions. To provide this service they began to publish auxiliary sets, all related to each other, and all aimed to assist lawyers in finding answers to all of their legal questions through the use of these publications. These sets gradually grew into what they now call *The Total Client-Service Library*,[1] which consists of nine distinctive sets of law books. This chapter will discuss its annotated law reports.

SECTION A. AMERICAN LAW REPORTS

1. Introduction

The *American Law Reports* is a selective reporter of appellate court decisions. Its editors scan all current decisions and select those

[1] *The Total Client-Service Library* consists of: *American Jurisprudence 2d; American Jurisprudence Legal Forms 2d; American Jurisprudence Pleading and Practice Forms, Annotated, Revised; American Jurisprudence Trials; American Law Reports Annotated (A.L.R.; A.L.R.***2***d; A.L.R.***3***d; A.L.R.***4***th; A.L.R.Fed.); American Jurisprudence; Proof of Facts; United States Code Service; United States Supreme Court Reports, Lawyers' Edition; and Federal Procedural Forms, Lawyers' Edition.*

that in their opinion have points of law of general interest. There are no advance sheets to this set and several volumes are published each year. A.L.R., however, is significant not for the decisions it reports but for the editorial service that follows each reported decision, or what the publishers call *Annotations*. These are encyclopedic essays or memoranda on the significant legal topics from each case selected for publication in the *American Law Reports*.

The manner in which the *American Law Reports* are published and the role of annotations can best be made clear by example.

In the case of *Gumenick v. United States*, decided in the Supreme Court of Virginia,[2] the plaintiff had been sitting on the back porch of a friend's apartment. Upon leaving, the plaintiff placed his hand on the porch's railing and turned to speak to his friend whereupon the railing collapsed, throwing the plaintiff to the ground, resulting in his being severely injured. He then brought suit against the owners of the apartment building alleging their failure to exercise reasonable care in the maintenance of the hand rail. The editors decided that this case was suitable for publication in A.L.R. but in terms of legal research this is not important, as this decision is also published in the official *Virginia Reports* and in the *South Eastern Reporter*. What is significant is what A.L.R. provides *in addition* to the decision, which is a 222-page annotation that immediately follows the decision as printed in the A.L.R. volume. In legal research, A.L.R. is used not for the reported decisions, but for the subsequent annotations. The case of *Gumenick v. United States*, in common with all reported cases, involves more than one point of law. For instance, this case in addition to the topic of landlord and tenant, dealt with the topics of evidence, damages, and trial procedure. It was chosen by A.L.R. for the issues involving the law of landlord and tenant and it is these issues which are covered in the Annotation. Thus, the Annotation immediately following *Gumenick v. United States* in 65 A.L.R. 3d is entitled:

LANDLORD'S LIABILITY FOR INJURY OR DEATH DUE TO DEFECTS IN AREA OF BUILDING (OTHER THAN STAIRWAYS) USED IN COMMON BY TENANTS

Although the decision itself consists only of ten pages, the annotation is not restricted to its limited fact situation, but rather it is written on the generalized topic. The editor assigned to write the annotation researched the entire area of law covered by the topic of the annotation and located all previous decisions from all jurisdictions that dealt with this topic. The annotation cites and summarizes the

[2] 213 Va. 510, 193 S.E.2d 788, 65 A.L.R.3d 1 (1973).

facts and holdings of all reported cases in point and presents an analysis and synthesis of the cases. As shown in Illustration 24, a volume of the *American Law Reports* contains annotations on many different topics. What A.L.R. designates as an "Annotation" is in fact a legal memorandum on a particular aspect of the law which covers all sides of every question, presents general principles deduced from the cases, and gives their exceptions, qualifications, distinctions, and applications.

The usefulness of locating an A.L.R. annotation should be evident, since it presents in an organized fashion a commentary and discussion of all previously reported decisions and saves the searcher the task of locating the cases and then analyzing and synthesizing them.

A.L.R., in summary, consists of bound volumes containing selected appellate decisions, each of which has an annotation on a point of law decided in the case. An annotation may vary from one page to several hundred.

2. A.L.R. Series

The *American Law Reports* are published in five series.[3]
First Series (cited "A.L.R.") 1919–1948, 175 v.
Second Series (cited "A.L.R.2d") 1948–1965, 100 v.
Third Series (cited "A.L.R.3d") 1965–1980, 100 v.
Fourth Series (cited "A.L.R.4th") 1980 to date.
Federal (cited "A.L.R.Fed.") 1969 to date.

The latter set started in 1969 and includes only court decisions from the federal courts. As mentioned in Chapter 3, the Lawyers Co-operative Publishing Company publishes an annotated set of the *U.S. Reports*. Although decisions from the Federal Courts of Appeals previously have appeared in A.L.R., litigation has been increasing in both amount and importance and the publishers felt that federal cases now deserved special treatment.

A.L.R.Fed. is published in a format similar to A.L.R. Leading decisions of the federal courts are published followed by an annotation in the same manner as described *supra*.

SECTION B. ILLUSTRATIONS. A.L.R. ANNOTATIONS

23. Page from 94 A.L.R.3d

24. Sample page of subjects annotated in an A.L.R. volume

[3] The *American Law Reports Annotated* replaced the *Lawyers' Reports Annotated (L.R.A.)*. For a description of the set and other earlier sets of annotated reports, see E. POLLACK, FUNDAMENTALS OF LEGAL RESEARCH 116 (3d ed. 1967).

25–30. Pages from 65 A.L.R.3d

31. Excerpts from A.L.R.3d–4th Quick Index

[Illustration 23]

PAGE FROM 94 A.L.R.3d

SUBJECT OF ANNOTATION

Beginning on page 486

Relationship between victim and plaintiff-witness as affecting right to recover damages in negligence for shock or mental anguish at witnessing victim's injury or death

Troy S. LEONG, a minor, by his next friend, Gail M. Petagno, Plaintiff-Appellant,

v

Dennis TAKASAKI, Defendant-Appellee

Supreme Court of Hawaii
March 28, 1974

55 Hawaii 398, 520 SW2d 758, 94 ALR3d 471

SUMMARY OF DECISION

The Circuit Court, Hawaii, Masato Doi, J., entered summary judgment for the defendant in an action brought on behalf of a 10-year-old boy to recover damages for nervous shock and psychic injuries suffered when he witnessed his step-grandmother being struck and killed by an

In Chapter 6 it was demonstrated that by using the Key Number System and the various Key Number Digests, cases could be located which dealt with the right to recover damages for mental anguish caused by witnessing a personal injury to another.

This illustration shows how cases on the same subject could also be located in an A.L.R. annotation.

In the remaining chapters, it will be demonstrated how cases located by use of the Key Number System and by A.L.R. may be located in other sets of law books.

471

[Illustration 24]
SAMPLE PAGE OF SUBJECTS ANNOTATED IN AN A.L.R. VOLUME

x SUBJECTS ANNOTATED

LAUNDRIES OR DRY CLEANERS
Application of city ordinance requiring license for a laundry, to supplier of coin-operated laundry machines intended for use in apartment building—65 ALR3d 1296

LICENSES AND PERMITS
Application of city ordinance requiring license for a laundry, to supplier of coin-operated laundry machines intended for use in apartment building—65 ALR3d 1296

MALICIOUS PROSECUTION
May action for malicious prosecution be predicated on defense or counterclaim in civil suit—65 ALR3d 901

MALPRACTICE
Coverage and exclusions under hospital

M

A.L.R. annotations are written on many different topics.

MEDICAL TREATMENT OR CARE
Admissibility of evidence showing payment, or offer or promise of payment, of medical, hospital, and similar expenses of injured party by opposing party—65 ALR3d 932

MONEY ORDER
Falsifying of money order as forgery—65 ALR3d 1307

PARDON, PAROLE OR PROBATION
Propriety, in imposing sentence for original offense after revocation of probation, of considering acts because of which probation was revoked—65 ALR3d 1100

POLLUTION
Validity and construction of statute or ordinance allowing tax exemption for property used in pollution control—65 ALR3d 434

PREMISES LIABILITY
Landlord's liability for injury or death due to defects in areas of building (other than stairways) used in common by tenants—65 ALR3d 14

PUBLIC OFFICERS
Validity of requirement that candidate or public officer have been resident of governmental unit for specified period—65 ALR3d 1048

PUNITIVE DAMAGES
Intoxication of automobile driver as basis for awarding punitive damages—65 ALR3d 656

RELEASE OR DISCHARGE
Validity and effect of agreement with one cotortfeasor setting aside his maximum liability and providing for reduction or extinguishment thereof relative to recovery against nonagreeing cotortfeasor—65 ALR3d 602

ɩf 5 /- e)

Propriety, in imposing sentence for original offense after revocation of probation of considering acts because of which probation was revoked—65 ALR3d 1100

SCHOOLS
What constitutes a private, parochial, or denominational school within statute making attendance at such school a compliance with compulsory school attendance law—65 ALR3d 1222

SENTENCE AND PUNISHMENT
Propriety, in imposing sentence for original offense after revocation of probation, of considering acts because of which probation was revoked—65 ALR3d 1100

STARE DECISIS
Binding effect upon state courts of opinion of United States Supreme Court supported by less than a majority of all its members—65 ALR3d 504

[Illustration 25]

FIRST PAGE OF AN A.L.R.3d ANNOTATION

ANNOTATION

LANDLORD'S LIABILITY FOR INJURY OR DEATH DUE TO DEFECTS IN AREAS OF BUILDING (OTHER THAN STAIRWAYS) USED IN COMMON BY TENANTS

by

Allan E. Korpela, LL.B.

I. INTRODUCTION

§ 1. Prefatory matters:
 [a] Scope
 [b] Related matters
§ 2. General comment:
 [a] Summary
 [b] Practice pointers

II. BASIS OF LIABILITY IN GENERAL

§ 3. Landlord's duty:
 [a] Generally
 [b] Massachusetts' rule
§ 4. Retention of control of common areas; porches:
 [a] C
 [b] C
§ 5. —Roo
 [a] C
 [b] C

This is the first page of the annotation for 65 A.L. R.3d 14. Immediately preceding it is reprinted the case of Gumenick v. United States, 213 Va. 510, 193 S.E.2d 788, 65 A.L.R.3d 1 (1973). Although this case dealt specifically with the liability of a landlord for negligent maintenance of a porch railing, note how the annotation deals with the many aspects of the liability of a landlord.

TO

49 AM

16 AM
 40

2 AM J

6 AM JUR PROOF OF FACTS 527, Invitees; 7 AM JUR PROOF OF FACTS 239, Lights; 10 AM JUR PROOF OF FACTS 785, Slip and Fall

10 AM JUR TRIALS 255, Premises Liability—Trip and Fall

ALR DIGESTS, Landlord and Tenant §§ 174, 174.2, 174.4, 174.8

ALR QUICK INDEX, Landlord and Tenant; Premises Liability

Consult POCKET PART in this volume for later cases

14

[Illustration 26]

PAGE FROM 65 A.L.R.3d

65 ALR3d LANDLORD'S LIABILITY — COMMON AREAS
65 ALR3d 14

§ 6. —Other areas:
[a] Control retained
[b] Control not retained
§ 7. Requirement of notice of defect; generally
§ 8. Actual notice charged
§ 9. Constructive notice charged; generally
§ 10. Duration of defect; years
§ 11. —Less than year but more than month
§ 12. —Less than month

III. LANDLORD'S BREACH OF DUTY AS TO PARTICULAR CONDITION

A. CONSTRUCTION AND STRUCTURAL MAINTENANCE

1. LOBBIES, HALLS, AND PASSAGEWAYS

§ 13. Floors:

r of

§ 1

An outline of the topics covered in the annotation is set forth. This is the second page of the outline. Note how cases dealing with porch railings are covered at § 17 within the annotations. Thus, the researcher can immediately turn to this section to find cases for the matter being researched.

r of

§ 1

§ 1

[a] Finding of negligence held supported or supportable
[b] Finding of no negligence held supportable or required as matter of law
§ 17. Railings and posts:
[a] Finding of negligence held supported or supportable
[b] Finding of no negligence held supportable or required as matter of law
§ 18. Other parts or appurtenances:
[a] Finding of negligence held supported or supportable
[b] Finding of no negligence held supportable or required as matter of law

3. ATTICS, BATHROOMS, BASEMENTS, AND CHAMBERS

§ 19. Floors:
[a] Finding of negligence held supported or supportable
[b] Finding of no negligence held supportable or required as matter of law
§ 20. Other areas or appurtenances:
[a] Finding of negligence held supported or supportable
[b] Finding of no negligence held supportable or required as matter of law

15

[Illustration 27]

PAGE FROM 65 A.L.R.3d

After the outline, as shown in the previous illustration, a word index is provided to the various facts covered in the cases cited in the annotation.

[Illustration 28]

FIRST PAGE OF TEXT OF A.L.R. ANNOTATION

65 ALR3d LANDLORD'S LIABILITY — COMMON AREAS § 1[a]

65 ALR3d 14

Miss .... § 22[b]
Mo .... §§ 3[a], 4[a], 5[a], 7, 9–11, 14[a], 17[b], 19[a], 23[a], 25[a], 28[a, b], 30[b], 31[b], 32[a], 34, 35[a, b], 36[a], 37[b], 40[a], 47[a], 52[a], 56[b], 57[a], 59[a]
Mont .... §§ 22[b], 53[b]
Neb .... §§ 19[b], 31[b]
Nev .... § 6[a]
NH .... §§ 2[b], 4[b], 5[a], 6[a, b], 9, 16[a], 17[a], 19[a], 20[a], 21[a], 34, 37[a], 40[a], 48, 53[a]
NJ .... §§ 2[b], 4[a], 5[a], 6[b], 7, 13[a], 14[b], 17[a], 23[a],
NC .... §§ 4[b], 19[b]
ND .... §§ 32[a], 34, 55[a]
Ohio .... §§ 4[a, b], 6[a, b], 13[a], 17[a], 19[b], 20[a], 25[a], 29[a], 35[a], 36[a], 40[a], 52[b], 55[a, b], 56[a]
Or .... §§ 13[b], 17[b], 25[b], 26[a], 54[b]
Pa .... §§ 2[b], 3[a], 4[b], 6[a], 9, 12, 13[a], 14[b], 17[a], 22[a], 25[a, b], 26[b], 31[a, b], 33[a], 37[b], 39[a], 54[b], 57[a], 60[a]
RI .... §§ 5[b], 40[b], 44[b]
SD .... § 29[b]
Tenn .... §§ 6[a], 26[a], 35[a], 44[b]

Immediately before the text of the annotation, a Table of Jurisdictions Represented is set forth.

§ 1[a] always covers the scope of the annotation. While not illustrated, § 1[b] is always entitled Related Matters and summarizes other annotations on similar topics. It may also give citations to legal articles on the topic of the annotation. It should be carefully consulted.

Note how Footnote 1 indicates that this annotation supersedes previous ones.

I. Introduction

§ 1. Prefatory matters

[a] Scope

This annotation[1] collects those cases in which recovery is sought for personal injury or death which allegedly resulted from defects in common areas of a building (other than interior stairways) controlled by the landlord, where the ground of recovery is breach of a duty of care owed by the landlord with respect to such areas.[2] The annotation assumes the existence of such duty as one arising out of retention of control over areas used in common by tenants with the landlord's permission, or, in a few cases, used in common by a tenant and the landlord. The annotation is limited to cases in which recovery is sought for breach of such duty.[3]

1. It supersedes 25 ALR2d 444 and §§ 14–16, 25–38 of 26 ALR2d 468.

2. It should be noted that the definitive statement, or the statement of latest legal position in a particular jurisdiction, on some aspect of landlord liability arising by virtue of control of common areas may have involved a common area other than interior areas (other than stairways), discussed in this annotation. Thus the annotation does not purport to discuss in specific terms modern developments in landlord-tenant law.

3. Cases in which the duty of care is predicated on grounds other than the

25

[Illustration 29]

PAGE FROM 65 A.L.R.3d 14

§ 16[b] LANDLORD'S LIABILITY — COMMON AREAS 65 ALR3d
65 ALR3d 14

trolled by the landlord, a finding for defendant on the issue of defendant's negligence with respect to such condition was held required or supportable under the particular facts and circumstances of the case.[82]

§ 17 brings together and discusses all cases dealing with landlord's liability in reference to railings and posts.

a child of one of the defendant's tenants, who ventured upon the platform of the fire escape and was injured when a trap door in the platform, the hinges of which were defective, gave way.

Testimony by the plaintiff and his wife that they commonly used the fire escape on the defendant's building for the purpose of reaching the cellar was held in Aubrey v McCarthy (1926) 217 App Div 492, 217 NYS 161, not to justify a finding that it was a common passageway provided for this purpose, where there was an interior stairway provided from the ground floor into the cellar, and to reach it by the fire escape one had to climb through a window. It was therefore held that there could be no recovery for injuries to a tenant from a defect in a wooden platform which had been laid over a platform of the fire escape, where, at the time of the accident, the plaintiff tenant was using the fire escape to reach the ground to pick up a piece of clothing which had fallen from his apartment, the court pointing out that there was no claim of any defect in the fire escape itself.

§ 17. Railings and posts

[a] Finding of negligence held supported or supportable

In the following cases, where recovery was sought for injury or death allegedly caused by defective or improper mode of construction or a failure to perform proper structural maintenance of railings or posts of porches, balconies, fire escapes, and platforms used in common by tenants, or by a tenant and the landlord, and controlled by the landlord, a finding for plaintiff on the issue of defendant's negligence with respect to such condition was held supportable under the particular facts and circumstances of the case.

Allegations that the plaintiff, a tenant of part of the defendant's premises, was injured when a faultily constructed railing inclosing a rear stair landing used in common by the tenants and the defendant collapsed with the plaintiff when she was attempting to use a clothesline and pulley device attached to the railing for the joint use of the parties, and that the defect in the railing was a latent one not observable by the plaintiff in the exercise of due care, but known to the defendant at all the times in question, was held in Hassell v Denning (1927) 84 Cal App 479, 258 P 426, to state a cause of action as against general demurrer, either on the theory that the lessor through fraud or concealment allowed the lessee to occupy the premises in ignorance of a risk known to the landlord, or that the landlord reserved control of the part of the premises in question for the common use of himself and the tenants, or of different tenants, the court saying that liability under the latter theory might

82. For cases involving injuries suffered because of the allegedly rotten condition of the floors of porches, balconies, fire escapes, or platforms, see infra § 33.

88

[Illustration 30]

PAGE FROM 65 A.L.R.3d

contention that it was just as likely that the accident was caused by the decedent's defective eyesight or a sudden seizure of some kind, as by the defendant's negligence, saying that the plaintiff had only the burden of proving his cause of action by a preponderance of the evidence, and need not disprove other possible causes.

A landlord who permitted pickets in the railing of a common porch of his apartment house to be removed, leaving a gap about fifteen inches wide and twenty-five inches high, was held in Faro v College Town Bldg. & Loan Ass'n (1938) 119 **NJL** 289, 196 A 463, affd 121 **NJL** 76, 1 A2d 371, properly to have been liable for injuries received when a tenant's eight-year-old son, playing on a porch, saw a cat run down the steps below, leaned through the opening in order to watch it, and slipped and fell, the court rejecting the defendant's contention that the boy's act was without the scope of the invitation.

Where the plaintiff, an infant child of the tenant of an adjoining tenement house, was injured when, watching another child play on the second-story porch, he backed through an open space in the pickets of the railing around a common walkway which ran along the edge of the porch, it had actual knowledge that the plaintiff himself was in the practice of using the walk, since from the fact that there were eleven families living in the building he should have assumed that there would be some children using the passageway.

In Ludman v Miller (1938) 133 **Pa** Super 361, 3 A2d 32, the court sustained a jury's verdict for the tenant of a second-story rear apartment who was injured when, in the darkness, he fell from a ground-floor porch which was apparently a common passageway, the evidence showing that the defendant, in the course of repairs, had removed the porch railing without notifying the plaintiff or giving warning of any kind.

A jury verdict in favor of an injured guest of a tenant of defendant's apartment building was affirmed in Gumenick v United States (1973) 213 **Va** 510, 193 SE2d 788, 65 ALR3d 1, where there was evidence that the guest was injured when, while preparing to leave by way of a common rear porch and stairway of the apartment building, he placed his hand upon the railing of the porch which gave way and he fell to the ground; that examination of the railing established that it was composed of common pine which should not have been in unprotected use, be-

A typical page of an A.L.R. annotation. The researcher should <u>always</u> read the full text of cited cases.

After reading an A.L.R. annotation, a check should be made for later cases in the appropriate Up-Keep service. See Illustrations 32–34.

removed for over a year, the court holding that it was not necessary for the jury to find that the defendant

duty to maintain the porch and railings in a reasonable state of repair and that in the exercise of reasonable

SECTION C. FINDING A.L.R. ANNOTATIONS

With the understanding of the importance of A.L.R. annotations, it is now necessary to discuss how one determines if there is an A.L. R. annotation on the subject under research. The following methods may be used.

1. Index Method

Each of the four sets has a one-volume index entitled *Quick Index*. These are alphabetically arranged indexes to the annotations in the A.L.R. volumes, and are subdivided by topics and facts, and the annotations are listed by their titles. Presently, the indexes available are as follows:

Quick Index to A.L.R.3d and A.L.R.4th (with cumulative pocket supplement kept inside front cover). Second edition. [See Illustration 31]

Quick Index to A.L.R.2d.

Quick Index to A.L.R.

Quick Index to A.L.R.Fed. (with cumulative pocket supplement inside front covers.)[4]

2. Digest Method

A.L.R. and A.L.R.2d were both provided with additional sets entitled A.L.R. *Digests*. These are no longer provided for A.L.R.3d or 4th.

3. Table of Cases

An alphabetical listing of all cases reported in A.L.R. (first series) may be found in Volume 12 of the *A.L.R. Permanent Digest* and Volume 7 of the A.L.R.2d Digest. For A.L.R.3d, A.L.R.4th, and A.L.R.Fed. a *Table of Cases* appears in the bound volumes of the *Quick Index* for these sets and is supplemented in the pocket supplement. It is important to note that this Table lists decisions reported in A.L.R. and not the cases cited in the annotations.

4. American Jurisprudence and Shepard's Citations

The method of using these sets for finding A.L.R. annotations will be discussed in Chapters 15 and 16.

[4] This index is called *Federal Quick Index to the Total Client-Service Library*. It indexes *A.L.R.Fed.* as well as all matters on federal law in the other sets of *The Total Client-Service Library*. There are also published for the first and second series of A.L.R. separate indexes called *Word Indexes*. The annotations were indexed in much greater depth in these indexes. The *Word Index* for the first series is in four volumes and in three volumes for the second series. These have now been replaced by the *Quick Indexes*.

[Illustration 31]

EXCERPTS FROM A.L.R.3d–4th QUICK INDEX

Landlord and Tenant

Common areas
- animals: landlord's liability to third person for injury resulting from attack by dangerous or vicious animal kept by tenant, 81 ALR3d 638
- appliances: landlord's liability for personal injury or death due to defects in appliances supplied for use of different tenants, 66 ALR3d 374
- ice or snow: landlord's liability to tenant or tenant's invitees for injury or death due to ice or snow in areas or passageways used in common by tenants, 49 ALR3d 387
- lighting: liability of landlord for personal injury or death due to inadequacy or lack of lighting on portion of premises used in common by tenants, 66 ALR3d 202
- miscellaneous areas of building: landlord's liability for injury or death due to defects in areas of building (other than stairways) used in common by tenants, 65 ALR3d 14
- shopping center: liability of lessee of particu...

- step

- walk

Consti
pr
st
ALR3d 14, 5 Am Jur POF2d, pp 549–560

Contributory negligence
- children: landlord's liabiity to tenant's child for personal injuries resulting from defects in premises, as affected by tenant's negligence with respect to supervision of child, 82 ALR3d 1079
- common areas: landlord's liability for injury or death due to defects in areas of building (other than stairways) used in common by tenants, 65 ALR3d 14
- stairways: landlord's liability for injury or death due to defects in exterior steps or stairs used in common by tenants, 67 ALR3d 490
- proceeding in the dark across exterior premises as contributory negligence, 23 ALR3d 441
- proceeding in the dark across interior prem-

for later annotations **735**

QUICK INDEX

gamma ray, and neutron radiography, 10 Am Jur POF2d. pp 365–425

RAIDING OF EMPLOYEES

Liability for inducing employee not engaged for definite term to move to competitor, 24 ALR3d 821

RAILINGS

Landlord's liability for injury or death due to defects in areas of building (other than stairways) used in common by tenants, 65 ALR3d 14

RAILROADS

§ 1. Generally
§ 2. Liability for injury, loss or damage

§ 1. Generally.

Adjustment Board: judicial enforcement or review of decisions of National Railroad Ad-
...st,
...ent
LR

...ri-

...he
...ak-
...for

...ed
...3d

...or

"Permanent" location: construction of covenant or condition in conveyance of land relating to "permanent" maintenance of location of building or other structure, 7 ALR3d 650

Proof: railroads, 10 Am Jur POF, pp 1–47

Street Railways (this index)

Survey: right to enter land for preliminary survey or examination, 29 ALR3d 1104

Switching Operations (this index)

"Train" or "train movement": what is a "train" or "train movement" within the meaning of the brake provisions (45 USC §§ 1, 9) of the Federal Safety Appliance Act, 17 ALR3d 283

Urban Mass Transportation Act (this index)

993 **Consult POCKET PAR**

FINDING A.L.R. ANNOTATIONS

Use Quick Index to A.L.R. (1st), A.L.R.2d, A.L.R.3d and 4th, or Federal Quick Index for A.L.R.Fed.

For the problem under research, note how an annotation can be located under the entry LANDLORD–TENANT, or the more specific entry RAILINGS in the Quick Index for A.L.R.3d and 4th.

SECTION D. HOW A.L.R. IS KEPT CURRENT

1. Upkeep Service

Once an A.L.R. annotation has been found in a volume, further steps must be taken to determine cases subsequent to those found in the A.L.R. annotation. For example, after Volume 1 of A.L.R. was published in 1919, the publishers were immediately faced with the problem of providing their subscribers with a means of alerting them to cases that were handed down after Volume 1 was published and that related to the annotations in it, and would have been cited had they been handed down before Volume 1 had been published. They accomplished this by providing their subscribers a supplementary set to A.L.R. Each of the A.L.R. series is now supplemented as follows.

a. *A.L.R. (First)*

Volume 1 of A.L.R. was published in 1919. The publishers then started a companion set to A.L.R. which they called the *A.L.R. Blue Book of Supplemental Decisions.* This service is correlated to A.L.R. annotations and lists citations to all decisions on the same topic as the annotations. Thus, if one located an annotation in 117 A.L.R. 606–639, all that is necessary is to turn to that citation in *A.L.R. Blue Book of Supplemental Decisions* and find citations to all cases on that topic handed down after the annotation in 117 A.L.R. 606–639 was written. The *A.L.R. Blue Book of Supplemental Decisions* is now in five volumes and is kept current by an annual cumulative pamphlet. [See Illustration 34]

b. *A.L.R.2d*

After the publication of 175 A.L.R. in 1948, the publishers decided to stop this series and the next volume published was 1 A.L.R.2d, being the second series of the *American Law Reports.* Actually, each volume of the second series appears nearly the same as the first series. The most fundamental change was in the method of keeping annotations published in A.L.R.2d up to date. For this purpose it abandoned the use of the *A.L.R. Blue Book of Supplemental Decisions* (although still publishing it for use with A.L.R. [first series]). In its place, a new set called A.L.R.2d *Later Case Service* was started. This provides the same service for A.L.R.2d that *A.L.R. Blue Book of Supplemental Decisions* does for the first series, but instead of merely listing citations to later cases, it provides digests of these cases and then keys them directly to each section of the A.L.R.2d annotations. In using A.L.R.2d then, after the annotation has been read, the set of A.L.R.2d *Later Case Service* must be consulted. [See Illustration 33]

c. *A.L.R.3d and A.L.R.4th*

After 100 volumes of A.L.R.2d were published, the publishers again decided to change the method of upkeep. In 1965, A.L.R.3d began, and the most significant difference from the previous two series is that it is no longer necessary to examine an auxiliary set, such as the *A.L.R. Blue Book of Supplemental Decisions,* or A.L.R.2d *Later Case Service.* Rather, each volume of A.L.R.3d has an annual cumulative pocket supplement. When using A.L.R.3d and after reading the annotations, it is only necessary to check the pocket supplement to locate later cases. A.L.R.4th continues this method of upkeep. [See Illustration 32]

d. *A.L.R.Fed.*

This is kept up to date by pocket supplements the same as A.L.R. 3d and A.L.R.4th.

2. Supplementing and Superseding Annotations

a. *Superseding Annotations*

Frequently, a topic of law of an A.L.R. annotation is completely changed by later decisions. For example, an annotation in an early volume of A.L.R. may have dealt with the right to receive damages for emotional distress when there was no physical impact. Subsequently, this rule is changed and the courts start allowing damages in such instances. The editors may then decide to rewrite and publish in a later A.L.R. volume a superseding annotation. Sometimes only a part of a previous annotation will be superseded.

b. *Supplementing Annotations*

This method was used most frequently in A.L.R. (First) and A. L.R.2d. In such instances, a new annotation was written which served as a supplement to the orignal one. Both had to be read and then the upkeep service used for the citation to the supplementing annotation.

c. *Annotation History Table*

Whenever a researcher has a citation to an A.L.R. annotation, whether obtained from the A.L.R. *Quick Index* or elsewhere, it is good practice to check first to see if the annotation has been superseded. This may be done either by checking the citation in the appropriate A.L.R. upkeep service as described in Section D1 *supra,* or using the *Annotation History Table* located in the back of both the bound volume and pocket supplement of the A.L.R.3d & 4th *Quick Index* volume.[5] Its use may be best described graphically:

[5] These tables do not include supplementing or superseding annotations published in the first series of A.L.R. To determine if an annotation in 1–175 A.L.R. was supplemented or superseded in a subsequent volume of the first series, consult the *A.L.R. Blue Book of Supplemental Decisions.*

HISTORICAL TABLE

10 ALR 321-336 Superseded 75 ALR2d 633	**11 ALR 1325-1328** Superseded 50 ALR2d 143	**13 ALR 151-156** Superseded 46 ALR2d 1227
10 ALR 409-410 Superseded 84 ALR2d 1017	**11 ALR 1401-1402** Superseded 24 ALR2d 194	**13 ALR 225-247** Supplemented 43 ALR2d 1291
10 ALR 429-435 Superseded 17 ALR3d 705	**11 ALR 1405-1407** Superseded 20 ALR2d 1053	**13 ALR 324-340** Superseded 8 ALR3d 235
10 ALR 488-494 Superseded 92 ALR2d 570	**12 ALR 111-144** Supplemented 37 ALR2d 453	**13 ALR 346-355** Superseded 19 ALR3d 1227
10 ALR 783-809 Supplemented 40 ALR2d 1407	**12 ALR 333** Superseded 7 ALR2d 226	**13 ALR 372-383** Superseded 35 ALR2d 124

This means that 12 A.L.R. 111–140 and 37 A.L.R.2d 453 should be read together as if they were a single annotation, and then searching for later decisions as previously outlined in A.L.R.2d *Later Case Service.*

Suppose, however, that the researcher had found a citation to 25 A.L.R.2d 444, an earlier annotation on the subject of landlord-tenant liability for injury due to a defect in an area of building. By checking in the *Historical Table* in the *Quick Index* to A.L.R.3d & 4th, it would be noted that this annotation has been superseded as indicated below:

HISTORICAL TABLE

ALR3d

24 ALR2d 194-234 § 7 superseded 79 ALR3d 253	**29 ALR2d 911-920** Superseded 75 ALR3d 441	**36 ALR2d 1333-1336** Superseded 66 ALR3d 472
24 ALR2d 618-627 Superseded 77 ALR3d 735 § 6 superseded 83 ALR3d 1142	**29 ALR2d 1074-1140** § 4.135 superseded in 44 ALR3d 306	**37 ALR2d 7-149** §§ 39–52 superseded 70 ALR3d 630
24 ALR2d 1400-1403 Superseded 95 ALR3d 891	**29 ALR2d 1181-1185** Superseded 52 ALR3d 464	**37 ALR2d 169-188** Superseded 68 ALR3d 714
25 ALR2d 364-437 Superseded 67 ALR3d 587	**29 ALR2d 1279-1341** §§ 30, 31 superseded 9 ALR Fed 225	**37 ALR2d 737-746** Superseded 85 ALR3d 541
→ **25 ALR2d 444-487** Superseded 65 ALR3d 14	**30 ALR2d 1138-1141** Superseded 52 ALR3d 1118 & 97 ALR3d 421	**37 ALR2d 1125-1130** Superseded 25 ALR3d 1171 & 94 ALR3d 533
25 ALR2d 496-565 Superseded 66 ALR3d 202	**30 ALR2d 1233-1236** Superseded 74 ALR3d 637	**37 ALR2d 1136-1137** Superseded 97 ALR3d 1253
25 ALR2d 576-592 Superseded 66 ALR3d 374 § 2 superseded 35 ALR3d 1129	**30 ALR2d 1265-1298** § 17 Superseded 73 ALR3d 907	**38 ALR2d 778-784** Superseded 9 ALR Fed 457, 80 ALR3d 456

This means that the Annotation in 25 A.L.R.2d 444 should be ignored and only the annotation in 65 A.L.R.3d 14 has to be read, and its pocket supplement checked for later cases.

SECTION E. ILLUSTRATIONS. A.L.R. UPKEEP SERVICES

32. Page from A.L.R.3d volume. Pocket Supplement

33. Page from A.L.R.2d Later Case Service

34. Excerpts from A.L.R. Blue Book of Supplemental Decisions volume

[Illustration 32]

PAGE FROM POCKET SUPPLEMENT TO 65 A.L.R.3d

AMERICAN LAW REPORTS

THIRD SERIES

1980 Supplement

VOLUME 65 ALR3d

65 ALR3d 14–237

§ 1 [65 ALR3d 25]

[b] Related matters

Modern status of landlord's tort liability for injury or death of tenant or third person caused by dangerous condition of premises. 64 ALR3d 339.

Liability of landlord for personal injury or death due to inadequacy or lack of lighting on portion of premises used in common by tenants. 66 ALR3d 202.

Landlord's liability for personal injury or death due to defects in appliances supplied for use of c

Landl
defects
mon by

Land
by defe
ways u
587.

Land
defects
used in

Land
sonal i
ises, as
respect
1079.

After reading the annotation, a search should be made for later cases. When using A.L.R.3d, or A.L.R.4th, this is done by checking in the annual cumulative supplement in the back of the volume.

Note how this pocket supplement is keyed to the paragraph numbers of the main annotation.

Liability for injuries in connection with allegedly dangerous or defective doormat on nonresidential premises, 94 ALR3d 389.

§ 6 [65 ALR3d 51]

[b] Control not retained

Landlord was not liable for injuries sustained by tenant when he slipped and fell on wet basement laundryroom floor near leaky washer, where there was no evidence that landlord retained control over laundryroom which it had leased to another party under lease providing that party would control area, have title to, repair and maintain equipment, and maintain liability insurance, and where, though landlord retained duty to notify lessee when equipment had stopped working, evidence was insufficient to establish that landlord had failed to discharge duty. Macke Co. v Housing Management Co. (1978) 38 **Md** App 425, 381 A2d 313.

§ 7 [65 ALR3d 59]

See McCrorey v Heilpern, 170 **Conn** 220, 365 A2d 1057, infra § 29[b].

See Hornsby v Ray (**La** App) 327 So 2d 146,

accident,
ke sub-
ecise to
ndlord's
floor in
oot and
2d 898,

pporta-

liability in respect to premises leased to lessee who assumes responsibility for condition of premises but rendering landlord liable in respect to defects which landlord knew or should have noticed, trial court erred in finding landlord liable for injuries sustained by tenant's employee whose right leg slipped through rotten floorboard near back door, where lessee had entered into oral agreement to assume liability for condition of premises, evidence failed to show that landord either knew or should have known of defect in floor, and defect was latent. Hornsby v Ray (**La** App) 327 So 2d 146.

3

[Illustration 33]

PAGE FROM A.L.R.2d LATER CASE SERVICE

543 LATER CASE SERVICE **63 ALR2d 108–175**

63 ALR2d 108–175

Liability for injury occasioned by backing of motor vehicle from private premises into public street or highway.

§ 1. Scope, p. 114.

3 Am Jur Pl & Pr Forms, Automobiles and Highway Traffic, Forms 480, 481.

§ 3. Generally; lookout and right of way, p. 116.

[a] Generally.

Automobile operator who drives from private driveway onto highway must be

extremely careful, and if he is backing onto highway he must use an even higher degree of care. Morgan v Southern Farm Bureau Casualty Ins. Co. (DC La) 223 F Supp 996, affd (CA5) 339 F2d 755 (applying Louisiana law).

[b] Right of way and lookout.

Also recognizing duties of backing drivers:

Iowa.—Sayre v Andrews (Iowa) 146 NW2d 336 (duty to exercise high degree of care, keep proper lookout, stop, and yield right of way to approaching vehicles).

La.—State Farm Mut. Auto. Ins. Co. v C. & C. Oil Field Servicing Co. (La App) 168 So 2d 918 (statutory duty to yield right of way, and duty to exercise unusual degree of care); Deville v Aetna Ins. Co. (La App) 191 So 2d 324 (duty to exercise high degree of care, stop at curb or sidewalk, and yield right of way), writ refused 250 La 13, 193 So 2d 527.

Miss.—Baxter v Rounsaville (Miss) 193 So 2d 735 (statutory duty to yield right of way).

Okla.—Turner v Gallagher (Okla) 371 P2d 733 (duty to keep proper lookout while

imposed upon backing motorist; remaining half of duty is to maintain proper lookout during continuing maneuver. Smith v Hearn (La App) 181 So 2d 433.

§ 4. Warning signals; lights, p. 120.

Also recognizing duty to signal or to warn of presence:

Ky.—Nolan v Nally (Ky) 342 SW2d 400 (duty to warn that truck backed across highway at night near curve was blocking road).

§ 5. In general; action against owner or operator of backing vehicle, p. 122.

[b] Questions of negligence of one responsible for backing automobile.

In action for injuries to plaintiff when car she was driving was struck by defendant's car, being backed from private driveway into street, evidence supported finding that defendant's negligence proximately caused accident, and that plaintiff was not contributorily negligent. Alessi v Farkas (Fla App) 118 So 2d 658.

Where plaintiffs, motorist and passenger, testified that defendant backing from driveway at night had stopped car with its

When using an annotation in A.L.R.2d a different method of locating later cases must be used as A.L.R.2d did not use pocket supplements. Rather, a separate eleven volume set called A.L.R. 2d Later Case Service is provided. The citation of the A.L.R.2d annotation should be checked in this set. While not shown in this Illustration, the pocket supplement to A.L.R.2d Later Case Service must also be checked.

[Illustration 34]

EXCERPTS FROM A.L.R. BLUE BOOK OF SUPPLEMENTAL DECISIONS

VOL. 1

117 A.L.R. 606–639.

Richardson v. D. (Ala.) 187 So. 176.

Norgard v. N. 54 CalApp(2d) 82, 128 P(2d) 566.

Morrison v. N. 311 IllApp 411. 36 NE(2d) 581.

Loeser v. S. (Ind) 39 NE(2d) 945.

Re Gollobit (Iowa) 8 NW(2d) 191.

Crawford v. C. (Iowa) 15 NW (2d) 633.

Re Stephenson (Iowa) 14 NW (2d) 684.

Simpson v. S. 276 Ky. 223, 123 S.W.(2d) 816.

Feltner v. G. (Ky) 177 SW (2d) 903.

Re Boese (Minn) 7 NW(2d) 355.

VOL. 2

117 ALR 606–639

Livingston v. P. (Ala) 57 So2d 521.

Cross v. P. (Ark) 221 SW2d 24.

Guyot v. F. (Ark) 243 SW2d 630.

Black v. B. 91 Cal App2d 328. 204 P2d 950

Johnson v. B. (Ga App) 67 SE2d 189.

Re Conner's Estate (Iowa) 36 NW2d 833.

Boggess v. C. E. (Mo App) 207 SW2d 814.

Re Haas' Estate, 10 NJ Super 581, 77 A2d 523.

Santos v. M. (Tex Civ App) 193 SW2d 927.

Logan v. T. (Tex Civ App) 199 SW2d 210. error granted.

VOL. 3

117 ALR 583–599

General Motors Acceptance Corp. v M. (Kan) 311 P2d 339.

117 ALR 606–639

Berendsen v. Mcl. 126 Cal App2d 347, 272 P2d 76.

Seeba v B. (Fla) 86 So2d 432.

Fuller v F. (Ga) 97 SE2d 306.

Hays v I. I. H. (Ill) 147 NE2d 287.

Re Guardianship of Anderson (Iowa) 78 NW2d 788.

Reidinger v. A. (Mo) 266 SW2d 610

Grimm v G. (Mo) 303 SW2d 43.

Ellison v. S. (ND) 62 NW2d 95.

Theadgill v A. (Okla) 303 P2d 297.

Chandler v W. (Tex) 294 SW2d 801.

Leach v C. E. (Tex Civ App) 279 SW2d 630.

Chandler v W. (Tex Civ App) 282 SW2d 940

Chamberlain v R. (Tex Civ App) 303 SW2d 817.

VOL. 4

117 ALR 606–639

Ala.—Taylor v F. N. B. 189 So 2d 141

Alaska—Re Hewett's Estate. 358 P2d 579

Ky.—Cook v B. 346 SW2d 725

Neb.—Olsen v B. 92 NW2d 531

N. J.—Moss v G. (Co) 146 A2d 227

N. Y.—Lindsay v L. 22 Misc 2d 1071. 203 NYS2d 705

Tex.—Connor v P. (Civ App) 360 SW2d 438

117 ALR 649

Superseded 130 ALR 272◆

LATEST PAM. SUPPL.

117 ALR 470–484

Supplemented 168 ALR 581◆

117 ALR 496–498

Superseded 95 ALR2d 585◆

117 ALR 522–538

Mo.—Swiastyn v S. J. L. & P. Co. (App) 459 SW2d 24 (citing anno)

117 ALR 563–565

Superseded 53 ALR2d 224◆

117 ALR 571–572

U. S.—Doyle v N. J. Const. Co. (CA Wis) 382 F2d 735

117 ALR 606–639

Fla.—Roberts v B. (App) 201

Note how A.L.R. Blue Book of Supplemental Decisions also indicates when an Annotation has been supplemented or superseded. It is simpler to use the Historical Table.

After using an Annotation in A.L.R. (First Series), later cases may be found in the *A.L.R. Blue Book of Supplemental Decisions.* There are five *Blue Books* that contain references decided after the original annotation was written. Vol. 1 covers 1919–46; Vol. 2, 1946–52; Vol. 3, 1953–58; Vol. 4, 1959–67. Vol. 5 (not illustrated) covers the years 1968–75. An annual pamphlet lists citations since 1975.

SECTION F. SUMMARY

A.L.R. may be used to locate court decisions on a topic of law. If, through its indexes, an A.L.R. annotation is located, it will cite all previous court decisions on the topic, and the upkeep services provided will locate cases subsequent in time to the writing of the A.L.R. annotation.

It is important to keep in mind that A.L.R. is primarily a *case finding tool* and all decisions located through its use should be read.

Summary of Finding A.L.R. Annotations

Step 1. Start search in *Quick Index* to A.L.R.3d and A.L.R.4th.

(a) If reference in index to an appropriate annotation is located, proceed to Step 2; if not:

(1) search *Quick Index* to A.L.R.2d; if reference located, proceed to Step 2, if not,

(2) search *Quick Index* to A.L.R. (1st); if applicable reference found, proceed to Step 2, if not:

(a) subject being researched probably not covered by A.L.R.; start search for cases using other techniques outlined in Chapter 25.

Step 2. Check *Historical Table* in Pocket Supplement in *Quick Index* to A.L.R.3d and 4th to determine if annotation(s) located through Step 1 have been *superseded* or *supplemented*:

(a) If superseded, note superseding annotation, ignore original, and proceed to Step 3;

(b) if supplemented, note supplementary annotation and proceed to Step 3;

(c) if annotation not listed in *Historical Table*, proceed to Step 3.

Step 3. Read annotation(s) found through Steps 1 and 2.

After reading annotation(s) check for later cases:

(a) If A.L.R. (1st) annotation in *A.L.R. Blue Book of Supplemental Decisions;*

(b) If A.L.R.2d annotation in *Later Case Service* to A.L.R.2d;

(c) If A.L.R.3d or A.L.R.4th annotation in pocket supplement to that volume;

(d) If A.L.R.Fed. annotation in pocket supplement to A.L.R. Fed. volume.

Other methods of locating A.L.R. annotations will be discussed in Chapters 15 and 16.

Chapter 8

CONSTITUTIONS

This chapter will discuss the role of constitutions for both the federal and state governments. As these documents are the charters adopted by the people, they are the highest primary authority.

SECTION A. FEDERAL CONSTITUTION

The Constitution of the United States, in a formal sense, is the written document which was drafted at Philadelphia in the summer of 1787 plus the amendments that have since been added. It was not the intention of the framers that the Constitution be static but rather, as noted by Chief Justice Marshall, it should "endure for the ages to come and consequently, be adapted to various crises in human affairs."[1] More recently, a noted constitutional scholar commented that "The proper point of view from which to approach the task of interpreting the Constitution is that of regarding it as a living statute, palpitating with the purpose of the hour, reenacted with every waking breath of the American people, whose primitive right to determine their institutions is its sole claim to validity as law and as the matrix of laws under our system." [2]

It follows from this that to research problems in federal constitutional law, one must not only consult the document itself, but all of the sources that will assist in the interpretation of the Constitution. Such sources will include the background and record of the Constitutional Convention, the interpretation of the Constitution by the Supreme Court of the United States in the over 400 volumes of its reports, and the commentaries on the Constitution which appear in treatises, legal periodicals and encyclopedias.

Lawyers, when faced with grave constitutional questions of interpretation, frequently refer to the sources of constitutional interpretation.[3] How to locate and use such sources will be discussed in this chapter.

[1] McCulloch v. Maryland, 17 U.S. (4 Wheat.) 316, 415 (1819).

[2] U.S. LIBRARY OF CONGRESS. CONGRESSIONAL RESEARCH SERVICE, THE CONSTITUTION OF THE UNITED STATES OF AMERICA. S.DOC. NO. 92–82, 92d Cong., 2d Sess. VII (1973). This edition of the Constitution is supplemented biennially with pocket supplements and new hardbound editions are issued every ten years. 2 U.S.C. sec. 168 (1976).

[3] *See, e. g.*, United States v. Nixon, 418 U.S. 683, 705 at note 15 (1974).

1. Historical Sources

When faced with interpreting the meaning of a provision or clause of the Constitution, it is frequently useful to ascertain the meaning given to the words used by the "founding fathers." At times, it may be necessary to check into sources that preceded the adoption of the Constitution, such as documents of the Continental Congress or the Articles of Confederation. These may be easily located in *Documents Illustrative of the Formation of the Union of the American States*.[4]

While the Constitutional Convention did not keep official records of its secret session, several sources exist that provide an insight into the debates that took place and should be consulted when researching a historical interpretation of the Constitution.[5]

2. Judicial Interpretation: Annotated Editions of the Federal Constitution

When determining the meaning of the United States Constitution, it is also necessary to search for the interpretations of constitutional provisions by the courts, and especially those of the Supreme Court of the United States. Some of the most useful sources for these are the various annotated editions of the United States Constitution, which set forth each article, section and clause of the Constitution and provide digests (and, in some instances, commentary) on court decisions.

a. *United States Code Annotated. Constitution of the United States Annotated.* (West)

[4] U.S. LIBRARY OF CONGRESS. LEGISLATIVE REFERENCE SERVICE, DOCUMENTS ILLUSTRATIVE OF THE FORMATION OF THE UNION OF THE AMERICAN STATES, H.DOC.R. NO. 398, 69th Cong., 1st Sess. (1935). *See also* S. BLOOM, FORMATION OF THE UNION UNDER THE CONSTITUTION (1935). For background on the Articles of Confederation, *see* Swindler, Our First Constitution: The Articles of Confederation, 67 A.B.A.J. 166 (1981).

[5] J. MADISON, THE PAPERS OF JAMES MADISON (H. Gilpin ed. 1840); THE FEDERALIST (P. Ford ed. 1898) (This is one of several editions); U.S. BUREAU OF ROLLS AND LIBRARY OF THE DEPARTMENT OF STATE, DOCUMENTARY HISTORY OF THE CONSTITUTION OF THE UNITED STATES OF AMERICA, 1786–1870 (1894–1905); M. FARRAND, THE RECORDS OF THE FEDERAL CONVENTION OF 1787 (1934–1937); J. ELLIOT, THE DEBATES IN THE SEVERAL STATE CONVENTIONS OF THE ADOPTION OF THE FEDERAL CONSTITUTION TOGETHER WITH THE JOURNAL OF THE FEDERAL CONVENTION (1937, Supp.: DEBATES ON THE ADOPTION OF THE FEDERAL CONSTITUTION IN THE CONVENTION HELD AT PHILADELPHIA IN 1787, 123–565, Madison papers revised and newly arranged); THE DOCUMENTARY HISTORY OF THE RATIFICATION OF THE CONSTITUTION (to be completed in 12 volumes) (M. Jensen ed. 1976). When finished, this set will be the most complete and up-to-date source for the history of the United States Constitution. For evaluation of scholarship in this area since 1937 *see* Hutson, *Pierce Butler's Records of the Federal Constitutional Convention,* 37 Q.J. LIB. CONGRESS 64 (1980).

The United States Constitution volumes are a separate unit of the *United States Code Annotated* and consist of several unnumbered volumes, including a separate index to the Constitution. After each article, section or clause of the Constitution, digest headnotes from all cases that have interpreted a constitutional provision are organized into "notes of decisions." For example, Article I is followed by 103 notes while Article I, section 8, clause 3 is followed by 1187 notes. To assist in the location of these notes, indexes to them are provided. The means of locating a constitutional provision and the annotations to it are shown in Illustrations 35–37.

b. *United States Code Service. Constitution Volume*

These volumes are a separate unit of the *United States Code Service* published by the Lawyers Co-operative Publishing Company and the Bancroft-Whitney Company which is part of their *Total Client-Service Library.*[6] It is organized similarly to the *United States Code Annotated* and is used in a like manner.

c. *The Constitution of the United States of America* (Library of Congress ed., 1973)[7]

This one-volume edition of the annotated Constitution was prepared by the Congressional Research Service of the Library of Congress, as authorized by a Joint Congressional Resolution.[8] It sets forth each article, section and clause of the Constitution; immediately following each of them, in smaller typeface, appear an analysis and commentary prepared by the editorial staff. Important decisions of the Supreme Court of the United States are discussed in the analysis, and citations to them are given in the footnotes. [See Illustrations 38–39], Frequently, the commentary will quote from the proceedings of the Constitutional Convention, the opinions of dissenting justices, and other documents. This volume, unlike the ones discussed above, does not attempt to cite or comment on all decisions of the Supreme Court of the United States, but refers only to the significant ones. It has a detailed index and includes the following useful tables:

Proposed Amendments Pending Before the States.

Proposed Amendments Not Ratified by the States.

Acts of Congress Held Unconstitutional in Whole or in Part by the Supreme Court of the United States.

State Constitutional and Statutory Provisions and Municipal Ordinances Held Unconstitutional on Their Face or As Administered (1789–1972).

[6] See Chapter 7, Section A.

[7] For the complete citation of this *see* note 2.

[8] 2 U.S.C. § 168 (1976).

Supreme Court Decisions Overruled by Subsequent Decisions.

Table of Cases.

This is a very useful volume, and it is often the preferred starting point for research on constitutional questions. The Congressional Research Service plans to keep the volume up to date by biennial issuance of pocket supplements.

d. *Digests*

The following digests of federal cases provide additional judicial interpretations to the Constitution. These publications are discussed in detail in Chapter Six.

United States Supreme Court Reports Digest (Lawyers Co-operative Publishing Co.).

Volume 17 includes the text of the Constitution with references to related sections in the *Digest.*

United States Supreme Court Digest (West Publishing Co.).

Federal Digest, Modern Federal Practice Digest, and *West's Federal Practice Digest, 2d.*

e. *Annotations*

The annotations in A.L.R.Fed. and the *U.S. Supreme Court Reports* (L.Ed.) may contain discussion, with case analysis, on a phase of the Constitution which is being studied.

3. Treatises and Periodical Literature

Voluminous literature has been written by legal scholars on the interpretation of constitutional provisions, and research in constitutional law can seldom be completed successfully without consulting the writings of constitutional scholars in either treatises or legal periodicals.[9]

[9] A few useful titles are: P. BREST, PROCESSES OF CONSTITUTIONAL DECISION MAKING (1975); G. GUNTHER, CASES AND MATERIALS ON CONSTITUTIONAL LAW (10th ed. 1980); L. TRIBE, AMERICAN CONSTITUTIONAL LAW (1978). For a list of older titles *see* NEW YORK UNIVERSITY, SCHOOL OF LAW LIBRARY, A CATALOGUE OF THE LAW COLLECTION AT NEW YORK UNIVERSITY (1953), and ASSOCIATION OF AMERICAN LAW SCHOOLS, 2 LAW BOOKS RECOMMENDED FOR LIBRARIES: CONSTITUTIONAL LAW (1968). Periodical literature may be located through methods described in Chapter 17.

SECTION B. ILLUSTRATIONS: FEDERAL CONSTITUTION

Problem: What protection is given in the Constitution to speeches of the members of Congress?

Illustrations

35. **Page from Index to Constitution: U.S.C.A.**

36–37. **Pages from Constitution volume: U.S.C.A.**

38–39. **Pages from the Library of Congress Edition—Annotated Constitution**

[Illustration 35]

PAGE FROM INDEX TO CONSTITUTION: U.S.C.A.

CONSTITUTION OF THE UNITED STATES

The first step in researching a problem involving the U.S. Constitution is to look in an index to the Constitution. For the problem under research, Article 1, Section 6, Clause 1 should be examined. See next Illustration.

597

[Illustration 36]

PAGE FROM CONSTITUTION—U.S.C.A.

1 § 5, cl. 3 CONSTITUTION

Section 5, Clause 3. Journal; publication; recording of yeas and nays

Each House shall keep a Journal of its Proceedings, and from time to time publish the same, excepting such Parts as may in their Judgment require Secrecy; and the Yeas and Nays of the Members of either House on any question shall, at the Desire of one fifth of those Present, be entered on the Journal.

Notes of Decisions

Entries 1
Evidence 2

Library references

United States ⟹18.
C.J.S. United States §§ 21, 23.

not expressly require bills that have passed Congress to be attested by the signatures of the presiding officers of the two houses, usage, the orderly conduct of legislative proceedings, and the rules under which the two bodies have acted since the organization of the government require that mode of authenti-

Text of the constitutional provision covering speeches by members of the Congress as it appears in the Constitution volumes of the United States Code Annotated. This set and the United States Code Service are kept current by annual pocket supplements.

mode to that end which its wisdom suggests. Although the Constitution does

Morgenthau, 1939, 106 F.2d 330, 70 App D.C. 306.

Section 5, Clause 4. Consent of each house to adjournment

Neither House, during the Session of Congress, shall, without the Consent of the other, adjourn for more than three days, nor to any other Place than that in which the two Houses shall be sitting.

Section 6, Clause 1. Compensation of members; privilege from arrest

The Senators and Representatives shall receive a Compensation for their Services, to be ascertained by Law, and paid out of the Treasury of the United States. They shall in all Cases, except Treason, Felony and Breach of the Peace, be privileged from Arrest during their Attendance at the Session of their respective Houses, and in going to and returning from the same; and for any Speech or Debate in either House, they shall not be questioned in any other Place.

190

[Illustration 37]

PAGE SHOWING ANNOTATIONS: CONSTITUTION VOLUME: U.S.C.A.

COMPENSATION, ARREST, ETC. 1 § 6, cl. 1

Note 3

Notes of Decisions

Library references
United States ⚷12.
C.J.S. United States § 18.

1. Construction

This clause that for any speech or debate in either House, Senators and Representatives shall not be questioned in any other place is to be interpreted liberally and not narrowly. U. S. v. Johnson, C.A.Md.1964, 337 F.2d 180, affirmed 86 S.Ct. 749, 383 U.S. 169, 15 L.Ed.2d 681, certiorari denied 87 S.Ct. 44, 134, 385 U.S. 846, 889, 17 L.Ed.2d 77, 117.

This clause will be read broadly to effectuate its purpose. Id.

This clause, providing that congressmen should, except for treason, felony, and breach of peace, be privileged from arrest, and that they should not be questioned for any speech in either House, is to be liberally construed to free congressman from fear of prosecutions for words spoken, votes cast, or actions taken in pursuit of their lawful functions but lieved from absenting himself from his public duties during the session of Congress, for the purpose of defending his private suits in court, as that he should be exempt from imprisonment on execution. Doty v. Strong, 1840, 1 Pinn. (Wis.) 84.

2. Purpose

Purpose of this clause that for any speech or debate in either House, Senators and Representatives shall not be questioned in any other place, is to promote free expression on floor of each House by freeing Congressmen from fear of involvement in judicial proceedings. U. S. v. Johnson, C.A.Md.1964, 337 F.2d 180, affirmed 86 S.Ct. 749, 383 U.S. 169, 15 L.Ed.2d 681, certiorari denied 87 S.Ct. 44, 134, 385 U.S. 846, 889, 17 L.Ed.2d 77, 117.

Purpose of this clause giving to Senators and Representatives immunity from arrest, except in certain cases, during attendance at sessions and in going to and returning therefrom is not for benefit or even convenience of individual legislators but is to prevent interference with the legislative process, and it prevents judicial branch of government from effecting such interference by restricting power of courts. James v. Powell, 1966, 274 N.Y.S.2d 192, 26 A.D.2d 295, affirmed 277 N.Y.S.2d 135, 18 N.Y.2d 931, 223 N.E.2d 562, motion granted 279 N.Y.S.2d 972, 19 N.Y.2d 813, 226 N.E.2d 705.

3. Privilege from arrest—Scope of

Where attention given in evidence is to substance of defendant congressman's speech on floor of House and his motivation in making it was not incidental part of government's prosecution under charge of conspiracy to defraud United States, since conspiracy theory depended on showing that speech was made

Both *UNITED STATES CODE ANNOTATED* and *UNITED STATES CODE SERVICE* have digests of all cases that have involved interpretation of clauses of the Constitution.

191

[Illustration 38]

PAGE FROM LIBRARY OF CONGRESS EDITION—
ANNOTATED CONSTITUTION

116 ART. I—LEGISLATIVE DEPARTMENT

Sec. 6—Rights of Members **Cl. 1—Compensation, Privileges**

This one volume edition sets forth the text of each Section and Clause of the Constitution. Immediately following, in smaller type, is an analysis and commentary of the Clause.

SECTION 6. Clause 1. The Senators and Representatives shall receive a Compensation for their Services, to be ascertained by Law, and paid out of the Treasury of the United States. They shall in all Cases, except Treason, Felony and Breach of the Peace, be privileged from Arrest during their Attendance at the Session of their respective Houses and in going to and returning from the same; and for any Speech or Debate in either House, they shall not be questioned in any other Place.

Clause 2. No Senator or Representative shall, during the Time for which he was elected, be appointed to any civil Office under the Authority of the United States, which shall have been created, or the Emoluments whereof shall have been encreased during such time; and no Person holding any Office under the the United States, shall be a Member of either House during his Continuance in Office.

COMPENSATION, IMMUNITIES AND DISABILITIES OF MEMBERS

When the Pay Starts

A Member of Congress who receives his certificate of admission, and is seated, allowed to vote, and serve on committees, is *prima facie* entitled to the seat and salary, even though the House subsequently

[8] *Field* v. *Clark*, 143 U.S. 649 (1892); *Flint* v. *Stone Tracy Co.*, 220 U.S. 107, 143 (1911). A parallel rule holds in the case of a duly authenticated official notice to the Secretary of State that a state legislature has ratified a proposed amendment to the Constitution. *Leser* v. *Garnett*, 258 U.S. 130, 137 (1922); *see also Coleman* v. *Miller*, 307 U.S. 433 (1939).

[Illustration 39]

PAGE FROM LIBRARY OF CONGRESS EDITION— ANNOTATED CONSTITUTION

ART. I—LEGISLATIVE DEPARTMENT 117

Sec. 6—Rights of Members **Cl. 1—Privileges**

declares his seat vacant. The one who contested the election and was subsequently chosen to fill the vacancy is entitled to salary only from the time the compensation of such "predecessor" has ceased.[1]

Analysis of the privilege of speech clause by the editors of the volume. Footnotes contain citations to cases mentioned in the analysis.

Privilege of Speech or Debate

Members.—This clause represents "the culmination of a long struggle for parliamentary supremacy. Behind these simple phrases lies a history of conflict between the Commons and the Tudor and Stuart monarchs during which successive monarchs utilized the criminal and civil law to suppress and intimidate critical legislators. Since the Glorious Revolution in Britain, and throughout United States history, the privilege has been recognized as an important protection of the independence and integrity of the legislature." [6] So Justice Harlan explained the significance of the speech and debate clause, the ancestry of which traces back to a clause in the English Bill of Rights of 1689 [7] and the history of which traces back almost to the beginning of the development of Parliament as an independent force.[8] "In the American governmental structure the clause serves the additional function of reinforcing the separation of powers so deliberately established by the Founders." [9] "The immunities of the Speech or Debate Clause were not written into the Constitution simply for the personal or private benefit of Members of Congress, but to protect the integrity of the legislative process by insuring the independence of individual legislators." [10]

---

[1] *Pace* v. *United States*, 127 U.S. 67 (1888).

[2] *Long* v. *Ansell*, 293 U.S. 76 (1934).

[3] Id., 83.

[4] *United States* v. *Cooper*, 4 Dall. (4 U.S.) 341 (C.C. Pa. 1800).

[5] *Williamson* v. *United States*, 207 U.S. 425, 446 (1908).

[6] *United States* v. *Johnson*, 383 U.S. 169, 178 (1966).

[7] "That the Freedom of Speech, and Debates or Proceedings in Parliament, ought not to be impeached or questioned in any Court or Place out of Parliament." 1 W. & M., Sess. 2, c. 2.

[8] *United States* v. *Johnson*, 383 U.C. 169, 177–179, 180–183 (1966); *Powell* v. *McCormack*, 395 U.S. 486, 502 (1969).

[9] *United States* v. *Johnson*, 383 U.S. 169, 178 (1966).

[10] *United States* v. *Brewster*, 408 U.S. 501, 507 (1972). This rationale was approvingly quoted from *Coffin* v. *Coffin*, 4 Mass. 1, 28 (1808), in *Kilbourn* v. *Thompson*, 103 U.S. 168, 203 (1881).

SECTION C. STATE CONSTITUTIONS

Each of the fifty states has adopted its own constitution, and many states have adopted several different constitutions over the years. The procedure for adopting a new constitution is usually accomplished by the convening of a state constitutional convention.[10] The state constitution, except for those issues covered by the supremacy clause of the United States Constitution,[11] is the highest primary legal authority for the state.

When doing research involving a state constitution, it may also be necessary to check the historical documents that led to its adoption and to consult the state and federal court decisions interpreting it.

1. Texts of State Constitutions

a. The most common source for the text of a state constitution is the constitution volume of the state code.[12] This ordinarily will contain the current text, the text of previously adopted versions, and annotations similar in format to those of the United States Constitution as described in Section A *supra*. The volume or volumes containing the state constitution should be examined carefully, and distinctive bibliographic features should be noted. Many states also print and distribute an unannotated edition of the state constitution in pamphlet form.

b. Columbia University. Legislative Drafting Research Fund. *Constitutions of the United States: National and State* (2d ed. 1974).[13]

This multi-volume, looseleaf set collects the text of the Constitutions of all U.S. territories and fifty states and is kept current by supplements.

[10] A. STURM, A BIBLIOGRAPHY ON STATE CONSTITUTIONS AND CONSTITUTIONAL REVISION, 1945–1975 (1975).

[11] U.S.CONST. ART. VI; Gibbons v. Ogden, 22 U.S. (9 Wheat.) 1 (1824); National Labor Relations Bd. v. Jones & Laughlin Steel Corp., 301 U.S. 1 (1937); United States v. Darby, 312 U.S. 100 (1941); Perez v. United States, 402 U.S. 146 (1971).

[12] State codes are discussed in Chapter Eleven.

[13] The following older titles are also useful in tracing the historical development of state constitutions: B. POORE, CHARTERS AND CONSTITUTIONS (1877); F. STIMSON, THE LAW OF THE FEDERAL AND STATE CONSTITUTIONS OF THE UNITED STATES (1908); F. THORPE, FEDERAL AND STATE CONSTITUTIONS (1909); C. KETTLEBOROUGH, STATE CONSTITUTIONS (1918); NEW YORK CONSTITUTIONAL CONVENTION COMMITTEE, 3 REPORTS: CONSTITUTIONS OF THE STATES AND UNITED STATES (1938). Although Thorpe and Poore are out-of-date, they are useful for their parallel study of state constitutions. The last item, although never brought up-to-date, is still useful for its index volume to the constitutions of all of the states.

2. Historical Sources of State Constitutions

The records, journals, proceedings, and other documents relating to state constitutional conventions provide valuable information on the intended meanings and interpretations given to state constitutions by their framers.[14] Some state codes also contain historical introductions to the constitutions printed therein. Local encyclopedias and treatises should also be consulted.

3. Judicial Interpretation of State Constitutions

In addition to consulting the annotations to the constitution in the appropriate volumes of the state code, the state digest should also be consulted, using the index to the constitution to locate the relevant sections of the digest.

4. Comparative Sources of State Constitutions

Frequently, a provision of a particular state constitution may not have received any judicial interpretation. In such instances, judicial decisions on similar provisions in other state constitutions may be useful. One method of locating which state constitutions have similar provisions is through the use of one of the following:

a. *Index Digest of State Constitutions.* This set is a companion to the *Constitutions of the United States: National and State,* discussed in 1–b *supra.* It is arranged alphabetically by subject and under each subject are listed the various constitutional provisions of the states. Although this set has not been kept current since 1971, it is still useful, as many provisions of state constitutions do not change with great frequency.

b. Beginning in 1980, the publisher of *Constitutions of the United States: National and State* announced a new indexing service for this set. Rather than indexing the fifty state constitutions in one alphabetical index, it plans to issue a series of subject indexes. The first is entitled *Fundamental Liberties and Rights: A 50–State Index.* When this project is completed it will provide a comprehensive and current subject index to the constitutions of the fifty states.

SECTION D. FOREIGN CONSTITUTIONS

There are occasions when it is necessary to locate the constitutions of foreign countries. This may be accomplished by consulting the *Constitutions of the Countries of the World.*[15]

[14] *See* note 10. The Congressional Information Service has made most of these materials available in their collection "State Constitutional Conventions, Commissions, and Amendments on Microfiche" (1972–1980) with accompanying hard copy indexes.

[15] Edited by A. Blaustein and C. Flanz.

This set is published in looseleaf format, with a separate pamphlet for each country. For those countries where there is not an official English version, an English translation is provided. The constitutions for each country are preceded by a constitutional chronology and followed by an annotated bibliography.

Periodically supplements are issued, keeping each constitution up to date.

The Introduction in Chapter One should be consulted for bibliographical references to previous compilations of constitutions.

A companion set is *Constitutions of Dependencies and Special Sovereignties.*[16] This set contains pamphlets on the world's associated states, dependent territories, and areas of special sovereignty. Each pamphlet contains constitutional status data and an annotated bibliography. When a "territory" in this set achieves the status of a nation-state, it will be incorporated into the *Constitutions of the Countries of the World.*

SECTION E. SUMMARY

1. Federal Constitution

a. *Text in:*

(1) *United States Code.*

(2) *United States Code Annotated.*

(3) *United States Code Service.*

(4) *U. S. Supreme Court Reports Digest* (Lawyers Co-operative Publishing Co.).

(5) *Library of Congress, Constitution of the United States of America* (1973).

b. *Interpretation*

(1) Historical (*see supra*).

(2) Judicial.

(a) U.S.C.A.: (i) index is to the text of the Constitution; does not cover interpretative cases; (ii) topic analysis precedes digests of cases; (iii) digests of interpretative federal and state cases and Attorneys General opinions under constitutional provisions, subdivided by topic analysis (Notes to Decisions); (iv) parallel citation; and (v) cumulative annual pocket and subsequent pamphlet supplements.

[16] Edited by A. Blaustein and E. Blaustein.

(b) U.S.C.S.: (i) index is to the text of the Constitution; does not cover interpretative cases; (ii) topic analysis precedes digests of cases; (iii) digests of interpretative federal and state cases and Attorneys General opinions under constitutional provisions, subdivided by topic analysis (Notes to Decisions); (iv) parallel citation; and (v) cumulative annual pocket and later pamphlet supplements.

(c) *Library of Congress. Constitution of the United States of America* (1973): (i) partially indexes cases as well as the text of the Constitution; (ii) discussion of selected cases of the Supreme Court of the United States; documents; views of writers; (iii) no provision is made for keeping this publication up-to-date.

(d) *U. S. Supreme Court Reports Digest*: (i) volume 17 provides text and references to sections of the *Digest* covering the Constitution and (ii) volume 14 contains a Table of Constitutional Provisions with citations to U. S. Supreme Court decisions which construe them.

(e) Digests (*see* Section A2d, *supra*).

(f) Annotations: A.L.R.Fed. and the U. S. Supreme Court Reports (L.Ed.) may discuss the problem.

c. *Treatises and periodical literature* (*see* Section A3, *supra*)

2. State Constitutions

a. Published with state code.

b. Separate indexes and general indexes which are topically and not factually analyzed.

c. Annotated.

3. Sources of Comparative Information about State and Federal Constitutions

a. *See* Section C, *supra*.

b. *Index Digest of State Constitutions* (2d ed. 1959–1969)

Comparative statement of the provisions of all state constitutions arranged by subject.

c. *Constitutions of the United States: National and State*

(1) Looseleaf edition.

(2) Texts of the constitutions of the U. S. and the 50 states.

(3) Index volume has number of pamphlets, each devoted to indexing a broad subject area of the fifty state constitutions.

(4) Companion publication to the *Index Digest*.

Chapter 9

FEDERAL LEGISLATION

Article I, Section 8, of the *United States Constitution* enumerates the powers of Congress, and provides the authority for Congress to make all laws necessary and proper for carrying into execution the enumerated powers, as well as other powers vested in the Congress.

Congress meets in two-year periods, with each such period known as a *Congress*. The period in which Congress met, for example, during the years 1979–80, is known as the 96th Congress, the First Congress being 1789–91. Under the Constitution, Congress must meet at least once a year.[1]

SECTION A. THE ENACTMENT OF FEDERAL LAWS

Before discussing the various ways the laws of Congress are published, a brief description of the legislative process is necessary.[2] At the beginning of each Congress, representatives or senators may introduce legislation in their respective branch of Congress. Each proposed law is called a "bill"[3] when introduced. The first bill in the House of Representatives is labeled "H.R. 1" with all subsequent bills numbered sequentially. Similarly, the first bill introduced into the Senate is labeled "S. 1.". After a bill passes the house in which it was introduced, it is sent for consideration to the other house. If approved, it is then sent to the President for his signature. If he signs it, it then becomes a law. If the President vetoes it, it becomes law if approved by two-thirds of both houses of Congress.[4] Under the Constitution, a bill sent to the President also becomes law if

[1] U.S.Const., Art. I, § 4.

[2] For more detailed statements on the enactment of federal laws, *see* E. WILLETT, HOW OUR LAWS ARE MADE, H.DOC. NO. 96–352, 96th Cong., 2d Sess. (1980); ENACTMENT OF A LAW: PROCEDURAL STEPS IN THE LEGISLATIVE PROCESS, S.DOC. NO. 96–15, 96th Cong., 1st Sess. (1979). *See also* CONGRESSIONAL QUARTERLY SERVICE, GUIDE TO THE CONGRESS OF THE UNITED STATES, ORIGINS, HISTORY, AND PROCEDURE, Part III (2d ed. 1976).

[3] A *bill* is the form used for most legislation. *Joint resolutions* may also be used, but there is no practical difference between the two and the two forms are used indiscriminately. *Concurrent resolutions* are used for matters affecting both Houses, but are not legislative. *Simple resolutions* are used for matters concerning the operation of either house. The first three forms are published in the *Statutes at Large*, the latter in the *Congressional Record*. HOW OUR LAWS ARE MADE, *supra* note 2 at 6–8.

[4] U.S.Const., Art. I, § 7.

the President does not either sign or veto it within ten days of receiving it.[5] Bills introduced but not passed during a specific Congress do not carry over to the next Congress. If the sponsors wish the bill to be considered by the new Congress, it must be submitted as a new bill.

After a bill has been approved in identical form by both houses and signed by the President (or approved over a Presidential veto,[6] or the President does not sign or veto it within ten days), it becomes a law. It is then sent to the Administrator of General Services who is directed to publish all laws so received.[7] The Administrator classifies each law as either a public law or a private law. The former is one that affects the nation as a whole, or deals with individuals as a class and relates to public matters. A private law benefits only a specific individual or individuals. Such laws deal primarily with matters relating to claims against the government or with matters of immigration and nationalization.[8]

The first law to pass a Congress is designated as either Public Law No. 1 or Private Law No. 1. Each succeeding public or private law is then numbered in sequence throughout the two-year life of a Congress. The *Federal Register* publishes cumulative lists of all public laws during, and at the conclusion of, each session of Congress for public laws passed during that session. The laws are listed chronologically by date of approval with references to original bill number, public law number, *Statutes at Large* number, and subject matter.[9]

SECTION B. PUBLICATION OF FEDERAL LAWS

1. Current Laws

During a session of Congress, each law as passed is first issued by the U. S. Government Printing Office as a *slip law*. [See illustration 40]. This means that each law is separately published and may be one page or several hundred pages in length. There are four sources commonly consulted for the text of current laws.

[5] *Ibid.*

[6] For a list of Presidential vetoes, *see* U.S. CONGRESS, SENATE LIBRARY, PRESIDENTIAL VETOES, 1789–1976 (1978).

[7] 1 U.S.C. Secs. 106(a), 112 (1976).

[8] For a complete discussion of private bills and laws, *see* CONGRESSIONAL QUARTERLY SERVICE, *supra* note 2, at 299–310.

[9] 44 FED.REG. viii (July 18, 1979).

a. *Slip laws*

These are available at all libraries that are depositories for U. S. Government publications [10] and in certain law libraries.

b. *U. S. Code Congressional and Administrative News Service*

This set is published by the West Publishing Co. in connection with the *United States Code Annotated.* During each session of Congress it is issued monthly in pamphlet form and prints in full text all of the public laws. Each issue contains a cumulative subject index and a cumulative *Table of Laws Enacted.* After each session of Congress the pamphlets are re-issued in bound volumes.

c. *Advance Sheets, United States Code Service, Lawyers' Edition*

This is published by the Lawyers Co-operative Publishing Company in connection with the *United States Code Service, L.Ed.* It contains similar information to that described in b. *supra.*

d. *U. S. Law Week*

This weekly looseleaf service, which is published by the Bureau of National Affairs, includes the text of the more important laws passed during the previous week.

2. U. S. Statutes at Large

At the end of each session of Congress, all of the slip laws are published in numerical order as part of the set called the *United States Statutes at Large.* Thus all of the laws enacted since 1789 are contained in the many volumes of this set.[11]

It is important to keep in mind that the laws are arranged in chronological order rather than by subject. Moreover, amendments to a previously passed law will appear in different volumes from the law being amended. For example, a law passed in 1900 is in volume 31 of the *Statutes at Large.* If Congress amended it in 1905, the amendment will appear in the volume for that year. Some laws have been amended many, many times and in order to obtain the full and current text of such a law, the *Statutes at Large* volume containing the original law must be examined in context with subsequent volumes in which amendments to the law appear.

[10] JOINT COMM. ON PRINTING, 96th Cong. 1st Sess., GOVERNMENT DEPOSITORY LIBRARIES (Comm.Print 1979).

[11] Until 1936, each volume of the Statutes at Large covered the two-year period for each Congress. *See also* CHECKLIST OF U.S. SESSION LAWS, 1789–1873 (U.S. Library of Congress 1979).

Each volume of the *Statutes at Large* has its own subject index and contains tables listing how each public law in it affects previous public laws.

SECTION C. CODIFICATION OF FEDERAL LAWS

The chronological method of publication of Congressional laws created obvious problems for the process of determining the statutory provisions on any given subject. In order to better accomplish this, the laws passed by Congress have to be rearranged in a manner that will do three things: (1) collate the original law with all subsequently passed amendments by taking into consideration the deletion or addition of language changed by the amendments; (2) bring all laws on the same subject or topic together, and (3) eliminate all repealed, superseded, or expired laws. This process is called codification.[12]

1. United States Revised Statutes

The first codification [13] of the *Statutes at Large* was authorized by the Congress in 1866 and resulted in the publication of the *Revised Statutes of 1875*.

The Commissioners authorized by Congress to prepare this revision began by extracting from the volumes of the *Statutes at Large* all public laws that met the following two criteria: (1) they were still in force, and (2) they were of a general and permanent nature. They eliminated all appropriation laws and those that did not have general applicability. The next step was to take each public law and all its amendments and rewrite the law in one sequence by incorporating amending language and eliminating deleting language. All of the laws on one topic were then arranged in a chapter. Chapter 35, for example, contained all legislation passed by Congress, and still in force, on taxation; Chapter 70, all legislation in force on criminal law. All of the chapters were then bound in one volume, a subject index prepared, and the volume issued as the *Revised Statutes of 1875*.

This volume as prepared by the Commissioners was then submitted to Congress, introduced as a bill, and went through the legislative process of becoming a public law. Within the bill before Congress there was a section specifically repealing each previously passed pub-

[12] For articles dealing with codification *see* Tucker, *Tradition and Technique of Codification in the Modern World: The Louisiana Experience*, 25 LA.L.REV. 698 (1965); Zinn, *Revision of the United States Code*, 51 LAW LIB.J. 388 (1958); *A Code Odyssey, A Critical Analysis of the Alabama Recodification Process*, 10 CUM.L.REV. 119 (1979); Dowling, *The Creation of the Montana Code Annotated*, 40 MONT.L.REV. 1 (1979).

[13] Dwan and Feidler, *The Federal Statutes, Their History and Use*, 22 MINN. L.REV. 1008 (1938).

lic law that had been incorporated into the *Revised Statutes of 1875.*[14] Thus, when it passed Congress and was signed by the President, all of the laws passed since 1789, in force and of a general and public nature, were codified in the *Revised Statutes of 1875*. Moreover, as the act of codification repealed all the previous *Statutes at Large* citations, the *Revised Statutes of 1875* became *positive law* and it was no longer necessary to refer to the *Statutes at Large* volumes.

Unfortunately, this volume, known as the first edition, was subsequently discovered to contain many inaccuracies and unauthorized changes in the law.[15] In 1878, a second edition of the *Revised Statutes* was authorized to be published which would include legislation passed since 1873, delete sections that were repealed since 1873, and also correct the errors that had inadvertently been incorporated into the first edition.

The second edition indicated changes to the text of the first edition by the use of brackets and italics. It is important to note, however, that the second edition of the *Revised Statutes* was never re-enacted by Congress and all changes indicated in it are only *prima facie* evidence of the law. There was no further codification of federal laws until 1926.

2. United States Code

Prior to 1926, the positive law for federal legislation was contained in the one volume of the *Revised Statutes of 1875* and then in each of the twenty-four subsequent volumes of the *Statutes at Large*. Although several attempts were made to adopt a new codification, nothing further officially occurred until the publication of the *United States Code,* prepared under the auspices of special committees of the House of Representatives and the Senate. In this codification all sections of the *Revised Statutes of 1875* that had not been repealed were extracted and then all of the public and general laws from the *Statutes at Large* since 1873 that were still in force. These were then arranged into fifty titles and published as the *United States Code,* 1926 ed.[16] Between 1927 and 1931 cumulated bound supplements were issued each year. In 1932 a new edition was issued which incorporated the cumulated supplements to the 1926 edition, and this became the *United States Code,* 1932 edition. Every six years a new edition is published with cumulative supplements being issued during the intervening years.

[14] Revised Statutes of the United States, 1873–1874, Act of June 22, 1874, Title LXXIV, Repeal Provisions, 5595–5601, at 1091–1092 (1875).

[15] Dwan and Feidler, *supra* note 13.

[16] *See* Preface to Volume 44, Part One, *Statutes at Large* (1926).

The *United States Code* differs from the *Revised Statutes of 1875* in an important aspect. It was never submitted to Congress and reenacted in its entirety. Instead, Congress has created the Office of Law Revision Counsel [17] and directed it to revise the *United States Code* title by title. Each title is then submitted to Congress for enactment into law. To date, twenty-two titles have been enacted into law.[18] Thus, in using the *United States Code* it is important to ascertain if the title being consulted has been enacted into positive law. Those titles not yet enacted are *prima facie* evidence of the law.[19] Should there be a conflict between the wording in the *United States Code* and the *Statutes at Large,* the latter will govern.[20]

3. Annotated Editions of the U.S. Code

The *United States Code* is designated as the official edition, and is printed and sold by the U.S. Government Printing Office. As is frequently the case with such publications, it is slow in being published, particularly in the issuance of the supplements, which are seldom available until several months after a session of Congress is over. Furthermore, the meaning of a law passed by a legislative body is not always clear and the language used must frequently be interpreted by a court. Consequently, access to the court decisions interpreting

[17] The principal duty of this Office is "to develop and keep current an official and positive codification of the laws of the United States" and "to prepare * * * one title at a time, a complete compilation, restatement and revision of the general and permanent laws of the United States * * *." 1 U.S.C. § 204(a) (1976 ed.) The Law Revision Counsel has indicated that his office plans to reenact the remaining titles of the U.S.Code as soon as possible, but could not indicate an exact schedule. It will probably be several years before this assigned task is completed. (Memo of telephone conversation of authors with Mr. Edward Willett, September 13, 1976, on file at the Tarlton Law Library, University of Texas, Austin).

[18] These are 1, 3, 4, 5, 6, 9, 10, 11, 13, 14, 17, 18, 23, 28, 32, 35, 37, 38, 39, 44, 49, and the Internal Revenue Code (Tit.26). A list of enacted titles may be found in the following sources: (1) Preface to the Volumes of the U.S.Code; (2) after Section 203(e) of Title I in the U.S.C.A. and the U.S.C.S.; (3) inside front cover of the volumes of the U.S.C.S.

[19] 1 U.S.C. § 204(a) (1976 ed.) provides that "The matter set forth in the edition of the Code of Laws of the United States current at any time shall, together with the then current supplement, if any, establish prima facie the laws of the United States, general and permanent in their nature, in force on the day preceding the commencement of the session following the last session the legislation of which is included: *Provided, however,* that whenever titles of such Code shall have been enacted into positive law the text thereof shall be legal evidence of the laws therein contained in all the courts of the United States, the several States, and the Territories and insular possessions of the United States."

[20] *See* an interpretation of 1 U.S.C. § 204(a) (1976) in *U. S. v. Welden,* 377 U.S. 95, 98, n. 4 (1964).

statutes is frequently as important as the text of the statute itself. This has led to the publication of annotated codes where digests of court decisions interpreting a code section are given. There are two privately published annotated editions of the *United States Code*.

Both of these sets have many advantages over the official edition of the *United States Code* and are usually consulted in preference to it. These advantages are (1) each title is published in one or more separate volumes; (2) the entire set is kept up to date by annual cumulative pocket supplements and, when necessary, by recompiled volumes; (3) pamphlets are issued during the year bringing up to date the pocket supplements; (4) more detailed indexing is provided in both bound volumes and supplements; (5) each code section contains annotations of court decisions which have cited and interpreted it; (6) when applicable, citations to *Code of Federal Regulations*[21] are given.

a. *United States Code Annotated* (U.S.C.A.)

This set is published by the West Publishing Company. In addition to annotating relevant cases, the notes following each code section make reference to other West publications and frequently refer to the Topic and Key Numbers where additional cases may be located. In addition to a separate eight-volume index, each title has an individual, detailed index.

b. *United States Code Service, Lawyers' Edition* (U.S.C.S.)

This set is published by the Lawyers Co-operative Publishing Company and the Bancroft-Whitney Company[22] and is a unit of their Total Client-Service Library.[23] It includes a multi-volume index and a single-volume *U.S. Code Guide*. This volume is arranged by U.S.C. citation and indicates where the matter covered by a code section is discussed in the other units of their Total Client-Service Library. Two unnumbered volumes contain the rules of procedure governing practice before the Federal administrative agencies, and Volume I includes the text of the Universal Copyright Convention, the Convention on Enforcement of Foreign Arbitral Awards, and the Warsaw Convention.

[21] This set is discussed in Chapter 13.

[22] This set was originally published by another company as the *Federal Code Annotated*. After the present publishers acquired it, they began issuing replacement volumes with newly written annotations and editorial notes. Nearly all of the volumes have been replaced. Those not yet re-issued have a red label attached to the spine.

[23] *See* Chap. 7, note 1.

c. *Summary and Comparison: Annotated Editions of the United States Code*

Both the U.S.C.A. and the U.S.C.S. follow the same citation pattern as the official *United States Code.* Thus, a citation to U.S.C. may be located in either of the two annotated sets. Each of these contains exactly the same information as in the official *U.S. Code,* but in addition contains digests of decisions which have cited or interpreted a section of the Code. Each set is kept up to date by annual pocket supplements, monthly pamphlets, and, when necessary, by the issuance of replacement volumes. Each set has editorial matter which refers to their other publications. The *United States Code Annotated* will usually contain more annotations than the U.S.C.S., which makes frequent cross-references to one of their annotations in ALR–Fed. or in the *Lawyers' Editions* of the *U.S. Reports* for additional cases. Each is simple to use, more current, and better indexed than the *United States Code.* However, when only the text of the Code is needed, it may be simpler to consult the official unannotated edition. Illustrations 41–46 show the use of the various editions of the *United States Code.*

SECTION D. ILLUSTRATIONS

40. A public law in "slip" form

41. A page from the Index Volume to the U.S.C.A.

42. A page from the U.S. Code, 1952 ed.

43. A page from Volume 73, Statutes at Large

44. A page from the U.S. Code, 1976 ed.

45–46. Pages from Title 31, U.S.C.A.

[Illustration 40]

SLIP LAW—96th CONGRESS

PUBLIC LAW 96–73—SEPT. 29, 1979 **[1]** ⟶ 93 STAT. 537

Public Law 96–73
96th Congress

An Act

To amend the Rail Passenger Service Act to extend the authorization of appropriations for Amtrak for 2 additional years, and for other purposes. **[2]** ⟶ Sept. 29, 1979 [H.R. 3996]

Be it enacted by the Senate and House of Representatives of the United States of America in Congress assembled, Amtrak Reorganization Act of 1979.

TITLE I—AMTRAK REORGANIZATION

SHORT TITLE

SECTION 101. This title may be cited as the "Amtrak Reorganization Act of 1979" 45 USC 501 note.

PURPOSES

SEC. 102. Section 101 of the Rail Passenger Service Act (45 U.S.C. 502) is amended— 45 USC 502.

(1) by inserting "(a)" immediately before "The Congress";

(2) by striking out "and" after "this purpose;";

(3) by striking out the period after "Railroad Passenger Corporation" and inserting in lieu thereof the following: "; and that rail passenger service offers significant benefits in public transportation for the safe movement of passengers with minimum energy expenditure and represents a significant national transportation asset in time of national emergency or energy shortage."; and

(4) by adding at the end thereof the following new subsection:

"(b) The Congress further finds that—

"(1) inadequately defined goals for the Corporation have denied its board of directors an effective role in guiding the

This is a typical "slip" law. At the end of the year, all of the slip laws are published in a bound volume of the Statutes at Large.

Marginal notes are not part of the law but editorial aids. The code citations in the margin indicate where the Statute at Large citations in the text are found in the U.S.Code.

Notes: 1. Statute at Large citation
2. Bill number in House

to justify additional expenditure of public funds.".

GOALS

SEC. 103. (a) GOALS FOR AMTRAK.—The Rail Passenger Service Act (45 U.S.C. 501 et seq.) is amended by redesignating section 102 as 45 USC 502.

[Illustration 41]

PAGE FROM THE INDEX VOLUME TO THE U.S.C.A.

FINDING A FEDERAL STATUTE

Problem: Are stocks and bonds issued by the United States Government exempt from taxation by the states?

Step 1. Check index volumes to U.S.C., U.S.C.A., or U.S.C.S.

This will indicate that there is a code section covering this topic at Title 31, § 742.

[Illustration 42]

PAGE FROM U.S. CODE, 1952 EDITION

§ 741a. Sale and disposition of bonds, notes, and other securities.

(a) Notwithstanding the provisions of section 302 of Title 40, the Secretary of the Treasury is authorized to sell, exchange, or otherwise dispose of any bonds, notes, or other securities, acquired by him on behalf of the United States under judicial process or otherwise, or delivered to him by an executive department or agency of the United States for disposal, or to enter into arrangements for the extension of the maturity thereof, in such manner, in such amounts, at such prices, for cash, securities, or other property, or any combination thereof, and upon such terms and conditions as he may deem advisable and in the public interest. No such bonds, notes, or other securities of any single issuer having at the date of disposal an aggregate face or par value, or in the case of no-par stock an aggregate stated or book value, in excess of $1,000,000, which may be held by the Secretary of the Treasury at any one time, shall be sold or otherwise disposed of under the authority of this section.

(b) Nothing contained in this section shall be construed to supersede or impair any authority otherwise granted to any officer or executive department or agency of the United States to sell, exchange, or otherwise dispose of any bonds, notes, or other securities, acquired by the United States under judicial process or otherwise. (Apr. 3, 1945, ch. 51, § 5, 59 Stat. 48.)

REFERENCES IN TEXT

Section 302 of Title 40, referred to in the text, was repealed by act Oct. 31, 1951, ch. 654, § 1 (95), 65 Stat. 705, and is now covered by sections 483 and 484 of Title 40, Public Buildings, Property and Works.

This is a page from the United States Code 1952 edition. Ordinarily one would use the latest edition of the U.S.C., or one of the two annotated editions which are kept current by pocket supplements.

This edition is shown to illustrate how this section of the Code appeared before it was amended.

→**§ 742. Exemption from taxation.**

Except as otherwise provided by law, all stocks, bonds, Treasury notes, and other obligations of the United States, shall be exempt from taxation by or under State or municipal or local authority. (R. S. § 3701.)

DERIVATION

Act Feb. 25, 1862, ch. 33, § 2, 12 Stat. 346; act Mar. 3, 1863, ch. 73, § 1, 12 Stat. 710; act Mar. 3, 1864, ch. 17, § 1, 13 Stat. 13; act June 30, 1864, ch. 172, § 1, 13 Stat. 218; act Jan. 28, 1865, ch. 22, § 1, 13 Stat. 425; act Mar. 3, 1865, ch. 77, § 2, 13 Stat. 469; act July 14, 1870, ch. 256, § 1, 16 Stat. 272.

CROSS REFERENCES

United States obligations and evidences of ownership issued after March 27, 1942, as subject to Federal taxation, see section 742a of this title.

Note the reference to the Revised Statutes. All sections of the Revised Statutes not repealed are still in force.

After each code section, citation is given either to the Revised Statutes or the Statutes at Large where the section first appeared as passed by Congress.

[Illustration 43]

PAGE FROM VOLUME 73 OF THE STATUTES AT LARGE

622 PUBLIC LAW 86-346—SEPT. 22, 1959 [73 STAT.

bond shall be includible in gross income in the taxable year in which the obligation is finally redeemed or in the taxable year of final maturity, whichever is earlier."

Paying agents. Relief from liability. 57 Stat. 63.

SEC. 103. Subsection (i) of section 22 of the Second Liberty Bond Act, as amended (31 U.S.C., sec. 757c(i)), is amended by inserting after the third sentence thereof the following: "Relief from liability shall be granted in all cases where the Secretary of the Treasury shall determine, under regulations prescribed by him, that written notice of liability or potential liability has not been given by the United States, within ten years from the date of the erroneous payment, to any of the foregoing agents or agencies whose liability is to be determined: *Provided*, That no relief shall be granted in any case in which a qualified paying agent has assumed unconditional liability to the United States."

SEC. 104. The following provisions of law are amended by striking out the words "on original issue at par" and inserting in lieu thereof the words "on original issue at the issue price":

53 Stat. 1226.

(1) Section 6(g)(5) of the Act of March 24, 1934, as amended (22 U.S.C., sec. 1393 (g)(5)), relating to the trust account for

R.S. 3701 (31 U.S.C. 742) was amended in 1959. Frequently, as in this instance, a public law amends many different sections of the U.S.Code.

Account.

70 Stat. 397.

(5) Section 209(e)(2) of the Highway Revenue Act of 1956 (23 U.S.C., sec. 173(e)(2)), relating to the Highway Trust Fund.

23 USC 120 note. Tax exemption.

SEC. 105. (a) Section 3701 of the Revised Statutes (31 U.S.C., sec. 742) is amended by adding at the end thereof the following: "This exemption extends to every form of taxation that would require that either the obligations or the interest thereon, or both, be considered, directly or indirectly, in the computation of the tax, except nondiscriminatory franchise or other nonproperty taxes in lieu thereof imposed on corporations and except estate taxes or inheritance taxes."

Repeals.

(b) The following provisions of the Second Liberty Bond Act, as amended, relating to the tax-exempt status of obligations of the United States, are repealed, without changing the status of any outstanding obligation:

46 Stat. 19, 775.

(1) Subsections (b) and (d) of section 5 (31 U.S.C., sec. 754 (b) and (d));

40 Stat. 291, 1309.

(2) The second and third sentences of section 7 (31 U.S.C., sec. 747);

(3) Subsection (b) of section 18 (31 U.S.C., sec. 753(b));

55 Stat. 7.

(4) The first sentence of subsection (d) of section 22 (31 U.S.C., sec. 757c(d)).

TITLE II—INCOME TAX TREATMENT OF CERTAIN EXCHANGES OF UNITED STATES OBLIGATIONS

68A Stat. 302. 26 USC 1031-1036.

SEC. 201. (a) Part III of subchapter O of chapter 1 of the Internal Revenue Code of 1954 (relating to common nontaxable exchanges) is amended by adding at the end thereof the following new section:

[Illustration 44]

PAGE FROM U.S. CODE, 1976 EDITION

1945—Subsec. (c). Act Nov. 8, 1945, added "and also means any bond issued under section 780 of title 26".

1939—Subsec. (b)(4). Act Aug. 10, 1939 amended subsec. (b)(4) generally.

SECTION REFERRED TO IN OTHER SECTIONS

This section is referred to in section 528 of this title; title 40 sections 722, 726, 728, 729.

§ 739. Exchange of coupon for registered bonds

The Secretary of the Treasury is authorized to issue, upon such terms and under such regulations as he may from time to time prescribe, registered bonds in exchange for and in lieu of any coupon bonds which have been or may be lawfully issued; such registered bonds to be similar in all respects to the registered bonds issued under the Acts authorizing the issue of the coupon bonds offered for exchange.

(R.S. § 3706.)

CODIFICATION

R.S. § 3706 is from act June 30, 1864, ch. 172, § 7, 13 Stat. 220.

Here is 31 U.S.C. 742 as amended.

Note how citation is given to original R.S. citation and amending public law.

(R.S. § 3707.)

CODIFICATION

R.S. § 3707 is from act Aug. 10, 1846, ch. 180, § 2, 9 Stat. 107.

§ 741. Purchase or redemption of bonds

The Secretary of the Treasury may at any time apply the surplus money in the Treasury not otherwise appropriated, or so much thereof as he may consider proper, to the purchase or redemption of the United States bonds: *Provided*, That the bonds so purchased or redeemed shall constitute no part of the sinking fund, but shall be canceled.

(Mar. 3, 1881, ch. 133, § 2, 21 Stat. 457.)

§ 741a. Sale and disposition of bonds, notes, and other securities

(a) Notwithstanding the provisions of section 302 of title 40, the Secretary of the Treasury is authorized to sell, exchange, or otherwise dispose of any bonds, notes, or other securities, acquired by him on behalf of the United States under judicial process or otherwise, or delivered to him by an executive department or agency of the United States for disposal, or to enter into arrangements for the extension of the maturity thereof, in such manner, in such amounts, at such prices, for cash, securities, or other property, or any combination thereof, and upon such terms and conditions as he may deem advisable and in the public interest. No such bonds, notes, or other securities of any single issuer having at the date of disposal an aggregate face or par value, or in the case of no-par stock an aggregate stated or book value, in excess of $1,000,000, which may be held by the Secretary of the Treasury at any one time, shall be sold or otherwise disposed of under the authority of this section.

(b) Nothing contained in this section shall be construed to supersede or impair any authority otherwise granted to any officer or executive department or agency of the United States to sell, exchange, or otherwise dispose of any bonds, notes, or other securities, acquired by the United States under judicial process or otherwise.

(Apr. 3, 1945, ch. 51, § 5, 59 Stat. 48.)

REFERENCES IN TEXT

Section 302 of title 40, referred to in the text, was repealed by act Oct. 31, 1951, ch. 654, § 1(95), 65 Stat. 705, and is now covered by sections 483 and 484 of Title 40, Public Buildings, Property, and Works.

§ 742. Exemption from taxation

Except as otherwise provided by law, all stocks, bonds, Treasury notes, and other obligations of the United States, shall be exempt from taxation by or under State or municipal or local authority. This exemption extends to every form of taxation that would require that either the obligations or the interest thereon, or both, be considered, directly or indirectly, in the computation of the tax, except nondiscriminatory franchise or other nonproperty taxes in lieu thereof imposed on corporations and except estate taxes or inheritance taxes.

(R.S. § 3701; Sept. 22, 1959, Pub. L. 86-346, title I, § 105(a), 73 Stat. 622.)

CODIFICATION

R.S. § 3701 is from acts Feb. 25, 1862, ch. 33, § 2, 12 Stat. 346; Mar. 3, 1863, ch. 73, § 1, 12 Stat. 710; Mar. 3, 1864, ch. 17, § 1, 13 Stat. 13; June 30, 1864, ch. 172, § 1, 13 Stat. 218; Jan. 28, 1865, ch. 22, § 1, 13 Stat. 425; Mar. 3, 1865, ch. 77, § 2, 13 Stat. 469; July 14, 1870, ch. 256, § 1, 16 Stat. 272.

"Except as otherwise provided by law," was inserted by the Revisers in the 1926 general revision of the Code.

AMENDMENTS

1959—Pub. L. 86-346 added second sentence.

CROSS REFERENCES

State taxation of circulating notes of national banking associations and United States legal tender notes and other notes and certificates of the United States, see section 425 of this title.

United States obligations and evidences of ownership issued after March 27, 1942, as subject to Federal taxation, see section 742a of this title.

§ 742a. Application of other laws

(a) Exemption from taxation under Internal Revenue Code; exceptions

Interest upon obligations, and dividends, earnings, or other income from shares, certificates, stock, or other evidences of ownership, and gain from the sale or other disposition of such obligations and evidences of ownership

[Illustration 45]

PAGE FROM TITLE 31—U.S.C.A.

Ch. 12 **PUBLIC DEBT** **31 § 742**

(b) Nothing contained in this section shall be construed to supersede or impair any authority otherwise granted to any officer or executive department or agency of the United States to sell, exchange, or otherwise dispose of any bonds, notes, or other securities, acquired

> **This is the text of 31 U.S.C. 742 in an annotated code. Note how the text and notes are the same as in the U.S.C.**
>
> **The difference is the case annotations that are added. They start immediately after the notes.**
>
> **See next Illustration.**

Except as otherwise provided by law, all stocks, bonds, Treasury notes, and other obligations of the United States, shall be exempt from taxation by or under State or municipal or local authority. This exemption extends to every form of taxation that would require that either the obligations or the interest thereon, or both, be considered, directly or indirectly, in the computation of the tax, except nondiscriminatory franchise or other nonproperty taxes in lieu thereof imposed on corporations and except estate taxes or inheritance taxes.

R.S. § 3701; Sept. 22, 1959, Pub.L. 86–346, Title I, § 105(a), 73 Stat. 622.

Historical Note

Derivation. Act Feb. 25, 1862, c. 33, § 2, 12 Stat. 346; Act Mar. 3, 1863, c. 73, § 1, 12 Stat. 710; Act Mar. 3, 1864, c. 17, § 1, 13 Stat. 13; Act June 30, 1864, c. 172, § 1, 13 Stat. 218; Act Jan. 28, 1865, c. 22, § 1, 13 Stat. 425; Act Mar. 3, 1865, c. 77, § 2, 13 Stat. 469; Act July 14, 1870, c. 256, § 1, 16 Stat. 272.

1959 Amendment. Pub.L. 86–346 added second sentence.

Legislative History. For legislative history and purpose of Pub.L. 86–346, see 1959 U.S.Code Cong. and Adm.News, p. 2769.

Cross References

United States obligations and evidences of ownership issued after Mar. 27, 1942, as subject to federal taxation, see section 742a of this title.

Library References

Taxation ⚷7.

C.J.S. Taxation § 209.

Notes of Decisions

139

[Illustration 46]

PAGE FROM TITLE 31, U.S.C.A.

31 § 742 **PUBLIC DEBT** **Ch. 12**
Note 1

cision, has established the inherent nontaxability by the states of property held by the United States, and of bonds and obligations issued by the United States and held by individuals or corporations, except by permission of the United States. Howard Sav. Inst. v. Newark, 1899, 44 A. 654, 63 N.J.Law 547.

2. Purpose

This section generally exempting inter

One of the advantages of an annotated code is the digest of court decisions which is given after each section of the code.

Another advantage is the way the volumes are kept up-to-date by pocket supplements (not illustrated).

Both of these features are also available in the U.S.C.S.

---

1. Historical

From the time when McCulloch v. Maryland, 1819, 4 Wheat. 316, 4 L.Ed. 579, was decided, an unbroken line of cases adopting the principles of that de-

should not be expanded or modified in any degree by the judiciary. Smith v. Davis, Ga.1944, 65 S.Ct. 157, 323 U.S. 111, 89 L.Ed. 107.

3. Retroactive effect

This section exempting from state taxation United States securities did not apply to such securities held before the passage of this section. Bank of Commerce v. City and County of New York, N.Y.1863, 67 U.S. 620, 2 Black 620, 17 L. Ed. 451. See, also, People v. Commissioners of Taxes and Assessments, N.Y. 1862, 37 Barb. 635.

4. Generally

Obligations of federal government cannot be taxed, either directly or indirectly, by state, municipal or local authorities. Peter Kiewit Sons' Co. v. Douglas County, 1955, 72 N.W.2d 415, 161 Neb. 93.

5. Power of Congress

Congress has power to declare that bonds issued by the United States shall not be taxable by a state. Newark City Bank v. Assessor of Fourth Ward of City of Newark, 1862, 30 N.J.Law, 1 Vroom 13.

Congress cannot withdraw from state taxation securities issued by the United States already subject to such taxation, and Act Feb. 25, 1862, incorporated in this section, so far as it exempts from

140

SECTION E. POPULAR NAMES OF FEDERAL ACTS

It is common practice to refer to a federal act by a popular name. Generally, this is the name which the public or media gives the statute, and it may describe its subject matter (e. g., Gold Clause Act) or refer to its authors (e. g., the Taft-Hartley Act).

The tables of popular names of federal acts are designed to provide the citations to acts when only the popular names are known.

There are a number of such tables. They are:

1. *Shepard's Acts and Cases by Popular Names*, Vol. 1, 1968 and Cumulative Supplement. [See Illustration 47]

2. *United States Code Annotated* contains a table of acts cited by popular name in an index volume. [See Illustration 48]

3. Many of the titles of the U.S.C.A. have in the first volumes of the title a Popular Name Table for the principal laws included in the title. [See Illustration 49]

4. The popular names for federal acts for those still in force are also listed alphabetically in the general indexes to the *U.S. Code Annotated* and the *United States Code Service*.

5. The *United States Code* in the *General Index* volume has an *Index of Acts by Popular Name*.

6. *United States Code Service*. Table volumes contain a *Table of Acts by Popular Name*.

7. *U.S. Code Congressional and Administrative News* provides tables of *Popular Name Acts* for each session of Congress, beginning with the 77th Congress, 2d Session, 1942. These tables are for each session, are not cumulated, and cite the acts in the pages of the *News*.

[Illustration 47]

PAGE FROM SHEPARD'S FEDERAL AND STATE ACTS CITED BY POPULAR NAMES

FEDERAL AND STATE ACTS CITED BY POPULAR NAMES Bon

Bond Act of 1915 (Improvement Bonds)
Cal. Streets and Highways Code §8500 et seq.

Bond Act of 1918
N. J. Rev. Stat. 1937, 2:60-207 to 2:60-211

Bond Act of 1935 (Revenue)
N. C. Public Laws 1935, Ch. 473

Bond Act of 1938 (Revenue)
N. C. Gen. Stat. 1943, §160-413 et seq.

All laws are listed in this volume by popular name.

Cal. Military and Veterans Code §996 et seq.

Bond Act of 1962 (State Construction Program)
Cal. Statutes 1962, 1st Ex. Sess., Ch. 23, p. 193

Bond Act of 1962 (State School Building Aid)
Cal. Education Code 1959, §19891 et seq.

Bond Act of 1962 (Veterans)
Cal. Military and Veterans Code §996.87 et seq.

Bond and Coupon Collection Law
Cal. Government Code §16311

Bond and Coupon Registration Law
Cal. Statutes 1935, p. 994

Bond and License Act (Citrus Fruits)
Fla. Stat. 1965, 601.55 et seq.

Bond and Lien Collateral Act of 1949
Az. Rev. Stat. 1956, §30-191 et seq.

Bond and Mortgage Act
N. J. Rev. Stat. 1937, 2A:50-1 et seq.

Bond and Warrant Acts
N. J. Rev. Stat. 1937, 2:27-266 to 2:27-277, 22:1-13
Tex. Rev. Civ. Stat. 1948, Art. 2368a

Bond Assumption Acts (Highways)
Tex. Rev. Civ. Stat. 1948, Arts. 6674q-1 to 6674q-11a

Bond Certification Law
Cal. Water Code §20000 et seq.

Bond Compromise Law (Municipal)
Cal. Statutes 1903, p. 164

Bond Curative Act (Municipalities)
Wis. Stat. 1965, 67.02

Bond for Deed Act
La. Rev. Stat. 1950, 9:2941 et seq.

Bond Guarantors Protection Law
Cal. Government Code §5100 et seq.

Bond Investment Act
Ohio Rev. Code 1953, 3949.01 et seq.

Bond Issue Acts (Roads)
Ill. Rev. Stat. 1965, Ch. 121, §6-510 et seq.

Bond Limitation Act
U. S. Code 1964 Title 31, §757b
May 26, 1938, c. 285, 52 Stat. 447
Kan. Stat. Anno. 10-301 et seq.

Bond Plan Enabling Act (Industrial Locations)
Ala. Code 1958, Title 37, §511(20)

Bond Purchase Act
U. S. Code 1964 Title 31, §741
Mar. 3, 1881, c. 133, §2, 21 Stat. 435

Bond Refinancing Act (Revenue)
W. Va. Code 1931, Ch. 13, Art. 2A, §1 et seq.

Bond Refinancing Act of 1937
Ark. Stat. 1947, 19-4301 et seq.

Bond Refunding Act
Ark. Pope's Digest 1937, §§11237-11367

Bond Refunding Act (Municipal)
Mich. Comp. Laws 1948, 136.1 et seq.

Bond Refunding and Special Assessment Law of 1939
Cal. Government Code §59100 et seq.

Bond Registration Act
Mo. Rev. Stat. 1959, 108.240 et seq.

Bond Registration Act (Municipal)
Kan. Stat. Anno. 10-601 et seq.
N. C. Gen. Stat. 1943, §160-406 et seq.

Bond Retirement Fund Act
Okla. Stat. 1961, Title 62, §217.1 et seq.

Bond Sinking Fund Law of 1943
Cal. Statutes 1943, Ch. 611, p. 2225

Bond Surrender Act
Okla. Stat. 1961, Title 62, §341 et seq.

Bond Trust Fund Act
Nev. Rev. Stat. 1957, 282.230 et seq.

Bond Validating Acts
Fla. Stat. 1965, 75.01 et seq.
Ida. Laws 1935, First Extra Session, Ch. 3
Ida. Laws 1937, Ch. 232

Continued

91

[Illustration 48]

PAGE FROM THE POPULAR NAME TABLE U.S.C.A.

POPULAR NAME TABLE **616**

Legislative Reorganization Act of 1970
Pub.L. 91–510, Oct. 26, 1970, 84 Stat. 1140 (**Title 2, §§ 28, 29, 60–1, 61–1, 72a, 88b–1, 166, 190a–190d, 190f, 190h–190k, 198, 281–281b, 282–282e, 331–336, 411–417, 2107, 8332; Title 5, §§ 2107, 5533, 8332; Title 8, § 1106 note; Title 31, §§ 11, 1151–1157, 1171–1176; Title 40, §§ 166 note, 166b–1a–166b–1f, 184a, 193m–1, 851**)
Pub.L. 91–522, § 1(1), (3)–(5), Dec. 16, 1970, 84 Stat. 1440

Leprosy Act
Mar. 3, 1905, ch. 1443, 33 Stat. 1009

Lesinski Pension Increase Act
June 6, 1940, ch. 246, 54 Stat. 237

Lever Act (Food Control)
Aug. 10, 1917, ch. 53, 40 Stat. 276
Oct. 22, 1919, ch. 80, 41 Stat. 297

Liberty Loan Acts
(First)
Apr. 24, 1917, ch. 4, 40 Stat. 35 (**Title 31, §§ 745, 746, 755, 755a, 759, 764, 768, 774, 804**)
(Second)
Sept. 24, 1917, ch. 56, 40 Stat. 288 (**Title 31, §§ 745, 747, 752–754b, 757, 757b–757e, 758, 760, 764–766, 769, 771, 773, 774, 801**)
(Third)
Apr. 4, 1918, ch. 44, 40 Stat. 502 (**Title 31, §§ 752, 752a, 754, 765, 766, 771, 774**)
(Fourth)
July 9, 1918, ch. 142, 40 Stat. 844 (**Title 31, §§ 750, 752, 772, 774**)
(Supplement to Second)
Sept. 24, 1918, ch. 176, 40 Stat. 965 (**Title 12, §§ 84, 95a; Title 31, §§ 757, 774; Title 50 App., § 5**)
(Victory)
Mar. 3, 1919, ch. 100, 40 Stat. 1309 (**Title 31, §§ 750, 753, 754, 763, 767, 774, 802, 803**)
Mar. 2, 1923, ch. 179, 42 Stat. 1427 (**Title 31, § 767**)

Library of Congress Police Act
Aug. 4, 1950, ch. 561, §§ 1 to 11, 64 Stat. 411 (**Title 2, §§ 167 to 167j**)
June 17, 1970, Pub.L. 91–281, 84 Stat. 309 (**Title 2, § 167j**)

Library of Congress Trust Fund Board Act
Mar. 3, 1925, ch. 423, 43 Stat. 1107 (**Title 2, §§ 154–163**)

Library Services Act

> **This Popular Name Table is from the U.S.C.A.**
>
> **There is a similar Table in the U.S.C. and the U.S.C.S.**

Pub.L. 91–600, § 2(b), Dec. 30, 1970, 84 Stat. 1660–1669 (**Title 20, §§ 351–354, 355a–355c, 355e to 355e–2**)

Library Services and Construction Act Amendments of 1966
Pub.L. 89–511, July 19, 1966, 80 Stat. 313 (**Title 20, §§ 351–353, 355–355b, 355e to 355e–3, 355f to 355f–7, 356–358**)

Library Services and Construction Amendments of 1970
Pub.L. 91–600, Dec. 30, 1970, 84 Stat. 1660 (**Title 20, §§ 351–354, 355a–355c, 355e to 355e–2, 1204, 1211**)

[Illustration 49]

POPULAR NAME TABLE FROM TITLE 29, U.S.C.A.

POPULAR NAME ACTS

This table lists the principal laws included in Title 29, designated as they are popularly known, and shows the classification of each within the title.

Popular Name	Sections
Age Discrimination in Employment Act of 1967	621–634
American Samoa Labor Standards Amendments of 1956	206, 213, 216
Anti-Injunction Act (Labor Disputes)	101–115
Barden-LaFollette Act (Vocational Rehabilitation)	31–41
Black-Connery Fair Labor Standards Act	201–216, 217–219
Child Labor Act (Fair Labor Standards)	212, 213
Clayton Act (Trusts)	52, 53
Combination and Conspiracies Acts	52, 53
Connery-Black Fair Labor Standards Act	201–216, 217–219
Connery-Wagner Labor Relations Act	151 et seq.
Cooper Labor Jurisdiction Amendment	164(c)
Department of Labor Acts	1 et seq.; 551 et seq.
Employment Service Act	49 et seq.
Equal Pay Act of 1963	206, 206 notes
Fair Labor Standards Act of 1938	201–216, 217–219
Fair Labor Standards Amendments of 1949	201 note, 202, 202 note, 203–208, 208 note, 211–216, 216 note, 216b, 217
Fair Labor Standards Amendments of 1955	204–206, 208, 210
Fair Labor Standards Amendments of 1961	203–208, 212, 213, 213 note, 214, 216, 217
Fair Labor Standards Amendments of 1966	203, 203 note, 206, 207, 213, 214, 216, 218, 255
Fess-Kenyon Act (Vocational Rehabilitation)	31–41
Fitzgerald Act (Apprentice Labor)	50, 50a, 50b
Griffin-Landrum Labor Reform Act	153, 158–160, 164, 186, 187, 401 et seq.
Gwynne Act (Portal to Portal)	216(b), 251–262
Hartley-Taft Act	141 et seq.
Hour-Wage Act	201–216, 217–219
Industrial Productivity and Labor Costs Act	2b
Injunction Act (Labor Disputes)	101–110, 113–115
Kennedy-Douglas Welfare and Pension Plans Disclosure Act	301–309
Kenyon-Fess Act (Vocational Rehabilitation)	31–41
Labor Disputes Acts	51, 101 et seq.
Labor Injunction Act	101–115
Labor Management Relations Act, 1947	141 et seq.
Labor-Management Reporting and Disclosure Act of 1959	153, 158–160, 164, 186, 187, 401 et seq.
Labor Standards Act	201–216, 217–219
LaFollette-Barden Act (Vocational Rehabilitation)	31–41

SECTION F. TABLES FOR FEDERAL STATUTES

As has been noted, federal laws are first published in chronological order in the volumes of the *Statutes at Large.* A particular law may be on one topic, or may include matters on several different topics. Another law may amend one or several previously passed laws. Some are public laws of a general and permanent nature and are codified in the *U.S. Code.* This method of enacting and publishing laws makes it necessary to have tables so that a researcher may be able to trace each section of a law as it appears in the *Statutes at Large* and find out if it has been codified and, if so, its citation in the *U.S. Code.* For example, assume a researcher has a citation to Section 103 of Public Law 96–73 and wishes to find out where this section is in the *U.S. Code.* To do so, the appropriate table of statutes has to be consulted. [See Illustration 50]

From time to time, a particular title in the *U.S. Code* is completely revised with entirely new section numbers. One having a citation to the old title must then consult a table to find out the section number in the new title. [See Illustration 51]

Each of the three sets of U.S. Codes described *supra* has a volume or volumes containing transfer tables of one kind or another. These include the following:

Revised Titles: These tables show where former section titles of the *United States Code,* which have been revised, are now incorporated within the U.S.C.

Revised Statutes of 1878: This shows where *Revised Statutes* (R.S.) citations are found in the U.S.C.

Statutes at Large: This table shows where the Acts of Congress as they appear in the *Statutes at Large* are found in the U.S.C.

[Illustration 50]

PAGE FROM TABLES VOLUME—U.S.C.A.

STATUTES AT LARGE 1979

1979–96th Cong.–93 Stat.				USCA		
Sept.	**P.L.**	**Sec.**	**Page**	**Tit.**	**Sec.**	**Status**
		1(g)	501	12	1715z–10	
		1(h)	501	12	1748h–1	
		1(i)	501	12	1748h–2	
		1(j)	501	12	1749bb	
		1(k)	501	12	1749aaa	
		2	501	12	1709–1	
		3	502	12	1723e nt	
		4	502	42	1452b	
		5(a)	502	42	1483	
		5(b)	502	42	1485	
		5(c)	502	42	1487	
		5(d)	501	42	1490c	
29	96–72	1	503	50 App.	2401 nt	
		2 to 19(a)	503	50 App.	2401 to 2418	
		19(b)(1)	535	50 App.	2409 nt	
		19(b)(2)	535	50 App.	2406 nt	
		20, 21	535	50 App.	2419, 2420	
		22(a)	535	22	2778	
		22(b)(1)	535	42	6212	
		22(b)(2)	535	42	6274	
		22(c)	535	26	993	
		23(a)	536	22	3108	
		23(b)	536	22	3108 nt	
		24	536	7	1732	
	96–73	101	537	45	501 nt	
		102	537	45	501	
		103	537	45	502	
		103	538	45	501a	
		104	538	45	502	
		105 to 111(a)	539	45	545	
		111(b)	541	45	641	
		112	541	45	546	
		113	542	45	548	
		114 to 120(a)	542	45	562 to 565	
		120(b)	548	45	565 nt	
		121	548	45	566	
		122(a)	550	45	601	
		122(b)(1)	551	45	601	
		122(b)(2)	551	45	602	
		123 to 126	551	45	647 to 650	
		127	552	45	521 nt	
		128	553	49	1653	
		129	553	45	602 nt	

This Table lists all Public Laws and indicates where each section has been codified in the U.S.Code.

For example, Section 103 of Public Law 96–73 may be located in Title 45 § 502 in the U.S.C., or the U.S.C.A. or the U.S.C.S.

Sec.	Page	Tit.	Sec.
111	580	42	297–1
112	580	42	297b
113	581	42	296 nt
201	582	42	294b
202(a), (b)	582	42	294u

329

[Illustration 51]

PAGE FROM TABLES VOLUME—U.S.C.A.

23 **REVISED TITLES** **Title 23**

TITLE 23. HIGHWAYS

This title was enacted into law by Pub.L. 85–767, § 1, August 27, 1958, 72 Stat. 885. This table shows where sections of former Title 23 have been incorporated in revised Title 23.

Title 23 Former Sections	Title 23 New Sections
1	Omitted
2	101
2a	101(a)
2b	101(a)
3	Omitted
3a	Omitted
3b	Omitted
4	Omitted
5	Omitted
6	103(b), 103(e), 105(c), 121(c)
6—1	103(c)
6a	103(d)
6a—1	105(d)
6a—2	310
6b	Omitted
6c	Omitted
7	110(a)
8	109(a)
8a	109(a), 112(a)
9	301
9a	129(a)
9a—1	Omitted
9b	129(a)
10	109(a)
10a	Omitted
17	316
18	317(a) (b) (c)
19	315
20	Omitted
20a	Omitted
21	104(a), 104(b) (1)
21—1	307(a), 307(b)
21a	104(b), 105(a), 106 (a), 114(a), 118(a), 118(c)
21a—1	Omitted
21a—2	Omitted
21b	Omitted
21c	311
21d	Omitted
21e	122
22	104(e)
23	101(a), 202(b), 204(a), 204(b), 204(c), 205(a), 205(b), 205(c)
23a	Omitted
23b	Omitted
23b—1	Omitted
23c	205(c)
24	Omitted
24a	109(e)
25	Omitted
26	Omitted
41	101(a), 105(e) (Rep.)
41a	101(a), 103(b)
41b	101(a), 103(b)
42	Omitted
43	Omitted
44	Omitted
45	Omitted
46	See T. 18, § 1020
47	Omitted
48	Omitted
49	See T. 40, §§ 483, 484
62	318
63	109(d)
64	320(a)
65	320(b)
66	320(c)
67	320(d)
68	320(e)
69	320(f)
70	313
71	303(a)
72	See § 303 note
73	303(a)
101	Omitted
101a	Omitted
102	Omitted
103	Omitted
104	Omitted
105	Omitted
106	210(a), 210(b)
107	Omitted
108	Omitted
109	Omitted
110	Omitted
111	Omitted
112	Omitted
113	Omitted
114	210(e)
115	308(a)
116	315
117	312
151	104(c), 117(a), 117(b), 117(c), 118(b)
152	204(f), 205(d)
153	206(a), 207(a), 208 (a), 208(b)
154	209(a)
155	203
156	101(b), 103(f) (Rep.), 104(b) (1), 116(d)
165	Omitted
166	113(a), 113(b)
167	101(b), 128(a), 128(b), 304
168	Omitted
169	Omitted
170	305
171	306
172	Omitted
173	See § 120 note
174	See § 307 note
175	Omitted

Whenever a Title of the U.S.Code is revised with new section numbering, a table similar to this is prepared and may be consulted in the Tables Volumes of the various editions of the U.S. Code.

SECTION G. FEDERAL LEGISLATION: RESEARCH PROCEDURE

1. Laws in Force—The *United States Code*

To determine whether there is federal legislation on any given topic, the following procedures may be used:

a. *Index Method.* Check first the general index to one of the sets of the code. As both U.S.C.A. and U.S.C.S. have more detailed indexes, it is usually better to start with either of these rather than the official U.S. Code. The index will lead to the title under which the subject being researched will be found. Next, check the index to the individual title which may be in either of the annotated editions. The individual title indexes will provide a better guide to the subject matter of the title than the entries located in the general index.

b. *Topic or Analytic Method.* If one is familiar with the title which includes the topic under research (for example, bankruptcy or copyright), it is then useful to obtain the volumes covering the title and consult the analysis which precedes the section numbers. The annotated editions will have digests of decisions following each section.

c. *Definition Method.* The general indexes of all three sets of the U.S. Code have a main entry, "Definitions" and list under it all terms that have been defined within the Code. In the U.S.C.A., over thirty pages are devoted to entries under the main heading, "Definitions." Similar coverage is given in the U.S.C. and the U.S.C.S.

This method can be a quick entry into the Code. For example, if one were doing research in labor relations and wanted to determine if the term "supervisor" was defined in the U.S. Code, the following entries would be noted:

DEFINITIONS

Supervisor

Labor Management Relations Act, 29 § 142.

At times it may be useful to consult the text of an act as passed by Congress and not as it appears in the Code. The *Statutes at Large* citations may always be located by referring to the parenthetical reference following the code section. [See Illustration 44]

When only a *Statute at Large* citation is at hand, the table volumes will indicate if it has been codified and whether or not it is still in force.

2. Public Laws No Longer in Force

a. *Public Laws*

When interested in locating federal laws that are no longer in force, the following indexes should be consulted:

a. *Index Analysis of Federal Statutes, 1789–1873.*

b. *Index to the Federal Statutes, 1874–1931,* compiled by W. McClenon and W. Gilbert.

c. Superseded editions of the *United States Code.* As indicated, since 1926, the U.S. Code is published every six years with cumulated supplements issued between editions. Many law libraries keep the superseded editions and they may be consulted for laws no longer in force.

3. Private, Temporary and Local Laws

Occasionally there will be the need to locate a private or temporary or local law which was never included in the U.S. Code. They all, however, have been published in the *Statutes at Large* and may be consulted there if the date of enactment is known. If the date is not known, it becomes more difficult to locate such acts. The *Consolidated Index to the Statutes at Large* covers the period 1789 to 1903. After that period the volumes of the *Statutes at Large* must be individually checked.

The *United States Code Service* has an *Uncodified Laws* volume which contains annotations to private and temporary acts.

SECTION H. SUMMARY

1. Statutes at Large

a. Published after each session of Congress.

b. Arrangement—by chapters and chronologically by date of passage of act.

c. Grouped into public and private laws.

d. Volumes 1–8 were published some time after the acts were passed.

(1) Volumes 1–5 contain public laws and are arranged in chronological order.

(2) Vollume 6 consists of private laws.

(3) Volume 7 relates to Indian treaties.

(4) Volume 8 contains foreign treaties.

e. For various periods, public and private laws were published in two parts. Part Two covered private laws and resolutions, concurrent resolutions, treaties and proclamations.

f. Since 1950, treaties are not published as part of the *Statutes at Large.*

g. Marginal notes since Volume 33 give House or Senate bill number, Public Law number and date.

h. Each volume includes a chronological and numerical list of laws and a very complete subject index.

2. Methods of Codification (see Section C *supra*)

3. Features Common to Codes

a. Constitutions.

b. Text of statutes.

c. Historical notes.

d. Annotations.

e. Tables.

f. Indexes.

g. Popular names of acts.

h. Pocket and pamphlet supplementation.

4. United States Revised Statutes

a. 1875 edition—rewritten and reenacted, with inaccuracies and unauthorized changes.

b. 1878 edition—evidence of the law to December 1, 1873.

(1) Rewritten and classified.

(2) Some case annotations and marginal notes.

5. United States Code, Current Edition

a. Current official code.

b. Covers public and permanent laws in force.

c. Arranged alphabetically under 50 titles.

d. Supplemented by cumulative bound volumes.

e. Complete index.

f. Many tables.

g. *Prima facie* evidence of law; is a recompilation of the law and not a re-enactment, except for titles listed in 1 U.S.C. sec. 204.

h. New editions every six years.

6. United States Code Annotated (West)

a. Text of public, permanent laws in force.

b. Arranged under the 50 titles of U.S.C.

c. Annotations are complete, covering federal and state court decisions and Attorney General's opinions.

d. Historical notes.

e. About 135 volumes with one or more separate volumes for each code title.

f. Kept current by cumulative pocket and pamphlet supplements and replacement volumes.

g. Multi-volume index and title indexes in recompiled volumes.

h. Table volumes.

i. Index includes a *Table of Acts* by popular names.

7. United States Code Service (Lawyers Co-operative Publishing Co.)

a. Formerly called *Federal Code Annotated*, new publication replacing older volumes title by title.

b. Covers public and permanent laws in force.

c. Annotations include federal and state court decisions and Attorney General's opinions.

d. Historical notes.

e. Volume of Uncodified Laws.

f. Tables volumes.

g. General Index and each volume also has an index covering its subject matter.

h. Research aid references.

i. Federal acts by popular names.

j. Kept up to date by cumulative annual pocket and pamphlet supplements and replacement volumes.

k. Federal court rules.

l. Advance pamphlets issued for current materials.

8. Tables for Federal Statutes

Tables translating *Statutes at Large* citations into U.S.C. citations are found in U.S.C., U.S.C.A., and U.S.C.S. Tables also contain transfer tables for revised titles and for statutes repealed.

9. Popular Names of Federal Acts

Tables found in U.S.C., U.S.C.A., and U.S.C.S. Also listed under popular name in general indexes.

Shepard's Acts and Cases by Popular Name—Federal and State. Kept current by cumulated pamphlets.

Chapter 10

FEDERAL LEGISLATIVE HISTORIES

SECTION A. LEGISLATIVE HISTORIES IN LEGAL RESEARCH

A law is the means by which a legislative body expressed its intent to declare, command, or prohibit some action. A legislative history is the term used to designate the documents that contain the information considered by the legislature prior to reaching its decision to enact a law. A legislative history of a statute is consulted in order to better understand the reasons for the enactment of the statute. Since an act of the legislature is usually prospective and is not always drafted with the most precise language, courts constantly look to extrinsic aids in determining the intent of a legislative body.[1] This intent may be found in the language of the bill introduced into the legislature, the subsequent amendments to the bill, the reports of legislative committees to which the bill was assigned, and other legislative documents issued in consideration of the submitted bill.

There has been some difference of opinion as to the extent to which legislative histories should be used to determine the meaning of legislation.[2] But this conflict is more academic than it is practical,

1 "But, while the clear meaning of statutory language is not to be ignored, 'words are inexact tools at best,' *Harrison v. Northern Trust Co.*, 317 U.S. 476, 479 (1943) and hence it is essential that we place the words of a statute in their proper context by resort to the legislative history." *Tidewater Oil Co. v. United States*, 409 U.S. 151, 157 (1972).

2 Note, *e. g.*, the language of Mr. Justice Jackson: "Resort to legislative history is only justified where the face of the Act is inescapably ambiguous, and then I think we should not go beyond Committee reports, which presumably are well considered and carefully prepared * * *. Moreover, it is only the words of the bill that have presidential approval, where that approval is given. It is not to be supposed that, in signing a bill, the President endorses the whole Congressional Record." Schwegmann Bros. v. Calvert Distillers Corp., 341 U.S. 384, 395–396 (1951). Note also the language in National Small Shipments Traffic Conference Inc. v. Civil Aeronautics Board, 618 F.2d 819, 828 (D.C.Cir. 1980): "Courts in the past have been able to rely on legislative history for important insights into congressional intent. Without implying that this is no longer the case, we note that interest groups who fail to persuade a majority of the Congress to accept particular statutory language often are able to have inserted in the legislative history of the statute statements favorable to their position, in the hope that they can persuade a court to construe the statutory language in light of these statements. This devel-

for the use of legislative histories is a very essential technique of contemporary litigation.

Once the concept of what is contained in a legislative history is understood, the location and compilation of the history of a federal act becomes relatively simple. The techniques for locating legislative documents which assist in the interpretation of a statute or statutory provision will be discussed in the following sections of this chapter.

SECTION B. THE ELEMENTS OF A LEGISLATIVE HISTORY

Before compiling a legislative history, it is necessary to be familiar with the documents that are relevant to establishing the legislative intent of a federal law.[3]

1. Congressional Bills

Prior to its enactment as law, a proposed piece of legislation is first introduced as a bill into either the House of Representatives or the Senate and is assigned either an H.R. or S. number. This number stays with the bill until passed or until the adjournment of the Congress. When a bill is amended, it is usually reprinted with the amending language. The comparison of the language of the bill as introduced with that of the final language of the law as passed may frequently reveal legislative intent.[4]

2. Committee Reports

After a bill is introduced into either the House or the Senate, it is assigned to a committee which has jurisdiction over the subject matter of the bill. It is then the committee's obligation to consider the bill and to decide whether or not to recommend its passage. If passage is not recommended or if no action is taken during the life of the Congress in which the bill was introduced, the latter "dies in committee." If the committee recommends passage it does so in a written report which usually sets forth the rationale behind the recommendations. When the bill is approved by the house in which it was introduced, it is then sent to the other house and again assigned to an appropriate committee where it receives similar consideration. When

opment underscores the importance of following unambiguous statutory language absent clear contrary evidence of legislative intent." *See also*, F. DICKERSON, *The Uses* * * * *Histories*, in THE INTERPRETATION * * * STATUTES (1975).

[3] As legislative histories consist primarily of documents produced during the consideration of the bill or law by Congress, the documents cited in Chapter 9, footnote 2, should be consulted.

[4] United States v. St. Paul M. & M. R. Co., 247 U.S. 310, 318 (1918).

a bill has been passed by both houses, but in different versions, a "conference" committee is appointed which consists of Representatives and Senators who must reconcile differing language in the respective versions of the bill. Their recommendation is issued in a conference report.

Committee reports are usually considered the most important documents in determining the legislative intent of Congress.[5]

3. Congressional Debates

After a bill has been reported out of the committees to which it had been assigned, it may be debated upon the floor of the House or Senate.[6] Some authorities claim that floor statements of Congressmen on the substance of a bill under discussion are not to be considered by courts as determinative of Congressional intent.[7] The courts, however, generally do give some merit to such statements, especially when they are made by the bill's sponsors, whose stated intention is to clarify or explain the bill's purpose.[8] Such statements are published in the *Congressional Record* and are usually included as an integral part of legislative histories.[9]

4. Committee Hearings

After a bill is assigned to a Congressional committee, a hearing is frequently scheduled. The primary function of a hearing is to provide committee members with information which may be useful in their consideration of the bill. Interested persons or experts on the subject of the bill may be requested to express their opinions on the bill's purpose or effect and may suggest changes or amendments to its language. In most instances transcripts of the hearings are published. Committee hearings are technically not part of a legislative history since they do not contain Congressional deliberations but rather the views of non-legislators of what the bill under consideration should accomplish. But in practice, hearings should be consulted when available because they frequently contain information helpful to

[5] G. FOLSOM, LEGISLATIVE HISTORY: RESEARCH FOR THE INTERPRETATION OF LAWS 33 (1972). *See also,* Zuber v. Allen, 396 U.S. 168, 186 (1969), and Stevenson v. J. C. Penney Co., 464 F.Supp. 945 (N.D.Ill.1979).

[6] Most public laws are passed without ever being debated on the floor of Congress. It is usually only bills of great public interest which receive such debate.

[7] S. & E. Contractors, Inc. v. United States, 406 U.S. 1, 13 and note 9 (1971).

[8] Jacques Islar Corp. v. United States, 306 F.Supp. 452, 454 (Cust.Ct. 1st Div. 1969).

[9] The *Congressional Record* may not reflect what was said on the floor. *See* Morehead, *Record Redux,* 4 SERIALS LIBRARIAN 355 (1979).

understanding why Congress adopted or did not adopt certain language.

5. Other Documents

There are occasions when other documents are relevant to obtaining the legislative intent of a law. These may consist of Presidential messages, committee hearings on other bills, or reports and documents of other federal agencies. The location and use of these, however, are beyond the scope of this chapter. Ordinarily, the documents discussed are sufficient to help determine the legislative intent of a federal statute. When not sufficient, the researcher must then pursue the matter further.[10]

SECTION C. THE SOURCES OF LEGISLATIVE HISTORIES

A legislative history consists of all or some of the following documentary sources:

1. Bills

a. The bill as originally introduced in the House or Senate.

b. The bill, with any amendments.

c. The bill as it passed in the originating body and as introduced into the other. (At this point, it is called an "act").

d. The "act", with any amendments.

e. The "act" as amended by Joint Conference Committee of the House and Senate.

2. Reports

a. The reports of the committee to which the bill was assigned.

b. The reports of the committee to which the "act" was assigned.

c. The report of the Joint Conference Committee of the House and Senate. This is usually issued as a House report.[11]

3. Debates

The debates, if any, on the floor of Congress that appear in the *Congressional Record.*

[10] G. Folsom, *supra* note 5.

[11] Under the rules of Congress, the Conference Report is also to be printed as a Senate Report. This requirement is frequently waived by the unanimous consent of the Senate. ENACTMENT OF A LAW: PROCEDURAL STEPS IN THE LEGISLATIVE PROCESS, S.DOC. NO. 96–15, 96th Cong., 1st Sess. (1979).

4. Hearings

The hearings, if any, held by the committees to which the bill or "act" had been assigned.

5. The Public Law resulting from all of the above

SECTION D. COMPILED LEGISLATIVE HISTORIES

The process of identifying and then locating all of the various documents that are needed in compiling a legislative history can be a time-consuming and laborious task. As compiled legislative histories may be available for some public laws, researchers may save considerable time and effort by ascertaining if one is available for the statute or statutes involved in their research. This may now be easily accomplished by consulting the *Sources of Compiled Legislative Histories*.[12] This is a looseleaf publication which lists all the sources of compiled legislative histories. It also includes a chart of legislative histories for all public laws starting with the first Congress in 1789, with an indication of where they have been published. *Sources of Compiled Legislative Histories* should be carefully consulted before one attempts the task of compiling a legislative history.

Beginning with the 96th Congress, CCH has published *Public Laws—Legislative Histories: Microfiche.* This service makes available the House or Senate bill as introduced; the reported House bill, Senate bill, or both; committee reports; conference reports, if any; and relevant legislative debate as reported in the *Congressional Record.* All enactments are indexed by subject, by public law number and by bill number. Information Handling Services has a similar microfiche legislative history file of selected enactments only, from the 61st Congress. For the 61st to 82nd Congress, tax legislation only is included.

SECTION E. HOW TO COMPILE A LEGISLATIVE HISTORY

There are frequent occasions when a legislative history has to be compiled during the course of one's research. This may be due to the sources described in Section D not being available, or for a public law for which there is not a previously compiled history. Moreover, it is also frequently necessary to examine the Congressional documents for a bill considered by Congress but not enacted into a public law.

[12] N. JOHNSON, SOURCES OF COMPILED LEGISLATIVE HISTORIES (AALL Pub.Ser.No.14, 1979 and Supp.1981).

The method of compiling a legislative history is described in this section.

1. Legislative Histories, 1970–

The publication of a set commencing in 1970 by the Congressional Information Service, Inc., called CIS, has simplified the method of compiling legislative histories. This service is first issued in monthly pamphlets and then each year is reissued in two cumulative bound volumes. Part (Volume) One contains abstracts of hearings, reports, committee prints,[13] and other Congressional publications such as House and Senate documents. This part is cumulated annually. Part (Volume) Two contains detailed indexes of the subjects of reports, documents, and hearings, lists of witnesses, official and popular names of laws, reports, and bills, and names of committee and subcommittee chairmen. This index section is cumulated quarterly, annually and quadrennially (the 1970–1974 and 1975–1978 cumulations are multi-volume sets).

Each CIS Annual volume has a section on legislative histories for the public laws passed during the year. Each public law is listed and citations are given to the bill number, the committee reports, hearings, the *Congressional Record,* and other documents that may be relevant to a legislative history such as committee prints, Congressional documents and hearings held under related bills.[14] References are also given to the abstracts of these documents within CIS. Through the use of the indexes in Part Two, references to public laws may be found by the name or title of a public law, by the subject matter of the law, or by bill number.

Because of the frequency of publication, the thoroughness of the indexing and the citation to all relevant documents, the CIS, since 1970, is now the quickest and most efficient method of locating citations to documents that make up a legislative history.

[13] Special studies in specific subject areas are often prepared for Congressional committees. These are known as committee prints. Often, only limited numbers, for the use of the committee members, are printed. Recently they have become more available through the Depository Program though indexing is often incomplete. The Depository Program is a system whereby approximately 1400 libraries throughout the country are issued a copy of selected U.S. government publications. For further information, *see,* GOVERNMENT DEPOSITORY LIBRARIES, JOINT COMM. ON PRINTING, 96th CONG., 1st SESS. (Comm. Print 1979). Since 1970, committee prints have been made available on microfiche by the Congressional Information Service, Inc.

[14] In order to speed measures through, identical or similar bills are frequently introduced into both houses, so that House and Senate committees may work on the measure at the same time. Ordinarily, at some point in the legislative process, one house agrees to drop its bill and the legislative process continues on the other bill. The Companion Bills Table should be consulted in the CCH Congressional Index. It lists all companion bills.

2. Legislative Histories, before 1970

Prior to 1970, or when CIS may not be available, the key to locating the citations of the various documents is the bill number under which a public law was introduced into either the House or Senate. This bill number may be located by the use of one of the following sources:

a. *Daily Digest. Annual Cumulation*

The *Daily Digest* appears in each issue of the *Congressional Record* and highlights the daily activities of Congress. After each annual session of Congress, it is cumulated and contains a *History of Bills Enacted into Public Law,* arranged by public law number.

b. *Guide to Legislative History of Bills Enacted Into Public Law*

Beginning with Volume 77 (1963) of the *Statutes at Large,* each volume contains this guide which lists all laws passed during the year with corresponding bill number, report numbers, and citations to consideration and passage in the *Congressional Record.*

c. *CCH Congressional Index*

This is a privately published looseleaf service which issues weekly supplements while Congress is in session and covers its legislative work. New volumes are issued for each Congress. One section contains a list of public laws passed and gives the bill number for each. This set lists all bills introduced, contains a history of all Senate and House bills introduced, and includes a detailed subject index. Because of its weekly supplements, this is the best set to use to obtain information about current laws.

d. *Digest of Public General Bills and Resolutions*

This is published by the Library of Congress and contains brief summaries of public bills for each Congress. The *Digest* is normally issued in five cumulative issues during each session of Congress. Among its many tables is a Public Law listing with corresponding bill numbers for each law.

After the bill number has been ascertained, it is then necessary to check a status table, which presents a chronological history of the bill as it has moved through the various legislative steps toward enactment. From such tables it is possible to determine if committee reports were issued, if debates on the bill took place in Congress, and if hearings were held and printed. Tables of histories of bills may be found in all of the publications listed *supra.*

SECTION F. ILLUSTRATIONS

When compiling a legislative history for a congressional statute, there are ordinarily two different procedures to follow. The first is to identify those documents which are part of a legislative history. This is accomplished by consulting indexes or tables which indicate the steps taken during the consideration of a bill by Congress. The end result is a list of citations to bills, reports, hearings and other documents.

The second procedure is to actually locate the documents for the citations which were found from the indexes and tables consulted.

For purposes of demonstration, illustrations are shown in this Section for the procedures involved in compiling a legislative history for the Justice System Improvement Act of 1979, P.L. 96–157.

Illustrations of Indexes and Tables

52. **Page from 1979 Volume—Congressional Information Service (CIS)**
53. **Page from 1979 Commerce Clearing House (CCH) Congressional Index—Senate Bills Status Table**
54. **Page from Digest of Public General Bills and Resolutions (Library of Congress)**
55. **Page from 1979 History of Bills and Resolutions, Congressional Record Index**

Illustrations of Documents

Legislative History of Public Law 96–157

56. **First Page of S. 241—96th Cong., 1st Sess.**
57. **First Page of Hearings on S. 241**
58. **First Page of Senate Report No. 96–142 on S. 241**
59. **First Page of S. 241 as Amended by Senate Committee**
60. **Fifth Page of S. 241 as Amended by Senate Committee**
61. **First Page of H.R. 2061 as Amended by House Committee**
62. **First Page of House of Representatives Report No. 96–163 on H.R. 2061**
63. **Page from Congressional Record—Senate Debate on S. 241**
64. **First Page of S. 241 as Passed by the Senate**

65. **Page from Congressional Record—Debate on H.R. 2061**

66. **First Page of Joint Conference Report on S. 241**

67. **First Page of Public Law 96–157—Justice System Improvement Act of 1979**

[Illustration 52]

PAGE FROM 1979 VOLUME—CONGRESSIONAL INFORMATION SERVICE (CIS)

PL96–157 JUSTICE SYSTEM IMPROVEMENT ACT OF 1979.
Dec. 27, 1979. 96-1. 57 p.
• CIS/MF/3 •Item 575.
93 STAT. 1167.

"To restructure the Federal Law Enforcement Assistance Administration, to assist State and local governments in improving the quality of their justice systems, and for other purposes."

Amends the Omnibus Crime Control and Safe Streets Act of 1968 to extend through FY83 and revise LEAA programs for State and local criminal justice system improvement. Also establishes within the Justice Dept a National Institute of Justice (NIJ) and a Bureau of Justice Statistics (BJS) for criminal justice research and statistics activities, and an Office of Justice Assistance, Research, and Statistics to coordinate NIJ, BJS, and LEAA programs.

Legislative history: (S. 241 and related bills):
1979 CIS/Annual:
Senate Hearings: S521-51.
House Reports: H523-9 (No. 96-163, accompanying H.R. 2061); H523-22 (No. 96-655); H523-25 (No. 96-695, Conference Report).
Senate Report: S523-6 (No. 96-142).
Congressional Record Vol. 125 (1979):
May 21, considered and passed Senate.
Oct. 12, H.R. 2061 considered and passed House; passage vacated and S. 241, amended, passed in lieu.
Dec. 11, Senate agreed to conference report.
Dec. 13, House agreed to conference report.

PL96–158 LITTLE SISTERS OF THE POOR, D.C., land conveyance.
Dec. 27, 1979. 96-1. 1 p.
• CIS/MF/3 •Item 575.
93 STAT. 1224.

"To grant to the Little Sisters of the Poor all right, title, and interest of the United States in the land comprising certain alleys in the District of Columbia."

expected to adversely impact wildlife, encourages international cooperation in the conservation of endangered and threatened plants, establishes an advisory commission to act as

Locating Legislative History Documents Using CIS

The CIS/INDEX volumes have a section containing legislative histories for all public laws. For each law, citations are given to all related documents. The citations refer to the pages in CIS where they are abstracted. In most instances, the researcher will need to examine the full documents.

This set is only useful for public laws. For congressional bills considered but not enacted, the tables shown in subsequent illustrations should be consulted.

amendment.
Dec. 28, 1979. 96-1. 1 p.
• CIS/MF/3 •Item 575.
93 STAT. 1232.

"To amend the District of Columbia Self-Government and Governmental Reorganization Act with respect to the borrowing authority of the District of Columbia."

Extends D.C. authority to obtain Treasury loans to cover FY81 capital projects for which funding is authorized or appropriated.

Legislative history: (H.R. 5537 and related bill):

Also amends the Federal Deposit Insurance Act, National Housing Act, Small Business Investment Act, Federal Reserve Act, and Federal Home Loan Bank Act to exempt financial insti-

in House amendment.
Weekly Compilation of Presidential Documents Vol. 15, No. 52 (1979):
Dec. 28, Presidential statement.

PL96–162 YAKIMA RIVER BASIN WATER ENHANCEMENT PROJECT, feasibility study.
Dec. 28, 1979. 96-1. 1 p.
• CIS/MF/3 •Item 575.
93 STAT. 1241.

"To authorize the Secretary of the Interior to engage in a feasibility study."

Volume 10, Number 1-12 **CIS/INDEX 1093**

[Illustrations 53 and 54]

PAGES FROM CCH CONGRESSIONAL INDEX AND DIGEST OF PUBLIC GENERAL BILLS AND RESOLUTIONS

Illustration 53

* 241

Hearing in S. 2/9/79
Reptd., amended, S. Rept. No. 96-142 . . . . 5/14/79
Amended on S. floor (Voice) 5/21/79
Passed S. as amended (Roll-call) . . . 5/21/79
Amended to contain text of H. 2061 as passed (Voice) 10/12/79
Passed H. as amended (Voice) 10/12/79
H. amends. rejected by S. 10/18/79
Conferees appointed by S. 10/18/79
Conferees appointed by H. 10/19/79
Conf. Rept. filed, H. Rept. No. 96-655 . . . . 11/16/79
Conf. Rept. recommitted to Conference Committee (Voice) 11/29/79
Conf. Rept. filed, H. Rept. No. 96-695 . . . . 12/10/79
Agreed to by S. (Voice) 12/11/79
Agreed to by H. (Roll-call) 12/13/79
To President 12/17/79
Approved (P.L. 96-157) 12/27/79

Locating Legislative History Documents Using CCH Congressional Index—96th Congress

The Status Tables in this Index list all bills and give citations to all relevant documents, including hearings, but not to the debates in the Congressional Record.

Illustration 54

5-14-79 Reported to Senate from the Committee on the Judiciary with amendment, S. Rept. 96-142
5-21-79 Measure called up by unanimous consent in Senat
5-21-79 Measure considered in Senate
5-21-79 Measure passed Senate, amended, roll call # 102 (67-8)
10-12-79 Measure called up by special rule in House
10-12-79 Measure considered in House
10-12-79 Measure passed House, amended, in lieu of H. R. 2061
10-18-79 Conference scheduled in Senate
10-19-79 Conference scheduled in House
11-16-79 Conference report filed in House, H. Rept. 96-65
11-29-79 Conference report recommitted to the Committee of Conference
12-10-79 Conference report filed in House, H. Rept. 96-69 (Second Conference Report)
12-11-79 Senate agreed to conference report
12-13-79 House agreed to conference report, roll call # 730 (304-83)
12-17-79 Measure enrolled in House
12-17-79 Measure enrolled in Senate
12-17-79 Measure presented to President
12-27-79 Public Law 96-157

Locating Legislative History Documents Using the Digest of Public General Bills and Resolutions

This publication of the Library of Congress gives a substantive digest for public bills considered by Congress and then, as shown, gives citations to all relevant documents, except hearings.

[Illustration 55]

PAGE FROM 1979 CONGRESSIONAL RECORD INDEX

History of Bills and Resolutions

SENATE BILLS

S. 157—For the relief of Anibal Hadad, his wife Alicia Hadad, and his son Daniel Hadad.
Mr. Bumpers and Mr. Pryor; Committee on the Judiciary, S373.
Reported (S. Rept. 96-510), S19036.
Passed Senate, S19399.
Referred to Committee on the Judiciary, H12522.

S. 207—For the relief of Dr. Herman Sardjono and his wife, Erlanda Sardjono.
Mr. Danforth; Committee on the Judiciary, S555.
Reported (S. Rept. 96-511), S19036.
Passed Senate, S19399.
Referred to Committee on the Judiciary, H12522.

S. 219—To amend the Internal Revenue Code of 1954

Examined and signed, H12133, S18877.
Presented to the President, S18877.

S. 299—To amend sections 551 and 553 of title 5, United States Code, to improve Federal rulemaking by creating procedures for regulatory issuance in two or more parts, and for other purposes.
Mr. Culver, Mr. Nelson, Mr. Thurmond, Mr. Wallop, Mr. Baucus, Mr. Nunn, Mr. Tower, Mr. Pressler, and Mr. Leahy; Committee on the Judiciary, S854.
Cosponsors added, S1475, S2225, S2541, S3610, S4721, S13211, S14262, S16778, S19489.

S. 328—For the relief of Mr. Oliver O. Ratajczek and his wife, Christine Diane Ratajczek.
Mr. Hatch; Committee on the Judiciary, S987.
Reported (S. Rept. 96-451), S17853.
Passed Senate, S18580.

Senate concurs in House amendment with an amendment, S19119.
Examined and signed, H12500.

S. 493—To promote the orderly development of hard mineral resources in the deep seabed, pending adoption of an international regime relating thereto, and for other purposes.
Mr. Matsunaga, Mr. Jackson, Mr. Church, Mr. Long, Mr. Bumpers, Mr. Ford, Mr. Inouye, Mr. Melcher, Mr. Weicker, and Mr. Wallop; Committees on Energy and Natural Resources; Commerce, Science and Transportation; Foreign Relations; if and when reported, jointly to the Committee on Finance to consider title V only, and Committee on Environment and Public Works for not to exceed 60 calendar days; and that such latter committees be required to file separate

Locating Legislative History Documents Using History of Bills and Resolutions Table in the Congressional Record.

This Table gives the history of all Senate bills introduced into each session of Congress. It gives citations to all relevant documents, except hearings.

These Tables are located in the bound annual Index volumes of the Congressional Record, and in the bi-weekly indexes of the unbound issues.

Conference report (H. Rept. 96-606), submitted in House and agreed to, H10493, H11369.
Conference report submitted in Senate and agreed to, S16432.
Examined and signed, S17670, H11471.
Presented to the President, S17670.
Approved [Public Law 96-143, S18599.

S. 241—To restructure the Federal Law Enforcement Assistance Administration, to assist State and local governments in improving the quality of their justice systems, and for other purposes.
Mr. Kennedy, Mr. Thurmond, Mr. DeConcini, Mr. Glenn, Mr. Javits, Mr. Leahy, Mr. Bayh, and Mr. Baker; Committee on the Judiciary, S763.
Cosponsors added, S1278.
Reported with amendments (S. Rept. 96-142), S5789.
Debated, S6196.
Amended and passed Senate, S6230.
Amended and passed House (in lieu of H.R. 2061), H9114.
Senate disagreed to House amendments and asked for a conference. Conferees appointed, S14802.
House insisted on its amendment and agreed to a conference. Conferees appointed, H9444.
Conference report (H. Rept. 96-655) submitted in House, H10988.
Senate recommitted to committee of conference the conference report, S17540.
Conference report (H. Rept. 96-695) submitted in House and agreed to, H11709, H11957.
Conference report submitted in the Senate and agreed to, S18272.

tional goal for the development and maintenance of effective, fair, inexpensive, and expeditious mechanisms for the resolution of consumer controversies, and for other purposes.
Mr. Ford, Mr. Kennedy, Mr. Danforth, Mr. Bayh, and Mr. Metzenbaum, S1429.
Ordered placed on the calendar, S1411.
Cosponsors added, S1593.
Amended and passed Senate, S4091.
Referred to Committee on Interstate and Foreign Commerce, H2150.
Reported with amendment (H. Rept. 96-492), H8786.
Reported with amendment (H. Rept. 96-492 pt. II), H9586.
Made special order H. Res. 488, H10795.
Debated, H11695, H11806.
Amended and passed House, title amended, H11841.
House insisted on its amendments and asked for a conference, conferees appointed, H11858.

S. 440—To revise and extend the Comprehensive Alcohol Abuse and Alcoholism Prevention Treatment and Rehabilitation Act of 1970.
Mr. Riegle, Mr. Williams, and Mr. Hatch; Committee on Labor and Human Resources, S1578.
Reported with amendment (S. Rept. 96-103), S4926.
Debated, S5366, S5386.
Amended and passed Senate, S5392.
Referred to Committee on Interstate and Foreign Commerce, H2946.
Amended and passed House (in lieu of H.R. 3916), H9234.
House concurs in Senate amendment to House amendment, H12317.

Examined and signed, S17670, H11471.
Presented to the President, S17670.
Approved [Public Law 96-142, S18599.

S. 521—To provide for the payment of losses incurred as a result of the ban on the use of the chemical Tris in apparel, fabric, yarn, or fiber, and for other purposes.
Mr. Thurmond, Mr. Kennedy, and Mr. Hollings; Committee on the Judiciary, S1935.
Reported (S. Rept. 96-528), S19036.
Passed Senate, S19343.
Referred to Committee on the Judiciary, H12522.

S. 523—To amend chapter 5 of title 37, United States Code, to revise the special pay provisions for certain health professionals in the uniformed services.
Mr. Hart; Committee on Armed Services, S1935.
Cosponsors added, S2225, S3361, S11500, S17971.
Reported with amendment (S. Rept. 96-507), S18877.
Debated, S19359.
Indefinitely postponed (H.R. 5235 passed in lieu), S19364.

S. 525—To amend the Drug Abuse Office and Treatment Act of 1972, and for other purposes.
Mr. Riegle and Mr. Williams; Committee on Labor and Human Resources, S1935.
Cosponsors added, S2764.
Reported with amendment (S. Rept. 96-104), S4926.
Debated, S5418, S5424, S5426.
Amended and passed Senate, S5428.
Referred to Committee on Interstate and Foreign Commerce, H2946.

H.B. 1

[Illustration 56]

FIRST PAGE OF S. 241—96th CONGRESS, 1st SESSION

96TH CONGRESS
1ST SESSION

S. 241

To restructure the Federal Law Enforcement Assistance Administration, to assist State and local governments in improving the quality of their justice systems, and for other purposes.

IN THE SENATE OF THE UNITED STATES

JANUARY 29 (legislative day, JANUARY 15), 1979

Mr. KENNEDY (for himself, Mr. THURMOND, Mr. DECONCINI, Mr. GLENN, Mr. JAVITS, Mr. LEAHY, Mr. BAYH, and Mr. BAKER) introduced the following bill; which was read twice and referred to the Committee on the Judiciary ←

A BILL

To restructure the Federal Law Enforcement Assistance Administration, to assist State and local governments in improving the quality of their justice systems, and for other purposes.

From the indexes or tables shown in previous illustrations the researcher should now have citations to (1) Bill number, (2) Reports, (3) Hearings, (4) Congressional Record. These must all be separately obtained and examined.

This illustration shows the first page of S. 241 as first introduced during the 96th Congress.

Streets Act of 1968, as amended, is amended to read as follows:

II—E●

[Illustration 57]

FIRST PAGE OF SENATE HEARINGS ON S. 241

LAW ENFORCEMENT ASSISTANCE REFORM

HEARINGS

BEFORE THE

COMMITTEE ON THE JUDICIARY UNITED STATES SENATE

NINETY-SIXTH CONGRESS

FIRST SESSION

ON

S. 241

FEBRUARY 9, 15, 28, AND MARCH 7, 13, 1979

Serial No. 96–5

Printed for the use of the Committee on the Judiciary

The Committee to which a bill is referred will usually hold hearings in which interested parties are invited to testify. Hearings are usually (but not always) printed. In many instances, similar hearings are held by the other house either on a companion bill or on the same bill after it has passed the first house.

This volume of the hearings contains 880 pages. Frequently, hearings on a bill will be printed in multi-volume sets.

U.S. GOVERNMENT PRINTING OFFICE

44-116 WASHINGTON : 1979

[Illustration 58]

FIRST PAGE OF SENATE REPORT NO. 96-142 ON S. 241

96TH CONGRESS *1st Session* } SENATE { REPORT No. 96-142

LAW ENFORCEMENT ASSISTANCE REFORM ACT OF 1979

MAY 14 (legislative day, APRIL 9), 1979.—Ordered to be printed

Mr. KENNEDY, from the Committee on the Judiciary, submitted the following

REPORT

[To accompany S. 241]

The Committee on the Judiciary, to which was referred the bill (S. 241) to restructure the Federal Law Enforcement Assistance Administration, to assist State and local governments in improving the quality of their justice systems, and for other purposes, reports favorably thereon, with amendments, and recommends that the bill as amended do pass.

AMENDMENTS AND PURPOSE OF AMENDMENTS

The committee made a number of technical and substantive amendments to S. 241, as introduced.[1] These amendments are usually identified and discussed throughout this report. Among the more significant

After the Committee has held hearings and agrees to send the bill for consideration by the full Senate, it issues a report setting forth the purposes of the bill and why it reported favorably on it. This report consists of 68 pages.

be under the general authority and policy control of the Attorney General.

[1] In the interest of economy, the committee decided not to list and number the amendments. The amendments are described in the report, with exact language indicated in the bill as reported by inserts in italics and deletions by linetype.

(1)

[Illustration 59]

FIRST PAGE OF S. 241 AS AMENDED BY COMMITTEE

Calendar No. 150

96TH CONGRESS
1ST SESSION

S. 241

[Report No. 96–142]

To restructure the Federal Law Enforcement Assistance Administration, to assist State and local governments in improving the quality of their justice systems, and for other purposes.

IN THE SENATE OF THE UNITED STATES

JANUARY 29 (legislative day, JANUARY 15), 1979

After a bill has been introduced, it may be amended several times. This is the bill reprinted with the amendments made by the Senate Committee on the Judiciary.

A BILL

To restructure the Federal Law Enforcement Assistance Administration, to assist State and local governments in improving the quality of their justice systems, and for other purposes.

Be it enacted by the Senate and House of Representatives of the United States of America in Congress assembled,

[Illustration 60]

FIFTH PAGE FROM S. 241, AS AMENDED

When a bill is amended it is frequently reprinted with the new version indicating the new language added by the amendments in italics, and the deleted words indicated by the lines drawn through the amended language.

ment to reduce and prevent delinquency by developing and implementing effective programs to improve the quality of juvenile justice in the United States.

"Congress further finds that the victims of crime should be made a more integral part of the criminal justice system.

"Congress further finds that there is an urgent need to encourage basic and applied research, to gather and disseminate accurate and comprehensive justice statistics, and to evaluate methods of preventing and reducing crime.

~~"Congress further finds that although crime is essentially a local problem that must be dealt with by State and local governments, the financial and technical resources of the Federal Government should be made available to support such State and local efforts.~~ *"Congress further finds that crime is essentially a State and local and community problem that must be dealt with by State and local governments. Congress further finds that the financial and technical resources of the Federal Government should be made available to support such State and local and community-based efforts.*

[Illustration 61]

FIRST PAGE OF H.R. 2061, AS AMENDED

Union Calendar No. 88

96TH CONGRESS
1ST SESSION

H.R. 2061

[Report No. 96–163]

To restructure the Federal Law Enforcement Assistance Administration, to assist State and local governments in improving the quality of their justice systems, and for other purposes.

Frequently, when a bill is introduced in one house of Congress, a similar bill is introduced in the other and both start proceeding through the legislative process. Shown here is H.R. 2061 after it has been reprinted with the amendments made by the House Committee on the Judiciary.

[Strike out all after the enacting clause and insert the part printed in italic]

A BILL

To restructure the Federal Law Enforcement Assistance Administration, to assist State and local governments in improving the quality of their justice systems, and for other purposes.

Be it enacted by the Senate and House of Representatives of the United States of America in Congress assembled,

[Illustration 62]

FIRST PAGE OF HOUSE OF REPRESENTATIVES REPORT NO. 96–163 ON H.R. 2061

96TH CONGRESS, *1st Session* } HOUSE OF REPRESENTATIVES { REPORT No. 96–163

JUSTICE SYSTEM IMPROVEMENT ACT OF 1979

MAY 15, 1979.—Committed to the Committee of the Whole House on the State of the Union and ordered to be printed.

Mr. RODINO, from the Committee on the Judiciary, submitted the following

REPORT

together with

SEPARATE, SUPPLEMENTAL, ADDITIONAL, AND DISSENTING VIEWS

[To accompany H.R. 2061]

The report of the House Committee on the Judiciary on H.R. 2061. This report contains 128 pages.

The House Committee on the Judiciary also held hearings on this bill.

H.R. 2061 would amend the Omnibus Crime Control and Safe Streets Act of 1968, as amended (42 U.S.C. 3701 et seq.) to restructure the Law Enforcement Assistance Administration (LEAA) and to reauthorize LEAA for four years. The bill would restructure LEAA by (1) eliminating the requirment that States submit an annual comprehensive plan for the use of the federal funds, substituting therefor a requirement that a three-year application be submitted; (2) providing for a similar simplified application process by which local units of government and state agencies receive federal funds from the State administering agency; (3) modifying the formula by which each State's share of formula grants (formerly called "block grants") is computed by including, in addition to the population distribution factor used under present law, provision for an alternative formula tak-

39–006 O

[Illustration 63]

PAGE FROM DEBATES ON S. 241—CONGRESSIONAL RECORD

May 21, 1979 CONGRESSIONAL RECORD—SENATE S 6203

tion" insert "under this title other than part L";

On page 133, line 19, strike "and";

On page 133, line 20, after "1983" insert "; and $750,000,000 for the fiscal year ending September 30, 1984";

On page 133, line 22, after the period, insert "There is authorized to be appropriated in each fiscal year such sums as may be necessary to carry out the purposes of part L.";

On page 134, beginning with line 7, strike through and including page 136, line 2;

On page 136, line 3, strike "1004" and insert "1003";

On page 136, line 8, strike "and";

On page 136, line 9, after "1983" insert "; and $25,000,000 for the fiscal year ending September 30, 1984";

On page 145, line 13, strike "or under sections 4351 to 4353 of title 18, United States Code";

On page 145, line 18, strike "and sections 4351 to 4353 of title 18, United States Code,";

On page 145, line 22, strike "(h)" and insert "(g)";

On page 145, line 24, strike "and the National Institute for Corrections";

On page 146, line 6, after the period, strike through and including line 10;

On page 146, line 11, strike "(i)" and insert "(h)";

On page 146, line 17, strike "(j)" and insert "(i)";

On page 147, line 4, strike "(k)" and insert "(j)";

On page 147, line 9, strike the colon and "Provided, That they meet" and insert

dealing with unique State and local needs.

Strengthened role for local governments.—Large cities and counties are guaranteed a fixed allotment of funds and localities are granted greater control over the use of LEAA funds in their communities.

Elimination of match requirements.—Funds for criminal justice use no longer require any State or local matching contribution.

New grant formulas.—Designed to target LEAA funds to urban, rural and suburban areas of greatest need.

More effective use of funds.—Limita-

The discussion of a pending bill by members of Congress may be useful in determining Congressional intent. The researcher should ascertain such discussion in both houses of Congress.

of the benefits received under this part.

On page 141, line 14, after "Puerto Rico," insert "the Virgin Islands, Guam, American Samoa, the Trust Territory of the Pacific Islands, the Commonwealth of the Northern Mariana Islands,";

On page 142, line 20, strike "—REPEALER";

On page 142, line 23, strike "and the National Institute of Corrections";

On page 142, line 3, strike "or";

On page 142, line 4, after "the" insert "Director of the";

On page 142, line 5, strike "and" and insert "or";

On page 142, line 14, after "Act," insert "and title II(c) of the Juvenile Justice and Delinquency Prevention Act,";

On page 142, line 16, strike "that Act" and insert "those Acts";

On page 143, beginning with line 19, strike through and including page 144, line 3;

On page 144, line 4, strike "(d)" and insert "(c)";

On page 144, line 6, strike "previously" and insert "funds";

On page 144, line 7, strike "unused or reversionary funds" and insert "for fiscal years prior to 1980";

On page 144, line 8, strike "the continuation of";

On page 144, line 11, strike "and the provisions of sections 4351 to 4353 of title 18, United States Code,";

On page 144, line 13, strike "these Acts" and insert "this Act";

On page 144, line 16, strike "(e)" and insert "(d)";

On page 144, line 20, strike "previously" and insert "funds";

On page 144, line 20, after "appropriated" insert "for fiscal years prior to 1980";

On page 144, line 21, strike "unused or reversionary funds or funds" and insert "and";

On page 144, line 23, strike "the continuation of" and insert "programs or";

On page 144, line 23, after "projects" insert "to be expended";

On page 144, line 24, strike "sections 4351 to 4353 of title 18, United States Code, and";

On page 145, line 4, strike "(f)" and insert "(e)";

On page 145, line 7, strike "(g)" and insert "(f)";

under this Act."

Mr. KENNEDY. I yield myself such time as I may use.

Mr. President, S. 241, the Law Enforcement Assistance Reform Act of 1979, would reauthorize the Law Enforcement Assistance Administration for an additional 5-year period. But more importantly, it makes long overdue reforms in the structure and administration of the LEAA program. S. 241 constitutes the most ambitious effort yet undertaken by the U.S. Senate to reform an agency which has often been sharply criticized.

This program is of critical importance to the American people; LEAA remains the major Federal vehicle to assist localities in their struggle against crime. S. 241 has enjoyed broad bipartisan support, was unanimously reported out of the Senate Judiciary Committee, and has the personal endorsement of President Carter, Attorney General Bell, and this administration. A companion bill—sponsored by Chairman RODINO—was favorably reported out of the House Judiciary Committee last week.

S. 241 is the culmination of a decade of debate over the nature and scope of the LEAA program. This bill is designed to deal with the problems which have plagued the agency and limited its impact. Band-Aid reforms have been rejected; major surgery has been performed. I am convinced that S. 241 will go a long way in making LEAA the type of Federal agency contemplated by the Congress when it first enacted the LEAA program over 10 years ago.

The major reforms proposed in S. 241 include:

Reduced redtape.—Burdensome annual planning requirements are eliminated and replaced by simplified 3-year applications.

Greater local flexibility.—Earmarking of funds in all but a few areas is eliminated, thus allowing more flexibility in

contract making authority, is established with new independence.

Improved Statistics.—A Bureau of Justice Statistics, with grant and contract-making authority, is established to collect, analyze and disseminate reliable and uniform statistics on criminal and civil justice.

National Priority Grant Program.—Provides an opportunity for States and localities to invest in programs which, on the basis of research and evaluation, have been shown to be particularly effective in improving and strengthening the administration of justice. Under this approach, the Federal Government suggests, but does not mandate, certain LEAA priorities; local governments are encouraged, but not forced, to participate in these programs.

Finally, Mr. President, the Judiciary Committee unanimously accepted an amendment of critical importance offered by Senator BIDEN. This amendment would mandate the type of careful evaluation and priority-setting that has for too long been absent from the LEAA program. The amendment is designed to focus LEAA spending practices on eighteen long-standing, measurable problems confronting our criminal justice systems. The Biden amendment goes a long way in answering widespread criticism that LEAA's grant activities have been excessively diffuse, misguided, and undirected. Although a straight-forward categorical grant program as a solution to these problems was considered by the committee to be too rigid to take into account the varying needs of different localities, the Biden amendment requires an evaluation, an explanation of the effectiveness of LEAA assistance in 18 specific problem areas itemized in the bill.

Mr. President, the Senate Judiciary Committee conducted 8 days of hearings on the reauthorization and reform of the LEAA program. S. 241 reflects the type of

[Illustration 64]

FIRST PAGE OF S. 241 AS PASSED BY THE SENATE

96TH CONGRESS
1ST SESSION

S. 241

IN THE SENATE OF THE UNITED STATES

MAY 21 (legislative day, APRIL 9), 1979

Ordered to be printed as passed

AN ACT

To restructure the Federal Law Enforcement Assistance Administration, to assist State and local governments in improving the quality of their justice systems, and for other purposes.

After the house in which a bill has been introduced has voted to enact the bill, it is reprinted with all amendments and labeled an "Act" and sent to the other house for consideration.

In this instance, S. 241 was sent to the House of Representatives for its consideration.

Streets Act of 1968, as amended, is amended to read as follows:

"TABLE OF CONTENTS

"Sec. 2. Title I—Justice system improvement.

[Illustration 65]

PAGE FROM HOUSE OF REPRESENTATIVES DEBATE ON H.R. 2061—CONGRESSIONAL RECORD

H 9114 CONGRESSIONAL RECORD—HOUSE *October 12, 1979*

Sawyer	Stark	White
Schulze	Stockman	Whitehurst
Sharp	Stokes	Whitley
Shelby	Stratton	Whittaker
Skelton	Studds	Whitten
Smith, Iowa	Swift	Williams, Mont.
Smith, Nebr.	Tauke	Wilson, Bob
Solomon	Trible	Wolpe
Spellman	Udall	Yates
Spence	Vanik	Young, Fla.
Staggers	Walgren	Zablocki
Stanton	Weiss	

NOES—54

Archer	Frenzel	Petri
Ashbrook	Gephardt	Roth
Bauman	Hance	Rudd
Beilenson	Hansen	Russo
Bereuter	Holt	Satterfield
Burgener	Hubbard	Schroeder
Carney	Hughes	Seiberling
Cavanaugh	Ichord	Sensenbrenner
Collins, Tex.	Jeffries	Shumway
Conyers	Jones, Okla.	Shuster
Dannemeyer	Kelly	Simon
Daschle	Kramer	Stangeland
Duncan, Oreg.	Leath, Tex.	Steed
Early	Lewis	Symms
Edwards, Okla.	Luken	Taylor
English	Marlenee	Volkmer
Erlenborn	Moffett	Weaver
Ertel	Pease	Wirth

NOT VOTING—159

Albosta	Garcia	Pursell
Alexander	Gibbons	Quayle
Anderson, Ill.	Ginn	Quillen
Anthony	Glickman	Railsback
Applegate	Gradison	Regula
Aspin	Gramm	Reuss
Badham	Gray	Richmond
Barnard	Guyer	Roberts
Beard, R.I.	Harkin	Rodino
Bedell	Harsha	Roe
Biaggi	Hefner	Rose
Bingham	Heftel	Rosenthal
Boggs	Hightower	Rousselot
Boland	Hillis	Runnels
Bolling	Holland	Sabo
Bonior	Hollenbeck	Scheuer
Brinkley	Holtzman	Sebelius
Brooks	Hopkins	Shannon
Brown, Calif.	Horton	Slack
Burton, John	Hutto	Snowe
Butler	Ireland	Snyder
Byron	Jacobs	Solarz
Campbell	Jenkins	St Germain
Chappell	Johnson, Colo.	Stack
Chisholm	Jones, N.C.	Stenholm
Clausen	Kemp	Stewart
Clay	LaFalce	Stump
Cleveland	Latta	Synar
Coelho	Leach, La.	Thomas
Coleman	Lee	Thompson

the Senate bill (S. 241), to restructure the Federal Law Enforcement Assistance Administration, to assist State and local governments in improving the quality of their justice systems, and for other purposes, and ask for its immediate consideration.

The Clerk read the title of the Senate bill.

MOTION OFFERED BY MR. GUDGER

Mr. GUDGER. Mr. Speaker, I offer a motion.

The Clerk read as follows:

Mr. GUDGER moves to strike out all after the enacting clause of the Senate bill, S. 241, and to insert in lieu thereof the provisions of the bill, H.R. 2061, as passed, as follows:

That this Act may be cited as the "Justice System Improvement Act of 1979".

SEC. 2. Title I of the Omnibus Crime Control and Safe Streets Act of 1968, as amended, to read as follows:

"TITLE I—JUSTICE SYSTEM IMPROVEMENT

"The Congress finds and declares that the high incidence of crime in the United States is detrimental to the general welfare of the Nation and its citizens, and that criminal justice efforts must be better coordinated, intensified, and made more effective and equitable at all levels of government.

"Congress further finds that juvenile delinquency constitutes a growing threat to the national welfare requiring immediate and comprehensive action by the Federal Government to reduce and prevent delinquency by developing and implementing effective programs to improve the quality of juvenile justice in the United States.

"Congress further finds that there is an urgent need to encourage basic and applied research, to gather and disseminate accurate and comprehensive justice statistics, and to evaluate methods of preventing and reducing crime.

"Congress further finds that although crime is essentially a local problem that must be dealt with by State and local governments, the financial and technical resources of the Federal Government should be made available to support such State and local efforts.

"Congress further finds that the future welfare of the Nation and the well-being of

toward the improvement of civil, criminal, and juvenile justice systems and new methods for the prevention and reduction of crime and the detection, apprehension, and rehabilitation of criminals; (9) encourage the collection and analysis of statistical information concerning crime, juvenile delinquency, civil disputes, and the operation of justice systems; and (10) support manpower development and training efforts. It is further the policy of the Congress that the Federal assistance made available under this title not be utilized to reduce the amount of State and local financial support for criminal justiçe activities below the level of such support prior to the availability of such assistance.

"PART A—LAW ENFORCEMENT ASSISTANCE ADMINISTRATION

"SEC. 101. There is hereby established within the Department of Justice under the direct authority of the Attorney General, a Law Enforcement Assistance Administration (hereinafter referred to in this title as the 'Administration'). The Administration shall be under the direction of an Administrator, who shall be appointed by the President, by and with the advice and consent of the Senate, and such other Deputy Administrators as may be designated by the Attorney General. The Administrator shall have final authority over all grants, cooperative agreements, and contracts awarded by the Administration.

"SEC. 102. The Administrator shall—

"(a) provide funds to eligible States and units of local government pursuant to part D of this title in order to finance programs approved in accordance with the provisions of this title;

"(b) recognize national criminal justice priorities established by the Office of Justice Assistance, Research, and Statistics in accordance with parts E and F of this title, inform States and units of local government concerning such priorities and award and allocate funds among the eligible States, units of local government, and public and private nonprofit organizations according to the criteria and on the terms and conditions determined by the Administration to be consistent with parts E and F of this title;

"(c) publish and disseminate information on the condition and progress of the criminal justice system and establish and carry on a specific and continuing program of cooperation with the States and units of local gov-

When a bill has passed one house and is sent to the other house while the latter is still considering a companion bill, the other house may adopt the "Act" and then amend it to contain its language. In this instance, the House amended and then passed S. 241 and then sent it to the Senate with its amendments.

☐ 1920

Mr. SIMON changed his vote from "aye" to "no."

So the bill was passed.

The result of the vote was announced as above recorded.

A motion to reconsider was laid on the table.

Mr. GUDGER. Mr. Speaker, pursuant to the provisions of House Resolution 351, I call up from the Speaker's table

their criminal justice and juvenile justice systems; (2) develop and fund new methods and programs to enhance the effectiveness of criminal justice agencies; (3) support the development of city, county, and statewide priorities and programs to meet the problems confronting the justice system; (4) reduce court congestion and trial delay; (5) support community anticrime efforts; (6) improve and modernize the correctional system; (7) encourage the undertaking of innovative projects of recognized importance and effectiveness; (8) encourage the development of basic and applied research directed

Law Enforcement Assistance Administration the Office of Community Anti-Crime Programs (hereinafter in this section referred to as the 'Office'). The Office shall be under the direction of the Administrator and shall—

"(1) provide appropriate technical assistance to community and citizens groups to enable such groups to—

"(A) apply for grants which encourage community and citizen participation in crime prevention and criminal justice activities;

"(B) participate in the formula grant ap-

[Illustration 66]

FIRST PAGE OF CONFERENCE REPORT ON S. 241

96TH CONGRESS } HOUSE OF REPRESENTATIVES { REPORT
1st Session } { No. 96–695

JUSTICE SYSTEM IMPROVEMENT ACT OF 1979

DECEMBER 10, 1979.—Ordered to be printed

Mr. RODINO, from the committee of conference, submitted the following

CONFERENCE REPORT

[To accompany S. 241]

The committee of conference on the disagreeing votes of the two Houses on the amendment of the House to the bill (S. 241) to restructure the Federal Law Enforcement Assistance Administration, to assist State and local governments in improving the quality of their justice systems, and for other purposes, having met, after full and free conference, have agreed to recommend and do recommend to their respective Houses as follows:

That the Senate recede from its disagreement to the amendment of the House, and agree to the same with an amendment as follows:

In lieu of the matter proposed to be inserted by the House amendment, insert the following:

That this Act may be cited as the "Justice System Improvement Act of 1979".

SEC. 2. Title I of the Omnibus Crime Control and Safe Streets Act of 1968 is amended to read as follows:

S. 241 as passed by the House differed from the version as passed by the Senate. In such instances, a joint Conference Committee is appointed. This committee then agrees to new language and issues a Conference Report explaining the changes agreed to. If both houses accept the Conference Report, the "Act" is then sent to the President.

[Illustration 67]

FIRST PAGE OF PUBLIC LAW 96-157

PUBLIC LAW 96-157—DEC. 27, 1979 93 STAT. 1167

Public Law 96-157
96th Congress

An Act

To restructure the Federal Law Enforcement Assistance Administration, to assist State and local governments in improving the quality of their justice systems, and for other purposes.

Dec. 27, 1979
[S. 241]

Be it enacted by the Senate and House of Representatives of the United States of America in Congress assembled, That this Act may be cited as the "Justice System Improvement Act of 1979".

Justice System Improvement Act of 1979. 42 USC 3701 note.

SEC. 2. Title I of the Omnibus Crime Control and Safe Streets Act of 1968 is amended to read as follows:

"TITLE I—JUSTICE SYSTEM IMPROVEMENT

"TABLE OF CONTENTS

"Declaration and purpose.

"PART A—LAW ENFORCEMENT ASSISTANCE ADMINISTRATION

"Sec. 101. Establishment of Law Enforcement Assistance Administration.
"Sec. 102. Duties and functions of Administrator.

This is Public Law 96-157, the product of all of the documents previously illustrated. It consists of 56 pages. Note how citation is given to where it is published in the Statutes at Large, the date it became a law, and the reference to S. 241.

As with many public laws, the various sections of this law will be codified in different titles of the U.S. Code. To locate where a specific section is codified, a Table has to be consulted. See Illustration 50.

"Sec. 404. Review of applications.
"Sec. 405. Allocation and distribution of funds.

"PART E—NATIONAL PRIORITY GRANTS

"Sec. 501. Purpose.
"Sec. 502. Percentage of appropriation for national priority grant program.
"Sec. 503. Procedure for designating national priority programs.
"Sec. 504. Application requirements.
"Sec. 505. Criteria for award.

"PART F—DISCRETIONARY GRANTS

"Sec. 601. Purpose.
"Sec. 602. Percentage of appropriation for discretionary grant program.

SECTION G. HOW TO OBTAIN ACCESS TO THE DOCUMENTS OF LEGISLATIVE HISTORIES

After using the indexes previously described, the bills with amendments, the committee reports, the debates on the bills, and the committee hearings now have to be located and consulted. The means of access to these will vary because libraries shelve U.S. government documents in different ways.[15] The various documents that must be consulted, and the tools for gaining access to them are set forth below:

1. **Bills.** These are usually kept together by Congress, with all different stages of each bill collected together.

2. **House and Senate Reports** are included as part of the "Serial Set" [16] and assistance from the library staff is usually needed to locate them. Some law libraries maintain these reports in separate series. Many reports are also reprinted in both the pamphlets and bound volumes of the *United States Code Congressional and Administrative News Service.*[17]

3. **Transcripts** of debates on the floor of Congress are found in the *Congressional Record.* For each session of Congress there is an Index volume which contains a *History of Bills Table.* Under the bill number, one is directed to the pages in the *Congressional Record* where the bill was debated.

4. **Hearings.** The *CCH Congressional Index, CIS,* the *Monthly Catalog of Government Publications,* and *Cumulative Index of Committee Hearings* (issued by the Library of the United States Senate) all indicate when Committee hearings have been printed.

[15] If the research for the compilation of a legislative history is being done in a law library, the researcher should ascertain how the law library organizes and indexes government documents. If a researcher is not near a law library, or the law library does not collect government documents, access to needed documents may be had at any public or college libraries which are depositories for the publications of the U.S. Government Printing Office. Any such depository collection may be consulted by the public.

Many libraries now receive on microfiche one or more of the items described in this Section, either from the U.S. Government Printing Office or from certain publishing companies.

[16] The "Serial Set" is a bound compilation of *House Documents, Senate Documents, House Reports,* and *Senate Reports.* They are arranged in numerical sequence.

[17] This set is issued bi-weekly during a session of Congress, and then reissued in bound volumes and has a section entitled "Legislative Histories." However, it only reprints either a House Report or a Senate Report, and in some instances the Conference Report. It does not include all of the other elements which are part of a legislative history.

Hearings are usually shelved according to the Government Printing Office classification scheme. This number is always given in the *Monthly Catalog of United States Government Publications.* In some law libraries hearings are cataloged separately and may be located either through the name of the committee or by subject.

SECTION H. SUMMARY

A legislative history for a law passed by Congress consists of all or some of the following documents:

Bills as introduced, with any amendments

"Act" with any amendments

Reports of committee to which bill or "Act" was referred

Debates and discussions on floor of Congress, if any

Hearings before committees considering the bill or "Act"

When in need of a legislative history, the following steps should be taken:

1. Check *Sources of Compiled Legislative Histories.* If this gives reference to a compiled legislative history, obtain, if possible, and examine the various documents.

2. If *Sources of Compiled Legislative Histories* is not available, or if the compiled legislative history cited is not available, obtain citations to relevant documents by checking one or more of the following:

CIS Indexes

CCH Congressional Index

History of Bills and Resolutions, Congressional Record Index

Digest of Public General Bills and Resolutions

3. Obtain documents cited in above sources.

Chapter 11

STATE AND MUNICIPAL LEGISLATION

There is much similarity between the organization and publication of federal and state statutes. While there are differences between the fifty states, this is mostly in nomenclature rather than substance. Each state has a state legislature, and with the exception of Nebraska, each has an upper and lower house similar to the House of Representatives and the Senate of the United States Congress. In general, the legislative process for the passage of state laws is similar to that previously described for federal laws.

State legislatures meet in either annual or biennial sessions.[1] Information for individual states as to nomenclature, frequency of session, and other pertinent information on state legislatures may be obtained by consulting the latest edition of *The Book of the States*.[2]

SECTION A. SESSION LAWS

Each state publishes all of the laws passed during each session of its legislature in volumes with the generic name, "session laws," although in some states they may have other names, such as acts and resolves, or statutes or laws. The session laws are published in chronological order comparable to those in the *U. S. Statutes at Large*. [See Illustrations 68 and 69] Most states also publish their laws in "slip" form soon after they are passed. In many states current laws are found in the pamphlet or advance sheet services to privately published state codes.

SECTION B. CODIFICATION OF STATE LAWS

Since each volume of the session laws for a state contains the laws passed by the state legislature during an annual, biennial or special session, and since the laws passed are arranged chronologically in

1 The monthly issues of *State Government News*, published by the Council of State Governments, have a section on Legislative Session Dates.

2 COUNCIL OF STATE GOVERNMENTS, THE BOOK OF THE STATES (biennial). This chapter is devoted to the location of state statutes. It must be noted, however, that after a relevant statute has been located, it is frequently necessary to determine its proper application. For these purposes, consult F. DICKERSON, THE INTERPRETATION AND APPLICATION OF STATUTES (1975); J. SUTHERLAND, STATUTES AND STATUTORY CONSTRUCTION (4th ed. C. Sand 1972–1975).

each volume, it is necessary to have the laws rearranged by title or subject as they are in the *United States Code.* Each state does, in fact, have a set of statutes which have been extracted from its session laws. The terms "revised," "compiled," "consolidated," and "code" are often used indiscriminately to describe such sets of books.[3] In some instances compilations are accomplished under the official auspices of a state, in others by private publishers, and in some states there are both official and unofficial sets of codes. Some are unannotated, while others are fully annotated. Some state codes have been enacted into positive law, others are only *prima facie* evidence of the law with the positive law being in the volumes of the session laws. The important thing to note is that each state has a set of session laws and a current code. The set or sets for the state being used should be carefully examined to note its features, its method of publication, and the way it is kept up to date.

The following features are common to most sets of state statutes:

1. Constitutions

The constitution of the state currently in force as well as the text of previous constitutions.

2. Text of Statutes

Each state code contains the public laws of a general nature and still in force, arranged by subject.

3. Historical Notes

Historical references showing the derivation of each section of the code appear at the end of each statutory section. As many state codes have several completely new codifications during the history of the state, citations are frequently given to the present provision in a previous codification.

4. Annotations

Most state codes have an annotated edition. Some are very similar in appearance to the U.S.C.A. or the U.S.C.S. Frequently, citations are given to law review articles and to legal encyclopedias.

5. Tables

Each state code will have tables that cross reference from session law to the code and many will have tables that refer from an old-

[3] Methods of compilation differ from state to state. One state may simply reissue the session laws in chronological order but with temporary and repealed acts not included. A second may arrange the laws still in effect in a classified order but with the text kept intact as originally enacted. A third may rewrite, rearrange, and re-enact the laws in a new classified order. *See* Chapter 9, note 12.

er codification to the current one. [See Illustrations 71–74 for examples of a state annotated code.]

SECTION C. INDEXES AND GUIDES TO STATE LEGISLATION

There is no comprehensive indexing service comparable to the Key Number System for state statutes. When comparative state statutes are needed it is necessary at times to consult the indexes to the fifty sets of state codes. As this can be a time-consuming and difficult task, the following sources [4] which frequently provide citations or digests of all state statutes on a particular subject, should be consulted.

1. Looseleaf Services

These are described in detail in Chapter 14. Many looseleaf services provide either full texts, digests, or tables of citations to state laws on a specific subject. For example, the CCH *All-State Tax Reporter* provides charts and digests of comparative state tax provisions; the Prentice-Hall *Wills, Trusts, and Estates Reporter* reproduces the text of all state laws on these subjects.

2. Martindale-Hubbell Law Directory

This is an annual publication which includes a volume titled *Law Digests* providing a digest of state laws on many subjects.

SECTION D. FINDING STATE LEGISLATION

1. Current State Law

When researching state legislation, one is usually attempting to ascertain if there is a current state statutory provision on a particular legal subject, *e. g.*, at what age may one be issued a driving license? The first step is to examine carefully the code for the state in question and familiarize oneself with the way the code is organized. Consulting the index provided should lead to the citation of a provision in the code which will set forth the current statutory law on the subject. Next, all of the notes set forth below the statutory provision should be consulted. Many annotated codes have references to legislative reports and give citations to law reviews and other secondary

[4] There are also two excellent bibliographies which list other sources for locating state statutes on similar topics. *See* J. SCHULTZ, COMPARATIVE STATUTORY SOURCES (2d ed. 1978), Boast and Foster, *Current Subject Compilations of State Laws: Research Guide and Annotated Bibliography.* 72 LAW LIB. J. 209 (1979).

sources. The method of supplementation should then be noted (*e. g.*, pocket supplements, bound cumulative supplements, or advance pamphlets). If the set is annotated, the appropriate case annotations should be checked. Frequently it will also be helpful to use the appropriate Shepard's Citator. This will be discussed in Chapter 15.

2. Inoperative State Law

At times the problem being researched may involve an act which has been repealed or is no longer in force. It will then be necessary to consult this law in the code volume that was available when the law was in force, or to consult the session volumes which contain the text of the act as originally passed by the legislature.

SECTION E. ILLUSTRATIONS

68. Page from 1979 Minnesota Session Laws

69. Page from 1978 Pennsylvania Session Laws Amending a Previous Session Law

70. Page from Tables Volumes—Purdon's Pennsylvania Statutes Annotated

71. Page from an Index Volume of West's Wisconsin Statutes Annotated

72–74. Pages from West's Wisconsin Statutes Annotated

[Illustration 68]

PAGE FROM THE 1979 MINNESOTA SESSION LAWS

Ch. 281 LAWS of MINNESOTA for 1979 617

CHAPTER 281—H.F.No.699

An act relating to labor; increasing the minimum wage; providing for future increases; amending Minnesota Statutes 1978, Sections 177.23, Subdivision 7; and 177.24, Subdivision 1.

BE IT ENACTED BY THE LEGISLATURE OF THE STATE OF MINNESOTA:

Section 1. Minnesota Statutes 1978, Section 177.23, Subdivision 7, is amended to read:

Subd. 7. "Employee" means any individual employed by an employer but shall not include

(1) any individual employed in agriculture on a farming unit or operation employing less than the equivalent of two full time workers and on any given day employing no more than four employees. For the purpose of this clause, equivalent of a

A typical state session law. Minnesota is a state that has re-enacted its codification. When amending it, the session law can then cite directly to the Minnesota Statutes, which is its codification. Note how this is done.

(4) any individual employed in a bona fide executive, administrative, or professional capacity, or a salesman who conducts no more than 20 percent of his sales on the premises of the employer, as such terms are defined and delimited by regulations of the department;

(5) any individual who renders service gratuitously for a nonprofit organization as such terms are defined by regulations of the department;

(6) any individual who serves as an elected official for a political subdivision or who serves on any governmental board, commission, committee or other similar body, or who renders service gratuitously for a political subdivision;

(7) any individual employed by a political subdivision to provide police or fire protection services or who is employed by an entity whose principal purpose is to provide police or fire protection services to a political subdivision;

(8) any individual employed by a political subdivision who is ineligible for membership in the public employees retirement association by reason of the provisions of

Changes or additions indicated by underline **deletions by** ~~strikeout~~

[Illustration 69]

PAGE FROM 1978 PENNSYLVANIA SESSION LAWS

62 Act 1978-31 LAWS OF PENNSYLVANIA

No. 1978-31

AN ACT

HB 1761

→ Amending the act of July 25, 1961 (P.L.857, No.372), entitled "An act regulating the manufacture of stuffed toys intended for sale, gift, or use in Pennsylvania; providing for registration of such manufacturers, the paying of a fee for such registration, the issuance of a seal of approval to such manufacturers; providing that material used in such toys shall be new and free from dangerous or harmful substances; providing for disinfection of such material containing products of animal origin; and prescribing penalties," changing certain registration fees, exempting charitable and nonprofit organizations from payment of the registration fee and making editorial changes.

The General Assembly of the Commonwealth of Pennsylvania hereby enacts as follows:

Section 1. The title and sections 2, 3, 4 and 6, act of July 25, 1961 (P.L.857, No.372), entitled "An act regulating the manufacture of stuffed

Another typical state session law. Note, however, how this law refers to and amends a previous session law rather than a specific section of the Purdon's Pennsylvania Statutes (its codification of session laws). With only a citation to this session law, a transfer table must be used to find where this session law has been codified. See next Illustration.

the paying of a fee for such registration, the issuance of a **[seal of approval]** ***certificate of registration*** to such manufacturers; providing that material used in such toys shall be new and free from dangerous or harmful substances; providing for disinfection of such material containing products of animal origin; and prescribing penalties.

Section 2. As used in this act—

[(1)] The term "Department" shall mean the Department of Labor and Industry.

The term "manufacturer" shall mean any person engaged in the producing or making of stuffed toys for use outside the maker's household.

[(2)] The term "new" shall mean any article or material which has not been subjected to a previous manufacturing process, or which has not been previously used for any purpose.

[(3)] The term "person" shall include individuals, **[partnership]** ***partnerships***, associations, trusts, corporations, and any other individual or any other business entity.

[Illustration 70]

PAGE FROM TABLES VOLUME OF PURDON'S PENNSYLVANIA STATUTES ANNOTATED

CHRONOLOGICAL TABLE OF LAWS

1978—Cont'd

Apr 18—Cont'd
PL 61, No 30
§ 1—62 PS § 2265
§ 2—Effective date
PL 62, No 31
§ 1—35 PS § 5201 note, 5202, 5203, 5204, 5206
§ 2—Effective date
PL 64, No 32
§ 1 to 5—72 PS § 3946.20 note
§ 6—Effective date
Apr 24, PL 67, No 33
§ 1—24 PS 9—960
§ 2—Effective date
PL 69, No 34—Special act
Apr 28, PL 74, No 35
§ 1—61 PS § 408 note
§ 2—61 PS § 408
§ 3—Effective date
PL 76, No 36
§ 1—53 PS § 46724
§ 2—Effective date
PL 77, No 37
§ 1—20 PaCS § 712

1978—Cont'd

Apr 28, PL 108, No 47—Cont'd
§ 10—11 PS § 2410
§ 11—11 PS § 2411
§ 12—11 PS § 2412
§ 13—11 PS § 2413
§ 14—11 PS § 2414
§ 15—11 PS § 2415
§ 16—11 PS § 2416
§ 17—11 PS § 2417
§ 18—11 PS § 2418
§ 19—11 PS § 2419
§ 20—11 PS § 2420
§ 21—11 PS § 2421
§ 22—11 PS § 2422
§ 23—11 PS § 2423
§ 24—11 PS § 2424
§ 25—General repealer
§ 26—Effective date
PL 118, No 48
§ 1—53 PS § 57005
§ 2—Effective date
PL 119, No 49
§ 1—72 PS § 5453.701, subsec (b)
§ 2—72 PS § 5453.701 note

This Table indicates where each separate session law is located in Purdon's Pennsylvania Statutes Annotated.

§ 2—35 PS § 7002
§ 3—35 PS § 7003
§ 4—35 PS § 7004
§ 5—35 PS § 7005
§ 6—35 PS § 7006
§ 7—Effective date
PL 93, No 43
§ 1—73 PS § 261 note
§ 2—73 PS § 262, clauses (b), (f), (g), (p), (q)
§ 3—73 PS §§ 266, 267, 268
§ 4—71 PS § 335, 510—1, 510—15, 669, 73 PS § 262, 266, 267, 268 note
§ 5—Effective note
PL 97, No 44
§ 1—53 PS § 23851, subsecs A, B
§ 2—Effective date
PL 93, No 45
§ 1—16 PS § 11301
§ 2—Effective date
PL 106, No 46
§ 1—62 PS § 2043.32
§ 2—62 PS § 2043.35, subsecs. (e), (f)
§ 3—Repealing section
§ 4—Effective date
PL 108, No 47
§ 1—11 PS § 2401
§ 2—11 PS § 2402
§ 3—11 PS § 2403
§ 4—11 PS § 2404
§ 5—11 PS § 2405
§ 6—11 PS § 2406
§ 7—11 PS § 2407
§ 8—11 PS § 2408
§ 9—11 PS § 2409

54, 6780—55, 6780—56, 6780—57, 6780—58, 6780—59
Art III
§ 8—53 PS prec § 6780—101
§ 9—53 PS § 6780—101, 6780—102, 6780—103
§ 10—53 PS § 6780—104
§ 11—53 PS § 6780—105, 6780—106, 6780—107
§ 12—53 PS § 6780—108
§ 13—53 PS § 6780—109
Art IV
§ 14—53 PS prec § 6780—151
§ 15—53 PS § 6780—151, 6780—152, 6780—153, 6780—154, 6780—155, 6780—156, 6780—157, 6780—158
§ 16—53 PS § 6780—159
§ 17—53 PS § 6780—160
§ 18—53 PS § 6780—161
§ 19—53 PS § 6780—162, 6780—163, 6780—164, 6780—165
Art V
§ 20—53 PS prec § 6780—201
§ 21—53 PS § 6780—201, 6780—202
§ 22—53 PS § 6780—203
§ 23—53 PS § 6780—204
§ 24—53 PS § 6780—205
§ 25—53 PS § 6780—206
§ 26—53 PS § 6780—207, 6780—208
§ 27—53 PS § 6780—209
§ 28—Repealing section
§ 29—53 PS § 6780—210

307

[Illustration 71]

A PAGE FROM THE INDEX TO WEST'S WISCONSIN STATUTES ANNOTATED

L

319

[Illustration 72]

A PAGE FROM WEST'S WISCONSIN STATUTES ANNOTATED

111.17 **EMPLOYMENT RELATIONS**

Library References

Statutes ⚷223.2(19). C.J.S. Statutes §§ 366, 368.

Notes of Decisions

1. In general

This section did not apply to subsequently enacted section 108.02 where it did not appear that it was legislative intent that prior law should prevail over later enacted law. Salerno v. John Oster Mfg. Co. (1967) 155 N.W.2d 66, 37 Wis.2d 433.

Employment relations board had jurisdiction to determine union's demand for order to pay money in connection with alleged unfair labor practice arising by reason of claimed breach of expired employment contract and had power to make order for payment of money notwithstanding fact that claimed practice arose after termination of contract which was allegedly violated. General Drivers and Helpers Union Local 662 v. Wisconsin Employment Relations Bd. (1963) 124 N.W.2d 123, 21 Wis.2d 242.

This subchapter and National Labor Relations Act, 29 U.S.C.A. § 151 et seq., are not so inconsistent on their face as to require holding that the state act has been suspended by the national act. International Brotherhood of Electrical Workers, Local No. 953, A. F. of L., v. Wisconsin Employment Relations Board (1944) 15 N.W.2d 823, 245 Wis. 532.

After locating the citation in the Index, the Section cited to must be read carefully.

Care must be taken to check any supplement that may have been published. In this set, annual pocket supplements are available.

SUBCHAPTER II

FAIR EMPLOYMENT

→ **111.31 Declaration of policy**

(1) The practice of denying employment and other opportunities to, and discriminating against, properly qualified persons by reason of their age, race, creed, color, handicap, sex, national origin or ancestry, is likely to foment domestic strife and unrest, and substantially and adversely affect the general welfare of a state by depriving it

388

[Illustration 73]

A PAGE FROM WEST'S WISCONSIN STATUTES ANNOTATED

EMPLOYMENT RELATIONS **111.31**

of the fullest utilization of its capacities for production. The denial by some employers, licensing agencies and labor unions of employment opportunities to such persons solely because of their age, race, creed, color, handicap, sex, national origin or ancestry, and discrimination against them in employment, tends to deprive the victims of the earnings which are necessary to maintain a just and decent standard of living, thereby committing grave injury to them.

(2) It is believed by many students of the problem that protection by law of the rights of all people to obtain gainful employment, and other privileges free from discrimination because of age, race, creed, color, handicap, sex, national origin or ancestry, would remove

Note how citations are given to the session laws from which Section 111.31 was codified.

Also note cross reference to the Sections of the code where discrimination is prohibited.

Source:

L.1945, c. 490, § 3.
St.1945, § 111.31.
L.1959, c. 149, § 1.
L.1961, c. 529, § 1.
L.1965, c. 230, § 1.
L.1967, c. 234, § 1, eff. Dec. 21, 1967.

Cross References

Civil rights, generally, see 42 U.S.C.A. § 1981 et seq.
Discriminations prohibited,
- Accommodations or amusements, see § 942.04.
- Automobile insurance, see §§ 631.36, 942.04.
- Blighted area law, see § 66.43.
- Civil service, see § 16.14.
- Handicapped teachers, see § 118.195.
- Housing, see §§ 66.432, 101.22.
- Housing authorities, see § 66.395 et seq.
- Metropolitan transit authority, see § 66.94.
- National guard, see §§ 21.145, 21.35.
- School pupils, see § 118.13.
- Teacher employment, see § 118.20.
- Urban redevelopment projects, see § 66.405.
- Veterans' housing, see § 66.39.

Equal protection, see U.S.C.A.Const. Amend. 14, § 1.
Equal rights for women, see § 246.15.
Equality and inherent rights of man, see Const. Art. 1, § 1.
Maintenance of free government, see Const. Art. 1, § 22.
Religious tests for public office prohibited, see Const. Art. 1, § 19.

389

[Illustration 74]

A PAGE FROM WEST'S WISCONSIN STATUTES ANNOTATED

111.31 EMPLOYMENT RELATIONS

Law Review Commentaries

Discrimination concerning migrant farm workers in Wisconsin. 1951 Wis. L.Rev. 344, 349.

Effect of state statute upon federal requirement for collective bargaining. 1966 Wis.L.Rev. 538 (Spring).

Racial discrimination in denial of union membership. 1958 Wis.L.Rev. 294.

Library References

Civil Rights ⚷9.10 et seq.
Labor Relations ⚷1 to 8.

C.J.S. Master and Servant § 14.

Notes of Decisions

In general 1
Racial discriminations 2
Remedies, in general 3

1. In general

Purpose of the Fair Employment Practices Act would clearly not be effectuated if Industrial Commission could do no more than enter an order to cease and desist. Murphy v. Industrial Commission (1968) 155 N.W.2d 545, 37 Wis. 2d 704, rehearing 157 N.W.2d 568, 37 ....

objection, on racial grounds, of members already there. Ross v. Ebert (1957) 82 N.W.2d 315, 275 Wis. 523.

3. Remedies, in general

Agreement whereby employer was to reemploy complainant conditioned on his ability to perform duties of available work and complainant was to dismiss complaint as to Equal Rights Division of state of Wisconsin did not encompass liability under federal law so as to bar complainant from bringing an action in

At the end of each Section of the Code, citations are given to Law Review articles published in the state; to the Topic and Key Numbers where cases on this subject are digested, and annotations of all Federal and Wisconsin cases which cited and interpreted this Section.

Most annotated codes are similar to this one.

2. Racial discriminations

The Fair Employment Code did not give to a colored applicant an enforceable right to union membership over

tion by female employees against employer for back pay based on employer's alleged discrimination because of sex. Murphy v. Miller Brewing Co. (1971) 184 N.W.2d 141, 50 Wis.2d 323.

390

SECTION F. MUNICIPAL OR LOCAL GOVERNMENT LEGISLATION

Traditionally the various forms of local government are known as "municipal corporations". Municipalities are instruments of the state and have only such power as granted to them by the state. This will vary from state to state,[5] and the constitution and statutes of the state wherein the municipality is located must be examined.

1. Municipal Charters

In general, municipalities operate under a charter which is the basic document setting forth their power. Usually the charter has been adopted by the voters of a municipality and is analogous to a state constitution. The form of publication will vary, and in the larger cities, may include bound volumes.

a. *Ordinances*

Ordinances are the legislative enactments of local jurisdictions, as passed by their legislative body, *e. g.*, the city council or board of supervisors. They are to municipalities what acts are to the state legislatures and the United States Congress. In larger cities, ordinances are first published in an official journal and may be separately published in "slip" form. In smaller communities they are frequently published in the local newspaper.

b. *Codes*

Municipal codes are codifications of ordinances. As with state codes, they generally contain only those ordinances in force at the time of publication and are usually classified and arranged according to a logical plan.

2. Features Common to Most City Codes

a. *City Charters*

Most city codes include the text of city charters. They usually are unannotated.

b. *Text of Ordinances*

The texts of city ordinances are the basic information contained in municipal codes. They are rarely annotated with digests of cases.

c. *Topical Analyses; Historical Notes; Cross References*

In some of the new city codes a topical analysis may precede each chapter. The history of the sections, references to pertinent

[5] C. ANTIEAU, MUNICIPAL CORPORATION LAW § 12 (1975).

state law and notations to related provisions in the city code may be given after the text of each ordinance or in footnotes.

d. *Indexes*

The codes are indexed according to various schemes. Some index the charter and ordinances together and some contain separate indexes to each of these units. In a few cities, where the codes are divided into separately bound parts, each part may have a detailed index and/or a broad general index covering all the ordinances.

e. *Tables*

In some municipal codes, tables are included which show the disposition of the sections of an earlier code and the location of earlier provisions in the current compilation.

3. Interpretations of Municipal Charters and Ordinances

Most city codes are unannotated and do not include annotations of cases interpreting the charters and ordinances. The following are useful in obtaining court decisions for municipal legislation:

a. *State Digests*

The reported cases interpreting an ordinance or a charter are included in a state digest. The location of the appropriate key number or paragraph numbers under which such cases are digested may be located through the use of the index or topical outlines to the digest.

b. *Treatises*

Both *E. McQuillin, Law of Municipal Corporations* and *C. Antieu, Municipal Corporation Law* will be helpful in locating court decisions.

c. *Shepard's State Citations* [6]

This is most useful for finding court decisions which have cited and interpreted municipal laws. [See Illustrations 75–76]

d. *Shepard's Ordinance Law Annotations*

This set is arranged by subject and has annotations on court decisions arising out of city charters and ordinances. [See Illustration 77]

SECTION G. ILLUSTRATIONS FOR MUNICIPAL LEGISLATION

75–76. Pages from Shepard's North Carolina Citations

77. Page from Shepard's Ordinance Law Annotations

[6] Shepard's Citations are discussed in Chapter Fifteen.

[Illustration 75]

PAGE FROM SHEPARD'S NORTH CAROLINA CITATIONS—
ORDINANCE SECTION

I-O **INDEX TO ORDINANCES**

Each state unit of Shepard's has a section, with an index, on charters and ordinances.

If, for example, one is interested in locating regulations on the licensing of massage parlors, the index will indicate which cities have ordinances on this subject.

See Chapter 15 for a detailed description of Shepard's Citations.

See note on first page of this division. See 1957 and 1957-1974 Bound Volumes for additional references

582

[Illustration 76]

PAGE FROM SHEPARD'S NORTH CAROLINA CITATIONS— ORDINANCE SECTION

Employees–Regulations
7WFL193

Housing
Code–Provisions
420FS709

Licenses
Taxation–Exemption–Religious Organizations
465FS576

Massages
Treatment–Opposite Sex–Prohibition–Exceptions
285NC530
21NCA102
203SE411
206SE203
399FS133
423FS761
C457FS391

Motor Vehicles
Towing–Inventory–Procedure
298NC573
39NCA278
250SE309
260SE629
Wreckers–License–Duties–Charges
97A2504n

Nuisan
Definiti
7WFL
Persona
Propert
Trash–
Abaten
41NCA
255SE2

Sidewa
Protrudi
S
80A2697
80A2702n
80A2712n
80A2714n

Sunday
Business–Regulations
283NC165
195SE496

Taxicabs
Regulation
30NCA657
228SE43

Television
Cable–Franchise–Nonexclusive–Authorization
546F2d570

Vehicles
Impoundment–Procedure
297NC216
254SE586

Zoning
Classification–Uses
39LCP161
Districts–Business
36NCA410
244SE469
–Business–Signs–Regulations
81A2496n
81A2533n
81A2553n
–Residential–Restricted Uses
24NCA231
210SE498

CONOVER

Annexation
Notice of

Sunday
Stores–Closing
C17NCA99
–Closing–Exceptions
C283NC165
C195SE496

CURRITUCK COUNTY

Subdivisions
Improvements–Performance Bond
1976DuL18
Public Utilities–Dedication
1976DuL13
Recreational Areas–Dedication
1976DuL13
Streets–Dedication
1976DuL13

Water and Sewer
Outer Banks–Nonparticipation
299NC270
261SE899

Zoning
Beach Access–Regulations
1976DuL12
Classification
1976DuL11
Districts–

Mobile Homes–Prohibition
19NCA45
197SE883
–Residential–Agricultural–Uses
19NCA45
197SE883
Mobile Homes–Licenses–

Conditions
1976DuL12
Planned Unit Development–Design Scheme
299NC270
261SE899

DARE COUNTY

Subdivisions
Setback–Sideline–Requirements
37NCA557
43NCA703
246SE541
260SE172

DAVIE COUNTY

Zoning
Regulations
28NCA717
222SE910

DURHAM

City Code

255SE739

§ 18-13
Water Connection
–Provisions
41NCA649
255SE739

§ 18-30
Water and Sewer
Service Rates

41NCA649
255SE739

(Not in or prior to their inclusion in the Durham City Code, 1964 as Amended)

Massage Parlor
Licensing–Regulations
29NCA502
224SE661
C399FS133
410FS399
423FS761
460FS152

Offenses
Massage–Restrictions
C399FS133
423FS761

Urban Renewal Project
Land Exchange
298NC476
259SE558

Water
Family Unit–Minimum Charge
41NCA649
255SE739

–Residential District
39NCA117
250SE68

EDENTON

Definitions
Planning Board

294NC679
242SE877
Town Board
294NC679
242SE877

Zoning
Amendment–Application–Restriction
31NCA648
230SE695
–Petition–Initiation
294NC679
242SE877
–Planning Board–Recommendation–Requirement
31NCA648
230SE695
–Regulations
294NC679
242SE877
Official Map-Ordinance–Incorporation
294NC679
242SE877
Proposed Amendments–Planning Board–Submission–Requirement
294NC679

ment–Approval–Time Limit
294NC679
242SE877
–Residential Agricultural to Highway Commercial
Va31NCA [648

Va230SE [695
–Residential Agricultural to Shopping Center
V31NCA648
V230SE695

ELIZABETH CITY

Zoning
Districts–Residential–Structure–Nonconforming Use
31NCA118
228SE525

ELKIN

Zoning
Districts–Residential–Rezoning
290NC608
227SE576

FAYETTE

Licenses
Businesses–Requirements
C285NC530
C21NCA102
C203SE411
C206SE203

Massages
Business License–

Regulations
C285NC530
C21NCA102
C203SE411
C206SE203
543F2d570
423FS761
–Revocation
C285NC530
C21NCA102
C203SE411
C206SE203
423FS761
454FS597
Treatment–Opposite Sex–Prohibition–Exceptions
C285NC530
C21NCA102
C203SE411
C206SE203
578F2d1002
423FS761
482FS681

Prostitution
Provisions
43NCA76
257SE690
Soliciting–Prohibition
43NCA76
257SE690

FORSYTH COUNTY

Zoning
tional
al
ermits
A361
E770
n-
ng
Uses
A361
E770
ersion
A361
E770
Regulations
19NCA361
198SE770

GARNER

Zoning
Nonconforming
Continued

This illustrates how Shepard's Citations enables a researcher to locate court decisions interpreting a city ordinance.

See Index to Ordinances. See 1957 and 1957-1974 Bound Volumes for earlier citations

[Illustration 77]

PAGE FROM SHEPARD'S ORDINANCE LAW ANNOTATIONS

MASSAGE PARLORS

This multi-volume set, published by Shepard's, is actually a digest rather than a citator.

It is topically arranged and digests appellate court decisions that have interpreted a provision of a city charter or ordinance.

For example, if research involved the regulation of massage parlors, this set, under that heading, will digest all cases wherein such regulation was the subject of litigation.

It is kept current by annual pocket supplements.

I. REGULATING THE BUSINESS OR PERSONS

§1. Requiring License or Permit

Licensing of massage parlors has not been preempted by the state licensing of any professional art of healing. A massage parlor is not such an art of healing and is subject to control by the city. The control may include the right to grant and revoke licenses on notice and hearing.

NC Smith v Keator (1974) 21 NCApp 102, 203 SE2d 411; affd (1974) 206 SE2d 203.

A licensing provision for massage parlors requiring photographing and fingerprinting of personnel as well as physical examination is reasonable. The intimate physical contact provides a rational basis to support the requirements for physical examination and resubmission on reasonable belief of the applicant having contacted a communicable disease.

NC Brown v Brannon (1975) 399 F Supp 133.

A business in which male customers are given massages by topless females is a massage parlor rather than a health club. As such it is not permitted use when the ordinance only provides for health clubs.

Pa Berger v Bethel Park (1974) 14 PaCmwlth 13, 321 A2d 389.

486

SECTION H. STATE LEGISLATIVE HISTORIES

Generally, state legislatures do not publish their debates, committee reports, or transcripts of hearings held before legislative committees.[7] It is therefore difficult to compile legislative histories of most state laws as was described in Chapter 10 for federal laws. Yet the need for them is just as great since state laws often have provisions which are vague and ambiguous. The most accessible official documents are the Senate and House Journals. These Journals usually contain only brief minutes of the proceedings and the final votes on legislation.[8] A few states may have reports of a State Law Review Commission or the reports of special committees of the legislature for selected laws. If a state has an annotated code, the notes should be carefully examined to see if reference is made to such documents. Often, guidance for research in state legislative history is available from state legal research guides[9] or from librarians with extensive experience within a state. In many instances, however, extrinsic aids for determining legislative intent are not available and reliance must be made on the language of the act by using the ordinary rules of statutory construction.

SECTION I. SUMMARY

1. Session laws are published after adjournment of the state legislatures for the regular or special sessions and cover the laws enacted during that period.

2. State statutes are compiled, in single or multi-volume editions, under a logical arrangement with the obsolete and revoked laws eliminated.

3. **Features Common to Most State Statutes**

   a. Constitutions.

      (1) State—usually annotated.

      (2) Federal—usually unannotated.

[7] To determine those state documents which are available, *see* M. FISHER, GUIDE TO STATE LEGISLATIVE MATERIALS [AALL Pub. Ser. 15, 1979] (Periodic supplements are issued).

[8] However, Maine and Pennsylvania have legislative journals which record actual legislative debate and parallel the *Congressional Record* in form of content.

[9] See a list of these guides in Appendix A. *See also* Marke, *Finders Guide to Legislative History, Intent in New York*, N.Y.LAW J., Nov. 20, 1979, at 4, col. 5, and Nov. 21, 1979, at 6, col. 1–4.

b. Text of statutes.

c. Historical notes.

d. Comparative legislation.

e. Annotations.

f. Tables.

g. Research aids.

h. Cross references to related sections.

i. Indexes.

j. Forms.

k. Popular names of state acts.

l. Supplementation—cumulative annual pocket parts, pamphlet supplements and replacement volumes.

4. Martindale-Hubbell Law Directory

a. *Law Digests* volume contains brief synopses of some statutory laws of all states and selected statutory laws of many foreign countries.

b. Revised annually.

5. Inoperative State Law

Consult earlier state code or session laws.

6. Popular Names of State Acts

a. In *Shepard's Acts and Cases by Popular Names.*

b. General index of the state code.

7. Private, Temporary, Local and Appropriation Acts

Generally, consult session laws.

8. Municipal Charters—variously published

9. Municipal Ordinances are the legislative enactments of local jurisdictions

10. Municipal Codes are codifications of ordinances

11. Features Common to Most City Codes

a. Classified.

b. City charters.

c. Text of ordinances.

d. Topical analysis; historical notes; cross references.

e. Indexes.

f. Tables.

g. Supplementation—not always up-to-date.

h. Annotations in codes are a rarity.

12. Interpretations to Municipal Charters and Ordinances

a. Shepard's State Citations.

b. *Shepard's Ordinance Laws Annotated.*

13. Status and History of a City Charter and Ordinances

a. Check Shepard's State Citations.

b. Check city code and its supplement.

Chapter 12

COURT RULES AND PROCEDURE

This chapter is concerned with the procedures and rules for the conduct of lawsuits in the courts. After the substantive rights of a party have been determined, the lawyer involved may then decide it is necessary to institute an action in court on behalf of the client. The publications discussed herein deal with the procedures for bringing and defending a court suit, and the procedures and methods of appellate courts. Such publications include legislation pertaining to judicial proceedings, the rules promulgated by courts for the conduct of their business, and legal forms used in court proceedings.

SECTION A. COURT RULES IN GENERAL

Rules of courts are legislative in effect, since they control the operation of the court and the conduct of the litigants appearing before it. Court rules relate to such matters as the issuance of complaints, assignment of cases, method of appeal, and the proper method of making motions which are required during the many phases of a court proceeding. In general, the purposes of court rules are (1) to aid the court in performing its business, (2) to establish uniform procedures, and (3) to provide the parties to a lawsuit with information and instruction on matters pertaining to judicial proceedings.

The power of a court to promulgate court rules is found either in its inherent authority or in a constitution or statutory provision.

SECTION B. FEDERAL COURT RULES OF GENERAL APPLICABILITY

Federal court rules are in three categories: (1) the rules of general application such as the Rules of Civil Procedure, the Rules of Criminal Procedure; (2) the Federal Rules of Appellate Procedure; and (3) the individual rules of the various federal courts.

1. Rules of General Application: Unannotated

The Supreme Court of the United States has the authority to issue rules for the other federal courts. The Supreme Court, pursuant to this authority, has promulgated rules of criminal and civil procedure for use in the federal district courts and rules pertaining to proceedings in matters of bankruptcy, admiralty, and copyright. The text of the Rules of Criminal Procedure may be found in 18 U.S.C. Appendix. The Rules of Civil Procedure and Appellate Procedure are in 28 U.S.C. Appendix, as well as in the Rule volumes of the *U.S. Supreme Court Digest* (Lawyers Co-operative Publishing Co.).

2. Federal Rules: Annotated

After the promulgation of rules, there frequently is litigation concerning the meaning of the rules and their applicability to specific fact situations. When involved in research on federal procedure, one must often locate court decisions which interpret the rules. The following are useful for this purpose:

a. *Federal Rules Decisions* (F.R.D.)

This is a unit of the *National Reporter System* and contains cases of the federal district courts since 1940 which construe the Rules of Civil Procedure and cases since 1946 decided under the Rules of Criminal Procedure. Similar to other units of the *National Reporter System,* it first appears in the form of advance sheets and then in bound volumes with headnotes which are classified to the West Key-Number System. In addition to court decisions, it also includes articles on various aspects of federal courts and federal procedure.

b. *Federal Rules Service* (Callaghan & Co.)

This is a most useful service to use when searching for court decisions construing the Federal Rules of Civil Procedure and the Federal Rules of Appellate Procedure. It is in four sections:

(1) *Federal Rules Service* (First and Second Series). This contains the full text of all federal court decisions construing the Federal Rules of Civil Procedure.

(2) *Federal Rules Digest* (3d ed. 1973).

This multi-volume set digests all court decisions from 1955 to date which appear in the *Federal Rules Service.* Digests of decisions from 1938 to 1954 are located in the four volumes of *Federal Rules Digest* (2d ed.).

(3) *Federal Local Court Rules.*

(4) *Finding Aids Volume.* This includes a Word Index to the Federal Rules of Civil Procedure and the full text of all the rules This volume also contains an outline on how to use the entire *Federal Rules Service* set.

3. Annotated Codes

Both the U.S.C.S. and the U.S.C.A. have volumes which contain the Rules of Federal Procedure, Civil and Criminal.

a. *United States Code Service*

This set has several unnumbered volumes of Court Rules. In organization they are similar to the other volumes of the set. The text of each rule is given and then followed by annotations of decisions under the rule. The notes include comments from the Advisory Committee of the Federal Rules, and references to other appropriate sections in other sets of the *Total Client Service Library.*

b. *United States Code Annotated*

The Rules of Civil Procedure are in volumes following Title 28, and the Rules of Criminal Procedure are in volumes following Title 18. Each rule is followed by editorial annotations and Advisory Committee notes.

4. Treatises

There are many treatises pertaining to the practice and procedure of the federal courts. They generally contain the text of appropriate statutes and the Rules of Federal Civil and Criminal Procedure. The text of each rule is followed by an analysis of the rules, and citations to court decisions are given in the footnotes. The following multi-volume sets are most useful in obtaining commentary on federal practice:

a. *Cyclopedia of Federal Procedure*

b. *Moore's Federal Practice*

c. *West's Federal Practice Manual*

d. Wright and Miller, *Federal Practice and Procedure*

5. Form Books

Model instruments or forms used in federal practice have also been published and keyed to the Federal Rules. They contain proper terms, phrases, and other essential details needed by an attorney to compose formally correct legal documents. These are practice form books. Other types of form books are discussed in Chapter Nineteen.

a. *Bender's Federal Practice Forms*

This is a looseleaf publication with annotations and cross references to *Moore's Federal Practice.* The forms cover civil and criminal rules.

b. *Nichols Cyclopedia of Federal Procedure Forms*

The forms are annotated and cover civil and criminal rules and some administrative agencies.

c. *West's Federal Forms*

d. U.S.C.S. *Federal Procedural Forms*

Additional treatises and books of forms may be located by checking the catalog in a law library.

SECTION C. LOCAL COURT RULES FOR FEDERAL COURTS

All federal district courts, the eleven courts of appeal, and the Court of Appeals for the District of Columbia have promulgated court rules. These rules apply only to the court issuing them and are mainly concerned with its operation. They contain rules for filing motions and the preparation of briefs, as well as other rules dealing with the procedure of the court. Rules for the federal courts may be found in the following publications:

1. Federal Rules Service. Local Rules Volume

This is a looseleaf volume which contains all of the rules of federal district courts currently in force. It is arranged in alphabetical order by state, and the volume is kept up to date as amendments and new rules are issued.

Many of the federal district courts also issue their court rules in pamphlet form.

2. Rules for the Courts of Appeal

(a) *Federal Rules Service. Local Rules Volume.*

(b) Rules volume following 28 U.S.C.A.

(c) Rules volumes of the U.S.C.S. and the *U.S. Supreme Court Digest* (Lawyers Co-operative ed.)

(d) Each court also issues its rules in pamphlet form.

(e) Certain courts of appeal have privately published guidebooks which include their rules, i. e. the *Second Circuit Redbook* (4th ed. 1980), G. Rahdert & L. Roth, *Appeals to the Fifth Circuit Manual* (1977).

SECTION D. FEDERAL RULES OF EVIDENCE

In 1974, the United States Congress enacted Public Law 93–595, which created for the first time a uniform code of evidence providing uniform standards for the admission of evidence in all United States courts. Prior to this enactment, the law of evidence was scattered throughout the court decisions, with the law varying from circuit to circuit. The Federal Rules of Evidence may be found in the following publications:

1. Appendix, Title 28 U.S.C.

2. Federal Rules of Evidence volume, Appendix, Title 28 U.S.C.A.

3. Appendix, Title 28 U.S.C.S.

4. Pike and Fischer's *Federal Rules of Evidence Service.*

5. J. Weinstein and M. Berger, *Weinstein's Evidence.*

SECTION E. COURT RULES FOR STATE COURTS

The method of publication of the rules of court varies from state to state.[1] In most states, they are published in the state code or in the state reports.

Treatises on state civil and criminal practice have been published for a number of states. They may be located in the catalog of a local law library.

SECTION F. SUMMARY

1. Purposes of court rules

a. Aid the court in expediting and performing its business.

b. Establish uniform procedure for the conduct of the court's business.

c. Provide parties to a suit with procedural information and instructions on matters pertaining to judicial proceedings.

2. Publication of Federal Court Rules

a. *Rules of General Application*

U.S.C., 18 Appendix and 28 Appendix

U. S. Supreme Court Digest, Rules Volumes (not annotated)

Federal Rules Service

b. *Rules and Annotations*

Federal Rules Service (Callaghan)

Federal Rules Decisions (West)

U.S.C.A. and U.S.C.S.

c. *Treatises*

Cyclopedia of Federal Procedure

Moore's Federal Practice

[1] Checklists of state court rules are found in Klein, *Rules of Court,* 52 LAW LIB. J. 206 (1959) and Blau & Clark, *Sources of Rules of State Courts,* 66 LAW LIB. J. 37 (1973). *See also:* J. Weinstein, REFORM OF COURT RULE-MAKING PROCEDURE (1977).

West's Federal Practice Manual

Wright and Miller, *Federal Practice and Procedure*

d. *Form Books*

Bender's Federal Practice Forms

Nichols Cyclopedia of Federal Procedure Forms

West's Federal Forms

U.S.C.S. *Federal Procedural Forms*

e. *Local Federal Court Rules*

Federal Rules Service. Local Rules Volume

f. *Courts of Appeal Rules*

28 U.S.C.A. Rules Volumes

g. *Federal Rules of Evidence*

See Section D

h. *State Courts*

Check local library catalog

Chapter 13

ADMINISTRATIVE LAW

SECTION A. FEDERAL ADMINISTRATIVE REGULATIONS AND DECISIONS: INTRODUCTION

Administrative law has been defined as:

"[T]he law concerning the powers and procedures of administrative agencies, including especially the law governing judicial review of administrative action. An administrative agency is a governmental authority, other than a court and other than a legislative body, which affects the rights of private parties through either adjudication, rule-making, investigating, prosecuting, negotiating, settling, or informally acting. An administrative agency may be called a commission, board, authority, bureau, office, officer, administrator, department, corporation, administration, division or agency." [1]

The purpose of this chapter is to explain the manner in which the rules and the adjudication of federal administrative bodies are published and how they may be located.

The power of issuing regulations [2] and of adjudication is delegated to administrative bodies by Congress.[3] The increasingly complex problems of security and the economy in the last forty years have brought about a tremendous increase in the number of administrative agencies and in the documents produced by them for publication. The normal procedure is for Congress to delegate to an administrative office or agency the power to issue rules or regulations, and in some instances the power to hear and settle disputes arising from the statute. Once an administrative body has been established, the issuance of rules or regulations is fairly simple, unlike the enactment of a statute which must go through the legislative process of Congress. Some agencies, such as the National Labor Relations Board, not only

[1] 1 K. DAVIS, ADMINISTRATIVE LAW AND GOVERNMENT 6 (2d ed. 1978).

[2] For a discussion of Congressional authority to delegate legislative power to administrative agencies, *see* 1 B. MEZINES, J. STEIN, AND, J. GRUFF, ADMINISTRATIVE LAW § 3.03[1] (1980).

[3] For example, 16 U.S.C. § 824(f) (1976) provides that whenever the Federal Power Commission "* * * shall find that any interstate service of any public utility is inadequate * * *, the Commission shall determine the * * * adequate * * * service to be furnished, and shall fix the same by its order, rule, or regulation * * *."

promulgate regulations, but are also authorized to adjudicate disputes between management and labor unions, and the results of their adjudications are published in a format similar to court reports.

All regulations by administrative agencies are issued either under authority delegated to them by a federal statute or by a Presidential Executive Order.

The types of actions taken by federal agencies may be classified as: (a) rules or regulations, (b) orders, (c) licenses, (d) advisory opinions, and (e) decisions. Each of these may be defined as follows: [4]

> a. Rules or regulations. These are statements by an agency of general or particular applicability which are designed to implement, interpret, prescribe law or policy. Properly promulgated rules and regulations have the same legal effect as statutes.
>
> b. Orders. These are used to describe the final dispositions of any agency matters (other than rule making but including licensing).
>
> c. Licenses. These include any permits, certificates, or other forms of permission.
>
> d. Advisory opinions. Although containing advice regarding contemplated action, they are not binding and serve only as authoritative interpretations of statutes and regulations.
>
> e. Decisions. Federal agencies authorized by law use decisions to adjudicate controversies arising out of the violation or interpretation of statutes and administrative regulations or rules. This function is performed by special boards of review, hearing examiners, and other officers through administrative decisions.

SECTION B. PUBLICATION OF FEDERAL RULES AND REGULATIONS

1. Federal Register

Before 1936, there was no official source for publication of rules and regulations of federal agencies nor indeed were such agencies required to make them available to the public. This resulted in much confusion, as there was no way of determining if a proposed action by a person or company was prohibited by some federal agency. In fact, in one well-known instance, the federal government prosecuted a corporation for violations of an administrative regulation. This

[4] 5 U.S.C. § 551 (1976).

case [5] reached the Supreme Court of the United States before the Attorney-General realized that the action was based on a regulation that had been revoked prior to the time the original action had begun.[6]

As a result of the *Panama* case, Congress passed the *Federal Register Act,* 49 *Stat.* 500, 44 U.S.C. § 1504 *et seq.* (1976). This provided for the publication of the *Federal Register.* It started in 1936 and is published daily (except Saturday, Sunday, or days following official holidays). For any administrative ruling or regulation to be legally effective it must be published in the *Federal Register.* The definition of what is considered to have general applicability and legal effect is as follows:

> * * * any document issued under proper authority prescribing a penalty or a course of conduct, conferring a right, privilege, authority, or immunity, or imposing an obligation, and relevant or applicable to the general public, members of a class, or persons in a locality, as distinguished from individuals or organizations * * *. (1 C.F.R. 1.1, January 1, 1980).

Thus, since 1936, the *Federal Register* contains within it every regulation having legal effect, and amendments thereto, that have been issued by any federal agency authorized by Congress or the President to issue rules or regulations. It now consists of several hundred volumes.

Although the *Federal Register* is the source for publication of regulations, it alone is insufficient to locate the present status of a particular regulation. It is analogous to the *Statutes at Large.* Although the latter contains every law ever passed by Congress, it is not useful in locating a statute on a particular subject. For this, of course, the *U.S. Code* must be consulted. In order to give subject access to federal regulations in a similar manner, the *Code of Federal Regulations* was also established. This bears the same relationship to the *Federal Register* as the *U.S. Code* does to the *Statutes at Large.*

2. Code of Federal Regulations (C.F.R.) [7]

This set is a codification of the *Federal Register* wherein all regulations, and amendments thereto, in force, are codified and brought

[5] Panama Ref. Co. v. Ryan, 293 U.S. 388 (1935).

[6] K. DAVIS, ADMINISTRATIVE LAW TREATISE § 2.06 n. 5 (1958); *see also "The Federal Register And The Code of Federal Regulations—a Reappraisal,"* 80 HARV.L.REV. 439 (1966).

[7] For a more detailed history of the publication of the earlier editions of the *Code of Federal Regulations, see* E. POLLACK, FUNDAMENTALS OF LEGAL RESEARCH 366–72 (3d ed. 1967).

together by subject. It is in fifty titles similar to the arrangement of the *U.S. Code* and published in pamphlet form. Each year, the pamphlet volumes of the *Code of Federal Regulations* are revised at least once and are issued on a quarterly basis approximately as follows:

Title 1 through Title 16	as of January 1
Title 17 through Title 27	as of April 1
Title 28 through Title 41	as of July 1
Title 42 through Title 50	as of October 1

Each new volume when issued contains the text of regulations still in force, incorporating those promulgated during the preceding twelve months, and deleting those revoked. Through this process, all of the regulations first published chronologically in the *Federal Register* and currently in force are rearranged by subject and by agency in the fifty titles of the *Code of Federal Regulations.* For example, all of the regulations issued by the Federal Communications Commission, and still in force, may be located in Title 47 of the *CFR* and are up-to-date through October 1st of the current year.

The contents of the *Federal Register* are required to be judicially noticed [8] while the *Code of Federal Regulations* is *prima facie* evidence [9] of the original documents which were published in the *Federal Register.*

3. Up-Dating The Code of Federal Regulations

After a title of the *CFR* has been newly published as explained above, an agency may issue new regulations or amend or revoke a regulation. These changes will be published in the *Federal Register.* Thus, whenever using a volume of the *CFR,* it is always imperative to ascertain if the section of the *CFR* being consulted has been changed in any way subsequent to the effective date of the regulations in the particular volume of the *CFR.* To accomplish this, three tables must be consulted:

a. *LSA: List of CFR Sections Affected*

This is a monthly pamphlet which indicates the changes made since the latest publication of the *CFR* volumes. The December issue cumulates all changes for Titles 1–16, the March issue contains all changes for Titles 17–27, the June issue changes for Titles 28–41, and the September issue for Titles 42–50.

[8] 44 U.S.C. sec. 1507 (1976).

[9] *Id.* sec. 1510(e).

b. *Cumulative List of Parts Affected*

As the list described in 3a above is issued monthly, a further check must be made for any later changes. This is accomplished by checking in the latest issue of the daily *Federal Register* in the section entitled *Cumulative List of Parts Affected.*

c. *Shepard's Code of Federal Regulation Citations*

The use of this set is explained in Chapter 15. However, the importance of using this set in order to obtain the most recent status of a CFR section is emphasized here.

SECTION C. FINDING FEDERAL REGULATIONS

1. New Regulations

As has been noted, newly promulgated regulations are first published in the *Federal Register*. There is frequently a period of several months before new regulations may appear in the appropriate volumes of the *Code of Federal Regulations*. These may be located by using either the monthly, quarterly, or annual indexes to the *Federal Register*.

Many current regulations are also published in the *United States Code Congressional and Administrative News Service* and in the Advance Pamphlets to the *United States Code Service*. Each of these sets has its own index.

2. Regulations in Force

a. *Index Method*

A new index volume to the CFR is issued semiannually. This index includes in one alphabet both subject entries and the names of administrative agencies. Consequently, one can consult it either under the name of an agency or under a specific subject heading. Since January 1980, the subject terms used are taken from a thesaurus developed by the Office of the Federal Register. This now assures that the same subject headings will be used in the Index if two or more agencies use different terms covering the same concept. For example, in its regulations, one agency may use the word, "compensation", another "pay" and a third "salaries". By the use of the thesaurus, references to all three of these regulations will appear in the CFR Index under the subject heading "Wages".[10]

The Index always refers to the appropriate Title of the CFR and then to the specific Part within the Title. [See Illustration 78]

[10] *Thesaurus of Indexing Terms* 45 Fed. Reg. 2999 (Jan. 15, 1980).

b. *Parallel Table of Statutory Authorities and Rules*

If the citation is known to a statute or Presidential Executive Order which authorized an agency or administrator to issue regulations, this Table will indicate where administrative regulations promulgated under such authority will be found in the CFR. This Table is located in the *Finding Aids* Section of the CFR Index. [See Illustration 79]

It should be noted that as the CFR volumes are revised annually on a quarterly schedule, the latest semiannual CFR Index will include reference to some material in the daily issues of the *Federal Register*. The tables described in B–3, a–b *supra* should always be consulted to bring the CFR up to date.

If none of the above techniques is successful in locating a desired regulation, the *Finding Aids* Section in the current CFR Index should be consulted for other possibilities.

3. Regulations No Longer in Force

At times it is necessary to locate regulations that are no longer in force. For example, a dispute may arise over the ownership of mineral leases on public lands in which the determination of the rights of the parties involved depends on the interpretation of the regulations that were in force at the time of signing the leases. To obtain the text of these regulations, it will be necessary to examine the title of CFR that contained the regulations at the time when the lease was signed. This may be accomplished by examining the index volume to CFR for the year involved and then the CFR volume which contained the regulations in force at the time.[11]

4. U. S. Government Manual

This is an annually published directory of general information about the federal government, with emphasis upon the executive branch and regulatory agencies. Each department and agency is described in concise form with citations to the statutes creating the department or agency; a description of functions and authority, names and functions of major officials; organization charts and bibliographies of major publications.

[11] Two private publishing companies have published, in microform, a cumulation of the CFR title by title. The Information Handling Services has published the CFR, title by title, in microfiche from 1938–78, with plans for periodic cumulations. It also has prepared an extensive index of the CFR for the years 1977–79, with plans to publish annual current indexes.

The Trans-Media Company has published, in roll microfilm, the CFR, cumulated title by title, for the years 1938–71, 1972–76, 1977–78. It also provides its subscribers with a detailed Guide to its microfilm edition of the CFR.

Appendix A lists all abolished and transferred agencies with an indication of what has happened to the functions for which they had responsibility. For example, under *United States Civil Service Commission*, it is noted that it has been redesignated as the *Merit System Protection Board* and its functions were transferred to the *Board and Office of Personnel Management* by the Reorganization Plan No. 2 of 1978.

Appendix B lists commonly used abbreviations and acronyms.

Appendix C contains the text of the Freedom of Information Act, the Privacy Act of 1974, and the Government in the Sunshine Act.

Appendix D lists the Standard Federal Regions, the Federal Regional Councils, and the Federal Executive Board.

Appendix E lists all agencies, in alphabetical order, which appear in the *Code of Federal Regulations.*

There are also separate indexes for names, subjects and agencies.

The *United States Government Manual* is a component unit of the *Federal Register* and the *Code of Federal Regulations.* It frequently will be useful to consult this volume before starting research on an administrative law problem.

5. Federal Regulatory Directory [12]

This is an annual publication which is helpful to use in connection with the *United States Government Manual.*

Part I discusses the topic of regulation and the current issues involving federal administrative agencies.

Part II contains extensive profiles of the largest and more important agencies.

Part III contains summary information on most of the other federal agencies.

SECTION D. ILLUSTRATIONS FOR FEDERAL REGISTER & CFR

Problem: Are licenses required in order to engage in whaling?

78. Page from Index Volume to CFR

79. Page from Finding Aids CFR Index Section

80–81. Pages from Title 50, CFR

82–83. Pages from issue of CFR: List of CFR Sections Affected Pamphlet

[12] Published by Congressional Quarterly, Inc. 1979/80–.

84. Page from Cumulative List of Parts Affected in an issue of the Federal Register

[Illustration 78]

PAGE FROM SEMI-ANNUAL INDEX VOLUME TO CFR

Step 1.

Consult the latest semi-annual index to the CFR. As in using any index, the most specific term should be used first. In this instance, it would be whales or whaling. While not shown, the CFR index has a reference under these terms to Marine Mammals.

Note the citation to 50 CFR 230 after the sub-entry, Whaling Provisions. This refers to Part 230 of Title 50 of the CFR.

[Illustration 79]

PAGE FROM PARALLEL TABLE OF STATUTORY AUTHORITIES AND RULES: CFR INDEX VOLUME

16 U. S. C. 826i CFR Index

United States Code	Code of Federal Regulations
16 U. S. C. 826i	18 CFR Part 2 Parts 33–35 Part 125 Part 141
831 through 831dd	18 CFR Parts 1300–1306 Part 1308
835 et seq	43 CFR Part 416
835c note	43 CFR Part 17
835c–1	43 CFR Part 17
835c–4	43 CFR Part 413
852c	50 CFR Parts 13–14
916 et seq	50 CFR Part 351
916a–1	50 CFR Part 230
916j	50 CFR Part 230
921	43 CFR Part 17
951	50 CFR Part 280
955	50 CFR Part 281

Step 1–a.

An alternative method of finding CFR Regulations.

There are times when the U.S.C. citation to the statutes which delegates to an agency the authority to issue regulations is known. In such instances the Parallel Table of Statutory Authorities and Rules Section in the Index Volume to CFR can be used to locate the citations to regulations in the CFR. For example, statutory authorization for issuing whaling licenses is found at 16 U.S.C. 916j.

United States Code	Code of Federal Regulations
1151 through 1187	50 CFR Part 215
1201 through 1205	43 CFR Part 17 50 CFR Part 254
1241 through 1249	36 CFR Part 251 43 CFR Part 8370
1241	43 CFR Part 8300 Part 8350
1241 et seq	36 CFR Part 212 43 CFR Part 8000 Part 8340
1246	36 CFR Part 261
1271 through 1287	36 CFR Part 251 43 CFR Part 8370
1271	43 CFR Part 8300 Part 8350
1271 et seq	43 CFR Part 8000
1277	43 CFR Part 2110
1281	36 CFR Part 261
1281c	43 CFR Part 8340
1301	23 CFR Part 771
1311	7 CFR Part 752
1317	50 CFR Part 216

602

[Illustration 80]

PAGE FROM TITLE 50 OF CFR

§ 230.1 **Title 50—Wildlife and Fisheries**

SUBCHAPTER D—WHALING

PART 230—WHALING PROVISIONS

DEFINITIONS

Sec.
230.1 Factoryship.
230.2 Land station.
230.3 Secondary processing land station.
230.4 Whale catcher.
230.5 Whales.
230.6 Whale products.

LICENSES AND SCIENTIFIC PERMITS

→230.10 Licenses required to engage in whaling.
230.11 Applications for licenses.
230.12 Schedule of fees.
230.13 Applications for scientific permits.

CLOSED SEASONS

230.20 Whale catchers attached to land stations taking baleen whales.
230.21 Whale catchers attached to land stations taking sperm whales.
230.22 Whale catchers attached to factoryships taking sperm whales.

CATCH QUOTAS

230.25 Fin and sei whale quotas for the

WITH WHALES

230.50 Molesting of whales prohibited.

INSPECTION AND ENFORCEMENT

230.60 Fish and Wildlife Service employees designated as enforcement officers.
230.61 State officers designated as enforcement officers.
230.62 Disposal of perishable seized whales and whale products.

SUBSISTENCE

Sec.
230.70 General.
230.71 Definitions.
230.72 Prohibited acts.
230.73 Licenses.
230.74 Quotas.
230.75 Salvage of stinkers.
230.76 Reporting by whaling captains.
230.77 Penalties.

AUTHORITY: Sec. 12, 64 Stat. 425; 16 U.S.C. 916j. ←

SOURCE: 33 FR 5953, Apr. 18, 1968, unless otherwise noted.

CROSS REFERENCE: For the regulations of the International Whaling Commission, see Part 351 of this title.

DEFINITIONS

§ 230.1 Factoryship.

The word "factoryship" means a vessel in which or on which whales are treated or processed, whether wholly or in part.

§ 230.2 Land station.

The words "whale catcher" mean a vessel used for the purpose of hunting, killing, taking, towing, holding on to, or scouting for whales.

§ 230.5 Whales.

(a) "Baleen whale" means any whale which has baleen or whale bone in the mouth, i.e., any whale other than a toothed whale.

372

Step 2.

Refer to the part indicated in the Index. After each part, a detailed list of sections of the part is given. In this instance, Section 230.10 appears to be relevant.

Note how at the end of the listing of the sections, the statutory authority for this regulation is given as well as the citation where this regulation originally appeared in the Federal Register.

This information is given for each part in the CFR.

[Illustration 81]
PAGE FROM TITLE 50 OF CFR

Chapter II—National Marine Fisheries Service **§ 230.11**

(b) "Blue whale" (Balaenoptera or Sibbaldus musculus) means any whale known by the name of blue whale, Sibbald's rorqual, or sulphur bottom.

(c) "Fin whale" (Balaenoptera physalus) means any whale known by the name of common finback, common rorqual, finback, finner, fin whale, herring whale, razorback, or true fin whale.

(d) "Gray whale" (*Rhachianectes glaucus* or *Eschrichtius gibbosus*) means any whale known by the name of gray whale, California gray, devil fish, hard head, mussel digger, gray back, or rip sack.

(e) "Humpback whale" (*Megaptera nodosa* or *novaeangliae*) means any whale known by the name of bunch, humpback, humpback whale, hump-backed whale, hump whale, or hunch-backed whale.

(f) "Minke whale" (*Balaenoptera acutorostrata, B. Davidsoni, B. huttoni*) means any whale known by the name of lesser rorqual, little piked whale, minke whale, pike-headed whale, or sharp-headed finner.

(g) "Right whale" (*Balaena mysticetus, Eubalaena glacialis, E. australis,* etc.; *Neobala:na marginata*) means any whale known by the name of Atlantic right whale, Arctic right whale,

LICENSES AND SCIENTIFIC PERMITS

§ 230.10 Licenses required to engage in whaling.

(a) No person shall engage in the taking or processing of any whales without first having obtained an appropriate license.

(b) No permit or license shall be issued except as provided in § 230.13 and §§ 230.70 through 230.77. Licenses issued under § 230.73 shall be governed solely by the requirements of §§ 230.70 through 230.77.

[36 FR 7432, Apr. 20, 1971, as amended at 44 FR 19409, Apr. 3, 1979]

§ 230.11 Applications for licenses.

(a) Applications for licenses to engage in the taking or processing of whales of the species listed in § 230.10, shall be submitted to the Bureau of Commercial Fisheries through the Regional Director, Pacific Northwest Region (Region 1), Bureau of Commercial Fisheries, 6116 Arcade Building, 1319 Second Avenue, Seattle, Wash. 98101. Such applications shall be accompanied by the affidavit or affidavits prescribed in sections 6(d) and (e) of the Whaling Convention Act of 1949 and by a check or U.S. Postal Money Order payable to the Bureau

Step 3.

Read the specific Section 230.10. This indicates that licenses are necessary and the next section indicates how they may be obtained.

When the cover of Title 50, from which this illustration is taken, is consulted, it will be seen that it is "Revised as of October 1 (of the current or past year)". Hence, it must be ascertained if any changes have subsequently occurred. This is accomplished by checking the pamphlet: LIST OF CFR SECTIONS AFFECTED.

See next illustration.

§ 230.6 Whale products.

The words "whale products" mean any unprocessed part of a whale and blubber, meat, bones, whale oil, sperm oil, spermaceti, meal, and baleen.

means of a letter to the Regional Director information specifying the names and addresses of the owner and operator of the vessel, the name, official number and home port of the vessel, its length, beam, and draft, its

373

[Illustration 82]

PAGE FROM AN ISSUE OF LIST OF SECTIONS AFFECTED PAMPHLET

Step 4.

After reading appropriate regulations in current CFR volume, research has to be made current by checking in this List.

It is issued monthly with the December, March, June, and September issues consisting of an annual cumulation for the titles indicated on the cover.

LSA

List of CFR Sections Affected

March 1980

SAVE THIS ISSUE
for Annual Cumulation
of Titles 17–27*

CONTAINING:

TITLES 1–16
Changes Jan. 2, 1980
through Mar. 31, 1980

TITLES 17–27
*Changes April 2, 1979
through Mar. 31, 1980

TITLES 28–41
Changes July 2, 1979
through Mar. 31, 1980

TITLES 42–50
Changes Oct. 1, 1979
through Mar. 31, 1980

PARALLEL TABLE OF U.S.C.–C.F.R.

[Illustration 83]

PAGE FROM CFR LIST OF CFR SECTIONS AFFECTED

146 **LSA—LIST OF CFR SECTIONS AFFECTED**

CHANGES OCTOBER 1, 1979 THROUGH MARCH 31, 1980

Title 50, Chapter I—Continued

Page

26.37 Added; interim ---------- *14194
32.11 Amended ---------------- 61969
32.12 Amended ---------------- 59910, 61966, 61967, 61970, 63106
32.21 Amended ---------------- 61969
32.22 Amended --------- 56940, 61966
32.31 Amended ---------------- 61969
32.32 Amended ---- 56941, 61966, 67670
Amended --------------- *3053, 7817
33.4 Amended ---------------- 61969
33.5 Amended ---------------- 59911, 62899, 74841, 75387–75391, 77172, 77174
Amended -------------------- *1027, 2046, 3589, 6948, 8307, 9939, 13093, 14866, 16195, 18011, 20485
Corrected ------------------ *18377

Chapter II—National Marine Fisheries Service, National Oceanic and Atmospheric Administration, Department of Commerce

216 Determination ------------ 57100
Temporary regulation --------- *7262
Determination --------- *9284, 13094
230 Temporary regulation ------ 59911
Removed ------------------ *11134
→ 230.10 (b) revised ------------ *20488
230.70—230.77 Undesignated
cen...
230.70
230.71
230.72
Revis
230.73
230.74
ne\
Revis
230.75
230.76
230.77
258.5
258.20–
ed -------------------------- 61547
258.22 (g) revised ------------ *17018
285 Temporary regulation ------ 62900
296 Added -------------------- *6069
Appendix 1 corrected --------- *19256

Chapter III—International Regulatory Agencies (Fishing and Whaling)

351.30 Added ------------------ 76536

Page

351.34 (a)(1)(iii) amended; (a)(4) and tables 1 and 2 revised ------------------ 76536
351.35 Revised ------------------ 76539
351.36 (a)(1) removed; (a)(2) and (3) redesignated as (a)(1) and (2); new (a)(1) revised ---------------------- 76539
351.38 Revised ------------------ 76539
351.51 (a) amended ------------ 76539
351.72 Amended ---------------- 76539
351.75 Redesignated as 351.76; new 351.75 added -------------- 76539
351.76 Redesignated from 351.75 -- 76539

Chapter IV—Joint Regulations (United States Fish and Wildlife Service, Department of the Interior and National Marine Fisheries Service, National Oceanic and Atmospheric Administration, Department of Commerce); Endangered Species Committee Regulations

402.05 Removed -------------- *13022
424 Added ------------------- *13022
451 Added ------------------- *8627

Chapter VI—Fishery Conservation and Management, National Oceanic and Atmospheric Ad... ...nt of

-- *1029
-- 70481
-- *3590
- *11498
- *15182
-- 64421
-- 65590
05, 14046
*14587
Appendix II amended -------- *15935
611.20 (c) table I amended ---- 57102, 64418
(a) and (b) amended; (c) table removed; (c) revised ------ 76541
Appendix I added ------------ 76542
Appendix I amended ---- *1037, 14588
Table amended --------------- *9941
611.21 Existing text designated as (a); (b) added ------------ 76297

Step 4 (cont.).

Note that Section 230.10(b) has been revised. Page 20488 of the Federal Register for 1980 should be read for the text of the revision.

Note: Symbol (*) refers to 1980 page numbers

[Illustration 84]

PAGE FROM CFR PARTS AFFECTED IN AN ISSUE OF THE FEDERAL REGISTER

Federal Register / Vol. 45, No. 182 / Wednesday, September 17, 1980 / Reader Aids iii

320 59871
Proposed Rules:
111 .... 60452, 61318
310 60453

40 CFR

51 59874
52 .... 58340, 58526–58528, 59313, 59314, 59577–59580, 61293
81 .... 59150, 59315, 61293
117 61617
122 59317
125 61617
180 .... 58121, 60430
261 60903
409 59152
423 61617
Proposed Rules:
Ch. I 59180
4 60929
52 .... 58146, 58598, 58599 58881, 58923, 59177, 59178 59329, 59334, 59339, 59591, 59597, 60930, 60931, 61319, 61644
55 58381
65 59341
81 .... 59179, 60941
86 61645
116 59907
117 59907
120 59598
122 59343
162 58600
180 .... 58497–58500, 58600
401 60942
415 58383
717 58384
763 61966

41 CFR

Ch. 18 58843–58857
Ch. 101 61304
5A–1 58341
Ch. 101 58122
3–7 60903

42 CFR

57 60431
122 59132
405 .... 58123, 59153
Proposed Rules:
405 .... 59734, 60945
442 60945
447 59734
483 60945

43 CFR

2880 59879
Proposed Rules:
4 61322

44 CFR

9 .... 59520, 59538
64 .... 58529–58531, 60904
65 .... 58341, 60905
67 .... 58342–58346, 60437
311 59880
Proposed Rules:
59 59346
60 59346
67 .... 58148, 58149, 58601 59348, 59599, 59602, 60453, 60946, 60953

360 59344

45 CFR

134 58362
233 58125
400 59318
1050 59153
1061 .... 58363, 58534
1068 59153
Proposed Rules
100a 59349
100b 59349
122b 60382
1010 60954
1060 60954

46 CFR

148 60913
Proposed Rules:
521 58923
536 58385

47 CFR

1 59880
2 59880
21 61305
68 61631
73 .... 58539, 58540, 59887 61305, 61632
74 61305
76 60186
83 .... 60438, 61306
90 59880
Proposed Rules:
Ch. I 58608
61 60955
63 61646
73 .... 58150, 58609–58629 59350, 59360, 59361, 59908, 61646

49 CFR

25 59154
173 59887
178 59887

1111 .... 58632, 61335
1136 61649
1137 61326
1138 61337
1311 61337
1331 58166

50 CFR

17 61944
20 .... 58540, 61532
32 .... 58552–58554, 58867, 58869, 59171, 59172, 59581, 60441–60444
33 58554
258 60913
285 59586
611 58870
651 61634
674 59172
Proposed Rules:
17 .... 58166, 58168, 58171, 59909
23 60455
32 .... 59602, 59603
33 59603
80 59914
222 60956
223 60956
224 60956
225 60956
226 60956
277 60956
601 58632
611 .... 59914, 60457, 60957
652 61341
656 60457
662 60957
672 59914
680 60957
810 60455

Step 5.

Check the table of CFR Parts Affected in the latest available issue of the Federal Register. This supplements the List of CFR Parts Affected pamphlets.

In this instance, no changes have been made to Section 230.10 of Title 50 of the CFR.

Depending on the title being searched and the month in which the search is taking place, it may be necessary to check the cumulative table in the previous month's issues of the Federal Register.

SECTION E. PRESIDENTIAL DOCUMENTS

Although most of the contents of the *Federal Register* and the *Code of Federal Regulations* result from the activities of federal agencies operating under delegated powers from Congress, the President also has the authority to issue regulations that have legal effect. This authority is both constitutional and statutory. The publications of Presidential documents are issued in the following forms.

1. Proclamations

While there is no legal difference between Presidential Proclamations and Executive Orders, the former is customarily used for Presidential action that has no legal effect, such as Proclamation 4579 in which the President [see Illustration 85] designated a Citizenship Day and Constitution Week.

Proclamations appear in:

a. *Statutes at Large.*

b. *Federal Register.*

c. *Weekly Compilation of Presidential Documents.*

d. C.F.R. Title 3 and compilation volumes of Title 3.

e. *U.S. Code Congressional and Administrative News.*

f. *U.S. Code Service. Advance Pamphlets.*

2. Executive Orders [13]

These are generally used by the President to direct and govern activities of government officials and agencies.

Executive Orders are published in all the sources publishing Proclamations except the *Statutes at Large.*[14]

3. Codification of Presidential Proclamations and Executive Orders

This publication was started in 1979 by the Office of the Federal Register. Its purpose is to provide in one source Proclamations and Executive Orders which have general applicability and continuing effect. This codification has taken all of the previously published Proclamations and Executive Orders which were first separately published as issued and has brought them together by subject. Additionally, in each instance, amendments to the original documents have

[13] For a detailed study, *see* HOUSE COMM. ON GOVERNMENT OPERATIONS, 85th CONG., 1st SESS., EXECUTIVE ORDERS AND PROCLAMATIONS: A STUDY OF A USE OF PRESIDENTIAL POWERS (Comm. Print 1957).

[14] To locate Executive Orders issued prior to the publication of the *Federal Register* in 1936, *see* HISTORICAL RECORDS SURVEY, PRESIDENTIAL EXECUTIVE ORDERS (1944).

been incorporated in the text. This codification is arranged in fifty titles corresponding to those of the Code of Federal Regulations and covers the period from January 20, 1961 to January 20, 1977. Annual supplements are planned.

4. Reorganization Plans

By the provisions of 5 U.S.C. 901 *et seq.* (1976) the President is authorized to examine the organization of all agencies and make changes that provide for the better management of the executive branch of the government. The President is authorized to submit proposed reorganization plans to both houses of Congress. If after 60 days neither house has passed a resolution opposed to the plan, it goes into effect.

The President issues his proposed changes as Executive Orders. In addition to their publication in the sources indicated at 1 *supra,* reorganization plans are published as approved in 5 U.S.C., Appendix.

5. Weekly Compilation of Presidential Documents

This Office of the Federal Register publication is published every Monday and contains statements, messages and other presidential materials released by the White House. It includes an Index of Contents at the front of each issue for documents in it and a quarterly cumulative index at the back. The quarterly indexes are cumulated semiannually. Other finding aids are: lists of laws approved by the President, nominations submitted to the Senate, and a checklist of White House releases.

6. Public Papers of the Presidents

This set starts with the administration of President Herbert Hoover. The papers of Franklin Roosevelt and certain earlier Presidents were privately published. Now published annually in one or more volumes, the set includes a compilation of the Presidents' messages to Congress, public speeches, news conferences, and public letters. The final volume of each year contains a cumulative index to the volumes of that year. After all the volumes for an administration are published, a cumulative index for that President is privately published.[15]

Beginning with the 1977 volumes, which cover the first year of President Carter's administration, the set includes *all* of the material printed in the *Weekly Compilation of Presidential Documents.*

[15] The Cumulated Indexes to the Public Papers of the Presidents of the United States (KTO Press 1977–).

7. Shepard's Code of Federal Regulations Citations

This set should always be consulted to obtain the latest status of Proclamations, Executive Orders, and Reorganization Plans.

SECTION F. ILLUSTRATIONS FOR PRESIDENTIAL DOCUMENTS

85–86. Examples of Presidential Proclamations

87–88. Examples of Presidential Executive Orders

[Illustration 85]

PAGE FROM TITLE 3, 1979 CODE OF FEDERAL REGULATIONS

Proclamations **Proc. 4579**

Proclamation 4579 • **July 19, 1978**

Citizenship Day and Constitution Week, 1978

By the President of the United States of America

A Proclamation

September 17, 1978, will mark the 191st anniversary of the signing, in Independence Hall, Philadelphia, of the Constitution of the United States. That great document has endured, with but few changes, as the finest foundation of government in the history of mankind.

By a joint resolution of February 29, 1952 (36 U.S.C. 153), Congress designated September 17 as Citizenship Day, in commemoration of the signing of the Constitution and in recognition of all who, by coming of age or by naturalization, have ... :nt to issue ... ay the flag c ... ust 2, 1956, ... eriod begin ... :ution Week

A Presidential Proclamation issued under the inherent authority of the President.

N ... es of America, call upon appropriate government officials to display the flag of the United States on all government buildings on Citizenship Day, September 17, 1978, the 191st anniversary of the signing of the Constitution. I urge Federal, State, and local officials, as well as leaders of civic, educational and religious organizations, to conduct suitable ceremonies and programs on that day.

I also designate as Constitution Week the period beginning September 17 and ending September 23, 1978, and urge all Americans to observe that week with ceremonies and activities in their schools, churches and in other suitable places in order to foster a better understanding of the Constitution and of the rights and duties of United States citizens.

IN WITNESS WHEREOF, I have hereunto set my hand this nineteenth day of July in the year of our Lord nineteen hundred seventy-eight, and of the Independence of the United States the two hundred and third.

JIMMY CARTER

35

40-002 O—79——4

[Illustration 86]

PAGE FROM TITLE 3, 1979 CODE OF FEDERAL REGULATIONS

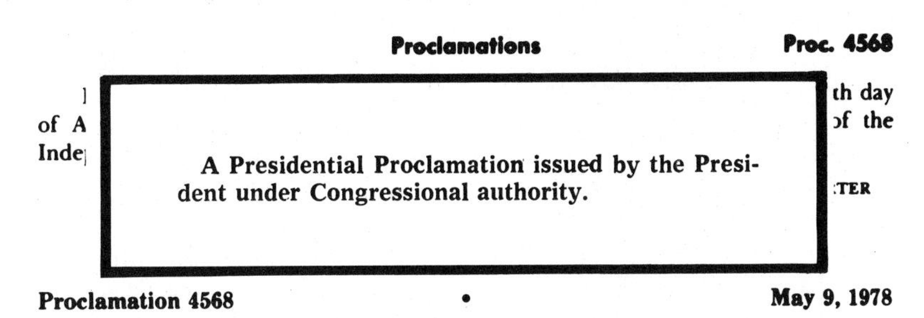
] ... th day of A ... of the Inde ... TER

A Presidential Proclamation issued by the President under Congressional authority.

Proclamation 4568 • **May 9, 1978**

Application of Certain Laws of the United States to the Northern Mariana Islands

By the President of the United States of America

A Proclamation

The Northern Mariana Islands, as part of the Trust Territory of the Pacific Islands, are administered by the United States under a Trusteeship Agreement between the United States and the Security Council of the United Nations (61 Stat. 3301). The United States has undertaken to promote the political development of the Trust Territory toward self-government or independence and to protect the rights and fundamental freedoms of its people.

In accordance with those obligations, the United States and the Northern Mariana Islands have entered into a Covenant to Establish a Commonwealth of the Northern Mariana Islands in Political Union with the United States of America (Public Law 94-241; 90 Stat. 263). Section 1004(a) of the Covenant provides that if the President finds a provision of the Constitution or laws of the United States to be inconsistent with the Trusteeship Agreement, the application of that provision to the Northern Mariana Islands may be suspended.

Certain provisions of law restrict jury service in Federal District Courts to United States citizens. The vast majority of the inhabitants of the Northern Mariana Islands are not citizens of the United States and consequently may not participate as jurors in proceedings before the United States District Court for the Northern Mariana Islands. They may also be deprived of the right to have their cases heard before juries selected at random from a fair cross-section of their community. These results would be contrary to the obligations assumed by the United States in the Trusteeship Agreement.

NOW, THEREFORE, I, JIMMY CARTER, President of the United States of America, by the authority vested in me by the Constitution and laws of the United States, including Section 1004(a) of the Covenant to Establish a Commonwealth of the Northern Mariana Islands in Political Union with the United States of America, do hereby find, declare and proclaim as follows:

Any provision of the Constitution or laws of the United States which prescribes United States citizenship as a qualification for service on a grand or petit jury in the District Court for the Northern Mariana Islands, including that provision contained in Section 1865(b)(1) of Title 28 of the United States Code, would be inconsistent with the Trusteeship Agreement if applied to a citizen of the Trust Territory of the

[Illustration 87]

PAGE FROM TITLE 3, 1979 CODE OF FEDERAL REGULATIONS

the information necessary for setting procurement targets and recording achievement. They shall keep the Administrator informed of plans and programs which affect labor surplus procurements, with particular attention to opportunities for minority firms.

1-303. In accord with Section 6 of the Office of Federal Procurement Policy Act (41 U.S.C. 405), the Administrator for Federal Procurement Policy shall be responsible for the overall direction and oversight of the policies affecting procurement programs for labor surplus areas.

JIMMY CARTER

THE WHITE HOUSE,
August 16, 1978.

A Presidential Executive Order issued under the inherent power of the President.

Executive Order 12074 • **August 16, 1978**

Urban and Community Impact Analyses

By the authority vested in me as President by the Constitution of the United States of America, and in order to establish an internal management procedure for identifying aspects of proposed Federal policies that may adversely impact cities, counties, and other communities, it is hereby ordered as follows:

1-1 *Urban and Community Impact Analyses.*

1-101. The Director of the Office of Management and Budget shall: (a) develop criteria for identifying major policy proposals to be analyzed; (b) formulate standards regarding the content and format of impact analyses; and (c) establish procedures for the submission and review of such analyses.

1-102. The Director of the Office of Management and Budget and the Assistant to the President for Domestic Affairs and Policy shall review the analyses.

1-2. *Agency Responsibilities.*

1-201. Executive agencies shall prepare urban and community impact analyses for major policy initiatives identified by the Office of Management and Budget, the Assistant to the President for Domestic Affairs and Policy, or the agencies themselves.

1-202. Each Executive agency shall, to the extent permitted by law, cooperate with the Director of the Office of Management and Budget and the Assistant to the President for Domestic Affairs and Policy in the performance of their functions

[Illustration 88]

PAGE FROM TITLE 3, 1979 CODE OF FEDERAL REGULATIONS

(b) In carrying out the functions in this Order, the Secretary of Commerce shall coordinate activities as appropriate with the Federal Communications Commission and make appropriate recommendations to it as the regulator of the private sector. Nothing in this Order reassigns any function vested by law in the Federal Communications Commission.

6-304. This Order shall be effective March 26, 1978.

A Presidential Executive Order issued by the President under Congressional authority.

Imported Objects of Cultural Significance

By virtue of the authority vested in me by the Act of October 19, 1965, entitled "An Act to render immune from seizure under judicial process certain objects of cultural significance imported into the United States for temporary display or exhibition, and for other purposes" (79 Stat. 985, 22 U.S.C. 2459), and as President of the United States of America, it is hereby ordered as follows:

SECTION 1. The Director of the International Communication Agency is designated and empowered to perform the functions conferred upon the President by the above-mentioned Act and shall be deemed to be authorized, without the approval, ratification, or other action of the President, (1) to determine that any work of art or other object to be imported into the United States within the meaning of the Act is of cultural significance, (2) to determine that the temporary exhibition or display of any such work of art or other object in the United States is in the national interest, and (3) to cause public notices of the determinations referred to above to be published in the FEDERAL REGISTER.

SEC. 2. The Director of the International Communication Agency, in carrying out this Order, shall consult with the Secretary of State with respect to the determination of national interest, and may consult with the Secretary of the Smithsonian Institution, the Director of the National Gallery of Art, and with such other officers and agencies of the Government as may be appropriate, with respect to the determination of cultural significance.

SEC. 3. The Director of the International Communication Agency is authorized to delegate within the Agency the functions conferred upon him by this Order.

SEC. 4. Executive Order No. 11312 of October 14, 1966 is revoked.

SEC. 5. Any order, regulation, determination or other action which was in effect pursuant to the provisions of Executive Order No. 11312 shall remain in effect until changed pursuant to the authority provided in this Order.

SECTION G. FEDERAL ADMINISTRATIVE DECISIONS

1. Agency Decisions

Many federal administrative agencies also serve in a quasi-judicial manner and in performing this function issue decisions. The Federal Communications Commission, for example, is authorized by Congress to license radio and television stations. It also has the authority to enforce its regulations covering the operations of these stations. When stations allegedly violate the terms of the statute or the regulations, the Federal Communications Commission will hear the charges and issue decisions.

Decisions of administrative agencies are not published in the *Federal Register* but in separately published sets of volumes. They are available in two forms: (1) official publications of the Government Printing Office and (2) unofficial publications of commercial publishers. The latter will be discussed in Chapter 14.

Official Publications of Federal Administrative Agencies. These are available in most law libraries, and in public and university libraries that are official depositories of the U. S. Government Printing Office. The format, frequency, and method of publication vary from agency to agency. Generally, they are issued on an infrequent schedule and poorly indexed. Some sets have separate volumes of indexes and digests and it is often necessary to check the indexes in the individual volumes of decisions. Some sets of federal administrative agencies do provide an advance sheet service.

2. Judicial Review of Agency Decisions

After an agency has issued a decision, it may, in most instances, be appealed to the federal courts. These decisions may be found by consulting the following sets:

a. *West's Federal Practice Digest, 2d; Modern Federal Practice Digest; Federal Digest.*

b. *U. S. Supreme Court Digest.*

c. *American Digest System* in the absence of the preceding digests.

d. *Shepard's U. S. Administrative Citations.* (Discussed in Chapter 15).

e. Treatises on administrative law. (Discussed in Chapter 18).

3. Representative Examples of Currently Published Official Decisions of Federal Administrative Tribunals

a. Civil Aeronuatics Board. *Reports,* vol. 1 *et seq.* (1939 to date).

b. Comptroller General. *Decisions,* vol. 1 *et seq.* (1921 to date).

c. Federal Communications Commission. *Reports,* vol. 1 *et seq.* (1934 to date).

d. Federal Trade Commission. *Decisions,* vol. 1 *et seq.* (1915 to date).

e. National Labor Relations Board. *Decisions and Orders,* vol. 1 *et seq.* (1935 to date).

f. Securities and Exchange Commission. *Decisions,* vol. 1 *et seq.* (1934 to date).

SECTION H. FEDERAL REGISTER: OTHER FEATURES

In addition to the publication of the rules and regulations from the Office of the President and the executive agencies, issues of the *Federal Register* contain the following features.

1. *Highlights.* On the front page of each issue, the more important documents are summarized.

2. *Reminders.* This lists *Rules Going Into Effect Today, Next Week's Deadlines for Comments on Proposed Rules, Next Week's Public Hearings,* and *Next Week's Meetings.*

3. *Proposed Rules.* This section contains notices of proposed issuance of rules and regulations. Its purpose is to give interested persons an opportunity to participate in the rule-making process prior to the adoption of final rules.

4. *Notices.* This section of the *Federal Register* contains documents other than rules or proposed rules that are applicable to the public.

5. *Consumer Subject Listing.* At the end of the Table of Contents in each issue, items are listed which have been identified by the issuing agency as documents of particular interest to consumers.

6. *List of Public Laws.* Each issue lists those public bills from the current session of Congress which have recently become Federal law.

7. *Calendar of Federal Regulations.* This Calendar is published semiannually. It is produced by the Regulatory Council and it is designed to be a comprehensive listing of proposed important regulations and will give information on their objectives and benefits, the sectors of the economy affected, the economic implications, and major alternatives under study.

SECTION I. OTHER METHODS OF FINDING FEDERAL REGULATIONS

As discussed in the previous sections of this chapter, the rules and regulations and other documents that serve as the written sources for administrative law can all be located through the use of the *Federal Register*, the *Code of Federal Regulations*, and other publications of administrative agencies. But it is frequently an awkward and time-consuming task necessitating the constant checking of these sources. In the next chapter, looseleaf services are discussed. Most of these services consist primarily of documents that appear in the *Federal Register*, or in the publications of administrative agencies. They are usually better indexed and contain other features facilitating the location of information. Consequently, when the necessity to research a problem of administrative law arises, it is frequently better practice to ascertain if a looseleaf service covering the topic under research exists and to use that service rather than the official publications discussed above.

SECTION J. STATE ADMINISTRATIVE REGULATIONS AND DECISIONS

1. State Regulations

The regulations and decisions of state agencies are variously published by the states. In most states,[16] the administrative regulations are officially codified and published in sets similar to the *Code of Federal Regulations*. In other states, each agency issues its own regulations and it is necessary that inquiries be directed to the pertinent agency.

2. State Administrative Decisions

Many state agencies also publish their decisions.[17] These more commonly are those of the Unemployment Compensation Commissions, Tax Branches, and Public Utility Commissions.

3. Research in State Administrative Law

a. Check the state code to determine if the state has an Administrative Procedure Act, and if the method of publication for regulations is prescribed.

[16] Tseng and Pederson, *Acquisition of State Administrative Rules and Regulations—Update 1979*, 31 ADMIN.LAW REV. 405 (1979).

[17] Allen, *State Administrative Decisions: A Very Preliminary Listing*, 72 LAW LIB.J. 276 (1979).

b. Check the state's organization manual to determine the agencies which issue regulations or decisions.

c. Many states have local legal encyclopedias or local administrative law treatises. These should be consulted.

SECTION K. SUMMARY

1. Federal Register

a. Types of federal documents published in it

(1) Regulations and Rulings of Federal Agencies.

(2) Proposed Regulations and Rules.

(3) Notices of Agencies.

(4) Presidential Executive Orders.

b. Indexes

(1) Monthly, Quarterly, Annually.

(2) *Cumulative List of Parts Affected.*

This table brings up to date the monthly issues of *Cumulative List of CFR Sections Affected.*

c. Frequency of Publication

Began in 1936. Published Monday through Friday, except on the day following an official federal holiday.

d. Publications in the *Federal Register* must be judicially noted.

2. Code of Federal Regulations

a. Contains all regulations which first appeared in the *Federal Register,* are of a general and permanent nature, and are still in force.

b. Arranged by subject in 50 titles similar to the *U. S. Code.*

c. Each title is subdivided into Chapters, Subchapters, Parts, and Sections. It is cited by Title and Section.

d. Each title is in separate pamphlets. Each title is re-published once a year, in which new material is added, and repealed or obsolete regulations are deleted.

e. Regulations published in CFR are *prima facie* evidence of the text.

f. Indexes.

(1) Annual subject and agency index.

(2) *Monthly List of CFR Sections Affected.*

This list indicates any changes in the semi-annual volumes of the CFR.

g. The *finding aids* section in the semiannual index has Parallel Tables of Authorities or Rules, and other aids for assisting in the location of federal administrative documents.

3. U. S. Government Manual

a. Annual Handbook.

b. Describes administrative organizations whose regulations are published in the *Federal Register*.

c. Information on Congress, the federal judiciary and important agency personnel.

d. Subject index.

4. Federal Administrative Decisions

a. Official publications published by U. S. Government Printing Office.

b. Unofficially published by commercial publishers.

5. State Administrative Regulations and Decisions

a. Most states have codified their administrative rules.

b. Some states publish the decisions of administrative agencies.

Chapter 14

LOOSELEAF SERVICES

SECTION A. INTRODUCTION TO LOOSELEAF SERVICES

The rapid growth of statutory and case law has caused a major change in the literature of the law, but it is the expansion of the administrative agency as an arm of the executive branch that has created the greatest obstacle to effective legal research. This is especially true in the area of public law where administrative regulations and rulings play so large a role. Over the past forty years such rules and regulations have shown phenomenal growth, both in numbers and complexity. Thus while cases and statutes can still be located through the traditional means of digests, annotations and citators, research that involves the publications of administrative agencies demands a broadening of the research focus. For example, to adequately research a problem in the law of taxation, a researcher must locate not only relevant statutes and court decisions, but regulations of the Internal Revenue Service and the Treasury Department, rulings of the Commissioner of Internal Revenue, news releases, technical information bulletins, Tax Court decisions, and other agency documents. A researcher attempting to find the answer to a tax problem using only the *U. S. Code,* the digests, the *Federal Register* and the *Code of Federal Regulations* would find it not only cumbersome but at times impossible.

It was the inaccessibility, complexity and bulk of administrative regulations and decisions that prompted the publication of looseleaf services or reporters by private publishers.[1] As the name indicates, looseleaf services consist of separate, perforated pages in special binders that simplify the insertion, removal and substitution of individual pages. This characteristic allows the publisher to update continuously the material in a process of constant editing, introducing what is new, removing what is superseded. The speed and accuracy afforded by this on-going revision are two of the looseleaf services' greatest values.

The looseleaf format allows for creativity in organizational approach. Most, however, attempt to consolidate into one source the statutes, court decisions and commentary on a particular legal topic. By this means a researcher can find all relevant material, both pri-

[1] Neal, *Loose-Leaf Reporting Services,* 62 LAW LIB.J. 153 (1969).

mary and secondary, in one place. Further, most services provide current awareness notices on the topic, which can include news of proposed legislation, pending agency decisions and even informed rumor.

The convenience, currentness, and excellent indexing of looseleaf services make them the best place to begin researching most administrative law problems. It should be noted that in many rapidly developing areas of the law, like privacy, the environment, consumer protection and others, the looseleaf service may be the only research tool available.

Looseleaf services vary in content and coverage, reflecting both the subject area of the service and the editorial policy of the publisher. This chapter can describe only those features that are common to most services. When using any looseleaf service, one should be alert to its individual characteristics, and special attention should be paid to the introduction and prefatory materials supplied by the publisher.[2]

SECTION B. USING LOOSELEAF SERVICES

1. In General

Most looseleaf services have the following common elements:

a. Full text of the statutes on the topic, with significant legislative history.

b. Full text of administrative regulations, and either full text or digests of all relevant court and agency decisions.

c. Editorial comment and explanatory notes.

d. Subject or Topical indexes.

e. Tables of cases and statutes.

f. Indexes to current materials.

g. Current Reports summarizing recent developments. Such reports are issued either weekly, bi-weekly, or monthly.

2. Using Commerce Clearing House or Prentice-Hall Looseleaf Services

Commerce Clearing House (CCH) and Prentice-Hall (P–H) are two of the major publishers of looseleaf services. Although their publications run the full spectrum of form and content, the underly-

2 This is particularly necessary when using looseleaf services on taxation or labor law because the magnitude of materials on these subjects makes the looseleaf services very complex. For more detailed information on taxation *see* Chapter 24.

ing organizational principle of each publisher is the same. This allows them to be discussed together.

CCH and P–H services range from those complete in one binder to those that fill a dozen or more. Regardless of size, they commonly share similar features. They begin with an introductory section that discusses the use and organization of the service. The importance of this feature cannot be over-emphasized. A careful reading of it may save the researcher both time and frustration. The volume(s) will be divided into sections by tab cards. These offer quick access to major topic headings. Typically there will be a comprehensive index to the entire service (Topical Index in CCH, Master Index in P–H). In addition, some services have special indexes to particular topics or volumes. The quality of the indexing is generally quite high, since both publishers strive to provide as many access points as possible.

The indexes are made more useful by the unique, dual numbering system employed in these services. Under this system, in addition to normal pagination, there is a "paragraph" number assigned to each topic area. These numbers may encompass one paragraph or fifty pages. This flexibility of format allows for constant additions and deletions to the text without a total disruption of the indexing system. Research can begin by consulting one of the indexes, which will refer to the appropriate paragraph number. By turning to the correct paragraph number one can locate the pertinent material. In looseleaf services, page numbers are often used only for filing purposes.

The full texts of new court decisions and agency rulings, often supplied as part of the looseleaf service, are generally placed in a separate volume or section. Each case or ruling is commonly assigned its own paragraph number, and can be located in any one of several ways. Most services have tables of cases, statutes, and administrative regulations. When a citation to one of these is encountered, research can begin by consulting the appropriate table and obtaining the paragraph number where the citation is discussed. Both services have special indexes which cross-reference from materials found under the paragraph numbers to materials concerning current developments.

Materials on current developments are generally presented in the form of weekly bulletins that accompany the pages to be filed. These bulletins are often retained as part of the service, and constitute valuable research tools in themselves.

In general, the successful use of CCH or P–H looseleaf services requires the following three steps:

a. Locate where topic or topics under research are dealt with in the service by consulting the Topical or Master Index.

b. Read carefully all materials under paragraph numbers referred to by the Index. When digests of cases are given, note citations to cases so that the full text of decisions may be read.

c. Consult appropriate index or indexes to current materials.

Illustrations 89–94 demonstrate the use of a CCH Service.

3. Bureau of National Affairs, Inc.

The Bureau of National Affairs (BNA) is the third major publisher of looseleaf services. Its organizational principle differs from that of CCH and P–H. BNA's typical format consists of one or more three-ring binders in which periodic issues (or releases) are filed. Unlike CCH and P–H, the issues do not contain individual pages to be interfiled with existing text, but instead consist of pamphlet-size inserts numbered sequentially and filed chronologically. Thus there is no provision for revision of earlier issues. This format allows for greater speed of issue generation, at the expense of the comprehensiveness guaranteed by the interfiling system.

Each issue contains several separate components, usually including a summary and analysis of major developments, the text of pertinent legislation, and the text or a digest of court and agency actions. Such features as important speeches, government reports, book reviews and bibliographies may also be included. Each of these components is generally filed behind its own tab card. Thus each issue is an attempt to keep the practitioner fully informed of all developments in the subject area of the service.

BNA services feature cumulative indexes which offer topic access to the material. Since current issues supplement earlier ones there is no need for paragraph numbers, and simple pagination is used. There are also case tables for each service. BNA periodically supplies special storage binders for old issues, so that the main volumes can always contain current material.

BNA also has one large service which differs in arrangement from its other looseleaf services. This is its *Labor Relations Reporter*. This set has separate looseleaf volumes for the following areas of labor relations:

Labor Management Relations (Federal)

Labor Arbitration

Wages and Hours

Fair Employment Practices

State Labor Laws

Each of the looseleaf volumes for these units of the *Labor Relations Reporter* contains relevant statutes and regulations and court decisions. Periodically, court decisions are removed from the looseleaf volumes and reprinted in bound series of cases (e. g. *Labor Arbitration Cases, Wage and Hour Cases*).

Each set of cases also has its own index and digest where the cases are classified to BNA's classification scheme.

The entire set is unified by a *Master Index* looseleaf volume and a *Labor Relations Expediter* looseleaf volume. [See Illustrations 95–97]

4. Other Features of Looseleaf Services

Looseleaf services aim at providing complete information on a subject. Thus they frequently contain forms, reports on current Congressional activities, summaries of professional meetings, and other news deemed relevant to the researcher or practicing attorney. Those services which include state laws are generally arranged by states with the same paragraph number being assigned uniformly to the same topic for each state. In some instances, "all-state" charts are published which give citations to the various state codes. [See Illustration 98]

Many looseleaf services, as already indicated, report the full text of current court decisions that fall within the scope of a particular service. These are filed in a separate section or volume since they usually arrive with each mailing. In many instances, at the end of the year, the publisher will send to the subscriber a bound volume of the decisions for permanent reference. The looseleaf pages containing the decisions for the year can then be discarded. As an example, subscribers to Commerce Clearing House *Standard Federal Tax Reports* will receive bound volumes with the title *U. S. Tax Cases.* The latter contain decisions previously sent in looseleaf format. Similiarly, subscribers to BNA's *Labor Relations Reporter* will receive bound volumes called *Labor Relations Reference Manual(s),* which contain all cases on federal labor law. In all cases, headnotes and other editorial aids are prepared by the publishers. Some of these case series have come to be recognized as standard reference units. Of course, the decisions usually can also be found in official reporters or the *National Reporter System,* but some of these looseleaf sets have become so widely recognized for the speed, accuracy and ease of access that they are cited by the courts.[3]

[3] As was noted in Chapter 4, the decisions of the Federal District Courts are reported selectively. Some decisions not reported in the *Federal Supplement* are published in one of the subject looseleaf services. Consequently, it is frequently worthwhile to check the Table of Cases of these services for opinions not reported in the *Federal Supplement* or the *Federal Reporter.*

CCH, BNA and P–H are not the only publishers of looseleaf services, but most services will conform to either the interfiled or supplemented format. If the principles that underlie these forms are understood, any service should be usable. The most vital step will always be a careful reading of the publisher's introductory material. Section C lists looseleaf services by subject.

SECTION C. SELECTED LISTING OF REPORTER SERVICES BY LAW SCHOOL COURSE [4]

Note: This selected listing of looseleaf reporting services and specialized newsletters has been prepared as an aid to students wishing to see the types of information available for some law school courses. Omission from this list or inclusion in it does not indicate lack of recognition or endorsement.

1. Accounting

a. *Accountancy Law Reports* (CCH) monthly

2. Administrative Law

see also: Regulated Industries

a. *Administrative Law Service* (P&F) second series; bimonthly

b. *The United States Law Week* (BNA) weekly, Supreme Court decisions when rendered

3. Admiralty

a. *Benefits Review Board Service* (MB) biweekly

b. *Federal Maritime Commission Service* (Hawkins) periodically supplemented

c. *Shipping Regulation* (P&F) bimonthly

4. American Indian Law

a. *Indian Law Reporter* (Amer. Indian Lawyer Training Program, Inc.) monthly

5. Antitrust

includes: Unfair Competition; Trade Regulation

see also: Regulated Industries;

a. *Antitrust & Trade Regulation Report* (BNA) weekly

b. *FTC: Watch* (Wash. Regulatory Reporting Group) biweekly

c. *Trade Regulations Reports* (CCH) weekly

6. Arbitration

see: Labor Law

7. Aviation Law

a. *Aviation Cases in the Courts* (Hawkins) periodic supplementation

b. *Aviation Law Reports* (CCH) monthly

c. *Civil Aeronautics Board Service* (Hawkins) monthly

d. *National Transportation Safety Board Service* (Hawkins) monthly

[4] From *Reporter Services and Their Use* (© 1980). (Reprinted with permission of the Bureau of National Affairs).

8. Banking

see: Regulated Industries

9. Bankruptcy

a. *Bankruptcy Court Decisions* (CRRI) weekly

b. *Bankruptcy Law Reports* (CCH) biweekly

10. Civil Procedure

a. *Class Action Reporter* (Plus Publications, Inc.) bimonthly

b. *Federal Rules of Evidence News* (CAL) monthly

c. *Federal Rules Service* (CAL) monthly

d. *The United States Law Week* (BNA) weekly; Supreme Court decisions when rendered

11. Civil Rights

includes: Employment Discrimination; Fair Housing, Sex Based Discrimination

see also: Constitutional Law, Poverty Law, Women and the Law

a. *EEOC Compliance Manual* (BNA) periodic supplementation

b. *EEOC Compliance Manual* (CCH) periodic supplementation

c. *The Equal Employer* (FP) biweekly

d. *Equal Opportunity in Housing* (P–H) monthly

e. *Fair Employment Practice Series* (BNA) weekly

f. *Housing & Development Reporter* (BNA) weekly

g. *Mental Disability Law Reporter* (ABA) periodic

h. *The United States Law Week* (BNA) weekly; Supreme Court decisions when rendered

12. Collective Bargaining

see: Labor Law

13. Commercial Law

a. *Secured Transactions Guide* (CCH) biweekly

b. *The United States Law Week* (BNA) weekly; Supreme Court decisions when rendered

c. *Uniform Commercial Code Law Letter* (WGL) monthly

d. *Uniform Commercial Code Reporting Service* (CAL) monthly

14. Communications Law

see: Regulated Industries

15. Computers

see: Law and Science

16. Constitutional Law

a. *Media Law Reporter* (BNA) weekly

b. *The United States Law Week* (BNA) weekly; Supreme Court decisions when rendered

c. *U.S. Supreme Court Bulletin* (CCH) monthly

17. Consumer Law

a. *Consumer & Commercial Credit Guide* (P–H) monthly

b. *Consumer Credit & Truth-in-Lending Compliance Report* (WGL) monthly

c. *Consumer Credit Guide* (CCH) biweekly

d. *Consumer Product Law Guide* (P–H) biweekly

e. *Consumer Product Safety Guide* (CCH) weekly

f. *Consumer Protection Reporting Service* (CSG Press) Semiannual

g. *Fair Credit Reporting Manual* (WGL) monthly

18. Corporations

includes: Business Planning; Corporate Finance

a. *Corporate Practice Series* (BNA) portfolios and weekly memoranda

b. *Corporation Law Guide* (CCH) biweekly

c. *Corporation Service* (P–H) biweekly

d. *Professional Corporation Guide* (P–H) biweekly

19. Creditors' Rights

see: Bankruptcy; Commercial Law

20. Criminal Law and Procedure

a. *Arrest Law Bulletin* (Quinlan) monthly

b. *Criminal Law Reporter* (BNA) weekly

c. *The Criminal Law* (Nedrud) monthly

d. *The Law Officer's Bulletin* (BNA) biweekly

e. *Narcotics Law Bulletin* (Quinlan) monthly

f. *Search & Seizure Law Report* (CB) monthly

21. Domestic Relations

includes: Family Law; Juvenile Law

a. *Abortion Law Reporter* (National Abortion Rights Action League) irregular

b. *Family Law Reporter* (BNA) weekly

c. *Juvenile Law Newsletter* (Natl. Juvenile Law Cntr.) bimonthly

22. Education Law

a. *College & University Reports* (CCH) weekly

b. *College Law Digest* (Natl. Assn. College & Univ. Attorneys) bimonthly

c. *Education for the Handicapped Law Report* (CRR) biweekly

d. *Higher Education Admission Law Service* (Educational Testing Service) periodic supplementation

e. *Nolpe School Law Reporter* (Natl. Org. on Legal Probs. in Education) bimonthly

f. *School Law Bulletin* (Quinlan) monthly

23. Election Law

a. *Federal Election Campaign Financing Guide* (CCH) periodic supplementation

b. *Campaign Practices Reporter* (Plus Publications, Inc.) twice monthly

24. Energy Law

see: Environmental Law

25. Entertainment Law

includes: Sports Law

see also: Patents, Copyrights and Trademarks

a. *Entertainment Law Reporter* (E.L.R. Publishing Co.) twice monthly

26. Environmental Law

see also: Land Use Planning

a. *Chemical Regulation Reporter* (BNA) weekly

b. *Energy Controls* (P–H) weekly

c. *Energy Law Service* (CAL) monthly monographs

d. *Energy Management* (CCH) weekly

e. *The Energy Regulation Manual* (Aspen) quarterly

f. *Energy Users Report* (BNA) weekly

g. *Environmental Law Reporter* (Environmental Law Institute) monthly

h. *Environment Reporter* (BNA) weekly

i. *Environment Regulation Handbook* (EIC) monthly

j. *Hazardous Materials Transportation* (BNA) monthly

k. *International Environment Reporter* (BNA) monthly

l. *Noise Regulation Reporter* (BNA) weekly

m. *Pollution Control Guide* (CCH) weekly

27. Estate Planning

see also: Taxation

a. *Estate Planning & Taxation Coordinator* (RIA) biweekly

b. *Estate Planning Library* (P–H) periodic supplementation

c. *Inheritance, Estate & Gift Tax Reports* (CCH) weekly

d. *Tax Management: Estates, Gifts, Trusts* (BNA) portfolios supplemented periodically; biweekly memorandum

28. Family Law

see: Domestic Relations

a. *The Family Law Reporter* (BNA) weekly

29. Government Contracts

a. *Contract Appeals Decisions* (CCH) biweekly

b. *Extraordinary Contractual Relief Reporter* (FP) periodic supplementation

c. *Federal Contracts Reports* (BNA) weekly

d. *The Government Contractor* (FP) biweekly

e. *Government Contracts Reports* (CCH) weekly

30. Insurance

a. *Automobile Law Report* (CCH) biweekly

b. *Fire & Casualty Insurance Law Reports* (CCH) biweekly

c. *Insurance Guide* (P–H) monthly

d. *Life, Health & Accident Law Reports* (CCH) biweekly

e. *Loss Prevention and Control* (BNA) biweekly

f. *Unemployment Insurance—Social Security* (CCH) weekly

31. International Law

a. *International Environment Reporter* (BNA) monthly

b. *International Law Perspective* (Intnl. Lw. Perspective) monthly

32. International Transactions

a. *Balance of Payments Report* (CCH) monthly

b. *Common Market Reports* (CCH) biweekly

c. *International Trade Reporter* (Export Shipping Manual; U.S. Export Weekly; U.S. Import Weekly) (BNA) weekly

d. *Tax Management: Foreign Income* (BNA) portfolios supplemented periodically; biweekly memorandum

33. Juvenile Law

see: Domestic Relations

34. Labor Law

includes: Arbitration; Collective Bargaining; Economic Controls; Occupational Safety and Health; Pensions; Public Employment

a. *Collective Bargaining, Negotiations & Contracts* (BNA) biweekly

b. *Construction Labor Report* (BNA) weekly

c. *Daily Labor Report* (BNA) daily

d. *Employment & Training Reporter* (BNA) weekly

e. *Employment Practices Guide* (CCH) twice monthly

f. *Employment Safety & Health Guide* (CCH) weekly

g. *Fair Employment Practice Series* (BNA) biweekly

h. *Federal Controls* (BNA) daily

i. *Government Employee Relations Report* (BNA) biweekly

j. *The Government Manager* (BNA) biweekly

k. *Health Care Labor Manual* (Aspen) bimonthly

l. *Job Safety & Health Manual* (BNA) biweekly

m. *Job Safety & Health Reporter* (Business Publishers, Inc.) biweekly

n. *Labor Arbitration Awards* (CCH) weekly

o. *Labor Arbitration Reports* (BNA) weekly

p. *Labor Law Reports* (CCH) weekly

q. *Labor Relations Reporter* (BNA) weekly

r. *National Public Employment Reporter* (Labor Relations Press) monthly

s. *Occupational Safety & Health Reporter* (BNA) weekly

t. *Pension & Profit Sharing* (P–H) biweekly

u. *Pension Plan Guide* (CCH) weekly

v. *Pension Reporter* (BNA) weekly

w. *Policy and Practice Series* (BNA) weekly

x. *Public Employee Bargaining* (CCH) biweekly

y. *Public Personnel Administration* (P–H) biweekly

z. *Public Sector Arbitration Awards* (Labor Relations Press) periodic

aa. *Retail Services Labor Report* (BNA) weekly

bb. *Union Labor Report* (BNA) weekly

cc. *White Collar Report* (BNA) weekly

35. Land Use Planning

see also: Environmental Law

a. *Housing & Development Reporter* (BNA) weekly

b. *Land Development Law Reporter* (Land Development Institute, Ltd.) monthly

c. *Land Use Law & Zoning Law Digest* (Amer. Soc. of Planning Officials) monthly

d. *Zoning and Planning Law Report* (CB) monthly

36. Law and Poverty

a. *Poverty Law Reports* (CCH) biweekly

37. Law and Science

includes: Computers

a. *Computer Law Service* (CAL) quarterly

38. Legal Profession

includes: Professional Responsibility

a. *Ethics in Government Reporter* (Washington Service Bureau)

b. *Professional Liability Reporter* (Prof. Liability Rptr. Co.) monthly

39. Legislation

a. *Congressional Index* (CCH) weekly

b. *Congressional Monitor* (Cong. Monitor, Inc.) daily and weekly editions

c. *Daily Report for Executives* (BNA) daily

40. Military Law

a. *Military Law Reporter* (Public Law Education Institute) periodic supplementation

41. Natural Resources

see: Environmental Law

42. Occupational Safety and Health

see: Labor Law

43. Patents, Copyrights, and Trademarks

see also: Entertainment Law

a. *Copyright Law Reporter* (CCH) monthly

b. *Patent, Trademark & Copyright Journal* (BNA) weekly

c. *United States Patents Quarterly* (BNA) weekly

44. Pensions

see: Labor Law

45. Product Liability

includes: Consumer Product Safety

a. *Products Liability Reports* (CCH) biweekly

b. *Product Safety & Liability Reporter* (BNA) weekly

46. Professional Responsibility

see: Legal Profession

47. Public Employment

see: Labor Law

48. Public Utilities

see: Regulated Industries

49. Real Property

see also: Land Use Planning

a. *National Property Law Digest* (NPLD, Inc.) monthly

b. *Resort Timesharing Law Reporter* (CHB Co. & Land Development Institute, Ltd.) quarterly

50. Regulated Industries

includes: Banking; Communications; Energy; Food, Drug & Cosmetics; Public Utilities; Transportation see also: Administrative Law; Aviation Law

a. *Drug Research Reports* (Werble) weekly

b. *Energy Users Report* (BNA) weekly

c. *F-D-C Reports* (Werble) weekly

d. *Federal & State Carriers Reports* (CCH) biweekly

e. *Federal Banking Law Reports* (CCH) weekly

f. *Federal Carriers Reports* (CCH) biweekly

g. *Federal Power Service* (MB) biweekly

h. *Food Drug Cosmetic Law Reports* (CCH) weekly

i. *Medical Devices Reports* (CCH) periodic supplementation

j. *Motor Carrier—Freight Forwarder Service* (Hawkins) monthly

k. *Media Law Reporter* (BNA) weekly

l. *Nuclear Regulation Reports* (CCH) weekly

m. *Radio Regulation, 2d* (P&F) weekly

n. *Rail Carrier Service* (Hawkins) monthly

o. *Utilities Law Reports* (CCH) weekly

p. *Washington Financial Reports* (BNA) weekly

51. Securities Regulation

a. *Blue Sky Law Reports* (CCH) monthly

b. *Commodity Futures Law Reports* (CCH) twice monthly

c. *Federal Securities Law Reports* (CCH) weekly

d. *Mutual Funds Guide* (CCH) biweekly

e. *SEC No-Action Letters* (WSB) periodic supplementation

f. *Securities & Federal Corporate Law Report* (CB) monthly

g. *Securities Regulation & Law Report* (BNA) weekly

h. *Securities Regulation & Transfer Report* (WGL) twice monthly

i. *Securities Regulation & SEC Compliance Manual* (P–H) biweekly

52. Taxation

see also: Estate Planning

a. *Daily Tax Report* (BNA) daily

b. *Federal Tax Citator* (P–H) weekly

c. *Federal Tax Guide* (CCH) weekly

d. *Federal Tax Coordinator, 2d.* (RIA) weekly

e. *Federal Tax Library* (P–H) weekly

f. *Standard Federal Tax Reports* (CCH) weekly

g. *The Tax Barometer* (FP) biweekly

h. *Tax Court Decisions Reports* (CCH) weekly

i. *Tax Court Reports* (CCH) weekly

j. *Tax Management: Primary Sources* (BNA) monthly

k. *Tax Management: U.S. Income* (BNA) portfolios supplemented periodically; biweekly memorandum

53. Torts

a. *Hospital Law Manual* (Aspen) bimonthly

b. *Personal Injury Newsletter* (MB) biweekly

54. Trade Regulation

see: Antitrust;
Consumer Law;
Regulated Industries

55. Unfair Competition

see: Antitrust

56. Urban Law

a. *Housing & Development Reporter* (BNA) weekly

b. *Urban Affairs Reports* (CCH) weekly

57. Wills

see: Estate Planning

58. Women and the Law

a. *Women's Rights Law Reporter* (Rutgers Law School) quarterly

59. Workers' Compensation

a. *Workmen's Compensation Law Bulletin* (Quinlan) monthly

b. *Workmen's Compensation Law Reports* (CCH) biweekly

60. Zoning

see: Land Use Planning

Abbreviations—Major Publishers

ABA American Bar Association
BNA The Bureau of National Affairs, Inc.
CAL Callaghan & Company
CB Clark Boardman Company, Ltd.
CCH Commerce Clearing House, Inc.
CRRI Corporate Reorganization Reporter, Inc.
EIC Environment Information Center, Inc.
FP Federal Publications, Inc.
P&F Pike & Fischer
P–H Prentice-Hall, Inc.
RIA Research Institute of America, Inc.
WSB Washington Service Bureau, Inc.
WGL Warren, Gorham & Lamont, Inc.

SECTION D. ILLUSTRATIONS

89–94. Illustrations Using CCH Standard Federal Tax Reports

Problem: After two years, an Associate at a law firm was notified that her services were being terminated. Although the firm, under an agreement in force at the time of hiring, was obligated to pay her 1/10 of her salary upon termination, or $3,500 in this instance, they actually paid her $20,000. The Associate treated the $16,500 difference as a gift. The Internal Revenue Service was claiming that it was income. What is the law?

95–97. Illustrations Using BNA Fair Employment Practices

Problem: May an employer pay a higher salary to men on the theory that there are more women available in a particular field and therefore women are willing to take a lower salary?

98. Page From CCH Food Drug Cosmetic Law Reports

[Illustration 89]

INDEX PAGE FROM CCH STANDARD FEDERAL TAX REPORTS

8 2-14-79

Topical Index **6807**

References are to paragraph (¶) numbers.

Semi-monthly withholding tables 160; 162

Seminar attendance, travel expenses 1350.0839

Seminar tour costs, educational expenses 1360.59

Senator-elect, expenses 1330.652

Senior citizens—see Sixty-five-or-over

Separability clause 6037; 6037.01

Separate accounting for collected taxes 4977A.01-4977A.04

Separate accounting for withheld taxes ..... 5921A-5921 I 15

SEPARATE ENTITIES
. anonymous companies 324.74
. basis 324.743
. corporation 5017.265; 5017.286
. corporation and stockholder
. . dividends received 2377.55
. . dummy corporation 324.78
. . recognition requirements 324.01
. . taxable income of affiliates combined 324.75

Step 1.

If the IRC Section Number is known, the research could start in the Finding Aids which would lead to a paragraph number. If Code Section is not known, start in Topical Index. In this instance, looking under "Severance pay" indicates a reference to "Dismissal pay."

See next Illustration.

SEP...
. community property status, effect on 325.08
. payments—see Alimony and separate maintenance
. taxes paid on wife's property 1449.166

Septic tank, damage by tractor 1566.595

Sequestration—see Seizure of property

Series E bonds—see Savings bonds

Series of transactions—see Reorganizations: series of transactions

Servants—see Domestic servants

SERVICE CENTERS, INTERNAL REVENUE SERVICE 5975.08; 5987; 6056
. offers in compromise, authority to accept 5697.0255

Service charges, year income taxable ... 2769.3666

Service contracts, depreciation 1717.1205

Service of Tax Court petition—see Tax Court

Service of Tax Court pleadings—see Tax Court

Servicemen—see Armed Forces of the U.S.

Set-aside deduction of charitable contributions, estates and trusts ... 3621.015

SET-OFF
. claim for, suits by taxpayers 5781.3955
. Court of Claims procedure 5766B; 5769I

Settlement payment, capital loss v. business loss 2907.52

Settlements—see Compromises

Seventy-five-day rule, disallowance of deductions for unpaid expenses and interest 2239

Severance damages, condemned property 4625.054

Severance damages to property 680.0862

→**Severance pay**—see Dismissal pay←

. tax-option corporation 4846N.74

Sharecroppers, meals and lodging ... 1191.0675

Shareholders—see Stockholders

Sheep, livestock status 4729.0769

Sheep raisers expenses 1332.25

Sheetpiling costs 2219.2783

SHIPOWNERS' PROTECTION AND INDEMNITY ASSOCIATIONS 3297; 3299.01
. amounts allocable to exempt income 2232.05
. return of excess due 3299.84

Shipping companies, additions to reserves, year income taxable 1198.05

Shipping profits, foreign base company income 4383; 4383EA; 4383EB; 4383F.02

SHIPS, SHIPBUILDERS AND SHIPBUILDING
. capital construction fund 4656A-4657.15

SHI

[Illustration 90]

INDEX PAGE FROM CCH STANDARD FEDERAL TAX REPORTS

8 2-14-79

Topical Index **6477**

References are to paragraph (¶) numbers.

DISCLOSURES—continued
. written determinations of IRS—continued
. . availability of documents 5229K.15; 5229K.16
. . background file documents 5229K.09
. . civil remedies 5229K.20
. . definition of written disclosure ... 5229K.07
. . deletions proposed, ways for expressing disagreement 5229K.50
. . determination letters 5229K.05
. . disposal of records 5229K.35
. . excepted documents 5229K.27
. . exemptions from disclosure 5229K.10
. . Freedom of Information Act 5229K.55
. . notice of intent to make available 5229K.17; 5229K.50
. . notice requirements 5229K.26
. . pre-November 1, 1976 requests 5229K.25
. . private rulings 5229K.05
. . public inspection 5229D
. . request for disclosure 5229K.75
. . scope of disclosure rule 5229K.06
. . Tax Court actions 5825A-5825K
. . technical advice memoranda 5229K.05
. . third party contacts 5229K.30
. . time limits 5229K.18
. . timing requirements 5229K.26

Discount coupons, redemption costs, accounting 237.078; 2926A-2926M.05

Discounted receivables, amounts withheld in reserve 2830.732

DISCOUNTS—continued
. non-interest bearing obligations issued at 2891.01
. notes issued or sold
. . bad debts 1619.638
. . gain or loss recognition 2475.05
. . interest deduction 1416.0957; 2907.3265
. obligations issued at
. . interest deduction 2907.3265
. . sale or exchange 4730; 4733; 4735.02; 4735.03
. percentage depletion affected by ... 3558.49
. short-term obligations issued 2893.01
. speculative obligations, cost recovery method 2769.3668
. state securities purchased at, interest received, taxability 947.016; 947.30
. stock issued at
. . failure to repurchase 4616.055
. . interest paid, deduction 1416.2628
. trade 2916.652
. . deductions allowed 2916.664
. . gross sales reduced 652.14
. . reserves, deductibility 2916.652
. unrealized
. . incorporation in principal of extended or renewed loan 2769.3662

Discovery
. enforcement of summons 5924.033
. injunction dismissal suit 5779.6399
. purpose of summons 5924.084
. suits by taxpayers 5770.0842; 5781.4935
. summons, purpose 5924.084
. Tax Court proceedings—see Tax

Step 2.

Under index entry "Dismissal Pay", note the various sub-entries. "Income . . . 644.195" seems the most relevant to the problem under research. This refers to Paragraph Number in one of the compilation volumes.

See next Illustration.

. discount value of notes 4400.4507
. employee discounts, tax savings through 203C.037
. FHA loan discount 1416.15
. income accruable, only item of 2769.16
. inventory, deduction from 2940.07-2940.0762
. lien for taxes discharged at, effect on basis 4516.9665
. life insurance premiums paid in advance, deductibility as interest paid 4009.335
. loans, interest 1416.01; 1416.1325
. mining supplies purchased, effect on computation of taxable income from the property 3560.16
. mortgage purchase discounts, life insurance company's treatment ... 4033.15
. mortgages purchased at
. . accrual basis 2769.41
. municipal securities 947.30-947.305

personnel 644.026

Dismantling property, expense 1330.196

Dismissal of Tax Court petition, effect of 5477.33

Dismissal of tax suit, compromise of tax effected by 5697.14

→ **DISMISSAL PAY**
. deductibility 1370.1048
. . employer 1379
. employees' trust providing, contributions, year deductible ... 2643.4787
→ income .... 644.195 ←
. withholding 4933; 4934.1515; 4958.15

Dispatch hall, exempt status 3037.0447

Display space rental, unrelated business income 3237.016

Displays, cost, deductibility 1330.30

[Illustration 91]

PAGE FROM CCH STANDARD FEDERAL TAX REPORTS

12,090 **GROSS INCOME DEFINED—Sec. 61 [page 12,005]** 23 5-23-79

[¶ 643]—Continued

(5) *Property transferred on or before June 30, 1969, subject to restrictions.* Notwithstanding paragraph (d)(1), (2), or (4) of this section, if any property is transferred after September 24, 1959, by an employer to an employee or independent contractor as compensation for services, and such property is subject to a restriction which has a significant effect on its value at the time of transfer, the rules of § 1.421-6(d)(2) shall apply in determining the time and the amount of compensation to be included in the gross income of the employee or independent contractor. This (5) is also applicable to transfers subject to a restriction which has a significant effect on its value at the time of transfer and to which § 1.83-8(b) (relating to transitional rules with respect to transfers of restricted property) applies. For special rules relating to options to purchase stock or other property which are issued as compensation for services, see § 1.61-15 and section 421 and the regulations thereunder.

(6) *Certain property transferred, premiums paid, and contributions made in connection with the performance of services after June 30, 1969*—(i) *Exception.* Paragraph (d)(1), (2), (4), and (5) of this section and § 1.61-15 do not apply

to ... 969,
ur ... nal
ru ... rty
is ... ket
va ... and
en ...
se ... bu-
tic ... (a),
se ...
... 272.
Ar ... for
th ... ross
ref ... ded

Step 3.

Obtain volume that contains Paragraph Number 644. Although the Index referred to 644.195, one should always turn first to the whole number to the left of the decimal point. This usually contains editorial explanatory matter. In this instance, "CCH Explanation" is continued on two more pages.

7/21/78 by T. D. 7554. The Preamble to T. D. 7554 is at 789 CCH ¶ 6789. Amended 5/14/79 by T. D. 7623 by deleting in paragraph (d)(2)(ii)(*a*) the phrase "group-term life insurance on the employee's life as defined in paragraph (b)(1) of § 1.79-1" and inserting the phrase "certain group-term life insurance on the employee's life." The Preamble to T. D. 7623 is at 79(10) CCH ¶ 6610.

[¶ 644] Compensation for Services

• • *CCH Explanation*

.015 Compensation as income.—All compensation for personal services, regardless of the form of payment (whether cash, notes, stock, or other property), is taxable. This includes maintenance, food and lodging where they are compensatory in character. See ¶ 1191.01 et seq. It might include also the rental value of property, such as a residence or an automobile, furnished to an employee. See ¶ 1370.313. The gross amount of compensation, before reductions for such items as income tax withholding, Social Security or Railroad Retirement Act contributions, pension fund or insurance, is the amount treated as income. For cases involving the question of whether payments received were compensation, taxable as ordinary income, or whether they were capital gains, see ¶ 4717.01 et seq. For the treatment of compensation paid other than in cash, see ¶ 646.

[Illustration 92]

PAGE FROM CCH STANDARD FEDERAL TAX REPORTS

12,108 GROSS INCOME DEFINED—Sec. 61 [page 12,005]

[¶ 644.18]—Continued

books and records of personal expenditures and prevented the corporation from keeping adequate books and records of its alleged expenditures.

J. Zukin v. Riddell, (DC Cal.) 55-2 USTC ¶ 9688.

No income results to bank officers when the bank pays premiums on insurance policies to cover its liability for wrongful acts committed by its officers and to reimburse the officers for expenses arising from such acts.

Rev. Rul. 69-491, 1969-2 CB 22.

.183 **Debts paid for services.**—Payments made by a client directly to his lawyer's mortgagee were compensation paid to the lawyer for services.

K. C. Davis, 15 TCM 879, Dec. 21,850(M), TC Memo. 1956-166.

The amount received by a teacher from his employer to repay a scholarship loan from a state is additional compensation for services rendered and includible in gross income.

Rev. Rul. 70-282, 1970-1 CB 16.

.1835 A stockholder did not receive income from his corporation by virtue of its repayment of a loan borrowed by the stockholder from a third person. The proceeds of the loan had been "reloaned" to the corporation with the understanding that it be repaid directly to the third party.

W. T. Pettit, 19 TCM 679, Dec. 24,239(M), TC Memo. 1960-130.

.185 **Debts recovered in excess of basis.**—Amounts received on a certificate of indebtedness after its cost basis had been reduced to zero were taxable.

Est. of B. L. Rosset, 13 TCM 1193, Dec. 20,740(M), TC Memo. 1954-241.

.195 **Dismissal pay** is taxable.

Duskis, BTA memo., Dec. 8575-B.

See also .297 below.

.205 **Dissolution of joint venture.**—In settlement of a suit by the taxpayer to declare the existence of a joint venture and partition its property, he received a tract of land. The value of the property was not taxable as compensation for services, since the nature of the controversy settled was controlling. The property plainly was a distribution in the nontaxable dissolution of a joint venture.

U. S. Nat. Bank of Portland (Ore.), Exr. of S. J. Wilson, (CA-9) 57-1 USTC ¶ 9276, 239 F. 2d 475.

Step 4.

After reading the CCH explanation, turn to the numbers to the right of 644. These contain a digest of decisions all dealing with the definition of gross income. Note that after .195 reference is made to the Duskis decision and to .297.

See next Illustration.

.215 Amounts received by an individual, representing 10 per cent of the amount of dividends on corporate stock received by a family trust of which he was a member, are taxable as compensation and not as dividends. The payments were received under a contract entered into in order to induce the individual to retain his position as director of the corporation, and were to continue until he had acquired a certain number of the shares from the trust.

Lihme v. Reinecke, (CA-7) 1932 CCH ¶ 9361, 59 F. 2d 633.

.216 Fees paid to attorneys for successfully terminating litigation to determine the ownership of stock which had been held in escrow are taxable as compensation and not dividends although paid from the dividends accumulated on the stock.

Thorp et al., 32 BTA 767, Dec. 8989.

.217 Corporate funds used by the sole stockholder for his own purposes were taxable to him as dividends, even though he had placed his stock in trust, naming himself as co-trustee and beneficiary. The funds were not embezzlement proceeds.

Buff, 4 TCM 1130, Dec. 14,926(M).

[Illustration 93]

PAGE FROM CCH STANDARD FEDERAL TAX REPORTS

Sec. 61 [page 12,005]—EMPLOYERS **12,121**

employees in recognition of services are includible in the gross income of the recipients and constitute wages subject to withholding for income tax purposes.

T. I. R. No. 527, December 12, 1963, 647 CCH ¶ 6327, distinguishing I. T. 3726, 1945 CB 63.

See also .2905, above.

Termination of Employment

.297 Additional compensation.—Regardless of an employer's description of informal payments made to an employee upon termination of employment, whether for age, dismissal for cause, ill health, dissolution of the employer, compensation for lost benefits under a pension plan, surrender or cancellation of employment contract, sale of part of an employer's operating property accompanied with a transfer of some of its employees, release of claims against the employer, or because the payments are required by law, if the payments are actually for past services, they will usually be treated as taxable compensation. Application of this rule in the cases listed below resulted in a finding that the pay-

Severance of employment contract.—

Rev. Rul. 74-252, 1974-1 CB 287, distinguishing Rev. Rul. 58-301, 1958-1 CB 23, on another ground.

Rev. Rul. 55-520, 1955-2 CB 393.

R. I. Ingalls, Jr., (DC) 67-2 USTC ¶ 9482, 272 F. Supp. 10, rev'd and rem'd as to taxable year of inclusion, (CA-5) 68-2 USTC ¶ 9519. Cert. denied, 393 U. S. 1094.

A. A. Seserman, 21 TCM 1042, Dec. 25,604(M), TC Memo. 1962-191.

C. C. Blake, 20 TCM 1606, Dec. 25,124(M), TC Memo. 1961-311.

T. D. 2090 (1914).

D. L. Gordon, (CA-5) 59-1 USTC ¶ 9125, 262 F. 2d 413.

J. F. McManus, 23 TCM 245, Dec. 26,666(M), TC Memo. 1964-43.

J. R. Lockwood, 27 TCM 1462, Dec. 29,249(M), TC Memo. 1968-274.

Similarly, a lump-sum payment received by a railroad employee as consideration for relinquishing employment seniority rights and terminating his employment in a particular position is taxable income.

Rev. Rul. 59-227, 1959-2 CB 13, modified by Rev. Rul. 75-44.

A lump-sum payment received by a railroad employee as consideration for relinquishing employment seniority rights is

Step 5.

Note how 644.297 digests and summarizes decisions dealing with the question whether payments made in the course of termination of employment are considered gifts or income.

Note particularly the Ruestow case, a Tax Court Memorandum decision that seems relevant.

After noting relevant cases in the compilation volume, a check should be made next for new decisions.

See next Illustration.

dom, 15 TCM 1180, Dec. 21,961(M), TC Memo. 1956-224; *Deasy*, (DC Pa.) 56-1 USTC ¶ 9120.

Liquidating corporation.—

S. B. Carragan, (CA-2) 52-1 USTC ¶ 9317, 197 F. 2d 246.

D. T. Nattrass, 33 TCM 1389, Dec. 32,862(M), TC Memo. 1974-300.

Lost benefits under pension plan.—

Poorman, (CA-9) 42-2 USTC ¶ 9814, 131 F. 2d 946.

Release of claims.—

R. Jackson, 25 TC 1106, Dec. 21,591.

W. Miller, (DC) 73-2 USTC ¶ 9681, 362 FSupp 1242.

Severance pay received by a lawyer upon termination of his association with a law firm was not excludable from his gross income as a gift.

E. A. Ruestow, 37 TCM 639, Dec. 35,105(M), TC Memo 1978-147.

Statutory retirement gratuity.—

Williams, 36 BTA 974, Dec. 9821.

Stock purchase.—

L. Friend, 20 TCM 858, Dec. 24,883(M), TC Memo. 1961-167.

[Illustration 94]

PAGE FROM NEW MATTER VOLUME, CCH STANDARD FEDERAL TAX REPORTS

70,308 **Cumulative Index to 1979 Developments (For Reports 1-47)** 48 11-14-79

See also Cumulative Index at page 70,251.

From Compilation Paragraph No. **To New Development Paragraph No.**

631 .0335 *Florists' Transworld Delivery*—Nonacquiescence announced.
.0335 *North Carolina Oil Jobbers Assn., Inc.* (DC) (¶ 9001.7)—Insurance trust fund deposits benefiting members not income. Gov't won't appeal.
.04 *Davidson*—Taxpayer's appeal to CA-2 dismissed nolle pros. 7/2/79.
.064 *Keller Street Development Co.*, TCM—Amounts received as a settlement of a stockholder's derivative suit were includible in gross income 7035
.0715 *George*, TCM—Taxpayer did not meet burden of proof regarding unreported income 7502
.0715 *Malmstedt*—Taxpayer on appeal to CA-4.
.0715 *Malmstedt*, TCM—Remanded on other issues 7631
.073 *Lakeside Garden Development, Inc.* (here Murry) aff'd, CA-5—Rental value from recreational facilities connected to sale of condominiums 9565
.073 *Mangurian*, TCM—Excessive ground rent not capitalized, and attributed to taxpayer as dividend 7445
.077 Condominiums—Illustrative Case 8321

Step 6.

Each week new materials are filed in a separate volume behind a "New Matter" tab. These are all correlated to materials in the main volume through a Cumulative Index keyed to the Paragraph numbers of the main volumes.

Note all the new matters relating to Paragraph 644. These will be found under the indicated paragraph numbers in the separate "New Matter" volume.

Note how at 644.297 it is indicated that the Ruestow case has been affirmed by the Court of Appeals and that there is a new case [Ramella] on the subject. Full text of both should be read.

While not illustrated, similar results would be obtained by using Prentice-Hall, Federal Taxes.

.30 IRS guidelines on tax protest activity—*Rewrite* 8272
643 Proposed amendment of Reg. § 1.61-2 8988
644 .01 *Garber*, CA-5—Sale of blood plasma is services and generates gross income 9212
.015 Nutrition Program for the Elderly benefits—Rev. Rul. 6909H
.015 Reemployed civil service annuitant—Rev. Rul. 6280
.0165 Discussion draft bill and report on employee fringe benefits 6156
.0165 Employee fringe benefits draft bill released—*Rewrite* 8247
.0165 Proposed legislation on prohibition on issuance of fringe benefit regulations 6156
.02 Allowances paid to Navy personnel—Rev. Rul. 6255C
.128 Honorarium transferred to charity included in gross income—Rev. Rul. 6548
.1411 Rev. Rul. 77-290 amplified—Rev. Rul. 6549
.142 Interest on investor's deposit—Rev. Rul. 6770
.17 Traveling expenses paid by employer includible in gross income—*Rewrite* 8255
.23 Educational benefits trust was deferred compensation plan—*Rewrite* 8248
.263 *Funk*, TCM—Farm produce was income 7902
.27 *Abram*, DC—Employee contributions to Civil Service Retirement Fund 9487
.27 Actions stayed for exclusion of mandatory employee retirement plan contributions—News Release 6364
.293 *Estate of J.S. Sweeney*, TCM—Honorarium was compensation for services 7844
.297 *Ramella*, TCM—Severance pay includable in gross income 7563
.297 *Ruestow* aff'd, CA-2—Payment upon involuntary termination income not gift 9173
.2988 *Deason* aff'd, CA-5—Payments to corporation from government were taxable compensation 9269
.329 Actions stayed for exclusion of mandatory employee retirement plan contributions—News Release 6364

[Illustration 95]

PAGE FROM FAIR EMPLOYMENT PRACTICES CUMULATIVE DIGEST AND INDEX, 1975–1979 VOLUME

FEP Cases OUTLINE OF CLASSIFICATIONS

Step 1.

Consult Classification Guide in FEP Cumulative Digest and Index (CDI). Note how 130.5091–95 may be relevant. Consult these paragraph numbers in the Digest section of the CDI. See next Illustration.

[Search could also have begun in the Master Index volume using a subject approach rather than the Classification approach.]

Age discrimination

.701 —In general
.705 —Retirement

.75 Handicap discrimination [See also ▶108.4401.]

.80 Reprisal; retaliation
.83 Educational and testing requirements
.85 EEO regulations, compliance with
.89 Attorneys' fees
.90 Costs

Remedies

.910 —In general
.917 —Preliminary, temporary relief

▶ **130. Equal Pay Act**

[Includes rulings under state equal pay acts. For limitations period see ▶108.6925. For pleadings and motions see ▶108.7201 et seq. For class actions under Act, see ▶108.7555.]

.01 In general
.05 Conflict with other laws, regulations, etc.
.07 Jurisdiction
.08 Coverage; exemptions
.20 Burden of proof [For Defenses, see ▶130.25.]

.25 Defenses

Elements of equal pay standard

.301 —In general

▶ **130. — Contd.**

.315 —"Substantially equal," what constitutes
.318 —Performance; effort
.320 —Job content; additional duties
.326 —Primary v. subsidiary tasks
.327 —Shift differentials
.328 —Working conditions
.329 —Job classification systems

Wage differentials

.341 —In general
.343 —Evidence of; manner of determining; standard of comparison

.345 "Red circling;" prohibition against reduction in wage rates

Exceptions to equal pay standard

[See also ▶130.25.]

.501 —In general
.503 —Merit system
.505 —Seniority system
.507 —Quantity or quality of pro-

—Other factors other than sex

.5091 ——In general

.5093 ——Economic benefit to employer

.5095 ——Availability of employees of both sexes

.70 Union liability; joint employer-union liability
.80 Compliance

REMEDIES FOR DISCRIMINATION

▶ **200. Remedies**

[See also ▶106.7001 et seq.]

.01 In general

▶ **205. Injunctions; Declaratory Relief**

Injunctions

[See also ▶106.09.]

.011 —In general

Appropriateness of injunctions

.101 —In general
.105 —Defenses

64

[Illustration 96]

PAGE FROM FAIR EMPLOYMENT PRACTICES CUMULATIVE DIGEST AND INDEX, 1975–1979 VOLUME

Ind.-Dig. OTHER FACTORS OTHER THAN SEX ►130.5091

tory merit review plan —Federal National Mortgage Assn.; Brennan v. [DC Calif (1975)] 12 FEP Cases 490

Labor Secy.'s Equal Pay Act action against employer that claims that it acted pursuant to merit system at its Atlanta, Ga., headquarters is which employer's executives meet every three or four months to discuss each employee's job performance, is merit system within meaning of Equal Pay Act —Ibid.

Step 2.

Note how 130.5091 digests cases dealing with factors other than sex in instances where there are discrepancies in pay between males and females.

Full text of the decisions will be found in the volume of Fair Employment Practices (FEP) cases.

The search must now be brought up to date.

See next Illustration.

Employer did not violate Title VII or Equal Pay Act when it paid certain female draftsmen less than it paid certain male draftsmen where pay differences have been result of merit system within meaning of Equal Pay Act —Ibid.

Employer is not violating either Title VII or Equal Pay Act by its policies of granting annual percentage salary increase to all employees plus constant dollar cost of living allowance and of giving only certain percentage of prior salary in merit increases to employees in order to prevent inequitable rise or reduction in salary —Wheeler v. Armco Steel Corp. [DC Tex (1979)] 20 FEP Cases 1594

►130.505—130.507 *

—Other factors other than sex

►130.5091 ——In general

U.S. Supreme Court

Gender-neutral pension plan does not violate Title VII or Equal Pay Act despite disproportionate heavy impact on male employees —Manhart v. City of Los Angeles, Dept. of Water & Power [US SupCt (1978), sub nom City of Los Angeles, Dept. of Water & Power v. Manhart, aff 13:1625; 14:1233; see also 10:101] 17 FEP Cases 395

Bennett Amendment to Title VII, which makes compensation differentials lawful under Title VII if authorized by Equal Pay Act, does not shield employer from Title VII liability for pension plan requiring female employees to make larger contributions than male employees —Ibid.

U.S. Courts of Appeals

Mere existence of separate state licensing schemes for professions of barber and beautician that perform work of substantially similar job content is not "factor other than sex" within meaning of EPA that would justify county hospital's payment of higher pay to barbers than to beauticians —Allegheny County Institution District dba John J. Kane Hospital; Dunlop v. [CA 3 (1976), sub nom Usery v., revs'g and reman'g 13:1185] 13 FEP Cases 1188

Burden of proving that factor other than sex is basis for wage differential is a heavy one; requirements for exceptions are not met unless factor of sex provides no part of basis for wage differential —Owensboro-Daviess County Hospital; Hodgson v. [CA 6 (1975), sub nom Brennan v., revs'g and reman'g 9:872] 11 FEP Cases 600

Lower court erred when, after finding that bank did not maintain training program, it took into account possibility of future promotion in concluding that bank had not violated Act by its payment of higher wages to male tellers and supervisors than to female tellers and supervisors —Security Bank & Trust Co.; Usery v. [CA 10 (1978), sub nom Marshall v., aff, rem in part 16:1121] 17 FEP Cases 631

Airline that paid male pursers more than stewardesses failed to prove that part of purser salary was justified by factor other than sex, as compensation for foreign flying, since pursers are used substantially on pure domestic flights and on domestic segments of international flights, and they received same pay regardless of whether they were engaged in foreign flying —Laffey v. Northwest Airlines, Inc. [CA DC (1976) vac'g and reman'g in part 6:902, 7:687] 13 FEP Cases 1068

U.S. District Courts

Title abstract company unlawfully paid female head abstract examiner less than male employee; male employee's alleged "flexibility" does not constitute factor other than sex —Lambert v. Beach Enterprises, Inc. [DC Ark (1978)] 20 FEP Cases 1169

Starting salary to female conventional loan representative, who has no college experience and whose prior employment history was as loan clerk, loan counselor, and loan assistant lower than that paid male conventional loan representatives with relevant business experience and college education, no violation —Federal National Mortgage Assn.; Brennan v. [DC Calif (1975)] 12 FEP Cases 490

University sued by female former administrator paid less than male assistant dean may not have action dismissed, despite premature claim that because male is Jesuit priest, he is paid more in return for services as priest than for services as administrator —National Organization for Women, Inc., San Jose Chapter v.

For Guidance see Introduction 1111

[Illustration 97]

PAGE FROM BNA MASTER INDEX LOOSELEAF VOLUME

D-II A886 FEP Cases▸ MASTER INDEX BINDER

employee's duties cannot be equated with hers despite his temporary assignment [Ibid.]

Employer did not violate Equal Pay Act when it paid lower wage rates to female duplicator operator than to male operators, where skill and duties required of female operator was not substantially equal [DC NC (1979)] 23 FEP Cases 1772

Employer that paid female customer correspondents less than male correspondents whose jobs involved equal skill, effort, and responsibility violated Equal Pay Act, where not only has employer failed to show that pay differential was result of application of sex-neutral determinant, but its pay system served to perpetuate earlier established sex-determined pay differential among customer correspondents [Ibid.]

▸**130.328** Prohibition against "downward equalization" of benefits precludes airline, which had been ordered to provde female cabin attendants with single-occupancy hotel rooms on layovers and with periodic uniform cleaning allowances, from implementing provisions of new contract authorizing airline to apply double-occupancy room layover policy to all attendants and

male teachers on theory it was relying on market forces of greater supply of female prospective faculty members and of willingness of women to accept lower beginning salaries than men [DC Ga (1980)] 23 FEP Cases 451

City that paid female cell block attendants more than it paid male cell block turnkeys who performed same duties and services violated Equal Pay Act, even though female attendants' wage was established by state court in sex discrimination action brought by policy matrons who formerly performed attendants' duties, since wage differential resulting from that action was not caused by factor other than sex [DC NY (1980)] 23 FEP Cases 1448

▸**130.5093** Factors other than sex, including seniority and special usefulness, justified nursing home's payment of higher wages to male orderly to female nurse's aides, despite contention that there was no demonstrated seniority "system" applicable to both men and women [CA 1 aff 16:1137] 23 FEP Cases 1797

Research organization that uses subjective evaluation system to determine salaries has not discriminated against black female scientist

Step 3.

After noting citations to relevant cases in the 1975–79 bound CDI, check in the Master Index looseleaf volume under classification number for later cases. Note here the case under 130.5091. Be sure to read the full text.

discrimination remedies supplement each other [Ibid.]

▸**130.501** Employer that paid female customer correspondents less than male correspondents whose jobs involved equal skill, effort, and responsibility violated Equal Pay Act, where not only has employer failed to show that pay differential was result of application of sex-neutral determinant, but its pay system served to perpetuate earlier established sex-determined pay differential among customer correspondents [DC NC (1979)] 23 FEP Cases 1772

▸**130.503** Alleged merit system does not justify state college's payment of lower salaries to female teachers for substantially equal work [DC Ga (1980)] 23 FEP Cases 451

▸**130.505** Factors other than sex, including seniority and special usefulness, justified nursing home's payment of higher wages to male orderly to female nurse's aides, despite contention that there was no demonstrated seniority "system" applicable to both men and women [CA 1 aff 16:1137] 23 FEP Cases 1797

→ ▸**130.5091** State college may not justify, under Equal Pay Act, its payment of higher salaries to

ty under Equal Pay Act to seek contribution from unions that allegedly participated in alleged discrimination, and because right of contribution would simply entitle employers to pass off onto third parties their own liability for violations of Act, no right of contribution will be implied under Act [DC Mich (1980)] 23 FEP Cases 434

Fact that Equal Pay Act precludes contribution actions by employers against unions deprives court, hearing EEOC's action against state university, of jurisdiction to entertain under FRCP 14 university's third-party action against unions based on common tort laws [Ibid.]

▸**200.01** Individual claim that has merit, even though it directly relates only to one position of employment, is proper basis for equitable relief under Title VII with regard to all of employer's practices [DC Ark (1980)] 23 FEP Cases 1266

Relief to be afforded class will not be fashioned by district court until court of appeals makes determination of issues on appeal [DC Miss (1976) proc foll 12:770] 23 FEP Cases 1076

▸**205.101** To extent that court finds racial discrimination by county, it should grant injunction against future discrimination despite county's af-

[Illustration 98]

PAGE FROM CCH FOOD DRUG COSMETIC LAW REPORTS

FOOD DEFINITIONS

¶ 10,011

"Food" is defined in most state food laws to mean: (1) articles used for food or drink for man or other animals, (2) chewing gum, and (3) articles used for components of any such article.

A few states impose special restrictions on the use of "food additives," "color additives," and "pesticide chemicals" in or on food and define these terms.

Definitions of "food," "food additive," "color additive," and "pesticide chemical" that appear in the basic laws are referred to in the chart below.

State	"Food"	"Food Additive"	"Color Additive"	"Pesticide Chemical"
Ala.	¶ 11,013			
Alas.	¶ 11,624			
Ariz.	¶ 12,011	¶ 12,011	¶ 12,011	¶ 12,011
Ark.	¶ 12,512			
Cal.	¶ 13,023	¶ 13,024	¶ 13,015	¶ 13,036
Colo.	¶ 13,512	¶ 13,512	¶ 13,512	¶ 13,512
Conn.	¶ 14,012	¶ 14,012	¶ 14,012	¶ 14,012
Del.				
D. C.[1]				
Fla.				13
Ga.				
Haw.				11
Ida.				
Ill.				29
Ind.				03
Iowa				
Kan.	¶ 19,012	¶ 19,012	¶ 19,012	¶ 19,012
Ky.	¶ 19,512	¶ 19,512	¶ 19,512	¶ 19,512
La.	¶ 20,012			
Me.	¶ 20,542			

Several looseleaf services include coverage for state laws. In some, the sections containing the full text of the state laws are preceded with a chart outlining where the laws on a topic may be found for the various states.

[1] Provisions of the Federal Act also are applicable to commerce within the District of Columbia.

Food Drug Cosmetic Law Reports ¶ 10,011

SECTION E. SUMMARY

1. Each service relates to a special subject.

2. Includes all relevant sources—both primary and secondary.

3. Frequent reports keep contents up-to-date.

4. Contents.

a. Text of statutes on the topic, with significant legislative history.

b. Text of relevant administrative regulations as published in the *Federal Register* and *Code of Federal Regulations.*

c. Full text, or digests, of all court or agency decisions on the subject. Some services also provide permanent bound volumes for decisions.

d. Tables of cases, statutes and regulations.

e. Indexes to subjects—including indexes to the most current material.

f. Some services cover state law, with comparative analysis.

5. Best place to start research for subjects governed by administrative regulations and rulings.

Chapter 15

SHEPARD'S CITATIONS

SECTION A. CASE CITATORS

The previous chapters were directed toward enabling one to locate court decisions relevant to a particular point of law. In most instances, this is a preliminary step toward a more concrete goal—a trial or appellate brief has to be written, or an opinion letter composed, or an article authored. Locating cases is undertaken to find rules of law as determined from the reading of the cases, which can then be cited in another document as authority. But before this can be done with any degree of confidence, one further step must be taken. This is to determine that any given case that is to be relied on as authority is indeed still good authority. The decision must be checked to make certain that it has not been reversed by a higher court, or overruled by a subsequent decision of the same court.[1] This is accomplished by the use of *Shepard's Citations.*

These sets of law books provide a means by which any reported case (cited decision) may be checked to see when and how another court (the citing decision) has cited the first decision. For example, assume the problem under research is the constitutionality of a state statute which imposed criminal sanctions on newspapers for disclosing the confidential proceedings of a state's Judicial Inquiry and Review Commission. During the course of the research, the case of *Landmark Communications, Inc. v. Commonwealth,* 217 Va. 699, 233 S.E.2d 120 (1977) has been found. Although this is exactly on point it cannot be cited yet as authority. One must first determine if this case has been appealed to the Supreme Court of the United States,

[1] The failure to *Shepardize* properly can lead to embarrassing situations. One court commented on such an instance as follows: "* * * unfortunately, counsel for the defendant quoted extensively from * * * the Matter of Newins' Will, 29 Misc. 614, 213 N.Y.S.2d 255 (Sur.Ct., Suffolk County 1961); that case was cited as the authority which required plaintiff herein to prove every possible and conceivable fact imaginable before a court of law will declare a marriage null and void. *The court was astounded to find that that case upon which so much reliance was placed by defendant's counsel was reversed by the Appellate Division * * * on the point in question and this reversal was affirmed by the Court of Appeals * * *.*" (emphasis added) Rosenstiel v. Rosenstiel, 43 Misc.2d 462, 475, 251 N.Y.S.2d 565, 578 (Sup.Ct.1964).

and if so, whether it was affirmed or reversed. If the latter, it is no longer authority and must not be cited as if it were.

Another factor that must be ascertained is whether the Virginia Supreme Court in a subsequent case overruled its decision in the *Landmark Communications* case (assuming it had not been reversed). Again, if it did so, the case can no longer be cited as authority.

This is determined by checking in the *Shepard's Virginia Citations* or *Shepard's Southeastern Citations*. As they list every case subsequently written in which the cited case was mentioned, it can be determined easily if the cited case has been affirmed, reversed or overruled.

As *Shepard's Citations* presents all citing cases for a cited case, it is evident that its usefulness goes beyond only checking to see if a cited case has been reversed or overruled. The value of a precedent for any given decision also depends to a large extent on the treatment subsequently given to it by courts deciding whether the cited case is in fact applicable to the case under consideration. Whether a cited case has subsequently been followed, distinguished, limited, or questioned may be of vital importance in determining the present value of the cited case as a precedent. Thus, *Shepard's* may be used to determine how a given case has been treated in subsequent decisions.

The court decisions are listed by volume and page in black letter (bold face) type. Under the citation of the case in point subsequent decisions, which have cited the case, are listed by volume and page with letter-form abbreviations indicating the *judicial history* of the case in point and its *treatment* by subsequent decisions. [See Illustrations 102–103]

The *history of the case* is indicated by abbreviations showing whether the case was affirmed, reversed, dismissed or modified on appeal. Parallel citations of the cited case in the standard reports are also provided. In like manner, the nature of the *treatment of the case* in point in subsequent decisions is indicated by abbreviations. The introductory pages of each *Shepard's Citations* explain the abbreviations used in the volume. Some illustrative abbreviations of case citations are given below:

History of Case [2]

a (affirmed)	Same case below affirmed on appeal.

[2] These abbreviations and their descriptions are embodied in the pamphlet HOW TO USE SHEPARD'S CITATIONS, published by Shepard's Citations, Inc.

cc (connected case)	Different case from case cited but arising out of same subject matter or intimately connected therewith.
D (dismissed)	Appeal from same case below dismissed.
m (modified)	Same case below modified on appeal.
r (reversed)	Same case below reversed on appeal.
s (same case)	Same case as case cited.
S (superseded)	Substitution for former opinion.
v (vacated)	Same case vacated.
US cert den	Certiorari denied by U.S. Supreme Court.
US cert dis	Certiorari dismissed by U.S. Supreme Court.
US reh den	Rehearing denied by U.S. Supreme Court.
US reh dis	Rehearing dismissed by U. S. Supreme Court.

Treatment of Case

c (criticized)	Soundness of decision or reasoning in cited case criticized for reasons given.
d (distinguished)	Case at bar different either in law or fact from case cited for reasons given.
e (explained)	Statement of import of decision in cited case. Not merely a restatement of the facts.
f (followed)	Cited as controlling.
h (harmonized)	Apparent inconsistency explained and shown not to exist.
j (dissenting opinion)	Case cited in dissenting opinion.

L (limited)	Refusal to extend decision of cited case beyond precise issues involved.
o (overruled)	Ruling in cited case expressly overruled.
p (parallel)	Citing case substantially alike or identical with law or facts of cited case.
q (questioned)	Soundness of decision or reasoning in cited case questioned.

There is a separate set of *Shepard's Citations* for every set of court reports. Consequently, there are sets of *Shepard's* for each of the fifty states, the District of Columbia and Puerto Rico; separate sets for each of the Regional Reporters of the *National Reporter System*; one set for the *Federal Reporter* and the *Federal Supplement*; and one for the reports of the Supreme Court of the United States.

As most court decisions are reported in two sets, one has to make a determination of which set of *Shepard's* is to be used in *Shepardizing* [3] a case. For example, the case reported in 217 Va. 699, is also reported in 233 S.E.2d 120. It can be *Shepardized* in the *Shepard's Virginia Citations* or the *Shepard's Southeastern Citations.* When one should be selected over the other will be discussed *infra.*

1. Shepard's State and Territorial Citations

These are used in connection with the state reports. As most reported decisions cover more than one point of law, *Shepard's,* through the use of superscript figures, keys each citing case to the headnotes of the cited case. For example, the case of *Landmark Communications, Inc. v. Commonwealth* as published in the *Virginia Reports* has three headnotes, each on a different point of law. A citing case may cite *Landmark Communications* only for the point in its third headnote. In order to allow a researcher to find all citing cases which cite *Landmark Communications* for the point of law covered in its third headnote, *Shepard's* adds the superscript "3" to the citing case. By this means, one can find in *Shepard's Virginia Citations* all subsequent cases that cited *Landmark Communications* for that point of law. [See Illustration 102]

The state *Shepard's* gives citing cases only from courts within the jurisdiction or cases that originated in a federal court within the

[3] The term *Shepardizing* is the trademark property of Shepard's/McGraw-Hill, Inc., and is used here with reference to its publications only and with its express consent.

state. Additionally, state *Shepard's* gives citations to any legal periodical published in the state (plus 20 national law reviews) that cite the cited cases. It also gives a citation to the reports of the state Attorney General's opinions that cite the cited cases. State *Shepard's* also have a section or a separate volume arranged by the regional reporter citation. By this means, when only a state unit *Shepard's* is available, it may be *Shepardized* under the state citation, or the regional reporter citation. In both instances, citing cases are given only for the courts within the state.

2. Shepard's Citations for the Regional Reporters

In the example of *Landmark Communications, Inc. v. Commonwealth,* this case could also be *Shepardized* in the *Southeastern Reporter* under 233 S.E.2d 120. In such instances, that volume has to be examined to determine which headnote or headnotes are of interest. In the *Southeastern Reporter,* there are nine headnotes and each can be followed in citing cases in the same manner as described *supra.* In our example, if the *Shepard's Virginia Citations* is used, all of the citing cases given are to the *Virginia Reports* or to federal cases heard in Virginia. In *Shepard's Southeastern Citations,* all citations to the same citing cases are to the *Southeastern Reporter.* The regional *Shepard's,* unlike the state *Shepard's,* also give citations to any case throughout the *National Reporter System.* Thus, if a Texas case cited *Landmark Communications, Inc. v. Commonwealth,* it can be found in *Shepard's Southeastern Citations* but not in *Shepard's Virginia Citations.* However, the regional *Shepard's* do not give citations to legal periodicals or Attorney General's opinions.

The choice, then, of when to use a state or regional *Shepard's* depends on the research in hand. Illustrations 102–103 demonstrate the *Shepardizing* of the *Landmark Communications* case in both sets of reports.

3. Shepard's Citations for Federal Cases

a. *Shepard's United States Citations*

This unit is divided into four separate parts:

(1) *Cases and Statutes.* The Cases Volumes consist of a main volume and bound supplements. The main volume contains citations to the *U.S. Reports* through 1943 and the history and treatment of the cases appear only under the official (U.S.) citations. The *Lawyers' Edition* and the *Supreme Court Reporter* sections only provide parallel references from their citations to the *U.S. Reports.* The cases must then be *Shepardized* under the official citations.

In all volumes after the 1943 volume, citations to the citing cases are given under both the official set and the two unofficial sets. It should be noted, however, that when *Shepardizing* under either of the two unofficial sets (*S.Ct.Rep.* or *L.Ed.*), citations are given exclusively to cases from the federal courts. When a state court cites a U.S. Supreme Court decision, it is listed only under the U.S. citation. Moreover, it is only under the U.S. citation that references are made to specific justices when a decision has concurring or dissenting opinions. Also, under the U.S. citations, the heading "first" is used. This refers to the summary which appears at the beginning of opinions in the *U.S. Reports.*

(2) *Constitutions, Statutes, Treaties and Court Rules.* These volumes *Shepardize* all cases citing the U.S. Constitution, the U.S. Code, the U.S. Treaties Series, and the court rules of the U.S. Supreme Court.

(3) *Administrative.* These volumes show citations to the decisions and orders of selected federal administrative departments, courts, boards, and commissions.

(4) *Patents and Trademarks.* This unit of the *Shepard's United States Citations* is a compilation of citations to U.S. patents, trademarks, and copyright.

The patents section lists each patent by number and then lists all citations to a patent by a court or administrative agency.

The copyright section. This lists titles of copyrighted works and lists citations to all court and administrative decisions involving the title.

The trademark section lists all trademarks alphabetically and then lists all citations to court and administrative decisions involving the trademark.

A separate section contains all citations to decisions published in the *United States Patents Quarterly.*

b. *Shepard's Federal Citations*

These volumes *Shepardize* cases reported in the *Federal Reporter* (F., F.2d); *Federal Supplement* (F.Supp.); *Federal Rules Decisions* (F.R.D.); and the United States Court of Claims Reports.

SECTION B. OTHER USES FOR SHEPARD'S CITATIONS—CASES

1. Citations to Articles in Legal Periodicals

The state units of *Shepard's Citations,* in addition to indicating every time a cited case has been cited by a citing case, will also indicate when the cited case has been cited in a legal periodical published within the state and in twenty other national legal periodicals.[4]

2. A.L.R. Annotations

When *Shepardizing* a case citation, *Shepard's* will indicate when the case has been cited in the body of an A.L.R. annotation. [See Illustration 102]

3. Using Shepard's Citations to Find Parallel Citations

In Chapter 5 it was pointed out how, given a state report citation, the *National Reporter System* regional citations could be found through the use of the *National Reporter Blue Book*. *Shepard's* may also be used for this and, additionally, to find the state citation from the regional reporter citation. It always includes the parallel citation as the first citation under the page number the first time the case is listed.[5] When a case has also been reported in *A.L.R.* that is also listed.

[4] These are:
American Bar Association Journal
California Law Review
Columbia Law Review
Cornell Law Review
Georgetown Law Journal
Harvard Law Review
Law and Contemporary Problems
Michigan Law Review
Minnesota Law Review
New York University Law Review
Northwestern University Law Review
Stanford Law Review
Texas Law Review
University of California at Los Angeles Law Review
University of Chicago Law Review
University of Illinois Law Forum
University of Pennsylvania Law Review
Virginia Law Review
Wisconsin Law Review
Yale Law Journal

[5] As cases are frequently reported earlier in the units of the *National Reporter System* than in the official reports, the parallel state citation is frequently not available at the time a citation first appears in a regional *Shepard's*. When a parallel citation is not the first citation under the page number, check the subsequent issues of the *Shepard's Citations* unit being used. If it still does not appear, it is likely that the state citation is from a state which has discontinued its official state reports.

4. Shepard's Citations as a Research Aid

Although *Shepard's Citations* are very useful research aids, they should not be stretched beyond their normal function.

The editors' use of the letter-form abbreviations to indicate the treatment of cases is intelligently conservative. The essence of a citing case may go beyond its expressed language. The inclusiveness of a case is not identified by the abbreviations unless its expression is clearly stated in the opinion. Therefore, a case which implicitly overrules a cited case will not be marked with the symbol "o" for "overruled." This can be determined only by a careful reading of the case. In other words, although these guides immeasurably facilitate a lawyer's research, there are no substitutes for reading and "squeezing the juices" from cases.

In addition, cases dealing with the same subject matter, which do not cite each other, are not covered by *Shepard's Citations*. Or contrariwise, since the *Shepard's* editions are not selective, the citing cases may be so numerous as to create a formidable research problem. A further limitation is that *Shepard's Citations* perpetuate the inaccuracies created by judges who inappropriately cite cases. But these are minor defects which the general utility, comprehensiveness and accuracy of the *Citators* effectively overbalance.

SECTION C. ILLUSTRATIONS: SHEPARD'S CITATIONS: CASES

99. First page—217 Va. 699

100. First page—233 S.E.2d 120

101. Title page from Shepard's Shepardizing the Case Landmark Communications v. Commonwealth

102. Page from Shepard's Virginia Citations—Cases

103. Page from Shepard's Southeastern Citations

[Illustration 99]

FIRST PAGE FROM 217 Va. 699

LANDMARK COM. v. COMMONWEALTH, 217 VA. 699. 699

Opinion.

Richmond

LANDMARK COMMUNICATIONS, INC. v. COMMONWEALTH OF VIRGINIA.

March 4, 1977.

Record No. 760596.

Present, All the Justices.

(1) Statutory Construction—Person—Corporation.

(2) Penal Statute—Ambiguity—Construction.

(3) Constitutional Law — Freedom of Press — Confidentiality of Judicial Inquiry Proceedings.

1. Corporation is a "person" within meaning of statute.

2. While penal statute must be construed strictly, proscription of statute is so clear that it would be unreasonable to construe it to mean that only participants in Judicial Inquiry and Review Commission proceeding are subject to the proscribed sanctions, or that only the first disclosure of confidential information is actionable.

3. Freedom of press is not an absolute right and the state may punish its abuse. Code provision seeks to preserve confidentiality of Judicial Inquiry and Review Commission proceedings by providing for the imposition of criminal sanction *after* statute has been violated and does not impose a prior restraint upon publication. Code provision represents a legislative declaration by the General Assembly, fortified by a plain statement of public intent expressed in the Virginia Constitution, that a clear and present danger to the orderly administration of justice would be created by divulgence of the confidential proceedings of the Commission. Commonwealth need not produce other evidence by way of "actual facts" to show a clear and present danger. Matters involved are much more than minor matters of public inconvenience or annoyance. It can be said safely, without need of hard in-court evidence, that, absent a requirement of confidentiality, the Judicial Inquiry and Review Commission could not function properly or discharge effectively its intended purposes. Necessity of maintaining integrity of Commission outweighs any possible advantage of public disclosure.

Error to a judgment of the Circuit Court of the City of Norfolk. Hon. Alfred W. Whitehurst, judge presiding.

Headnotes of a case as published in the Virginia Reports. Shepard's shows the treatment of a cited case by a citing case by references to the headnotes.

CARRICO, J., delivered the opinion of the court.

[Illustration 100]

FIRST PAGE FROM 233 SOUTHEASTERN REPORTER 2d 120

120 Va. 233 SOUTH EASTERN REPORTER, 2d SERIES

LANDMARK COMMUNICATIONS, INC.

v.

COMMONWEALTH of Virginia.

Record No. 760596.

Supreme Court of Virginia.

March 4, 1977.

Same case as it appears in the Southeastern Reporter. Note how the headnotes differ from those in the Virginia Reports. The Shepard's Southeastern Citations is keyed to these headnotes.

es any information concerning a proceeding before the Commission, and it would be unreasonable to construe the statute to mean that only the participants in a Commission proceeding are subject to the prescribed sanctions or that only the first disclosure of confidential information is actionable; that the statute does not impose a prior restraint upon publication; and that the statute represented a legislative declaration by the General Assembly, fortified by a plain statement of public intent expressed in the Virginia Constitution, that a clear and present danger to the orderly administration of justice would be created by divulgence of the confidential proceedings of the Commission, and the sanction imposed thus sprung from a clear and well-defined legislative declaration.

Affirmed.

Poff, J., filed a dissenting opinion.

1. Disorderly Conduct ⚿1

Until a complaint against an allegedly disabled or unfit judge is filed with the Supreme Court, the proscription of statute, relating to the Judicial Inquiry and Review Commission, is applicable to punish any person, including a corporation, who divulges any information concerning a proceeding before the Commission, and the statute cannot be construed to mean that only the participants in a Commission proceeding are subject to the prescribed sanctions or that only the first disclosure of confidential information is actionable. Code 1950, § 2.1–37.13.

2. Constitutional Law ⚿90(3)

Freedom of the press is not an absolute right, and the state may punish its abuse. U.S.C.A.Const. Amend. 1.

3. Constitutional Law ⚿90.1(1)
Disorderly Conduct ⚿1

Statute providing that all proceedings before the Judicial Inquiry and Review Commission, including the identification of the subject judge, shall be confidential and shall not be divulged by any person to anyone except the Commission, except that the record of any proceeding filed with the Supreme Court shall lose its confidential character, does not impose a prior restraint upon publication. Code 1950, § 2.1–37.13; U.S.C.A.Const. Amend. 1.

4. Constitutional Law ⚿90.1(1)

Generally, prior restraints take the form of injunctions, requirements for licenses or permits, or censorship or previous review.

5. Disorderly Conduct ⚿1

Although, in prosecution of newspaper publisher for breach of the confidentiality of proceedings before the Judicial Inquiry and Review Commission, defendant could not be punished for the publication unless the revelation created a clear and present danger to a legitimate state interest, viz., the orderly administration of justice, and although the Commonwealth did not, beyond stipulated facts, produce other evidence by way of "actual facts" to show a clear and present danger, the subject statute represented a legislative declaration by the General Assembly, fortified by a plain statement of public intent expressed in the Constitution, that a clear and present danger to the orderly administration of justice

[Illustration 101]

TITLE PAGE: SHEPARD'S VIRGINIA CITATIONS

Vol. 69 OCTOBER, 1980 No. 3

SHEPARD'S VIRGINIA CITATIONS

A COMPILATION OF CITATIONS
TO
VIRGINIA CASES REPORTED IN THE VARIOUS SERIES OF VIRGINIA REPORTS AND IN THE SOUTHEASTERN REPORTER, TO THE UNITED STATES CONSTITUTION AND STATUTES, VIRGINIA CONSTITUTIONS, CODES, ACTS, ORDINANCES AND COURT RULES

THE CITATIONS

which include affirmances, reversals and dismissals by the United States Supreme Court and amendments, repeals, etc. of the Virginia Constitutions, Codes, Acts and Court Rules

APPEAR IN

VIRGINIA COLONIAL DECISIONS
JEFFERSON'S REPORTS
WYTHE'S CHANCERY REPORTS
HOWISON'S CRIMINAL TRIALS
PATTON, JR. AND HEATH, COURT OF APPEALS REPORTS
VIRGINIA DECISIONS
VIRGINIA REPORTS
WEST VIRGINIA REPORTS
SOUTHEASTERN REPORTER (Virginia and West Virginia Cases)
UNITED STATES SUPREME COURT REPORTS
LAWYERS' EDITION, UNITED STATES SUPREME COURT REPORTS
SUPREME COURT REPORTER
FEDERAL CASES
FEDERAL REPORTER
FEDERAL SUPPLEMENT
FEDERAL RULES DECISIONS
BANKRUPTCY REPORTER
UNIVERSITY OF RICHMOND LAW REVIEW
VIRGINIA LAW REVIEW
WASHINGTON AND LEE LAW REVIEW
WEST VIRGINIA LAW REVIEW
WILLIAM AND MARY LAW REVIEW
WILLIAM AND MARY REVIEW OF VIRGINIA LAW
CALIFORNIA LAW REVIEW
COLUMBIA LAW REVIEW
CORNELL LAW QUARTERLY
CORNELL LAW REVIEW
GEORGETOWN LAW JOURNAL
HARVARD LAW REVIEW
LAW AND CONTEMPORARY PROBLEMS
MICHIGAN LAW REVIEW
MINNESOTA LAW REVIEW
NEW YORK UNIVERSITY LAW REVIEW
NORTHWESTERN UNIVERSITY LAW REVIEW
STANFORD LAW REVIEW
TEXAS LAW REVIEW
UNIVERSITY OF CALIFORNIA AT LOS ANGELES LAW REVIEW
UNIVERSITY OF CHICAGO LAW REVIEW
UNIVERSITY OF ILLINOIS LAW FORUM
UNIVERSITY OF PENNSYLVANIA LAW REVIEW
WISCONSIN LAW REVIEW
YALE LAW JOURNAL
AMERICAN BAR ASSOCIATION JOURNAL
ACTS OF VIRGINIA

and in annotations of

LAWYERS' EDITION, UNITED STATES SUPREME COURT REPORTS
AMERICAN LAW REPORTS

also, for Virginia cases reported prior to the Southeastern Reporter, as cited in all units of the National Reporter System and in Vols. 1-283 Illinois Appellate Court Reports, Vols. 1-19 Ohio Appellate Reports and Vols. 1-101 Pennsylvania Superior Court Reports

SUBSCRIPTION $74.00 PER YEAR
Published Quarterly in January, April, July and October

SHEPARD'S/McGRAW-HILL
Post Office Box 1235
Colorado Springs, Colorado 80901
(303)475-7230

[Illustration 102]

PAGE FROM SHEPARD'S VIRGINIA CITATIONS

VIRGINIA REPORTS **Vol. 218**

-354-
63VaL1354
45A3581s

-360-
218Va[7]1049
219Va[2]467
220Va271
63VaL1352
73A2769s

-370-
63VaL1355

-376-
219Va[1]908

-381-
d218Va[1]611
63VaL1354
63VaL1400

-387-
219Va[1]26
219Va[1]96
219Va[1]754
219Va[2]755
35A2308s

-411-
84A31029n

4A2667s

-477-

-522-
f220Va[1]239
63VaL1472

-527-
218Va[2]929
63VaL1355
63VaL1397

-534-
d219Va[1]778
d219Va[3]778
218Va[3]137
460FS[3]416
75A3228s

-538-
63VaL1422

-548-
US cert den
in440US935
s219Va252
218Va[1]841
219Va[1]1071
63VaL1433

-552-
218Va154
218Va[1]299
63VaL1354

218Va[1]494

-637-

63VaL1402

-677-
63VaL1354

-680-
218Va[1]602

-682-
219Va1134
63VaL1353

-688-
63VaL1353
63VaL1401
64VaL1413

-699-
r435US829
r56LE21
r98SC1535
s434US887
s98SC259
63VaL1354
63VaL1385

-715-
63VaL1354

-740-
63VaL1456

-751-
219Va[3]980
599F2d[2]386
479FS[3]133
12RIC618
93A31268n

-763-
63VaL1495

-769-
14A3541s

-776-
63VaL1496

-782-
63VaL1369

-789-
591F2d[1]97
d463FS[1]907
63VaL1419

-847-
63VaL1353

-861-
220Va[1]416

-863-
64VaL53

-867-
218Va[1]925
63VaL1351

-869-
63VaL1473

220Va[1]407
63VaL1352
63VaL1436

-916-
220Va[3]320

-924-
218Va[1]356
63VaL1421

-929-
US cert den
in434US1016
218Va[4]101
63VaL1353
63VaL1411

-958-

Vol. 218

-1-
(235SE306)
63VaL1354

-4-
(235SE304)
d219Va[2]561
d219Va[3]561

-8-
(235SE307)

-12-

219Va[4]474
220Va[2]207
220Va[2]250
220Va[2]269
94A324n

-40-
(235SE325)
12RIC284
63VaL1418

-49-
(235SE432)
218Va[5]92
63VaL1354
63VaL1408

-59-
(235SE450)

-109-
(235SE346)

-115-
(235SE349)
219Va[1]78
63VaL1500

-124-
(235SE456)
86A31058n
87A31095n

-134-
(235SE354)

(237SE88)
cc619F2d327
f619F2d[2]332

-196-
(237SE89)
64VaL1442

-202-
(237SE92)
64VaL1537

-210-
(237SE97)

-216-
(237SE100)

-220-

-257-
(237SE120)
220Va[1]142
d459FS[2]733
482FS[2]1064
64VaL1387

-264-
(237SE124)

-270-
(237SE128)
64VaL1490
43LCP(2)47

220Va[2]67

-321-
(237SE157)

-333-
(237SE388)
219Va[1]938
218Va[8]255
64VaL1543

-346-
(237SE164)

-352-
(237SE167)
64VaL1443

-360-

-458-
(237SE777)
64VaL1410

-462-
(237SE779)
cc218Va453
cc100SC2814
64VaL1453

-467-
(237SE782)
95A3301n
95A3352n

(237SE799)

-511-
(237SE803)
219Va[1]402
219Va[2]402

-523-
(237SE810)

-529-
(237SE594)

-530-
(238SE799)
64VaL1384

-533-
(238SE800)

63VaL1352

219Va[2]923

Case appealed to U.S. Supreme Court, which reversed. Citations to all three sets are given.

Citations to same case in earlier proceedings.

217 Va. 699 cited in Virginia Law Review.

Note how in 217 Va. 751 Shepard's indicates when a case has been cited in an A.L.R. annotation.

Shepardizing the Landmark Communications Case in the Shepard's Virginia Citations.

Note how the first citation is <u>not</u> a parallel citation. This is because a parallel citation is only given the first time it appears in Shepard's. One will find the citation to the Southeastern Reporter in the 1978 bound volume, Case Edition of Shepard's Virginia Citations.

[Illustration 103]

PAGE FROM SHEPARD'S SOUTHEASTERN CITATIONS

Vol. 233 **SOUTHEASTERN REPORTER, 2d SERIES**

237SE[3]668
242SE[1]369
f242SE[2]370
243SE[1]263
– 40 –
(141GA184)
– 41 –
(141GA192)
252SE[1]430
– 42 –
(141GA193)
237SE[4]706
243SE[2]259
243SE[3]259
– 44 –

– 60 –
Case 2
(141GA241)
– 62 –
Case 1
(141GA224)
– 62 –
Case 2
(141GA96)
233SE284
– 62 –
Case 3
(141GA96)
– 63 –
Case 1

– 95 –
(268SoC276)
242SE[1]415
244SE[2]527
2. ⟶
– 98 –
(268SoC284)
– 101 –
(268SoC291)
235SE[1]293
464FS[4]885
– 105 –
(268SoC300)

– 151 –
(238Ga421)
239SE[3]677
240SE[1]847
240SE[3]875
f249SE[11]67
f250SE[3]475
251SE[9]288
– 154 –
(238Ga431)
– 155 –
(238Ga427)
233SE[1]157
236SE[3]647
249SE[2]573
249SE[1]610

251SE[3]360
– 178 –
(238Ga364)
e238SE439
243SE[4]72
– 180 –
(238Ga362)
– 182 –
1. ⟶
(238Ga351)
247SE[1]856
– 185 –

– 193 –
(238Ga413)
242SE[2]49
242SE[2]49
242SE[4]49
242SE[4]49
247SE[2]872
e250SE[2]462
251SE[2]546
251SE[4]546
446FS[2]1173
446FS[3]1173
Colo
570P2d522
– 195 –
Case 1
(238Ga416)

– 210 –
(238Ga432)
– 211 –
(238Ga444)
– 212* –
(141GA209)
234SE[4]820
234SE[5]820
257SE[5]41
– 215 –
(141GA258)
a236SE644
– 217 –
(141GA271)
253SE[1]564

– 243 –
(141GA254)
– 244 –
(141GA255)
– 245 –
(141GA256)
245SE[2]462
– 246 –
(141GA257)
242SE[1]368
– 247 –
(141GA265)
252SE[1]673
– 248 –

Shepardizing the Landmark Communications Case in the Shepard's Southeastern Citations. (233 S.E.2d 120) Note how the parallel citation is given and the symbol indicating the case has been reversed.

Notes:

1. In regional Shepard's, citations are given to citing cases from other states.

2. Under page 151 note how citing cases refer to headnotes, e. g., 249 S.E.2d 67 has cited 233 S.E.2d 151 for the point of law in its 11th headnote.

– 53 –
Case 1
(141GA207)
253SE[1]171
– 53 –
Case 2
(141GA208)
– 54 –
(141GA235)
246SE[1]423
246SE[1]425
250SE[1]553
– 56 –
(141GA236)
– 57 –
(141GA238)
– 58 –
(141GA238)
247SE[1]189
249SE[3]330
252SE[7]84
– 60 –
Case 1
(141GA240)

– 74 –
(32NCA588)
– 76 –
(32NCA548)
r240SE338
– 79 –
(32NCA593)
– 80* –
(32NCA565)
s235SE788
– 84 –
(32NCA584)
246SE[8]36
– 87 –
(32NCA591)
s220SE164
– 88* –
(32NCA499)
s235SE783
Colo
585P2d322
Mo
559SW206
559SW213

(268SoC329)
cc233SE118
– 120 –
(217Va699)
r435US829
r56LE1
r98SC1535
s431US964
s434US887
s53LE1059
s54LE172
s97SC2919
s98SC259
– 142 –
(238Ga277)
– 144 –
(238Ga480)
f233SE[2]150
235SE[1]32
235SE33
238SE[3]124
243SE[1]285
245SE[1]326
248SE[1]693
o251SE[1]244
256SE[3]611
– 149 –
(238Ga489)
243SE[1]604

Parallel citation to state reporter.

Case reversed by U.S. Supreme Court.

f238SE[1]286
f235SE[2]477
250SE[2]480
– 174 –
(238Ga372)
254SE[1]825
– 175 –
(238Ga367)
240SE[1]39
240SE[2]778
240SE[3]778
241SE219
246SE517
251SE359

243SE[2]265
f253SE[1]887
253SE[4]888
f254SE[1]463
f254SE[2]463
f254SE[4]463
f254SE[1]910
– 189 –
(238Ga490)
– 191 –
(238Ga454)
243SE[1]69

(238Ga437)
– 208 –
(238Ga435)
j234SE[2]415
238SE[2]76
– 209 –
(238Ga433)
240SE[1]53
255SE[1]58
Mich
267NW85

(141GA298)
– 236 –
(141GA245)
j246SE[5]654
254SE[7]475
– 240 –
(141GA249)
– 242 –
(141GA253)
246SE[1]353
248SE[1]511

246SE[1]459
– 264 –
Case 1
(141GA294)
– 264 –
Case 2
(141GA304)
– 267 –
(141GA306)

328 See note on first page of this division. See prior volume(s) of citator for earlier citations

SECTION D. STATUTE CITATIONS

Statutes are dealt with by *Shepard's Citations* in a manner similar to cases. The notations cover the form and operation of the law by the legislature and the courts. Its operation is identified by abbreviations denoting legislative changes (amendments, repeals, revisions, re-enactments, etc.) and judicial interpretations (constitutional, unconstitutional, invalid, etc.).

Some abbreviations used for notations in *Shepard's Citations* to statutes are given below: [6]

Form of Statute

Amend.	Amendment
App.	Appropriation Act
Art.	Article
C or Ch.	Chapter
Cl.	Clause
Ex.	Extra Session
Loc.	Local Acts or Laws
No.	Number
p.	Page
Res.	Resolution
Sp.	Special Session
Subd.	Subdivision
Subsec.	Subsection
Tit.	Title
§	Section
¶	Paragraph

The form of statutes vary, depending on the plan adopted by a jurisdiction. The Table of Abbreviations in each unit of *Shepard's Citations* should be examined specifically to determine the local scheme.

Operation of Statute

Legislative

A (amended)	Statute amended.
Ad (added)	New section added.
E (extended)	Provisions of an existing statute extended in their application to a later statute, or allowance of additional time for

[6] HOW TO USE SHEPARD'S CITATIONS, *supra* note 2.

	performance of duties required by a statute within a limited time.
L (limited)	Provisions of an existing statute declared not to be extended in their application to a later statute.
PA (proposed amendment)	Future action necessary to confirm or reject amendment.
PR (proposed repeal)	Future action necessary to confirm or reject repeal.
R (repealed)	Abrogation of an existing statute.
Re-en (re-enacted)	Statute re-enacted.
Rn (renumbered)	Renumbering of existing sections.
Rp (repealed in part)	Abrogation of part of an existing statute.
Rs (repealed and superseded)	Abrogation of an existing statute, and substitution of new legislation therefor.
Rv (revised)	Statute revised.
S (superseded)	Substitution of new legislation for an existing statute, not expressly abrogated.
Sg (supplementing)	New matter added to an existing statute.
Sp (superseded in part)	Substitution of new legislation for new part of an existing statute, not expressly abrogated.

Judicial

C	Constitutional
U	Unconstitutional
V	Void or invalid.
Up	Unconstitutional in part
Va	Valid
Vp	Void or invalid in part

The Citations to Statutes units of *Shepard's Citations* cover the following areas: citations to the United States Constitution and state constitutions; the United States Code and Acts of Congress (not included in the United States Code); the various state codes, legislative enactments and court rules; and various municipal charters and ordinances.

The information contained in the statutes units is presented in accordance with this arrangement: Statutory amendments, repeals, etc., are listed first, followed by state and federal court citations and citations in the attorneys general opinions, legal periodicals and acts of the legislature.

1. Constitutions

The federal and state constitutions are covered by the *Statute Editions to Shepard's Citations.* A constitution section in a *Statute Edition* is arranged under the articles and amendments to the constitution. Citing sources are listed under these provisions. [See Illustration 105]

2. City Charters and Ordinances

The municipal charters and ordinances are part of the *State Citations.* Reference should be made to the citator of the state in which the city is located for citations to the city's charter or ordinances.

The section under "Municipal Charters" in the *Statute Citations* is arranged alphabetically by cities in many state editions and subdivided by topics. The unit may have a separate *Index to Municipal Charters.* The Ordinances section also may be arranged alphabetically by cities and subdivided by topics. It, too, may have a separate *Index to Ordinances.* In some citators, the citations to the ordinances of the larger cities are separately arranged. To meet editorial requirements, the citations to ordinances may be indexed by section numbers as well as topically. [See Illustration 76]

3. Shepard's Ordinance Law Annotations

This six-volume set is actually a digest rather than a citator. It is arranged under broad subjects, with each subject subdivided into sub-entries. Under each sub-entry annotations of court decisions are listed. This set is useful when legal research requires the locating of cases on the same aspect of local government law in different cities. [See Illustration 77]

4. Court Rules

Citations to court decisions interpreting court rules are also covered by *Shepard's Citations.* The Court Rules section is arranged by courts (final, intermediate and original jurisdiction), and is subdivided by rule numbers.

SECTION E. ILLUSTRATIONS: STATUTE CITATIONS

104. Page from Shepard's U.S. Citations—Statutes

105. Page from Texas Constitution in the Shepard's Texas Citations—Statutes

106. Page from Shepard's Virginia Citations—Statute Section

107. Page from Shepard's Texas Citations—Court Rules Section

[Illustration 104]

PAGE FROM SHEPARD'S U.S. CITATIONS—STATUTES

T. 26 § 6401 UNITED STATES CODE '76 Ed. & '77 Supp.

§§ 6401 to 6407
594F2d1146
§ 6401
590F2d72
Subsec. c
590F2d68
Subsec. d
A94St209
R94St266
§ 6402
592F2d1047
609F2d1138
478FS309
480FS1239
Subsec. a
592F2d310
602F2d942
609F2d1136
478FS307
Subsec. b
588F2d342
592F2d1046
§ 6411
483FS593
Subsec. a
1. → A94St211
483FS593
Subsec. d
Subd. 2
A94St218
§ 6413
484FS182
Subsec. a
Subd. 1
465FS1118
Subsec. b
465FS1118
§ 6416
609F2d1138
Subsec. a
609F2d1138
Subd. 1
609F2d1138
¶A
609F2d1138
Subd. 2
¶B
609F2d1138
Subsec. b
609F2d1138
Subd. 2
609F2d1139
¶B
604F2d17
¶G
597F2d449
¶N
Ad94St227
Subd. 3
¶A
A94St227
¶B
609F2d1136
¶C
A94St227

Subd. 4
¶B
A94St227
§ 6421
Subsec. d
Subd. 2
(91St3190)
¶B
A94St226
§ 6427
Subsec. a
A94St278
Subsec. b
Subd. 1
A94St278
Subsec. c
A94St278
Subsec. d
A94St278
Subsec. e
(92St2758)
Subd. 1
A94St278
Subsec. f
(92St2758)
599F2d516
607F2d1303
614F2d1264
460FS1283
471FS1159
483FS592
41ALRF378n
Subsec. b
471FS1151
Subsec. c
602F2d135
614F2d1265
464FS716
Subd. 1
589F2d827
589F2d828
591F2d1244
614F2d1265
471FS1151

Subd. 2
471FS1151
Subd. 3
614F2d1265
Subd. 4
607F2d1300
Subsec. e
614F2d1267
471FS1159
Subd. 1
¶A
471FS1151
Subsec. h
483FS592
Subsec. q
RnSubsec o
[94St208
RnSubsec p
[94St210
Ad94St253
§ 6502
613F2d619
470FS280
41ALRF372n
41ALRF381n
41ALRF384n
A94St226
§ 6511
590F2d69
469FS759
Subsec. a
588F2d954
590F2d69
597F2d1354
603F2d503
606F2d536
613F2d519
484FS182
Subsec. b
588F2d954
613F2d525
Subd. 1
590F2d69
Subd. 2
613F2d519

¶A
590F2d68
¶B
590F2d69
613F2d519
Subsec. c
613F2d519
Subd. 1
613F2d524
Subd. 2
613F2d519
Subsec. f
A94St226
Subsec. g
(92St2819)
Subd. 2
A94St208
Subsec. h
RnSubsec i
[94St254
Subsec. h
Ad94St254
§ 6512
Subsec. a
A94St253
Subsec b
615F2d901
476FS1288
43ALRF141n
Subsec. 1
615F2d901
Subsec. 2
615F2d902
476FS1288
Subsec. 3
43ALRF141n
43ALRF144n
Subsec. 5
476FS1288
Subsec. 8
615F2d901
§ 6532
463FS842
469FS759

Subsec. a
611F2d1226
Subd. 1
440US475
59LE523
99SC1306
594F2d45
597F2d257
608F2d772
463FS842
471FS973
Subd. 4
594F2d45
§ 6601
602F2d734
607F2d1300
467FS30
Subsec. a
588F2d342
602F2d272
602F2d737
602F2d939
607F2d1302
Subsec. b
602F2d273
Subd. 1
602F2d945
Subsec. h
RnSubsec i
[94St254
Subsec. h
Ad94St254
§ 6621
602
46
473
Subsec. a
A93St1275
Subsec. c
482FS1320
§ 6651
592F2d1074
611F2d212
480FS813

Subsec. a
592F2d228
594F2d122
603F2d495
612F2d193
613F2d771
614F2d816
480FS809
483FS287
Subd. 1
594F2d1142
611F2d213
461FS1382
467FS30
480FS810
483FS285
Subd. 2
467FS30
480FS810
§ 6652
Subsec. a
A93St1277
Subd. 2
R93St1277
Subd. 3
RnSubd 2
462FS847
471FS1152
§ 6654
603F2d495
§ 6656
591F2d1144
2. → **§ 6658**
R93St1276
§ 6659
Subsec. a
437US308
469FS618
Subd. 1
591F2d1144

§§ 6671 to 6675
594F2d1313
§ 6671
591F2d1139
591F2d1153
592F2d156
602F2d921
Subsec. b
588F2d952
591F2d1139
598F2d1129
602F2d923
607F2d954
§ 6672
588F2d952
591F2d1136
591F2d1144
591F2d1151
592F2d156
593F2d4
594F2d220
594F2d1313
598F2d1129
600F2d87
[92St2938
§ 6695
Subsec. b
481FS812
§ 6698
Rn§6698*A
[94St223
§ 6699
A94St200
§ 6851
594F2d423
475FS297
11ALR359s
Subsec. a
482FS1228

Subd. 1
475FS298
482FS1228
§ 6861
et seq.
41ALRF377n
§ 6861 ← 3.
C462FS846
590F2d49
594F2d427
468FS461
475FS1101
Subsec. a
C462FS846
41ALRF377n
Subsec. b
590F2d51
Subsec. c
590F2d51
Subsec. e
590F2d51
§ 6862
A94St226
Subsec. a
¶A
614F2d870
Cl. 1
592F2d227
§ 6902
Subsec. a
592F2d227
§ 7122
611F2d500
469FS616
Subsec. a
437US312
611F2d503
465FS438
469FS614
82FRD19
§ 7201
et seq.

Continued

See note on first page of this division. See prior volumes for earlier citations

122

Shepardizing a U.S. Code section.

This unit gives citations to each court decision citing the U.S. Code. It also indicates when a Code section has been amended or repealed.

Notes:

1. **26 U.S.C. § 6411a has been amended by 94 Stat. 211.**
2. **26 U.S.C. § 6658 has been repealed by 93 Stat. 1276.**
3. **26 U.S.C. § 6861 has been held constitutional at 462 F.Supp. 846.**

[Illustration 105]

PAGE FROM TEXAS CONSTITUTION IN THE SHEPARD'S TEXAS CITATIONS—STATUTES

Art. 1 **TEXAS CONSTITUTION, 1876 AS AMENDED 1973**

Art. 1
588SW596
§ 1
582SW396
33SLJ589
§ 3
568SW357
569SW902
570SW124
570SW494
572SW526
586SW168
586SW487
589SW712
591SW560
484FS1005
15HUL549
32SLJ128
32SLJ219
33SLJ162
33SLJ838
19SoT411
§ 3a

582SW807
582SW848
586SW504
586SW513
588SW356
588SW369
589SW404
594SW75
33SLJ510
§ 10
568SW132
571SW911
572SW533
573SW19
573SW25
573SW809
574SW125
574SW770
576SW66
576SW621
576SW835
577SW700
577SW734
578SW394

§ 12
576SW148
§ 13
570SW494
578SW460
578SW468
580SW47
580SW849
582SW158
584SW918
590SW763
591SW560
594SW446
596SW303
596SW913
596SW928
33SLJ162
19SoT432
10TTR424
§ 14
569SW902
570SW929
574SW74
574SW620

590SW730
31BLR432
31BLR443
31BLR490
32SLJ415
§ 18
582SW625
584SW925
589SW792
590SW775
592SW47
594SW120
595SW846
597SW16
597SW500
33SLJ557
34SLJ155
§ 19
568SW329
568SW341
568SW357
568SW374
569SW902
570SW47

§ 28
571SW934
581SW672

Art. 2
579SW915
§ 1
568SW392
580SW350
582SW231
582SW395
582SW617
594SW163
454FS598
33SLJ552
34SLJ474

Art. 3
570SW417
§ 1
575SW60
§ 30
594SW435

Subd. d
Ad1979
[p3237
§ 52f
1979p3231
§ 56
572SW832
572SW937
586SW483
96$A^2$586n
§ 66
1979p3232

Art. 4
§ 1
591SW568
§ 11
571SW906
580SW350
591SW465
594SW103
63MnL73
§ 11A

A1979p3240
435US848
98SC1546
Subd. 12
1977p3362
A1979p3238
§ 2
1979p3223
§ 3
1979p3223
582SW396
589SW956
§ 3b
572SW291
§ 4
1977p3359
A1979p3240
16HUL364
32SLJ508
§ 5
1977p3359
1979p3223
A1979p3241

586SW564
589SW955
590SW597
591SW563
591SW648
592SW406
593SW134
593SW676
593SW796
596SW527
596SW849
477FS902
32SLJ20
33SLJ429
19SoT403
§ 10
571SW517
583SW665
592SW19
§ 11
570SW900
581SW251
582SW629
582SW774

In each Shepard's Citations state unit there is a statute section which includes a section on the state's constitution. This Illustration is from the Shepard's Texas Citations. Each time a section of the Texas constitution has been cited by a Texas court, or a federal court sitting in Texas, the citation appears in this section.

Note also how citations are given to amendments to the constitution.

90$A^2$164n
90$A^2$175n
90$A^2$178n
§ 6
569SW902
33SLJ171
§ 8
569SW902
577SW477
577SW547
16HUL593
34SLJ455
84$A^2$614n
84$A^2$632n
§ 9
569SW614
569SW902
573SW516
574SW765
576SW48
576SW376
576SW380
576SW819
577SW227
577SW709
578SW385
578SW419
578SW688
579SW8
582SW434
582SW467

591SW832
592SW620
593SW703
594SW425
596SW857
596SW894
597SW363
443US415
61LE644
99SC2923
15HUL4
16HUL364
33SLJ524
§ 11
573SW245
574SW166
594SW102
594SW450
32SLJ455
§ 11a
1977p3353
A1979p3233
574SW166
594SW449
32SLJ455
Subd. 1
32SLJ455
Subd. 2
32SLJ455
Subd. 3
32SLJ455

571SW517
576SW621
584SW945
591SW648
592SW19
§ 15a
569SW643
571SW58
592SW656
§ 16
569SW608
573SW502
577SW341
582SW235
584SW323
587SW422
591SW620
595SW906
481FS1254
32SLJ128
33SLJ846
33SLJ1000
34SLJ321
§ 17
570SW391
571SW518
572SW581
578SW496
582SW230
584SW545
589SW392

587SW58
589SW133
590SW144
590SW568
591SW485
591SW610
591SW895
592SW624
592SW655
594SW558
596SW928
578F2d1005
15HUL15
32SLJ123
33SLJ133
33SLJ162
34SLJ494
10SMJ44
19SoT411
92$A^2$1097n
§ 23
586SW501
34SLJ522
§ 26
583SW828
590SW730
615F2d345
§ 27
577SW477

§ 45
576SW66
§ 47
1979p3221
§ 49b
1977p3355
A1979p3234
33SLJ147
§ 49d-1
A1977p
[LXXV
§ 50c
1979p3219
AdNov6,
[1979
34SLJ82
§ 51
31BLR408
63MnL548
§ 51b
1977p3367
R1979p3237
§ 51f
584SW899
§ 52
31BLR408
Subd. a
33SLJ493
Subd. d
1977p3374

A1979p3237
569SW931
572SW938
582SW396
586SW483
591SW648
595SW202
§ 1a
575SW402
30BLR16
Subd. 2
1977p3362
A1979p3238
Subd. 5
1977p3362
A1979p3238
Subd. 6
¶ A
1977p3362
A1979p3238
Subd. 7
1977p3362
A1979p3239
Subd. 8
1977p3362
A1979p3239
Subd. 9
1977p3362
A1979p3239
Subd. 10
1977p3362

32SLJ508
33SLJ485
33SLJ520
§ 6
1977p3366
1979p3223
A1979p3241
569SW558
572SW293
576SW868
577SW386
580SW172
589SW812
591SW852
§ 7
578SW518
16HUL364
§ 8
568SW132
570SW454
571SW214
571SW877
572SW573
572SW752
573SW225
576SW148
577SW574
578SW809
580SW170
580SW635
585SW760

A1979p3242
572SW751
575SW346
577SW575
583SW665
591SW648
592SW407
593SW748
477FS902
34SLJ415
§ 17
572SW716
§ 18
587SW59
596SW575
616F2d106
454FS598
472FS976
477FS920
16HUL364
§ 19
1977p3372
A1979p3243
577SW575
586SW484
591SW872
34SLJ415
§ 21
581F2d560

202 **See 1974 and 1974-1979 Bound Volumes for earlier citations**

[Illustration 106]

PAGE FROM SHEPARD'S VIRGINIA CITATIONS— STATUTE SECTION

§ 1-10 **CODE OF VIRGINIA, 1950 (AS AMENDED BY REPLACEMENT**

§ 1-10
218Va473
219Va287
247SE400
14RIC157
§ 1-12
219Va143
219Va658
246SE613
250SE739
§ 1-13.3:1
567F2d263
§ 1-13.11
219Va1084
254SE108
§ 1-13.42
218Va134
219Va775
250SE365
Subsec. a
Subd. 2
13RIC663
Subsec. b
218Va134
13RIC695
§ 1-15.2
Ad1980C465
§ 1-16
218Va134
218Va473
219Va455
219Va775
248SE135
250SE365
460FS412
§§ 2-57.05 to 2-57.015
218Va739
241SE420
§ 2.1-1
A1978C219
A1979C272
§ 2.1-11
Rs1980C119

A1978C420
§ 2.1-37.3
A1978C452

§ 2.1-37.7
A1978C260
§ 2.1-37.8
A1978C452
A1979C316
§ 2.1-37.13
A1979C11
435US829
56LE1
98SC1535
454FS804
480FS199
63VaL1354
§ 2.1-38.1
R1979C455
§ 2.1-41.2
A1979C294
§ 2.1-42.1
L1978C653
A1978C834
L1980C621
§ 2.1-42.2
A1979C141
§ 2.1-51.9
A1978C32
A1979C294
§ 2.1-51.9:1
Ad1978C88
§ 2.1-51.15
A1978C635
§ 2.1-51.18
A1978C455
A1978C606
A1978C607
A1978C820
§ 2.1-51.18:2

A1980C620
§ 2.1-51.29
Ad1978C314
Rs1979C231

§ 2.1-51.30
Ad1978C753
A1980C273
§§ 2.1-64.4 to 2.1-64.14

← 1.

2.1-64.22
Rs1978C820
§ 2.1-64.23
A1979C644
A1980C728
§§ 2.1-64.28:1 to 2.1-64.28:4
Ad1978C455
§§ 2.1-64.29 to 2.1-64.31
R1979C455
§ 2.1-64.33
A1979C147
§ 2.1-70
R1978C449

← 2.

§ 2.1-71.1
Ad1978C641
§ 2.1-113
A1978C846
§§ 2.1-113.1 to 2.1-113.3
Ad1978C846
§ 2.1-113.2
A1980C728
§ 2.1-114.5

116.1 et seq.
484FS803

§§ 2.1-116.1 to 2.1-116.9
Ad1978C19
§ 2.1-116.1
A1979C592
§ 2.1-116.2
484FS803
§ 2.1-116.4
484FS803
§ 2.1-116.5
A1980C191
484FS803
Subsec. 2
484FS803
§ 2.1-116.6
484FS803
§ 2.1-116.7
484FS803
§§ 2.1-116.10 to 2.1-116.14
Ad1979C355

A1980C255
12RIC543
§ 2.1-124
486FS311
§ 2.1-125
A1980C269
§ 2.1-127
A1979C266
§ 2.1-133.1
218Va589
219Va1023
239SE94
254SE73

218Va739
241SE420
§ 2.1-190.1
Ad1979C173

§ 2.1-204
A1978C195
A1979C509
§ 2.1-206.1
A1978C726
A1979C19
A1979C151
Rs1980C672
§ 2.1-208
R1979C215
§ 2.1-209
A1979C215
§ 2.1-210
A1978C52
A1979C215
§ 2.1-225
A1980C672
§ 2.1-226
218Va739
241SE420
§ 2.1-227
218Va739
241SE420
§ 2.1-230
R1979C215
§§ 2.1-234.1 to 2.1-234.9
Ad1980C538
§ 2.1-328
A1980C596
§ 2.1-328.2
Ad1980C50
§ 2.1-329
A1978C53
§ 2.1-329.1
A1979C135
§§ 2.1-335.1 to 2.1-335.3
Ad1978C103
§ 2.1-

346.1
68CaL509
§ 2.1-341
A1978C573
A1978C826

A1979C369
A1979C687
A1980C754
§ 2.1-342
A1978C810
A1979C682
A1979C684
A1979C686
A1979C689
A1980C678
A1980C754
§ 2.1-344
A1979C369
A1979C684
A1980C221
A1980C475
A1980C476
A1980C754
§ 2.1-345
A1979C369
§ 2.1-346
A1978C826
§ 2.1-346.1
A1978C826
§ 2.1-348
A1980C552
§§ 2.1-349 to 2.1-351
L1978C537
§ 2.1-349.1
A1980C562
§ 2.1-353.1
A1978C243
§ 2.1-353.2
Ad1978C847
A1979C301
606F2d654
§ 2.1-354
A1978C847
§ 2.1-354.1
Ad1978C847

Ad1980C422
§§ 2.1-377 to 2.1-386
62MnL659

§ 2.1-380
L1978C409
§ 2.1-382
A1978C810
A1979C683
A1979C688
A1979C689
§ 2.1-383
A1979C683
§ 2.1-384
A1979C685
A1980C752
§ 2.1-384.1
Ad1978C409
§ 2.1-391
A1979C672
A1979C678
§ 2.1-392
R1978C802
§ 2.1-393
A1978C802
12RIC305
§ 2.1-394
A1979C283
§ 2.1-397.1
Ad1979C678
§ 2.1-398
A1978C570
A1979C319
A1979C320
§ 2.1-399
A1979C319
§ 2.1-405
Rs1979C672
§ 2.1-406
Rs1979C672
§ 2.1-407
A1978C84
§ 2.1-408
A1978C84
§ 2.1-409
A1978C84
§ 2.1-410
A1978C84
A1979C678
A1980C628
§ 2.1-420

§§ 2.1-437.1 to 2.1-437.3
Ad1979C519

§ 2.1-440
A1980C357
§ 2.1-441
A1980C357
§ 2.1-442
A1979C508
A1980C357
§ 2.1-447
A1980C357
§ 2.1-450.1
Ad1978C24
§ 2.1-454
A1978C653
A1980C620
§ 2.1-458
A1980C357
§ 2.1-467.2
A1979C403
§ 2.1-467.4
A1979C403
§ 2.1-467.5
A1979C403
§§ 2.1-469 to 2.1-479
Rs1978C653
§ 2.1-482
A1978C139
A1978C770
§ 2.1-483
A1978C770
R1979C678
§ 2.1-484
A1978C770
§ 2.1-486
A1978C770
A1978C811
§§ 2.1-488.1 to 2.1-488.6
Ad1978C580
§ 2.1-488.1

Ad1978C545
Rs1980C525
§ 2.1-521.1
A1979C243

Shepardizing a state statute

1. § 2.1–37.13 of the Code of Virginia amended by 1979 Virginia session laws, Chapter 11. Note that this is the statute involved in the Landmark Communications Case and the citations to the U.S. Supreme Court Reports.

2. § 2.1–70 is repealed by 1978 Virginia session laws, Chapter 449.

See note on first page of this division. See 1978 Bound Volume, Statute Edition for earlier citations

70

[Illustration 107]

PAGE FROM SHEPARD'S TEXAS CITATIONS— COURT RULES SECTION

TEXAS COURT RULES

Rules of Civil Procedure

As Amended 1977

Rule 1
579SW459
589SW493
589SW860
590SW605
592SW58
596SW178
20SoT2

Rule 2
596SW178

Rule 4
569SW877

Rule 11
568SW131
568SW442
569SW536
573SW839
576SW670
580SW902
582SW209
582SW615
583SW433
586SW941
587SW518
588SW599
589SW143
589SW514
589SW671
590SW187
596SW178
596SW212
597SW22
34SLJ435

590SW155
590SW561
592SW27
593SW766
593SW856
595SW634
595SW636
596SW266
596SW572
30BLR20
32SLJ112
32SLJ423
33SLJ476
34SLJ445
Subd. 1
576SW170
581SW700
33SLJ477

Rule 22
573SW833
585SW679
597SW520

Cl. 2
593SW376

Rule 40
569SW928
Subd. a
579SW56

Rule 41
576SW137
576SW908
580SW30
581SW305
583SW653
584SW516
586SW664
586SW688
591SW909
33SLJ120

Rule 42
577SW778

577SW353
581SW791
587SW675
589SW157
590SW206
591SW583
592SW678
595SW586
19SoT415
Subd. b
576SW773
581SW523
596SW316

Rule 47
570SW218
578SW886
581SW789
589SW157
591SW583
595SW586
597SW388
32SLJ413

592SW678
597SW34

Rule 60
581SW305
586SW701
586SW704

Rules 62 to 65
593SW809

Rule 62
569SW928
578SW525
597SW50

Rule 63
569SW614
569SW934
571SW409
573SW257

574SW641
574SW795
577SW291
577SW341
577SW347
578SW681
578SW886
580SW444
580SW673
580SW932
586SW909
591SW583
595SW207
596SW937
34SLJ264
34SLJ445
11SMJ16

Rule 68
574SW808
578SW469

Rule 71

Rule 87
578SW491
582SW215
32SLJ264

Rule 88
585SW340

Rule 89
568SW410
570SW138
578SW491

Rule 90
568SW668
570SW81
570SW180
570SW463
570SW512
571SW72
572SW557

Each state unit of Shepard's Citations has a section in the Statutes Division which Shepardizes the Court Rules of the state appellate courts.

Rule 5
568SW410
577SW559
579SW545
579SW911
581SW269
582SW492
583SW645
583SW899
584SW506
585SW680
586SW137
586SW699
586SW847
589SW164
597SW346
33SLJ378
34SLJ339
34SLJ447
Subd. b
581SW272

Rule 7
573SW257
574SW808

Rule 8
573SW263

Rule 10
573SW263

Rule 21a
568SW410
575SW361
578SW834
587SW715
592SW24
592SW70
596SW569
30BLR29
32SLJ274

Rule 21c
570SW212
572SW86
572SW105
572SW358
575SW319
576SW168
577SW561
577SW579
577SW795
578SW529
580SW127
581SW700
581SW714
581SW777
581SW779
582SW605
583SW442
583SW645
584SW710
586SW701
590SW153

Rule 31
585SW769
591SW931
32SLJ218
34SLJ272

Rule 38
10TTR934
Subd. a
596SW296
Subd. c
83A3355n
Subd. d
10TTR957

Rule 39
574SW180
581SW300
586SW956
591SW322
593SW374
594SW548
596SW569
32SLJ416
Subd. a
581SW302
596SW569
10TTR940
¶ 1
593SW375
¶ 2
Cl. 1
593SW375

34SLJ426
11TTR21
Subd. a
591SW933
594SW484
Subd. b
577SW778
578SW171
¶ 1
594SW174
¶ 2
594SW174
¶ 3
594SW174
¶ 4
594SW174
Subd. c
582SW601
¶ 1
578SW169
34SLJ426
Subd. f
32SLJ415

Rule 44
570SW458
576SW140
33SLJ160
Subd. 2
570SW459

Rule 45
570SW180
575SW376

577SW353
581SW710
19SoT424

Rule 51
581SW710
584SW954
442US425
60LE1004
99SC2378
10TTR934
Subd. a
585SW352
Subd. b
83A3355n

Rule 52
568SW413

Rule 54
570SW193
574SW174
576SW874
578SW866

Rule 56
580SW25
581SW789

Rule 59
586SW149
591SW590

597SW349
597SW411
597SW525
33SLJ432
34SLJ438

Rule 65
597SW444

Rule 66
571SW409
574SW795
581SW793
582SW556
585SW818
586SW688
588SW406
588SW645
588SW664
592SW56
595SW207
596SW301
597SW50
597SW351
11SMJ16

Rule 67
570SW81
570SW180
570SW222
570SW512
571SW214
572SW568

32SLJ422

Rule 83
580SW620

Rule 84
578SW827
582SW538

Rules 86 to 89
585SW359

Rule 86
568SW411
570SW193
571SW344
577SW769
580SW896
581SW269
582SW492
582SW534
582SW537
584SW582
585SW786
589SW790
590SW721
591SW953
594SW465
597SW464
32SLJ264
10TTR958

588SW626
588SW643
589SW863
590SW940
591SW590
591SW910
592SW14
593SW380
593SW774
593SW813
593SW857
594SW515
596SW941
34SLJ437

Rule 91
591SW910
593SW380
593SW774

Rule 92
584SW919
590SW750
593SW415

Rules 93 to 95
33SLJ219

Rule 93
570SW559
572SW110
Continued

346

See note on first page of this division. See 1974 and 1974-1979 Bound Volumes for earlier citations

SECTION F. OTHER UNITS OF SHEPARD'S CITATIONS

Some units of *Shepard's Citations* have additional or different features from those previously described. These are discussed below:

1. Acts and Cases by Popular Name, Federal and State

[See Illustration 21]

2. Bankruptcy Citations

This includes citations to bankruptcy decisions in *American Bankruptcy Reports,* in the various federal reporters, and in looseleafs such as *Bankruptcy Court Decisions* (CRR) and *Bankruptcy Law Reporter* (CCH).

3. Code of Federal Regulations

Contains citations to the *Code of Federal Regulations,* Presidential Proclamations, Executive Orders, and reorganization plans.

4. Criminal Justice Citations

The American Bar Association has adopted and published[7] the *Standards for Criminal Justice.* There are presently seventeen *Standards,* with titles such as "Urban Police Functions," "Providing Defense Services," "Fair Trial and Fair Press," and "Trial by Jury." While these *Standards* have no official status, they are frequently cited by courts. *Criminal Justice Citations* lists each of the *Standards* and then gives citations to those cases which have cited sections of the *Standards.*

5. Federal Circuit Table

In order to determine the circuit or district for *Federal Reporter* or *Federal Supplement* citations, *Shepard's Federal Circuit Table* has been published. This Table identifies the circuit or district of any reference since 1960 to the *Federal Reporter* or the *Federal Supplement* shown in any edition of *Shepard's Citations.*

6. Federal Labor Law Citations

This contains citations to the decisions and orders of the National Labor Relations Board. It also provides cross reference tables to citations from labor law looseleaf services. The statutes volumes contain citations to the various federal statutes dealing with labor.

7. Federal Law Citations in Selected Law Reviews

This unit will be discussed in Chapter 17.

[7] Little, Brown and Co. (1980). (4 vols.).

8. Federal Tax Locator

This multi-volume set started publication in 1974. It is unlike other *Shepard's* publications in that it is not a citator. Rather, it is an index to current sources of law relating to federal taxation. It attempts in one alphabet to cite all sources of federal tax law. Main entries are listed on the top of the page, and sub-entries are then alphabetically listed under each main entry. Each sub-entry cites to the relevant Internal Revenue Code provision, Treasury regulations, Tax Court Rules, Treatises, Treasury decisions and other applicable administrative regulations. It also cites court decisions, the various tax looseleaf services, and articles from over 120 legal periodicals.

It is kept up to date by quarterly cumulative pocket supplements.

9. Law Review Citations

This unit will be discussed in Chapter 17.

10. Military Justice Citations

This citator covers citations to decisions of the U.S. Court of Military Appeals and the Boards and Courts of Military Review, to the Uniform Code of Military Justice, the Manual for Courts Martial, and to military court rules and regulations. The citing material includes cases in the *Military Justice Reporter*, in the other federal and state reporters, and in Opinions of the Attorneys General of the United States.

11. New York Codes, Rules and Regulations Citations

The New York Codes, Rules, and Regulations is a set containing the administrative regulations and rules for the State of New York. Shepard's publication is part digest, part index. It contains annotations of selected cases which cite the New York administrative code. It also provides a citator function for those cases selected for annotations.

12. Professional Responsibility Citations

This unit gives coverage to all citations to the American Bar Association, *Code of Professional Responsibility* and *Code of Judicial Conduct*.

13. Restatement Citations

This unit will be discussed in Chapter 18.

SECTION G. ILLUSTRATIONS: OTHER UNITS OF SHEPARD'S

108. Excerpts from Shepard's United States Citations: Patents

109. Excerpts from Federal Circuit Identification Table and Standards Relating to the Administration of Criminal Justice

[Illustration 108]

EXCERPTS FROM SHEPARD'S UNITED STATES CITATIONS: PATENTS

UNITED STATES PATENTS (Original) **No. 3,714,696**

3,713,523
co913OG794

3,713,524
co916OG3

3,713,541
co911OG1132

3,713,554
co913OG794

3,713,556
co914OG4

3,713,557
co911OG113

3,713,55
co916OG3

3,713,699
co910OG1457

3,713,710
co912OG397

3,713,711
co911OG3
co919OG404

3,713,713
Re28,431

3,713,876
co911OG762

3,713,883
co913OG5

3,713,908
co917OG4

3,713,910
co915OG1562

3,714,077
co913OG1044

3,714,078
co912OG2

3,714,079
co923OG806

3,714,080
co914OG394

3,714,151
co928OG888

3,714,156
co913OG794

3,714,160
co913OG794

3,714,165
co913OG4

3,714,243
co913OG5
co920OG1020

3,714,245
co913OG4

3,714,249
co914OG394

3,714,259
co911OG762

3,714,375
co910OG1457

3,714,378
co915OG2

3,714,385
co912OG397

3,714,391
920OG286
920OGT88

3,714,501
co915OG1166

3,714,510
co913OG5

3,714,512
co911OG365

3,714,515
co915OG380

3,714,518
co913OG5

3,714,537
co913OG4
co915OG1166

3,714,545
co913OG4

An excerpt from Shepard's United States Citations: Patents.

This illustrates how decisions on a specific patent may be located.

Basketmaster **TRADEMARKS**

Basket-master
924OGT
[151

Basodur
942OGT
[403

Basol
902OGT
[100

Bass Anglers Sportsman Society
185PQ43

Bass Bagger
185PQ192

Bass Buggy
898OGT
[412

Bass Buster
185PQ192

Bass-Buzzer
185PQ192

921OGT
[109

Batchelors
917OGT
[234

Batch-Pak
913OGT
[136

Bathanal
917OGT53

Bath Buddy
938OGT
[142

Bath-Gard
907OGT
[112

Bathhouse Brass
925OGT68

Bathtub Buddies
895OGT
[306

Bath-Valet
943OGT57

Bath Wand
942OGT
[404

Batik
918OGT
[152

Batman
937OGT
[191
919OGT
[181

Bat-Man, The
928OGT

Bauder Fashion College
181PQ275

Bauer
932OGT
[332

Bavarian
345FS1402
173PQ421

Bavarian Alpine Inn
941OGT
[197

Baybrook
932OGT80

Bay City Sight Sound Bay

B. B.
918OGT
[152

B B i
927OGT
[330

B Bonded
902OGT
[250

BBQ-Lites
927OGT
[330

B C
893OGT60
927OGT
[266

B C A
912OGT
[307

Beach Party
914OGT71

Beach Peach
901OGT
[266

Beachville U S A
924OGT73

Beach-wagon
923OGT
[141

Beach Warmer
909OGT
[322

Beacon
930OGT

"'Beanie" Beans
938OGT
[142

Bear
58PA982
178PQ428

Bear Brand
902OGT
[250

Bearcat
177PQ344

Be a Social Lion
903OGT
[307

Beast Brand
941OGT

Beau
923OGT
[200

Beau-Bra
909OGT
[322

Beau Breck
936OGT
[206

Beau-Bunt
888OGT
[218

Beauchaine
929OGT
[247

Beau Chalet
931OGT52

Beau/Craft
903OGT
[306

Beau de Cologne
909OGT
[251

An excerpt from Shepard's United States Citations: Patents.

This is from the Trademarks Section and illustrates how a trademark may be Shepardized.

[Illustration 109]

EXCERPTS FROM OTHER UNITS OF SHEPARD'S CITATIONS

FEDERAL CIRCUIT IDENTIFICATION TABLE

Pages	Circ	Pages	Circ	Pages	Circ	F2d Vol. 466 Pages	Circ	Pages	Circ	Pages	Circ
379–380	5	891–928	PT	1338–1350	5			573–577	7	1163–1177	7
380–381	7	929–932	9	1350–1366	10			577–578	6	1177–1191	6
381–382	9	933–933	5	1366–1369	8			578–583	5	1191–1193	9
382–388	5	934–939	9	1369–1372	2			583–588	10	1193–1194	5
388–392	8	940–943	5	1373–1376	6			588–593	3	1194–1200	9
392–395	7	943–950	9	1376–1382	9	1–6	10	593–600	7	1200–1201	5
396–402	9	950–956	5	1382–1389	8	6–11 ←	7	601–611	3	1201–1202	8
402–406	7	956–958	10	1389–1394	10	11–17	5	611–612	9	1203–1205	10
406–407	9	958–964	9	1394–1395	5	17–24	2	613–618	7	1205–1206	9
408–415	5	964–966	10	1395–1397	9	24–35	6	618–621	10	1206–1209	8
416–418	8	966–969	9	1398–1398	2	35–42	10	621–625	8	1209–1210	10
419–420	5	969–970	6	1398–1398	3	42–53	9	626–672	7	1210–1212	8
420–421	10	970–973	5	1398–1399	5	53–59	6	672–674	9	1213–1226	5
422–423										1229	3
423–425										1233	5
425–427										1239	3
427–428										1246	5
428–432										1249	6

Excerpt from Shepard's Federal Circuit Identification Table.

This Table may be used to determine the circuit or district for F., F.2d, or F.Supp. citations.

Note how 466 F.2d 6 is indicated that it was heard in the Seventh Circuit.

SPEEDY TRIAL (1968)

1.1
et seq.
Iowa
195NW356
1.1
255Ark545
16MdA312
457Pa508
Ark
502SW484
Iowa
215NW264
Md
295A2d782
Pa
327A2d18
1.2
373FS827
210Kan556
448Pa322
66Wis2d361
Kan
502P2d742
Pa
292A2d402
Wis
225NW465
1.3

Kan
502P2d742
Mich
194NW138
Mont
516P2d375
Nebr
202NW609
Pa
303A2d486
2.2(a)
468F2d1134
391FS121
456Pa428
Alk
486P2d946
Iowa
207NW776
Pa
321A2d640
2.2(c)
163Mt214
4TnCr669
Iowa
224NW235
Mont
516P2d375
Tenn
475SW206

2.3(1)
Colo
525P2d469
Pa
329A2d265
3.1
36CA3d114
176Col292

Excerpt from Shepard's Criminal Justice. This unit compiles citations to the American Bar Association's Standards Relating to the Administration of Criminal Justice.

This illustrates how citations to court decisions which have cited Section one of the Standard on Speedy Trial may be located.

SECTION H. KEEPING SHEPARD'S CITATIONS CURRENT

1. Supplements

As with any set of law books, there must be a method of keeping the set up to date. Since *Shepard's Citations* are used to determine current status of a case or statute, the method of supplementation is of utmost importance. Nearly every unit of *Shepard's* is available in at least one bound volume. Every three months a cumulative paper supplement is issued, covering all changes since the date of the bound volume. For some sets, in addition to the quarterly cumulative supplement, an interim advance sheet is issued in the form of a white pamphlet. Some sets now have a bound volume, one or more bound supplements, and then an annual cumulative supplement with periodic supplements provided during the year. Before using *Shepard's Citations,* it is extremely important to ascertain that all of the volumes and supplements are at hand. The latest paper supplement usually contains a box entitled "What Your Library Should Contain." This should be examined carefully and all of the volumes and supplements should be consulted.

In all instances, the bound volume or volumes plus the available paper supplement or supplements must be used.

2. Shepard's Special Citation Service

A special updating service is now available to subscribers of any unit of *Shepard's Citations.* By writing or calling the publisher, information to citing cases subsequent to the latest supplement may be obtained. Detailed information about this service is available upon request.

SECTION I. SUMMARY

1. Shepard's Citations. Cases

a. *States*

(1) There is a separate *Shepard's* unit for each of the fifty states, the District of Columbia and Puerto Rico. In some states there are separate volumes for cases and statutes; in others they are combined.

(2) In each state unit, all of the sets of reports are listed in separate sections. For each state case listed in dark type, the columns thereunder reveal (a) the history of the case in the same or higher courts, and (b) citations to all cases within the state that have cited the cited case.

(3) Citations are given to legal periodicals published within the state and to 20 national law reviews.

(4) Citations in Attorney General's opinions to state cases are given.

b. *National Reporter System*

There is a *Shepard's* unit corresponding to each of the units of the *National Reporter System.*

For any given *National Reporter* decision, citations to it are listed whenever the given citation is cited in any unit of the *National Reporter System.*

c. *Shepard's Citations for Federal Cases*

(1) *United States Citations*

Separate volumes for (a) Supreme Court reports; (b) Constitution, *U. S. Code* and *Statutes at Large,* (c) Administrative agency decisions, and (d) *Patents and Trademarks.*

(2) *Federal Citations*

Separate volumes for (a) *Federal Reporter, First and Second Series,* (b) *Federal Supplement,* (c) *Federal Rules Decisions,* and (d) *Court of Claims Reports.*

2. Shepard's Citations. Statutes

States

a. Each state unit of *Shepard's Citations* has either separate volumes or separate sections in which the state constitutions and the current code are listed, with citations to cases that have cited each section.

b. Reference is also made to any constitutional amendment, or statutory clause which has been cited in court decisions.

c. City Charters and Ordinances. These are in separate parts of the statute volumes or sections of the state units.

d. Court Rules. These are in separate sections in the statute volumes or sections of the state units.

3. Other Units of Shepard's Citations

a. *Acts and Cases by Popular Name*

b. *Bankruptcy Citations*

c. *Code of Federal Regulations Citations*

d. *Criminal Justice Citations*

e. *Federal Circuit Table*

f. *Federal Labor Law Citations*

g. *Federal Law Citations in Selected Law Reviews*

h. *Federal Tax Locator*

i. *Law Review Citations*

j. *Military Justice Citations*

k. *New York Codes, Rules, and Regulations Citations*

l. *Ordinance Law Annotations*

m. *Professional Responsibility Citations*

n. *Restatement Citations*

4. Other Uses of Shepard's Citations

a. Indicates when a case is cited in:

(1) A.L.R. annotations

(2) Legal periodical articles (state and U.S. editions only)

b. Finds parallel citations.

Chapter 16

LEGAL ENCYCLOPEDIAS

SECTION A. INTRODUCTION

In the previous chapters we have discussed the primary sources of the law: court decisions, constitutions, statutes, legislative histories, court rules, and the indexes, digests, and other sets of law books which enable a researcher to find both the source and status of the law. In the remaining chapters we shall discuss the secondary sources of the law. The mass of primary source materials has reached such voluminous proportions that secondary publications have assumed significant roles in identifying and explaining the law. As will be pointed out, it is frequently much better practice to start one's research with secondary publications rather than the sets containing the primary sources which were studied in the previous chapters. The secondary sources to be discussed consist of legal encyclopedias, treatises, periodicals, Restatements, and other miscellaneous sets of law books.

Legal encyclopedias are written in narrative form, arranged by subject and containing supporting footnote references to cases in point. In most instances, they are noncritical in approach and do not attempt to be analytical or evaluative. Instead, they simply state the propositions of law, with introductory explanations of an elementary nature. The legal encyclopedia, because of these features, is a popular and useful research tool. Its utility, however, as a secondary source, has frequently been abused by both courts and attorneys. In particular, it is often cited as a final authoritative source rather than as an expository introduction to case authority.

In many research problems, it is necessary to go beyond such rudimentary sources. It is not wise to stop one's research without reading the cases cited in the footnotes because cited references frequently will not fully reflect the propositional ramifications for which they stand, or because the facts of the immediate problem will be distinguishable and different from those in the cited cases.

This criticism should not be interpreted as being directed at the function of the encyclopedia. It is an excellent index and introductory guide to the law, and as long as this is kept in mind, and it is not relied upon as the final authority for a proposition of law, it is a valuable publication to be consulted initially. In most instances, the cases cited will have to be read, analyzed and Shepardized; statutory sources must be checked to ascertain whether the rules of law have changed in any particular jurisdiction.

Three types of legal encyclopedias are distinguished by dealing with: (1) general law, (2) local or state law, and (3) special subjects. Each is discussed below.

SECTION B. CURRENT GENERAL ENCYCLOPEDIAS

1. Corpus Juris Secundum (cited "C.J.S.")

Corpus Juris Secundum, published by the West Publishing Company, is an attempt to restate the entire body of American law in encyclopedic form from the first reported case to the present. It includes both procedural and substantive law, and it aims at citing all reported cases in its footnotes. *Corpus Juris Secundum* contains 101 volumes (or about 150 actual volumes counting supplements) and supersedes its predecessor, *Corpus Juris.*[1]

Cross references from C.J.S. titles and sections to corresponding West topics and Key-Numbers also are provided, permitting easy entry to the *American Digest System.* The West topics and Key-Numbers and other secondary authority sources are noted under "Library References," which precede the texts of the sections in the C.J.S. replacement volumes published since 1961 and in the annual cumulative pocket supplements.

C.J.S. has a five-volume general index. Each volume also has a separate index to the topics contained in it. Where the topic is covered in more than one volume, the Topic Index appears in the concluding volume of the topic.

The set is kept up-to-date by replacement volumes and annual cumulative pocket supplements. Replacement volumes appear when significant sections of the text require rewriting or when the recent pocket references become very extensive and unwieldy. The pocket references may cover rewritten text, citations to cases rendered since the publication of the original volume, and secondary sources.

Judicial and other definitions of *words and phrases* and *legal maxims* are interfiled alphabetically with the essay topics. They also are listed in each appropriate volume preceding the index, with references to the pages containing the definitions.

[1] Although *Corpus Juris Secundum* supersedes *Corpus Juris,* occasionally the footnotes in *Corpus Juris Secundum* will refer to *Corpus Juris* rather than repeating the citations that appeared in that set.

Corpus Juris Secundum provides some discussion of federal and local statutory law, including court interpretation of these enactments.

A "Law Chart" of the topical arrangement of *Corpus Juris Secundum* is included at the beginning of the first volume of the General Index and a "List of the Titles in Corpus Juris Secundum" precedes the text of each volume of the set. The Law Chart is a guide to the titles under seven major divisions with numerous subheads. All related titles are so grouped as to enable comparison and discrimination in their correct selection. To use a topical approach when you do not know the title under which your question is discussed, first select the major division in the Law Chart that covers the problem. Then choose the pertinent subhead and the most specific title under that subhead. The last step is to consult the text of C.J.S. under the selected title.

2. American Jurisprudence 2d (Am.Jur.2d)

American Jurisprudence 2d is published by the Lawyers Co-operative Publishing Company and the Bancroft-Whitney Company. It is a textual statement of substantive and procedural law, arranged alphabetically under 400 topics. It contains 82 volumes plus an eight-volume index and supersedes *American Jurisprudence.*

It differs from *Corpus Juris Secundum* in that this set does not cite all reported decisions in support of its textual statements of the law. Rather, *American Jurisprudence 2d* cites only selected decisions in its footnotes but does give citations to *A.L.R.* annotations. In using *American Jurisprudence 2d,* reported cases may be located through its footnotes and by consultation of the cited *A.L.R.* annotations.

American Jurisprudence 2d also gives in its footnotes references to treatment of a topic in the other sets of the *Total Client-Service Library.* Since *American Jurisprudence 2d* has a detailed multi-volume index, it is much more inclusive in entries than the indexes to *A.L.R.* It is frequently easier to locate an A.L.R. annotation by starting in the *American Jurisprudence 2d* index, reading the section cited to, and then locating the appropriate *A.L.R.* citation in *American Jurisprudence 2d*'s footnotes.

The publishers describe *American Jurisprudence 2d* as giving the law in breadth and *A.L.R.* as the law in depth. The former is very useful to obtain a quick answer to a problem which then may be explored in depth through the use of *A.L.R.* In use one may go directly to the volume containing the topic being researched. For example, if one is interested in the law of *Copyright,* the index volumes may be by-passed and the search started immediately by consulting the volume that contains the title *Copyright.* If the broad topic of the law under which the subject is included is not familiar to the researcher (e. g., restrictive covenants), the search should start first in the index volumes.

Some features of *American Jurisprudence 2d* are:

(1) Greater emphasis is placed on statutory law, federal procedural rules, and uniform state laws. The federal statutory law germane to a topic is covered, while state statutory law is covered in general but without reference to the specific laws of each state. There is a separate volume of *Table of Statutes and Rules Cited.* This *Table* covers the *United States Code Service,* the Federal Rules of Procedure, the Federal Rules of Evidence, and the Uniform Laws. When a citation to one of these is at hand, this *Table* may be consulted to find out where the subject matter of such citations is discussed in *American Jurisprudence 2d.*

(2) *Federal Taxation.* Volumes 33 and 34 are replaced annually and contain substantially the same text found in the current year editions of the Research Institute of America (RIA) *Tax Guide.* This is a looseleaf service with weekly supplements. The volumes as printed in *American Jurisprudence 2d* are supplemented during the year only for major Federal tax law changes. As rules, regulations, and new court decisions occur so frequently in tax law, the user of these *Am. Jur.2d* volumes should always check for the most current materials in the RIA *Tax Guide,* or the other taxation services described *supra* in Chapter 14, Section B, or in Chapter 24, *infra.*

(3) *Am.Jur.2d* New Topic Service.

This looseleaf volume started in 1973 and covers (1) new topics of the law which have developed after the printing of the main volumes and (2) new and substantial changes in already published articles. For example, this *Service* contains articles on No-Fault Divorce and Right to Die. The pocket supplements to the multi-volume Index includes references to this *Service.*

(4) *Am.Jur.2d* Desk Book. Another feature of Am.Jur.2d is its *Desk Book,* which functions as a "legal" almanac, containing miscellaneous data and information. The *Desk Book* is divided into seven main categories: (1) governmental documents and historical matters, (2) the courts (the canons of judicial ethics and the business and organization of the courts), (3) lawyers and the legal profession (the canons of professional ethics, minimum requirements for admission to legal practice in the U. S. and professional data), (4) statutes and statutory material (text of the ancient statutes and tabulated statutory material—e. g., marriage laws, record of passage of Uniform and Model Acts), (5) statistical matters (financial and mathematical tables, etc.), (6) tables of law reports (abbreviations),

and (7) miscellaneous information (selected legal (Latin) maxims and phrases, freely translated, etc.).

(5) *American Jurisprudence 2d* is kept up to date by annual pocket supplements.

(6) Words, phrases and definitions are interfiled alphabetically in the index to each volume.

3. American Jurisprudence Proof of Facts, 1st and 2d Series

The purpose of this set is to provide a compilation of materials that will guide a lawyer in organizing his or her fact material in preparing for trial, and in the examination of witnesses. It attempts to show the elements required in presenting or defending a *prima facie* case. This is done through a text discussion of the area followed by an outline in question-and-answer form, demonstrating the facts discussed in the text. It is designed to assist a lawyer in obtaining information from his client, in interviewing witnesses, in preparing for the taking of depositions, in preparation of briefs, and in other steps lawyers need to take in preparing a case for trial.

The first series is in 30 volumes and new volumes are periodically published for the second series. Both sets are kept current by pocket supplements. The main part of the Index volume indexes articles in the First Series and the cumulative pocket supplement indexes the Second Series.

4. American Jurisprudence Trials (Am.Jur. Trials)

This set, which started in 1964 and is now in 227 volumes, is essentially a treatise on trial practice. The first six volumes cover what the publishers describe as practice, strategy and control, and include matters that are common to all types of problems in trial practice. The remaining volumes are called *Modern Trials* and deal with the handling of trials for a specific topic. *American Jurisprudence Trials* is written by over 250 experienced trial lawyers. As with *American Jurisprudence Proof of Facts 2d* it has its own index and is referred to in the footnotes of the other sets of the *Total Client Service Library.*

5. American Jurisprudence Pleading and Practice Forms, Annotated (Am.Jur. P & P)

This set is essentially a collection of forms designed to assist a lawyer in preparing the procedural aspects of a law suit. Aside from the references in its footnotes to the other sets of the publisher, it is typical of other sets containing legal forms.

6. American Jurisprudence Legal Forms 2d

This set is similar to *American Jurisprudence* P & P, but contains forms lawyers need in their practice other than pleading and practice forms.[2]

SECTION C. ILLUSTRATIONS: ENCYCLOPEDIAS CORPUS JURIS SECUNDUM

In Chapter 6, Section A, in discussing the use of the *Key Number System* and the *American Digest System,* we had the problem of finding cases dealing with the question of whether one accompanying a third person who is injured can receive damages for mental distress. We found cases using the *Key Number System.*

Another approach would have been to start the search in *Corpus Juris Secundum* as shown in the following illustrations.

110. Page from General Index to C.J.S.

111. Page from Index to Topic: Damages

112. Page from Topic: Damages, Vol. 25, C.J.S.

113. Page from Cumulative Supplement, Vol. 25, C.J.S.

AMERICAN JURISPRUDENCE 2d

In Chapter 7, it was shown how cases dealing with the liability of a landlord for failure to keep a porch railing in good condition could be located in an A.L.R. annotation by using the *Quick Index* to A.L.R. Another approach would be to use *American Jurisprudence 2d,* as shown in the following illustrations.

114. Page from Index to American Jurisprudence 2d

115. Page from Volume 49, American Jurisprudence 2d

116. Page from Pocket Supplement to Vol. 49, Am.Jur.2d

[2] Form books will be discussed in more detail in Chapter 19.

[Illustration 110]

PAGE FROM GENERAL INDEX TO C.J.S.

PADLOCK

PADLOCK—Continued
Nuisances—Continued
Duration of order padlocking building to prevent use for prostitution, **Nuis § 125, p. 903, n. 80**
Intoxicating liquor,
Abatement, relief by way of padlocking, **Int Liq § 424, p. 706**
Interlocutory order closing premises, **Int Liq § 418**
Punishment, violation of injunction, **Nuis § 135, p. 943, n. 29**

PADRE
Defined, **Vol. 67, p. 550**

PADRINO
Defined, **Vol. 67, p. 550**

PADRON
Defined, **Vol. 67, p. 550**

PAGA (PAGO)

PAID-UP INSURANCE
Generally, see **Title Index to Insurance**
Assignments for benefit of creditors, assignment of as constructive assignment, **Assign for Cred § 24**
Defined, **Ins § 27, p. 490**

PAID-UP STOCK
Building and loan associations, see **Title Index to Building and Loan Associations**
Corporations,
Assessments on, stockholders' liability, **Corp § 486, p. 1159**
Representation by seller, **Corp § 410, p. 980**
Defined, **Corp § 215**

PAIN AND SUFFERING
Generally, see **Title Index to Damages**
Animals, item of damage by trespassing animals, **Anim § 206, p. 1322**
Appeal and review, discretion in respect to damages for, **App & E § 1650, p. 375, n. 68**

This is a page from the General Index to C.J.S. These volumes index the entire 101 volumes of C.J.S. and thus must be more general than specific in their entries. For example, there is no entry under "mental distress" although there is one for "Pain and suffering." Note how under that entry there is the reference "Generally, see Title Index to Damages."

See next Illustration.

Size printed record, **App & E § 1078**
Transcript, statement of case, reference deficiencies, **App & E § 1108, n. 46**
Defined, **Vol. 67, p. 551**
Wills,
Separate pages as single instrument, burden of proof, **Wills § 384, p. 269, n. 7**
Subscribing witnesses, signing each, **Wills § 195**

PAGETS' DISEASE
Workmen's compensation,
Aggravation, **Work C § 175**
Exertion, **Work C § 182, p. 615, n. 47**
Payment from special fund, **Work C § 837, p. 156, n. 41**

PAID
Defined,
Int Rev §§ 239, 274
Vol. 67, p. 551

PAID-IN SURPLUS
Surplus, this index

Banks and banking, damages for refusal to pay check, **Banks § 365, p. 782**
Breach of marriage promise, damages, **Breach of M P § 40**
Carriers, see **Title Index to Carriers**
Civil rights, discrimination, damages, **Civil R § 21**
Collision, crew members, damages recoverable, **Collision § 210**
Constitutional law,
Due process of law as violated by creation, **Const Law § 632**
Telegraph companies for, imposition of as denial of equal protection, **Const Law § 556**
Contracts, capacity to contract as affected by, **Contracts § 133**
Dead bodies,
Consent to burial given under, removal of remains in case of, **Dead Bodies § 4, p. 1024**
Damages for violation of right to bury and preserve remains, **Dead Bodies § 8, p. 1030**
Death, see **Title Index to Death**
Defined, **Vol. 67, p. 552**

480

[Illustration 111]

PAGE FROM INDEX TO TOPIC: DAMAGES, IN VOL. 25A, C.J.S.

DAMAGES

This is the Index to the Topic "Damages." These indexes to the individual titles are more specific than the entries contained in the General Index.

Note here the sub-entry, "Pain and suffering" and the sub-entry, "Third persons, suffering accompanying injury to," and the reference to § 67. This refers to section 67 under the Topic, Damages. See next Illustration.

1078

[Illustration 112]

PAGE FROM TOPIC: DAMAGES, VOL. 25, C.J.S.

25 C.J.S. **DAMAGES § 67**

§ 67. —— Accompanying Injury to Another

As a general rule, distress caused by sympathy for another's suffering, and fright due to a wrong against a third person, are not compensable.

Library References

Damages ⟹51.

Subject to some exceptions,[75.50] as where the injury is a willful or malicious one,[75.55] although even as to this exception there is some authority to the contrary,[75.60] as a general rule, the right of recovery for mental suffering resulting from bodily injuries is restricted to the person who has suffered the bodily hurt,[76] and there can be no recovery for anguish or distress caused by sympathy for another's suffering,[77] or for fright due to a wrong against a third person.[78] It has also been held that the anguish of mind arising as to the safety of others who may be in personal peril from the same cause cannot be taken into consideration.[79]

Ind.—Harrod v. Bisson, 93 N.E. 1093, 48 Ind.App. 549.
17 C.J. p 835 note 74.

Mental suffering or sense of shame or humiliation resulting from consciousness of disfiguring marks is not an element of damage.
R.I.—Halladay v. Ingram, 82 A.2d 875, 78 R.I. 464.

75.50 Husband's claim for loss of unborn child

In action brought against motorbus owner and its insurer to recover for damages allegedly sustained as result of jolting received by passenger as result of negligent operation of bus, where it was decided that no recovery could be had for passenger's loss of her unborn child, both passenger and her husband were nevertheless entitled to recover for worry and mental anguish.
La.—Valence v. Louisiana Power & Light Co., App., 50 So.2d 847.

75.55 R.I.—Bedard v. Notre Dame Hospital, 151 A.2d 690, 89 R.I. 195.

Deliberate beating of father

Where defendant wrongfully beat plaintiff's father in plaintiff's sight and hearing, thereby causing her to be greatly frightened, and as consequence thereof she suffered miscarriage, defendant was liable to

Cal.—Amaya v. Home Ice, Fuel & Supply Co., 379 P.2d 513, 59 C.2d 295, 29 Cal.Rptr. 33.
Ind.—Boden v. Del-Mar Garage, 185 N.E. 860, 205 Ind. 59.
La.—Johnston v. Fidelity Nat. Bank of Baton Rouge, App., 152 So.2d 327—Vinet v. Checker Cab Co., App., 140 So.2d 252—Honeycutt v. American General Ins. Co., App., 126 So.2d 789—Covey v. Marquette Cas. Co., App., 84 So.2d 217—Alston v. Cooley, 5 La.App. 623.
Md.—Resavage v. Davies, 86 A.2d 879, 199 Md. 479.
N.H.—Barber v. Pollock, 187 A.2d 788, 104 N.H. 379.
N.Y.—Kalina v. General Hospital of City of Syracuse, 220 N.Y.S.2d 733, 31 Misc.2d 18, affirmed 235 N.Y.S.2d 808, 18 A.D.2d 757, affirmed 195 N.E.2d 309, 13 N.Y.2d 1023, 245 N.Y.S.2d 599—Adams v. Harry T. Mangurian, Inc., 126 N.Y.S.2d 167, 204 Misc. 890.
Davis v. William J. Burns Intern. Detective Agency, 135 N.Y.S.2d 59—Balestrero v. Prudential Ins. Co. of America, 126 N.Y.S.2d 792, affirmed 128 N.Y.S.2d 295, 283 App.Div. 794, affirmed 121 N.E.2d 537, 307 N.Y. 709.
Ohio.—Hapner v. Newman, Com.Pl., 6 Ohio Supp. 220.

Baur, D.C.Idaho, 143 F.Supp. 804, under Utah law—Gonzalez v. U. S., D.C.Puerto Rico, 140 F.Supp. 102—Maury v. U. S., D.C.Cal., 139 F.Supp. 532.
Cal.—Kelly v. Fretz, 65 P.2d 914, 19 C.A.2d 356.
Idaho.—Hayward v. Yost, 242 P.2d 971, 72 Idaho 415.
Ill.—McCullough v. Orcutt, 145 N.E.2d 109, 14 Ill.App.2d 513.
La.—Vinet v. Checker Cab Co., App., 140 So.2d 252—Hughes v. Gill, App., 41 So.2d 536—Alston v. Cooley, 5 La.App. 623.
N.Y.—Roher v. State, 112 N.Y.S.2d 603, 279 App.Div. 1116.

Corpus Juris Secundum cited in Adams v. Harry T. Mangurian, Inc., 126 N.Y.S.2d 167, 168, 204 Misc. 890.
Berg v. Baum, 224 N.Y.S.2d 974.
N.C.—Helmstetler v. Duke Power Co., 32 S.E.2d 611, 224 N.C. 821.
Okl.—Van Hoy v. Oklahoma Coca-Cola Bottling Co., 235 P.2d 948, 205 Okl. 135.
17 C.J. p 835 note 76.

78. U.S.—Angst v. Great Northern Ry. Co., D.C.Minn., 131 F.Supp. 156.
Cal.—Amaya v. Home Ice, Fuel & Supply Co., 379 P.2d 513, 59 C.2d 295, 29 Cal.Rptr. 33.
Reed v. Moore, 319 P.2d 80, 156

First page of section 67 of the Topic "Damages" which deals with the matter of damages for mental distress caused by observing an injury to another. Note the proportion of text in relation to footnotes.

Text should be carefully read with notes made of seemingly relevant cases. These cases must then be examined.

[illegible] tling Co. of California, D.C.Cal., 44 F.Supp. 10—Grier v. Tri-State Transit Co., D.C.La., 36 F.Supp. 26.
Ala.—Tyler v. Brown-Service Funeral Homes Co., 34 So.2d 203, 250 Ala. 295.

77. U.S.—Rogers v. Hexol, Inc., D.C.Or., 218 F.Supp. 453—Mahaffey v. Official Detective Stories, Inc., D.C.La., 210 F.Supp. 251—Beaty v. Buckeye Fabric Finishing Co., D.C.Ark., 179 F.Supp. 688—Preece v.

physical injuries sustained by one out of the range of ordinary physical peril as a result of the shock of witnessing another's danger.
Wis.—Waube v. Warrington, 258 N.W. 497, 216 Wis. 603, 98 A.L.R. 394.

825

[Illustration 113]

PAGE FROM CUMULATIVE SUPPLEMENT, VOL. 25, C.J.S.

25 CJS 79 **DAMAGES § 68**

Pages 823–826

72. U.S.—Downie v. U. S. Lines Co., C.A.Pa., 359 F.2d 344, cert. den. 87 S.Ct. 201, 385 U.S. 897, 17 L.Ed.2d 130.
N.M.—Rutledge v. Johnson, 465 P.2d 274, 81 N.M. 217.

§ 66. —— Disfigurement

page 824

73. U.S.—Rapisardi v. United Fruit Co., C.A.N.Y., 441 F.2d 1308.
Hernandez v. U. S., D.C.Tex., 313 F.Supp. 349.
La.—Orfanello v. Pepsi Cola Bottling Co., App., 290 So.2d 353, application den., Sup., 293 So.2d 178.
N.C.—C.J.S. cited in King v. Britt, 148 S.E.2d 594, 598, 267 N.C. 594.

74. N.C.—C.J.S. cited in King v. Britt, 148 S.E.2d 594, 598, 267 N.C. 594.

§ 67. —— Accompanying Injury to Another

page 825

75.50 Statutory right
U.S.—Commercial Union Ins. Co. v. Gonzalez Rivera, C.A.Puerto Rico, 358 F.2d 480.

76. U.S.—Lula v. Sivaco Wire & Nail Co., D.C.N.Y., 265 F.Supp. 222.
Fla.—City Stores Co. v. Langer, App., 308 So.2d 621.
Ga.—Cotton States Mut. Ins. Co. v. Crosby, 254 S.E.2d 485, 149 Ga.App. 450.
La.—Reid v. Clearfield Cheese Co., Inc., App., 307 So.2d 115.
N.J.—Gilborges v. Wallace, 379 A.2d 269, 153 N.J.Super. 121, affd. in part, remd. in part 396 A.2d 338, 78 N.J. 342.
N.Y.—Tobin v. Grossman, 249 N.E.2d 419, 24 N.Y.2d 609, 301 N.Y.S.2d 554.
Wash.—Smith v. Rodene, 418 P.2d 741, 69 Wash.2d 482, am. on oth. grds. 423 P.2d 934—Grimsby v. Samson, 530 P.2d 291, 85 Wash.2d 52, 77 A.L.R.3d 436.

Overruled case
To the extent that it is inconsistent with the opinion of the court, Amaya v. Home Ice, Fuel & Supply Co., 379 P.2d 513, 59 C.2d 295, 29 Cal.Rptr. 33, was overruled.

Cal.—Archibald v. Braverman, 79 Cal. Rptr. 723, 275 C.A.2d 253.

Determination of existence of duty
Cal.—Archibald v. Braverman, 79 Cal. Rptr. 723, 275 C.A.2d 253.

Injury must be subject of sensory perception
Cal.—Jensen v. Children's Hospital Medical Center of East Bay, 106 Cal. Rptr. 883, 31 C.A.3d 22.

Zone of danger
Cal.—Hoyem v. Manhattan Beach City School Dist., 150 Cal.Rptr. 1, 585 P. 2d 851, 22 C.3d 508.
N.D.—Whetham v. Bismarck Hospital, 197 N.W.2d 678.

Fear for own safety
U.S.—Young v. Caribbean Associates, Inc., D.C.Virgin Islands, 358 F.Supp. 1220.

Absence of blood relationship no bar to recovery
Hawaii—Leong v. Takasaki, 520 P.2d 758, 55 Haw. 398.

Knowledge of plaintiffs presence not necessary
Hawaii—Leong v. Takasaki, 520 P.2d 758, 55 Haw. 398—Kelley v. Kokua Sales and Supply, Ltd., 532 P.2d 673, 56 Haw. 204.

Defendants conduct is proximate cause of plaintiffs injury
Hawaii—Leong v. Takasaki, 520 P.2d 758, 55 Haw. 398.

Factors considered
Conn.—D'Amicol v. Alvarez Shipping Co., Inc., 326 A.2d 129, 31 Conn.Sup. 129.
Mich.—Gustafson v. Faris, 241 N.W.2d 208, 67 Mich.App. 363.
Tex.—Landreth v. Reed, Civ.App., 570 S.W.2d 486.

Visual perception not required
Cal.—Krouse v. Graham, 137 Cal.Rptr. 863, 562 P.2d 1022, 19 C.3d 59.

No damages where tort committed at noncontemporaneous time
Mich.—Miller v. Cook, 273 N.W.2d 567, 87 Mich.App. 6.

77. U.S.—Beanland v. Chicago, R. I. & P. Ry. Co., C.A.Mo., 480 F.2d 109—Owens v. Childrens Memorial Hospital, Omaha, Neb., C.A.Neb., 480 Garfield v. U. S., D.C.Wis., 297 F.Supp. 891—Welsh v. Davis, D.C.Mont., 307 F.Supp. 416—F.2d 465—Young v. Caribbean Asso-

Tenn.—Burroughs v. Jordan, 456 S.W.2d 652, 224 Tenn. 418.
Vt.—Guilmette v. Alexander, 259 A.2d 12, 128 Vt. 116.

78. U.S.—Garfield v. U. S., D.C.Wis., 297 F.Supp. 891.
Cal.—Mobaldi v. Board of Regents of University of California, 127 Cal. Rptr. 720, 55 C.A.3d 798.
Conn.—Anonymous v. Hospital, 398 A.2d 312, 35 Conn.Sup. 112.
La.—Duet v. Cheramie, App., 176 So.2d 667.
N.Y.—Tobin v. Grossman, 291 N.Y.S.2d 227, 30 A.D.2d 229, affd. 249 N.E.2d 419, 24 N.Y.2d 609, 301 N.Y.S.2d 554.
Pa.—Bowman v. Sears, Roebuck & Co., Super., 369 A.2d 754, 245 Pa.Super. 530.

Overruled case
To the extent that it is inconsistent with the opinion of the court, Amaya v. Home Ice, Fuel & Supply Co., 379 P.2d 513, 59 C.2d 295, 29 Cal.Rptr. 33, was overruled.
Cal.—Dillon v. Legg, 69 Cal.Rptr. 72, 441 P.2d 912, 68 C.2d 728, 29 A.L.R.3d 1316.

No strict liability
Ill.—Woodill v. Parke Davis & Co., 374 N.E.2d 683, 15 Ill.Dec. 900, 58 Ill. App.3d 349.

page 826

79.5 Mass.—Dziokonski v. Babineau, 380 N.E.2d 1295.
N.Y.—Bessette v. St. Peter's Hospital, 381 N.Y.S.2d 339, 51 A.D.2d 286.

Factors to be considered
Cal.—Dillon v. Legg, 69 Cal.Rptr. 72, 441 P.2d 912, 68 C.2d 728, 29 A.L.R.3d 1316.

Necessity of physical symptoms
U.S.—D'Ambra v. U. S., D.C.R.I., 354 F.Supp. 810, affd., C.A., 481 F.2d 14, cert. den. 94 S.Ct. 592, 414 U.S. 1075, 38 L.Ed.2d 482, affd., 518 F.2d 275.

§ 68. —— Accompanying Injury to Property

79.50 U.S.—Griffin v. Hunt Tool Co., D. C.La., 286 F.Supp. 402, affd., C.A., 412 F.2d 328.
Cal.—Crisci v. Security Ins. Co. of New Haven, Conn., 58 Cal.Rptr. 13, 426

Each volume of C.J.S. is kept current by cumulative annual pocket supplements. In the supplement to Vol. 25, note the reference to Leong v. Takasaki. This was the case located in Chapter 6 by use of the Descriptive-Word Indexes and the use of Key Numbers in the American Digest System.

Hair v. Monterey County, 119 Cal. Rptr. 639, 45 C.A.3d 538.
Ga.—Cotton States Mut. Ins. Co. v. Crosby, 254 S.E.2d 485, 149 Ga.App. 450.
La.—Hymel v. Tom Alexander Brokerage Co., App., 348 So.2d 104, writ den., Sup., 350 So.2d 894.
Mich.—Toms v. McConnell, 207 N.W.2d 140, 45 Mich.App. 647.
N.J.—Friel v. Vineland Obstetrical and Gynecological Professional Ass'n, 400 A.2d 147, 166 N.J.Super. 579.
R.I.—D'Ambra v. U. S., 338 A.2d 524, 114 R.I. 643.

Right of recovery extended to relative arriving immediately after injury

chester Ins. & Indem. Co., App., 299 So.2d 517, writ den., Sup., 302 So.2d 617, 618—Hickman v. East Baton Rouge Parish, App., 314 So.2d 486, writ den., Sup., 318 So.2d 59.
Md.—Dageforde v. Potomac Edison Co., 369 A.2d 93, 35 Md.App. 37.
Mich.—Perlmutter v. Whitney, 230 N.W. 2d 390, 60 Mich.App. 268.
N.H.—Jelley v. Laflame, 238 A.2d 728, 108 N.H. 471.
N.Y.—Tobin v. Grossman, 249 N.E.2d 419, 24 N.Y.2d 609, 301 N.Y.S.2d 554.
Pa.—Knaub v. Gotwalt, 220 A.2d 646, 422 Pa. 267.
Knaub v. Gotwalt, 79 York 188. Affd. 220 A.2d 646, 422 Pa. 267.

Or.—Fredeen v. Stride, 525 P.2d 166, 269 Or. 369.
W.Va.—Jarrett v. E. L. Harper & Son, Inc., 235 S.E.2d 362.

Recovery denied
(2) Other statements.
La.—Hayward v. Carraway, App., 180 So.2d 758, writ ref. 182 So.2d 662, 248 La. 909—Farr v. Johnson, App., 308 So.2d 884, application not considered, Sup., 310 So.2d 854, consideration den. 315 So.2d 143.

Flood damage
Hawaii—Rodrigues v. State, 472 P.2d 509, 52 Haw. 156, 283.

[Illustration 114]

PAGE FROM INDEX TO AMERICAN JURISPRUDENCE 2d

AMERICAN JURISPRUDENCE 2d

Step 1.

Use index volumes to Am.Jur.2d. Note the sub-entry "Porches" under the main entry "Landlord and Tenant", and the references to the various sections where this topic is discussed in the Am.Jur.2d volume which contains the title "Landlord and Tenant".

400

[Illustration 115]

PAGE FROM VOLUME 49, AMERICAN JURISPRUDENCE 2d

lord is liable for injuries due to the defective condition of parts of premises used by several tenants and retained in his control, even though the defect is an open and obvious one, or was a pre-existing defect. His liability is

Step 2.

Examine the Sections referred to in the Index. Section 806 seems most relevant to the problem under research. Note the citations in the footnotes to A.L.R. Annotations. The next step is to check the cumulative pocket supplement.

See next Illustration.

It has been held that the duty of the owner of an office building to keep in proper condition the common portions retained in his possession does not extend to keeping outer doors unlocked on Sunday to enable tenants to remove large pieces of furniture in case of fire.[7]

§ 806. When premises deemed in landlord's control and maintained by him for tenants' use.

The view has been taken that a landlord is to be presumed to have retained control over premises used in common by different occupants of his property.[8] The parts of leased premises used in common by several tenants are to be considered as under the landlord's control even though it is not shown that he exercised any specific acts of control.[9] Where approaches

Annotation: 25 ALR 1273, 1292, s. 39 ALR 294, 299, 58 ALR 1411, 1416, 75 ALR 154, 161, 97 ALR 220, 226.

As to the view that the landlord's duty is confined to keeping the premises in the condition in which they were when the tenant took possession, see § 818, infra.

3. Primus v Bellevue Apartments, 241 **Iowa** 1055, 44 NW2d 347, 25 ALR2d 565.

4. United Shoe Machinery Corp. v Paine (CA1) 26 F2d 594, 58 ALR 1398; Ziulkowski v Kolodziej, 119 **Conn** 230, 175 A 780, 96 ALR 1065; Primus v Bellevue Aparments, 241 **Iowa** 1055, 44 NW2d 347, 25 ALR2d 565; Consolidation Coal Co. v Zarvis, 222 **Ky** 238, 300 SW 615, 58 ALR 1430; Richmond v Standard Elkhorn Coal Co. 222 **Ky** 150, 300 SW 359, 58 ALR 1423; Estes v Aetna Casualty & S. Co. (**La App**) 157 So 395, 158 So 25; Rosenberg v Chapman Nat. Bank, 126 **Me** 403, 139 A 82, 58 ALR 1405; Whitcomb v Mason, 102 **Md** 275, 62 A 749; Looney v McLean, 129 **Mass** 33; Olson v Schultz, 67 **Minn** 494, 70 NW 779; Roman v King, 289 **Mo** 641, 233 SW 161, 25 ALR 1263; Siggins v McGill, 72 **NJL** 263, 62 A 411; Wilson v Woodruff, 65 **Utah** 118, 235 P 368, 43 ALR 1269; Wool v Larner, 112 **Vt** 431, 26 A2d 89; Schedler v Wagner, 37 **Wash** 2d 612, 225 P2d 213, 230 P2d 600, 26 ALR2d 604.

Annotation: 25 ALR2d 364, 366–437, §§ 1–20 (inside steps or stairways); 25 ALR2d 444, 446–487, §§ 1–16 (inside passageways and chambers); 26 ALR2d 468, 476–603, §§ 1–38 (exterior stairs, passageways, areas, or structures); 25 ALR 1273, 1292, s. 39 ALR 294, 299, 58 ALR 1411, 1416, 75 ALR 154, 161, 97 ALR 220, 226.

5. Miles v Tracey, 28 **Ky** LR 621, 89 SW 1128.

6. Gobrecht v Beckwith, 82 **NH** 415, 135 A 20, 52 ALR 858.

7. Whitcomb v Mason, 102 **Md** 275, 62 A 749.

8. Primus v Bellevue Apartments, 241 **Iowa** 1055, 44 NW2d 347, 25 ALR2d 565.

9. Primus v Bellevue Apartments, supra, in which the evidence was held sufficient to show that control over a laundry room in

[Illustration 116]

PAGE FROM POCKET SUPPLEMENT TO VOL. 49, AM.JUR.2d

LANDLORD AND TENANT § 808

§ 804. Premises leased to other tenants

Additional case authorities for section:

Landlord could be held responsible to tenant for its maintenance of a nuisance if noises arising in an adjacent garage infringed upon rights of tenants residing in their apartment, even though garage and apartment were under same roof, where they were separately let and separately occupied, and tenants complained, not of condition of premises which they occupied, but of a condition permitted by landlord to exist elsewhere in building. Zamzok v 650 Park Ave. Corp., 80 Misc 2d 573, 363 NYS2d 868.

§ 805. Generally

Practice Aids: Landlord's liability for injury or death due to defects in areas of building (other than stairways) used in common by tenants. 65 ALR3d 14, superseding 25 ALR2d 444, 26 ALR2d 468, §§ 14–16, 25–38.

Liability of landlord for personal injury or death due to inadequacy or lack of lighting on portion of premises used in common by tenants. 66 ALR3d 202 (superseding 25 ALR2d 496).

Landlord's liability for personal injury or death due to defects in appliances supplied for use of different tenants. 66 ALR3d 374 (superseding 25 ALR2d 576).

Landlord's liability for injury or death due to defects in exterior steps or stairs used in common by tenants. 67 ALR3d 490 (supplementing 26 ALR2d 468).

Landlord's liability for injury or death caused by defective condition of interior steps or stairways used in common by tenants. 67 ALR3d 587 (superseding 25 ALR2d 364).

Landlord's liability for injury or death due

enforceable. The record indicated that the lease met the sixth criteria used to identify the kind of agreements in which an exculpatory clause is invalid as contrary to public policy, in light of the facts that leases are increasingly the subject of governmental regulation, that the lease concerned shelter, a basic necessity of life, that the landlord offered his units to all members of the public, that the parties had unequal bargaining strength, that the landlord had not made any provision whereby a tenant could pay additional fees and obtain protection against negligence, and that the tenant was exposed to the risk of injury through the landlord's carelessness. Henrioulle v Marin Ventures, Inc. (1978) 20 **Cal** 3d 512, 143 Cal Rptr 247, 573 P2d 465.

Trial judge properly instructed jury that landlord had general continuing duty toward tenant to exercise reasonable care in keeping stairway in safe condition, and judgment for tenant who sustained injury when she caught slipper on nail protruding from step and fell down stairs whose railing was gone was affirmed. King v G & M Relaty Corp. (1977, **Mass)** 1977 Adv Sheets 2372, 370 NE2d 13 (retreating from prior rule that landlord's duty to tenant was limited to exercise of reasonable care to maintain common areas in condition not less safe than they were or appeared to be at time of letting to particular tenant).

§ 806. When premises deemed in landlord's control and maintained by him for tenant's use

Practice Aids: Landlord's liability for injury or death due to defects in areas of building (other than stairways) used in common by tenants. 65 ALR3d 14, superseding 25 ALR2d 444, 26 ALR2d 468, §§ 14–16, 25–38.

Step 3.

Check same section in Pocket Supplement. Note here the reference to 65 A.L.R.3d 14. This is the same Annotation that was located in Chapter 7 by using the Word Index to A.L.R.3d.

If the problem under research is to result in litigation, the researcher should also examine the relevant sections of the other Am.Jur. sets, such as Proof of Facts and Trials. References to these may be located on the first page of the A.L.R.3d Annotation.

See Illustration 25.

SECTION D. STATE ENCYLOPEDIAS

Some states have encyclopedias devoted to their own laws. Five states have encyclopedias published by the Lawyers Co-operative Publishing/Bancroft-Whitney Co., and they follow the format of *American Jurisprudence 2d* while covering only the laws of a specific state. These are:

California Jurisprudence 3d
Florida Jurisprudence 2d
New York Jurisprudence 2d
Ohio Jurisprudence 3d
Texas Jurisprudence 3d

Three states have encyclopedias published by the West Publishing Co. and these follow the format of *Corpus Juris Secundum*. These are:

Illinois Law and Practice
Maryland Law and Practice
Michigan Law and Practice

A few other states have sets by other publishers.

1. Common Features of State Encyclopedias

a. *Scope:* case and statutory law (substantive and procedural). The cases include both state and federal courts interpreting state law.

b. *Arrangement:* alphabetically by topics.

c. *Index:* general index and individual volume indexes. In some local encyclopedias, the titles included in a volume are separately indexed in the volume.

d. *Supplementation:* cumulative annual pocket parts and replacement volumes.

e. *Table of Statutes:* shows where code sections are cited in the local encyclopedia.

f. *Words and Phrases:* definitions of words and phrases are indexed.

g. *Research aids:* references to other secondary aids, such as A.L.R. annotations, periodical articles, etc., are often provided.

2. Shepard's Law Locators

See Chapter 15, Section F for a description of these sets.

3. New York Law Finder

This publication of the West Publishing Company is a subject arrangement of references, relevant cases, laws, forms and secondary materials.

SECTION E. SUMMARY

1. Corpus Juris Secundum

a. *Scope*

(1) Attempts to restate the entire body of American case law citing all reported cases since publication of *Corpus Juris*. Where there are earlier cases in point, footnote references are given to C.J. The text supersedes the text of C.J.

(2) Includes some discussion of federal and state statutory law.

(3) Definitions of words and phrases and legal maxims are interfiled alphabetically with the essay topics.

b. *Arrangement*

(1) Alphabetically by titles.

(2) "Law Chart" is an outline of the titles, with all related topics grouped together under seven major divisions. (General Index, vol. 1.)

(3) Scope-note—delimits and identifies the content of a title.

(4) Analysis—appears after scope-note, giving conceptual breakdown of the topic.

c. *Indexes*

(1) General Index—arranged alphabetically by broad descriptive and legal terms.

(2) Volume Indexes—more detailed subject and fact indexes.

d. *Supplementation*

(1) Cumulative annual pocket supplements to volumes.

(2) Replacement volumes.

2. American Jurisprudence 2d

a. *Scope*

(1) Textual statement of substantive and adjective law, with selected case references. Supersedes *Am.Jur.*

(2) Greater emphasis on federal statutory laws, federal procedural rules and Uniform State Laws.

(3) State statutory law is treated broadly.

(4) Definitions of words and phrases are noted under the words and phrases which are interfiled alphabetically in a Volume Index.

(5) Footnote references to *A.L.R. annotations and research aids.*

(6) Table of Statutes and Rules Cited.

(7) Desk Book (See Section B2(4)).

b. *Arrangement*

(1) Alphabetically by titles.

(2) A scope-note, cross references, notations to federal aspects of the law and an analysis of the section headings precede the text pertaining to a title.

c. *Indexes*

(1) Multivolume Index.

(2) Volume Indexes arranged by topics in a volume with sub-headings under each topic.

d. *Supplementation*

(1) Cumulative annual pocket supplements.

(2) Replacement volumes.

(3) *New Topic Service* in looseleaf binder.

e. *Citations to other sets of the Total Client-Service Library*

3. Local Encyclopedias

For an outline of the generally applicable features of local encyclopedias, see Section D.

Chapter 17

LEGAL PERIODICALS

Legal periodicals are an important secondary source in legal research. During the nineteenth century they greatly contributed to improving the image of the legal profession in America.[1] With the ever increasing proliferation of legislation and court decisions, legal periodicals in the twentieth century are playing an increasingly important role in keeping lawyers current in developing areas of the law and in providing information on the specialized areas of the law. The function of a legal periodical may be described as "recording and critici[zing] of doings of legislators and judges, discussion of current case law, narration of lives of eminent lawyers, and the scientific study of * * * jurisprudence."[2] Legal periodicals may be classified into three groups: (1) law school publications, (2) bar association publications and (3) special subject and interest periodicals.

SECTION A. LEGAL PERIODICALS

1. Law School Reviews

The periodical publications of law schools are generally called "reviews" (as the *Harvard Law Review* or *Michigan Law Review*). Law school reviews play a unique role in legal research. One distinctive feature of law school reviews is the control of their editorial policy and management by student editors. As one legal scholar has noted:

> There is not so far as I know in the world an academic faculty which pins its reputation before the public upon the

[1] M. BLOOMFIELD, AMERICAN LAWYERS IN A CHANGING SOCIETY 1776–1876, at 142–143 (1976). For a brief account of legal periodicals in nineteenth-century America *see* L. FRIEDMAN, A HISTORY OF AMERICAN LAW 546–548 (1973). Some additional references that deal with the early history of legal periodicals in the United States are as follows:

Brainerd, *Historical Sketch of American Legal Periodicals*, 14 LAW LIB.J. 63 (1921).

Pound, *Types of Legal Periodicals*, 14 IOWA L.REV. 257 (1929).

Digest of American Reports and American Law Periodicals, 23 AM.JURIST 128 (1840).

A complete list of legal periodicals of the last century and their dates of publication may be found in L. JONES, INDEX TO LEGAL PERIODICALS TO 1886, at vii–xiii (1888), and 1887–1899, at vii–xii.

[2] F. HICKS, MATERIALS AND METHODS OF LEGAL RESEARCH 210 (3d rev. ed. 1942).

work of undergraduate students—there is none, that is, except in the American law reviews.[3]

The students forming the board of editors are chosen entirely on the basis of their scholarship record or, in some instances, through a writing competition. Each year a new board is chosen and has the responsibility for the publication of the next volume.

The typical law review is in two or more sections. The first consists of solicited leading articles, usually written by law professors, on various legal topics. These articles are usually scholarly in nature and frequently have a substantial impact in changing the law or in charting the course for newly developing fields of law.[4] The second section is written entirely by the students and is devoted to surveys of selected subjects and critical analyses of current court decisions. In many law reviews the former are called "comments" and the latter "notes". Many reviews also publish book reviews. There are now published more than 200 law school reviews. The majority of law reviews are general in nature with no emphasis placed on any specific subjects,[5] but some continue to stress only the law of the state where they are published. A new trend in law schools is to publish more than one review; in such instances the publications are on specialized subjects, such as civil rights, constitutional law, environmental law or international law.[6]

3 K. LLEWELLYN, THE BRAMBLE BUSH 105 (2d ed. 1951).

4 *E. g.*, Warren & Brandeis, *The Right to Privacy*, 4 HARV.L.REV. 193 (1890).

5 During the 1950's and 1960's there was a trend for law reviews to change their format and devote their efforts toward covering a single area of the law. More recently, this trend appears to be abating. The following journals have changed titles and formats: *Wyoming Law Journal* to *Land and Water Law Review* (with v. 1, no. 1, 1966); *University of Detroit Law Journal* to *Journal of Urban Law* (with v. 44, no. 1, Fall 1966); *Journal of Public Law* to *Emory Law Journal* (with v. 23, no. 1, Winter 1974); *Law and the Social Order* to *Arizona State Law Journal* (with v. 1974, no. 1).

6 The following are representative titles from seven American law schools:
Columbia University Law School:
Columbia Human Rights Law Review
Columbia Journal of Environmental Law
Columbia Journal of Law and Social Problems
Columbia Journal of Transnational Law
Columbia Law Review

Harvard University Law School:
Harvard Civil Rights–Civil Liberties Law Review
Harvard Environmental Law Review
Harvard International Law Journal
Harvard Journal of Law and Public Policy

In general, the objectives of law school reviews are these: "(1) To serve the practicing bar and the profession, and through them the nation as a whole; (2) to educate students in the method of legal research, analysis, and expression." [7]

Harvard Journal on Legislation
Harvard Law Review
Harvard Women's Law Journal

University of California, Hastings College of Law:
COMM/ENT: A Journal of Communications and Entertainment Law
Hastings Constitutional Law Quarterly
Hastings International and Comparative Law Review
Hastings Law Journal

University of California School of Law (Berkeley):
California Law Review
Ecology Law Quarterly
Industrial Relations Law Journal

University of Michigan Law School:
Michigan Law Review
Michigan Yearbook of International Legal Studies
University of Michigan Journal of Law Reform

University of Texas School of Law:
American Journal of Criminal Law
Review of Litigation
Texas International Law Journal
Texas Law Review
Urban Law Review

Yale University Law School:
Yale Law Journal
Yale Studies in World Public Order

The following international legal periodicals are edited at American law schools:
Boston College International and Comparative Law Review
Brooklyn Journal on International Law
California Western International Law Journal
Case Western International Law Journal
Columbia Journal of Transnational Law
Cornell International Law Journal
Denver Journal of International Law and Policy
Fordham International Law Forum
Georgia Journal of International and Comparative Law
Harvard International Law Journal
Hastings International and Comparative Law Review
Houston Journal of International Law
International Trade Law Journal (University of Maryland)
Journal of International Law and Economics (George Washington University)
Journal of Space Law (University of Mississippi)
Law and Policy in International Business (Georgetown University)
Lawyer of the Americas (University of Miami)
New York Law School Journal of International and Comparative Law

7. See note 7 on page 312.

The law school reviews have had a high degree of success in meeting these goals.[8] The foremost legal scholars of this century have written for law reviews, and their articles have been instrumental in molding the course of many legal doctrines. Increasingly, courts have cited law review articles and student comments.[9] It is interesting to note that only as recently as the 1920's did the Supreme Court of the United States begin citing law review articles in its opinions,[10] while presently many decisions of the Court cite or quote from law review articles.

But law school reviews have not been without their critics.[11] The substance of the criticism is aimed at their pedantic style and their similarity to each other. Indeed, some members of Congress have even attacked law reviews as having an insidious influence on the Supreme Court of the United States.[12]

Law school reviews do, however, play a significant role in the growth of the law and remain important to legal research. The typical review may be summarized as being subsidized by its parent institution, with its circulation usually limited to law libraries, its alumni,

New York University Journal of International Law and Politics
North Carolina Journal of International Law and Commercial Regulation
Northwestern Journal of International Law & Business
Stanford Journal of International Studies
Suffolk Transnational Law Journal
Syracuse Journal of International Law and Commerce
Texas International Law Journal
Vanderbilt Journal of Transnational Law
Virginia Journal of International Law
Yale Studies in World Public Order

7 Cribbett, *Experimentation in the Law Reviews*, 5 J.LEGAL ED. 72, 74 (1952).

8 *See, e. g.*, Douglas, *Law Reviews and Full Disclosure*, 40 WASH.L.REV. 227 (1965); Warren, *Upon the Tenth Anniversary of the UCLA Law Review*, 10 U.C.L.A.L.REV. 1 (1962); Hughes, *Foreward*, 50 YALE L.J. 737 (1940); Edmunds, *Hail to Law Reviews*, 1 JOHN MAR.J.PRAC. & PROC. 1 (1967); M. HALL, SELECTED WRITINGS OF BENJAMIN NATHAN CARDOZO 190–192 (1947).

9 For a scientific study of the citation patterns of the "major" law reviews, *see* Maru, *Measuring the Impact of Legal Periodicals*, 1 A.B.F.RES.J. 227 (1976). *See also:* Johnson, *Legal Periodical Usage Survey: Method and Application*, 71 LAW LIB.J. 177 (1978).

10 Newland, *The Supreme Court and Legal Writing: Learned Journals as Vehicles of an Anti-Trust Lobby?*, 48 GEO.L.J. 105, 127 (1959).

11 *See, e. g.*, Rodell, *Goodbye to Law Reviews*, 23 VA.L.REV. 38 (1936), and *Goodbye to Law Reviews—Revisited*, 48 VA.L.REV. 279 (1962); Miller, *The Law Journals*, 5 CHANGE 64 (1973).

12 103 CONG.REC. 16159–16162 (1957) (remarks of Representative Patman). *See also*, Douglas, *supra* note 8.

and members of the bar within the jurisdiction where it is published.[13] It is edited by a select group of law students and serves as an important vehicle for the publication of significant legal research as well as an incisive and effective teaching tool.

2. Bar Association Periodicals

Each state and the District of Columbia have bar associations. In some states membership is voluntary; in other states it is a prerequisite to the practice of law within the state. The latter have what is called an "integrated bar." [14] In addition, many counties and larger cities have their own local bar associations. Most of the state bar associations and many of the local ones publish periodicals. They vary in scope from such distinguished periodicals as the *American Bar Association Journal* [15] or the *Record of the Association of the Bar of the City of New York,* to those that are little more than newsletters. The primary purposes of bar association publications are to inform the membership of the associations' activities, to comment on pending and recent legislation, and to review current local court decisions. When they do publish articles, they tend to stress the more practical aspects of the law, with emphasis upon problem-solving, rather than the theoretical ones. They are concerned more with the law as it is rather than with what it should be. Thus, they perform different functions than the law school reviews, where the emphasis is upon reform and scholarly legal research. As a consequence, bar association publications have less historical value but are more useful when researching subjects of current interest to practitioners.

3. Subject and Interest Legal Periodicals

As the literature of the law grows and reflects the increasing complexity of society, it has become ever more difficult for lawyers to keep current not only with the general development of the law, but also with their particular legal interests. Concurrently with this law explosion, there has been developing a movement in the legal profession towards the interest of one particular sub-group within the legal profession. Some are published by law schools, edited by students, and follow the format of the traditional law review; others are published by non-profit associations; and still others are published by private publishing companies. Another recent development has been the publication of periodicals devoted to law and its interaction with another discipline. These reflect the increasing emphasis many law

[13] The *Harvard Law Review* has the largest circulation at 10,000.

[14] For a complete list *see*: latest American Bar Association Directory.

[15] Allen, *A Preliminary Listing of Current Publications of A.B.A.—Approved Law Schools and Their Libraries,* 67 LAW LIB.J. 79 (1974).

schools and legal scholars are placing on integrating the findings of the social and behavioral sciences with the legal process.

a. *Subject Journals*

Journals devoted to one area of law vary in scope from the very practical to the very scholarly.[16] The *Insurance Law Journal* or *Trusts and Estates,* both published by private companies, are examples of periodicals aimed primarily at the practicing attorney specializing in particular fields of law. They contain articles written by well-known practitioners interpreting the impact of recent legislation and court decisions and may contain reviews of books within their subject area. The *American Journal of Legal History* and the *American Journal of Comparative Law* are examples of periodicals published under the auspices of learned societies, while the *Ecology Law Quarterly,* published at the University of California, Berkeley, School of Law, and the *Urban Law Review,* published at the University of Texas School of Law, are typical of subject journals that are similar to law school reviews.

b. *Special Interest Periodicals*

These periodicals are aimed at those members of the bar who have similar interests and serve as a means to encourage writing and research within the special area of interest. They include such journals as *Black Law Journal,* the *Women Lawyers Journal,* the *Catholic Lawyer,* the *Christian Lawyer,* and the *Judges' Journal.*

c. *Interdisciplinary Journals*

Perhaps the most distinguished of this group is the *Journal of Law and Economics,* published by the faculty of the School of Law at the University of Chicago. Other representative titles are the *University of Michigan Journal of Law Reform,* the *Journal of Psychiatry and Law, Law and Society Review,* and the *Journal of Legal Medicine.*

4. Legal Newspapers

Many larger cities[17] publish newspapers devoted to legal affairs of their metropolitan area. Most are published daily, Monday

[16] A few publishers have begun the practice of collecting the best articles written and published over the course of each year, and combining them into a single volume which measures the development of the law in a particular subject area over the period. ADVERTISING LAW is an example of one such annual. Another annual which changed its approach to include original articles which update the law is the CRIMINAL JUSTICE REVIEW.

[17] A complete list of legal newspapers is available in the *annual Ayer Directory of Publications,* One Bala Ave., Bala Cynwyd, Pennsylvania 19004.

through Friday, and contain primarily information on court calendars and dockets, changes in court rules, news about recent changes in legislation, new administrative rules, and stories about local judges and lawyers. Some of the larger ones, such as the *New York Law Journal* or the *Los Angeles Daily Journal* also publish current court opinions and articles on various legal topics.

There are also two weekly legal newspapers that are national in scope. These are the *Legal Times of Washington* and the *National Law Journal*. A monthly legal newspaper, *The American Lawyer,* contains similar national coverage and features.

SECTION B. COMPREHENSIVE PERIODICAL INDEXES

As described in Section A the usefulness of legal periodicals to legal research depends almost entirely on the ability to find out what articles have been written and where they have been published. Generally, it is necessary to rely on indexes to the legal periodical literature for this purpose.

1. Jones-Chipman Index to Legal Periodicals, 1888–1937, 6 vols.

This was the first index that attempted to provide a comprehensive and systematic index to English language legal periodicals. It is still necessary to consult this set to locate articles published prior to 1908.

2. Index to Legal Periodicals

This index, first published in 1908 by the American Association of Law Libraries, was purchased in 1961 by the H. W. Wilson Co. From 1961 until 1979, the Committee on the *Index to Legal Periodicals* of the American Association of Law Libraries served in an advisory capacity to the publisher on indexing and editorial policy. This *Index* includes legal periodicals published in the United States, Canada, Great Britain, Ireland, Australia and New Zealand, if they regularly publish legal articles of high quality and of permanent reference value. It includes only articles which are at least five ordinary pages or two folio pages in length. Case notes, bibliographies, biographies, and book reviews must be at least two ordinary pages or one folio page in length. Over four hundred and forty periodicals are included with new titles added when they meet the criteria for inclusion in this *Index*.

Authors are listed only as cross-references to subjects, the only headings under which articles are fully indexed. Current issues are published monthly, except for September, and are cumulated quarterly, annually, and triennially. Each of the cumulations contains a "List of Subject Headings." In addition to indexing articles, there is a "Table of Cases Commented Upon" which gives the names of all cases (for the time period of the issue) that have had a note or comment written on them. Under the name of the case, citations are given to the periodicals. Each issue and cumulative volume also has a "Book Review Index," which lists by author all books reviewed in the periodicals indexed by the *Index to Legal Periodicals.* Under the author's name is the title of the book, followed by the citations to periodicals where the reviews appeared. Each issue contains a "Table of Statutes Commented Upon" listing statutes by subject under each jurisdiction.

When consulting the *Index to Legal Periodicals* the following limitations should be noted.

a. Includes periodicals from limited number of countries (Australia, Canada, Great Britain, Ireland, New Zealand, and the United States).

b. The limitations placed on length of articles indexed.

c. Case notes in law school reviews are not listed by title.

[See Illustrations 117–119 for sample pages from the *Index to Legal Periodicals.*]

3. Current Law Index and Legal Resource Index

These two indexes began publication in 1980 by the Information Access Corporation. Both are published under the auspices of the American Association of Law Libraries. They are computer-produced and each has the following features:

Author/Title Index: This Section lists all articles by author with full title and periodical citation given. It also lists all articles by title giving the periodical citation.

Book Reviews: Book reviews which appear in the periodicals covered by the Indexes are listed under both the author and title of the book in the *Author/Title Index* section. An interesting feature is the rating of books from A–F, recording the opinion of the reviewer.

Coverage: Over 680 legal periodicals, selected by an Advisory Board of the American Association of Law Libraries, are indexed. All are in the English language (except for a few in French from Quebec, Canada) published throughout the world. Coverage begins with the 1980 imprint for each periodical. All materials of value are indexed without any limitation as to number of pages. Subject headings are selected from the Library of Congress *Subject Headings* as augmented by additional or alternative terms as recommended by the Advisory Board.

Table of Cases: All substantive cases cited in articles are listed, both under plaintiff and defendant.

Table of Statutes: Lists all statutes cited in articles, both by official and popular citation.

a. *Current Law Index (CLI)*

This is a printed index issued monthly with quarterly and annual cumulations. Each issue contains a list of the periodicals indexed with their addresses. [See Illustrations 120–122 for sample pages from the *Current Law Index*]

b. *Legal Resource Index (LRI)*

This index has all of the features of the *Current Law Index*. It also has the following added features: It is produced on microfilm and read on a specially designed automated reader. Each month a new cumulated reel of microfilm is sent to subscribers. Thus, it is never necessary to look at several separate issues as with printed indexes.

In addition to the 680 legal periodicals, it includes relevant legal material from the following:

Magazine Index, which indexes over 370 popular periodicals.

National Newspaper Index, which indexes the *Christian Science Monitor*, the *New York Times*, and the *Wall Street Journal.*

Books and government documents.

Six legal newspapers (*Legal Times of Washington*, *Los Angeles Daily Journal*, *National Law Journal*, *New Jersey Law Journal*, *New York Law Journal*, and the *Pennsylvania Law Journal*).

Computer searching: Since the LRI is produced by computer, its information is available in machine-readable form. It may be computer-searched through the DIALOG Information Systems.[18]

SECTION C. OTHER INDEXES TO PERIODICAL LITERATURE

There are other periodical indexes less comprehensive than those discussed in Section B which may be useful in legal research.

1. Index to Periodical Articles Related to Law [19]

This publication is issued quarterly and indexes all articles of a legal nature in English that, in the judgment of the editors, are of re-

[18] Lockheed Missiles & Space Company, Inc., Palo Alto, CA.

[19] Index to Periodical Articles Related to Law, Glanville Publishers, Inc., Dobbs Ferry, N.Y. 10522. Edited by R. M. Mersky and J. M. Jacobstein, this index started publication in 1958.

search value and appear in periodicals that are not covered by the *Current Law Index*, the *Index to Foreign Legal Periodicals*, or the *Index to Legal Periodicals*. It is arranged in three parts: an Index to Articles, an Author Index, and a List of Journals Indexed. The last issue of each volume is a cumulative one. There is a ten-year cumulative volume covering the years 1958–68, followed by five-year cumulative volumes, updating the index through 1978.

Since legal subjects are assuming greater prominence in a variety of non-legal journals, this *Index* is particularly useful in locating timely articles on newly developing areas which often first appear in non-legal periodicals. With fifteen or more different periodical indexes being brought together in this publication, it is a useful tool as a companion to the comprehensive legal periodical indexes.

2. Annual Legal Bibliography

This is published by the Harvard Law School Library. It is issued first in a monthly pamphlet called *Current Legal Bibliography*, which is then cumulated annually. It is an index to selected books and articles received at the Harvard Law School Library. Unlike most indexes, it is arranged in a classified, rather than alphabetical, manner. Section A covers Common Law Jurisdictions; Section B, Civil Law and Other Jurisdictions; Section C, Private International Law; and Section D, Public International Law. Each section is classified hierarchically, i. e., there is a main class such as "Corporations," and then all of the subdivisions within corporations are arranged under it. Since the Harvard Law Library is the largest law school library in the world and since this *Index* includes books as well as periodical articles, it is an extremely useful bibliographic reference tool, especially when searching for materials in international and comparative law. Its classified arrangement makes it more difficult to use and the lack of any cumulation of the annual volumes makes it cumbersome for retrospective searching.

3. Index to Foreign Legal Periodicals

Since 1960, the Institute of Advanced Legal Studies of the University of London, in cooperation with the American Association of Law Libraries, has published an *Index to Foreign Legal Periodicals*. It covers a wide range of journals dealing with International Law (Public and Private), Comparative Law and the Municipal Law of all countries of the world other than the United States, the British Isles and nations of the British Commonwealth whose legal systems are based on the common law.

The *Index to Foreign Legal Periodicals* is published quarterly with triennial cumulations. Articles and book reviews of two or more pages in length are indexed in this publication. Titles of articles are given in the language of publication, transliterated for those languages not using the Roman alphabet.

The publication is divided into the following units: (1) subject index; (2) geographical index, grouping, by country or region, the topics of the articles listed in the subject index; (3) book review index; and (4) author index. The author-index entries refer to the subject index where the notations are complete.

4. Index to Indian Legal Periodicals

Since 1963 the Indian Law Institute (New Delhi, India) has issued this publication which indexes periodicals (including yearbooks and other annuals) pertaining to law and related fields published in India. Articles, case comments, notes and other material are included irrespective of the length of the material. Unbound issues appear semi-annually with bound, annual cumulations.

5. Index to Canadian Legal Periodical Literature

This Index was started by the Canadian Association of Law Libraries in 1961 to cover the growing number of Canadian legal journals and to give access to two systems of law, Civil and Common, in two languages, English and French. This is published in quarterly and annual cumulative volumes.

6. Index to Commonwealth Legal Periodicals

This index is published bi-monthly with annual cumulations by the Sir James Dunn Law Library, Dalhousie University, Halifax, Canada.

7. Current Australian and New Zealand Legal Literature Index

This is a quarterly non-cumulating index of Australian and New Zealand legal periodicals. It contains subject, name and case indexes.

8. Contents of Current Legal Periodicals

Published now by the Corporation Services Company, this monthly service reprints the table of contents for most currently issued legal periodicals and includes an index of articles by field of law.

SECTION D. INDEXES TO SPECIAL SUBJECTS

1. Index to Federal Tax Articles

This index, compiled by Gersham Goldstein, and published by Warren, Gorham and Lamont, is a computer-produced bibliography first published in 1975. It covers the literature on federal income, estate, and gift taxation contained in legal, tax and economic journals, as well as non-periodical publications. Consisting of separate subject and author indexes, all of the entries are arranged in reverse chronological order. It is kept current by quarterly supplements.

2. Commerce Clearing House, Federal Tax Articles

This monthly looseleaf reporter of the Commerce Clearing House, Inc., which began publication in 1962, contains summaries of articles on federal (income, estate, gift and excise) taxes appearing in legal, accounting, business and related periodicals. Proceedings and papers delivered at major tax institutes are also noted. The contents are arranged by Internal Revenue Code section numbers.

Articles may be located also by subject by consulting the "Index to Subjects" and by author in the "Index to Authors."

As the looseleaf volume becomes full, material is removed and placed in bound volumes for permanent reference.

3. Criminal Justice Periodical Index

This quarterly index, published by University Microfilms International, covers approximately 100 criminal justice and law enforcement periodicals published in the United States, England and Canada. There is an author index and a subject index which includes case names.

4. Kindex

Subtitled, "An Index to Legal Periodical Literature Concerning Children," *Kindex* is published six times each year with annual cumulations by the National Center for Juvenile Justice. The indexers emphasize practical information for those involved in the juvenile justice system.

SECTION E. PERIODICAL DIGESTS AND ABSTRACTS

1. Criminology and Penology Abstracts

Formerly *Excerpta Criminologica* (Volumes 1–8: 1961–68), this is an international abstracting service covering the etiology of crime and juvenile delinquency, the control and treatment of offenders, criminal procedure and the administration of justice. It is prepared by the Criminologica Foundation in cooperation with the University of Leiden, The Hague, Netherlands.

2. Law Review Digest

This bi-monthly digest contains selected, condensed articles from the legal periodical literature.

3. Monthly Digest of Legal Articles

Selected legal articles from 200 periodicals are condensed and published monthly, closely following the words and style of the original writers.

4. Monthly Digest of Tax Articles

This monthly periodical presents significant current tax articles in abridged form.

5. National Law Review Reporter

This started in 1980 and reprints in their entirety articles selected from currently published law reviews. It is issued six times a year.

6. Law Review Ink

This weekly list copies contents pages of major law reviews and annuals and selected edited books.

SECTION F. OTHER SOURCES

References to periodical articles may frequently be found in other reference books. Many state codes and the annotated editions of the *United States Code* will cite relevant articles in the notes preceding the annotations. Additionally, many of the West Digests will, under each Topic and Key Number, give citations to pertinent law review articles.

1. Shepard's Law Review Citations

This Citator lists, since 1957, over 180 law reviews and legal periodicals. It is arranged similarly to other units of *Shepard's Citations*. By using the *Shepard's Law Review Citations*, a researcher may *Shepardize* a periodical article and find citations to it by courts or in other articles. A footnote reference is given for periodicals added more recently and indicates the year the coverage begins.

2. Federal Law Citations in Selected Law Reviews

This unit of Shepard's indicates when the United States Supreme Court Reports, Federal Reporter 2d, Federal Supplement, Federal Rules Decisions, the United States Constitution, and the United States Code have been cited in the following law reviews beginning with the volume shown:

61 California Law Review (1973)

73 Columbia Law Review (1973)

58 Cornell Law Review (1973)
61 Georgetown Law Journal (1973)
86 Harvard Law Review (1973)
37 Law and Contemporary Problems (1972)
71 Michigan Law Review (1973)
57 Minnesota Law Review (1973)
48 New York Univ. Law Review (1973)
68 Northwestern Univ. Law Review (1974)
25 Stanford Law Review (1973)
51 Texas Law Review (1973)
20 Univ. Of Calif. at Los Angeles Law Review (1973)
40 Univ. of Chicago Law Review (1973)
1973 Univ. of Illinois Law Forum
121 Univ. of Penna. Law Review (1973)
59 Virginia Law Review (1973)
1973 Wisconsin Law Review
82 Yale Law Journal (1973)

3. Legal Periodical Citation in Other Units of Shepard's Citations

As indicated in Chapter 15, the state units of *Shepard's Citations* indicate when a case or statute has been cited in a legal periodical published in the state or the twenty law reviews covered by all of the state *Shepard's Citations.*

SECTION G. ILLUSTRATIONS FOR LEGAL PERIODICALS

117–119. Pages from Index to Legal Periodicals

120–122. Pages from Current Law Index

123. Page from 51 University of Colorado Law Review

124. Page from 55 Texas Law Review

125. Excerpt from Shepard's Law Review Citations

126. Excerpt from Shepard's Federal Law Citations in Selected Law Reviews

[Illustration 117]

PAGE FROM INDEX TO LEGAL PERIODICALS, 1976–1979 VOLUME

FREEDOM of the press—*Continued*

Federalization of state defamation law. Washburn L J 15:290-310 Spr '76

Firestone (Time, Inc. v. Firestone, 96 Sup Ct 958) case: a judicial exercise in press censorship. Emory L J 25:705-36 Summ '76

First amendment—freedom of the press: special symposium issue. Protection or censorship. D. B. Finkel; The British are coming! The British are coming! Is the bicentennial celebration to include imposition of the British contempt rule? R. S. Warren; Freedom to choose. D. K. Davis; Mr. Justice Douglas on sex censorship. S. Fleishman. LAB J 51:534-8+ My '76

First amendment: freedom, philosophy, and the law. W. H. Rehnquist. Gonzaga L Rev 12:1-18 Fall '76

First amendment, high school students, and the possibility of psychological harm. Buffalo L Rev 27:375-94 Spr '78

First amendment limitations on public disclosure actions. U Chi L Rev 45:180-217 Fall '77

First amendment: media's broadcast of performer's "entire act" not privileged. Loyola L Rev 24:111-16 Wint '78

→First amendment rights—Libel. Ann Survey Am L 1976:541-68 '76

First amendment rights to free speech and a free press: change and continuity—a symposium. Unwanted publicity, the news media, and the constitution: where privacy rights compete with the first amendment. E. G. Giglio; Comment, the Supreme Court and the press: freedom or privilege? FCC v. Pacifica Foundation (98 Sup Ct 3026). First amendment, freedom of speech, broadcasting, obscenity: Houchins v. KQED, Inc (98 Sup Ct 2588): first amendment, freedom of the press, access of news media to county jail. Metpath, Inc. v. Imperato (450 F Supp 115): first amendment, freedom of speech, commercial speech and advertising. Pinkus v. United States (98 Sup Ct 1808): first amendment, freedom of speech, obscenity. Akron L Rev 12:229-316 Fall '78

First amendment theory applied to the right of publicity. BC L Rev 19:277-94 Ja '78

Free press—fair trial dilemma: new dimensions in a continuing struggle. Hofstra L Rev 6:1013-40 Summ '78

Free press v. fair trial. Fair trial v. free press. S. A. Bennett; Free press boon: a stop to direct gag orders? J. C. Landau; Fair trial blow: an end run around Miranda? M. Shapiro. Trial 12:24-9+ S '76

Free press v. fair trial in Nebraska: a position paper. M. R. Larson. Neb L Rev 55:543-71 '76

Freedom of the press and public access: toward a theory of partial regulation of the mass media. L. C. Bollinger, jr. Mich L Rev 75:1-42 N '76

Freedom of the press—civil contempt—incarceration of newsperson for refusal to disclose confidential sources does not abridge first amendment. Santa Clara L Rev 16:379-90 Spr '76

Gag orders on criminal defendants. Hastings L J 27:1369-99 Jl '76

Gag orders on the press: a due process defense to contempt citations. Hastings Const L Q 4:187-218 Wint '77

[Gertz] (Gertz v. Robert Welch, Inc. 94 Sup Ct 2997) and Firestone (Time, Inc. v. Firestone, 96 Sup Ct 958): a study in constitutional policy-making. G. G. Ashdown. Minn L Rev 61:645-90 Ap '77

[Gertz] v. Robert Welch, Inc. 94 Sup Ct 2997. Rev Jur UPR 44:175-94 '75

Hazards to the press of claiming a "preferred

Invasion of privacy and the first amendment: Zacchini (Zacchini v. Scripps-Howard Broadcasting Co. 97 Sup Ct 2849) makes the press pay. U Pitt L Rev 39:561-77 '78

Invasion of privacy—constitutional privilege—the first amendment does not protect the publicizing of unnewsworthy private facts. Vand L Rev 29:870-80 Ap '76

Invasion of privacy: new guidelines for the public disclosure tort. Capital U L Rev 6:95-110 '76

Iowa libel law and the first amendment: defamation displaced. Ia L Rev 62:1067-107 Ap '77

Kuczo v. Western Connecticut Broadcasting Company (566 F 2d 384): broadcasting, licensee discretion and governmental action. Capital U L Rev 8:129-48 '78

Law and the media—Leaked information as property: vulnerability of the press to criminal prosecution. E. E. Dennis; Time, Inc. v. Firestone (96 Sup Ct 958): more than a new public figure standard? D. J. McKenna; Free press-fair trial: an introduction. Free press-fair trial controversy: using empirical analysis to strike a desirable balance. S. Nagel, T. Elmerman [sic]; Nebraska Press Association v. Stuart (96 Sup Ct 2791): have we seen the last of prior restraints on the reporting of judicial proceedings? E. B. Prettyman, jr. St Louis U L J 20:610-62 '76

Legal foundations of the right to know. T. I. Emerson. Wash U L Q 1976:1-24 '76

Legal pitfalls in the right to know. J. C. Goodale. Wash U L Q 1976:29-36 '76

Libel—a private individual may recover actual damages for a statement libelous per se published by the public media if the defendant knew, or in the exercise of reasonable care, should have known that the statement was false or would create a false impression in some material respect. Drake L Rev 26:464-71 '76-'77

Libel and slander: the constitution and the private figure in Oklahoma. Okla L Rev 30:686-99 Summ '77

→Libel and the first amendment. Neb L Rev 56:366-81 '77

→Libel—first amendment—story defaming lower level official must reveal that it refers to his official conduct before New York Times privilege applies; paid consultant is not automatically a public official or a public figure for project undertaken; and private plaintiff in defamation action must prove negligence by defendant. Tex L Rev 55:525-40 F '77

Libel law today. D. A. Anderson. Trial 14:18-21+ My '78

Making the first amendment as real as sex. N. Hentoff. Civil Liberties Rev 4:51-4 Mr/Ap '78

Maryland court of appeals: state defamation law in the wake of [Gertz v Robert] Welch, Inc (94 Sup Ct 2997) Md L Rev 36:622-52 '77

Media conglomerates, antitrust law, and the marketplace of ideas. Memphis St U L Rev 9:257-80 Wint '79

Media liability for libel of newsworthy persons: before and after Time, Inc. v. Firestone (96 Sup Ct 958) Fla St U L Rev 5:446-62 Summ '77

Media reporting and privacy claims—decline in constitutional protection for the press. G. G. Ashdown. Ky L J 66:759-99 '77-'78

Möbius strip of the first amendment: perspec-

Using the Index to Legal Periodicals:

Find articles dealing with the First Amendment and libel.

Note how under each subject heading in the Index to Legal Periodicals articles are listed alphabetically by title. Each title has to be read to determine if it deals with the subject under research.

Note also how articles dealing with the case of Gertz v. Robert Welch, Inc., are found in different places. Articles under Freedom of Press heading are listed in over three and a half pages in this three-year cumulation.

[Illustration 118]

PAGE FROM INDEX TO LEGAL PERIODICALS, 1976–1979 VOLUME

SUBJECT AND AUTHOR INDEX

REHABILITATION of criminals—*Continued*

Problems of achieving rehabilitation and punishment in special school environments. D. K. Wiles. E. Rockoff. J L & Educ 7:165-76 Ap '78

Prosecutor's office: the need for a fresh look at resource allocation. R. E. Gerstein. T. K. Peterson. Fla B J 51:512-14 O '77

Psychiatry, the inmate and the law. A. W. Cragg. Dalhousie L J 3:510-27 O '76

Rebuttal to the attack on the indeterminate sentence. S. T. Reid. Wash L Rev 51:565-606 Jl '76

Removal of the public inebriate from the California criminal justice system: a sociological solution to a penal problem. UWLA L Rev 9:49-72 Spr '77

Representing the addict defendant. J. C. Weissman. Crim L Bull 12:389-409 Jl-Ag '76

Returned to the streets: legal issues raised by juvenile diversion programs. K. E. O'Brien. New England J Prison L 3:381-436 Spr '77

Right to treatment: case developments in juvenile law. A. Volenik. J System J 3:292-307

S
S
S
S
T
T
T
T

1. Note that the ILP does not have a separate listing of authors. Rather, it lists each author and then the subject headings under which the author's articles may be found. The parenthesis indicates the first letter of the title. To find all of the articles of Mr. Justice Rehnquist, one would have to look under 13 different subject headings.

2. Case comments are listed as a subdivision under the subject. However, it is not possible to know what aspect of the subject the case note covers.

VASAP: a rehabilitation alternative to traditional DWI penalties. Wash & Lee L Rev 35:673-94 Spr '78

Valentine v. Gray (410 F Supp 1394): incarceration and the right to free enterprise. New England J Prison L 3:549-87 Spr '77

Victory at sea: a marine approach to rehabilitation. R. S. Berry. A. N. Learch. Fed Prob 43:44-7 Mr '79

When criminals repay their victims: a survey of restitution programs. J. Hudson. B. Galaway. S. Chesney. Judicature 60:312-21 F '77

Why jurisdiction over status offenders should be eliminated from juvenile courts. O. W. Ketcham. BU L Rev 57:645-62 Jl '77

Work release in North Carolina—a program that works! A. D. Witte. Law & Contemp Prob 41:230-51 Wint '77

Working paper 7. Diversion. J. L. Clendenning; A. Grant; J. Hackler. Ottawa L Rev 8:275-89 Summ '76

Wyoming penitentiary work release act. Land & Water L Rev 13:997-1019 '78

See also
Parole

Cases

Brown v. Carlson. 431 F Supp 755
New England J Prison L 4:207-9 Fall '77
Morgan v. Sproat. 432 F Supp 1130
New England J Prison L 4:220-2 Fall '77

2. ←

REHABILITATION of offenders. See Rehabilitation of criminals

REHBINDER, Eckard
Environ law (C)
Germany (Fed Republic) (C)
Judicial rev (C)

REHKOPF, Donald G., Jr
Fishing: int law (L)
High seas (L)
Territorial waters (L)

REHMET, Vincent W.
Advertising (L)
Legal ethics (L)

REHNQUIST, William H.
Adm of just (T)
Adm proc—US (N)
Arb and award (J)
Biog (Hastings)
Biog: coll (C)
Const hist (A)
Freedom of speech (F)
Freedom of the press (F)
Judges (W)
Judicial rev (N, T)
Jurisprudence (T)
US: Congress (N)
US: Sup Ct (C, S, W)

1. ←

REIBEN, Stanley J.
Adm of crim just (I)
Dist and prosecuting attorneys (A)
Grand jury (A)
Sentencing (I)

Courts—Local (R)
Judges (R)
Probation (W)

REICHLER, Richard
Corp: taxation (E)
Inc tax: employee benefits—US (E)
Profit sharing (E)
Securities (E)

REICHMAN, Uriel
Easements (J)
Real property: covenants (J)

REID, Donald J.
Dividends (P)
Inc tax: corp distr—PR (P)

REID, Hubert
Civil proc (Q)
Class actions (R)
Language (Q)

REID, Inez Smith
Const law—US (O)
Discrimination: race (O)
Minorities (O)
Poverty (O)

REID, John Phillip
Adm of crim just (P)
Const hist (G, I)
Contracts (B)
Customary law (I)
Government (G)
Legal hist (B, D, G, I, K, P, S)
Partnerships (S)
Property (D, K, S)
Stamp duties (I)
Stock cos (D)
Trials (P)

[Illustration 119]

PAGE FROM INDEX TO LEGAL PERIODICALS, 1976–1979 VOLUME

1502 INDEX TO LEGAL PERIODICALS 1976–1979

GERTZ v. Robert Welch, Inc. 94 Sup Ct 2997
Brooklyn L Rev 43:123-46 Summ '76
Creighton L Rev 10:351-61 D '76
Md L Rev 36:622-52 '77
Minn L Rev 61:645-90 Ap '77
Rev Jur UPR 44:175-94 '75
St Louis U L J 21:374-84 '77
Vand L Rev 29:1431-47 N '76

GIAMBANCO v. Immigration & Naturalization Serv. 531 F 2d 141
Seton Hall L Rev 8:250-87 '77

GIBLIN, In re Petition of (Minn) 232 N W 2d 214
Minn L Rev 60:820-38 Ap '76

GIBSON v. Jackson, 443 F Supp 239
New England J Prison L 4:378-82 Spr '78

GIBSON Products of Ariz., In re, 543 F 2d 652
Santa Clara L Rev 17:967-76 Fall '77
Washburn L J 16:738-44 Spr '77

GILBERT v. Allied Chem. Corp. 411 F Supp 505
DePaul L Rev 26:185-96 Fall '76

GILBERT v. General Elec. Co. 519 F 2d 661
SC L Rev 28:219-33 Je '76

GOLDIE v. Bauchet Properties (Cal) 540 P 2d 1
Calif L Rev 65:367-82 Mr '77
Pepperdine L Rev 3:377-85 Spr '76

GOLDMAN v. First Natl Bank, 532 F 2d 10
U Pa L Rev 125:635-64 Ja '77

GOLDSTEIN v. California, 93 Sup Ct 2303
Sup Ct Rev 1975:147-87 '75

GOLDSTEIN v. Goldstein (1976) 67 D L R (3d) 624
Ottawa L Rev 9:406-17 '77

GOLDWATER, Estate of v. C I R, 539 F 2d 878
Notre Dame Law 52:702-32 Ap '77
Rutgers Camden L J 8:556-61 Spr '77
Trusts & Es 116:784-8 D '77

GOLDY v. Beal, 429 F Supp 640
U Pitt L Rev 38:535-49 Spr '77

GOLZ v. Children's Bureau of New Orleans, Inc (La) 326 S 2d 865
J Family L 15:123-9 '76-'77

GONIN, In re [1977] 2 All E R 720
Convey 41:350-3 S-O '77
L Q Rev 93:485-6 O '77

When it is known that a particular case deals with the subject under research, law review citations on the subject can be located in the Table of Cases section of the Index to Legal Periodicals. E.g., if the Gertz v. Welch case had already been found, this Table indicates which periodicals have articles or comments on it during 1976–79. Later issues of the ILP should be consulted for later law review citations.

Calif L Rev 65:472-82 Mr '77

GLENN v. Conner (Tenn) 533 S W 2d 297
Tenn L Rev 43:511-17 Spr '76

GLICKMAN v. Collins (Cal) 533 P 2d 204
J Family L 14:484-8 '75-'76

GLOVER v. Natl Bank of Commerce (Ark) 529 S W 2d 333
Ark L Rev 30:544-50 Wint '77

GOFFINET v. County of Christian (Ill) 357 N E 2d 442
Ill B J 65:666-70 Je '77
Loyola U L J (Chicago) 8:642-64 Spr '77

GOLCONDA Mining Corp. v. C I R, 507 F 2d 594
Gonzaga L Rev 11:271-93 Fall '75
U Colo L Rev 47:325-62 Spr '76

GOLDBERG v. Meridor, 567 F 2d 209
Brooklyn L Rev 44:1271-93 Summ '78
Geo L J 66:1593-612 Ag '78
Geo Wash L Rev 46:861-76 Ag '78
Va L Rev 64:765-77 Je '78

GOLDBERG v. U.S. 96 Sup Ct 1338
ABA J 62:1334 O '76

GOLDEN v. Biscayne Bay Yacht Club, 530 F 2d 16
Mercer L Rev 28:395-400 Fall '76
Miss L J 47:1011-22 N '76
Neb L Rev 56:207-15 '77
U Fla L Rev 28:850-8 Spr '76
U Miami L Rev 31:198-216 Fall '76

GOLDEN v. Biscayne Bay Yacht Club, 521 F 2d 344
Cumb L Rev 7:157-68 Spr '76
St Mary's L J 8:188-95 '76

GOLDEN Enterprises, Inc. In re, 566 F 2d 1207
Miss L J 49:505-17 Je '78

GOLDER v. United Kingdom, Judgment of Feb. 21, 1975 (European Ct of Human Rights)
Aust L J 50:229-45 My '76

GOLDEX Mines Ltd. v. Revill (1974) 54 D L R (3d) 672
Modern L Rev 39:331-5 My '76

GOLDFARB v. Virginia State Bar, 95 Sup Ct 2004
Ala L Rev 29:317-37 Fall '77
Colum L Rev 77:898-933 O '77
Drake L Rev 25:763-72 Summ '76
Duke L J 1977:1047-68 D '77
How L J 19:149-58 Spr '76
Ia L Rev 63:367-91 D '77
Loyola L Rev 22:390-6 Wint '75-'76
ND L Rev 52:585-92 Spr '76
NY L S L Rev 22:699-737 '77
Real Prop Prob & Tr J 13:238-52 Spr '78
U Miami L Rev 30:464-75 Wint '76
UCLA L Rev 24:475-522 F '77
Washburn L J 15:485-90 '76

Loyola U L J (Chicago) 7:830-50 Summ '76

GORRELL v. City of Parsons (Kan) 576 P 2d 616
Washburn L J 18:182-9 Fall '78

GOSS v. Lopez, 95 Sup Ct 729
Capital U L Rev 5:327-38 '76
J Contemp L 3:85-101 Wint '76
J L & Educ 4:565-621 O '75
NY L F 21:633-46 Spr '76
Ore L Rev 56:137-49 '77
Pepperdine L Rev 5:523-46 Spr '78
Santa Clara L Rev 16:147-57 '75
Stan L Rev 29:627-62 Ap '77
Sup Ct Rev 1975:25-75 '75
Urban L Ann 12:233-43 '76
Wis L Rev 1976:934-74 '76

GOTLIEB v. Commissioner of Taxation (Minn) 245 N W 2d 244
Minn L Rev 61:887-900 My '77

GOURIET v. Union of Post Off Workers [1977] 3 All E R 70
Camb L J 36:201-5 N '77
Can B Rev 56:331-46 Je '78
F L Rev 9:113-23 Mr '78
L Q Rev 94:4-9 Ja '78
Modern L Rev 41:63-7 Ja '78
UBC L Rev 12:320-42 '78

GOURIET v. Union of Post Off Workers [1977] 1 All E R 696
Can B Rev 56:331-46 Je '78
L Q Rev 93:162-5 Ap '77
Modern L Rev 41:58-62 Ja '78

GOUZENKO v. Harris et al (1976) 72 D L R (3d) 293
Can B Rev 56:116-21 Mr '78

GRACE v. State Farm Mut. Automob. Insur. Co (Neb) 246 N W 2d 874
Creighton L Rev 11:222-34 O '77

GRAHAM v. Graham (Colo) 574 P 2d 75
Conn L Rev 11:62-74 Fall '78
J Family L 17:182-5 N '78
Tulsa L J 13:646-57 '78

GRAND Bahama Petroleum Co. v. Asiatic, In re 550 F 2d 1320
Brooklyn L Rev 44:1323-4 Summ '78

GRAND Bahama Petroleum Co. v. Canadian Transp. Agencies, Ltd. 450 F Supp 447
Va J Int L 18:829-37 Summ '78

GRAND Jury Proceedings, In re, 517 F 2d 666
Mercer L Rev 27:1213-18 Summ '76

GRAND Jury Proceedings, In re, 563 F 2d 577
Duquesne L Rev 16:667-78 '77-'78
Memphis St U L Rev 8:694-702 Spr '78

[Illustration 120]

PAGE FROM QUARTERLY ISSUE—CURRENT LAW INDEX

SUBJECT INDEX

LAND grants
The Mexican land grants of John Sutter. by Jerome Curtis Jr.
55 Cal. St. B.J. 118-125 March '80
-CASES
Mineral and surface rights under the doctrine of accretion: property law - doctrine of accretion. (case note) Smith v. United States 593 F.2d 982 (10th Cir. 1979) by M.H. Schwarz
20 Nat. Resources J. 199-203 Jan '80
LAND, Liability for condition and use of *see* Liability for condition and use of land
LAND tax *see* Real property tax
LAND tenure
Les terres du clerge. (Quebec) by Andre Cossette
82 Rev. Notariat 272-280 Jan-Feb '80
see also Rent
LAND titles
Moot point: Caveat caveator! (validity of caveats against real property in New South Wales) by Peter Butt
54 Austl. L.J. 166-172 March '80
Possessory title and the torrens system in New South Wales. by R.A. Woodman and Peter Butt *54 Austl. L.J. 79-88 Feb '80*
see also
Adverse possession
Conveyancing
Insurance, Title
Leases
Mortgages
-CASES
Title insurance - reasonable expectation doctrine applied to incorporate survey of land into title insurance policy. (case note) MacBean v. St. Paul Title Insurance Corp. 405 A.2d 405 (N.J. Super. App. Div. 1979)
10 Seton Hall L. Rev. 762-764 Spr '80
LAND trusts
The foreclosure of mortgages executed by land trustees. by Lawrence E. Varsek
68 Ill. B.J. 462-464 March '80
LAND use
Areas of critical state concern: some unresolved issues. (environmental law in Florida) by Robert W. Martin Jr.
54 Fla. B.J. 381-385 May '80
Police power, compensation, and property rights in Florida. by Frank E. Catalina
8 Real Est. L.J. 333-336 Spr '80
Prosecutions under section 27 of the Town and Country Planning Act 1971 for inaccurate certificates. (Great Britain) by Arthur Ward
J. Plan. & Envt'l L. 166-168 March '80
Notes of cases: highway law. (diversion of footpath ... ning Act
J. Pla[...]
Notes of c[...] (expiratic[...] Great Br[...]
J. Pla[...]
Planning [...] (British [...] ry
J. Pla[...]
Temporary [...] Samuels
J
The Comi[...] (Great B[...]
J
Evaluating [...] recapture [...] control o[...] B.W. Schoivinick

Open spaces
Public lands
Real estate business
Rent
-CASES
Contract for the sale of land: clause 17 and disclosure. (disclosure of land use restrictions in New South Wales) (case note) Beverly Manufacturing Co. Pty. Ltd. v. A.N.S. Nominees Ltd. 52 A.L.J.R. 760 (High Ct. 1978) by Marcelle Lawrence
9 Sydney L. Rev. 210-218 Jan '80
An aggrieved party - loss of inverse condemnation actions in zoning ordinance disputes. (case note) Agins v. City of Tiburon 598 P.2d 25 (Cal. 1978) by Walter R. Luostari
7 Pepperdine L. Rev. 457-468 Wntr '80
LAND use, rural
Property taxes and farmers in Ohio: the Park Investment story. by Theodore R. Finnarn
53 Ohio St. B.A. Rep. 505(4) March 31 '80
see also
Agriculture
Farms
LAND use, urban
Planning control and the property market. (English planning law) by Martin Loughlin *3 Urb. L. & Pol'y 1-22 March '80*
Stop notices. (urban planning enforcement in Great Britain) by Henry E. Markson
124 Solicitor's J. 56(2) Jan 25 '80
Constitutional and judicial limitations on the community's power to downzone. by C. Thomas Williamson III
12 Urb. Law. 157-182 Wntr '80
-CASES
Zoning - governing body may modify or reverse board of adjustment final decision only upon finding that board acted arbitrarily and capriciously. (case note) Evesham Township Zoning Board v. Evesham Township Council 404 A.2d 1274 (N.J. Super. Law Div. 1979)
10 Seton Hall L. Rev. 764-765 Spr '80
LANDLORD and tenant
see also
Apartment houses
Commercial leases
Eviction
Leases
Real covenants
Rent
-ANECDOTES, FACETIAE, SATIRE, ETC
A garden-variety opinion on tenant-landlord law. by Howard Zaharoff
8 Student Law. 13-14 April '80
-LAW AND LEGISLATION
The Illinois landlord's obligation to protect persons on his premises against the

The implied warranty of habitability: a dream deferred. by Jeffrey Hiles
48 U.M.K.C.L. Rev. 237-257 Wntr '80
The Connecticut housing court: an initial evaluation. by Kathleen Eldergill
12 Conn. L. Rev. 296-323 Wntr '80
-LITIGATION
Pro bono bulletin. (housing) by Charles F. Palmer and Carol Kuntz Lysaght
3 L.A. Law. 42-43 April '80
Landlord-tenant - landlord's duty in tort held fulfilled where hazard causing injury to tenant was open and obvious. by Eugene A. Cordaro
8 Real Est. L.J. 354 Spr '80
Commercial lease - shopping center - tenant held not under duty to install fire prevention system. by Eugene A. Cordaro
8 Real Est. L.J. 351 Spr '80
Landlord-tenant - warranty of habitability - tenant entitled to a rent abatement for lack of service despite landlord by Eugene A. Cordaro
8 Real Est. L.J. 354-355 Spr '80
Commercial lease - rights of landlord in bankruptcy - assignment of lease. by Eugene A. Cordaro
8 Real Est. L.J. 350 Spr '80
Clear the way, landlord. (Great Britain) by Trevor M. Aldridge
124 Solicitor's J. 39-40 Jan 18 '80
Joram Developments v. Sharratt: Helby v. Rafferty. (unmarried cohabitee's right to succeed to statutory tenancy in Great Britain) by C.H. Sherrin
43 Mod. L. Rev. 77-80 Jan '80
-REMEDIES
Retaliatory eviction: a national perspective. by William Bush and Karen Shoos
8 Law & Housing J. 26-55 Spr '80
-RULES AND REGULATIONS
A new administrative rule on landlord-tenant agreements. by Mary K. Ryan
53 Wis. B. Bull. 24-28 May '80
LANDRAM, C.J.
C.J. Landrum. (obituary)
43 Tex. B.J. 490 May '80
LANGDON, Jim C.
J.C. Langdon. (obituary)
43 Tex. B.J. 389 April '80
LANGUAGE and languages
Of silk shirts and common usage. (language) (column) by Flora Johnson
8 Student Law. 10-11 April '80
see also
Bilingualism
Programming languages (Electronic computers)
LANGUAGES
Validity of Manitoba laws after Forest: what is to be done by Joseph Eliot Magnet
[...] *-257 Spr '80*
[...]its. by Ste-
[...] *94 Wint '79*
[...]c computers)
[...] computers)
[...]ormation is [...]t Act 1968.
[...]y
[...]-10 Feb '80
[...] rev by D.T.
[...]45 April '80

A typical page from the Current Law Index. Note under the subject heading "Landlord and Tenant," the various sub-headings. It is by the use of such sub-headings as well as many specific entries that this Index avoids the problem of having too many entries under one subject heading.

Note also how under the subdivision "Cases" under "Land grants" the title of the case note is given so that the researcher can know what subject the case notes cover.

[Illustration 121]

PAGE FROM QUARTERLY ISSUE—CURRENT LAW INDEX

AUTHOR/TITLE INDEX

PICKRELL, Robert W.
Family disputes mediation - a new service for lawyers and their clients. by Robert W. Pickrell and Alice L. Bendheim *7 Barrister 27-28 Wntr '80*

PIEHLER, Henry R.
Products liability and the reasonably safe product. by Alvin S. Weinstein, Aaron D. Twerski, Henry R. Piehler and William A. Donaher rev by R. Matthew Neff grade B *13 Ind. L. Rev. 627-635 March '80*

PIERCE, James L.
The competitive implications of EFT. by James L. Pierce *2 Computer L.J. 133-151 Wntr '80*

PIERCE, James R.
Admissibility of evidence of other crimes - emphasis on use in pros crimes - for which the defe acquitted, under similar subsequent trial. (case note) by James R. Pierce *7 N. Ky. L. Rev. 133-144 Wntr '80*

PIERCE, James Winston, Jr.

1. →

PLATT, John C.
May a state say no to nuclear power? Pacific Legal Foundation gives a disappointing answer. (case note) by Judith C. Bauman and John C. Platt *10 Envt'l L. 189-212 Fall '79*

PLECK, Joseph H.
Conflicts between work and family life. (research summary) by Joseph H. Pleck, Graham L. Staines and Linda Lang *103 Month. Lab. Rev. 29-32 March '80*

PLUECKHAHN, Vernon D.
Road traffic accidents and the prevention of injury and death of vehicle occupants. by Vernon D. Plueckhahn *20 Med. Sci. & L. 28-34 Jan '80*

POHL, Geoffrey V.
Comparative contribution and strict tort liability: a proposed reconciliation. by Geoffrey V. Pohl *13 Creighton L. Rev. 889-907 Spr '80*

Points of choice. by Roger Fisher rev by D.W.

PONTECORVO, Giulio
Economic rationalization of fisheries: the problem of conflicting national interests on Georges Bank. by John Donaldson and Giulio Pontecorvo *8 Ocean Dev. & Int'l L.J. 149-169 Spr '80*

POPE, Richard S.
One day - one trial or a one week term of jury service: the misleading marketing of modern jury management systems. by Michael H. Graham and Richard S. Pope *45 Mo. L. Rev. 255-280 Spr '80*

POPKO, Daniel A.
Workmen's compensation: new cause of action for retaliatory discharge. by Roland K. Filippi and Daniel A. Popko *68 Ill. B.J. 329-332 Jan '80*

PORTER, Linda S.
Constitutional law - due process of law - prisons and prisoners - parole - due process does not apply to a parole release proceeding unless state law creates a reasonable expectation that parole will be

A typical page from the Author-Title Section of Current Law Index. Note the following:

1. **Authors are listed alphabetically with complete title and citation.**
2. **Articles are also listed under title.**
3. **Book reviews are included in this section under both the author and title of the book. Books are rated A–F according to the opinion of the reviewer.**

Pioneer conservationists of Western America. by Peter Wild rev by Channing Kury grade B *20 Nat. Resources J. 208 Jan '80*

PIORE, Michael J.
Comment. (reply to Foge policy and unsanctioned Michael J. Piore *33 Indus. & Lab. Rel. Rev. 31*

3. →

PISANO, R.V.
The comparison of alcohol concentrations in postmortem fluids and tissues. by R.C. Backer, R.V. Pisano and I.M. Sopher *25 J. For. Sci. 327(5) April '80*

PITOFSKY, Robert
Improving the administrative process - time for a new APA? Improving the process: views from the agencies. (A.B.A. National Conference on Federal Regulation) by Joan Z. Bernstein, Robert Pitofsky, Howard C. Anderson and Clark Byse *32 Ad. L. Rev. 327-347 Spr '80*

Plain English for lawyers. by Richard Wydick rev by Jill Switzer grade A *55 Cal. St. B.J. 164 April '80*

PLAINE, Daniel J.
Technical barriers to trade (standards) and licensing. (U.S. Ct. of Customs and Patent Appeals, Judicial Conference, 1979) (transcript) by David Busby, Thomas Graham, Alexander Sierck and Daniel J. Plaine *84 F.R.D. 564-573 March '80*

Planning ambulatory health care. rev by Peter T. Ittig grade A *4 J. Health Pol. Pol'y & L. 706-708 Wntr '80*

Planning in practice (with specimen documents). by G.N.D. Jones and J.W. Davies grade A *124 Solicitor's J. 132 Feb 22 '80*

← 2.

Cyril D. Robinson grade C *26 Crime & Delinquency 261-263 April '80*

Political leadership in NATO. by Robert S. Jordan rev by Inis L. Claude Jr. grade B *74 Am. J. Int'l L. 247-248 Jan '80*

The politics of justice. by Kermit L. Hall rev by Lawrence M. Friedman grade B *33 Vand. L. Rev. 1017-1026 May '80*

The politics of the budgetary process. by Aaron Wildavsky rev by James P. Pfiffner grade B *40 Pub. Ad. Rev. 194-200 March-April '80*

POLITO, Joseph M.
Real property, natural resource and environmental law. (survey of Michigan law) by Joseph M. Polito *26 Wayne L. Rev. 769-808 Jan '80*

POLLOCK, Earl E.
Panel discussion interview with John Shenefield, Assistant Attorney General, Antitrust Division. by Allen C. Holmes, Earl E. Pollock, Ira M. Millstein and James T. Halverson *48 Antitrust L.J. 637-655 Spr '80*

POLLOCK, Ellen Joan
Beverly Hills's Hirsch hangs a new shingle. by Ellen Joan Pollock *2 Am. Law. 9 June '80*

POMERANTZ, Roy E.
Products liability insurance in the new industrial revolution. by Roy E. Pomer- *Ins. L.J. 129-137 March '80*
nages: an insurer's view. by Roy ntz *684 Ins. L.J. 21-32 Jan '80*
orton

by C. Paul Rogers III grade B *93 Harv. L. Rev. 1039-1050 March '80*

POST, Joseph
Federal common law suits to abate interstate air pollution. by Joseph Post *4 Harv. Envt'l L. Rev. 117-144 Wntr '80*

POTTER, Paul
Se habla Espanol? by Paul Potter *3 L.A. Law. 34(5) April '80*

POTUTO, Josephine R.
A model proposal to avoid ex-offender employemnt discrimination. by Josephine R. Potuto *41 Ohio St. L.J. 77-106 Wntr '80*

POULET, N.
Copyright in international relations. by Mark M. Boguslavsky, N. Poulet and David Catterns rev by igor I. Kavass grade A- *8 Int'l J.L. Lib. 75-76 April '80*

POWELL, William Jay
The right to treatment - a fabled right receives judicial recognition in Missouri. (case note) by William Jay Powell *45 Mo. L. Rev. 357-369 Spr '80*

POWER, Craig E.
Securities. (Fifth Circuit survey of cases) by Craig E. Power *11 Tex. Tech. L. Rev. 515-534 Wntr '80*

POWER, D.J.
Principles of forensic psychiatry. by D.J. Power grade A- *124 Solicitor's J. 308 May 2 '80*

POWERS, Lonnie A.
Tax incentives for historic preservation: a survey, case studies and analysis. by Lonnie A. Powers

[Illustration 122]

PAGE FROM QUARTERLY ISSUE—CURRENT LAW INDEX

TABLE OF CASES

BELLOTTI v. Baird,
99 S. Ct. 3035 (1979) Restrictions on the abortion rights of minors. (case note)
3 Harv. Women L.J. 119-139 Spr '80
99 S. Ct. 3035 (1979) Constitutional law - parental and judicial consent restrictions on a minor's decision to have an abortion. (case note)
14 Suffolk U.L. Rev. 48-59 Wntr '80
99 S. Ct. 3035 (1979) Statute requiring pregnant minor who seeks abortion to obtain parental consent or judicial approval following parental notification found to unconstitutionally burden her right to abort. *18 J. Fam. L. 403-408 Feb '79-'80*
BENEFICIAL Finance Corporation Ltd., Elder's Trustee and Executor Co. Ltd. v,
(1979) 21 S.A.S.R. 216 (S. Ct. S. Austl.) Companies - debenture stock in foreign currency - whether such stock ranks pari passu with other stock. (Australia)

BENJAM
Assn
(New
Yorl
unc
disa
4 Men
BENNE
68 C
imp
BERKEY
603
She
no duty to predisclose information on innovations. (case note)
55 Notre Dame Law. 554-573 April '80
603 F.2d 263 (2d Cir. 1979) An economic and legal analysis of physical tie-ins.
89 Yale L.J. 769-801 March '80
603 F.2d 263 (2d Cir. 1979) Recent antitrust developments - 1979.
80 Colum. L. Rev. 1-42 Jan '80
BESUNDER v. Coughlin,
422 N.Y.S.2d 564 (Nassau County Sup. Ct. 1979) Critical N.Y. court orders proper care for two MR patients, upholds standing of advocacy agency to sue.
4 Mental Disab. L. Rep. 97-98 March-April '80
BETTIS, Nolan v,
577 S.W.2d 551 (Tex. App. 1979) Jury award of punitive damages upheld.
97 Banking L.J. 373-374 April '80
BEVERLY Manufacturing Co. Pty. Ltd. v. A.N.S. Nominees Ltd.,
52 A.L.J.R. 760 (High Ct. 1978) Contract for the sale of land: clause 17 and disclosure. (disclosure of land use restrictions in New South Wales) (case note)
9 Sydney L. Rev. 210-218 Jan '80
BIG Mama Rag, Inc. v. United States,
79-1 U.S. Tax Cas. 9362 (D.D.C. Apr. 30, 1979) Tax exemptions for educational institutions: discretion and discrimination. (case note)
128 U. Pa. L. Rev. 849-882 April '80
BOARD of Curators of the University of Missouri v. Horowitz,
435 U.S. 78 (1978) Student suspensions and expulsions. (case note)
17 Am. Bus. L.J. 526-531 Wntr '80

BOARD of Education v. Nyquist,
408 N.Y.S.2d 606 (Sup. Ct. 1978) The constitutionality of public school financing laws: judicial and legislative interaction.
8 Fordham Urb. L.J. 673-693 Summ '79-'80
BOARD of Education v. Walter,
390 N.E.2d 813 (1979) Equal educational opportunity and public school finance reform in Ohio. (case note)
41 Ohio St. L.J. 179-210 Wntr '80
390 N.E.2d 813 (Ohio 1979) Education - equal protection - schools and school districts: finance. (case note)
48 U. Cin. L. Rev. 1126-1135 Fall '79
BOARD of Regents of the University of California v. Bakke,
438 U.S. 265 (1978) Some post-Bakke-and-Weber reflections on reverse discrimination.
14 U. Rich. L. Rev. 373-388 Wntr '80
BOARD of Tax Appeals, State ex. rel. Park Investment Co. v,

260 S.E.2d 338 (Ga. 1979) Will violates perpetuities rule but charitable bequest upheld. *7 Est. Plan. 184-185 May '80*
BOLES, Califano v,
99 S. Ct. 2767 (1979) Denial of mother's insurance benefits under the Social Security Act to mother of illegitimate child does not violate the fifth amendment equal protection requirement.
18 J. Fam. L. 618-623 Spr '80
BORDEN, Inc., In re,
92 F.T.C. 669 (1978) The FTC and the generic doctrine: a new RX for pharmaceutical trademarks.
15 Tulsa L.J. 327-347 Wntr '80
BORDEN (U.K.) Ltd. v. Scottish Timber Products Ltd.,
(1979) 3 W.L.R. 672 (C.A.) Another Romalpa case; resin used in the manufacture of chipboard. (tracing rights in Great Britain) (editorial) *J. Bus. L. 5-7 Jan '80*
BORG-WARNER Corp., Melton v,
467 F. Supp. 983 (W.D. Tex. 1979) Jurisdiction - tort action - choice of foreign or United States law - most significant contacts test.
74 Am. J. Int'l L. 192-193 Jan '80
BRITISH Broadcasting Co., Attorney-General v,
(1979) 3 All E.R. 45 Criminal contempt of a civil court. (British law)
44 J. Crim. L. 26-28 Feb '80
BRITISH Columbia v. Gilbertson,
597 F.2d 1161 (9th Cir. 1979) Foreign judgments - enforcement - revenue rule - reciprocity.
74 Am. J. Int'l L. 190-191 Jan '80
BRITISH Railways Board, Waugh v,
(1979) 3 W.L.R. 150 (H.L.) Evidence and discovery - legal professional privilege - test of dominant purpose in preparation of

441 U.S. 1 (1979) Price fixing and the per se rule: a redefinition. (case note)
5 Del. J. Corp. L. 73-96 Spr '80
BROOKS, Flagg Brothers v,
436 U.S. 149 (1978) Creditors' remedies as state action. *89 Yale L.J. 538-560 Jan '80*
BROOKS, Hamel v,
No. 78-115 (D. Or. Dec. 1979) Preliminary hearing necessary before trial release of patient can be revoked.
4 Mental Disab. L. Rep. 97 March-April '80
BROOKS v. A.M.F., Inc.,
278 N.W.2d 310 (Minn. 1979) Workers' compensation - intervenors' right to reimbursement. (case note)
6 Wm. Mitchell L. Rev. 228-241 Wntr '80
BROWN,
73 T.C. No. 15 Multiple motives okayed for child care credit.
8 Tax. for Law. 299 March-April '80
BROWN, Chrysler Corp. v,
441 U.S. 281 (1979) The trade secret status of health and safety testing information:
rch '80
idential
agency
own.
Jan '80
eaty -
of 1968
Jan '80
all and
Board
of Education. (transcript)
55 Notre Dame Law. 471-484 April '80
BROWN v. Inter-Ocean Insurance Company,
438 F. Supp. 951 (N.D. Ga. 1977) Life insurance - coverage not established.
29 Def. L.J. 200-201 Spr '80
BUCHAN v. Swan,
(1979) 1 N.S.W.L.R. 19 Discrimination in employment - purported revocaton of appointments of teachers - compensation for loss of office - Teaching Service Act 1970 (N.S.W.) - Interpretation Act 1897 (N.S.W.) - Anti-Discrimination Act 1977 (N.S.W.) (case note)
54 Austl. L.J. 161-165 March '80
BUCK, State v,
275 N.W.2d 194 (Iowa 1979) Buck should stop here: consecutive sentencing of multiple offenders in Iowa.
65 Iowa L. Rev. 468-491 Jan '80
BULMAN, Bates v,
(1979) 1 W.L.R. 1190 Assault with offensive weapon? (British law)
44 J. Crim. L. 5-6 Feb '80
BURCH, Jech v,
466 F. Supp. 714 (D. Haw. 1979) Parents have a constitutionally protected right to choose any surname for their child. (case note)
18 J. Fam. L. 408-411 Feb '79-'80
BURD, Sinn v,
404 A.2d 672 (Pa. 1979) Parent and child - a mother who witnesses the act which causes death or serious injury to her child has a cause of action for negligent infliction of mental distress. (case note)
18 J. Fam. L. 643-648 Spr '80
BURMAH Oil Co. Ltd. V. Bank of England,
(1979) 3 W.L.R. 722 (H.L.) The House of Lords inspects the Burmah Oil documents. (editorial) *J. Bus. L. 7-8 Jan '80*
BURNETTE v. Wahl,

The Table of Cases in the Current Law Index lists all cases commented on in articles indexed and gives citation of the case, and full title of the casenote.

[Illustration 123]

PAGE FROM 51 UNIVERSITY OF COLORADO LAW REVIEW

EDITORIAL PRIVILEGE AND FREEDOM OF THE PRESS: *HERBERT v. LANDO* IN PERSPECTIVE

GERALD G. ASHDOWN*

The Supreme Court's 1972 decision refusing to recognize a privilege on behalf of news reporters to withhold their sources of information in criminal investigations[1] has proven to be the harbinger of a decided anti-press sentiment on the part of a majority of the

A typical leading article in a typical law review.

preme Court toward freedom of the press from the perspective of the Court's media decisions. Examination of these decisions exposes the Court's narrow philosophy of free press and illuminates the potential effect of *Herbert v. Lando* on the editorial process and the news media in general. Once the decision is placed in this perspective and critically evaluated it, it will be suggested that the States recognize a privilege protecting the editorial process from compelled judicial disclosure.

THE BURGER COURT'S RESTRICTIVE FREE PRESS PHILOSOPHY

There are basically three facets to the performance of the constitutional function of the press in fostering informed self-government and serving as a check on the exercise of public and private concentrations of power:[3] (1) the acquisition of information (2) the

---

* Associate Professor of Law, West Virginia University College of Law. B.A., J.D. University of Iowa.

1. Branzburg v. Hayes, 408 U.S. 665 (1972).
2. 441 U.S. 153 (1979).
3. Unlike freedom of speech which serves a dignitary, self-fulfillment function in addition to fostering the distribution of ideas, freedom of the press is designed exclusively to facilitate the dissemination of information to the public. The press enjoys no inherent right to speak outside of this function. *See* Meiklejohn, *The First Amendment Is An Absolute*, 1961 SUP.

[Illustration 124]

PAGE FROM 55 TEXAS LAW REVIEW

LIBEL—FIRST AMENDMENT—STORY DEFAMING LOWER LEVEL OFFICIAL MUST REVEAL THAT IT REFERS TO HIS OFFICIAL CONDUCT BEFORE *NEW YORK TIMES* PRIVILEGE APPLIES; PAID CONSULTANT IS NOT AUTOMATICALLY A PUBLIC OFFICIAL OR A PUBLIC FIGURE FOR PROJECT UNDERTAKEN; AND PRIVATE PLAINTIFF IN DEFAMATION ACTION MUST PROVE NEGLIGENCE BY DEFENDANT. *Foster v. Laredo Newspapers, Inc.*, 541 S.W.2d 809 (Tex. 1976), *cert. denied*, 45 U.S.L.W. 3562 (U.S. Feb. 22, 1977).

A civil engineer brought a libel action against the *Laredo Times*, alleging that a story in the newspaper attributed to him responsibility for a severe flooding problem in a local subdivision and intimated that he was guilty of impropriety by serving as both the elected county surveyor and a paid

A typical law review student note. The purpose of student notes or comments is to provide critical analyses of recent cases or topics of law. Most notes or comments are from two to twelve pages in length.

the alleged libel related to his official capacity as an elected county surveyor. Furthermore, a private plaintiff who seeks damages for a defamatory falsehood can recover on a showing that the publisher or broadcaster knew or should have known that the statement was false, although liability may not result from a misstatement whose content does not reveal its defamatory potential.

Foster v. Laredo Newspapers, Inc.[4] represents the Texas Supreme Court's initial reaction to the landmark 1974 Supreme Court decision of *Gertz*

1. The alleged defamation was contained in these paragraphs from the news story:

> The Rice development official said the flooded area in question was platted by Jack Foster, who doubles as a consultant engineer for Webb County.
>
> Foster has been handling numerous engineering jobs for the Commissioners Court on a consultant basis involving road improvements, some paving, park recreational work and drainage problems in Del Mar Hills.

Foster v. Laredo Newspapers, Inc., 541 S.W.2d 809, 811 (Tex. 1976), *cert. denied*, 45 U.S.L.W. 3562 (U.S. Feb. 22, 1977).

2. Foster v. Laredo Newspapers, Inc., 530 S.W.2d 611 (Tex. Civ. App.—San Antonio 1975).

3. 376 U.S. 254 (1964).

4. 541 S.W.2d 809 (Tex. 1976), *cert. denied*, 45 U.S.L.W. 3562 (U.S. Feb. 22, 1977). The United States Supreme Court denied certiorari because the Texas decision lacked finality. *See* Cox Broadcasting Corp. v. Cohn, 420 U.S. 469 (1975).

525

[Illustration 125]

EXCERPT FROM SHEPARD'S LAW REVIEW CITATIONS

MISSOURI LAW REVIEW Vol. 27

Vol. 18	Vol. 19	Vol. 21	Vol. 22	Vol. 24	Vol. 26	Vol. 27
-1-	-214-	-105-	-14-	-137-	-1-	-1-
1974LF599	23A[illegible]	2Akr76	Mo	6CnL235	Mo	Mo
					9	531SW546
-215-	-					-354-
26FLR654						74WLQ231
39MoL489	518					
-249-						-406-
31MB333						Mo
						502SW35
						-533-
						Mo
						501SW557

This unit of Shepard's provides a means for "Shepardizing" law review articles cited since 1957. Through its use, one can find every time a law review article has been cited by another law review or in a court decision.

[Illustration 126]

EXCERPT FROM SHEPARD'S FEDERAL LAW CITATIONS IN SELECTED LAW REVIEWS

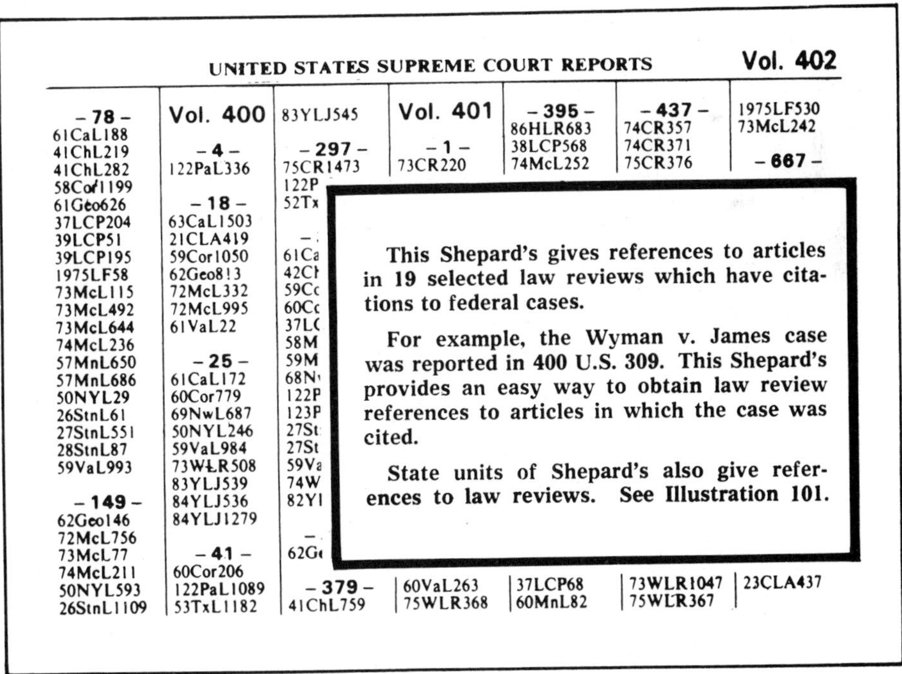

UNITED STATES SUPREME COURT REPORTS Vol. 402

-78- 61CaL188 41ChL219 41ChL282 58Cor1199 61Geo626 37LCP204 39LCP51 39LCP195 1975LF58 73McL115 73McL492 73McL644 74McL236 57MnL650 57MnL686 50NYL29 26StnL61 27StnL551 28StnL87 59VaL993

-149- 62Geo146 72McL756 73McL77 74McL211 50NYL593 26StnL1109

Vol. 400

-4- 122PaL336

-18- 63CaL1503 21CLA419 59Cor1050 62Geo813 72McL332 72McL995 61VaL22

-25- 61CaL172 60Cor779 69NwL687 50NYL246 59VaL984 73WLR508 83YLJ539 84YLJ536 84YLJ1279

-41- 60Cor206 122PaL1089 53TxL1182

83YLJ545

-297- 75CR1473 122P 52Tx

-: 61Ca 42Ch 59Cc 60Cc 37LC 58M 59M 68N 122P 123P 27St 27St 59Va 74W 82YI

-: 62G

-379- 41ChL759

Vol. 401

-1- 73CR220

60VaL263 75WLR368

-395- 86HLR683 38LCP568 74McL252

37LCP68 60MnL82

-437- 74CR357 74CR371 75CR376

73WLR1047 75WLR367

1975LF530 73McL242

-667-

23CLA437

This Shepard's gives references to articles in 19 selected law reviews which have citations to federal cases.

For example, the Wyman v. James case was reported in 400 U.S. 309. This Shepard's provides an easy way to obtain law review references to articles in which the case was cited.

State units of Shepard's also give references to law reviews. See Illustration 101.

SECTION H. SUMMARY

1. Legal Periodicals

a. *Law school reviews*

Contains leading articles, student-written articles and case comments. Over 200 law school reviews are published. Many cover the developments of the law for their particular state; others are national in scope.

b. *Bar association periodicals*

Emphasis is more on the practical aspects of the law.

c. *Special and subject periodicals*

These are devoted to a single subject, such as labor law or insurance law, or to the relationship of law with another subject, or are published for a particular class of lawyers.

2. Indexes to Legal Periodicals and Articles

a. *Periodical articles published prior to 1908*

Jones-Chipman Index to Legal Periodicals. Indexes English language periodicals published prior to 1908.

b. *Periodical articles published 1908 to 1979*

Index to Legal Periodicals. Indexes articles from most legal periodicals published in Australia, Canada, Great Britain, Ireland, New Zealand, and the United States.

3. Periodical Articles Published After 1979

Current Law Index

Index to Legal Periodicals

Legal Resource Index

4. Articles Published in Non-legal Journals

Index to Periodical Articles Related to Law

5. Articles in Foreign Legal Periodicals

Index to Foreign Legal Periodicals
Index to Indian Legal Periodicals
Index to Canadian Legal Periodical Literature
Index to Commonwealth Legal Periodicals
Current Australian and New Zealand Legal Literature Index

6. Locating Articles from Legal Periodicals Cited in Other Articles or in Court Decisions

Shepard's Law Review Citations

Federal Law Citations in Selected Law Reviews

Chapter 18

TREATISES, RESTATEMENTS, MODEL CODES, AND UNIFORM LAWS

SECTION A. TREATISES

Legal treatises are another important category of the secondary sources of the law. Treatises or textbooks are usually able to treat a subject in greater depth and with more analysis than a legal encyclopedia or periodical article. The first treatises were written by legal scholars during the early development of the common law. As there were few court decisions available as precedent, the early text writers such as Lord Coke or William Blackstone played a significant role in the development of the law. As the growth of the law resulted in an ever-increasing number of law reports, treatises were needed to organize the diffuse principles of case law. As one commentator has noted, treatises were first written because of the lack of precedents and then subsequently because there were too many precedents.[1]

During the eighteenth and the early nineteenth centuries in the United States, English treatises were an integral part of an American lawyer's library. But, gradually, American lawyers and legal scholars began publishing treatises devoted entirely to American law.[2] Moreover, the American system of federalism has resulted in an increasing number of published treatises dealing with the law of a particular state.

1. Nature of Treatises

Treatises may be defined as expositions by legal writers on case law and legislation. Generally, treatises are more exhaustive in their coverage of particular fields of law than legal encyclopedias. Treatises may be broadly classified into five types: (1) critical, (2) interpretative, (3) expository, (4) textual (for law students), and (5) educational (for practitioners keeping up in their fields). In most instances, however, treatises do not neatly fall into such a classification, and they frequently may include some features of all five types.

[1] G. PATON, A TEXTBOOK OF JURISPRUDENCE 231–232 (3d ed. 1964).

[2] For a discussion of the development and influence of treatises on American law, *see* L. FRIEDMAN, A HISTORY OF AMERICAN LAW 538–546 (1973).

a. *Critical Treatises*

These examine an area of law in depth and constructively criticize, when necessary, rules of law as presently interpreted by the courts. They often include historical analyses in order to show that current rules actually had different meanings or interpretations from those presently given by the courts. The author may include a thoughtful examination of the policy reasons for one or more such rules.[3] Critical treatises are not common, but their numbers are increasing.

b. *Interpretative Treatises*

These provide an analysis and interpretation of the law. Authors of such works do not attempt to evaluate rules in relation to underlying policy but rather to explain the terminology and meaning of the rules as they exist. Emphasis is placed upon understanding the law and not upon proposing what the law should be.

c. *Expository Treatises*

These exist primarily as substitutes for digests and are principally used as case finders. They consist primarily of essay paragraphs arranged under conventional subject headings with profuse footnote citations. Usually minimal analysis and synthesis of conflicting cases are the most a researcher can expect to find in them.

A real danger exists if one relies exclusively upon the expository treatise or encyclopedia article without verifying the writer's synopsis of the cases.

d. *Student Textbooks*

These may also be classified expository because they are usually elementary treatments and omit comprehensive and critical features of other works. In fact, the term "hornbook[4] law," frequently used by a judge to describe simple and well-settled points of law, comes from the "Hornbook" series of student treatises published by the West Publishing Company.

Student hornbooks, however, are useful as case finders as their references are usually selective and limited to landmark cases.

[3] For example, Professor Richard Powell in his treatise on real property in discussing the interests of a lessor and lessee in a condemnation proceeding criticizes the current rule as follows: "*This is the regrettable position taken by the majority of the jurisdictions* (emphasis ours). It is a regrettable position because it embodies a rigidly conceptualistic survival of the historical idea that the lessee 'owns the land for his term' * * *. It would be more businesslike and reasonable to hold * * *." R. POWELL, 2 POWELL ON REAL PROPERTY ¶ 247[2], at 372.144 (1977).

[4] For the derivation of the word "hornbook", *see* THE NEW ENCYCLOPAEDIA BRITANNICA: 5 MICROPAEDIA 135 (1975).

e. *Continuing Legal Education Handbooks*

In recent years, continuing education for lawyers has become increasingly important. The American Law Institute—American Bar Association Joint Committee on Continuing Legal Education and the Practising Law Institute hold seminars and symposiums on many current subjects and are all directed toward practicing lawyers to keep them up-to-date on new developments in the law. Many states have their own continuing legal education institutes.[5] It is quite common for such institutes to publish handbooks and texts in connection with their programs. These volumes usually furnish analyses of the law, practical guidance, forms, checklists, and other time-saving aids. Very frequently, these publications deal with such subjects as business transactions, personal injuries, commercial and corporate practice, trial practice, and other subjects of primary interest to practicing attorneys.

2. The Characteristics of Treatises

The fundamental characteristics of treatises are essentially the same. They contain the following elements:

a. *Table of Contents*

The table of contents shows the topical division of the treatise which is usually arranged by chapters and subdivisions thereof.

b. *Table of Cases*

The table of cases provides references as to where decisions discussed by the author are cited in the text.

c. *Subject Matter*

The subject matter of the text is contained in the main body of the publication.

d. *Supplementation*

The current trend is to provide pocket parts at the back of the volumes to supplement the text and indicate recent statutory and case developments.

Some current treatises are looseleaf in format, providing for the addition of current material, usually by interfiling.

e. *Index*

The index, embodying an alphabetical arrangement of the topics, sub-topics, fact and descriptive words, and cross references, is the last feature.

[5] For a listing of Continuing Legal Education courses, *see* the monthly issues of the CLE REGISTER, published by the ALI/ABA Committee on Professional Education.

SECTION B. ILLUSTRATIONS: TREATISES

Using Treatises to Find Cases

127. Page from Reuschlein and Gregory, Handbook on the Law of Agency and Partnership

128. Page from Dooley, Modern Tort Law

[Illustration 127]

PAGE FROM REUSCHLEIN AND GREGORY, HANDBOOK ON THE LAW OF AGENCY AND PARTNERSHIP

CHAPTER 10

DUTIES OF THIRD PERSON TO PRINCIPAL

TOPIC 1. LIABILITY IN CONTRACT

§ 102. Disclosed or Partially Disclosed Principal

A disclosed or partially disclosed principal is a party to simple contracts made on his behalf by his agent unless the specific terms of the contract or its form exclude him.[1] Of course, this rule presupposes that the agent has been authorized or acts under apparent authority or within his inherent powers as agent. In that situation, the principal is clearly a party to the contract and so the third party is liable to the principal just as fully as if he had contracted personally and directly with the principal.

A typical treatise written primarily for law students. Such textbooks usually do not have as many footnotes as other types. Law review articles are frequently cited in the footnotes.

party.[3] When a negotiable instrument is given by his agent, the principal may not maintain suit upon such instrument if he is not named therein as a party unless he later endorses it or becomes a holder in due course. If the agent is acting for a number of principals separately and joins their orders and enters upon a single transaction with a third party without authority, none of the principals become a party to the contract and consequently no one of them may enforce it separately.

§ 103. Defenses

The usual defenses arising out of the transaction are available to the third party in an action brought against him by the principal on a contract made by his agent and to which he is a party, such as

1. Lake Shore Management Co. v. Blum, 92 Ill.App.2d 47, 235 N.E.2d 366 (1968); Cavaness v. General Corp., 155 Tex. 69, 283 S.W.2d 33 (1955).

2. Barker v. Keown, 67 Ill.App. 433 (1896).

3. Standard Steel Car Co. v. Stamm, 207 Pa. 419, 56 A. 954 (1904).

[Illustration 128]

PAGE FROM DOOLEY, MODERN TORT LAW

§ 15.08. Emotional Injury from Apprehension of Harm to Another.

§ 15.09. — Traditional Rule Denying Recovery.

Many jurisdictions that allow recovery for fright caused by fear of negligently induced injury to the plaintiff himself deny it where the plaintiff's fear was of harm not to himself, but to another person.[1] The principle is applied even where the other person actually sustains physical injury witnessed by plaintiff.

In a recent New York case,[2] defendant negligently struck and injured a two-year-old child. Plaintiff, the child's mother, did not actually see the collision, but she heard the screech of brakes and immediately ran outside, where she found her injured child lying on the ground. The New York Court of Appeals discussed the prior cases in which it had allowed recovery for harm from negligently induced fear of injury to oneself,[3] and it took note of the celebrated case of Dillon v. Legg,[4] but then denied recovery on the ground of want of foreseeability:

> The risks of indirect harm from the loss or injury of loved ones is pervasive and inevitably realized at one time or another. Only a very small part of that risk is brought about by the culpable acts of others. This is the risk of living and bearing children. It is enough that the law establishes liability in favor of those directly or intentionally harmed.[5]

Another method of finding cases on the problem outlined in Chapter 6. It is frequently easier and quicker to start the research in a treatise. The cases noted in the footnotes must then be read and Shepardized. This set, as with many treatises, is kept current with pocket supplements.

Parents have similarly been denied recovery for their shock and anguish upon seeing a house burn with their children inside,[6] or

SECTION C. THE RESTATEMENTS OF THE LAW

In the 1920's concern was being shown by prominent American judges, lawyers, and law professors over two main defects in case law —its growing uncertainty and undue complexity. Finally, in 1923, the American Law Institute was founded by a group of these leaders to overcome such weaknesses.[6] The objectives of the Institute were focused on the reduction of the mass of legal publications which had to be consulted by the bench and bar, on the simplification of case law by a clear systematic restatement of it, and on diminishing the flow of judicial decisions. It was feared that the increasing mass of unorganized judicial opinions threatened to break down the system of articulating and developing case law.[7]

To remedy this, the American Law Institute undertook to produce a clear and precise restatement of the existing common law that would have "authority greater than that now accorded to any legal treatise, an authority more nearly on a par with that accorded the decisions of the courts." [8]

Procedurally, this was accomplished by the engagement of eminent legal scholars to be Reporters for the various subjects that were to be restated. Each Reporter prepared tentative drafts which were then submitted to and approved by the members of the Institute.

Between 1923 and 1944, Restatements were adopted for the law of agency, conflict of laws, contracts, judgments, property, restitution, security, torts, and trusts. Since 1952, Restatements, Second Series, have been adopted for agency, contracts, conflict of laws, foreign relations law, judgments, property, landlord and tenant, torts and trusts.

[6] This discussion on the Restatements is based on the following sources: Lewis, *History of the American Law Institute and the First Restatement of the Law* in AMERICAN LAW INSTITUTE, RESTATEMENT IN THE COURTS (Permanent ed. 1945); Goodrich, *The Story of the American Law Institute*, 1951 WASH.U.L.Q. 283; H. GOODRICH & P. WOLKIN, THE STORY OF THE AMERICAN LAW INSTITUTE, 1923–1961 (1961); THE AMERICAN LAW INSTITUTE 50TH ANNIVERSARY (1973); AMERICAN LAW INSTITUTE ANNUAL REPORTS. *See also* M. PIMSLEUR, CHECKLISTS OF BASIC AMERICAN LEGAL PUBLICATIONS, AALL PUBLICATIONS SERIES NO. 4, § 5: AMERICAN LAW INSTITUTE, RESTATEMENTS OF THE LAW (1976). This checklist updates all previous checklists and lists all Restatements, preliminary and tentative drafts published through 1975.

[7] Lewis, *supra* note 6, at 1.

[8] *Report of the Committee on the Establishment of a Permanent Organization for the Improvement of the Law Proposing the Establishment of an American Law Institute*, February 23, 1923, THE AMERICAN LAW INSTITUTE 50TH ANNIVERSARY 34 (1973).

The current status of the revision of specific Restatements and of proposed new Restatements may be ascertained from the latest *Annual Report* of the American Law Institute.

There are two aspects of the Restatements which limit their scope and function. First, they lack legislative sanction. It has been recommended that state legislatures be required to approve the Restatements, not as formal legislative enactments, but as aids and guides to the judiciary so that they would feel free to follow the "collective scholarship and knowledge of our profession." [9] But this proposal was not adopted by the Institute. Nevertheless, many courts began to give greater authority to the Restatements than that accorded to treatises and other secondary sources. In many instances, an authority is given to the Restatements nearly equal to that accorded to court decisions.[10]

The First Series of the Restatements reflected the desire of the American Law Institute founders that the Restatements would be admired and adopted by the courts. To this end they deliberately omitted the Reporters' citations and tentative drafts upon which the Restatement rules were based.

With publication of the Second Series of the Restatements, it was decided to abandon the idea of the Restatements serving as a substitute for the codification of the common law. The Second Series will also at times indicate a new trend in the common law and attempt to predict what a new rule will or should be.[11] This change in policy is also reflected in the appearance of citations to court decisions and to the Notes of the Reporters.

Further debate over the value of the Restatements may be left to others.[12] As a legal researcher, however, one must be familiar with the publications of the American Law Institute and their method of use.

1. The Features of the Restatements

The frequency with which the Restatements are cited by the courts merit their study in legal research. As of April 1, 1980, the

[9] Mason, *Harlan Fiske Stone Assays Social Justice*, 1912–1923, 99 U.PA.L.REV. 887, 915 (1951).

[10] For a discussion of the precedential authority of the Restatements, *see* Byrne, *Reevaluation of the Restatements as a Source of Law in Arizona*, 15 ARIZ. L.REV. 1021, 1023–1026 (1973).

[11] *Id.*

[12] An exhaustive list of articles on all aspects of the work of the American Law Institute may be found in each *Annual Report* in a section entitled "The Institute in Legal Literature, A Bibliography."

[Illustration 131]

PAGE FROM RESTATEMENT IN THE COURTS, POCKET SUPPLEMENT TO RESTATEMENT OF TORTS, 2d

§ 361 RESTATEMENT IN THE COURTS

cause they were composed of materials susceptible to destruction by fire. Magnotti v. Hughes, 57 Ill.App.3d 1000, 15 Ill.Dec. 455, 373 N.E.2d 801, 803.

Kan.App. 1977. Quot. in case cit. in disc. Plaintiff was social guest of defendant's tenants when he fell on the defective front porch steps of the premises. Plaintiff sued defendant landlord to recover for personal injuries sustained as a result. Judgment for the landlord was appealed, and the court affirmed, holding, inter alia, that the landlord's general obligation to make repairs, including repairs to steps, was not a contract

mary tenant terminated his lease with the city Redevelopment Authority brought a trespass action against the Redevelopment Authority for damages from a fire in a vacant store located on the floor below the apartment. Although the subtenants did not pay rent after the primary tenants terminated their lease, they remained in the apartment with the knowledge and consent of the Redevelopment Authority and continued to pay for heat, gas and electricity for the apartment. Prior to the fire, the subtenants notified the Authority of numerous acts of vandalism in the vacant store below, but the Au-

This set indicates each time a Restatement rule has been cited by a court, and further indicates whether the court supported, or did not support the rule.

The Restatement in the Courts was published in separate volumes until 1976. Since then, pocket supplements have been issued every two years and placed in the subject Restatement volumes.

was negligent conduct causing the plaintiff's injuries, and that the automobile driver could not be considered a superseding cause. The court also stated that the owner of the subsidiary had sufficient control over the restaurant to be held liable, and that the lessor, who had no control over the construction and design of the building, could not be held liable. Pushnik v. Winky's Drive-In Restaurants, 363 A.2d 1291, 1297.

Pa.Super. 1977. Cit. and quot. in part in disc. and quot. in ftn.; com. (a) cit. in disc. The subtenants of a second floor apartment who remained in possession after the pri-

and that any conflicting evidence must be resolved in the plaintiff's favor, and further that the plaintiff must be given the benefit, first, of all evidence favorable to him and, second, of every reasonable inference of fact arising from the evidence. The court held that, in viewing the evidence in a light most favorable to the plaintiffs, a jury might reasonably have found that after the primary tenant moved out of the store, the relationship between the Redevelopment Authority and the plaintiffs was that of landlord and tenant, and that, as landlord, the Authority violated its duty

See also cases under division, chapter, topic, title and subtitle that includes section under examination. For earlier citations see Restatement in the Courts, Perm Ed. and the 1948, 1954, 1965, 1967, 1968–1969, 1970–1971, 1972–1973, 1974–1975 and 1976 Supplements.

208

[Illustration 132]

PAGE FROM SHEPARD'S RESTATEMENT OF THE LAW CITATIONS

Alk
555P2d40
Ariz
601P2d285
611P2d550
Calif
134CaR33
148CaR809
151CaR732
159CaR847
602P2d767
Mass
362NE935
Md
407A2d345
Mich
287NW181
NJ
369A2d42
NY
429S2d613
Okla
593P2d1105
Ore
550P2d1231
580P2d1018
605P2d299
Pa
367A2d1109
393A2d772
So C
238SE168
Tex
546SW118
553SW649
558SW61
580SW625
Utah
565P2d78
72A31274n
75A3446n
75A3469n
93A3168n

Ore
550P2d1232
580P2d1018
605P2d299
So C
238SE169
Tex
553SW650
Utah
565P2d78
Wis
279NW211
93A31000n
§ 345
54IlA984
66IlA817
363Mas701
282Md246
24OrA401
146Su360
Ill
370NE127
384NE458
Md
384A2d81
NJ
369A2d986
Ore
545P2d1389
Pa
409A2d39
Comment d
Pa
409A2d40
Illustration 3
571F2d781
Comment e
146Su360
NJ
369A2d987

§ 352
586F2d720
441FS743
46IlA649
48IlA921
71Il2d428
44NCA140
Ill
360NE1351
362NE812
376NE995
Ind
408NE148
NC
260SE670
Tex
532SW365
Comment a
441FS744
§ 353
586F2d720
441FS743
46IlA649
48IlA921
50IlA385
74IlA938
71Il2d428
21WAp155
Ill
360NE1351
362NE812
365NE929
376NE995
393NE592
Ind
408NE148
Mass
385NE531
Pa
409A2d430
Tex

Wis
284NW59
Wyo
611P2d847
64A3344n
§ 356
543F2d275
55CA3d955
83IlA726
43MdA681
38NY617
271Or128
483Pa89
91W2d741
Calif
128CaR73
Ill
404NE843
Ind
408NE148
Md
407A2d351
NY
345NE325
381S2d854
Ore
530P2d1242
Pa
394A2d553
Wis
284NW59
64A3344n
Comment a
55CA3d961
91W2d740
Calif
128CaR78
Idaho
595P2d1092
Wis
284NW59

Mass
403NE374
Mich
242NW489
258NW33
NJ
397A2d360
NY
345NE325
381S2d854
Ore
530P2d1242
Pa
384A2d1239
405A2d902
Comment b
83IlA726
38NY618
Ill
404NE843
NY
345NE326
381S2d854
Illustration 1
1KA2d25
Kan
561P2d883
Comment d
309Min121
Minn
243NW729
§§ 358 to 362
64A3342n
§ 358
80McA251
271Or129
43OrA507

429S2d613
Pa
394A2d553
Comment a
543F2d493
43MdA682
Md
407A2d352
Comment e
43MdA683
Md
407A2d352
Comment i
43MdA683
Md
407A2d352
§§ 360 to 362
242PaS334
Pa
363A2d1297
§ 360
543F2d275
123Az550
55CA3d958
74IlA925
29U2d431
16WAp451
Ala
361So2d88
372So2d858
Ariz
601P2d313
Calif
128CaR75
Idaho
595P2d1091
Ill
393NE584

§ 361
295Ala12
55CA3d958
57IlA1003
249PaS311
Ala
321So2d653
342So2d353
361So2d88
Calif
128CaR76
Ill
373NE803
Pa
376A2d1003
Tex
572SW3
Comment a
249PaS317
Pa
376A2d1006
§ 362
478FS827
58H508
171Mt104
Haw
573P2d111
Idaho
595P2d1090
Mont
555P2d743
Comment d
Idaho
595P2d1090
§ 363 et seq.
Scope Note
195Col94

§§ 364 to 386
195Col94
Colo
575P2d422
§§ 364 to 371
623F2d1015
§ 364
549F2d990
146Su174
Idaho
595P2d1086
NJ
369A2d52
Wash
578P2d21
94A31166n
94A31170n
95A3787n
95A3797n
Comment j
273Or152
§ 365
474Pa593
Mass
402NE1049
Pa
379A2d113
§ 366
262Ark125
195Col89
46IlA178
146Su175
Ark

"Shepardizing" § 362 of the Restatement of Torts, 2d, in Shepard's Restatement of the Law Citations.

d

87CA3d52
75McA342
275Or304
282Or639
44OrA63
269SoC485
89Wis2d551
Alk
555P2d40
Calif
150CaR725
Mich
254NW670
NY
429S2d613
Okla
593P2d1105

§ 350
304Min566
§§ 351 to 353
441FS744
§ 351
441FS744

483Pa89
242PaS334
91W2d741
Idaho
595P2d1090
Mass
402NE1049
Md
407A2d351
NY
345NE325
381S2d854
Ohio
402NE1206
Pa
363A2d1297
394A2d553

571F2d1390
588F2d358
478FS827
71DC2d160
13DC3d431
42IlA647
83IlA726
67McA687
401Mch311
38NY617
271Or128
486Pa283
253PaS85
164Su514
Ill
356NE577
404NE843

§§ 359 to 362
91W2d741
Wis
284NW59
§ 359
543F2d493
588F2d358
43MdA681
483Pa89
Ind
408NE149
Md
407A2d351
NY

123Az550
249PaS317
Ariz
601P2d313
Pa
376A2d1006
Comment e
Ala
372So2d859
Comment f
Ala
372So2d859

Comment a
71IlA692
Ill
390NE524
Comment e
71IlA692
282Or347
Ill
390NE524
Ore
578P2d781

553SW837
Comment e
262Ark134
Ark
553SW837
Comment f
262Ark134
Ark
553SW837
Comment g
273Or152

See 1976 Bound Volume for earlier citations

SECTION E. UNIFORM LAWS AND MODEL CODES

1. Uniform Laws

The Restatements, as mentioned, have as their aim the restating of the common law as developed by the courts. The movement for law reform has also focused on statutory law and the need, in many instances, for similar statutes among the states. Toward this aim, the American Bar Association passed a resolution recommending that each state and the District of Columbia adopt a law providing for the appointment of Commissioners to confer with Commissioners of other states on the subject of uniformity in legislation on certain subjects. By 1912, all of the states, the District of Columbia, and Puerto Rico had passed such a law, and the National Conference of Commissioners on Uniform State Laws was formed. Its object is to "promote uniformity in state laws where uniformity is deemed desirable and practicable." [15]

The National Conference meets once a year and considers drafts of proposed uniform laws. When such a law is approved, it is the duty of the Commissioners to try to convince their state legislatures to adopt it. The National Conference has approved over two hundred acts.

A complete list of acts approved by the National Conference of Commissioners on Uniform State Laws appears each year in the Appendices in its annual *Handbook*. These tables also list which states have adopted each uniform law.

a. Laws approved by the National Conference of Commissioners on Uniform State Laws are published in the following forms.

(1) Separate pamphlet form.

(2) In the annual *Handbook of the National Conference.*

(3) *Uniform Laws Annotated. Master Edition,* 1969–

This edition, published by the West Publishing Co., replaces all former editions. After each section of a uniform law, pertinent official comment of the Commissioners is given. This is followed by a list of law review commentaries and then by digests of federal and state court decisions citing the particular section of the uniform law. It is kept up-to-date by annual pocket supplements.

2. Model Codes

The National Conference of Commissioners on Uniform State Laws has determined that it will designate an act as a "Uniform

[15] NATIONAL CONFERENCE OF COMMISSIONERS ON UNIFORM STATE LAWS, Handbook, 269 (1978).

Act" when it has "a reasonable possibility of ultimate enactment in a substantial number of jurisdictions." [16] Acts which do not have such possibility are designated as "Model Acts." As a general rule, "Model Acts" embrace subject areas which do not have substantial interstate implications.

The American Law Institute also occasionally will draft and approve a Model Act,[17] and will participate jointly with the National Conference of Commissioners on Uniform State Laws as it did in the compilation of the *Uniform Commercial Code.*

3. Indexes to Uniform Laws and Model Codes

a. *Handbook of the National Conference of Commissioners on Uniform State Laws*

A complete list of acts appears in the annual *Handbook.* Information is given for all of the Acts and Model Codes promulgated by the National Conference. There are also charts showing which states have adopted specific Acts or Codes, and the date of adoption.

b. *Directory of Acts and Tables of Adopting Jurisdictions*

This is a pamphlet, frequently reissued, which is published as part of the *Uniform Laws Annotated.* It lists all Acts in alphabetical order and indicates where they are printed in *Uniform Laws Annotated.* There is also a table for each state listing all of the Acts adopted.

SECTION F. ILLUSTRATIONS: UNIFORM LAWS

133–135. Pages from Uniform Laws Annotated, Master Edition

136. Page from Uniform Laws Annotated—Directory of Uniform Acts

137. Page from Uniform Laws Annotated—Tables of Adopting Jurisdictions

[16] Id. at 302–304.

[17] *See* AMERICAN LAW INSTITUTE, ANNUAL REPORTS.

[Illustration 133]

PAGE FROM VOLUME 1, UNIFORM LAWS ANNOTATED MASTER EDITION

§ 2—609 UNIFORM COMMERCIAL CODE

Typical Uniform Law adopted by the National Conference of Commissioners on Uniform State Laws.

buyer to provide cash or satisfactory security; however seller's dissatisfaction with defendant's financial standing must not be false or arbitrary. James B. Berry's Sons Co. v. Monark Gasoline & Oil Co., C.C.A.8, 1929, 32 F.2d 74 (cited in Official Comment, supra).

Where a vendor contracts to deliver goods, and allows a buyer credit for with the buyer's financial responsibility is to be settled by the seller before he parts with the goods; but there must be a real want of satisfaction with the buyer's financial responsibility, and the refusal to ship without payment or security must be based on that reason alone. Corn Products Refining Co. v. Fasola, 1920, 109 A. 505, 94 N.J.Law 181 (cited in Official Comment, supra).

§ 2—610. Anticipatory Repudiation

When either party repudiates the contract with respect to a performance not yet due the loss of which will substantially impair the value of the contract to the other, the aggrieved party may

(a) for a commercially reasonable time await performance by the repudiating party; or

(b) resort to any remedy for breach (Section 2—703 or Section 2—711), even though he has notified the repudiating party that he would await the latter's performance and has urged retraction; and

(c) in either case suspend his own performance or proceed in accordance with the provisions of this Article on the seller's right to identify goods to the contract notwithstanding breach or to salvage unfinished goods (Section 2—704).

→ **Action in Adopting Jurisdictions**

Variations from Official Text:

Kentucky. In paragraph (b), should refer to 2—703, not to 7—703.

Official Comment

Prior Uniform Statutory Provision: See Sections 63(2) and 65, Uniform Sales Act.

For text of prior provision, see Appendix in end volume.

400

[Illustration 134]

PAGE FROM VOLUME I, UNIFORM LAWS ANNOTATED, MASTER EDITION

SALES **§ 2—610**

Purposes: To make it clear that:

1. With the problem of insecurity taken care of by the preceding section and with provision being made in this Article as to the effect of a defective delivery under an installment contract, anticipatory repudiation centers upon an overt communication of intention or an action which renders performance impossible or demonstrates a clear determination not to continue with performance.

After each Section the official comment of the Commissioners explaining the Section is given.

he cannot recover resulting damages which he should have avoided.

2. It is not necessary for repudiation that performance be made literally and utterly impossible. Repudiation can result from action which reasonably indicates a rejection of the continuing obligation. And, a repudiation automatically results under the preceding section on insecurity when a party fails to provide adequate assurance of due future performance within thirty days after a justifiable demand therefor has been made. Under the language of this section, a demand by one or both parties for more than the contract calls for in the way of counter-performance is not in itself a repudiation nor does it invalidate a plain expression of desire for future performance. However, when under a fair reading it amounts to a statement of intention not to perform except on conditions which go beyond the contract, it becomes a repudiation.

3. The test chosen to justify an aggrieved party's action under this section is the same as that in the section on breach in installment contracts—namely the substantial value of the contract. The most useful test of substantial value is to determine whether material inconvenience or injustice will result if the aggrieved party is forced to wait and receive an ultimate tender minus the part or aspect repudiated.

4. After repudiation, the aggrieved party may immediately resort to any remedy he chooses provided he moves in good faith (see Section 1—203). Inaction and silence by the aggrieved party may leave the matter open but it cannot be regarded as misleading the repudiating party. Therefore the aggrieved party is left free to proceed at any time with his options under this section, unless he has taken some positive action which in good faith requires notification to the other party before the remedy is pursued.

Cross References:

Point 1: Sections 2—609 and 2—612.
Point 2: Section 2—609.
Point 3: Section 2—612.
Point 4: Section 1—203.

1 U.L.A.-U.C.C.—26 401

[Illustration 135]

PAGE FROM VOLUME I, UNIFORM LAWS ANNOTATED, MASTER EDITION

§ 2—610 UNIFORM COMMERCIAL CODE

Definitional Cross References:

"Aggrieved party". Section 1—201.
"Contract". Section 1—201.
"Party". Section 1—201.
"Remedy". Section 1—201

Cross References

Assurance of performance, see section 2—609.
Good faith, enforcement of contracts, see section 1—203.
Installment contracts, defective delivery, see section 2—612.
Letters of credit
  Anticipatory repudiation for wrongful disposition of, see section 5—115.
  Application of remedies under this section for wrongful repudiation, see section 5—115.
Recovery of damages by seller for wrongful repudiation, see section 2—708.

Law Review Commentaries

Anticipatory breach of contract: a comparison of the Texas law and the Uniform Commercial Code. 30 Tex. L.Rev. 744 (1952).

Remedies under law of sales in the proposed Commercial Code. Samuel Williston. 63 Harvard L.Rev. 584 (Feb. 1950).

Remedies under this title. William C. Jones. 30 Mo.L.Rev. 212 (Spring 1965).

Repudiation of a contract under the Code. Arthur Anderson. 14 DePaul L.Rev. 1 (Autumn-Winter 1964).

Sales: "from status to contract". Howard L. Hall. 1952 Wis.L.Rev. 209.

Library References

Sales ⇨84, 98, 116, 370, 405.

C.J.S. Sales §§ 79, 98-100, 464, 520.

Notes of Decisions

Construction with other laws 1
Executory contracts, limitation to 2
Insolvency of parties 4
Remedies available on breach 5
Suspension of performance 3
Tender of delivery 6

---

1. Construction with other laws

This section and sections 2—709, 2—718 and 2—719 relating to anticipatory repudiation of a sales contract, and action for price, liquidation or limitation of damages, and modification or limitation of remedy, must be read and interpreted together, and unconscionable modification or limitation of remedial provisions must be deleted. Denkin v. Sterner, 1956, 10 Pa.D. & C.2d 203, 70 York Leg.Rec. 105.

2. Executory contracts, limitation to

Theory of an anticipatory breach cannot be invoked where contract, at time of fraud claimed as basis for re-

At the end of each Section, references to additional research aids are given.

Also, annotations to all court decisions citing the Section are indicated.

Pocket supplement should also be checked.

402

[Illustration 136]

PAGE FROM UNIFORM LAWS ANNOTATED—DIRECTORY OF UNIFORM ACTS

DIRECTORY OF UNIFORM ACTS

List of Uniform Acts or Codes, in alphabetical order, showing where each may be found in Uniform Laws Annotated, Master Edition.

The designation "Pocket Part" under the page column indicates that the particular Act or Code is complete in the Pocket Part. The user should always, of course, consult the Pocket Part for changes and subsequent material when an Act or Code appears in the main volume.

This Table lists all Uniform Acts and shows where the text may be found in the Uniform Laws Annotated. Similar information may also be found in the annual Handbook of the National Conference of Commissioners on Uniform State Laws.

t
t

[Illustration 137]

PAGE FROM UNIFORM LAWS ANNOTATED—TABLES OF ADOPTING JURISDICTIONS

TABLE OF JURISDICTIONS LISTING UNIFORM ACTS ADOPTED

List of jurisdictions, in alphabetical order, listing the Uniform Acts or Codes adopted by that particular jurisdiction, and where each may be found in Uniform Laws Annotated, Master Edition.

Each Uniform Act or Code in the Master Edition contains a Table showing the statutory citations of each of the adopting jurisdictions.

ALABAMA

Title of Act	Uniform Laws Annotated Volume	Page
Anatomical Gift Act	8	15
Brain Death Act	12	Pocket Part
Certification of Questions of Law Act	12	49
Commercial Code	1 to 3	
Common Trust Fund Act	7	83
Controlled Substances Act	9	187
Criminal Extradition Act	11	51
Declaratory Judgments Act	12	109

This Table lists all of the states alphabetically and then indicates whether uniform acts or codes have been adopted by the individual states.

Title of Act	Volume	Page
Motor Vehicle Certificate of Title and Anti-Theft Act	11	421
Partnership Act	6	1
Photographic Copies of Business and Public Records as Evidence Act	14	145
Principal and Income Act (1931 Act)	7A	461
Reciprocal Enforcement of Support Act (1950 Act)	9A	747
Securities Act	7A	561
Simplification of Fiduciary Security Transfers Act	7A	709
Simultaneous Death Act	8	605
Testamentary Additions to Trusts Act	8	629

9

SECTION G. INTERSTATE COMPACTS

The United States Constitution provides that "No state shall, without the consent of Congress * * * enter into any Agreement or Compact with another state * * *." [18]

In an early interpretation of this clause, the Supreme Court of the United States held that it prohibited all agreements between states unless consented to by Congress.[19] But in a subsequent decision,[20] the Court changed its position and held that Congressional consent was not necessary for agreements or compacts which did not increase the political powers of the states or interfere with the supremacy of the United States. Normally, interstate agreements or compacts are formally enacted by the legislatures of the states involved, and are then submitted to Congress for its consent.[21]

Until about 1900, most interstate compacts dealt with boundary disputes between states. Since then, the compacts have more commonly been used as a means of cooperation for solving problems common to two or more states, such as flood control, control of pollution, or the establishment of a port authority.

1. Publication of Interstate Compacts

As interstate compacts ordinarily do not come into effect until agreed to by the states involved, and with the consent of Congress, the text of agreements or compacts will be found in the session laws of the respective states and in the U. S. Statutes at Large.[22]

A complete listing of compacts may be found in *Interstate Compacts and Agencies*, published periodically by the Council of State Governments. It contains the following information:

List of compacts involving boundaries;

Subject arrangement of all other compacts, with short annotations;

[18] U. S. CONST. art. I, § 10, cl. 3.

[19] Holmes v. Jennison, 14 Pet. (39 U.S.) 540 (1840).

[20] Virginia v. Tennessee, 148 U.S. 503, 518 (1893). *See also* U. S. Steel v. Multistate Tax Commission, 434 U.S. 794 (1978).

[21] Interstate agreements do not have to be formally enacted. *See* the annotation to art. I, § 10, cl. 3, in THE CONSTITUTION OF THE UNITED STATES OF AMERICA, ANALYSIS AND INTERPRETATION 419–423 (Lib. of Cong. ed. 1973). *See also:* F. ZIMMERMAN and M. WENDELL, THE LAW AND USE OF INTERSTATE COMPACTS (2d ed. 1976); Comment, Federal Question Jurisdiction to Interpret Interstate Compacts, 64 GEO.L.J. 87 (1975).

[22] E. g., The North Dakota-Minnesota Boundary Agreement is published in 1961 Minn.Sess.Laws, ch. 236; 1961 North Dakota Sess.Law, ch. 319 and Congressional consent is given in Pub.Law No. 87–162, 75 Stat. 399.

Index of defunct or dormant compacts;

Index to compacts.

Each biennial edition of the *Book of States* has a chapter on current developments in interstate compacts, and a selective listing of the more significant ones.

2. Locating Court Decisions on Interstate Compacts

a. *Digests*

Cases involving interstate compacts are digested under *States* ⚷6 in the Key Number digests and under *States* § 52 in the *Digest of the U. S. Supreme Court.* (Lawyers Co-operative ed.)

b. *Annotated Statutes*

The practice of including the text of compacts in state codes varies. The indexes to the codes of the states concerned should be checked.

c. *Citators*

The Statutes section of the appropriate Shepard's Citations may be used to "Shepardize" the state code or session law citation, or the U. S. Statutes at Large citation.

SECTION H. TREATISES: RESEARCH PROCEDURE

1. Methods of Research

a. *Case Method*

If the name of a leading decision in point is known, consult the *table of cases* of the treatise to ascertain whether it is discussed in the book. If so, an examination of the cited pages in the text will reveal a discussion of the subject matter with additional cases in point.

b. *Index Method*

Consult the *index* in the back of the book if a case in point is not known. Select an appropriate fact or descriptive word or legal topic to use the index. References will be to the text of the publication.

c. *Topic Method*

The Topic Method can be used through the *table of contents*; however, its effectiveness in locating the pertinent text depends on the researcher's understanding of the structural subdivisions of the subject matter in that table.

d. *Definition Method*

The *index* to the treatise may list words or phrases which are defined and explained in the text.

2. Location of Treatises

a. *Library Catalog*

To locate treatises on a subject, consult the *catalog* in the law library.

b. For a comprehensive list of legal treatises, with book review annotations, see:

(1) New York University, School of Law Library, *A Catalogue of the Law Collection at New York University* (Julius J. Marke, ed. 1 vol. 1953). This is an excellent source for older treatises.

(2) *Law Books in Print* (4 vols. 1976). Supplemented by *Law Books Published,* a quarterly publication with an annual cumulation.

(3) Association of American Law Schools, *Law Books Recommended for Libraries.*

This set is a compilation of lists intended to provide carefully selected lists of books for law libraries. It is in six looseleaf volumes with each of the 46 topics in separate pamphlets. No. 47 is an author and subject index to the entire set. It is not being kept current.

(4) Harvard Law School Library, *Annual Legal Bibliography* (vol. 1—July 1, 1960 to date).

This is a subject classified list of selected United States and foreign books and periodical articles that are currently acquired by the Harvard Law Library. It covers all fields of law and is subdivided under some 40 jurisdictions. The *Annual* includes (1) an Analytical Table of Contents, subdivided into common law and civil law jurisdictions and private international and public international law, (2) subject indexes in Spanish, German and French, and (3) an Alphabetical Subject Index, covering the topics appearing in the *Annual.*

It is kept up-to-date by a *Current Legal Bibliography* which is published nine times a year, October to June. The material in the *Current* numbers of a year is cumulated into the bound *Annual* volume.

SECTION I. THE RESTATEMENTS: RESEARCH PROCEDURE

1. Index Method

Consult the index to the appropriate Restatement, *e.g., Contracts.* If the precise Restatement covering the problem is not known, refer to the *General Index to the Restatement of the Law.*

For cases which have cited the applicable rules of the Restatement, examine both (1) the *Restatement in the Courts* and its *Sup-*

plements and (2) if the Restatement has been revised, the *Appendix* to the Restatement, Second.

The tentative drafts and the *Restatements Second's* Appendix provide annotated Reporter's notes, with interpretations and citations to leading cases.

To compare the rule in a *Restatement* with the law of a specific state, consult the annotations to it for that state, if one was published, or consult the *Restatements in the Courts.* A specific section of a *Restatement* may also be *Shepardized* in *Shepard's Restatement of the Law Citations.*

2. Topic Method

The table of contents, rather than the index, to a specific Restatement can be examined to locate the appropriate rule.

3. Definition Method

To determine the meaning of words and phrases used in the Restatements, examine the Glossary of Terms Defined in the *Restatement,* which is included in the *Restatement in the Courts.*

SECTION J. SUMMARY

1. Treatises

a. *Scope*

(1) Expositions, some of which are critical, by legal writers on case law and legislation.

(2) More exhaustive in scope than encyclopedias, but periodical articles are usually more detailed and critical.

(3) Functions:

(a) Views of the writer as to what the law ought to be —critically evaluative.

(b) Interpretation of statutory and case law.

(c) Case finder.

(d) Presents a general view of the principles on a topic.

b. *Arrangement*

Treatises usually include these features:

(1) Table of contents.

(2) Table of cases.

(3) Subject matter—text.

(4) Index.

c. *Supplementation*

The current practice of publishers is to keep treatises current by cumulative pocket supplements. Some publications are furnished with replacement (revision) volumes.

2. Restatements

a. *Scope*

(1) Simplifies and restates case law on selected subjects.

(2) Weaknesses:

(a) Absence of legislative endorsement and sanction.

(b) Statements treat the subject matter antecedently and not prospectively.

(c) Inconsistency of terminology among Restatements.

b. *Arrangement and Supplementation*

(1) Tentative drafts—includes Reporter's notes and case discussion.

(2) Restatements—text.

(3) Revisions—Restatements, Second.

(4) *Annotations*—comparison of state case law with Restatement.

(5) *Restatement in the Courts*—digest-reference to cases citing the Restatements.

(6) *Glossary of Terms Defined in the Restatement*—included in the *Restatement in the Courts.*

(7) *Supplements*—amendments and additions to text and supplements to the *Restatement in the Courts.*

c. *Indexes, First Series*

(1) *General Index*—covers the several Restatements.

(2) Each Restatement also has an individual index.

d. *Indexes, Second Series*

Each Restatement has its own index.

3. Uniform Laws

a. *National Conference of Commissioners on Uniform State Laws*

(1) Uniform laws adopted by the Conference are published in its annual *Handbook* and in *Uniform Laws Annotated.*

(2) The annual *Handbook* lists all uniform laws and those states which have adopted them.

b. *Model Codes*

Drafted by National Conference of Commissioners on Uniform State Laws, or the American Law Institute. Some Model Codes and Uniform Acts are drafted jointly by both associations.

Chapter 19

OTHER RESEARCH AIDS

Attorney General Reports, Dictionaries, Directories, Form Books, Briefs and Records on Appeal, and Ethics Opinions

This chapter covers sets of law books that are useful in legal research but which fit into none of the categories previously discussed. They are: (1) attorneys general opinions, (2) law dictionaries, (3) directories, (4) form books, (5) briefs and records, and (6) opinions on legal ethics.

SECTION A. OPINIONS OF THE ATTORNEYS GENERAL

The opinions of the attorneys general have the characteristics of both primary and secondary authority.[1] As the legal advisor to the executive officials of the government, the attorney general renders requested legal advice to them, generally in the form of written opinions. Although these opinions are the official statements of an executive officer, issued in accordance with his authority, they are merely advisory statements and are not mandatory orders. Therefore, the inquirers and other officials are not bound to follow such recommendations and conclusions. However, the opinions are strongly persuasive and are generally followed by executive officers. Also, they have significant influence on the courts in their deliberations.

The opinions, as a general rule, relate to: (1) the interpretations of statutes or (2) general legal problems. Some attorneys general limit their advice and will not render opinions as to the constitutionality of proposed legislation.

1. Attorney General of the United States

a. *Opinions of the Attorney General*

These have been published in forty-two volumes covering the years 1789–1974.[2] Each volume contains the opinions covering sever-

[1] For more detailed information on the role of Attorneys General, *see* Thompson, *Transmission or Resistance: Opinions of State Attorneys General and the Impact of the Supreme Court,* 9 VAL.U.L.REV. 55 (1974). *See also* NATIONAL ASSOCIATION OF ATTORNEYS GENERAL, THE OFFICE OF ATTORNEY GENERAL (1974), and POWERS, DUTIES, AND OPERATIONS OF STATE ATTORNEYS GENERAL (1977).

[2] For a history of the publications of U. S. Attorney General opinions, *see* Rhodes, *"Opinions of the Attorney General" Revived,* 64 ABA J. 1374 (1978).

al years. In between the publication of the bound volumes, opinions are made available in slip opinion format. There are also digest volumes to the bound volumes of the U. S. Attorney General's opinions.

b. *Opinions of the Office of Legal Counsel*

Volume one contains selected opinions of the Office of Legal Counsel for the year 1977. The opinions selected are those useful to all branches of the government and the private bar.

The *United States Code Annotated* and *United States Code Service* include digests of U. S. Attorney General opinions in their annotations. They are also included in the United States and federal *Shepard's Citations* when cited in a court decision.

2. State Attorneys General Opinions

Nearly every state publishes the opinions of its Attorney General.[3] They are included in the annotations of many state annotated codes, and *Shepard's Citations* (state units) indicate when an attorney general's opinion has been cited by a court. Selected opinions appear in the *A–G Report*, a newsletter published by the National Association of Attorneys General.[4]

SECTION B. LAW DICTIONARIES

Law dictionaries are useful for locating the definition of words in their legal sense or use. For each word or phrase a short definition is given. Most legal dictionaries also provide a citation to a court decision or other reference tracing the source of the word or phrase. In Chapter 6, Section G, the set entitled *Words and Phrases* was discussed. This set includes digests from all court decisions in which a word or phrase has been interpreted. *Words and Phrases* may also be used as a dictionary, but as it is limited to those words which were involved in litigation, it is not a true dictionary. Moreover, most dictionaries are much more compact and are published in one or two volumes. Listed below are some of the more commonly used American and English law dictionaries.

[3] A checklist of all published opinions of state Attorneys General may be found in M. PIMSLEUR, CHECKLISTS OF BASIC AMERICAN LEGAL PUBLICATIONS sec. III (1962). For the availability of individual states' attorney general opinions *see* M. FISHER, GUIDE TO STATE LEGISLATIVE MATERIALS (AALL Pub. Ser. No. 15, 1979).

[4] From 1937–1969, the Council of State Governments published an annual digest of state Attorneys General opinions. From 1970–1979 a *Newsletter and Digest of State Attorneys General Opinions* was also published.

1. American Law Dictionaries

a. *Ballentine's Law Dictionary,* with Pronunciations, 3d ed., Lawyers Cooperative Publishing Co. 1969. 1429 p.

b. *Black's Law Dictionary,* 5th ed., West Publishing Co. 1979. 1511 p. Includes: Guide to Pronunciation of Latin Phrases and a Table of Abbreviations.

c. Bouvier, *Law Dictionary* (3rd revision), 8th ed., West Publishing Co. 1914. 3 vols.

This edition is now out of date in some respects. It is a particularly scholarly work, however, and many of its definitions are encyclopedic in nature. It still is very useful for many historical terms.

d. *Cochran's Law Lexicon:* Pronouncing Edition, 4th ed. (rev. by Gilmore), W. H. Anderson. 1973. 428 p.

e. Redden and Veron, *Modern Legal Glossary,* Michie Company. 1980. 576 p.

2. English Law Dictionaries

a. Jowitt, *Dictionary of English Law,* Sweet & Maxwell, 2d ed. 1977. 2 vols.

b. Mozley and Whitley, *Law Dictionary,* 8th ed., Butterworths. 1970. 389 p.

c. *Stroud's Judicial Dictionary,* 4th ed. (J. S. James), Sweet & Maxwell. 1971. 5 vols.

d. Walker, *The Oxford Companion to Law,* Clarendon Press. 1980. 1366 p.

3. Special Law Dictionaries

There are also dictionaries devoted to specific subjects, such as labor law or taxation. These may be located by checking the catalog of a library under the subject and then subdivision—*e. g.,* Taxation —U.S.—Dictionaries.

4. Legal Abbreviations

The Dictionary of Legal Abbreviations Used in American Law Books (1979) by Doris Bieber contains a comprehensive listing of abbreviations used in legal publications. While there have been several shorter lists, such as in the appendices to law dictionaries, this book is a compilation of abbreviations, acronyms, and symbols, both foreign and domestic, appearing in legal literature published in the United States, including government publications. Among the 16,000 entries are listed foreign and domestic government agencies, organizations, legislation, judicial reports—both early and contemporary, official and unofficial—and legal periodicals.

SECTION C. LAW DIRECTORIES

Law directories vary in the scope of their coverage. Some attempt to list all lawyers; others are limited to a region, state, municipality, or to a specialty. Law directories are useful in locating information about a particular lawyer and are used by many lawyers when they have to refer a case to a lawyer in another city.

In 1935 the American Bar Association appointed a Special Committee on Law Lists to investigate the law list business. This Committee developed "Rules and Standards as to Law Lists" [5] which were adopted by the American Bar Association in 1937. The American Bar Association has taken the position that "* * * A law list is conclusively established to be reputable if it is certified by the American Bar Association as being in compliance with its rules and standards." [6] As a result, nearly all lists and directories now seek to receive the certification of the American Bar Association.

1. General Directories

a. *Martindale-Hubbell Law Directory*

This multi-volume annual publication is the most comprehensive directory of lawyers. All lawyers admitted to the bar of any jurisdiction are eligible for listing without cost. The volumes are arranged alphabetically by state. Each of these volumes is in two parts. The first part consists of two alphabetical lists, one of the cities within each state, and a second of the lawyers within each city. For each listed attorney, information is given for date of birth, date of admission to the bar, college and law school attended, American Bar Association membership, and specialty. Confidential ratings [7] are also given which estimate legal ability, recommendations and promptness in paying bills. The second part is another double alphabetic arrangement, this time done by cities within the state and law firms within each city. This entry may include the address and telephone number of the firm, names and short biographies of its members, representative clients and areas of practice. Since this form of advertising carries a charge, the list is selective.

[5] The text may be found in the Martindale-Hubbell Law Directory.

[6] AMERICAN BAR ASSOCIATION, CODE OF PROFESSIONAL RESPONSIBILITY DR 2–102–A–6.

[7] A "Confidential Key" to their ratings is included in the inside covers of the volumes.

The following items are also included. As their location may change from year to year, the Table of Contents pages should be consulted for their location.

List of Canadian Lawyers

Government Lawyers Roster

Patent Lawyers Roster

Foreign Lawyers Section

Law digests of the statutory law for the fifty states, Canada, and over 50 of the more important foreign countries

American Bar Association Information

b. *The Lawyers Directory*

The Lawyers Directory is an annual publication which lists the following:

Part I, Leading lawyers and law firms in the United States and Canada and a list of foreign lawyers; Part II, Corporate law department counsel roster; Part III, Complete list of foreign embassies and legations in Washington D.C., and U.S. embassies, legations and consular offices throughout the world.

c. *Who's Who in American Law*

This semi-annual compilation contains biographical information on approximately 34,000 attorneys selected for their prominence as judges, educators, or practitioners. Despite the large number of entries there is no claim to comprehensiveness in any of the above areas of the profession. The format is similar to that used in other Marquis *Who's Who* publications.

d. *The American Bar, The Canadian Bar, The International Bar*

This is an annual biographical directory of ranking United States and foreign lawyers. It provides sketches of the North American law offices listed and individual biographical data. The third unit is a professional international directory of "the finest lawyers in the world."

e. *Other International Directories*

Many other companies publish directories which are to be used to locate a "recommended" attorney in a particular country and city to deal with any general legal questions. Included in this group are *The International List, The International Lawyers, and Kime's International Law Directory.*

2. State and Regional Directories

The Legal Directories Publishing Co., Inc.[8], produces 25 directories which are approved by the American Bar Association and list attorneys in specific states or regions. Examples of the state directories are the *Florida Legal Directory*, the *Illinois Legal Directory* and the *Texas Legal Directory*. The regional directories include the *Mountain States Legal Directory*, the *New England Legal Directory*, and the *Virginias, Maryland, Delaware and District of Columbia Legal Directory*. Each of these directories contains sections on:

a. Federal and state officials (including members of the state legislatures);

b. Federal, state and local courts; and

c. Attorneys practicing in the state (arranged by county and city). This section also contains some biographical data on law firms and their members.

3. Specialty Directories

Some directories have been published which contain only the attorneys who practice law in a particular specialty. These are useful for one who wishes reference to a lawyer in a specific city on a legal problem common to the specialty. Examples of such directories include *The Probate Counsel, American Bank Attorneys*, and *Markham's Negligence Counsel*. Specialty directories may be located by consulting a library catalog under the heading of "Lawyers—Directories".

4. Judicial Directories

There are three annual directories which list addresses and telephone numbers of federal judges and other court personnel. These are the *Federal Court Directory* (published by Lawyer's Diary & Manual, Newark, N. J.); *Federal Court Directory* (sometimes entitled *United States Court Directory*, published by the Legal Reporters Associates, Washington, D. C.); and the *United States Court Directory* (published by the Administrative Office of the United States Courts). There are two biographical directories which give short biographical sketches for all federal judges. The *Biographical Dictionary of the Federal Judiciary* (published by Gale Research Co.) covers federal judges from 1789 to 1974 and is based on material from *Who's Who in America* and *Who Was Who in America*. It has not been updated. *Judges of the United States* (published by the Bicentennial Committee of the Judicial Conference of the United

[8] Legal Directories Publishing Co., Inc., Suite 201, 1314 Westwood Blvd., Los Angeles, California 90024.

States) covers federal judges from 1780 to 1978 with updates planned.

5. Academic Directories

Certain directories are compiled to serve the academic world and provide a ready reference to those wishing to make use of the law schools' facilities. *The Directory of Law Teachers* [9] allows one to find biographic information on law school faculty as well as indexing by subject or specialty. Law libraries of the United States and Canada are indexed geographically in the *Directory of Law Libraries.*[10] An alphabetical listing of library personnel is also provided in this directory.

SECTION D. FORM BOOKS

Form books are used as aids in drafting legal documents. Much of a lawyer's time is spent in drafting forms. To assist lawyers in this aspect of their practice, there are available many different types of form books. When using form books it should be kept in mind that they are all general in nature and that before using a form, extreme care should be exercised to make sure that the language is entirely suitable for the purpose for which it is to be used. Books of forms may be classified as follows:

1. General form books

This type provides forms for all aspects of legal practice and varies from one volume to multi-volume sets. They generally are annotated and each form contains references to cases which have favorably construed provisions within the form. Editorial comment is also frequently given. Examples are:

American Jurisprudence, Legal Forms 2d 1971–74. 20 vols. with pocket supplements.

Modern Legal Forms (West Publishing Co.). 1950–1972. 17 vols. with pocket supplements.

Nichols, Cyclopedia of Legal Forms, Annotated. 1955–1964. 14 vols. with pocket supplements.

Rabkin and Johnson, *Current Legal Forms with Tax Analysis.* 1968. 22 vols. Looseleaf.

Warren, *Forms of Agreement.* 1966. 1 vol. Looseleaf.

[9] *Directory of Law Teachers,* West Publishing Co., 50 West Kellogg Blvd., St. Paul, Minn. 55102.

[10] *Directory of Law Libraries,* Commerce Clearing House, Inc., 420 Lexington Ave., New York, N. Y. 10017.

Most large states also have general form books that are keyed to local practice. These are published both by commercial publishers and state bar association programs. They contain the same features as the form books discussed above, but are designed for local use, and hence may be more useful to the practitioner. Examples are:

California Legal Forms, Transaction Guide (Matthew Bender). 1968. 1 vol. Looseleaf.

Legal Form Manual for Real Estate Transactions (State Bar of Texas). 1976. 1 vol.

2. Subject Form Books

Many form books are published which are devoted to a special subject. These are similar in format to the general form books but contain more forms on the aspect of the subject covered than will usually be found in the general ones. Examples are:

H. Lavien, *Bankruptcy Forms* (West Publishing Co.) (with supplements).

M. Melville, *Forms and Agreements on Intellectual Property* (Clark Boardman) 1 vol.

A. Arnold, *Modern Real Estate and Mortgage Forms* (Warren, Gorham and Lamont) (Looseleaf).

3. Other Sources of Forms

a. *Forms in Treatises*

Many multi-volume sets of treatises will include forms, either integrated with the text, or in separate volumes.

b. *State Codes*

Some state codes include both substantive and procedural forms. For any particular state code, consult the general index under "Forms."

c. *Procedural Forms*

These were discussed in Chapter 12.

SECTION E. BRIEFS AND RECORDS ON APPEAL

After a case has been decided by a trial court or an intermediate court of appeal, the case may be appealed to a higher court. When this happens, the attorneys for each side submit written briefs in which they set forth the reasons why the appellate court should either affirm or reverse the decision below. Such briefs contain the theories upon which arguments hinge and a discussion and analysis of the law, with citations to the authorities. Where available, the record of trial court action is submitted with the brief. This record usually contains forms of the preliminary motions and pleadings in the case; examination and cross-examination of witnesses; the instructions to the jury; the opinion of the lower court; and various other exhibits.

Briefs and records provide an attorney who has a similar case with much of his research and a list of arguments which have or have not impressed an appellate court.

1. Briefs and Records of the Supreme Court of the United States

A small number of libraries receive copies of the briefs and records which are submitted to the Supreme Court.[11] Most law school libraries and larger bar association libraries also have these briefs and records available on microform.

Oral arguments presented before the Court have been tape-recorded since 1955. They are available for purchase after three years have elapsed and must be used for scholarly or instructional purposes. Further information may be obtained from the Office of the Marshal of the U. S. Supreme Court.

Starting with the 1980 term, oral arguments are being made available by University Publications of America.

2. Federal Courts of Appeal

Most large law libraries receive the briefs and records for the federal court of appeals for the circuit in which they are located. Others may frequently be obtained from a local law library on interlibrary loan.

SECTION F. PROFESSIONAL RESPONSIBILITY

The national standard of conduct for lawyers is set forth in the *Code of Professional Responsibility* promulgated by the American Bar Association in 1970.[12] This Code "is designed to be adopted by appropriate agencies both as an inspirational guide to the members of the profession and as a basis for disciplinary action when the conduct of a lawyer falls below the required minimum standards stated

[11] *See* Charpentier, *Appellate Records—A Beginning Union List.*, 62 LAW LIB. J. 273 (1969).

[12] CODE OF PROFESSIONAL RESPONSIBILITY AND CODE OF JUDICIAL CONDUCT (American Bar Association 1975). This is published as a separate pamphlet and is reprinted in the *Martindale-Hubbell Law Directory*. This Code replaces the *ABA Code of Professional Ethics* adopted in 1908.

* * *."[13] The *Code of Professional Responsibility* consists of three parts: Canons, Ethical Considerations, and Disciplinary Rules.

The American Bar Association, as a voluntary association, has no means for enforcing its Code. Only the state legislatures or the highest court of each state has the power to discipline lawyers. Each state has adopted either its own code or that of the American Bar Association.

1. Discipline of Lawyers

The procedure for the discipline of lawyers varies from state to state. The rules governing discipline may be located by consulting the indexes of the state codes. The common practice is for the highest court of the state to appoint a committee of lawyers who hear complaints and make recommendations to the court.[14]

2. Opinions on Legal Ethics

The American Bar Association and most state bar associations have Committees on Legal Ethics. Lawyers submit to these Committees a situation they are facing and request an opinion as to whether or not their suggested action may be a breach of the *Code of Professional Responsibility*. The Committee on Legal Ethics of the American Bar Association issues its opinions in two series: *Formal Opinions* and *Informal Opinions*. Committees of state bar associations usually publish their opinions in their bar journal or other publications.[15]

3. Disciplinary Law and Procedure Research System

Published by the American Bar Association, this looseleaf volume provides subject and name access to decisions regarding professional responsibility. It is supplemented by monthly advance sheets.

4. Shepard's Professional Responsibility Citations

This citator is devoted to the coverage of citations to the *Code of Professional Responsibility* by both the federal and state courts.

[13] Id. at IC

[14] T. MORGAN AND R. ROTUNDA, PROBLEMS AND MATERIALS ON PROFESSIONAL RESPONSIBILITY 143–59 (1976).

[15] *e. g.*, ASSOCIATION OF THE BAR OF THE CITY OF NEW YORK, OPINIONS/COMMITTEES OF PROFESSIONAL ETHICS, THE ASSOCIATION OF THE BAR OF THE CITY OF NEW YORK, THE NEW YORK COUNTY BAR ASSOCIATION, NEW YORK BAR ASSOCIATION (1980). (Looseleaf)

Chapter 20

INTERNATIONAL LAW

SECTION A. INTRODUCTION

Research in international law is neither esoteric nor limited to the practice of the specialist. American treaties, as primary law,[1] are frequently determinative of the rights and duties of Americans. To illustrate this point, a resident of one state may leave a will devising her property to a relative in a foreign country. The state may have a statute prohibiting an alien from taking property by succession or testamentary disposition. The United States Supreme Court has held that such a state statute must give way when it conflicts with the terms of a United States treaty.[2] Similarly, another court has held that a Washington State statute regulating the fishing rights of certain Indian tribes is not enforceable when the statute is in violation of a treaty between the United States and the Indian tribes.[3]

These are not isolated illustrations, for they occur more frequently than is generally realized. It is essential, therefore, for the legal researcher to have some knowledge of the sources of international law and the tools available for locating them.

International law has been defined as

> "* * * [A] body of rules governing the relations between states * * *. Customary, as distinguished from conventional, international law is based upon the common consent of the nations extending over a period of time of sufficient duration to cause it to become crystalized into a rule of conduct. When doubt arises as to the existence or nonexistence of a rule of international law, or as to the application of a rule to a given situation, resort is usually had to such sources as pertinent treaties, pronouncements of foreign offices, statements by writers, and decisions of interna-

1 "* * * [A]ll treaties made or which shall be made under the Authority of the United States, shall be the Supreme Law of the Land." U.S.Const. art. VI, § 2, cl. 2.

2 Zschernig v. Miller, 389 U.S. 429 (1968).

3 United States v. State of Washington, 520 F.2d 676 (9th Cir. 1976).

tional tribunals and those of prize courts and other domestic courts purporting to be expressive of the law of nations." [4]

Another international law scholar has defined international law in terms of how it is made.

"When contrasted with national or 'domestic' law, we think of international law as that which is created of two or more states, whether such action is in the form of treaty-making or the formation of international customs." [5]

International law as so stated is usually known as *public* international law as distinguished from *private* international law, which is defined as:

"* * * [T]hat branch of the law of municipal law which determines before the courts of what nation a particular action or suit should be brought, and by the law of what nation it should be determined." [6]

This chapter will be devoted to public international law and specifically to the researching of the conventional international law of the United States as represented in the treaties and other international agreements entered into between the United States and other countries.[7]

SECTION B. RESEARCH IN INTERNATIONAL LAW IN RELATION TO THE UNITED STATES

1. Treaties and International Agreements Between the United States and Other Countries

Under the Constitution of the United States, the President ". . . shall have Power, by and with the Advice and Consent of the Senate, to make Treaties, provided two-thirds of the Senators

[4] 1 G. HACKWORTH, DIGEST OF INTERNATIONAL LAW 1 (1940); *see also*: The Paquette Habana, 175 U.S. 677, 700 (1899).

[5] H. KELSEN, PRINCIPLES OF INTERNATIONAL LAW 300 (2d ed. R. Tucker 1966).

[6] 1 JOWITT'S DICTIONARY OF ENGLISH LAW 999–1000 (2d ed. J. Burke 1977). In the United States the term "conflict of laws" is generally used rather than private international law.

[7] For additional information on the substantive aspect of international law, *see* the latest editions of J. BRIERLY, THE LAW OF NATIONS, or C. FENWICK, INTERNATIONAL LAW; for bibliographies *see* Marke, *International Law; An Annotated Bibliography* in 1978 ANN. SURVEY AM. L. Supplement 55–159 and PUB. INT'L. L.; A CURRENT BIBLIOGRAPHY (semi-annual).

present concur; . . . ."[8] An international agreement is one that the President may enter into under his constitutional power as President or as authorized by an act of Congress and which does not need the consent of Congress.[9] The actual power of the President to enter into international agreements rather than treaties is not entirely clear and has long been a matter of dispute.[10] But nevertheless, international agreements are entered into by Presidents much more frequently than treaties.

2. Restatement of the Law, Second. Foreign Relations Law of the United States

This *Restatement* was adopted by the American Law Institute in 1962. Its purpose, as stated in the introduction, is to set forth the foreign relations law of the United States, which consists of those rules the United States conceived to be established by international law and those parts of the domestic law which give effect to rules of international law. It is a useful place to start research for matters involving the interpretation of U. S. treaties or statutes and for cases interpreting them. Note that this Restatement is currently undergoing revision, and that parts of this revision may be available in "tentative draft" form.

SECTION C. SOURCES FOR UNITED STATES TREATIES

1. Current Publications

a. *Prior to Ratification by the Senate*

After the President has negotiated and signed a treaty, it has to be submitted to the Senate for advice and consent. The text of the treaty along with the Presidential message and other documents are published in the *Senate Executive Documents* series. Prior to 1945, these were almost always printed as confidential documents and were not generally available. Since 1946, the Senate has ordered them printed without the confidential classification.

[8] U.S.CONST. art. II, § 2, cl. 2. The Constitution does not mention how a treaty may be terminated, and whether the advice and consent of the Senate is needed. For a detailed study of this question, *see* UNITED STATES SENATE, TERMINATION OF TREATIES: THE CONSTITUTIONAL ALLOCATION OF POWER, MATERIALS COMPILED BY THE COMMITTEE ON FOREIGN RELATIONS, 95th CONG., 2d SESS. (Comm.Print 1978).

[9] RESTATEMENT (SECOND) OF FOREIGN RELATIONS LAW OF THE UNITED STATES sec. 115(a) (1965). *See also* A. GILBERT, EXECUTIVE AGREEMENTS AND TREATIES, 1946–1973 (1973).

[10] For an excellent discussion and bibliography of executive agreements, *see* Leary, *International Executive Agreements: A Guide to the Legal Issues and Research Sources*, 72 LAW LIB.J. 1 (1979).

Treaties submitted to the Senate by the President are assigned to the Committee on Foreign Affairs. This Committee may hold hearings and then after consideration issue a report recommending that the treaty be or not be ratified. These reports are published in the *Senate Executive Reports* series and may be located through either the *Monthly Catalog* or the *CIS Index*.[11]

b. *After Ratification*

Since December 27, 1945, all treaties and international agreements are first published in pamphlet form in the *Treaties and Other International Acts Series* (T.I.A.S.). This Series starts with Treaty Number 1501, since it combines and continues the numbering of two previous publications of treaties and international agreements, i.e. 994 numbers of the *Treaty Series* and 506 numbers of the *Executive Agreement Series*.[12] It contains all treaties which have been proclaimed during the calendar year, to which the United States is a party, and all international agreements other than treaties to which the United States is a party that have been signed, proclaimed, or with reference to which any other final formality has been executed during each calendar year.[13] The documents are literal prints of the originals with marginal notes and footnotes.

c. All of the pamphlets issued in the *Treaties and Other International Acts Series* since 1950 are published in bound volumes under the title *United States Treaties and Other International Agreements*

[11] These Documents and Reports are collected in M. MABRY, CHECKLIST OF SENATE EXECUTIVE DOCUMENTS AND REPORTS . . . 1947–AUGUST 1970 (1970), and since 1969 in each annual volume of *CIS-Abstracts*, under "Senate Committees—Foreign Relations—Executive Reports and Executive Documents" (S384 & S385).

[12] The T.I.A.S. replaces the *Treaty Series*, 1908–45, and the *Executive Agreement Series*, 1929–45. The *Treaty Series* consists of separate treaty prints in pamphlet or slip form, arranged numerically in chronological order of proclamation or publication. The publication of this Series was commenced in January 1908 with Treaty Number 489 by the Department of State. Prior to October 1, 1929 (Treaty Number 813) the *Treaty Series* includes both treaties and executive agreements. From October 1, 1929 (Treaty Number 813) to the end of the publication in December 1945 (Treaty Number 994), however, the *Treaty Series* is limited to treaties and international agreements submitted to the Senate. Another series, also by the Department of State, called the *Executive Agreement Series*, started its publication on October 1, 1929, and ended on March 16, 1945. This series contains 506 numbers and picks up the executive agreements, exchanges of notes, etc., excluded from the *Treaty Series* for that period. For a fuller explanation of these two series and for the treaties prior to Number 489, see H. MILLER, 1 TREATIES AND OTHER INTERNATIONAL ACTS OF THE UNITED STATES OF AMERICA 35–38, 99–135 (1931).

[13] 1 U.S.C. sec. 112a (1976).

(UST). By statute,[14] the treaties contained in the *Statutes at Large* and *United States Treaties and Other International Agreements* are evidence admissible in all federal courts, state courts, and courts of the Territories and insular possessions of the United States.

d. *Status of Pending Treaties*

The *CCH Congressional Index* has a section which contains a status table for all treaties which have been submitted to the Senate Committee on Foreign Affairs and are awaiting action by the committee or the full Senate.

e. *Commerce Clearing House, Tax Treaties*

This service provides looseleaf reporting on income and estate tax treaties between the United States and foreign countries. The Reporter contains interpretative regulations, news on treaties in preparation, significant court decisions and editorial comment. A special section of the publication features *CCH Treaty Charts* which show in graphic style the contents of each treaty relating to some 200 major tax aspects.[15]

2. Collections of United States Treaties

U. S. Treaties have from time to time been published in separate sets. These are:

a. *Malloy's Treaties.* 4 vols. (vol. 3 often cited as 3 *Redmond*; vol. 4 as 4 *Trenwith*). This set contains all treaties, *etc.*, between 1776 and 1937 with some annotations. Volume 4 includes an index to the set and a chronological list of treaties.

b. *Treaties and Other International Acts of the United States*, edited by Hunter Miller. This is a more recent compilation of treaties. However, only 8 volumes covering the years 1776 to 1863 were published.

c. From 1789 to 1950, many treaties were published in the *Statutes at Large*, but until volume 32 (1903) their publication in this set had been irregular. With volume 47, 1931–32,[16] the *Statutes at Large* started to include international agreements as well.

d. *Treaties and Other International Agreements of the United States*, 1776–1949, edited by C. E. Bevans, and published by the Department of State. Includes all treaties and international agreements which were published in the *Statutes at Large* between 1776 and

[14] *Id.*

[15] A similar service is published by Prentice-Hall.

[16] For a detailed study of the inclusion (and exclusion) of treaties in the U.S. *Statutes at Large*, *see* Miller, *supra*, vol. 1, at 33–35.

1949. It includes the English text or in cases where no English text was signed, the official United States Government translations. The first four volumes contain multilateral treaties and agreements, arranged chronologically according to date of signature. The next eight volumes (volumes 5–12) list bilateral treaties and agreements arranged alphabetically by country. Each volume includes a brief index which is consolidated into volume 13, a cumulative analytical index arranged in one alphabet by country and subject. Although the set is annotated, its essential value rests in its collection of documentary texts. The current status of a treaty or an agreement in this set may be determined by consulting the latest annual volume of *Treaties in Force* and the monthly *Department of State Bulletin.*

e. *Unperfected Treaties of the United States, 1776–1976,*[17] edited by C. Wiktor. This multi-volume set is an annotated collection of the texts of all treaties to which the United States was a signatory but which never went into force.

f. *Extradition Laws and Treaties of the United States,*[18] edited by I. Kavass and A. Sprudzs. This set, published in looseleaf volumes, contains all operative extradition treaties arranged in alphabetical sequence of countries with which the United States entered into extradition arrangements.

g. *Indian Affairs, Laws and Treaties,* compiled and edited by C. Kappler. This set has been recently reprinted by the U. S. Government (1976), and the treaties volume (volume 11) has been separately reprinted as *Indian Treaties 1778–1883* (Interland Publishing Inc. 1972). Though the last treaty with an Indian tribe was ratified in 1868, this volume cannot be considered comprehensive because the U. S. Government continued to sign "Agreements" (which have the same force as treaties) with Indian tribes until 1909. Earlier compilations of Indian treaties, such as the one found in volume 7 of the *Statutes at Large,* are not as comprehensive or well indexed as *Kappler.* Agreements not found in *Kappler* can usually be found in the *U. S. Statutes at Large* using the sources described below in Section C4. For treaties concluded with Indian tribes prior to the formation of the United States, *see* A. Vaughan (ed.), *Early American Indian Documents: Treaties and Laws 1607–1789* (1979).

3. Indexes to U. S. Treaties

a. *Treaties in Force.* This is an annual publication of the U. S. Department of State, listing all treaties and agreements, by country and by subject, that are still in force.

[17] Oceana Publications, Dobbs Ferry, N.Y. (1976–).

[18] W.S. Hein, Buffalo, N.Y. (1979).

b. I. Kavass and M. Michael, *United States Treaties and Other International Agreements Cumulative Index,* 1776–1949 (1975).[19] This 4-volume work indexes all treaties and international agreements from 1776–1949 which were published in the *Statutes at Large,* the *Malloy's,* the *Miller's,* the *Bevans'* and other relevant sources. Each volume is devoted to a particular type of arrangement: numerical by treaty number, chronological by date of signature, by country and by topic.

c. I. Kavass and A. Sprudzs, *UST Cumulative Index,* 1950–1970 (1973, Supp. 1971–75).[20] This work also has four volumes and indexes all treaties and international agreements from 1950 to 1970 which were published in the *United States Treaties and Other International Agreements* and the *Treaties and International Acts Series.* The arrangements are again numerical, chronological, by country and by topic. This set is kept current by a looseleaf volume, with bound five-year cumulations.

d. *U. S. Statutes at Large,* Vol. 64, pt. 3, at B 1107 *et seq.* This section lists alphabetically by country all treaties and agreements that were included in volumes 1–64, 1789–1949, except those treaties signed with Indian tribes.

e. A. Sprudzs, *Chronological Index to Multilateral Treaties in Force for the United States* (as of Jan. 1, 1972). This is a useful adjunct to *Treaties in Force* which lists multilateral treaties only under subject.

f. *Department of State Bulletin.* This is a monthly publication of the Department of State. Each issue has a section entitled "Treaty Information" which gives current information on treaties. This should be used to supplement *Treaties in Force.* There are monthly and annual indexes to the *Department of State Bulletin* which may be used to locate current information either by subject or country.

4. Special Subject Indexes

American Indians. A checklist and bibliography of Indian treaties appears in *List of Indian Treaties,* House Committee on Interior and Insular Affairs, 88th Cong., 2d Sess. (Comm. Print No. 33, 1964). This print consists of a chronological list of all ratified Indian treaties from 1778 to 1868, a list of treaties and agreements alphabetically by tribe from 1778 to 1881, and the index to the *Kappler* collection of Indian treaties (2g *supra*). The first two lists cite to the *U. S. Statutes at Large.*

[19] (1975).

[20] (1973).

A Chronological List of Treaties and Agreements Made by Indian Tribes with the United States (Institute for the Development of Indian Law, 1973) attempts to list all treaties and agreements between 1778 and 1909 whether ratified or unratified. For each ratified treaty or agreement, a citation to the *U. S. Statutes at Large* is given. Also, the uncodified volume of the *United States Code Service* lists, by year, Indian treaties which have been cited or construed by the courts, with digests of the decisions.

5. Interpretations of Treaties

a. Digests. These are more than case digests and include excerpts from treaties, periodical articles, and court decisions from various countries, and documents of the various international organizations. These digests have been published by the Department of State and the editors have all been distinguished scholars: [21]

(1) *Wharton's Digest of International Law.* 3 vols. 1886.

(2) *Moore's Digest of International Law.* 8 vols. 1906.

(3) *Hackworth's Digest of International Law.* 8 vols. 1940–1944.

(4) *Whiteman's Digest of International Law.* 15 vols. 1963–1973. Supplements *Hackworth's.*

(5) *Digest of United States Practice in International Law.* This is an annual publication which started in 1973.

(6) *Contemporary Practice of the United States Relating to International Law.* This appears in each quarterly issue of the *American Journal of International Law.* It digests current materials under the same headings as used in the *Digest of United States Practice in International Law.*

6. Citators For Treaties

After the text of a treaty or agreement has been located, steps should be taken to ascertain the interpretations given to it by the courts. The language of treaties, as that of statutes, may not be clear in meaning, or there may be doubt if it was the intent of the treaty to cover certain situations. Two methods of locating court decisions involving treaties are:

a. *Shepard's United States Citations, Statutes Volumes.* Treaties entered into before 1950 may be *Shepardized* in the usual manner in the section for *Statutes at Large (not included in the U. S. Code).*

[21] *See* Rovine, *U.S. International Law Digests: Some History and a New Approach,* 67 AM.J.INT'L.LAW 314 (1973), for a discussion of these digests.

Treaties entered into after 1950 may be *Shepardized* in the section for *United States Treaties and Other International Agreements.*

b. *United States Code Service.* The unnumbered volume for uncodified laws and treaties lists treaties by year of ratification and gives annotations to court decisions.

SECTION D. ILLUSTRATIONS: UNITED STATES TREATIES AND INTERNATIONAL AGREEMENTS

Problems: Do the United States and France have an agreement or treaty in reference to the origin of bourbon whiskey?

Is the United States a signatory to an International Convention on the regulation of whaling?

Illustrations

138–140. Pages from an Annual Issue of Treaties in Force

141. Page from a Monthly Issue of the Department of State Bulletin

142. Page from Treaty Status Table—CCH Congressional Index

143–144. Pages from Shepard's U.S. Citations—Statutes Volume

[Illustration 138]

TITLE PAGE FROM ANNUAL ISSUE OF TREATIES IN FORCE

TREATIES IN FORCE

A List of Treaties and Other International Agreements of the United States

This publication is reissued each year. It lists treaties and other international agreements of the United States on record in the Department of State on January 1, which had not expired by their terms or which had not been denounced by the parties, replaced or superseded by other agreements, or otherwise definitely terminated.

It is in two sections: Part 1 lists all countries for which the U.S. has bilateral agreements; Part 2 is arranged alphabetically by subject and lists all multilateral agreements to which the United States is a signatory.

Compiled by the Treaty Affairs Staff,
Office of the Legal Adviser,
Department of State.

[Illustration 139]

PAGE FROM ANNUAL ISSUE OF TREATIES IN FORCE

FRANCE (Cont'd)

Agreement respecting maritime claims and litigation. Signed at Washington March 14, 1949; entered into force March 14, 1949.
63 Stat. 2499; TIAS 1935; 7 Bevans 1300; 84 UNTS 225.

Agreement regarding settlement of certain residual financial claims and accounts. Signed at Washington March 14, 1949; entered into force March 14, 1949.
63 Stat. 2507; TIAS 1936; 7 Bevans 1304; 84 UNTS 237.

Agreement on postponement of installations pursuant to paragraph 3 of the lend-lease agreement of May 28, 1946, and paragraph 2 of the surplus property agreement of December 6, 1947. Signed at Washington January 30, 1958; entered into force January 30, 1958.
9 UST 67; TIAS 3979; 304 UNTS 9.

LIQUOR

Agreement providing for the recognition and protection by France of the appellation of origin of bourbon whiskey and continued protection by the United States of appellations of origin of the French brandies, cognac, armagnac and calvados. Exchange of notes at Paris December 2, 1970 and January 18, 1971; entered into force March 20, 1971.
22 UST 36; TIAS 7041; 777 UNTS 77.

MAPPING

Agreement for the mapping of certain French territories in the Pacific. Exchange of notes at Paris November 27, 1948; entered into force November 27, 1948.
3 UST 491; TIAS 2407; 168 UNTS 119.

MILITARY CEMETERIES AND MONUMENTS

Agreement concerning the interment in France and in territories of the French Union, or removal to the United States, of the bodies of American soldiers killed in the war of 1939-1945. Signed at Paris October 1, 1947; entered into force October 1, 1947.
61 Stat. 3767; TIAS 1720; 7 Bevans 1215; 148 UNTS 303.

Agreement regarding the transport, burial, and embalming of bodies of members of United States forces dying in France. Signed at Paris July 1, 1955; entered into force July 1, 1955.
6 UST 3787; TIAS 3380; 270 UNTS 19.

Agreement relating to the grant of plots of land located in France for the creation of permanent military cemeteries or the construction of war memorials, with annexes. Signed at Paris March 19, 1956; entered into force March 19, 1956.
7 UST 561; TIAS 3537; 275 UNTS 37.

MUTUAL SECURITY

Mutual security agreement. Exchange of notes at Paris January 5, 1952; entered into force January 5, 1952.
3 UST 4559; TIAS 2606; 181 UNTS 177.

NARCOTIC DRUGS

FINDING BILATERAL TREATIES

1. Use Part 1 of latest edition of Treaties in Force. All treaties or international agreements which the U.S. has entered into with other countries are listed under the name of the other country.

Note citations where text of treaty may be found.

Agreement relating to the fulfillment of military obligations during the wars of 1914-1918 and 1939-1945 by persons with dual nationality. Exchange of notes at Paris December 22, 1948; entered into force December 22, 1948.
62 Stat. 3621; TIAS 1876; 7 Bevans 1294; 67 UNTS 38.

Extension:
November 18 and December 31, 1952 (3 UST 5345; TIAS 2741; 185 UNTS 396).

OCEANOGRAPHY

Memorandum of understanding on the participation of France in the international phase of ocean drilling of the deep sea drilling project. Signed at Paris January 15, 1976; entered into force January 15, 1976.
28 UST 5026; TIAS 8610.

PACIFIC SETTLEMENT OF DISPUTES

Treaty to facilitate the settlement of disputes. Signed at Washington September 15, 1914; entered into force January 22, 1915.
38 Stat. 1887; TS 609; 7 Bevans 883.

Treaty of arbitration and exchange of notes dated March 1 and 5, 1928. Signed at Washington February 6, 1928; entered into force April 22, 1929.
46 Stat. 2269; TS 785; 7 Bevans 968; 91 LNTS 323.

PATENTS

Agreements to facilitate

exchange of parcel post. Signed at Paris December 7 and at Washington December 30, 1935; operative August 1, 1935.
49 Stat. 3322; Post Office Department print; 171 LNTS 117.

Convention relating to the initiation of reciprocal express mail/postadex service. Signed at Washington and Paris June 6 and 24, 1975; entered into force June 24, 1975; effective June 16, 1975.
TIAS 8841.

PUBLICATIONS

Agreement relating to exchange of official publications. Exchange of notes at Paris August 14, 1945; entered into force January 1, 1946.
60 Stat. 1944; TIAS 1579; 7 Bevans 1095; 73 UNTS 237.

[Illustration 140]

PAGE FROM PART 2, ANNUAL ISSUE OF TREATIES IN FORCE

Weights and Measures (Cont'd)

Convention amending the convention relating to weights and measures.
Dated at Sevres October 6, 1921; entered into force for the United States October 24, 1923.
43 Stat. 1686; TS 673; 2 Bevans 323; 17 LNTS 45.
States which are parties:
Australia
Austria
Belgium
Brazil
Bulgaria
Cameroon
Canada
China, People's Rep.
China (Taiwan)
Czechoslovakia
Denmark
Dominican Rep.
Egypt
Finland
France
Germany
Hungary
India
Indonesia
Iran
Ireland
Italy
Japan
Korea
Mexico
Netherlands
Norway
Pakistan
Poland
Portugal
Romania
South Africa
Spain
Sweden
Switzerland
Thailand
Turkey
Union of Soviet Socialist Reps.
United Kingdom
United States
Uruguay
Venezuela
Yugoslavia

Convention establishing an International Organization of Legal Metrology.
Done at Paris October 12, 1955 and amended January 18, 1968; entered into force for the United States October 22, 1972.
23 UST 4233; TIAS 7533; 560 UNTS 3.
Parties:
Arab Organization of Standardization and Metrology[1]
Australia
Austria
Belgium
Bulgaria
Cameroon
Cuba
Cyprus
Czechoslovakia
Denmark
Egypt
Ethiopia
Finland
France[2]
German Dem. Rep.
Germany, Fed. Rep.
Greece[1]
Guinea
Hungary
India
Indonesia
Iran
Israel
Italy
Jamaica[1]
Japan
Jordan[1]
Korea, Dem. People's Rep.
Korea, Rep.
Lebanon
Luxembourg[1]
Monaco
Morocco
Nepal[1]
Netherlands
New Zealand
Norway
Pakistan
Poland
Romania
Spain
Sri Lanka
Sweden
Switzerland
Turkey[1]
Union of Soviet Socialist Reps.
United Kingdom[3]
United States
Venezuela
Yugoslavia

NOTES:
[1]Corresponding Member.
[2]Extended to the French overseas territories.
[3]Extended to the British Virgin Islands, Gibraltar, Montserrat, Turks and Caicos Islands.

WHALING

Convention for the regulation of whaling.
Concluded at Geneva September 24, 1931; entered into force for the United States January 16, 1935.
49 Stat. 3079; TS 880; 3 Bevans 26; 155 LNTS 349.
States which are parties:
Austria
Bahamas, The[1]
Barbados[2]
Brazil
Canada
Cyprus[3]
Czechoslovakia
Denmark, including Greenland
Dominica[4]
Ecuador
Egypt
Fiji[5]
Finland
France
Gambia, The[6]
Ghana[7]
Grenada[8]
Guyana[9]
Indonesia
Ireland
Italy[10]
Jamaica[11]
Kenya[12]
Latvia
Malaysia[13]
Malta[14]
Mauritius[15]
Mexico
Monaco
Netherlands[16]
New Zealand
Nicaragua
Nigeria[17]
Norway
Poland
Seychelles[18]
Sierra Leone[19]
Solomon Is.[20]
South Africa
Spain
Sri Lanka
Sudan
Switzerland
Tanzania[4]
Tonga[21]
Trinidad & Tobago[22]
Turkey
Tuvalu[4]
United Kingdom[23]
United States ←
Yugoslavia

NOTES:
[1]See footnote 5 under Automotive Traffic (3 UST 3008;

FINDING MULTILATERAL TREATIES

PROBLEM: Is the United States a signatory to an International Convention on the regulation of whaling?

Check in Part 2 of Treaties in Force under subject: Whaling.

Note citations to where text of treaty may be located.

As additional countries become signatories, they are listed in the monthly Department of State Bulletin and then included in the next annual edition of Treaties in Force.

[Illustration 141]

PAGE FROM MONTHLY ISSUE OF THE DEPARTMENT OF STATE BULLETIN

Treaties

Satellite Communications System
Agreement relating to the International Telecommunications Satellite Organization (INTELSAT), with annexes. Done at Washington Aug. 20, 1971. Entered into force Feb. 12, 1973. TIAS 7532.
Accession deposited: Niger, Apr. 14, 1980.

Operating agreement relating to the International Telecommunications Satellite Organization (INTELSAT), with annex. Done at Washington Aug. 20, 1971. Entered into force Feb. 12, 1973. TIAS 7532.
Signature: Niger, Apr. 14, 1980.

Sugar
International sugar agreement, 1977, with annexes. Done at Geneva Oct. 7, 1977. Entered into force provisionally, Jan. 1, 1978; definitively Jan. 2, 1980. TIAS 9664.
Notification of provisional application deposited: Colombia, Apr. 14, 1980.
Ratification deposited: Costa Rica, Mar. 27, 1980.

Terrorism
International convention against the taking of hostages. Adopted at New York Dec. 19, 1979.[1]
Signatures: Bolivia, Mar. 25, 1980; Haiti, Apr. 21, 1980; Italy, Apr. 18, 1980; Lesotho, Apr. 17, 1980.

Trade
Protocol extending the arrangement regarding international trade in textiles of Dec. 20, 1973 (TIAS 7840). Done at Geneva Dec. 14, 1977. Entered into force Jan. 1, 1978. TIAS 8939.
Acceptance deposited: Argentina, Feb. 18, 1980.[6]

Agreement on trade in civi
at Geneva Apr. 12, 1979. E
force Jan. 1, 1980. TIAS 9(
Ratification deposited: Swi
Apr. 2, 1980.

U.N. Industrial Developm
Organization
Constitution of the U.N. I
velopment Organization, w
Adopted at Vienna Apr. 8,
Ratification deposited: Nic
1980.
Signatures: Malaysia, Apr. 10, 1980; Somalia, Mar. 21, 1980; Trinidad and Tobago, Apr. 14, 1980.

Wheat
Protocol modifying and further extending the wheat trade convention (part of the international wheat agreement), 1971 (TIAS 7144). Done at Washington Apr. 25, 1979. Entered into force June 23, 1979, with respect to certain provisions, July 1, 1979, with respect to other provisions.
Ratification deposited: Egypt, Apr. 22, 1980; Guatemala, Apr. 28, 1980.

Food aid convention, 1980 (part of the International Wheat Agreement), 1971, as extended (TIAS 7144). Done at Washington Mar. 11, 1980. Enters into force July 1, 1980, if by June 30, 1980 the governments referred to in paragraph (3) of Article III have deposited instruments of ratification, acceptance, approval or accession, or declarations of provisional application, and provided that the 1979 protocol for the fifth extension of the Wheat Trade Convention, 1971, or a new Wheat Trade Convention replacing it, is in force.
Signatures: Argentina, Australia, Belgium, Canada, Denmark, European Economic Community, France, Federal Republic of Germany, Ireland, Italy, Luxembourg, Netherlands, U.K., Apr. 30, 1980; Austria, Switzerland, U.S., Apr. 29, 1980; Finland, Japan, Apr. 22, 1980; Norway, Apr. 24, 1980; Sweden, Apr. 9, 1980.

BILATERAL

Bangladesh
Agreement amending the agreement for sales of agricultural commodities of Aug. 2, 1978 (TIAS 9389), with agreed minutes. Effected by exchange of notes at Dacca Mar. 7, 1980. Entered into force Mar. 7, 1980.

Botswana
Agreement providing for a radio facility for the purpose of relaying Voice of America programs to areas in Africa. Signed at Gaborone Mar. 28, 1980. Entered into force Mar. 28, 1980.

Canada
Protocol to amend the convention for the protection, preservation, and extension of the sockeye salmon fisheries in the Fraser River System of May 26, 1930, as amended (50 Stat. 1355. TIAS 3867). Signed at

The Department of State Bulletin is published monthly. Each issue has a section on Treaty Information which serves as "advance sheets" to Treaties in Force.

President: Mar. 31, 1980.

Colombia
Agreement amending the agreement of Aug. 3, 1978, as amended (TIAS 9515, 9645), relating to trade in cotton, wool, and manmade fiber textiles and textile products. Effected by exchange of letters at Bogota Jan. 2 and 31, 1980. Entered into force Jan. 31, 1980.

Cyprus
Convention for the avoidance of double taxation and the prevention of fiscal evasion with respect to taxes on income, with related exchange of notes. Signed at Nicosia Mar. 26, 1980. Enters into force upon the exchange of instruments of ratification.

Haiti
Agreement amending the agreement of Aug. 17, 1979 (TIAS 9595), relating to trade in cotton, wool, and manmade fiber textiles and textile products. Effected by exchange of notes at Port-au-Prince Jan. 28 and Mar. 3, 1980. Entered into force Mar. 3, 1980.

Indonesia
Agreement for sales of agricultural commodities, with agreed minutes. Signed at Jakarta Mar. 6, 1980. Entered into force Mar. 6, 1980.

Kenya
Agreement for sales of agricultural commodities, with minutes of negotiation. Signed at Nairobi Mar. 6, 1980. Entered into force Mar. 6, 1980.

Malaysia
Agreement amending the agreement of May 17 and June 8, 1978, as amended (TIAS 9180, 9602), relating to trade in cotton, wool, and manmade fiber textiles and textile products. Effected by exchange of letters at Washington and New York Jan. 8 and Mar. 27, 1980. Entered into force Mar. 27, 1980.

Malta
Agreement with respect to taxes on income, with related exchange of notes. Signed at Valletta Mar. 21, 1980. Enters into force upon the exchange of instruments of ratification. Provisions shall have effect in respect of income or profits arising on or after the first day of January of the year in which the agreement enters into

Pakistan
Agreement for sales of agricultural commodities, with minutes. Signed at Islamabad Mar. 25, 1980. Entered into force Mar. 25, 1980.

Poland
Agreement amending the agreement of Jan. 9 and 12, 1978, as amended (TIAS 9064, 9213, 9640), relating to trade in cotton, wool, and manmade fiber textiles and textile products. Effected by exchange of notes at Warsaw Jan. 22 and Mar. 17, 1980. Entered into force Mar. 17, 1980.

Agreement amending the agreement of Jan. 9 and 12, 1978, as amended (TIAS 9064, 9213, 9640), relating to trade in cotton, wool, and manmade fiber textiles and textile products. Effected by exchange of

[Illustration 142]

PAGE FROM TREATY STATUS TABLE—CCH CONGRESSIONAL INDEX

91 10-9-80 **Treaties** **7013**

taxation and provides for administrative cooperation between tax authorities to avoid double taxation and prevent fiscal evasion with respect to taxes on income.

Injunction of secrecy removed, 5/9/79.
In Foreign Relations Committee, 5/9/79.
Reported (Ex. Rept. 96-8), 6/18/79.
Ratified 7/9/79.

Executive Y—Arms Control and Disarmament—SALT II

The Treaty on the Limitation of Strategic Offensive Arms (SALT II) and Protocol were signed at Vienna, Austria on June 18, 1979.

Each Party to SALT II, by the terms of the treaty, undertakes to limit strategic offensive arms quantitatively and qualitatively, to exercise restraint in the development of new types of strategic offensive arms, and to adopt other measures relating to testing, notification and circumvention.

Injunction of secrecy removed, 6/25/79.
In Foreign Relations Committee, 6/25/79.
Reported (Ex. Rept. 96-14), 11/19/79.

Executive Z—Crimes—Sentences—Home Country

The Treaty with the Republic of Panama on the Execution of Penal Sentences, signed at Panama on January 11, 1978, would permit citizens of

After the President has signed a Treaty, it must be ratified by the Senate. This Table lists treaties awaiting ratification by the Senate.

It is arranged by Number of Congress and gives information as to the present status of such pending treaties. Weekly supplements are issued to this Service. Treaties not ratified in one Congress are held over for subsequent Congresses.

of cooperation, such as: (1) executing requests relating to criminal matters, (2) taking testimony; (3) preserving documents; (4) returning objects obtained by offenders; (5) serving documents; (6) effecting appearance before court; (7) locating persons; and (8) providing records and information.

Injunction of secrecy removed, 8/2/79.
In Foreign Relations Committee, 8/2/79.
Reported (Ex. Rept. 96-18), 11/20/79.
Ratified, 11/28/79.

Executive BB—Crimes—Sentences—Home Country

The Treaty between the United States and Turkey on the Enforcement of Penal Judgments would permit citizens of either country to serve their sentences in their home country.

Injunction of secrecy removed, 8/2/79.
In Foreign Relations Committee, 8/2/79.
Reported (Ex. Rept. 96-24), 11/20/79.
Ratified, 11/30/79.

Congressional Index—1979-1980

[Illustration 143]

PAGE FROM SHEPARD'S U.S. CITATIONS—STATUTES VOLUME

UNITED STATES STATUTES AT LARGE (Not in United States Code) **1946**

§ 5 70St116 **Aug.** **Ch. 9** **60 St. 1** 329US 91LE2 67SC1 329US 91LE6 67SC3 329US 91LE6 67SC3 **§ 2** 152FS 70St54 **Aug.** **Ch. 962** **60 St. 1057** Rs70A St1 61St798 **§§ 1** to **20** Rs70A St1 **Aug. 14** **Ch. 963** **60 St. 1062** **§ 1** R74St726 61St214 **Aug. 14** **Ch. 964** **60 St. 1062** 68St526 **§ 2** Subd. a ¶ 3 61St955 Subd. d A61St55 61St694 Subd. f R64St100 **§ 3** Subsec. 44 60St1099 **Aug. 14** **Ch. 966** **60 St. 1082** **Title 1** **§ 11** A61St694	**Aug. 14** 5UST2493 **Aug. 24** **Ch. 210** **60 St. 121** 79St285 **Aug. 30** **61 St. 1236** 64St B33 3UST3922 3UST3927 4UST2058 **Protocol** **Art. 1** Sg1UST626 62St1654 **Art. 2** Sg1UST626 62St1654 3UST3922 3UST3927 **Sept. 6** **61 St. 4121** 2UST460 **Art. 8** 9UST1468 **Schedule 1** Rs9UST [1468 **Schedule 2** Rs9UST [1468 **Sept. 12** **61 St. 2688** E13UST [2266 E14UST359 158FS64 78St1248 13UST408	**Art. 1** 158FS67 [1022 **Art. 11** R14UST [1022 78St1248 **Art. 12** R14UST [1022 78St1248 ¶ 1 158FS64 ¶ 2 158FS64 **Art. 15** ¶ 1 A13UST409 A14UST [1023 **Art. 17** A14UST [1022 78St1248 ¶ 2 13UST410 **Schedule 1** R14UST [1022 78St1248 **Schedule 2** R14UST [1022 78St1248 **Notes** Rp14UST [1022 **Sept. 13** **61 St. 3750** **Art. 3** A62St1889 **Sept. 23** **61 St. 2903** 62St3575	**Sept. 25** [1376 **Sept. 25** **61 St. 3524** Rs2UST [1423 **Sept. 25** **61 St. 3540** Rs2UST [1458 **Sept. 30** **61 St. 2495** A6UST6157 **Art. 2** A6UST6157 ¶ 3 Rn ¶ 4 10UST966 ¶ 3 Ad10UST [966 ¶ 4 Rn ¶ 5 10UST966 **Art. 4** ¶ 2 A10UST969 ¶ 3 Rs10UST [969 ¶ 5 A10UST970 ¶ 8 A10UST963 ¶ 9 Rs10UST [970 ¶ 10 A10UST959 ¶ 14 Ad10UST [961	**Art. 5** A6UST6157 ¶ 4 10UST961 **Oct. 1** **61 St. 1222** 62St1659 **Oct. 7** **61 St. 2398** E3UST351 Sg11UST [1982 6UST3771 15UST2489 **Art. 3** 3UST352 **Art. 9** 6UST3771 **Art. 10** 6UST3771 **Art. 12** 11UST1982 **Art. 14** 11UST1982 **Art. 15** 11UST1982 **Art. 16** 11UST1982 **Art. 17** 11UST1982 **Art. 20** 11UST1982 **Art. 21** 11UST1982 **Art. 22** 11UST1982 **Art. 24** 11UST1982 **Art. 25** 11UST1982 **Art. 29** 11UST1982 **Art. 32** 11UST1982	**Oct. 9** 10UST745 **Art. 11** 10UST745 **Art. 12** 10UST745 **Art. 13** 10UST745 **Art. 14** 10UST745 **Art. 15** 10UST745 **Art. 17** 10UST745 **Art. 18** 10UST745 **Art. 19** 10UST745 **Art. 20** 10UST745 **Art. 21** 10UST745 **Art. 25** 10UST745 **Oct. 18** **64 St. B3** Sg8UST843 **Art. 7** Subd. a A8UST847 **Art. 17** A8UST848 **Protocol** E8UST843 **Art. 1** Subd. 3 A8UST845 **Oct. 23** **61 St. 2876** 13UST1918 **Oct. 25** **61 St. 1044** A61St1073	**Oct. 30** **Annex** ¶ 2 A12UST847 **Nov. 16** **61 St. 2479** 62St3023 **Annex to Air Transport Agreement** **§ B** A62St3023 **Nov. 20** **61 St. 2795** A61St3777 **Dec. 2** **61 St. 2475** E62St3645 Sg1UST540 109FS343 62St2283 62St3600 63St2630 63St2654 64St B84 ¶ 4 A61St3614 ¶ 5 A61St3614 ¶ 6 Sub ¶ e Sg1UST541 ¶ 8 A61St3614 ¶ 12 61St3608 **Dec. 2** **62 St. 1716** 3UST3001	6UST645 8UST69 11UST32 UST1690 **Art. 2** ¶ 2 ST507 ¶ 3 UST953 **Art. 5** ST507 ST2999 ST645 UST331 UST33 UST494 ¶ 1 UST953 ¶ 3 ST509 ST658 UST331 UST33 UST494 13UST497 14UST112 14UST1690 **Art. 7** 8UST70 **Art. 11** 3UST3003 **Schedule** A13UST493 A13UST497 A14UST112 A14UST [1691 A15UST [2547 ¶ 1 Subd. a A11UST32 A14UST [1691 ¶ 2 4UST2184 ¶ 4 A4UST2181 A6UST647 ¶ 4 (6UST645) Cl. 1 A11UST33 Cl. 2 R7UST657 ¶ 5 A4UST2181 Sd7UST657 A8UST2204 A11UST33 A14UST [1691 ¶ 6 A1UST506 A2UST11 A3UST3001 A3UST5094 A4UST2180 A6UST647 ¶ 6 (6UST645) A10UST330 Cl. 1 A13UST498 *Continued*

See note on page 1219 **1645**

After locating a treaty or other agreement, it may be Shepardized to find subsequent amendments, other changes, or court decisions which have cited or interpreted the treaty or agreement.

For treaties or agreements entered into before the publication of the United States Treaties Series, the "Shepardizing" is done under the U.S. Statutes at Large citation.

[Illustration 144]

PAGE FROM SHEPARD'S U.S. CITATIONS—STATUTES VOLUME

UNITED STATES TREATIES AND OTHER INTERNATIONAL AGREEMENTS **Vol. 8**

-597-
11UST388
-609-
13UST288
-617-
A12UST240
¶ 4
A12UST240
-625-
8UST26
8UST77
-637-
8UST279
-657-
8UST680
22UST508
13UST2650
Art. 1
A9UST1416
¶ 1
A9UST1417
Art. 2
A9UST1417
¶ 1
Cl. d
A14UST
[1066
Art. 3
12UST508
¶ 1
A9UST1419
¶ 2
A9UST1419

Art. 3
12UST1045
-721-
E8UST1392
Art. 1
A8UST1392
Art. 2
¶ 1
Cl. c
A9UST1167
-738-
A12UST155
Art. 4
¶ A
A12UST155
Art. 7
A12UST156
-753-
14UST2222
-764-
E10UST25
A10UST
[1383
E11UST
[1455
¶ 6
10UST25
-771-
9UST1264
-773-
R10UST
[1418

¶ 7
Rn¶8
[12UST
[2947
-859-
9UST397
-863-
12UST1195
-866-
A8UST1427
8UST821
-869-
10UST2050
-890-
71St C51
76St1468
77St972
-894-
13UST2178
¶ 3
13UST2178
Annex A
A9UST1334
-899-
11UST2165
Art. 8
11UST2165
-933-
71St C50
76St1468
77St972
Schedule
¶ 907

10UST200
10UST1033
10UST1638
11UST2515
12UST728
-1063-
8UST1069
-1069-
8UST1063
-1073-
8UST1063
8UST1069
-1093-
71St454
10UST1425
14UST1265
14UST1489
Art. 6
¶ A
Cl. 3
A14UST135
Art. 12
10UST87
13UST416
¶ A
Cl. 1
13UST423
14UST1274
¶ C
14UST1269
Art. 14
¶ D
71St454

Art. 14
A10UST
[1818
-1265-
A10UST
[1659
8UST213
8UST1225
Art. 6
13UST1770
¶ A
A10UST
[1659
Art. 8
¶ A
A10UST
[1660
13UST1770
¶ B
A10UST
[1660
¶ C
A10UST
[1660
A13UST
[1770
-1289-
A11UST
[1872
8UST799
9UST1
10UST1049
-1343-

-1421-
8UST869
10UST2049
-1425-
10UST2081
-1427-
8UST821
8UST866
-1431-
8UST367
9UST237
12UST3176
-1435-
A11UST
[1783
A13UST
[1494
A15UST
[2007
-1442-
Sg10UST
[1997
-1445-
A15UST
[1539
-1457-
10UST1182
-1534-
8UST1629
9UST1416
21UST508
-1537-
A13UST

-1633-
A13UST
[1482
-1725-
Sg12UST
[904
-1741-
Sg11UST
[1405
Art. 2
¶ 7
11UST1406
¶ 8
11UST1405
-1757-
15UST167
-1767-
77St971
10UST272
13UST2757
13UST2823
13UST2891
15UST2590
¶ I
13UST2679
¶ L
13UST2606
¶ N
13UST2679
¶ R
13UST2678
¶ W

First Memorandum of Understanding
§ 1
A9UST1355
E10UST159
9UST1003
-1903-
13UST2645
14UST1424
-1937-
10UST2208
-2021-
A15UST289
-2043-
186FS300
46ABA24
Art. 1
186FS320
Art. 5
288F2d375
Art. 6
¶ 2
186FS320
-2205-
Sg9UST967
13UST2068
Art. 1
13UST2070
¶ 1
A9UST305

Treaties and other agreements that are published in the United States Treaties Series may be Shepardized under those citations in this section of Shepard's U.S. Citations.

9UST1379
11UST401
-680-
8UST657
-683-
Sg11UST
[1982
-691-
E10UST22
E11UST210
15UST1523
¶ 6
10UST22
-697-
A10UST
[1233
Art. 2
¶ 1
Cl. a
A10UST
[1233
Cl. b
A10UST
[1233
-715-
A9UST1025
12UST1044
Art. 1
12UST1045

Art. 3
¶ 2
Cl. d
A8UST1289
A11UST
[1872
-821-
8UST866
Art. 1
A8UST866
A8UST1427
-832-
A11UST
[1874
13UST1776
-835-
A12UST
[2947
E14UST
[1178
¶ 4
A9UST1547
¶ 6
Rn¶7
[12UST
[2947
¶ 6
Ad12UST
[2947

[1074
-957-
8UST963
Art. 1
¶ 3
8UST963
Art. 5
11UST2382
-963-
8UST957
-965-
A13UST
[1033
10UST3185
-970-
8UST721
-973-
9UST1444
-979-
9UST131
9UST1073
9UST1075
-993-
A11UST
[2532
A11UST
[2559
9UST1015
9UST1474

Art. 12
¶ C
15UST1459
-1225-
A13UST
[1486
8UST213
Art. 4
¶ 3
A13UST
[1486
Art. 5
A13UST
[1487
Art. 11
A13UST
[1487
-1245-
A10UST
[1815
Art. 4
¶ A
A10UST
[1815
Art. 7
A10UST
[1815

-1363-
15UST2209
-1367-
A13UST
[1812
Art. 6
A13UST
[1812
Art. 8
A13UST
[1813
Art. 10
¶ B
A13UST
[1815
Art. 12
A13UST
[1816
-1386-
12UST1659
-1391-
8UST721
8UST970
-1395-
10UST970
-1410-
14UST337
-1413-
E9UST1146

Cl. e
R13UST
[1878
Cl. f
R13UST
[1878
¶ 10
Cl. b
A13UST
[1878
Cl. d
A13UST
[1878
-1561-
10UST1620
-1567-
9UST1379
-1593-
E10UST
[3026
-1604-
11UST2337
-1626-
12UST718
13UST2598
-1629-
8UST1534
9UST1416
12UST508

13UST879
13UST898
13UST907
13UST1037
13UST1218
13UST1818
13UST2889
¶ Z
Art. 35
11UST1543
-1862-
Sg11UST
[2249
10UST1730
Art. 1
A10UST
[1733
-1869-
14UST1210
-1879-
10UST385
-1885-
A9UST1003
13UST1953
Art. 1
13UST1953
Art. 3
13UST1953

A9UST305
9UST968
9UST1343
-2213-
9UST1113
-2283-
A15UST317
80St1091
Art. 2
¶ 2
RnCl i
[15UST317
Cl. g
Ad15UST
[317
Cl. h
Ad15UST
[317
¶ 3
A15UST317
Art. 3
A15UST318
80St1092
Art. 5
80St1093
¶ 2
Cl. e
A15UST318
Continued

See note on page 1713
1729

SECTION E. UNITED STATES COURT DECISIONS ON INTERNATIONAL LAW

Litigation frequently arises involving the principles and rules of international law, including the effect and interpretations of treaties to which the United States is or was a signatory. These decisions are reported in the standard set of court reports discussed in previous chapters. All cases published in the various sets of the *National Reporter System* have been reprinted in the *American International Law Cases 1793–1978*.[22]

SECTION F. SOURCES OF INTERNATIONAL LAW FOR COUNTRIES OTHER THAN THE UNITED STATES

Most countries have collections of their treaties and indexes to them, but their description is beyond the scope of this book. There are, however, more general works published by international organizations which are useful when searching for information on treaties to which the United States is not a signatory. These are briefly discussed below: [23]

1. Multinational Collections of Treaties [24]

a. *The Consolidated Treaties Series* [25]

This series is a reproduced collection of world treaties in their original languages and existing translations in English or French from the foundation of the modern system of states, 1648, to the date of the commencement of the *League of Nations Treaty Series* (approximately 1918–1920). When completed, this set will be approximately 250 volumes and will be accompanied by volumes containing a chronology listing general treaties, postal treaties, and colonial and like treaties.

This set is now complete in 231 volumes plus one index volume.

[22] Oceana Publications (1971–). Volumes 1–20 (1793–1968) edited by F. Deak with separate index volume. Volumes 21–24 (1968–1978) edited by F. Ruddy.

[23] For a detailed discussion of locating treaties between countries for which the United States is not a signatory, *see* Parry, *Where to Look for Your Treaties*, 8 INT'L.J.LAW LIB. 8 (1980). *See also* A. SPRUDZS, TREATY SOURCES IN LEGAL AND POLITICAL RESEARCH: TOOLS, TECHNIQUES, AND PROBLEMS—THE CONVENTIONAL AND THE NEW (1971).

[24] For difficulties in searching for multilateral treaties, *see* Sprudzs, *Status of Multilateral Treaties—Researcher's Mystery, Mess, or Muddle?*, 66 Am.J.Int'l Law 365 (1972).

[25] C. Parry, ed. (1969–) Oceana Publications.

b. *League of Nations Treaty Series*

This set covers the period of 1920 to 1945, and contains treaties of member and nonmember nations registered with the Secretariat.

c. *United Nations Treaty Series,* 1946 to date

This set contains the text of all treaties registered with the Secretariat by its member states, or filed and recorded by nonmember states or international organizations. Each volume also includes a list of notifications of ratifications, accessions, successions, extensions, denunciations, etc., concerning published treaties. The *Series* is published in accordance with Article 102 of the United Nations Charter. The texts are given in their original language with English and French translated editions. Cumulative Indexes to the *United Nations Treaty Series* are published. Each Cumulative Index covers from 50 to 100 volumes and consists of three sections: (1) chronological index of all treaties; (2) chronological index of multilateral treaties; and (3) alphabetical index by country and subject.[26]

d. United Nations, Office of Legal Affairs, *Multilateral Treaties in Respect of Which the Secretary-General Performs Depository Function*

This is an annual publication started in 1968, which covers all multilateral treaties which have been concluded under the auspices of the United Nations and which have been deposited with the Secretary-General.

A loose-leaf volume (Annex) contains final clauses of the treaties deposited. It serves as a reference bank to the annual volumes.

e. *Keesing's Treaties and Alliances of the World*

This single-volume publication is designed to present the state of affairs with regard to groupings of States and their important treaties with each other, noting treaties in force as of early 1968. It covers several thousand agreements, mainly bilateral, which deal with trade, economic and technical aid, cultural relations and extradition.

f. *Major Peace Treaties of Modern History, 1648–1967*

This is the first comprehensive collection of peace treaties to appear in English. It consists of four volumes and is edited by Fred L. Israel. The official English translations, prepared by the British

[26] The official index to the UNTS is supplemented by *Cumulative List and Index of Treaties and International Agreements Registered and Recorded with the Secretariat of the United Nations, December 1969 to December 1974,* 2 vols. (J. & R. Vanberry, eds. 1977). Oceana Publications. This index contains information not included in the official index. For the difficulties and lacunae in the *League of Nations Treaty Series* and the *United Nations Treaty Series, see* Parry, note 23 *supra,* at 15–16.

Foreign Office, were used whenever available. When such English documents were nonexistent, private translations were used. The first document in the series is the peace treaty of Westphalia, concluded in 1648, and the last document in the set is the peace settlement concluded at Tashkent in 1966 between India and Pakistan through the intercession of the Soviet Union. The treaties are chronologically arranged, with a subject index in volume 4.

g. *Organization of American States Treaty Series* (formerly *Pan American Union Treaty Series*)

The General Secretariat of the Organization of American States is responsible not only for the receipt and custody of the instruments of ratification but also for the preparation and publication of the official texts of the Organization.

Since 1957, these texts, in English and Spanish, have been issued by the General Legal Division as part of its Treaty Series. The Series includes Organization treaties and other significant instruments. Treaty Series No. 1 covers the Charter of the Organization of American States, signed at the Ninth International Conference of American States, March 30–May 2, 1948.

No. 5 is a useful chart, revised at regular intervals, showing the Status of Inter-American Treaties and Conventions.

h. Harvard Law School Library, *Index to Multilateral Treaties (1965 and Supps.)*

This is a chronological list of multi-party, international agreements from the sixteenth century (1596) through 1963, with citations to their text. A subject and regional guide is also provided. The subject analysis does not include specific sections of a treaty; nor is the current status of each treaty given. Supplements were issued for 1964–1966.

i. *International Legal Materials: Current Documents*

This bi-monthly publication of the American Society of International Law is a collection of current official foreign and United States documents relating to international legal affairs. It began publication in 1962. The documents include: (1) current materials that may not become available in more permanent collections until a later date and (2) recent materials that are not readily accessible in any other form in most law libraries.

j. *World Treaty Index* and *Treaty Profiles* [27]

The *Index* is a computerized index in five volumes of the *League of Nations Treaty Series*, the *United Nations Treaty Series*, and over

[27] Edited by P. Rohn (1974) American Bibliographical Center—Clio Press, Santa Barbara, CA. (*Treaty Profiles*, 1976).

6000 other treaties assembled from forty-two national collections from 1920 to 1972 which were not included in these two series. The data base for this index is in machine-readable form and the volumes are printed from it. *Treaty Profiles* is a companion volume with statistical analyses of the treaties in the data base.

Standard information given for each treaty includes: (1) parties; (2) date of signature; (3) topic; (4) citation; and (5) treaty number.

2. Yearbooks of International Law

Many countries now publish annual publications which usually contain articles on international law and international relations, decisions or digests of decisions from both international courts [28] and domestic courts, and other materials relevant to the practice of international law.[29]

SECTION G. INTERNATIONAL LAW: RESEARCH PROCEDURE

Research methodology relating to treaties can be reduced to these steps: (1) identification of a problem as being within the scope of a treaty and whether a treaty covers the problem, (2) if there is a treaty in point, ascertain its present status and (3) elicit interpretations of the treaty. The following procedure encompasses these steps.

Some individuals begin their research by checking a status table immediately to determine both the scope and the status of a treaty. Others start with a descriptive publication, such as *Whiteman's Digest*. Still others commence their research with a treaty collection or an index. The nature of the problem also influences research procedure. To facilitate our explanation of methodology, we will follow a conventional procedure.

1. Determination of the Existence or the Status of an American Treaty

a. *Treaties in Force*

Check the most recent edition of this annual publication for information as to the existence and status of an American treaty.

[28] For information on international courts, *see* items listed in bibliographies cited in Footnote 7 *supra*.

[29] For a complete listing, *see* Stepan & Chapman, *National and Regional Yearbooks: A Brief Survey*, 8 INT'L.J.L.LIB. 19 (1980).

b. *Department of State Bulletin*

The current issues of the *Bulletin* provide information as to recent developments of important pending treaties. This supplements *Treaties in Force.*

2. Location of the Treaty Text

Besides the authoritative lists mentioned above, which cite to the sources below, most of these compilations have their own indexes.

a. *U. S. Treaties and Other International Agreements (UST)*

This is the official source for treaties and agreements entered into since 1949. There is an exhaustive, privately published index. Prior to the publication of this set, the official source for this material was either the *Executive Agreement Series* (1929–1945), the *Treaty Series* (1929–1945) or the *Statutes at Large.*

b. *Treaties and Other International Acts Series*

This is the slip form in which treaties appear prior to their compilation in the UST. They are numbered in a single numerical series. Prior to their appearance in this series, the text of the treaties might be found in the Department of State Bulletin or in the Senate Executive Documents.

c. *Treaties and Other International Agreements of the United States of America 1776–1949*

This 13-volume set, edited by C. Bevans, collects all United States Treaties prior to the initiation of the UST series. Volume 13 is a country-subject index. This set supersedes *Treaties, Conventions, International Acts, Protocols, and Agreements Between the U. S.A. and Other Powers* (Malloy) and *Treaties and Other International Acts of the U. S. A.* (Miller).

The privately published *United States Treaties and Other International Agreements Cumulative Index* covers all of the sets above, as well as citing to the *U. S. Statutes at Large,* the *Executive Agreement Series,* and the *Treaties and Other International Acts Series.*

d. C. Wiktor, *Unperfected Treaties of the United States 1776–1976*

This is the only collection of treaties which never went into force. For more recent and current treaties under consideration consult the *Department of State Bulletin* and the *CIS Congressional Index.*

3. Interpretations of Treaties

Judicial and other interpretations of treaties may be located through the following publications:

a. United States Code Service, FCA ed. Uncodified Laws and Treaties Volume

b. Shepard's United States Citations

c. Shepard's State Citations

d. Wharton's Digest

e. Moore's Digest

f. Hackworth's Digest

g. Whiteman's Digest

h. Digest of the United States Practice in International Law (annual)

i. American International Law Cases, 1793–1978

j. U. S. Supreme Court Digests

4. Treaties by Popular Names

When the popular name of a treaty is known, the following publications provide references from that name to the *Statutes at Large* or *Treaties and Other International Agreements* citation:

a. Malloy's Treaties, Index in vol. 4 (Trenwith).

b. Shepard's Federal Acts and Cases by Popular Names.

5. Foreign Treaties

Treaties between foreign countries may be found in a number of publications. The most exhaustive sources for such materials are the *Consolidated Treaty Series,* the *League of Nations Treaty Series* and the *United Nations Treaty Series.* There may also be specialized collections of treaties such as the *International Tax Treaties of All Nations.*[30] It may also be useful to check the *United Nations List of Treaty Collections* for a list of treaty collections since the 18th Century.

SECTION H. SUMMARY

1. Treaties between the United States and other countries are published in:

a. 1789–1949—*U. S. Statutes at Large*; reprinted in *Treaties and Other International Agreements of the United States,* 1776–1949.

[30] W. Diamond (ed.) Oceana Publications (1975).

b. 1950–date. *United States Treaties and Other International Agreements* (UST); published first in slip format in *Treaties and Other International Acts Series* (T.I.A.S.).

c. Indian treaties, Kappler, *Indian Affairs, Laws and Treaties* (1903–1941, 5 vols.) Indian treaties are compiled in vol. II.

d. Malloy's *Treaties,* 1776–1937.

e. Miller's *Treaties,* 1776–1863.

f. *Treaty Series,* 1908–1944; replaced in 1945 by *Treaties and Other International Acts Series.*

g. *Executive Agreement Series.* 1929–1945; replaced by *Treaties and Other International Acts Series.*

h. *Tax Treaties.* Looseleaf volumes published by the Commerce Clearing House and Prentice-Hall.

2. Indexes to United States Treaties

a. *Treaties in Force.* Issued annually by U. S. Department of State.

b. I. Kavass and M. Michael. *United States Treaties and Other International Agreements Cumulative Index,* 1776–1949.

c. I. Kavass and A. Sprudzs. *UST Cumulative Indexes,* 1950–1979 and supplements.

3. Interpretations of United States Treaties

a. *United States Code Service,* Uncodified Laws and Treaties Volume

b. *Shepard's Citations*

(1) *United States Citations,* for federal cases construing or mentioning the treaties.

(2) *State Citations,* for state cases pertaining to treaties.

c. *Wharton's Digest*

d. *Moore's Digest*

e. *Hackworth's Digest*

f. *Whiteman's Digest*

g. *Digest of United States Practice in International Law.*
An annual digest which started publication in 1973. Serves as a supplement to Whiteman's.

h. *International Legal Materials: Current Documents*

(1) Collection of current official foreign and United States documents relating to international legal affairs, which are otherwise unavailable.

(2) 1962 to date; bi-monthly.

i. *American International Law Cases 1793–1978.* This set collects state and federal cases interpreting U. S. treaties.

4. Status of United States Treaties

a. *CCH Congressional Index: Treaty Section.*

b. *Department of State Bulletin: Treaties Section.*

5. Multinational Collections of Treaties

a. *Consolidated Treaty Series,* 1648–1919

b. *League of Nations Treaty Series,* 1920–1945

c. *United Nations Treaty Series,* 1946–date

6. Latin American Treaty Collections

a. *Pan American Treaty and Law Series,* succeeded by Organization of American States *Treaty Series.*

7. Indexes to Multinational Treaties

a. *United Nations List of Treaty Collections.* 1956.

List of some 700 treaty collections published since the latter part of the 18th century.

b. *World Treaty Index,* 5 vols.

c. Harvard Law School Library, *Index to Multilateral Treaties.* 1965 and Supps.

d. United Nations, Office of Legal Affairs, *Multilateral Treaties in Respect of Which the Secretary-General Performs Depository Function.*

Chapter 21

ENGLISH LEGAL RESEARCH

SECTION A. INTRODUCTION

The development of American law from that of England was discussed in Chapter One. Even today, English cases are cited as persuasive authority in American courts, and English statutes have served as models for many of our important laws. No book on legal research would be complete without at least an introduction to the methods of finding English primary legal sources. Many American law libraries have English law books in their collections and this chapter will present a brief survey of their organization and use.

1. The English Legal System [1]

The United Kingdom of Great Britain and Northern Ireland does not have a single body of law universally applicable within its boundaries. Although there has been a single Parliament since 1707, Scotland has its own distinctive legal system [2] and Northern Ireland has its own Parliament [3] (as well as being represented in the Parliament at Westminster) and its own courts. While a common court of appeals and common opinions on broad issues have resulted in a common identity, differences in legal procedure and practice exist in Scotland and Northern Ireland. Our discussion will be limited to legal materials of England and Wales.

Perhaps the most fundamental difference between English law and the law of the United States is the lack of a written constitution in England. This difference has been described as follows:

> Since Parliament is the supreme lawmaking body in the United Kingdom, Acts of Parliament are absolutely binding

[1] Much of this Section is based on information obtained from U.K. CENTRAL OFFICE OF INFORMATION, REFERENCE PAMPHLET NO. 141, LEGAL SYSTEMS OF BRITAIN (1976).

[2] For a discussion of Scottish law and legal resources, *see id.* at 40–61; *see also* D. WALKER, THE SCOTTISH LEGAL SYSTEM: AN INTRODUCTION TO THE STUDY OF SCOTS LAW (4th ed. rev. 1976).

[3] For an outline of the legal system of Northern Ireland *see* LEGAL SYSTEMS OF BRITAIN, *supra* note 1, at 61–70; for current status, *see* HALSBURY'S LAWS OF ENGLAND, *Northern Ireland* (4th ed.) and latest cumulative supplement.

on all courts, taking precedence over all other sources of law; they cannot be *ultra vires* (outside the competence of —in this case Parliment) for, although the principles of natural justice (broadly speaking, rules which an ordinary, reasonable person would consider fair) have always occupied an important position in the British constitution, they have never been defined or codified in the form of guaranteed rights. Thus rights, such as the right of personal freedom, the right of freedom of discussion, and the rights of association and public meeting, which are commonly considered more or less inviolate, are not protected against change by Act of Parliament, and the courts could not uphold them if Parliament decreed otherwise. Acts of Parliament are, in fact, formal announcements of rules of conduct to be observed in the future, which remain in force until they are repealed. *The courts are not entitled to question or even discuss their validity* (emphasis ours)—being required only to interpret them according to the wording used or, if Parliament has failed to make its intentions clear, according to certain canons of interpretation * * *.[4]

2. Sources of English Law

There is no code of English law. Rather, the law is contained in about 3,000 Acts of Parliament, thousands of statutory instruments (administrative regulations, rules, and orders) and over 300,000 reported cases.

SECTION B. STATUTES

1. Current Statutes

The acts passed each year by Parliament are classified as either private and local or public and general acts and are published annually, in separate sets, by the Public Printer. The public acts have been published since 1831 as *The Public General Acts and Measures* and the final volume each year contains an index and other tables listing the acts alphabetically by title, and chronologically. Other tables show "derivations and destinations" of the Consolidated Acts and the effect of each statute upon earlier measures.

2. Codification of Statutes

There has not been in England an official codification of all the enactments of Parliament that is comparable to the *United States Code*. There is, however, a current interest in codifying particular

[4] LEGAL SYSTEMS OF BRITAIN, *supra* note 1 at 7.

branches of the law, such as the criminal law and the law of landlord and tenant. For this purpose, a Law Reform Commission for England and Wales has been created.[5]

a. *Statutes in Force, Official Revised Edition* [6]

This set is the nearest equivalent to an official codification of English statutory law. It reprints all Acts since 1235 that have not been entirely repealed, and it incorporates all amendments that have added or changed the language of the original Act. The Acts are then published in loose-leaf volumes alphabetically according to the title of the Act. Each Act is in a separate pamphlet which is replaced when repealed or heavily amended.

b. *Halsbury's Statutes of England, 3d ed.*

This privately published set is an encyclopedic compilation of English statutes in force, arranged so that all Acts on the same subject are brought together under one title. A valuable feature of this set is its annotations. These follow each section of an Act and contain brief descriptions of cases citing an Act and other information necessary to the understanding of the Act. Subscribers to the set also receive the following:

(1) *Current Statutes Service,* which is issued five times a year in looseleaf format and prints the text of acts recently passed. A Noter Up is also provided which updates already published materials.

(2) *Continuation Volumes.* These volumes are published annually in bound form and contain the text of the Acts published during the past year and replace the materials from the *Current Statute Service.*

(3) *Cumulative Supplements.* Bound annual volumes are issued which take account of all developments during the year which affect the contents of already published volumes.

The entire set consists of forty main volumes plus the Continuation Volumes, the Cumulative Supplement Volumes, a General Index and Alphabetical and Chronological Lists of Statutes Volumes.

3. Early English Statutes

The early English laws were published in many editions. A few sets are:

a. Statutes of the Realm, 12 vols. 1225–1713.

b. Pickering's Statutes at Large, 109 vols. 1225–1869.

[5] A. KIRALFY, THE ENGLISH LEGAL SYSTEM 94–96 (6th ed. 1978).

[6] This set replaces the *Statutes Revised, 3d ed.* which contained all acts in force through 1948.

c. Chitty's Statutes of Practical Utility, 6th ed., 16 vols. 1235–1910, with supplements to 1948.

4. Acts and Ordinances of the Interregnum, 1642–1660

This is a selected three-volume integration of the laws enacted during the interregnum. Volume 3 includes a Chronological Table of Acts and Ordinances, an Index to Subjects, and an Index of Names, Places, and Things.

5. English Statutes on LEXIS

Researchers who have access to *Lexis* may use this service to research English statutes. *Lexis* has an English library which includes all general statutes and statutory instruments in force as well as certain Inland Revenue and industrial law material.

6. Citation of English Statutes

Prior to 1962, English statutes were cited by name, regnal year (the year of the sovereign's reign in which statute was passed) and chapter. E. g., *National Services Act, 11 & 12 Geo. 6,* c. 64. This method of citation made it necessary to consult a Table to determine the year of passage. As all legal writing on English law prior to 1962 cited to regnal year, a Table of Regnal Years is set forth for convenience.

TABLE OF REGNAL YEARS

Sovereign	Reign Began	Sovereign	Reign Began
William I	Oct. 14, 1066	Mary	July 6, 1553
William II	Sept. 26, 1087	Elizabeth I	Nov. 17, 1558
Henry I	Aug. 5, 1100	James I	Mar. 24, 1603
Stephen	Dec. 26, 1135	Charles I	Mar. 27, 1625
Henry II	Dec. 19, 1154	The Commonwealth	Jan. 30, 1649
Richard I	Sept. 3, 1189	Charles II	May 29, 1660
John	May 27, 1199	James II	Feb. 6, 1685
Henry III	Oct. 28, 1216	William & Mary	Feb. 13, 1689
Edward I	Nov. 20, 1272	Anne	Mar. 8, 1702
Edward II	July 8, 1307	George I	Aug. 1, 1714
Edward III	Jan. 25, 1327	George II	June 11, 1727
Richard II	June 22, 1377	George III	Oct. 25, 1760
Henry IV	Sept. 30, 1399	George IV	Jan. 29, 1820
Henry V	Mar. 21, 1413	William IV	June 26, 1830
Henry VI	Sept. 1, 1422	Victoria	June 20, 1837
Edward IV	Mar. 4, 1461	Edward VII	Jan. 22, 1901
Edward V	Apr. 9, 1483	George V	May 6, 1910
Richard III	June 26, 1483	Edward VIII	Jan. 20, 1936
Henry VII	Aug. 22, 1485	George VI	Dec. 11, 1936
Henry VIII	Apr. 22, 1509	Elizabeth II	Feb. 6, 1952
Edward VI	Jan. 28, 1547		

This method of citation was changed by the Acts of Parliament Numbering and Citation Act, 1962. Under it, citation is to the name of the Act and calendar year. Since 1898, each Act of Parliament has a section indicating the title of the Act under which it is to be cited. E. g., Section 87 of *Highways Acts of 1971* is entitled *Short Titles, Citations, and Commencement and Extent.*

SECTION C. ENGLISH ADMINISTRATIVE LAW

The English equivalent to the rules and regulations that are published in the United States in the *Federal Register* and compiled in the *Code of Federal Regulations* is the *Statutory Instruments* (formerly called *Statutory Rules and Orders*). These are orders, rules, and regulations, known as subordinate or delegated legislation, promulgated by a Minister of the Crown under the authority of a statute. By-laws made by local governmental or other authorities exercising power conferred upon them by Parliament are also included.

1. Publication of Statutory Instruments

a. *The Statutory Rules and Orders and Statutory Instruments Revised, 3d ed.*

This set was published in 1949 as the official English administrative code. It contains administrative rules of general applicability and a permanent nature. It is updated by annual volumes of *Statutory Instruments.*

(1) *Guide to Government Orders.* This biennial publication serves as an index to *Statutory Instruments.* It indicates which statutory instruments are still in force. In addition to its subject index, it has a Table of Statutes which refers readers to the appropriate heading in the subject index.

b. *Halsbury's Statutory Instruments*

This unofficial compilation of statutory instruments of general application, arranged by subject, is published as a companion set to *Halsbury's Statutes of England.* It is kept current by the issuance of replacement volumes and a looseleaf cumulative supplement. It is similar in format to the *Code of Federal Regulations.* It also has a separate, frequently replaced index volume.

SECTION D. COURT REPORTING

1. English Court Organization

Modern organization of English courts began with the *Judicature Act of 1873* and continued with subsequent Parliamentary Acts, the latest being the *Courts Act of 1971*. The present-day court organization is as follows: [7]

a. *House of Lords*

This body, in addition to its legislative function, serves as the supreme court of appeal for the United Kingdom in civil cases and the final court of appeal for criminal cases from England, Wales, and Northern Ireland.

b. *Supreme Court of Judicature*

This court is divided into two parts: the Court of Appeals and the High Court of Justice.

(1) Court of Appeals. This court has two divisions: civil and criminal. It hears appeals from the High Court and certain other inferior courts.

(2) High Court. This court [8] now consists of three divisions: the Queen's Bench Division (including the Admiralty Court and Commercial Court), the Chancery Division, and the Family Division. In practice, each division acts as a separate court.

c. *Crown Court*

This court was created by the *Courts Act of 1971*. It is a criminal court with unlimited jurisdiction. It assumes jurisdiction of all criminal cases above the Magistrates' Courts and appellate jurisdiction of the Quarter Session courts which have now been abolished.

d. *County Courts*

These have limited first instance civil jurisdiction.

e. *Local and Special Courts*

These are mainly Magistrates' Courts and courts of special jurisdiction such as the Restrictive Trade Practices Court and the Industrial Relations Court.

[7] For a more detailed description and history of English courts, *see* R. JACKSON, THE MACHINERY OF JUSTICE IN ENGLAND, 24–106 (7th ed. 1977).

[8] Previous to the enactment of the *Courts Act of 1971*, the High Court consisted of (1) Queen's Bench Division, (2) Probate, Divorce, and Admiralty Division, and (3) the Chancery Division.

2. Development of English Court Reports

The history of court reporting in England is long and confusing.[9] For our purposes, we can divide the reporting of English cases into three periods.

a. *The Year Books. 1272–1535*

The Year Books are the first available law reports with the original text in "Law French." Their purpose and function are still disputed by legal historians. Other than the fact that they are the sources of modern law reporting, they serve little purpose in most legal research today other than for the study of legal history.

b. *Private Names Reporters. 1535–1865*

During this period there was no officially recognized system of court reporting. Any barrister could publish court reports and several hundred different sets were published with many covering the same period of time and the same courts with varying accuracy. It has been customary to refer to these reports by the names of the reporters.

(1) *English Reports, Full Reprint.* This is a reprint of all English cases from 1220 to 1865. When there were competing sets of the reports, the editors included only the one they deemed most accurate. There are 176 volumes in this set, including a two-volume Table of Cases, and a chart which lists all of the named reports with reference to their location in the *Full Reprint.* Most law libraries have only this set, rather than the original reports.

(2) *The Revised Reports.* The *Revised Reports* are in 149 volumes and cover the period 1785–1865. Although this set largely duplicates the *English Reports, Full Reprint,* its value lies in the fact that the reports were edited by the distinguished legal historian, Sir Frederick Pollock.

c. *The Incorporated Council of Law Reporting. 1865–*

In 1865 the Incorporated Council of Law Reporting for England and Wales was formed. While not an official body, it has quasi-official status. In 1865 the Council started publication of the *Law Reports,* and this is the preferred set of reports.

3. Current Law Reports

As previously mentioned, cases reported before 1865 may be found in the *English Reports, Full Reprint* or *The Revised Reports.* Since 1865 the English cases are found in the following sets:

[9] For detailed treatment of the development of English court reporting, *see* R. WALKER and M. WALKER, THE ENGLISH LEGAL SYSTEM, 131–137 (2d ed. 1970).

a. The *Law Reports.*

This set reports decisions since 1865 and is selective in its reporting, covering decisions of permanent significance of the Court of Appeals and High Court. In addition to the opinions of the judges, it also includes the legal argument presented to the court. Although originally published in eleven different series, the *Law Reports* are now published in four series: (1) Appeal Cases (includes both cases from the Court of Appeals and the House of Lords), (2) Queen's Bench, (3) Chancery, and (4) Family Division.

b. *Weekly Law Reports*

This set is also published by the Incorporated Council of Law Reporting and includes most cases that will ultimately be published in the *Law Reports.*

It also publishes cases not intended for publication in the *Law Reports.* These appear in the first of the three volumes published each year.

c. *Other Sets of Reports*

Although the Incorporated Council of Law Reporting assumed responsibility for systematizing court reporting, there is no prohibition of private reporting and many such sets were published. Most have now ceased publication.[10] The most important of the private reports is the *All England Law Reports.* This set began in 1936, incorporating the *Law Journal Reports* and the *Times Law Reports.* It includes the decisions of the House of Lords, the Court of Appeals, the High Court, and courts of special jurisdiction. The opinions are released in advance sheets and then in bound volumes.

d. *All England Law Reports Reprint*

This set covers selected cases from 1558–1935 and is reprinted from the *Law Journal Reports* in thirty-six volumes plus an index.

e. *English Cases on Lexis*

Researchers who have access to *Lexis* may use this service to research English case law. *Lexis* supplies a library of English cases back to 1945, including all cases from the *All England Law Reports,* the *Law Reports,* and *Lloyds Reports,* as well as certain tax reporters.

[10] *Id.*

SECTION E. DIGESTS AND ENCYCLOPEDIAS

1. Digests

a. *The English and Empire Digest*

This is a comprehensive digest of English cases reported from the earliest times to date, and is in fifty-six volumes. It also includes cases from the courts of Scotland, Ireland, Canada, and other countries of the British Commonwealth and South Africa. Obsolete cases and cases of only historical interest are excluded from the publication. The *Digest* is arranged topically and has a detailed outline at the beginning of each major subject and an index at the end of each volume. Cases on a particular aspect of a general topic are grouped in chronological order and assigned case numbers.

The English and Empire Digest is an annotated digest which embodies the citator feature. Each case digest is followed by notes of subsequent cases, if any, showing whether the digested case has been approved, followed, distinguished, overruled or otherwise mentioned. Under each section or subsection of the digest, cross references and references to pertinent statutes and to *Halsbury's Laws* (an encyclopedia) are given. Volumes 52 through 54 contain a Consolidated Table of Cases, and volumes 55 through 56 comprise a Consolidated Index. The digest is updated with replacement volumes, multi-year continuation volumes, and annual cumulative supplements.

2. Encyclopedias

The standard English encyclopedia for both statutory and case law is *Halsbury's Laws of England.* The first volume of the fourth edition was issued in 1972 and until all volumes have been issued it may be necessary to also consult the third edition. This set should not be confused with *Halsbury's Statutes of England,* a previously described code.

Halsbury's Laws of England is alphabetically arranged by topic. Each topic is subdivided into parts, sections, subsections and paragraphs with appropriate footnote references to cases, statutes, statutory rules and orders or statutory instruments. *Halsbury's Laws* places great emphasis on statutory law and, unlike its American counterparts, has a Consolidated Table of Cases. This table contains references to the *English and Empire Digest,* indicating where a case is digested in that set.

There is a two-volume index to the third edition and a temporary index is periodically issued for the completed volumes of the fourth edition.

Both editions are kept current by monthly releases filed in a looseleaf volume.

3. Current Law: Being a Complete Statement of All the Law from Every Source

This set began publication in 1947 and provides a digest of all phases of English law. It is arranged topically and, under each topic, digests cases, statutes, and statutory instruments. It consists of the following:

a. *Current Law*

A monthly pamphlet advance sheet service.

b. *Current Law Year Book*

An annual cumulation which includes, among other information, a cumulative subject index, table of cases, tables of statutory instruments and instruments affected, and digests of unreported cases.

c. *Master Volume*

The *Current Law Year Books* were consolidated into a 1947–51 volume; since then, every fifth year, a five-year cumulative Year Book called the *Master Volume* is issued.

d. *Current Law Citators*

These will be discussed in the section on citators. *Current Law* is also available in a Scottish edition.

SECTION F. CITATORS

There is no service precisely similar to *Shepard's Citations* for England. There are, however, several methods of obtaining later citations, or, as the British express it, "noting up" cases or statutes.

1. Statutes

Citators for statutes are arranged chronologically. For a particular statute, citations are given for each subsequent statute which amends or repeals the cited statute, and for each case which cites the statute. Citators for statutes are contained in:

a. *Current Law Statute Citator*

b. *All England Law Reports*

c. *Halsbury's Statutes of England*

2. Cases

a. *English and Empire Digest*

Each case in this set is assigned a case number. After the digest of the case, citations are given to all subsequent decisions which cited the digest case. After consulting a case in the main volume, later cases citing the digested case can be found by checking the case number in the latest cumulative supplement.

b. *All England Law Reports*

Both the Consolidated Index and the supplementary Index and Noter-Up volume contain a Table of Cases Judicially Considered. All cases reported since 1936 are listed alphabetically. Under each case name, citations are given to all subsequent cases which construed the cited case.

c. *Current Law Citator*

These volumes contain a Case Citator which lists cases alphabetically by name. Subsequent cases citing and statutes affecting the original case appear beneath each case name entry. It is kept up to date by periodic supplements.

3. Authority of English Cases

Until 1966, the House of Lords regarded itself as strictly bound by its earlier decisions. Once the House of Lords had rendered an opinion the rules enunciated in it could only be changed by an Act of Parliament. In 1966 the House of Lords stated that in the future they proposed to depart from their own decisions where it appeared proper to do so.[11]

SECTION G. HOW TO FIND ENGLISH STATUTES AND CASES

1. Statutes

a. *Chronological Table of the Statutes* and *Index to the Statutes in Force*

This two-volume set is issued annually and serves as the index to the *Statutes Revised, Statutes in Force,* and *The Public General Acts and Measures.* Volume 1 contains a chronological table of all *Public General Acts* since 1235 with references to amendments and repeals. Volume 2 is a subject index to statutes in force.

b. *Halsbury's Statutes of England*

This set is now in its third edition. It is kept up to date by annual supplement volumes and a looseleaf volume for current statutes. This set is annotated and also contains references to *Halsbury's Laws of England.* It is comparable to the *United States Code Annotated* or the *United States Code Service.*

[11] [1966] 3 All E.R. 77.

2. Cases

a. *English and Empire Digest*

This is the most comprehensive English case digest. The following steps are involved in its use:

(1) Consult index volumes for topic under investigation. This will refer to volume and *case number* in main set.

(2) Consult continuation volumes for later cases.

(3) Consult *Cumulative Supplement* for later citations of cases found through (1) and (2).

Citations are given to all sets of court reports in which a case is reported. Frequently, English legal writing gives only one citation for a case. When that set is not available in the law library being used, check the *Consolidated Table of Cases* in the *English and Empire Digest* to locate other citations to the case.

b. *All England Law Reports*

There is a *Consolidated Table and Index* which includes a detailed subject index and a Table of Cases Reported and Considered. Frequent supplements are issued.

c. *Current Law Year Book*

Use *Master Year Book* volumes and then subsequent annual volumes. Citations are given to the location of case digests in the *Year Book.*

3. Secondary Sources

It should be mentioned that it is frequently easier in starting research for English law to commence the search, as described in the previous chapters on American law, with secondary sources. These include:

a. *Halsbury's Laws of England*

b. English treatises

c. English legal periodicals. The major ones are included in the *Current Index to Commonwealth Legal Periodicals, Current Law Index,* and the *Legal Resource Index.*

SECTION H. WORDS AND PHRASES

A number of the English publications include definitions of words and phrases. They are discussed in the preceding sections. In addition, several sources exclusively treat words and phrases.

1. Stroud's Judicial Dictionary, 4th ed., 1971–1974

This five-volume publication includes not only definitions but also references to cases and statutes from which they are derived. It is kept current by supplementation.

2. Words and Phrases Legally Defined, 2d ed., 1969–1970

A revision of Burrow's *Words and Phrases Judicially Defined,* this five-volume work has been expanded to include textbook and statutory as well as judicial definitions. A cumulative supplement is published annually.

SECTION I. ENGLAND AND THE EUROPEAN COMMUNITIES

On January 1, 1973, the United Kingdom became part of the European Communities. As a result, Community law in the form of treaty provisions and secondary legislation became part of English law. Moreover, it became necessary for England to change many aspects of its law to comply with its membership in the European Communities.

Researchers in English law are now faced with the problem of determining when Community law is applicable and of the possible conflict of English law with Community law.[12] To facilitate the location of relevant Community law, *Halsbury's Statutes of England* has published in volume 42A, the *European Continuations, Volume 1, 1952–72,* which includes either full text or digests, with annotations, of all European Communities legislation through 1972 with amendments "noted up" through January 1, 1974. Supplements to this volume will contain later legislation. It is arranged by topic according to the titles used in the main set. By this means it is fairly simple to ascertain which aspects of English law have been affected by Community law.

SECTION J. ILLUSTRATIONS

STATUTES

Problem: Find English statute dealing with a landlord's tort liability to visitors.

[12] For an explanation of the relationship of English law to the law of the European Communities, *see* L. COLLINS, EUROPEAN COMMUNITY LAW IN THE UNITED KINGDOM (1975), GREAT BRITAIN, CENTRAL OFFICE OF INFORMATION, REFERENCE DIVISION, BRITAIN AND THE EUROPEAN COMMUNITY (Reference Pamphlet No. 137, 1976).

Illustrations

145. Page from Annual Index to the Statutes

146. Page from Halsbury's Statutes of England, 3d ed.

CASES

Problem: Find English cases dealing with liability of owners for animals straying onto highways.

Illustrations

147. Page from English and Empire Digest

148. Page from Subject Index: All England Law Reports

149. Page from Halsbury's Laws of England, 3d ed.

CITATORS

150. Page from Current Law Statute Citator

151. Page from Consolidated Tables and Index: 1936–1976: All England Law Reports

[Illustration 145]

PAGE FROM ANNUAL INDEX TO THE STATUTES

1476 INDEX TO THE STATUTES

OATH *cont.*

3 General *cont.*

Parties, witnesses, etc., oath of—*cont.*

substitution of affirmation—
in certain cases (for false declaration *see* PERJURY, E&W; PERJURY, S): 1888 c.46 s.1
1961 c.21

in case of persons who are or have been Quakers or Moravians: S 1828 c.29 s.13
1833 c.49
1838 c.77

Commrs. for oaths, execution of dealings in Govt. stock before *See* NATIONAL DEBT, 1*(f)*
Perjury, trial and punishment of *See* PERJURY, E&W: PERJURY, S
Pope, no oath to be taken to *See* ROME, SEE OF
Matters relating to Supreme Court, NI, how far 'reserved matters' *See* SUPREME COURT
Universities, no oath for matriculation, exhibition, scholarship, or degree in *See* UNIVERSITY, E&W, 1,2
Universities, certain oaths at, illegal *See* UNIVERSITY, E&W, 1,2
See also AFFIDAVIT: AFFIDAVIT, S: AFFIDAVIT, NI: DECLARATION: ECCLESIASTICAL JURISDICTION: NOTARY PUBLIC: NOTARY PUBLIC, S: SWEARING

FINDING ENGLISH STATUTES

This volume, issued annually, indexes all English statutes in force. This illustration shows how a statute dealing with a landlord's liability may be located. This citation could also be found in the other sources listed at Section B of this chapter. For text of Act, see next illustration.

OATS Guaranteed prices *See* AGRICULTURAL MARKETING, 5 *See also* CEREALS

OBSCENE PUBLICATION *See* INDECENCY *See also* POST OFFICE, 2

OBSERVATORIES, protection of *See* ELECTRICITY, 4

OBSTETRICIAN

Royal College of Obstetricians and Gynaecologists, representation of, on General Medical Council *See* Medical Act 1956 c.76 s.3(1)

OCCASIONAL LICENCES *See* CUSTOMS AND EXCISE, 5*(j)*,6*(f)*: Licensing, E&W, 12: Licensing, S, 2*(i)*: TOWN GOVT., S, 2*(p)*

OCCUPATIONAL THERAPISTS Regulation of *See* MEDICAL PROFESSION, 8

→**OCCUPIERS' AND LANDLORDS' LIABILITY**

1957 c.31 Occupiers' Liability 1960 c.30 Occupiers' Liability (S)

In England—
tort, liability in—
→common law rules, variation of: 1957 c.31 s.1(1)(2)
application of principles to visitors, etc., to vessels, vehicles, aircraft, etc.: 1957 c.31 s.1(3)*(a)*

extension so as to include damage to property: 1957 c.31 s.1(3)*(b)*

[Illustration 146]

PAGE FROM HALSBURY'S STATUTES OF ENGLAND, 3d ED., VOL. 23

The reference in the previous Illustration was to the Occupiers' Liability Act 1957. This is a page from the act from Vol. 23 of Halsbury's Statutes of England, 3d ed. The same text can also be located in the 1957 volume of The Public General Acts and Measures, but it will not be annotated.

NOTES

Sub-s. (1): Occupier; visitors. As to the persons who are to be treated as an occupier and his visitors, see s. 1 (2), *ante*. With regard to damage to property, see s. 1 (3) (*b*), *ante*.

Premises. As to fixed and moveable structures, see s. 1 (3) (*a*), *ante*.

Bound by contract. With regard to tenancies, note sub-s. (4) of this section.

Duty of care which he owes to them as his visitors. The duty of care which an occupier owes to persons whom he is bound by contract (or under the terms of a tenancy) to permit to enter, but who are strangers to the contract, is now (subject to the provisions of this section) the common duty of care, as defined by s. 2 (2), *ante*; see s. 2 (1), *ante*.

Previously, where a person contracted with the occupier for the use of premises on the footing that he was to be entitled under the contract to permit third persons to use them, it appears that the duty owed by the occupier to such third persons in regard to the safety of the premises was the same as that which he owed to the other party to the contract; see *Fosbroke-Hobbes* v. *Airwork, Ltd.*, [1937] 1 All E.R. 108, at p. 112. In cases where the landlord of premises retained under his control the means of access to the premises when let, a lodger or customer of the tenant was merely a licensee *vis-à-vis* the landlord (*Fairman* v. *Perpetual Investment Building Society*, [1923] A.C. 74, H.L.; *Jacobs* v. *London County Council*, [1950] A.C. 361; [1950] 1 All E.R. 737, H.L.), and the standard of care required was limited accordingly.

Sub-s. (4): Statutory tenancy. *E.g.*, a tenancy under which the tenant retains possession by virtue of the Rent Act 1968. As to the terms and conditions governing such a statutory tenancy, see ss. 12–15, 18 (2) of that Act, Vol. 18, pp. 803–806, 808.

Sub-s. (5): Common duty of care. For meaning, see s. 2 (2), *ante*; see also s. 2 (3)–(5), *ante*.

Commencement of this Act. *I.e.*, 1st January 1958; see s. 8 (3), *post*.

---

4. Landlord's liability in virtue of obligation to repair

(1) Where premises are occupied by any person under a tenancy which puts on the landlord an obligation to that person for the maintenance or repair of the premises, the landlord shall owe to all persons who or whose goods may from time to time be lawfully on the premises the same duty, in respect of dangers arising from any default by him in carrying out that obligation, as if he were an occupier of the premises and those persons or their goods were there by his invitation or permission (but without any contract).

(2) Where premises are occupied under a sub-tenancy, the foregoing subsection shall apply to any landlord of the premises (whether the immediate or a superior landlord) on whom an obligation to the occupier for the maintenance or repair of the premises is put by the sub-tenancy, and for that purpose any obligation to the occupier which the sub-tenancy puts on a mesne landlord of the premises, or is treated by virtue of this provision as putting on a mesne landlord, shall be treated as put by it also on any landlord on whom the mesne landlord's tenancy puts the like obligation towards the mesne landlord.

(3) For the purposes of this section, where premises comprised in a tenancy (whether occupied under that tenancy or under a sub-tenancy) are put to a use not permitted by the tenancy, and the landlord of whom they are held under the tenancy is not debarred by his acquiescence or otherwise from

[Illustration 147]

PAGE FROM ENGLISH AND EMPIRE DIGEST

380 VOL. 2—ANIMALS : PART II

Sect. 2. *Liabilities : Sub-sect.* 1, cont.]

& had caused the accident to pltf., afforded evidence of negligence, & it was for deft. to displace this evidence by showing that the gate was not left open by any negligence on his part or on that of his

D. C.) the tendencies of sheep as found by the cty. ct. judge were not a vicious or mischievous propensity within the decided cases.—HEATH'S GARAGE, LTD. *v.* HODGES, [1916] 2 K. B. 370 ; 85 L. J. K. B. 1289 ; 115 L. T. 129 ; 80 J. P. 231 ; 32 T. L. R. 570 ; 60 Sol. Jo. 554 ; 14 L. G. R. 911,

FINDING ENGLISH CASES: ENGLISH AND EMPIRE DIGEST

Step 1 (not shown). Check Index Volume under appropriate headings. This will give citation to volume, page and case number.

Step 2. Examine volume referred to by index. The number 2146 is not a "key" number but the number assigned to this case in this digest.

Step 3 (not shown). Check case number in Continuation Volumes and Cumulative Supplement for additional annotations.

Wallbank, [1947] 1 All E. R. 12; Wright *v.* Callwood (1950), 66 (pt. 2) T. L. R. 72; Gomberg *v.* Smith, [1962] 1 All E. R. 725.

2144. Sheep—Defective fence—Natural propensity.]—An owner or occupier of land adjoining **an ordinary highway** (*i.e.*, **putting aside cases where, either by a local Inclosure Act, or by prescription, or otherwise, a duty to fence is imposed) is not bound to fence so as to prevent harmless animals like sheep straying upon the highway.**

While pltfs.' motor car was being driven along a highway in the daylight at the rate of 16–20 m.p.h. the driver saw in front of him on the road a number of sheep untended; he put on his brakes & almost immediately thereafter two sheep, which had apparently been left behind by the others, jumped from the bank on the near side, & one of them ran in the front of the car & broke part of the steering gear, in consequence of which the driver lost control, & the car ran into the bank & was damaged. The sheep were the property of deft., who was

Note how annotations are given to where case is reported in different sets of court reports.

Note also how annotations are given to cases citing the digested case. This is one way of "Shepardizing" English cases.

on a nuisance to the highway, it was no breach of duty by deft. not to keep his sheep from straying on to the highway ; (2) an animal like a sheep, by nature harmless, could not fairly be regarded as likely to collide with a motor car, & deft. could not be held liable on that footing ; (3) (AVORY, J. in

go. In either case the owner is liable for the conduct of the animal if he puts it in a position in which it is likely to cause damage to persons lawfully using the highway.—DEEN *v.* DAVIES, [1935] 2 K. B. 282 ; [1935] All E. R. Rep. 9 ; 104 L. J. K. B. 540 ; 153 L. T. 90 ; 51 T. L. R. 398 ; 79 Sol. Jo. 381, C. A.

Annotations:—**Consd.** Aldham *v.* United Dairies (London), Ltd., [1940] 1 K. B. 507. **Folld.** Gomberg *v.* Smith, [1962] 1 All E. R. 725. **Refd.** Lathall *v.* Joyce & Son, [1939] 3 All E. R. 854 ; Toogood *v.* Wright, [1940] 2 All E. R. 306 ; Brackenborough *v.* Spalding U.D.C., [1942] A. C. 310 ; Searle *v.* Wallbank, [1947] 1 All E. R. 12 ; Wright *v.* Callwood (1950), 66 (pt. 2) T. L. R. 72 ; Wormald *v.* Cole, [1954] 1 All E. R. 683 ; Ellis *v.* Johnstone, [1963] 1 All E. R. 286 ; Fitzgerald *v.* E. D. & A. D. Cooke Bourne (Farms), Ltd., [1963] 3 All E. R. 36 ; Bativala *v.* West (trading as Westways Riding Academy), [1970] 1 All E. R. 332.

2146. Duty of adjoining owner to fence.]—The owner of a field abutting on the highway is under no *prima facie* legal **obligation to users of the highway so to keep & maintain his hedges & gates along the highway as to prevent his animals from straying on to it nor is he under any duty as between himself & users of the highway to take reasonable care to prevent any of his animals, not known to be dangerous, from straying on to the highway.—SEARLE *v.* WALLBANK, [1947] 1 All E. R. 12 ; [1947] A. C. 341 ; [1947] L. J. R. 258 ; 176 L. T. 104 ; 63 T. L. R. 24 ; 91 Sol. Jo. 83, H. L.**

Annotations:—**Consd.** Wright *v.* Callwood (1950), 66 (pt. 2), T. L. R. 72. **Apld.** Brock *v.* Richards, [1951] 1 K. B. 529. **Consd.** Wormald *v.* Cole, [1954] 1 All E. R. 683 ; Gomberg *v.* Smith, [1962] 1 All E. R. 725. Ellis *v.* Johnstone, [1963] 1 All E. R. 286. Fitzgerald *v.* E. D. & A. D. Cooke Bourne (Farms), Ltd., [1963] 3 All E. R. 36 ; Bativala *v.* West (trading as Westways Riding Academy), [1970] 1 All E. R. 332 ; Draper *v.* Hodder, [1972] 2 All E. R. 210. **Refd.** Davies *v.* Davies, [1974] 3 All E. R. 817.

2147. ——.]—It must be taken as clearly established by authority that there is no obligation **on the owner or occupier of a field adjacent to a highway to maintain a fence on the border of the highway. The law is founded upon ancient social conditions & is in no way related to, or liable to be qualified by, such matters as the relative levels of field & highway, the nature of the highway or the**

[Illustration 148]

PAGE FROM SUBJECT INDEX: ALL ENGLAND LAW REPORTS

SUBJECT INDEX 53

ANIMAL (cont)
Dog (cont)—
Offence—
Suffering unmuzzled ferocious dog to be at large in a thoroughfare—Passer-by bitten by greyhound on lead—Whether greyhound 'at large'—Metropolitan Police Act 1839, s 54(2). **Ross v Evans** [1959] **2** 222, QBD.
Order for destruction of dangerous dog. *See* Dog—Dangerous dog—Order—Destruction, *ante*.
Right to kill—
Dog chasing cattle or sheep. *See* Dog—Chasing cattle or sheep—Right to kill, *ante*.
Domestic animal—
Animal not known in wild state—
Camel—Onus of proof of vicious propensity—Functions of judge and jury. **McQuaker v Goddard** [1940] **1** 471, CA.
Negligence—
Liability of owner or keeper. *See* Negligence—Domestic animal—Liability of owner or keeper, *post*.
Gift for animal—
Charitable purpose. *See* **Charity** (Benefit to community—Animals).
Highway—
Straying animals—
Negligence. *See* Negligence—Highway—Animal straying on to highway, *post*.
Offence. *See* **Highway** (Straying animals—Offence).
Horse—
Safe system of working—
Unmanageable horse. *See* **Safe system of working** (Reasonable care not to expose employee to unnecessary risk—Servant provided with unmanageable horse).
Maintenance of animals—
Lien for cost of maintenance. *See* **Lien** (Maintenance of animals).
→ Negligence—
Domestic animal—
Liability of owner or keeper—Liability for damage caused by animal—Owner bringing dog on to highway—Dog not under control—Collision with van—Negligence of owner. **Gomberg v Smith** [1962] **1** 725, CA.
Liability of owner or keeper—Liability in negligence for personal injuries caused by animal—Bull—Bull of known fierce disposition—Attack on owner's employee—Duty of owner. **Rands v McNeil** [1954] **3** 593, CA.
Liability of owner or keeper—Liability in negligence for personal injuries caused by animal—Bullock—Ordinary consequences of negligence—Scienter—Bullock being unloaded from lorry escaping on to highway—Deliberate attack on human being. **Lathall v A Joyce & Son** [1939] **3** 854, KBD.
Liability of owner or keeper—Liability in negligence for personal injuries caused by animal—Dog—Dog loose in street with long lead trailing—Pedestrian thrown—Negligence of owner. **Pitcher v Martin** [1937] **3** 918, KBD.

FINDING ENGLISH CASES: ALL ENGLAND LAW REPORTS

This set may be used for finding cases reported after 1935. Note the digest of the Searle v. Wallbank case below. This Index only gives citations to the All England Reports, unlike the English and Empire Digest. Its digests are also very brief compared to the latter.

party having right to place animals on common land—Whether third party liable for damage—Animals Act 1971, s 8(2). **Davies v Davies** [1974] **3** 817, CA.
Animal straying on to highway—Domestic animal—Liability of owner or keeper—Dog dashing across highway from owner's adjoining house on to common—Entrance to highway from house concealed—Nearby bend in highway—Owner knowing dog's propensity to cross highway unaccompanied—Collision with passing car—Driver of car driving carefully—Whether special circumstances—Whether owner of dog liable to driver of car. **Ellis v Johnstone** [1963] **1** 286, CA.
→ Animal straying on to highway—Domestic animal—Liability of owner or keeper—Horse escaping through gap in fence of field adjoining highway—Collision with cyclist—Duty so to maintain gates and fences that escape of animals impossible—Duty to take reasonable care to prevent escape. **Searle v Wallbank** [1947] **1** 12, HL.

[Illustration 149]

PAGE FROM HALSBURY'S LAWS OF ENGLAND, 3d ED.

1 *Dewell v Sanders* (1618) Cro Jac 490, where it was said that a dovecot is not a common nuisance, but that the court may take cognisance of it. Dicta in that case concerning a landowner's right to kill pigeons coming on his land were criticised and the accuracy of the report of the case was

2

3 ...ark ...ver

FINDING ENGLISH CASES: HALSBURY'S LAWS OF ENGLAND.

This set gives a textual treatment of the law and footnote citations to cases and statutes.

As it covers both cases and statutes, and has a good index, it is usually best to start the research for English law in this set. A loose-leaf volume keeps the set up-to-date and should always be consulted.

431 bri... of ... the ...

... on ... doi... hig... it, has been abolished by statute, and accordingly the ordinary principles of negligence now apply to such a situation[3].

Where damage is caused by animals straying from unfenced land on to a highway the person who placed them on the land is not to be regarded as being negligent in so doing if the land is either common land[4], or is situated in an area where fencing is not customary[5], or is a town or village green[6], and if he had a right to place them where he did[7].

Where animals are brought on to a highway a different principle applies[8].

If any horse[9], cattle, sheep, goats or swine are found straying or lying[10] on or at the side of any highway[11], except on such part of it as passes over any common or waste or uninclosed ground[12], the keeper of the animals[13] is liable to a penalty not exceeding 25p for each animal, or £20 in all for a first offence or £50 for a subsequent offence[14], together with the reasonable expenses, recoverable summarily as a civil debt, of removing the animals to his premises or the common pound or other place provided, and any proper charges of the pound-keeper[15]. This provision does not prejudice or affect any right of pasture which may exist on the side of a highway[16], but a keeper exercising his right must keep his animals from straying, except temporarily, or lying on the actual road[17]. These penalties are provided for the protection of the public, and do not render the keeper liable to an action at law[18]. The release, without lawful authority or excuse, of any animal so impounded or seized for the purpose of being so impounded, or the damaging of any place where it is impounded, is an offence punishable by a fine not exceeding £20[19].

Cattle[20] found at large in any street[21] in a district to which the Town Police Clauses Act 1847[22] applies, without any person having charge of them, may be impounded, by any constable or resident, in any common pound within the district[23] or in such other place as the local authority may appoint for the purpose; and may be detained until the owner pays the authority a penalty not exceeding £2 and the reasonable expenses of impounding and keeping them[24]. Provision is made for the sale of impounded cattle if the money is not paid within three days[25], and for punishing persons guilty of pound-breach[26].

1 *Stevens v Whistler* (1809) 11 East 51; *Cox v Burbidge* (1863) 13 CBNS 430 at 435, per Erle CJ; *Higgins v Searle* (1909) 100 LT 280, CA, per Cozens-Hardy MR and Buckley LJ; *Heath's Garage Ltd v Hodges* [1916] 2 KB 370 at 377, CA, per Cozens-Hardy MR. See also *Durrant v Child* (1611)

[Illustration 150]

PAGE FROM CURRENT LAW STATUTE CITATOR

1957 STATUTE CITATOR 1972–79

CAP.

5 & 6 Eliz. 2 (1957)—cont.

20. House of Commons Disqualification Act 1957.
repealed: 1975,c.24,sch.3; c.25,sch.3; c.26,sch.3.

21. Cinematograph Films Act 1957.
s. 1, amended: 1975,c.73,s.1.
s. 2, regs. 73/728; 75/1885; 77/1330; 78/1092; amended: orders 75/1884; 79/395.
s. 4, amended: 1979,c.2,sch.4.
s. 17, amended: 1974,c.22,sch.,pt.XI.
sch., amended: 1972,c.11,sch.8.

25. Rent Act 1957.
s. 16, repealed: 1977,c.43,sch.3; regs. 75/219(

26. National
repealed:

27. Solicitors
repealed:
s. 18, s
Watson
ss. 18,
Court
sham,
s. 20, s
3 All E
[1976]
E.R. 6
Stipend
(1977)
s. 23, s
Watson
s. 56, rul
Hailsha
S.J. 58
s. 60, see
Eastwo
[1973]
s. 64, see
& Co.

28. Dentists A...
s. 2, amended: order 79/289.
ss. 10, 17, amended: 1973,c.31,s.1.
s. 25, see *Peter Ziderman* v. *General Dental Council* [1976] 1 W.L.R. 330, P.C.; *McEniff* v. *General Dental Council, The Times*, December 1, 1979, P.C.
s. 32, amended: 1972,c.71,sch.6; repealed in pt.: order 74/2143.
ss. 36, 42, 43, 50, sch. 1, amended: 1973, c.32,schs.4,5.
ss. 34, 35, 37, amended: 1977,c.45,ss.15, 30,sch.1.
s. 41, regs. 74/544; 78/1128.
s. 42, amended: 1972,c.58,schs.6,7; 1977, c.49,sch.15; 1978,c.29,sch.16 (S.)
s. 51, amended: 1974,c.22,sch.,pt.XI; sch. 2, repealed: *ibid.*
s. 52, amended: 1973,c.36,sch.6.

29. Magistrates' Courts Act 1957.
s. 1, repealed in pt.: 1977,c.45,sch.13.
s. 1, see *R.* v. *Liskerrett JJ., ex p. Child* [1972] R.T.R. 141.

CAP.

5 & 6 Eliz. 2 (1957)—cont.

31. Occupiers' Liability Act 1957.
s. 2, see *Clare* v. *L. Whittaker & Son (London)* [1976] I.C.R. 1.
ss. 2, 5, see *Sole* v. *Hallt* [1973] 2 W.L.R. 171; [1974] 1 W.L.R. 1575, C.A.
s. 4, repealed: 1972,c.35,s.6.

32. Naval and Marine Reserves Pay Act 1957.
s. 2, amended: 1974,c.22,sch.,pt.XI; sch. 2, repealed: *ibid.*

36. Cheques Act 1957.
s. 6, amended: 1974,c.22,sch.,pt.XI.; sch., repealed: *ibid.*
s. 7, amended: 1973,c.36,sch.6.

...lopment (Scot-
972,c.46,sch.11;
bid.,s.69,sch.11.
1974,c.22,sch.,
: *ibid.*
5,sch.12.
of Births) Act
,sch.,pt.XI.
led: 1976,c.31,
trial Buildings)
4.
601.
1973,c.66,schs.
/601.
repealed: 1972,
, 8, amended:
2,sch.,pt.XI.

44. National Health Service (Amendment) Act 1957.
repealed: 1973,c.32,sch.5.

45. Exchequer and Audit Departments Act 1957.
s. 1, amended: 1976,c.48,s.6.
s. 3, amended: 1974,c.22,sch.,pt.XI.

46. Judicial Offices (Salaries and Pensions) Act 1957.
repealed: 1973,c.15,sch.5.
s. 1, order 72/1078.

48. Electricity Act 1957.
s. 1, repealed: S.L.R. 1977.
s. 5, regs. 78/963.
s. 15, order 74/1295.
s. 15, sch. 4, amended: 1972,c.17,s.1,sch.
ss. 15, 17, amended: 1974,c.8,sch.2.
ss. 16, 20, 25, repealed in pt.: S.L.R. 1977.
s. 19, amended: 1975,c.55,s.5.
s. 26, repealed: S.L.R. 1977.
s. 28, repealed: 1979,c.11,sch.12.
s. 29, repealed in pt.: *ibid.*

510

CITATORS FOR ENGLISH STATUTES:

This page from the Current Law Citator illustrates how citators are arranged chronologically and then alphabetically by title of Act. References in this Citator are to the Current Law Year Books. For later developments be sure to consult the Statute Citator Section of the Cumulative Supplement, Current Law Citator. Other citators listed in Section F can be used in a similar manner.

[Illustration 151]

PAGE FROM CONSOLIDATED TABLES AND INDEX: 1936–1976: ALL ENGLAND LAW REPORTS

438 CASES REPORTED AND CONSIDERED

Seabrook v British Transport Commission [1959] **2** 15, QBD
  Applied, Patch v United Bristol Hospitals Board [1959] **3** 876
  Followed, Britten v F H Pilcher & Sons [1969] **1** 491
  Applied, Alfred Crompton Amusement Machines Ltd v Comrs of Customs and Excise (No 2) [1972] **2** 353
  Distinguished, Alfred Crompton Amusement Machines Ltd v Commissioners of Customs and Excise (No 2) [1973] **2** 1169
Seabrook v Gascoignes (Reading) Ltd [1973] **1** 1023, ChD
Seabrook v Mervyn [1947] **1** 295, CA
  Distinguished, Stagg v Brickett [1951] **1** 152
  Applied, Klassnick v Allen [1969] **3** 1278
Seabrook Estate Co Ltd v Ford [1949] **2** 94, KBD
Seaford Court Estates Ltd v Asher. *See* sub nom Asher v Seaford Court Estates Ltd
Seaford (decd), Re [1967] **2** 458, Prob
  Reversed [1968] **1** 482, CA
Seager v Copydex Ltd [1967] **2** 415, CA
Seager v Copydex Ltd (No 2) [1969] **2** 718, CA
Seagull Autos Ltd, Calabar Properties Ltd v. *See* Calabar Properties Ltd v Seagull Autos Ltd
Sealby, R v. *See* R v Sealby
Seale, Bone v. *See* Bone v Seale
Seale's Marriage Settlement, Re [1961] **3** 136, ChD
  Distinguished, Re Weston's Settlements [1968] **1** 720
  Distinguished, Re Weston's Settlements [1968] **3** 338
  Applied, Re Windeatt's Will Trusts [1969] **2** 324
Sealey, Young v. *See* Young v Sealey
Sealey (otherwise Callan) v Callan [1953] **1** 942, Div
Searle v Wallbank [1947] **1** 12, HL
  Applied, Brock v Richards [1951] **1** 261
  Dictum not followed, Wormald v Cole [1954] **1** 683
  Considered, Gomberg v Smith [1962] **1** 725
  Rule applied, Ellis v Johnstone [1963] **1** 286
  Dictum considered, Fitzgerald v E D and A D Cooke Bourne (Farms) Ltd [1963] **3** 36
  Considered, Bativala v West (trading as Westways Riding Academy) [1970] **1** 332

CITATORS FOR ENGLISH CASES:

Note how cases are listed alphabetically rather than by citation as in Shepard's Citations. References in this Citator are to the All England Law Reports.

Other citators listed in Section F may be used in a similar manner.

Second Covent Garden Property Co Ltd, Killick v. *See* Killick v Second Covent Garden Property Co Ltd
Secretan v Hart (Inspector of Taxes) [1969] **3** 1196, ChD
Secretary of State for Air, Chivers & Son Ltd v. *See* Chivers & Son Ltd v Secretary of State for Air
Secretary of State for Air, Racecourse Betting Control Board v. *See* Racecourse Betting Control Board v Secretary of State for Air
Secretary of State for Air, Tull's Personal Representatives v. *See* Tull's Personal Representatives v Secretary of State for Air
Secretary of State for Air, University College, Oxford (Master and Fellows) v. *See* University College, Oxford (Master and Fellows) v Secretary of State for Air
Secretary of State for Air, Watson v. *See* Watson v Secretary of State for Air
Secretary of State for Defence v Warn [1968] **1** 339, C-MAC
  Affirmed [1968] **2** 300, HL
Secretary of State for Education and Science v Metropolitan Borough of Tameside [1976] **3** 665, HL
Secretary of State for Employment v Associated Society of Locomotive Engineers and Firemen (No 2) [1972] **2** 949, NIRC & CA
  Dictum applied, Secretary of State for Education and Science v Metropolitan Borough of Tameside [1976] **3** 665
Secretary of State for Employment v Wellworthy Ltd [1973] **3** 488, NIRC
Secretary of State for Employment and Productivity v C Maurice & Co Ltd [1968] **2** 1031, CA
  Affirmed [1969] **2** 37, HL
  Dicta followed, Fisher-Bendix Ltd v Secretary of State for Employment and Productivity [1970] **2** 286
  Dictum applied, Central Press Photos Ltd v Department of Employment and Productivity [1970] **3** 775

SECTION K. SUMMARY

1. Statutes

a. *Current*

(1) *The Public General Acts and Measures*
(2) Current Law, Statutes

b. *Codification*

(1) *Statutes in Force, Official Revised Edition.* Looseleaf.

(2) *Halsbury's Statutes of England,* 3d ed. Multi-volume collection of statutes in force arranged by topic. Most convenient set to locate English statutes.

2. Administrative Law

English regulations (delegated legislation) published separately as *Statutory Instruments.* Codified in the *Statutory Rules and Orders* and *Statutory Instruments.* Similar to *U. S. Code of Federal Regulations.* Also privately published in *Halsbury's Statutory Instruments.*

a. *Indexes*

(1) *Guide to Government Orders.* Issued biennially.

(2) Index volume to *Halsbury's Statutory Instruments.*

3. Courts

a. *Court Organization*

Under the *Courts Act of 1971,* English courts are organized as follows:

(1) House of Lords

(2) Supreme Court of Judicature

(a) Court of Appeals

(b) High Court

[1] Queen's Bench Division

[2] Chancery Division

[3] Family Division

b. *Court Reporting*

(1) *Law Reports.* Quasi-official, selective in cases reported.

(a) *Law Reports. Appeal Cases.* Decisions from House of Lords and Court of Appeals.

(b) *Law Reports. Queen's Bench Division.*

(c) *Law Reports. Chancery Division.*

(d) *Law Reports. Family Division.*

(2) *All England Law Reports.* Privately published comprehensive reporting of English cases, began publication in 1936.

4. Digests

a. *English and Empire Digest*

A comprehensive digest of English cases with selective digests from Scotland, Ireland, Canada, and other countries of the Commonwealth.

b. *Halsbury's Laws of England*

A comprehensive encyclopedic treatment of English law, cases, and statutes.

c. *Current Law: Being a Complete Statement of All the Law from Every Source*

Began publication in 1947.

Chapter 22

CANADIAN LAW [1]

SECTION A. CANADIAN LEGISLATIVE AND JUDICIAL STRUCTURES

1. Federal and Provincial Legislative Structures

Parliament, the federal legislature, consists of the House of Commons and the Senate. The Prime Minister of Canada is an elected member of Parliament and is leader of the political party holding the most seats in the House of Commons. Usually, other elected members from the House serve as heads (Ministers) of federal departments. Parliament and the provincial legislatures have authority to enact legislation as directed by the British North America Act (see Section E, Constitutions). Federal areas include criminal law and divorce, while areas such as education and real property are provincial. There are ten provincial, unicameral legislatures and, in each, one member serves as Premier of the province. The Yukon and Northwest Territories have territorial councils, but the chief executive officers are federally appointed. Powers not given specifically to the provinces remain within federal jurisdiction.

2. Federal and Provincial Court Structures

Although there are federal and provincial courts, the division does not create separate structures to the extent that they exist in the United States. Provincial courts interpret federal legislation such as the Criminal Code, and the Supreme Court of Canada can act as the highest appellate level for interpretation of provincial law. The Federal Court has an Appeal Division and a Trial Division (see Section B, Federal Case Reporting). English case law is now of persuasive authority, but until 1949 (1933 for criminal cases) the highest court to which a Canadian case could be appealed was the Judicial Committee of the Privy Council in England.

[1] This Chapter was prepared by Douglass T. MacEllven, Director of Libraries, Law Society of Saskatchewan.

The chapter is written primarily for those involved in research in Canadian law in American libraries. For more detailed information about Canadian legal research, *see* D. MacELLVEN, CANADIAN LEGAL RESEARCH HANDBOOK (1981).

Structures of provincial court systems vary in name from province to province but generally follow the arrangement consisting of:

a. The lowest tier of criminal courts (Provincial Court or Magistrate's Court) and civil courts (Small Claims Court, Family Court, Juvenile Court, etc.).

b. A middle tier or tiers having both civil and criminal jurisdiction designated as County, District, and/or Queen's Bench Court.

c. The highest provincial court is usually designated as the Court of Appeal or the Supreme Court.

With respect to provincial matters, Quebec operates a civil law system stemming from its French legal heritage. The remaining provinces and territories operate a common law system with strong roots in the English legal tradition.

SECTION B. FEDERAL CASE REPORTING

Federal court decisions are published in both official and unofficial reports.

1. Canada Supreme Court Reports (1877–) (Queen's Printer)

These report decisions of the Supreme Court of Canada on cases appealed from lower federal courts and provincial courts. In earlier years, not all Supreme Court cases appeared in this series. From 1923 to 1969, the title was *Canada Law Reports, Supreme Court.* The paperbound advance sheets and later bound volumes report each case fully in both English and French. Each advance sheet and bound volume has a subject index.

2. Canada Federal Court Reports (1971–) (Queen's Printer)

The Federal Court Act (S.C.1970–71, c. 1) created this court with an Appeal Division and a Trial Division. All Appeal Division cases are reported but only selected Trial Division cases are published. The court's jurisdiction includes matters formerly handled by the Exchequer Court plus some new areas including appeals from decisions of federal administrative bodies. All cases are printed in both languages, and the advance sheets and bound volumes have subject indexes.

3. Exchequer Court Reports (1875–1970) (Queen's Printer)

These reports have had several title variations including *Canada Law Reports, Exchequer Court* (1923–1970). The subject matter jurisdiction involved patents, copyright, expropriation, income tax appeals, admiralty, citizenship appeals, and cases where relief was claimed against the government. The cases were reported only in the language of the court's written decision.

4. National Reporter (1974–) (Maritime Law Books Ltd.[2])

This unofficial series reports all Supreme Court, and all Federal Court Appeal Division cases, but does not include Federal Court Trial Division cases. The series publishes cases several months in advance of the official reports. Headnotes are indexed in accordance with Maritime Law Books Ltd.'s Topical Index System (similar to West's Key Number System). After every ten volumes of the reports, a cumulative Digest and Indexes volume is published covering the ten volumes.

5. Other Sources of Federal Decisions

Slip decisions are available from both federal court divisions. Counsels' briefs (factums) from the Supreme Court are available from the Canadian Law Information Council (CLIC). Federal decisions also are published in unofficial multi-jurisdictional reports (*e. g., DLR's*) and in single jurisdiction reports which contain cases appealed from the provinces' courts to the Supreme Court of Canada.

SECTION C. PROVINCIAL CASE REPORTING

1. Multi-Provincial Reports

There are a number of past and current reports publishing decisions from all the common law provinces or from either the western or eastern regions of Canada. Because there are several major legal publishers of Canadian law reports, there is duplication of case reporting among and between multi-jurisdictional reports, subject reports, and individual provincial reports.

a. *Dominion Law Reports* (1912–) (Canada Law Book Co.)

This is the only series which contains cases from the higher courts of all provinces as well as selected Supreme Court and Federal

[2] Maritime Law Books Ltd. has its own Topical Index System used with nearly all of its publications. This system is modeled after West's Key Number System. Within each volume there is a Key Word Index which is analogous to the Descriptive-Word Index of West. Key words lead to a Topical Index Number (e. g., torts topic 321) which is analogous to the West's Key Number. In each volume, digests are arranged under the Topical Index Number System similar to arrangement in the *American Digest System* main volumes. The indexing system is not published as a separate set like the *American Digest System* but is included in each volume of each report series. Except in the *Atlantic Provinces Reports*, there is a separate Digest and Indexes volume covering every ten volumes.

Maritime publishes the *National Reporter* plus individual reports series for all provinces except Quebec, British Columbia and Ontario (e. g., *Alberta Reports, New Brunswick Reports*, etc.). These provincial reports publish a higher percentage of cases than that provided by traditional reports series. Hence, the percentage of cases from across the country which may be termed "reported" (covered in "reported" cases digests) is higher than it was before 1970.

Court cases. Each weekly advance sheet and later bound volume has a subject index. There is no cumulative subject index, but cumulative aids are in the form of an annual Annotation Service volume consisting of a consolidated table of cases and a case citator (see Section H, Citators).

b. *Western Weekly Reports* (1912–) (Burroughs)

This series contains cases from British Columbia, Alberta, Saskatchewan, Manitoba, the Yukon Territory, and the Northwest Territories as well as selected cases appealed from provincial courts to the Supreme Court or Federal Court. There is a separately published paperbound Key Word Index (1971 to date). The series superseded the *Western Law Reporter* (1905–1916).

c. *Atlantic Provinces Reports* (1975–) (Maritime Law Books Ltd.)

This series appears in bound volume form only and reproduces cases published in report series for the individual Maritime Provinces (Nova Scotia, New Brunswick, Newfoundland, and Prince Edward Island). The indexing is part of Maritime Law Book's Topical Index System. Earlier reports for the region were the *Maritime Provinces Reports* (1930–1968) and the *Eastern Law Reporter* (1906–1914).

2. Individual Provincial Reports

a. *Alberta Law Reports* (2d) (1977–). (Burroughs)

b. *Alberta Reports* (1977–). (Maritime Law Books Ltd.)

c. *British Columbia Law Reports* (1977–). (Burroughs)

d. *Manitoba Reports* (2d) (1980–). (Maritime Law Books Ltd.)

e. *New Brunswick Reports* (2d) (1969–). (Included in the *Atlantic Provinces Reports*)

f. *Newfoundland and Prince Edward Island Reports* (1971–). (Included in the *Atlantic Provinces Reports*)

g. *Nova Scotia Reports* (2d) (1970–). (Included in the *Atlantic Provinces Reports*)

h. *Ontario Reports* (2d) (1974–). (Canada Law Book Co.)

i. *Prince Edward Island Reports* (1971–). (Officially published)

j. *Recueils de jurisprudence du Quebec* (1892–). (This set is the official reporter for Quebec. There are also two unofficial sets: *Rapports de practique de Quebec* (1898–) and *La Revue Legale* (1895–))

k. *Saskatchewan Reports* (1980–). (Maritime Law Books Ltd.)

3. Subject Reports

While sets of reports limited to a specific subject, such as criminal law, bankruptcy, and patents, have long been published, many new sets have started publication within the past ten years.[3] Examples of subject reports are as follows:

a. *Canadian Cases on the Law of Torts* (1976–)

b. *Canadian Criminal Cases* (1898–1970), 2d series (1971–)

c. *Criminal Reports* (1946–1967), new series (1967–1977), 3d series (1978–)

d. *Carswell's Practice Cases* (1976–)

e. *Estates and Trusts Reports* (1977–)

f. *Land Compensation Reports* (1972–)

g. *Municipal and Planning Law Reports* (1976–)

h. *Motor Vehicle Reports* (1978–)

i. *Real Property Reports* (1977–)

SECTION D. DIGESTS

There are several long-established Canadian digests, but during the past decade the number of digests has more than doubled. For many years reporting of cases from the middle tier(s) of provincial courts and Courts of Appeal has been selective. Therefore, many of the recent digests which include unreported cases give coverage to a depth analogous to the *American Digest System*. There is no single digest which covers all of Canadian law, but choice of a particular digest in which to search involves considerations noted in the legend below.[4] All of the Canadian digests may not be available in the li-

[3] For a complete listing of subject reports, *see Canadian Abridgment 2d, Cumulative Supplement, Table of Abbreviations.*

It should be noted that many of the decisions reported in the subject reports are also reported in the sets of general reports; some, however, are reported in only a particular set of subject reports. In order to have a complete collection of reported Canadian cases, a library must have all of the published sets of court reports.

[4] Reported, Unreported—denotes whether the digest includes primarily cases reported in law reports or whether the digest is primarily a rapid service digesting most cases, many of which will never appear in law reports (remain unreported). Publishers of digests containing unreported cases usually provide a photocopy service of the full judgment as it would be obtained from the court.

Traditional, Recent—denotes whether the digest has been a fixture in Canadian legal research for many years or whether it has appeared in approximately the past decade.

brary where research is taking place. Care should be taken to examine the coverage of the digests available.

It should be noted that most substantive law areas have the same designation as in the U. S. but there are some differences—e. g. the subject area of anti-trust is termed combines or anticombines in Canada.

1. Canadian Abridgment (2d) (Reported/Traditional/National/Both/Own)

The *Canadian Abridgment* has long been the most comprehensive digest of cases from all provinces and the federal courts. Coverage extends back to the early 1800's. The set has several groupings of volumes with subtitles which fall into either of two categories: (1) digests of reported decisions from reports series such as those discussed in Section C (not unreported decisions which are summarized in other digests); or (2) volumes providing index access to the digest volumes.

a. *Digest Volumes*

These consist of 38 bound volumes of the main work with digests grouped under 120 subjects plus many subtopics and the Practice volumes (three bound volumes with digests of decisions relating to such practice areas as discovery, trials, pleading, etc.)

b. *Supplements*

As the volumes in the main work and the practice subdivision are bound without pocket parts, supplementation is provided by bound supplements plus a looseleaf binder supplement. The supplements also continue the divisions discussed below.

c. *Division*

The *Abridgment* is divided into several parts to facilitate access to it. These are:

(1) General Index. These volumes index the entire set. Individual volumes of the main set have a more comprehensive index for the subject titles.

(2) Consolidated Table of Cases.

Court, Report Series, National, Regional, or Jurisdiction—denotes the scope of coverage.

Criminal, Civil, Both—denotes the type of cases digested.

Own, Maritime, WLP—denotes whether digest has its own subject classification or whether it belongs to a system used throughout a publisher's series of digests (Maritime Law Book Ltd. or Western Legal Publications Ltd.)

(3) Citators.

(a) Cases Judicially Considered. This includes citations to American cases considered by Canadian courts.

(b) Statutes Judicially Considered.

(c) Words and Phrases.

2. Canadian Current Law

The looseleaf binder supplements to the *Canadian Abridgment* provide updates current to the past half-year to one year. Updating to the present is supplied by the separately titled publication, *Canadian Current Law,* which appears in monthly, paperbound issues. Since the same subject classification system is used in both publications, transition of research from *Can. Abr. (2d)* to *CCL* is facilitated. The digests in *CCL* are subsequently cumulated into *Can. Abr. (2d).*

Also included are digests of cases involving damages for personal injury and death, many of which remain unreported and do not appear subsequently in the *Canadian Abridgment.* These damage awards are cumulated in the supplement volume to Goldsmith's *Damages for Personal Injury and Death.*

3. Other Digests

a. *CCH Dominion Report Service* (Reported/Traditional/National/Both/Own)

b. *Butterworth's Ontario Digest Replacement Edition* (Reported/Traditional/Jurisdiction/Both/Own)

c. *Annuaire de jurisprudence du Quebec* (Reported/Traditional/Jurisdiction/Both/Own)

d. *Supreme Court of Canada Reports Service* (Reported/Traditional/Court/Both/Own)

e. *Supreme Court of Canada Decisions* (1978–) (Reported/Recent/Court/Both/WLP)

f. *Federal Court of Canada Service* (Reported/Traditional/Court/Both/Own)

g. *Federal Court of Appeal Decisions* (Reported/Recent/Court/Both/WLP)

h. *National Reporter Digest and Indexes* volumes and sections (Reported/Recent/Report Series/Both/Maritime)

i. *Chitty's Abridgment of Canadian Criminal Case Law* (1892–1970) (Reported/Traditional/National/Criminal/Own)

j. *All Canada Weekly Summaries* (1977–) (Unreported/Recent/National/Civil/Own)

k. *Weekly Criminal Bulletin* (1977–) (Unreported/Recent/National/Criminal/Own)

l. *Canadian Weekly Law Sheet* (1961–) (Reported/Recent/National/Both/Own)

m. *British Columbia Digest* (Reported-Unreported/Recent/Jurisdiction/Both/Own)

n. *Nova Scotia Law News* (1974–) (Unreported/Recent/Jurisdiction/Both/Own)

o. *Alberta Decisions* (Unreported/Recent/Jurisdiction/Both/WLP)

p. *British Columbia Decisions* (Unreported/Recent/Jurisdiction/Both/WLP)

q. *Manitoba Decisions* (Unreported/Recent/Jurisdiction/Both/WLP)

r. *Saskatchewan Decisions* (Unreported/Recent/Jurisdiction/Both/WLP)

s. *Ontario Decisions* (Unreported/Recent/Jurisdiction/as of 1981, Criminal only/WLP)

t. Digest and Index volumes and sections of the provincial reports series, *e. g., New Brunswick Reports (2d)*, by Maritime Law Books Ltd. (Reported/Recent/Jurisdiction/Both/Maritime)

4. Words and Phrases

a. The most complete treatment of words and phrases is provided by *The Encyclopedia of Words and Phrases, Legal Maxims, Canada* (1925–1978) (3d ed. 1979) Toronto, Richard DeBoo Ltd., 4 volumes. This set provides digests of portions of the cases defining the words and phrases.

b. The *Canadian Abridgment* and *Canadian Current Law* provide a separate volume and a separate section, respectively, listing words and phrases followed by citations of cases defining them. The encyclopedia, *CED (Western, 2d)* has a separate volume listing words and phrases in a manner similar to the *Canadian Abridgment.*

SECTION E. CONSTITUTIONS

Unlike the U. S., which has federal and state constitutions, Canadian jurisdictions do not have single constitutional documents. The documents are a combination of legislative enactments by both the British Parliament and Canadian Parliament. The first constitutional source is the *British North America Act 1867*, 30–31 Vict., c. 3 (U. K.) passed by the British Parliament, which establishes areas of federal and provincial jurisdiction in Canada. Amendments to that act by British Parliament and recently to some extent by Canadian Parliament also are part of the constitution.

Other constitutional documents would include the British *Statute of Westminster,* 1931, 22 & 23 Geo. V., c. 4 (U.K.) which grants Canada full power to legislate internal and extra-territorial matters, and the Canadian Bill of Rights, S.C.1960, c. 44.

The 1980's began with a national political debate about the manner in which Canada's constitution could be repatriated from England to Canada. Because this is a potentially changing field, reference may be made to Christian L. Wiktor and Guy Tanguay, *Constitutions of Canada, Federal and Provincial.*[5]

SECTION F. STATUTES

1. Revised Statutes: Federal and Provincial

Federal and provincial statutes in Canada are published in chronological order and then codified into revised format in a manner similar to and for the same reasons that the U. S. *Statutes at Large* are codified into *United States Code.* This codification is accomplished federally and provincially at irregular intervals which usually fall into the range of every 10 to 15 years. Each statute revision supersedes the prior revision and subsequent sessional law volumes, unless a table in the new revision shows that there might be specific laws or sections of acts not repealed.[6]

Statutes do not have comprehensive indexes, but rather index volumes which list each act alphabetically with each act having its own index. While there are no annotated codes except for the federal Criminal Code and selected legislation from some provinces, statute citators (see Section H, Citators) perform the function of annotating statutes.

The *Revised Statutes of Canada* are officially printed in bound volume form only; as they lack pocket parts, reference must be made to each subsequent annual volume for amendments to the revision and new acts. The Table of Public Statutes in the back of the latest annual volume will list those amendments. There is a privately published looseleaf edition of the *Revised Statutes of Canada* by a subsidiary of CCH Canadian Ltd. Some provinces officially publish a looseleaf edition of their statutes as well as the bound volume edition.

[5] Oceana Publications, Dobbs Ferry, N.Y. (4 vols. looseleaf).

[6] For detailed information on updating provincial statutes, *see* HOW TO UPDATE A STATUTE FOR ALL CANADIAN JURISDICTIONS (G. Dykstra ed. 1980).

2. Legislation "Coming into Force"

It is important to determine when a new statute becomes law. After a bill passes Parliament or a provincial legislature it must be approved federally by the Governor-General, who is formally the Queen's personal representative in Canada and acts on the advice of the Canadian government, or provincially by the Lieutenant-Governor (Queen's representative). This formality is termed Royal Assent. The statute then becomes law when it "comes into force" on a specific date. One of the final sections of a statute usually will state that it will come into force on a specific day, the date of Royal Assent, or when it is proclaimed. Proclamation dates may be a considerable time after passage of the bill, and the purpose is to allow the administrative structure which will enforce the bill to be created. Federal legislation may come into force at different dates for the various provinces. Federal proclamation dates can be located in the *Canada Gazette, Part I* or the *Canada Statute Citator.* If a statute does not state when it will come into force, the effective date will be in accordance with the federal or a provincial Interpretation Act.

Federal and Provincial bills are published in pamphlet form before they appear in bound statute annuals. Federal bills are also published in *Canada Gazette, Part III* upon Royal Assent.

3. Revised Statutes of Canada, 1970: Research Updating

The first seven volumes contain the revised statutes to the end of 1969 with the alpha-numeric designation relating to the alphabetical sequence of the titles of the acts. The First and Second Supplement volumes contain new legislation and legislation amending the revised statutes from the beginning of 1970 to the date of proclamation of the revision. Reference to the Table of Public Statutes in the latest statute annual precludes any difficulties in statutory research during the period covered by these two supplements. The Second Supplement volume also has a table, History and Disposal of Acts, showing location of older statutes in the new revision plus a Schedule listing acts repealed by the revision. The Appendix volume contains constitutional acts and documents. The Index volume lists statutes in the order that they appear in the revision with a separate index for each act.

Updating statutory research should include checking for amendments and new acts in the Table of Public Statutes in the latest bound volume of annual statutes and checking for even more recent coverage in the Table of Public Statutes appearing in the *Canada Gazette, Part III.* Search should be made for proclamation dates if necessary. For the progression of current bills through Parliament, sources such as the *Status of Bills Report* (prepared by Library of

Parliament and distributed by Canadian Law Information Council), Progress of Bills Section of *Canadian Current Law,* or a looseleaf service such as *CCH's Ottawa Letter* should be checked.

SECTION G. REGULATIONS AND ADMINISTRATIVE LAW

1. Federal Regulations

a. *Consolidated Regulations of Canada, 1978*

In a publication analogous to the U. S. *Code of Federal Regulations,* the 19-volume *Consolidated Regulations of Canada, 1978* prints the texts of regulations in force on December 31, 1977. The arrangement is alphabetical by enabling statute, and although there is no index, there is a Table of Contents with the titles of enabling statutes and their regulations. A two-volume *Canada Gazette, Part II Special Issue* (Dec. 31, 1978) was published to show amendments and revocations made in 1978 to the regulations printed in the consolidation. It does not include new regulations issued in 1978.

b. *Canada Gazette, Part II and the Consolidated Index of Statutory Instruments*

New regulations appear in the *Canada Gazette, Part II,* which is analogous to the U. S. *Federal Register.* Access to regulations printed in the consolidation, amendments, and new regulations is provided by the *Consolidated Index of Statutory Instruments* which is a quarterly issue of the *Canada Gazette, Part II.*

Updating regulations since the last quarterly consolidated index requires searching through each *Canada Gazette, Part II* to date. The Index in the back of each Part II lists regulations within the issue but does not give the portion of old regulations affected, which necessitates examination of each amending regulation.

c. *Other Publications*

The *Regulatory Reporter* (1980–) by CLIC provides looseleaf coverage of selected federal and provincial regulations and regulatory matters. The *Canadian Legislative Report* (1980–) by Micromedia provides comprehensive information on regulations, status of bills, and proclamation dates for the federal government, Ontario, Quebec, and Alberta.

2. Provincial Regulations

Each province's regulations are listed in officially published provincial gazettes.

3. Federal and Provincial Administrative Decisions

In a quasi-judicial function, many federal and provincial administrative agencies issue decisions. Because many of these decisions are not published, reference should be made to *Publication of Administrative Board Decisions in Canada: A Report* (1972) (A. H. Janisch, Canadian Association of Law Libraries), which lists publication sources of reported board decisions and how access can be gained to unreported decisions.

Some areas such as labor and tax are well covered by private publishers in cooperation with boards. The Federal Court judicially reviews federal board decisions.

SECTION H. CITATORS

There is not a comprehensive service similar to *Shepard's Citations* for either Canadian statutes or cases. Some Canadian aids performing this function appear as parts of publications such as digests, while some appear as separate volumes referred to as citators.

1. Statute Citators

The separately published citator for federal statutes is *The Canada Statute Citator, RSC 1970 Edition.* This looseleaf service shows amendments to statutes as well as cases which have considered statutes. The bound volume, *Canada Statute Annotations,* lists older cases considering statutes which were still in force in the 1970 federal statute revision. The Statutes Judicially Considered sections of the *Canadian Abridgment* and *Canadian Current Law* also serve as citators for the federal, provincial, and English statutes.

Separate loose-leaf statute citator services are available for Ontario, British Columbia, Alberta, Saskatchewan, Manitoba, and New Brunswick.

2. Case Citators

The Cases Judicially Considered sections of the *Canadian Abridgment* and *Canadian Current Law* provide a selected listing of significant citing cases considering the earlier cited cases. The selected citing cases are reported Canadian cases, while the cited cases are from Canadian, U. S., British and other Commonwealth cases.

The *Dominion Law Reports* and *Canadian Criminal Cases* Annotation services give cited cases only if they appeared in those two report series, but the citing cases are from any Canadian reports. The listing of citing cases is generally more complete than the listing in the *Canadian Abridgment.*

Index Gagnon is a citator which lists cited Quebec cases and includes page numbers where the citing cases mentioned the cited cases.

SECTION I. ENCYCLOPEDIAS

The two current encyclopedias separately cover the eastern and western regions of the country, and, commencing in 1982, there will be an encyclopedia covering the country as a whole.

1. Canadian Encyclopedic Digest (Ontario 3rd edition)

Appearing in looseleaf form, the volumes of the 3rd edition have almost all been published. Main access to the work is through the paperbound volume titled *CED (Ont. 3rd) Deskbook and Key.* This volume includes a Statutes Key giving the location of discussions about Ontario and federal statutes. The portion entitled Key Words Index provides a word index to the set. The Titles Key lists the location of titles in the new 3rd edition as well as cross referencing older titles from the 2nd edition now renamed or incorporated in the 3rd edition titles. The Titles Key also cross references many subject areas not used as title designations to actual titles.

Cases footnoted are primarily Ontario and federal, but there are selected cases from other provinces, England, and other common law jurisdictions.

2. Canadian Encyclopedic Digest (Western 3rd edition)

The looseleaf 3rd edition has recently begun publication, and so decreasing portions of the bound 2nd edition will be in use for a number of years. There is no separately published key. However, each volume has a Titles Key, and each article has a table of statutes, table of cases, and key word index. The publication stresses the federal law plus provincial law for British Columbia, Alberta, Saskatchewan, Manitoba, and the two territories.

3. The Laws of Canada (Encyclopedia scheduled for publication beginning in 1982)

The set will be produced by the publisher, Butterworths, which produces the encyclopedia, *Halsbury's Laws of England.* The older 3rd edition of *Halsbury's Laws of England* has separate volumes titled *Canadian Converters* which supply footnotes to Canadian law. The new 4th edition has no *Canadian Converters,* and when *Halsbury's* 4th edition and *The Laws of Canada* are completed, these will have no linking volumes or features.

SECTION J. PERIODICALS AND PERIODICAL INDEXES

Canada produces law reviews, some law society and local bar association periodicals, subject journals, and some interdisciplinary journals. Listings of these journals are found at the beginning of the periodical indexes mentioned below. Major Canadian legal periodicals are indexed in *Current Law Index,* the *Index to Legal Periodicals,* and *Legal Resource Index,* as well as in Canadian indexes.

The most comprehensive Canadian periodical index is the *Index to Canadian Legal Periodical Literature* (1961–). The subject headings are similar to those in the *Index to Legal Periodicals* except that some Canadian legal terminology is different from American, such as Quebec civil law, which receives broad coverage. The indexing covers legal journals as well as journals with only partial legal contents. The material indexed includes journal articles as well as articles which are annotations in Canadian law reports, separately published collected essays, and audio-visual materials.

The Canadian publication, *Index to Commonwealth Legal Periodicals,* gives broad index coverage, with little time lag, to Canadian and other Commonwealth legal periodicals. Cumulative issues are printed, and more Commonwealth journals are indexed than by *Current Law Index* or *Index to Legal Periodicals.*

SECTION K. LOOSELEAF SERVICES, TREATISES, AND OTHER RESEARCH AIDS

1. Looseleaf Services

Canadian looseleaf reporters are very similar to those in the U. S., and the major Canadian publishers are CCH and DeBoo. There is some overlap in coverage between the two publishers' services.

2. Treatises

Until the past two decades, publication of treatises was sparse relative to England and the U. S. Reliance is still made on British texts for many points and American texts for coverage of narrow topics. There are now at least five major legal publishers of treatises in Canada (Butterworths, Canada Law Book, Carswell, CCH, and DeBoo). More and more Canadian casebooks and textbooks are being published, with many of them appearing in looseleaf binder editions.

3. Other Research Aids

a. *Dictionaries*

Canadian Law Dictionary (1980) is the first legal dictionary specifically published for the Canadian legal profession.

b. *Directories*

The major legal directories published annually in Canada are the *Canadian Law List* and the *Canada Legal Directory.*

c. *Forms*

The Canadian form set is *O'Brien's Encyclopedia of Forms* which has nine bound volumes and a looseleaf supplement.

SECTION L. ILLUSTRATIONS

152. Page from General Index, Canadian Abridgment (2d)

153. Page from Canadian Abridgment (2d) Vol. 5

154. Page from Canadian Abridgment (2d), Cases Judicially Considered

155. Page from Revised Statutes of Canada, Index Volume

156. Page from Canada Statute Citator, R.S.C. 1970 Ed.

[Illustration 152]

PAGE FROM GENERAL INDEX, CANADIAN ABRIDGMENT (2d)

BROKER

broker—*cont.*
rights of—*cont.*
profits, limited to commissions 35.802, 804
reimbursement 35.800, 801, 803
wrongful pledge of customer's securities by 14.2041

Bubble Acts 2.2694

buggery
attempt
requirements 9.591
defence
physical incapacity based on age 9.1153
gross indecency, as distinct from 9.1166
indictment on two counts, Judge refusing to sever S2.17075
lesser offence, conviction for
attempt 9.1152
power of Appeal Court to examine evidence 10.5556
"psychopathy" as defence to S2.16226
punishment
long record of unnatural offences 9.1151

→ **building contracts**
abandonment—*see abandonment*
architects and engineers—*see architects and engineers*
bonds and sureties—*see bonds and securities*

negligence, for S1.7878
negligence of subcontractor, for 5.868
tenant, to 5.867
work outside scope of employment 5.863
→ damages for breach of
contractor, by
→ building never begun 5.393
by-law, breach of 5.392
condition precedent, failure to fulfill dependent covents 5.391
defective workmanship 5.425-7, 440, 441, 444-9; S1.7878
abatement of contract price, agreement for 5.451
approval given by architect, effect of 5.463
caused by others 5.461
contractor unable to obtain payment of work 5.436
correcting defects, need to have spent money on 5.458
defective material using 5.459
delay, additional damages for 5.450, 453
divisible contract 5.439
faulty design by architect S1.7877, 7879
indirect losses 5.432, 433
loss resulting from 5.457
measure of damages 5.428, 430, 431, 434
necessity for evidence as to

FINDING CANADIAN CASES: CANADIAN ABRIDGMENT

Problem: How may damages be determined for breach of building contract when construction never began.

Step 1.

Check General Index to Canadian Abridgment (2d). Note reference to Vol. 5: ¶ 393. See next illustration

failure to complete, for 5.761
new contract replaces original, where 5.767
without notice 5.759
liability of
dangerous work 5.865
failure to inform owner of inherent dangers S1.7877
invitee, to 5.864
hidden defects 5.869
limitation 5.866

soil conditions, liability for 5.454
statutory standards, failing to meet 5.469
subsequent appearance of defects 5.452, 460
subsequent personal injury claim 5.462
substantial completion 5.437, 438, 442, 443
supplementary agreement to repair defects 5.465

198

[Illustration 153]

PAGE FROM CANADIAN ABRIDGMENT (2d) VOL. 5

dependent, and that the working of the railway was a condition precedent to plaintiff's right to do the work. *Held,* plaintiff was entitled to succeed, for, under the circumstances in which the parties entered into the agreements, the agreements were independent of each other, and therefore plaintiff was entitled to damages for breach of the company's covenant to permit him to do the work, even though he had failed to carry out his agreement to operate the railway line.

TATE v. PORT HOPE, LINDSAY AND BEAVERTON RY., (1859) 17 U.C.Q.B. 354 (C.A.).

2. DAMAGES AGAINST CONTRACTOR

a. General

389. Failure to pay scheduled rate of wages — Liability of contractor — Amount of damages. A contractor who failed to comply with a provision in his contract with the owner requiring him to pay the workmen in accordance with a spe[illegible] of wages was held to be liable in damages for his breach of these damages would be p[illegible] unless the owner could show suffered some actual loss.

KELLY v. WINNIPEG, (1908) 18 Man. R. 269.

390. Building encroaching [illegible] land — Liability of contracto[r] [illegible] of damages. Plaintiff compa[ny] [illegible] to erect a building for defend[ant] [illegible] pletion it was found that the [illegible] croached one-half inch on the [illegible] Objections were made by d[illegible] plaintiff agreed to procure a t[illegible] ant's name to the land upon which the building encroached. A quit-claim deed to defendant of the one-half inch was obtained. In an action to obtain payment for the work, defendant contended that the contract to erect the building was an entire one, and since the building had encroached upon the adjoining lot, plaintiff company had no right to bring the action without first procuring for defendant title to the land involved. *Held,* the contract was not an entire one, and defendant's remedy, if any, was an action for such damages as he might sustain in consequence of the encroachment: but if the contract was an entire one, defendant had waived his right to object to the encroachment by making the agreement that plaintiff company should furnish the title to the land encroached upon.

LECKY & CO. v. CARMAN, (1914) 7 W.W.R. 691, 7 Sask. L.R. 360, 22 D.L.R. 225 (C.A.).

391. Dependent covenants — Failure of owner to fulfil condition precedent — Consequent refusal of contractor to complete — Owner not entitled to damages. Defendant covenanted to erect a house for plaintiff, and to have it completed by a stipulated time. Plaintiff covenanted to pay defendant monthly instalments of the contract price on the architect's certificates. Defendant began the work, but plaintiff failed to pay the instalments, and the architect refused to issue his certificates. Defendant thereupon left the work, which plaintiff completed at a cost in excess of the contract price. Plaintiff sought to recover damages for defendant's alleged breach of contract. *Held,* on the true construction of the con-[illegible]

Step 2.

Read ¶ 393 and then full decision in the cited report.

Step 3.

Check for later cases in the supplements to Can.Abr. (2) and the Canadian Current Law.

393. Building never begun — Measure of damages. Defendant company agreed to build a house for plaintiff at a certain price. Defendant broke its contract in that it never started construction of the house. In an action for damages, *held,* the measure of damages was the difference between the contract price and the cost of building, but not the cost of building at today's prices; it must be the cost of building as of the time when plaintiff first became aware of defendant's breach of contract. Plaintiff must proceed diligently.

ARMSTRONG v. ROSLYN PARK LAND CO. AND SIGMORE (1951), 4 W.W.R. (N.S.) 270 (B.C.).

[Illustration 154]

PAGE FROM CANADIAN ABRIDGMENT (2d), CASES JUDICIALLY CONSIDERED

CASES JUDICIALLY CONSIDERED

Bennett v. Bennett, [1951] 1 All E.R. 1088; [1952] 1 All E.R. 413.
Consd. Lord v. Fudge, 4 D.L.R. (2d) 100.
Dist. Burleigh v. Crocker, [1954] O.W.N. 248.
Consd. Campbell v. Campbell, 13 W.W.R. (N.S.) 252.
Dist. Main v. Main, [1955] 2 D.L.R. 588; 2 D.L.R. (2d) 341.
Folld. Walls v. Hanson, 49 D.L.R. (2d) 435.
Apld. Furlong v. Burns & Co., [1964] 2 O.R. 3.
Dist. Stern v. Sheps, 58 W.W.R. 612.
Apld. McKay v. McKay, [1971] 1 W.W.R. 487.

gary) Ltd. (1966), 57 W.W.R. 600.
Dist. Boss v. Robert Simpson Eastern Ltd., 2 D.L.R. (3d) 114.

Bennett v. Fraser, [1936] 2 W.W.R. 616.
Consd. R. v. MacDonald, 38 C.R. 104.

Bennett v. Fraser Valley Bldrs. Ltd., [1952] 4 D.L.R. 834; 13 D.L.R. (2d) 109.
Apld. Piper v. Geldart, [1954] 2 D.L.R. 97.
Apld. Tri-City Drilling Co. v. Velie, 30 W.W.R. 61.
Dist. Re Chapman, 18 D.L.R. (2d) 745.
Folld. A.I.M. Steel Ltd. v. Gulf of Georgia Towing Co., 50 W.W.R. 476.

Bennett v. Gaslight & Coke Co., 52 L.J. Ch. 98.
Folld. Osadchuk v. Nat. Trust Co., [1942] 1 W.W.R. 163.

Bennett v. Gilmour, 16 Man. R. 304.
Dist. Man. Farm Loans v. Chapple, 52 Man. R. 117.

Bennett v. G.T.P., 2 O.L.R. 425.
Consd. Barrett v. C.P.R., 16 Man. R. 556.
Consd. Leighton v. B.C. Elec. Ry. Co., 20 B.C.R. 183.

Bennett v. G.T.R., 3 O.R. 446.
Folld. Lamond v. G.T.R., 16 O.L.R. 365.
Dist. Hollinger v. C.P.R., 20 O.A.R. 244.
Apld. Stevenson v. C.P.R., 59 Man. R. 110.

Bennett v. G.T.R., 7 O.A.R. 470.
Consd. Preston v. Toronto Ry. Co., 11 O.L.R. 56.

Bennett v. Havelock Elec. Light & Power Co., 21 O.L.R. 120; 25 O.L.R. 200; 46 S.C.R. 640

208.

Bennett v. Jones, 10 N.B.R. 342.
Apld. Hovey v. Long, 33 N.B.R. 469.

Bennett v. O'Meara, 15 Gr. 396.
Dist. Hoeffler v. Irwin, 8 O.L.R. 740.

Bennett v. Peattie, 57 O.L.R. 233.
Apld. McLeod v. Tor. Gen. Trusts, [1936] O.R. 379.
Consd. Adare v. Fairplay, [1956] O.R. 188.

Bennett v. Peck, 15 N.B.R. 316.
Apld. Whittaker v. Welch, 15 N.B.R. 444.

Bennett v. Pharmaceutical Assn. of Que., 1 Dor. App. 336.
Consd., Huson v. South Norwich, 24 S.C.R. 161.
Consd. Re Coal Mines Regulation Amendment Act, 1890, 5 B.C.R. 318.

207

FINDING CANADIAN CASES: CANADIAN ABRIDGMENT (2d)

Step 4.

Check in Cases Judicially Considered volumes. This acts as a citator and is one way of "Shepardizing" Canadian cases. See Section H for other methods.

[Illustration 155]

PAGE FROM REVISED STATUTES OF CANADA, INDEX VOLUME

Revised Statutes Index

(References are to sections)

FINDING CANADIAN STATUTES: FEDERAL

Problem: How is "book" defined in the Copyright Statute?

Step 1.

Check Index volume to latest edition of the Revised Statutes of Canada. Definition may be found, R.S. Chap. C–30, Section 2.

144

[Illustration 156]

PAGE FROM CANADA STATUTE CITATOR, R.S.C. 1970 ED.

FINDING CANADIAN STATUTES: FEDERAL

Step 2.

After reading the text of the statute, check in the Canada Statute Citator to the Revised Statutes of Canada to determine if statute has been amended or repealed and to locate case annotations.

Corporation relating thereto, shall be kept separate and distinct from those arising from its operations under the *Canada Deposit Insurance Corporation Act*.

COPYRIGHT ACT

R.S.C. 1970, Chap. C-30

Amended R.S.C. 1970, c. 4 (2nd Supp.); proclaimed in force August 1, 1972
Amended R.S.C. 1970, c. 10 (2nd Supp.), s. 65; proclaimed in force August 1, 1972
Amended 1974-75, c. 50, s. 47; proclaimed in force September 6, 1977
Amended 1976-77, c. 28, s. 10; in force June 29, 1977
Administered by the Dept. of Consumer and Corporate Affairs

Generally

For cases 1941 to 1971, see *Canada Statute Annotations,* R.S.C. 1970 edition.

Section 2

For cases 1941 to 1971, see *Canada Statute Annotations,* R.S.C. 1970 edition.

Fly by Nite Music Co. Ltd. et al. v. Record Warehouse Ltd., [1975] F.C. 386, 20 C.P.R. (2d) 263 (T.D.).

A record is a work within the meaning of this statute.

Section 3

For cases 1941 to 1971, see *Canada Statute Annotations,* R.S.C. 1970 edition.

Section 4

For cases 1941 to 1971, see *Canada Statute Annotations,* R.S.C. 1970 edition.

Subsec. (3) repealed and the following subsecs. (3) and (4) substituted by R.S.C. 1970, c. 4 (2nd Supp.), s. 1:

(3) Subject to subsection (4), copyright shall subsist for the term hereinafter mentioned in records, perforated rolls, and other contrivances by means of which sounds may be mechanically reproduced, in like manner as if such contrivances were musical, literary or dramatic works.

(4) Notwithstanding subsection 3(1), for the purposes of this Act "copyright" means, in respect of any record, perforated roll or other contrivance by means

SECTION M. COMPUTERIZED LEGAL RESEARCH AND THE CANADIAN LAW INFORMATION COUNCIL (CLIC)

QUIC/LAW is a computerized legal retrieval system similar to *Westlaw*, which received its initial software programming from QUIC/LAW. Search is made of case headnotes, but full text retrieval is made of statutes. In early 1981, the data bases available for cases were *SCR, FCR, DLR, WWR, APR* (includes retrieval by topic number), *CCC*, plus the advance digest series of *ACWS* and *WCB*. Other data bases include the federal statutes, selected federal regulations, British Columbia and New Brunswick Statutes, Statute Citators for Alberta and Manitoba, and many legally related data bases.

The Canadian Law Information Council (CLIC) is a non-profit corporation funded by federal and provincial governments, provincial Law Societies and associations with legal interests. It covers a wide range of activities from promotion of publication of more Canadian legal literature to legal education for the lay public. One goal is to enhance access to legal research material. It is promoting the addition of more data bases to QUIC/LAW and the establishment of computer service centers across the country at law schools and Law Society libraries. The advantage of low costs to the user of approximately $5 per question per data base is consistent with the approach of providing equal access to legal research material by all members of the legal profession regardless of geographical location.

Law Society libraries are administered centrally at the provincial level. Lawyers in remote areas have immediate access to materials supplied by Law Society libraries through such means as the telecopier network between court house libraries in Saskatchewan.

SECTION N. HIGHLIGHTS AND RESEARCH APPROACH

1. Case Reports

a. Official federal reports are the *Canada Supreme Court Reports* and *Canada Federal Court Reports*, but the unofficial *National Reporter* provides more rapid reporting.

b. The unofficial national series for provincial cases is the *Dominion Law Reports*, while the *Western Weekly Reports* and *Atlantic Provinces Reports* give regional coverage.

c. All provinces have individual reports series, and the Table of Abbreviations in the looseleaf portion of the *Canadian Abridgment (2d)* gives an updated listing of special subject reports.

2. Search for Case Law in Digests

The chart below is a planning aid in selecting digests for research, and the bracketed numbers refer to numbered items in Section D.

Digest Title		Type of Coverage	Type of Law	Type of Indexing
REPORTED CASES				
1.	*Can Abr.(2d)*	National	Both	Own
2.	*CCL*	National	Both	*Can Abr 2d*
3a.	*DRS*	National	Both	Own
3*l*.	*C. W. L. S.*	National	Both	Own
3b.	*BOD*	Ontario	Both	Own
3c.	Annuaire . . . Quebec	Quebec	Both	Own
3t.	Maritime Law Books provincial reports	Newf., N.S., P.E.I., N.B., Man., Sask., Alta.	Both	Maritime
3d.	*SCCRS*	Supreme Court	Both	Own
3e. & g.	*S. C. C. D. & F. C. A. D.*	S. C. and F. C.	Both	WLP
3h.	*NR*	S. C. and F. C.	Both	Maritime
3i.	Chitty's	National	Criminal	Own
UNREPORTED CASES (and Reported)				
3j.	*ACWS*	National	Civil	Own
3k.	*WCB*	National	Criminal	Own
3m.	*B. C. Digest*	British Columbia	Both	Own
3n.	*N. S. L. News*	Nova Scotia	Both	Own
3*o*. to s.	Western Legal decisions services	B.C., Alta., Sask., Man., Ont.	Both	WLP
3f.	*FCCS*	F.C.	Both	Own

3. Search for Statute Law

a. Index volume to *RSC 1970* which indexes each act separately.

b. The Table of Public Statutes in the most recent *Canada Gazette, Part III* which lists amendments and new statutes.

c. The *Status of Bills Report* which covers pending legislation.

4. Search for Federal Regulations

a. *Consolidated Regulations of Canada 1978*, Table of Contents.

b. *Consolidated Index of Statutory Instruments* issue of the *Canada Gazette, Part II*, Table II, which lists statutes and their regulations since the consolidation.

c. Individual issues of the *Canada Gazette, Part II* since the consolidated index.

5. Search for Cases and Statutes in Secondary Literature and Index Sources

a. Canadian treatises and looseleaf services. See Section K.

b. Encyclopedias provide:

(1) Regional coverage in the *CED (Ont.3d)* or *CED (Western 3d)*.

(2) National coverage in the *Laws of Canada* (1982–).

c. Periodical Indexes for Canadian material are:

(1) Canadian Sources: *Index to Canadian Legal Periodical Literature* and *Index to Commonwealth Legal Periodicals.*

(2) Non-Canadian sources: *Current Law Index, Index to Legal Periodicals, Legal Resource Index.*

6. Updating Research in Citators

a. Statute Citators are:

(1) *The Canada Statute Citator, RSC 1970* for cases considering federal statutes.

(2) *Canadian Abridgment (2d)* and *CCL* for cases considering federal and provincial statutes.

b. Case Citators give:

(1) Broad but selected coverage as in the *Canadian Abridgment (2d)* and *CCL.*

(2) Narrow but detailed coverage as in the *DLR* and *CCC* Annotation Service volumes.

Chapter 23

COMPUTERS AND MICROTEXT IN LEGAL RESEARCH

SECTION A. LEGAL RESEARCH AND COMPUTERS

The foregoing chapters of this text (with the exceptions of Chapter 21, Sections B and D, and Chapter 22, Section M, which include computer access to English and Canadian law, respectively) have described the various printed indexes, digests, citators, abstracts and services used in manually searching for the law. Although in most instances these research tools provide an effective and economical approach to the retrieval of legal information, computer-assisted legal research is playing an increasingly important role in legal research.

There are presently two systems, *Lexis* and *Westlaw*,[1] which provide computer-based legal research. Both use data bases [2] consisting of the full text of court decisions and are on-line interactive systems.[3] In each system the texts of the court decisions have been converted to machine-readable data bases and are accessed through telephone connections between a terminal and a central computer where the data base is stored. The terminal has a typewriter keyboard with an attached screen upon which requested information from the computer is displayed. Each system also has additional features which will be discussed below.

1 Both Lexis and Westlaw offer extensive training programs to their subscribers. The explanation given in this chapter is only intended to present a simplified explanation of these two systems. Additional information may be obtained by writing to:

Lexis Mead Data Central 200 Park Avenue New York, N.Y. 10017	Westlaw West Publishing Co. 50 W. Kellogg Blvd. P.O. Box 3526 St. Paul, MN 55165

2 A data base is defined as an organized collection of information or data, recorded in machine-readable form.

3 On-line interactive searching permits the user, via a computer, to interrogate a machine-readable data base directly in a conversational mode, with the searcher and the system program taking turns in dialogue. An interactive search gives the user the ability to view the results of his search at various stages and to revise his request to conform to what the user discovers about the data base on-line.

1. Lexis

Lexis provides a system for locating court decisions and other sources of legal information. The system has available in its data base the reported decisions [4] for the federal courts and for the fifty states, although the data bases vary from jurisdiction to jurisdiction. For example, the decisions of the U. S. Supreme Court are available from 1925 to date, while for some states only more recent decisions are available. *Lexis* has divided the decisions into what it calls "Libraries", which contain either federal cases, the cases of a particular state, or cases and other materials for a special subject such as taxation, trade regulation, or securities regulation. Each "Library" is then divided into "Files" where the cases are separated according to the court structure of the jurisdiction. For example, the federal "Library" is divided into different files, including: Supreme Court decisions, Circuit Court decisions, District Court decisions, Court of Claims decisions, and the U. S. Code. The Wisconsin "Library" is divided into files including Wisconsin Supreme Court decisions and Wisconsin Appellate Court decisions.

a. Searching for Cases with *Lexis*. A researcher should first analyze carefully the problem to be researched as described in the second Chapter. Since Lexis is a full text system, it is necessary to think of all possible synonyms for the important terms involved in the research. For example, if the problem involves a child, and only that term is used in the search, cases which do not contain the word "child" but the words "juvenile", or "minor" or "infant" may not be retrieved. The *Lexis* system is programmed to search on words typed at the terminal and uses a series of connectors to link together the words or phrases used in the search. Each case entered into the *Lexis* system is called a document and each document is divided into various segments such as Name, Counsel, Judge, Majority Opinion, Minority Opinion, or Dissenting Opinion. Each segment may be separately searched.

Now, let us see how a problem would be researched using *Lexis*. The one in Chapter 6 will be used for this purpose.

PROBLEM:

A child is standing with her step-grandmother on a street corner when an automobile jumps the curb and severely injures the grandmother. The observation of this accident causes the child severe mental suffering. The child's parents wish to know if they may recover damages from the driver of the automobile for the child's emotional distress.

[4] Lexis also includes in some of its Libraries unreported slip decisions.

After the researcher has made a telephone connection between the *Lexis* terminal and the *Lexis* computer, the various "Libraries" are displayed on the *Lexis* terminal screen. Search can be made for cases in the federal courts, for a particular state, or for all the states. In this instance, the search has been made for all cases from the highest courts of the fifty states.

Step 1. Type in the words:

(MENTAL OR EMOTIONAL w/3 SUFFERING) AND DAMAGES

[This will cause the computer to search the data base for all cases that contain either the word "mental" or the word "emotional" within 3 words of "suffering," and also contain within the case the word "damages". The result of the search is then displayed on the terminal screen. 690 cases were located.]

Step 2. As this is obviously too many cases, the search is narrowed by adding:

AND CHILD OR INFANT

[The computer now searches among the cases previously located and selects out those that contain the words "child" or "infant." 190 cases were located.]

Step 3. The search is further modified by adding:

AND GRANDMOTHER OR GRANDFATHER

[The computer now searches the 190 cases for the words "Grandmother" or "Grandfather." This step reduces the cases located to 19 and includes the case of *Leong v. Takasaki* which was located in Chapter 6.

The researcher now has several options for reviewing those cases retrieved.

(1) Each search word may be displayed along with twenty-five words that appear on each side of the word.

(2) The full text of the case may be displayed.

(3) Only the citations may be displayed.

(4) Selected segments of each case may be displayed.

The method demonstrated for this search is not the only way it could have been accomplished. One of the advantages of a full text system is that the research strategy may be determined by the researcher.

b. Other Features of *Lexis*. Some other important research features of *Lexis* are:

(1) Locating all opinions written by a particular judge.

(2) Locating other citations to a particular case or statutory section.

(3) Locating cases decided on a certain date or before or after a certain date.

(4) Locating all cases in which a particular party has been involved in litigation.

(5) Attached printer which will copy information on the terminal screen.

(6) *Auto-Cite*. This data base has been developed by the Lawyers Co-operative Publishing Company. By inputting one case reference, *Auto-Cite* will display parallel citations and its disposition on appeal.

(7) *Shepard's Citations*. This data base will allow researchers to check further references to a given case by inputting the citation to that case. *See* Chapter 15.

(8) *Lockheed*. Lockheed is a major data base vendor that offers over 200 non-legal bibliographic data bases. These will be available to users of *Lexis* at extra cost.

2. Westlaw

Westlaw is the name given to the computerized legal data base of the West Publishing Company. It includes the headnotes of all reported cases since 1966 as well as the full text of cases as reported in the *National Reporter System*. The years of coverage for full text vary from jurisdiction to jurisdiction. It is possible to search in *Westlaw* using only the headnotes, or only full text, or by combining both of these. In some instances, the ability to search only the headnotes through the use of the Key Number System may be useful.

A typical search is shown below using the problem in Chapter 7 which demonstrated the finding of A.L.R. Annotations.

PROBLEM

Plaintiff had been sitting on the back porch of a friend's apartment. Upon leaving, the plaintiff placed his hand on the porch's railing and turned to speak to his friend, whereupon the railing collapsed, throwing the plaintiff to the ground, resulting in his being severely injured. He then brought suit against the owners of the apartment building

alleging their failure to exercise reasonable care in the maintenance of the handrail.

a. *Westlaw* Search Procedure. [Full text mode]

The following is inputted at the terminal for searching by the *Westlaw* computer:

RAIL HANDRAIL/P PORCH VERANDA DECK

[This instructs the computer to search the data base and locate all cases which contain the words "Rail" or "Handrail" and within the same paragraph also contain the words "Porch" or "Veranda" or "Deck". For the purposes of this search the *Southeastern Reporter* data base was used. Twenty cases were located.]

An alternate query could be made as follows:

RAIL HANDRAIL/P PORCH VERANDA DECK & INJURY & LANDLORD LANDOWNER OWNER

[This instructs the computer to search for cases that contain the words "Rail" or "Handrail" within the same paragraph as the words "Porch" or "Veranda" or "Deck", and in addition must have the words "Injury" and either "Landlord" or "Landowner" or "Owner" appear in the same case. This search located 8 cases. In both searches, the case of *Gumenick v. U. S.* is among the cases found. This is the case that was located in Chapter 7.]

The researcher now has several options for reviewing the retrieved cases. Among these are:

(1) Display only the headnotes.

(2) Display full text.

(3) Display citations.

If the researcher wishes to find cases for jurisdictions other than those in the *Southeastern Reporter*, each of the other units of the *National Reporter System* should be similarly searched.

It should be noted that *Lexis* displays cases located in reverse chronological order, that is the latest cases first, while *Westlaw* ranks the cases according to the number of search terms within each case and displays the cases in the order of this ranking.

b. Other Features of *Westlaw*.

(1) *Shepard's Citations*. An automated citation service based on *Shepard's Citations* is available,

(2) Special subject data bases,

(3) Attached printer which copies the information displayed on the terminal screen.

[Illustration 157]

SECTION B. OTHER DATA BASES

There are many other data bases [5] which may be useful in legal research. Unlike *Lexis* or *Westlaw*, most of these are not full text

[5] For a listing of available data bases, *see* latest edition of M. WILLIAMS, COMPUTER–READABLE DATA BASES: A DIRECTORY AND SOURCEBOOK (American Society for Information Science). *See also* Greguras & Carlive, *Data Bases for the Legal Profession.* 3 DATA BASE 46–50 (June, 1980).

but rather consist of abstracts or indexes of articles and documents. These data bases are made available to subscribers by companies specializing in providing on-line data bases. In some instances special terminals are needed; in others, access may be made through word processing systems now prevalent in many law firm offices. Most university libraries and some larger law libraries offer the services of searching these data bases.[6] A few most relevant to legal research are:

CIS Index (Congressional Information Service Index)

Legal Resource Index

The Information Bank

> [This data base consists of abstracts of items from the *New York Times* and selected materials from over sixty other newspapers and magazines. It is also made available to *Lexis* subscribers.]

Newspaper Index

> [This indexes the *Christian Science Monitor,* the *New York Times,* and the *Wall Street Journal.*]

Psychological Abstracts

> [Most psychological journals are included in this service. It is useful in locating articles on the study of juries, psychological studies of the problems of evidence and many other topics that relate to law.]

SECTION C. MICROTEXT

Microtext is the generic term for bibliographic materials that have been photographically reduced in size and which require magnification on a microtext reader for normal use. Various ratios of reduction are used, varying from 8X to 90X.[7] The most common reduction used for printed materials varies from 18X to 42X.

1. Microtext Format

There are many different formats used for microtext but those mostly used for printed or bibliographic materials are:

[6] In many cities there are private companies which will search the various data bases for individuals. They are generally listed in the Yellow Pages under "Library Research & Service."

[7] The reduction ratio is a measure of the number of times a given linear dimension of an object is reduced when photographed. The larger the "X" the smaller the reduction.

a. *Microfilm*

This is still the most common form of microtext. Microfilm is a roll of film packaged in either reels, cartridges, or cassettes. It is normally used for massive amounts of material such as long runs of newspapers or periodicals.

b. *Computer Output Microfilm* (COM)

In this format, COM is produced directly from information stored on computer tapes. It is economical and gaining widespread use as more and more information is computer-produced. One example of its use is in the production of the *Current Law Index* and *Legal Resource Index* described in Chapter 17. The indexing for these is done on a computer terminal which produces a computer tape. This tape is then used to print the issues of the *Current Law Index* and to cumulate the monthly issues of the *Legal Resource Index.* Many libraries are now substituting COM-produced catalogs for their card catalogs.

c. *Microfiche*

This is a sheet of film varying in size from 3 x 5 inches to 6 x 9 inches, with 4 x 6 inches becoming the standard size for materials in microtext for libraries. Depending on the reduction ratio used, up to 96 normal printed pages can be placed on one standard size microfiche.

d. *Ultrafiche*

This is essentially the same as microfiche, only a much higher reduction ratio is used. In some instances up to 1700 pages can be placed on a single sheet of ultrafiche.

e. *Micro-opaques*

This format is similar to microfiche, only the film is arranged on opaque stock rather than on transparent film. They require special reading machines and generally are more difficult to read than microfilm or microfiche.[8]

2. Microform Equipment

As previously indicated, due to the miniaturization process, special reading machines must be used when using microtext. Frequently, separate machines are needed for each of the various formats although some machines will adjust to two or more types of format. Microtext reading machines come in varying prices, sizes, and op-

[8] The micro-opaques' sizes vary by their trade names: "Microcard" in 3 x 5 inches and 4 x 6 inches; "Microprint" measuring 6 x 9 inches; "Microlex" in 6½ x 7½ inches; "Mini-Print" in 6 x 9 inches.

tions. One of the most useful is the reader-printer. This not only magnifies the text on the reading machine but will also allow for a full-size photocopy of the page on the screen to be made. Many libraries now have microtext reading rooms with various types of reading equipment available. Some libraries also have portable reading machines which a reader may borrow and use outside of the microtext room.

3. Legal Materials Available on Microtext

There is an increasing amount of legal materials available in microtext.[9] Some of the more useful for legal research are:

a. *Briefs and Records*

The briefs and records of the United States Supreme Court, some of the federal courts of appeal, and a few state supreme courts will be found in many law libraries.

b. *Congressional Documents*

Nearly all of the Congressional bills, committee reports and hearings are now available in one form or another of microtext. The U. S. Government Printing Office is also publishing an increasing amount of government documents and reports on microtext.

c. *Legislative Histories*

Both the U. S. Government Printing Office and private publishing companies are reprinting legislative histories in microtext.

3. Microtext Summary

Microtext materials are playing an increasingly important role in legal research. Due to the availability of microtext almost any law library may have in its collection research materials such as briefs and records, legislative histories, out-of-print treatises, and important but scarce periodicals which at one time were only available at the very largest law libraries. The rising cost of printed materials will undoubtedly result in the even greater availability and use of microtext.

[9] For a comprehensive bibliography of legal materials available in microtext, *see* H. TSENG, COMPLETE GUIDE TO LEGAL MATERIALS IN MICROFORM (1976 and supplements).

Chapter 24

FEDERAL TAX RESEARCH [1]

Problems involving federal taxation can usually be solved using techniques and materials discussed in other chapters of *Fundamentals of Legal Research* and *Legal Research Illustrated*. However, most libraries have available a collection of alternative materials, dealing solely with federal tax questions, from which the same solutions may be derived far more expeditiously and in greater detail. Such materials frequently are shelved together in a "tax alcove," but even when dispersed throughout the collection they are no more difficult to locate or use than the more traditional items.

This chapter presents descriptions of these sources of federal tax law. Also presented are methods for finding the relevant materials and assessing their usefulness. Many libraries will lack one or more of the items described in this chapter. Because so many different tools are available, researchers in such libraries are not seriously disadvantaged. Those using institutions with larger collections should find the methods described in this chapter helpful in dealing with any additional materials they may encounter.

Discussion in this chapter will be limited whenever possible to those materials not described elsewhere in *Fundamentals of Legal Research*. Unless specifically cross referenced to other parts of this volume, all research tools listed in Sections B–H are described fully when first mentioned.

SECTION A. RESEARCH TECHNIQUE

Depending upon the nature of the problem and one's familiarity with the underlying law, tax research may begin with primary or secondary sources of law. The former, discussed in Sections B–H, include the Constitution, statutes, treaties, Treasury regulations, IRS

[1] This chapter was prepared by Gail Levin Richmond, Associate Professor of Law, Nova University Center for the Study of Law, Fort Lauderdale, Florida.

This and all subsequent chapter references refer to Jacobstein and Mersky's *Fundamentals of Legal Research* (2d ed. 1981). As material described in Chapters 4, 6–10, 13–18, and 20 of that text is quite useful in tax research, extensive cross references will be made to those chapters. Researchers with access to computerized word-search systems or microforms will also find Chapter 23 quite useful. *See also* Chanin, *Sources and Tools for Federal Tax Research*, 2 AGR.L.J. 161–70 (Summer 1980).

pronouncements, and judicial decisions. While legislative history materials fall within this grouping, they are also quite similar in nature to such secondary materials as treatises and looseleaf services, periodical articles, and commentary in form books, all of which are discussed in Sections I–K.

The following brief example, adapted from a problem used in a tax practice seminar, should prove helpful in illustrating the various strategies which can be employed in doing tax research.

> A client, who made an installment sale in 1974 of property she had then held eleven months, received her first payment of the selling price in 1979. Largely because of his financial difficulties, the buyer had paid only interest during the intervening period. Among other questions, the client wishes to know if she can report her 1979 gain as long-term capital gain.

A researcher familiar with the capital gains provisions would probably go directly to the text of Internal Revenue Code section 1222, which differentiates between long- and short-term holding periods. On the other hand, someone with no knowledge of the area might be better advised to consult one of the treatises or looseleaf services described in section I, using the index to locate discussions of capital gains and holding period. Using this method, one soon locates a reference to section 1222 and proceeds to read the section.

A reading of section 1222 would reveal that the holding period for long-term gains was "greater than one year" in 1979. Nevertheless, the researcher should further determine if a shorter holding period was required in 1974 if the date of sale, rather than the date of reporting gain, governs. Indeed, this issue is the crux of the problem.

One would ascertain the rule in 1974 ("more than six months") by consulting a copy of the law as then in effect. Either textual reading or tracing the subsequent changes in section 1222 would eventually bring the researcher to the *Tax Reform Act of 1976*, Public Law No. 94–455. Section 1402(c) of that Act, which is not a part of the Internal Revenue Code, provides that the time period in effect on the date of sale is the governing period in installment transactions straddling the change in the law. Thus, the research ends with *United States Statutes at Large*,[2] and the client's question is answered in the affirmative.

[2] *U.S. Statutes at Large* is discussed in Chapter 9, Sec. B. Text of recent acts can also be located in the *P–H Federal Taxes* Code Volume discussed in Section I of this chapter. *See also* Section C *infra*.

For those readers interested in practising tax research techniques, the Appendix contains the full text of the installment sale problem. It can be used as an introduction to research involving regulations, rulings, and judicial decisions in addition to the statutory material involved in the excerpt printed here.

SECTION B. CONSTITUTION

The Constitution of the United States grants Congress the power to levy both direct and indirect taxes.[3] While cases challenging the constitutionality of taxing statutes were once relatively numerous, tax litigation today rarely involves the Constitution. Those cases that do raise constitutional claims frequently arise in the context of a provision which does not even mention taxation.[4] For these reasons, tax research materials for the Constitution itself have not proliferated, and research in this area is best done using traditional materials.[5]

SECTION C. STATUTES

Congress has enacted numerous statutes dealing with income, estate and gift, excise, and employment taxes. These separate statutes comprise Title 26 of the *United States Code,* more commonly referred to as the Internal Revenue Code of 1954.[6] Throughout this chapter these statutory materials will be referred to as the Code.

The first steps in tax research are locating and reading any relevant Code sections.[7] The topical indexes accompanying statutory

[3] U.S.Const. art. I, § 2, cl. 3; § 8, cl. 1; § 9, cls. 4–5; amend. XVI.

[4] Most commonly invoked are the fifth amendment's Due Process clause and the fourteenth amendment's Equal Protection clause. See, e. g., *Green v. Kennedy,* 309 F.Supp 1127 (D.D.C.1970) (racial discrimination); *Moritz v. Comm'r,* 469 F.2d 466 (10th Cir. 1972) (sex discrimination); *Darusmont v. United States,* 80–2 USTC para. 9671 (E.D.Cal.1980) (retroactivity).

[5] Chapter 8.

[6] The 1954 Code replaced that adopted in 1939. In earlier years tax statutes were re-enacted in their entirety as necessary. As several provisions in the current law can be traced back to the 1939 Code or earlier, cross references to these earlier materials are extremely useful and are noted in this chapter, particularly in Section D.

[7] The Code may not be the best starting point for particularly complex problems. Instead, one may wish to begin research using the textual materials discussed in Section I of this chapter. Those materials provide information about all the relevant sources of tax law—Code, legislative histories, regulations, rulings and procedures, and judicial decisions—in addition to extensive discussion of the law. See also Section A, dealing with Research Technique.

codifications can be used if one does not know which Code section is needed. Likewise, indexes cross referencing public law section numbers and Code section numbers are helpful when one is doing research involving a recent statute.

1. Current Statutes

Federal tax statutes, as other federal laws,[8] are first published as slip laws and then bound in numerical order into the appropriate volume of *United States Statutes at Large.* While many libraries will have the slip laws themselves or will have one or more of the services discussed in Chapter 9, Section B,[9] these laws can also be located in the following tax-oriented publications.

a. *Internal Revenue Bulletin* (discussed in Section N.1.)

b. *Cumulative Bulletin* (N.1.)

c. *Daily Tax Report* (N.7.)

d. *Internal Revenue Acts—Texts and Legislative History* (N.2.)

e. Mertens, *Law of Federal Income Taxation—Code* (I.2.)

f. *Federal Tax Coordinator 2d* (I.2.)

g. *Prentice-Hall (P–H) Federal Taxes—Code* (I.1.)

2. Codification of Statutes

While tax statutes are included in *United States Code, United States Code Annotated,* and *United States Code Service,*[10] several tax-only codifications exist, each of which has an index for facilitating the location of Code section references.

a. *Commerce Clearing House (CCH) Standard Federal Tax Reporter*[11] (I.1.)

b. *Prentice-Hall (P–H) Federal Taxes*[12] (I.1.)

[8] With one exception—revenue bills may be introduced only in the House of Representatives—the process involved in enacting a tax statute follows that described in Chapter 9, Sec. A.

[9] *U.S. Code Congressional and Administrative News Service; Advance Sheets, United States Code Service; U.S. Law Week.*

[10] Chapter 9, Sec. C.

[11] Although all federal taxes are covered in its two Code volumes, the *Standard Federal Tax Reporter* otherwise limits its coverage to income and employment taxes. CCH also publishes *Federal Estate and Gift Tax Reporter* and *Federal Excise Tax Reporter.* As their formats are almost identical to that of *SFTR,* separate references to these other services will not appear in this chapter.

[12] All federal taxes are covered in the *Federal Taxes* Code volume, but this service is otherwise limited to income and employment taxes. *Federal Taxes—Estate & Gift Taxes* and *Federal Taxes—Excise Taxes* cover their respective subject matters in the same format and will not be separately referred to in this chapter.

c. *U. S. Code Congressional & Administrative News—Internal Revenue Code* (N.2.)

d. Rabkin & Johnson, *Federal Income, Gift and Estate Taxation* (I.2.)

3. Citators for Statutes [13]

If a statute's validity has ever been passed upon by any federal court, including the Tax Court, one can ascertain this information using *Shepard's United States Citations—Statutes.* Although this citator does not indicate jurisdiction for District Court or Court of Appeals decisions, that information can be obtained from *Shepard's Federal Circuit Table.*

4. Pending Legislation

Because Congress frequently has given statutory provisions effective dates which precede their enactment dates,[14] the research effort for proposed transactions must include an investigation of pending legislation. The following materials can be used in finding proposed statutes.

a. *Daily Tax Report* (N.7.)

b. *Tax Management Primary Sources* (N.4.)

c. *CCH Standard Federal Tax Reporter* (I.1.)

d. *P–H Federal Taxes* (I.1.)

Only the *Daily Tax Report* lists all bills introduced in the current Congress, and its description of many bills is at best cursory. For this reason, research into pending legislation should also include the *CCH Congressional Index,* which contains a brief digest of all pending bills, and the *Congressional Information Service (CIS),* which follows a bill's progress through Congress. Those tools are discussed in Chapter 10, Section E.

SECTION D. LEGISLATIVE HISTORIES [15]

Because Treasury regulations rarely are issued immediately following the enactment of a particular Code section, legislative histo-

[13] Citators are described in Section M of this chapter. For a general discussion of these research tools, see Chapter 15.

[14] The Installment Sales Revision Act of 1980 was signed into law on October 19, 1980. Portions of Code § 453, as amended by that Act, apply to transactions occurring after March 31, 1980.

[15] See Chapter 10 for a discussion of the material comprising the legislative history of a federal law. *See also* Lang, *Selected Legislative History of the Federal Income, Estate and Gift Tax Laws Since 1913,* 73 LAW LIB.J. 382 (1980), which lists available materials through November 10, 1978 (Pub.L. No. 95–628).

ries—particularly committee reports—are frequently used by courts in ascertaining Congressional intent.[16] While the materials discussed in Chapter 10, Section E,[17] can be used in compiling a history, the following sources also furnish legislative histories for tax statutes.

1. *Internal Revenue Acts—Text and Legislative History* (N.2.)

2. Rabkin & Johnson, *Federal Income, Gift and Estate Taxation* (I.2.)

3. *Cumulative Bulletin* (N.1.)

4. *Federal Tax Coordinator 2d* (I.2.)

5. *CCH Standard Federal Tax Reporter* (I.1.)

6. *P–H Federal Taxes* (I.1.)

7. *Tax Management Primary Sources* (N.4.)

8. *Seidman's Legislative History of Federal Income and Excess Profits Tax Laws* (N.5.)

9. *The Internal Revenue Acts of the United States: 1909–1950* (N.6.)

10. *Daily Tax Report* (N.7.)

SECTION E. TREATIES AND OTHER INTERNATIONAL MATERIAL

1. Treaties

Research involving income earned (or property transferred) abroad by a United States citizen or resident, or transactions undertaken in the United States by a foreign national, cannot be limited to the Internal Revenue Code. One must be aware that treaty provisions frequently override the Code rules.[18] Such provisions can be found in many publications,[19] of which those limited to tax treaties (usually referred to as tax conventions) are considered here.

a. Diamond & Diamond, *International Tax Treaties of All Nations* (Oceana)

[16] Even after such regulations have been issued, Congressional intent may be important in a taxpayer challenge to their validity.

[17] *Congressional Information Service; Daily Digest (Congressional Record); Guide to Legislative History of Bills Enacted Into Public Law (Statutes at Large); CCH Congressional Index; Digest of General Bills and Resolutions.*

[18] See Code §§ 894(a) & 7852(d).

[19] *Treaties and Other International Acts Series* (T.I.A.S.) and several other publications are discussed in Chapter 20, Sec. C.

This multi-volume set contains the text of all tax treaties, whether or not they have been published by the United Nations. The index for each country's treaties indicates those treaties not yet in effect because instruments of ratification have not been exchanged. This service is not limited to United States treaties.

b. *P–H Tax Treaties*

This service prints the text of income and estate tax treaties between the United States and other countries, along with explanatory material and annotations. Also printed are the texts of various United States and O.E.C.D. model treaties. In the table of contents there is a list of former territories which have assumed a treaty entered into by their former parent country. These treaties are printed under the listing of the original signatory country.

c. *CCH Tax Treaties*

This service provides looseleaf reporting on income and estate tax treaties involving the United States. It includes editorial comment and annotations. There is a special section of CCH Treaty Charts, which show in graphic style the contents of each treaty relating to its major aspects.

d. *Tax Management—Foreign Income*

This service [20] is different from those listed previously, because it has a separate volume for each country. Tax treaties are reproduced in the Working Papers sections of most such volumes. The Analysis sections contain explanations and significant cases and other interpretations. Not all treaty countries are presently covered.

e. *Internal Revenue Bulletin; Cumulative Bulletin*

These services [21] print the text of treaties and Treasury Department Technical Explanations prepared for the Senate. Each *Cumulative Bulletin* contains only those treaties issued during the previous six-month period; current treaties appear in the weekly *Internal Revenue Bulletin.*

f. *Federal Tax Coordinator 2d*

Chapter 20 of this looseleaf service [22] contains the text of United States tax treaties and lists the countries signatory to each. There is also explanatory material and a Developments section for updating material.

[20] A more extensive discussion of the *Tax Management* service appears in Section I of this chapter.

[21] See Section N of this chapter for a detailed description of these services.

[22] This service is discussed in greater detail in Section I.

g. *Daily Tax Report*

Texts of current United States tax treaties are printed in this daily service.[23]

2. Citators for Tax Treaties

The *Shepard's* and *United States Code Service* materials discussed in Chapter 20 can be used in locating court decisions involving treaties. To locate Internal Revenue Service interpretations, however, the best source is the Service's own *Bulletin Index-Digest System*.[24] This service provides citations to currently applicable revenue rulings and procedures as well as to Supreme Court decisions and to Tax Court decisions adverse to the government. Digests of these items also appear in this service.

3. Other International Material

Textual material describing tax rules and business practices in other countries can be found in several services, including many published by national accounting firms. Among the available materials are the following:

a. Diamond & Diamond, *Tax Havens of the World* (Matthew Bender)

b. Diamond, *Foreign Tax and Trade Briefs* (Matthew Bender)

c. Arthur Andersen & Co., *Tax and Trade Guides*

d. Price Waterhouse & Co., *Information Guides for Doing Business*

e. Ernst & Whinney, *International Series*

f. *Tax Management—Foreign Income* (E. 2.)

Because the first five series are used exclusively for background information, they are not further described in this chapter.[25]

SECTION F. REGULATIONS

In Code section 7805(a), Congress authorized the Secretary of the Treasury to "prescribe all needful rules and regulations for the enforcement" of the tax statutes.[26] Regulations issued pursuant to

[23] See Section N for a general discussion of this service.

[24] See Section N.

[25] Directories of foreign lawyers are described in Chapter 19, Sec. C.

[26] Regulations are actually formulated by the IRS, but they are approved by the Secretary of the Treasury or his delegate. See Procedural Rules of the Internal Revenue Service, § 601.601(a)(1), 26 C.F.R. § 601(a)(1).

this authorization are referred to as interpretative. In contrast, there are so-called legislative regulations, issued for Code sections in which Congress has made a specific grant of authority, allowing tax experts to write the rules in certain technical areas.[27] Interpretative regulations will be upheld by a court unless they are clearly contrary to Congressional intent; legislative regulations are virtually unassailable.

Final regulations are issued as Treasury Decisions (T.D.'s).[28] Each T.D. contains a preamble in which appears a textual discussion and the name of the appropriate IRS employee to contact for further information. Regulations are numbered in the same manner as the Code sections to which they relate, preceded by a numerical prefix indicating which tax is involved.[29]

Like the Code itself, regulations are found in both current and codified formats.

1. Current Final Regulations

Recently adopted tax regulations can be found using the *Federal Register* [30] or the Advance Pamphlets of the *United States Code Service*.[31] These new regulations may also be found in the following tax-oriented publications.

a. *Daily Tax Report* (N. 7.)

b. *Internal Revenue Bulletin; Cumulative Bulletin* (N. 1.)

c. *Federal Tax Coordinator 2d* (I. 2.)

d. Mertens, *Law of Federal Income Taxation—Regulations* (I. 2.)

e. *U. S. Tax Week* (N. 3.)

[27] See, e. g., Code § 385(a): "The Secretary is authorized to prescribe such regulations as may be necessary or appropriate to determine whether an interest in a corporation is to be treated . . . as stock or indebtedness."

[28] T.D. numbers bear no relation to regulations section numbers.

[29] The prefix 1. is for income tax regulations; 20. is for estate tax regulations; and 25. is for gift tax regulations. Still other prefixes are used for excise taxes, employment taxes and procedural regulations. Temporary regulations have different prefixes than do final regulations. In this numbering system, regulations § 1.-109–1 would be immediately recognizable as a regulation involving income tax Code § 109.

[30] Chapter 13, Sec. B.

[31] Chapter 9, Sec. C.

2. Codification of Final Regulations

While the *Code of Federal Regulations* [32] contains the text of tax regulations as its Title 26, the following tax-oriented publications also present this information.

a. Rabkin & Johnson, *Federal Income, Gift and Estate Taxation* (I. 2.)

b. *U. S. Code Congressional & Administrative News—Federal Tax Regulations* (N. 2.)

c. *CCH Standard Federal Tax Reporter* (I. 1.)

d. *P–H Federal Taxes* (I. 1.)

3. Citators for Final Regulations

When a transaction is affected by an existing regulation, that regulation's success or failure in previous litigation is quite relevant. The Internal Revenue Service does not consider itself bound by adverse decisions in any tribunal other than the Supreme Court, and it will not withdraw a regulation merely because one or more lower courts have invalidated it.[33] A citator indicating judicial action on regulations is extremely useful as a tool in gauging the likelihood of government success when a regulation is being challenged.

The three citators listed below follow two basic patterns: they are arranged in either regulations section order or in Treasury Decision number order.[34]

a. *Shepard's Code of Federal Regulations Citations*

b. *CCH Standard Federal Tax Reporter*

c. *P–H Federal Taxes—Citator*

4. Proposed Regulations

Notice of proposed regulations appears in both the *Federal Register* [35] and the *Internal Revenue Bulletin*.[36] After the proposed regulations have undergone taxpayer comment, both written and oral, final regulations are promulgated as T.D.'s. Proposed regulations can be located in the following services.

[32] Chapter 13, Sec. B.

[33] See, e. g., regulations § 1.105–4(a)(3)(i) (1966), which had been invalidated by the Sixth and Tenth Circuits as well as the Court of Claims, and was finally amended by the IRS in T.D. 7352 (1975).

[34] All three citators are described in Section M of this chapter. Only *Shepard's* is arranged by regulations section.

[35] Chapter 13, Sec. B.

[36] Section N of this chapter.

a. *Federal Tax Coordinator 2d* (I. 2.)

b. Mertens, *Law of Federal Income Taxation—Regulations* (I. 2.)

c. Rabkin & Johnson, *Federal Income, Gift and Estate Taxation* (I. 2.)

d. *CCH Standard Federal Tax Reporter* (I. 1.)

e. *P–H Federal Taxes* (I. 1.)

f. *Daily Tax Report* (N. 7.)

5. Regulations Under Development

In addition to indicating regulations which have been formally proposed, the IRS Semiannual Agenda of Regulations indicates all Code sections for which new regulations are under development or existing regulations are to be reviewed. Extensive information is given about the status of each item within the IRS. This information includes an indication of the item's relative priority for the next six months. The Semiannual Agenda is published in the *Federal Register* every March 31 and September 30. It is also reprinted in Mertens, *Law of Federal Income Taxation—Regulations.*[37] A monthly version is published as a supplement to the *Daily Tax Report.*[38]

SECTION G. INTERNAL REVENUE SERVICE PRONOUNCEMENTS

1. Types of Pronouncements

a. *Rulings*

The Internal Revenue Service issues rulings designed to apply the law to particular factual situations taxpayers have presented. Unlike regulations, rulings are not published in proposed form for general comment, and they do not bear the approval of the Secretary of the Treasury. There are two types of rulings—revenue rulings and letter rulings.

Rulings which the IRS determines are of general interest[39] are published in the weekly *Internal Revenue Bulletin* as revenue rulings and are numbered chronologically.[40] Although a revenue ruling is

[37] Section I of this chapter.

[38] Section N of this chapter.

[39] See Procedural Rules of the Internal Revenue Service, § 601.601(d)(2)(iii), 26 C.F.R. § 601(d)(2)(iii), for a statement of information which is not published in the *Internal Revenue Bulletin.*

[40] Rev.Rul. 81–1 is the first revenue ruling issued in 1981. Each week's rulings are assigned numbers according to the Code sections they interpret. Al-

not as authoritative as a Treasury regulation, it can be relied upon by any taxpayer whose circumstances are substantially the same as those described in that ruling.

Letter rulings [41] are indicative of IRS policy, and the public has access to them under the Freedom of Information Act, but the IRS does not consider itself bound by them in its dealings with other taxpayers.[42] Letter rulings are given multi-digit file numbers, of which the first two digits indicate the year, and the next two the week, of issuance.

b. *Revenue Procedures*

Revenue procedures are published statements of IRS practices and procedures, numbered chronologically.[43] Procedures of general applicability are frequently added to the IRS *Statement of Procedural Rules* and published in the *Code of Federal Regulations.*

c. *Operating Policies*

In many instances a tax problem will require knowledge of IRS operating policies. Thus, one may need to know how the Service acts to comply with the Privacy Act of 1974, what audit techniques are applied to stock brokers, or if a particular issue is on the "Prime Issues List" and is likely to be litigated whenever it arises on audit.

The workings of the Internal Revenue Service are compiled in the *Internal Revenue Manual,* which Commerce Clearing House publishes in two looseleaf services. The six Administrative volumes contain the text of policies, procedures, instructions and guidelines involved in the organization, functions, administration and operations of the Service. The three Audit volumes contain policies and other information relating to the Service's audit function. Unimportant information, such as that dealing with secretarial procedures, is omitted. Volumes are updated whenever the IRS finalizes a change in existing policies.

The *Manuals* are divided into parts based upon IRS functions. Each part is further subdivided into chapters, sections and subsections. Publisher-generated topical indexes appear at the beginning of each part; there is no comprehensive index for the *Manual* as a whole. In those instances where the IRS has compiled topical index-

though Rev.Rul. 81–1 does not interpret Code § 1, it does involve a Code section with a lower number than does Rev.Rul. 81–2.

41 Letter rulings are often referred to as private rulings. In reality most rulings originate as letter rulings; those officially published by the IRS are thereafter referred to as revenue rulings.

42 *But see* Ogiony v. Comm'r, 617 F.2d 14, 17–18 (2d Cir. 1980) (Oakes, J., concurring).

43 Rev.Proc. 81–1 is the first revenue procedure for 1981.

es for chapters, these indexes are reproduced at the end of the material to which they relate.

Manual Supplements are issued in situations where the IRS chooses to amend a stated policy without revising the existing material directly. These Supplements, which appear at the end of the chapters being revised, are frequently used when a temporary change is planned or in situations where a change is being given a trial run. In some instances a Supplement will affect more than one chapter. In such cases, the Supplement will be printed in full text after the "primary" chapter to which it relates, but it will also be referred to after the other affected chapters. Each chapter which is affected by a Supplement will have a Cross Reference Table following its Table of Contents.

In addition to the main text and Supplements, several text sections are followed by Exhibits (reproducing forms or giving lists of places) and Handbooks (providing specific guidelines and procedures for IRS personnel). Some Handbooks are so lengthy that they have instead been issued to subscribers as separate pamphlets. Exhibits and Handbooks are listed in the topical index preceding each part of the *Manuals*.

2. Finding Lists for IRS Pronouncements

Rulings and procedures, unlike regulations, are not assigned numbers which correspond to the Code sections they discuss. While rulings are thus more difficult to locate than are regulations, the following publications can be used to locate relevant items.[44]

a. *Bulletin Index-Digest System* (N. 1.)

b. Mertens, *Law of Federal Income Taxation* (I. 2.)

c. Rabkin & Johnson, *Federal Income, Gift and Estate Taxation* (I. 2.)

d. *Federal Tax Coordinator 2d* (I. 2.)

e. *CCH Standard Federal Tax Reporter* (I. 1.)

f. *P–H Federal Taxes* (I. 1.)

3. Digests of IRS Pronouncements[45]

Digests can be used to locate appropriate rulings and procedures. In addition, the digests can be used to determine which of a long list of rulings should be read first.

[44] These services do not have finding lists for letter rulings. See subsection 5 of this section for materials concerning letter rulings.

[45] See subsection 5 of this section for materials providing digests of letter rulings.

a. *Bulletin Index-Digest System* (N. 1.)

b. *U. S. Tax Week* (N. 3.)

4. Texts of Revenue Rulings and Revenue Procedures

The following services contain texts of rulings and procedures.

a. *Internal Revenue Bulletin; Cumulative Bulletin* (N. 1.)

b. *Federal Tax Coordinator 2d* (I. 2.)

c. Mertens, *Law of Federal Income Taxation—Rulings* (I. 2.)

d. *CCH Standard Federal Tax Reporter* (I. 1.)

e. *P–H Federal Taxes* (I. 1.)

f. *Daily Tax Report* (N. 7.)

5. Texts of Letter Rulings

Every week the IRS releases letter rulings for inspection and copying. These can be obtained directly from the Service, but IRS personnel do not include headnotes or summaries.

Tax Analysts & Advocates *Tax Notes, P–H Private Letter Rulings,* and BNA *Daily Tax Report* [46] all publish digests of letter rulings and will furnish full texts to subscribers as needed.[47] *CCH Standard Federal Tax Reporter* publishes full texts but only of selected rulings.[48]

CCH IRS Letter Rulings Reports prints both digests and full texts of all letter rulings. Digests appear in Code section order; full texts are in ruling number order. There are Code section and topical indexes.

6. Citators for IRS Pronouncements

Revenue rulings and procedures are often reviewed for continued relevance by the IRS itself. In addition, some rulings have been subjected to judicial scrutiny. The status of these items can be determined from the following materials.

a. *Bulletin Index-Digest System* (N. 1.)

b. Mertens, *Law of Federal Income Taxation—Rulings* (I. 2.)

c. *CCH Standard Federal Tax Reporter* (I. 1. & M. 3.)

d. *P–H Federal Taxes—Citator* (M. 2.)

[46] Section N of this chapter.

[47] See also Section L, dealing with computerized tax research materials.

[48] Section I. 1. of this chapter.

SECTION H. JUDICIAL REPORTS

1. Court Organization

There are three courts of original jurisdiction for tax cases: the United States District Courts; the United States Court of Claims; and the United States Tax Court. As District Courts are courts of general jurisdiction, their judges rarely develop as high a level of expertise on tax law questions as do judges of the Tax Court or even of the Court of Claims. The District Court is the only tribunal where a jury trial is available in tax litigation, but a taxpayer cannot litigate his case in District Court unless he first pays the amount in dispute and then sues for a refund.

Trials in the Court of Claims are conducted by a Trial Judge (formerly called a Commissioner), whose decisions are reviewed by Court of Claims judges. Although the Court of Claims does not hear tax cases exclusively, the percentage of such cases it hears is greater than that heard in the average District Court. As in the District Court, a taxpayer must first pay the disputed amount before he can bring suit before this court.

Because Tax Court judges hear only tax cases, their expertise is substantially greater than that of judges in the other trial courts. In addition, a taxpayer is entitled to sue in the Tax Court without paying the amount in dispute prior to litigation.[49] Tax Court cases are tried by one judge, who submits an opinion to the chief judge for consideration. The chief judge will either allow the decision to stand or refer it to the full court for review. The published decision will indicate whether or not it has been reviewed; dissenting opinions, if any, will be included. There are two types of Tax Court decisions: [50] decisions presenting important legal issues are published by the court (regular decisions); decisions involving well-established legal issues (memorandum decisions) are not officially published, but are privately issued by several publishers.

When research uncovers conflicting decisions at the trial court level, these decisions should be traced to the appellate court level. In the event that no appeals have been taken, the Tax Court's specialized knowledge justifies according greater weight to its decisions than to a decision from either of the other trial courts. In addition, if the Tax

[49] Taxpayers also had this privilege in the Tax Court's predecessor, the Board of Tax Appeals.

[50] The Tax Court also has a Small Cases division. Decisions in such cases are not appealable, cannot be used as precedents, and are not published in any reporter service. Code § 7463(b).

Court has ruled against the government and the IRS has issued a notice of acquiescence, a taxpayer can consider the decision a strong precedent.

Decisions of District Courts and the Tax Court are appealed to the Courts of Appeals. Decisions of the Court of Claims, however, are reviewed only by the Supreme Court, which also reviews Courts of Appeals decisions. Because the Supreme Court selects so few cases for review, the Court of Claims offers a forum-shopping opportunity to taxpayers living in circuits where Courts of Appeals decisions involving similar issues are adverse.[51]

2. Finding Lists for Decisions

If decisions involving a particular statute, treaty, regulation, or ruling are desired, a preliminary list can be compiled using the annotated treatise materials discussed in Section I. In addition, the following services can be used for that purpose.

a. *Bulletin Index-Digest System* (N. 1.)

b. *Shepard's United States Citations—Statutes* (M. 1.)

c. *Shepard's Code of Federal Regulations Citations* (M. 1.)

d. *CCH Standard Federal Tax Reporter* (I. 2. & M. 3.)

e. *P–H Federal Taxes—Citator* (M. 2.)

3. Digests of Decisions [52]

Digests are useful in locating decisions omitted from the annotations discussed in Section I. In addition, they can be used to determine which of many cases should be read first. The following services contain digests of tax cases.

a. *Bulletin Index-Digest System* (N. 1.)

b. *Daily Tax Report* (N. 7.)

c. *P–H Federal Taxes* (I. 1.)

d. *CCH Standard Federal Tax Reporter* (I. 1.)

e. *U. S. Tax Week* (N. 3.)

f. *Tax Court Digest* (Bobbs-Merrill) [53]

g. *CCH Tax Court Reporter*

[51] See *Ginsburg v. United States,* 396 F.2d 983, 986 (Ct.Cl.1968), for a discussion of this phenomenon.

[52] Chapter 6 includes a discussion of other available digests. The *General Digest* and *West's Federal Practice Digest 2d,* discussed in that chapter, are particularly helpful if digests are desired for District Court, Court of Appeals, or Court of Claims decisions.

[53] Until publication was suspended in 1978, this service printed digests of all regular decisions as well as of memorandum decisions which were appealed. Di-

In a looseleaf volume and transfer binders, this service contains copies of the official Tax Court digests and its own digests of memorandum decisions. The digests are arranged by subject matter.

4. Texts of Decisions [54]

Federal court decisions involving taxation are printed in the following sets:

a. Supreme Court

(1) United States Reports (official)

(2) United States Supreme Court Reports, Lawyers' Edition

(3) Supreme Court Reporter

(4) American Federal Tax Reports (AFTR; AFTR2d)

(5) U.S. Tax Cases (USTC)

(6) Internal Revenue Bulletin; Cumulative Bulletin

(7) Daily Tax Report

b. Courts of Appeals

(1) Federal Reporter

(2) American Federal Tax Reports

(3) U. S. Tax Cases

c. District Courts

(1) Federal Supplement (since 1932) [55]

(2) Federal Reporter (until 1932)

(3) American Federal Tax Reports

(4) U. S. Tax Cases

d. Court of Claims

(1) Court of Claims Reports (official)

(2) Federal Reporter (until 1932; since 1960)

(3) Federal Supplement (between 1932 and 1960)

gests were arranged by topic, and the subsequent history was given for each case. Citations were made to official and other case reports.

The Table of Cases volume listed cases alphabetically, indicated acquiescences and nonacquiescences, and gave citations. The topical headings under which each case was digested were listed, and an indication was given if the particular case was cited and followed in any subsequent digested decision. The Index volume listed topical headings and provided an extensive word index cross referenced to these headings. Even though recent material does not appear, this service is still quite useful for earlier decisions.

[54] See Chapter 4 for an extensive discussion of case reports.

[55] The *Federal Supplement* prints selected District Court opinions only.

(4) American Federal Tax Reports

(5) U. S. Tax Cases

e. Tax Court

(1) Tax Court of the United States Reports; United States Tax Court Reports (official)

(2) CCH Tax Court Reporter (advance sheets)

(3) P–H Tax Court Reports (advance sheets)

(4) CCH Tax Court Memorandum Decisions

(5) P–H Tax Court Memorandum Decisions

f. Board of Tax Appeals

(1) Board of Tax Appeals Reports (official)

(2) P–H B.T.A. Reports

(3) P–H B.T.A. Memorandum Decisions

Most of the sets listed above are either official or are published by West Publishing Company and are used the same way for tax research as they are for non-tax. Two of the sets, *AFTR* and *USTC,* published by Prentice-Hall and Commerce Clearing House, are sufficiently different from the other sets that further discussion of each is appropriate.

The use of these sets can be coordinated with the use of each publisher's looseleaf reporting service, *AFTR* with *P–H Federal Taxes* and *USTC* with *CCH Standard Federal Tax Reporter.* Each service publishes decisions from all courts except the Tax Court, and each includes District Court decisions omitted from *Federal Supplement.* Each first includes the texts of these decisions in an Advance Sheets volume of the publisher's looseleaf reporting service. Because *AFTR* and *USTC* are initially published in conjunction with the looseleaf services, texts of recent tax decisions are available on a weekly basis. Moreover, these cases will appear in the listings of new material in the services' update volumes (*P–H Federal Taxes* Current Matter volume; *CCH Standard Federal Tax Reporter* New Matters volume). Because these listings are done in Code section order and are cross referenced to discussions in the services' compilation volumes, one can locate a recent case when one knows the Code section involved but not the taxpayer's name, and one can immediately find a discussion of the topic involved in the compilation volumes. Indeed, the *Daily Tax Report* is probably the only more current source of these cases, and it is not indexed on a weekly basis.

5. Parallel Citations

The existence of so many case reporters for each jurisdiction increases the probability that at least one copy of any decision will always be on the library shelves. Because many of these reporters print non-tax as well as tax decisions, several volumes of each are issued during the year. If the desired reporter volume is not on the shelf, one can look up the case citation in one of the tools listed below to obtain a parallel citation to the same case in another reporter.[56] This approach usually will be a faster method of transferring between reporters than looking up the case name in several volumes' tables of cases.

a. *CCH Standard Federal Tax Reporter* (M. 3.)

b. *P–H Federal Taxes—Citator* (M. 2.)

c. Rabkin & Johnson, *Federal Income, Gift and Estate Taxation* (I. 2.)

d. Mertens, *Law of Federal Income Taxation* (I. 2.)

e. *Federal Tax Coordinator 2d* (I. 2.)

6. Citators for Decisions

There are three commonly used citators for judging the relative authority of any tax decision, and many libraries will have all of them. Although there is substantial overlap in their coverage, each citator contains some information the others lack. All three are discussed in Section M of this chapter.

a. *Shepard's Citations*

b. *CCH Standard Federal Tax Reporter*

c. *P–H Federal Taxes—Citator*

7. Pending Litigation

Either the *P–H Federal Taxes* Current Matter volume or the *CCH Standard Federal Tax Reporter* New Matters volume can be used to determine if appeals have been filed in recent tax cases.[57] *Federal Taxes* has an alphabetical List of Current Decisions in which appeals are noted; the *SFTR* version is the current year's Case Table.

Cases pending decision by the Tax Court can be located in volume 3 of the *CCH Tax Court Reporter*, which contains digests of petitions. These digests identify cases whose eventual outcome might affect the results of a current research effort. Cases are arranged by docket number. These numbers can be obtained from the alphabetical Petitioners Table or from the topical Petitions Index.

[56] Sections I & M of this chapter.

[57] See also *United States Law Week*, discussed in Chapter 4, Sec. A.

The *Tax Court Reporter* also contains Motion and Trial Calendars and a section for New Tax Disputes. The Calendars indicate where each docketed item stands in the procession to trial. The Disputes section contains explanations of newsworthy petitions—those presenting novel theories or involving previously unexplored areas of the Code. This service is updated weekly.

SECTION I. LOOSELEAF SERVICES, ENCYCLOPEDIAS, AND TREATISES

Explanatory materials are frequently consulted early in the research effort, often before the relevant statutes are read.[58] The texts described in this section provide insight into the problem being researched, and their liberal use of citations can be drawn upon for a preliminary reading list of cases and administrative pronouncements.

While some of these materials would be listed elsewhere as looseleaf services, and others as legal encyclopedias or treatises,[59] those classifications are less significant in this context than classifications based upon their formats. Most of them take a subject matter approach, but the two most frequently used services are arranged in Code section order.

1. Code Section Arrangement

The Commerce Clearing House[60] and Prentice-Hall[61] looseleaf services take essentially the same approach.[62] The full text of Code sections and Treasury regulations are printed along with editorial explanations. An annotation section listing cases and rulings follows each section. Persons wanting ready access to the text of the law while they are reading explanations of it will appreciate the format of these compilations.

Because of the arrangement described above, however, problems involving multiple Code sections are not given comprehensive discussion in the Code compilations. The publishers solve this problem in

[58] In appropriate cases these textual materials can be used to ascertain which statutes are involved. In addition, these materials can be consulted at any point in the research process if additional textual information is desired.

[59] See Chapters 14, 16, and 18 for further discussion of these research tools. The annotated law reports discussed in Chapter 7 also provide textual material.

[60] *CCH Standard Federal Tax Reporter* (income tax); *CCH Federal Estate and Gift Tax Reporter; CCH Federal Excise Tax Reporter.*

[61] *P–H Federal Taxes* (income tax); *P–H Federal Taxes—Estate & Gift Taxes; P–H Federal Taxes—Excise Taxes.*

[62] Additional discussion of these services appears in Chapter 14.

two ways. Pamphlets containing in-depth discussions are issued periodically to subscribers.[63] In addition, the compilation volumes include special sections devoted to tax planning, problems of specific businesses, and other materials involving several Code sections.

These services have subject matter indexes; their format makes Code section indexes unnecessary. New material is sent to subscribers weekly for insertion in a separate volume. These new developments are indexed according to the paragraph in the main compilation to which they relate, i. e., in Code section order.

Most libraries have both of these services, and users eventually develop a preference for one or the other. As each service's annotations are editorially selected, use of both can reduce the risk of missing a valuable annotation although it may substantially increase research time. In most instances the extra material obtained will not justify the additional time involved.

The two services are discussed individually below.

a. *CCH Standard Federal Tax Reporter*

The discussion of this looseleaf service follows the format in which it is arranged. Several of its volumes, such as the Citator, are discussed in greater detail elsewhere in this chapter and appropriate cross references to such discussions are given here.

Code Volumes. These volumes print, in Code section order, all provisions involving income, gift and estate taxes (volume I) and employment and excise taxes as well as procedural provisions (volume II). Following each Code subsection is a reference to its 1939 Code counterpart, a very brief history, and an explanation of amendments (including their effective dates). One of the most helpful tables in this volume indicates every other section of the Code which refers to any particular section. As the Code itself is not fully cross referenced, the value of this table, particularly for researching an unfamiliar area, cannot be overstated. Unfortunately, there will be many situations where Code sections do not refer to each other; in such instances the annotated materials discussed in this section help fill the gap.

Index Volume. This volume contains an extensive topical index, using paragraph numbers, to all of the material in the nine compilation volumes discussed below. It also includes such helpful features as Tax Calendars and Rate Tables, Check Lists (for such topics as taxable and nontaxable items), Tax Planning (discussions involving various situations and occupations), Tax Terms (definitions and dis-

[63] *CCH Tax Analysis Series; P–H Tax-Saving Series.*

cussions of commonly used jargon), and a discussion involving the recurring topic, "Who Is the Taxpayer?"

The Finding Lists in this volume, which are discussed in Section M, can be used as citators for revenue rulings and procedures and other IRS pronouncements. The Committee Reports section at the end of these Lists indicates all committee reports which explain amendments to the 1954 Code. The reports are listed in Code section order; *Cumulative Bulletin* or *Internal Revenue Bulletin* citations are given.

Compilation Volumes. Volumes 1–9 of this service contain, in Code section order, the full text of the Code, final and temporary regulations, and annotations to revenue rulings and procedures as well as to judicial decisions. An alphabetical index is provided whenever the annotations section is lengthy. Immediately after each Code section, the editors indicate which Public Laws have amended it and give *Cumulative Bulletin* or *SFTR* citations to committee reports; a brief history is also given following regulations sections. There is an extensive editorial explanation, including citations to the annotations, for each Code provision.

New Matters Volume. The compilation volumes receive little updating during the year involved. Instead, recent material is published in the New Matters volume of this service. This volume's Cumulative Index is arranged according to the paragraph numbers assigned each item in the Compilation volumes, so it is very easy to use this volume to determine if a more recent ruling or decision has been issued in any area of interest. [See Illustration 158, Section *O*]

The updating material indexed in this volume is also reproduced therein (texts of rulings, procedures, and digests of Tax Court decisions) or in the *USTC* Advance Sheets volume (texts of proposed regulations and of decisions rendered by the District Courts, Court of Claims, Courts of Appeals, and Supreme Court).

The New Matters volume has several other helpful features. In addition to a topical index of current year developments, it contains lists of special reports and tax forms sent to subscribers, recent developments affecting Tax Analysis booklets, and a table cross referencing the 1939 Code to the 1954 Code as well as to the compilation volumes.

This volume also contains materials relating to selected pending tax bills, although major bills are issued in special pamphlet reports. There is a Code section index indicating sections affected by pending bills; this index does not distinguish between provisions amending existing sections and those adding new ones. There is also a Status table indicating each bill's effect and reporting its progress through

Congress. With the exception of those selected for special reports, bills covered in this service receive far less detailed coverage than do those reported upon in *Primary Sources*, discussed in Section N. 4.

The New Matters volume contains a Rewrite Bulletins section, in which appear editorial discussions of significant recent developments. These discussions are indexed in this volume and also contain their own cross references to the compilation volumes.

A Case Table, listing each year's decisions alphabetically, indicates (1) which trial court is involved and where the decision appears in the text; (2) appeals action by either side, including IRS acquiescence or nonacquiescence in unfavorable Tax Court decisions; and (3) the outcome at the appellate level. The Supreme Court Docket, which also lists cases alphabetically, includes a brief digest of the issues involved.

USTC Advance Sheets Volume. This volume contains the text of proposed regulations issued by the Treasury Department. It also contains the texts of court decisions rendered by the District Courts, Court of Claims, Courts of Appeals, and the Supreme Court. All of these items can be located using the Cumulative Index in the New Matters volume. Each type of item appears in the order in which it was issued rather than in Code section order. When proposed regulations are later issued in final regulations form, they will be integrated into the compilation volumes. Likewise, the court decisions printed in this volume will later be issued in hardbound volumes as part of the *USTC* reporter service discussed in Section H. 4.

Citator. This volume, which lists all decisions alphabetically, can be used to determine if subsequent decisions have affected the earlier items. A full discussion of the *CCH Citator* appears in Section M. 3. The citator is perhaps the weakest feature of the CCH service compared to the P–H service.

b. *P–H Federal Taxes*

The discussion of this looseleaf service follows the format in which it is arranged. Several of its volumes, as well as the *P–H Citator,* are discussed in greater detail elsewhere in this chapter and appropriate cross references to such discussions are given here.

Code Volume. This volume prints, in Code section order, all provisions involving income, gift and estate, employment, and excise taxes as well as procedural provisions. Following each Code subsection is a very brief history, including the effective date of amendments. Prior language is not included, however. This information can often be obtained from the Amending Acts section of this volume, which provides the text of acts since June 30, 1969. Unfortunately, this material is not indexed.

One of the most helpful tables in this volume indicates every other section of the Code which refers to any particular section. As the Code itself is not fully cross referenced, the value of this table, particularly for researching an unfamiliar area, cannot be overstated. Unfortunately, there will be many situations where Code sections do not refer to each other; in such instances the annotated materials discussed in this section help fill the gap. This volume also has a table showing effective dates for Code sections and another table indicating provisions of the Constitution and *United States Code* which affect federal taxation.

Index Volume. This volume contains extensive topical and transactions indexes, using paragraph numbers, to all of the material in the seven compilation volumes discussed below. It also includes such helpful features as a Federal Tax Calendar, checklists (for such topics as taxable and nontaxable items), lists of tax forms, and tax tables.

There are Tables, of Rulings and of Cases, which cross reference these items to discussions in the compilation volumes. There is also an Index to Tax Articles, arranged in Code section order, which is discussed further in Section J.

Compilation Volumes. Volumes 2–8 of this service contain, in Code section order, the full text of the Code, final and temporary regulations, and annotations to revenue rulings and procedures as well as to judicial decisions. Italicized material indicates changes in both Code and regulations sections. An index is provided whenever the annotations section is lengthy. There is an extensive editorial explanation, including citations to the annotations, for each Code provision. Volume 8 also includes the text of Proposed Regulations.

Current Matter Volume. The Compilation volumes receive little updating during the year involved. Instead, recent material is published in the Current Matter Volume of this service. This volume's Cross Reference Table is arranged according to the paragraph numbers assigned each item in the Compilation volumes, so it is very easy to use this volume to determine if a more recent ruling or decision has been issued in any area of interest.

The updating material indexed in this volume is also reproduced therein (texts of rulings, procedures, and digests of Tax Court decisions) or in the *AFTR 2d* Advance Sheets volume (texts of decisions rendered by the District Court, Court of Claims, Courts of Appeals, and Supreme Court).

The Current Matter volume has several other helpful features. In addition to a List of Current Decisions, which gives information about appeals, it indicates in a separate table all cases the Supreme Court has agreed to hear in the current term.

This volume also contains materials relating to selected pending tax bills, although major bills are issued in special pamphlet reports. There is a Code section index indicating sections affected by pending bills; different type faces are used to distinguish between provisions amending existing sections and those adding new ones. A Legislation Status table gives the title of each bill, but it does not indicate the bill's effect. This table also reports each bill's progress through Congress. With the exception of those selected for special reports, bills covered in this service receive far less detailed coverage than do those reported upon in *Primary Sources*, discussed in Section N. 4.

AFTR 2d Advance Sheets Volume. This volume contains the texts of court decisions rendered by the District Courts, Court of Claims, Courts of Appeal, and the Supreme Court. All of these items can be located using the Cross Reference Table in the Current Matter volume. Each type of item appears in the order in which it was issued rather than in Code section order. The court decisions printed in this volume will later be issued in hardbound volumes as part of the *AFTR* reporter service discussed in Section H. 4.

Citator. This volume, which lists all decisions alphabetically, can be used to determine if subsequent decisions have affected the earlier items. A full discussion of the *P–H Citator* appears in Section M. 2. The citator is perhaps the strongest feature of the P–H service compared to the CCH service.

2. Subject Matter Arrangement—Multiple Topics

The second group of materials is quite varied; many libraries will lack at least one of them. Each of them covers a wide range of topics using a subject matter arrangement.

a. *Federal Tax Coordinator 2d* (Research Institute of America)

This bi-weekly service contains excellent discussions of all areas of taxation other than social security and unemployment taxes. The text volumes (4–26) are arranged by chapters using a subject matter approach. Discussions in each chapter include liberal use of citations as well as cross references to topics of potential relevance discussed in other chapters. Analysis of as yet unresolved matters is included.

Each chapter has the following arrangement: a detailed topical index; discussion of each topic, including annotations; text of code and regulations sections which are applicable to the topic being discussed; a Current Developments section.

Material in the other volumes is discussed in the following paragraphs.

Volume 1 contains a detailed subject matter index, which can be used to locate appropriate discussion in the text volumes. This index, like the Code and regulations sections indexes in the same volume, has both a main and a current section.

Volume 2 contains three Rulings and Releases Tables (a main and a current Table, as well as one for obsolete items) giving cross references to discussions in the text volumes. These Tables use a chronological arrangement for IRS materials.

Volume 2 also contains three Parallel Reference Tables for cases decided since 1954. All three tables are cross referenced to *American Federal Tax Reports* and to *U. S. Tax Cases*. The first table lists cases by volume and page from *United States Reports*; the second, from *Federal Reporter, Second Series*; the last, from *Federal Supplement*. These tables are not updated regularly. There is also an alphabetical listing of cases with cross references to discussions in the text volumes. This list is divided into Current, Supplementary and Main tables. A Supreme Court Docket and a Court of Appeals Docket, indicating where discussion of currently pending cases appears in the text volumes, are also found in Volume 2.

Planning checklists and other practice aids are provided in Volume 3, which also has a table showing where tax return forms are discussed in the text. Volume 3 contains cross references to recent tax developments discussed in more detail in a companion volume, *Federal Tax Coordinator 2d Weekly Alert*. The final section of Volume 3 is a reproduction of IRS Audit Guidelines for various industries, including tax shelters.

Volume 20 contains the texts of United States tax treaties and lists of signatory countries in addition to textual material dealing with the treaties.

Volume 27 contains proposed regulations reproduced in the order in which they were issued, along with preambles and *Federal Register* citations. There is a cross reference table listing the proposed regulations in Code section order.

Volume 28 contains reprints of the weekly *Internal Revenue Bulletin*, so subscribers have access to texts of recently enacted tax statutes, committee reports, recently adopted treaties, new final regulations, IRS rulings, procedures and other releases, texts of Supreme Court decisions, and announcements of proposed regulations. Because the material in Volume 28 is not indexed by Code section or by subject matter anywhere in this service, it will be difficult to locate a particular item unless the *Internal Revenue Bulletin* citation is known. Transfer Binders are provided for filing prior years' *Bulletins* so that a complete set can be retained.

An unnumbered companion volume in this service contains Special Studies, such as analyses of pending legislation and proposed regulations. This volume also contains lists (by journal rather than by topic) of current tax articles.

Additional softbound pamphlets are frequently issued. These contain analysis of major legislation or sample completed tax returns.

b. *Tax Management* (Bureau of National Affairs)

Tax Management Portfolios are issued in four series: *United States Income; Foreign Income;*[64] *Estates, Gifts, and Trusts;* and *Compensation Planning.*[65] Each series is divided into several volumes, each of which deals in great depth with a very narrow area of tax law. In addition to a Table of Contents, each Portfolio includes a Detailed Analysis section with extensive footnoting (including references to IRS Letter Rulings); a Working Papers section, which includes checklists, forms which can be used as models in drafting documents, and texts of relevant IRS materials; and a Bibliography and References section. Pink Changes and Additions sheets containing new material are added to the beginning of each Portfolio whenever warranted by new developments. There are also cross references to other Portfolios which may contain information relevant to a particular problem.

The looseleaf Master Binder includes a list of Portfolios in each series arranged by major category, such as Life Insurance. The Binder also has key word and Code section indexes for each series as an aid in locating relevant Portfolios. IRS Forms are also cross referenced to appropriate Portfolios. The Binder includes Recent Developments which have not yet been incorporated into the separate Portfolios; this section must be consulted if *Tax Management* is being used as a research tool.

The final feature of the Master Binder is the Tax Management Memorandum, a biweekly analysis of current unsettled problems and other items of significance. Topical and Code section indexes are given for the Memorandum reports.

c. Mertens, *Law of Federal Income Taxation* (Callaghan & Co.)

The Mertens service consists of four sets of volumes: treatise; Code; regulations; and rulings. The treatise materials closely resemble *Am.Jur.* and *C.J.S.* in format.[66] Material is presented by sub-

[64] See also Section E of this chapter.

[65] Although *Compensation Planning* can be acquired separately, it is also received by all subscribers to *United States Income.*

[66] These encyclopedias are discussed in Chapter 16, Sec. B. Although each of them covers a wide variety of topics, discussions of taxation appear in separate volumes within each service and are thus quite accessible.

ject matter with extensive footnoting at the bottom of each page. There are also cross references to relevant materials found elsewhere in the service. Extensive historical background is presented in the discussion. Indeed, because of the thoroughness of its discussions, Mertens has frequently been cited in judicial decisions. However, that very thoroughness can be a drawback, as using the Mertens treatise materials for background knowledge is very time-consuming.

A detailed subject matter index appears in volume 12; there is also a Tables volume indicating where in the treatise various Code and regulations sections, IRS materials, and cases are discussed. Because citations for Supreme Court decisions listed in this volume are given to *United States Reports*, to *United States Supreme Court Reports, Lawyers' Edition*, and to *Supreme Court Reporter*, the alphabetical case table can be used to some extent to obtain parallel citations.

Code. Each of the Code volumes contains all income tax provisions enacted or amended during a particular time period (one or more years). The looseleaf current volume contains a subject matter index in which each topic is cross referenced to applicable Code sections. Because each volume contains only new or amended provisions, this set cannot be used as a complete Code.

One very helpful feature of this set is its looseleaf volumes of Code Commentary. These provide cross references to the discussions in the treatise materials as well as being useful short explanations of statutory provisions.

Regulations. These volumes include the texts of all income tax regulations issued or amended during a particular time period (two or more years). Publication is made in Code section order. The most recent regulations appear in the looseleaf current volume, which also has a Regulations Status Table indicating where in this set regulations adopted in prior years appear.

This set has several useful features. Textual notations (diamond shapes and brackets) are used to indicate deletions, additions, and other changes in amended regulations. A historical note, from which the regulation's prior wording can be determined, follows. This facilitates research into early administrative interpretations. Each volume also has a section in which is reproduced the preamble to the Treasury Decision announcing each regulation.

The looseleaf volume containing the most recent regulations also provides the texts of proposed regulations, again in Code section order. Preceding each proposed regulation is a *Federal Register* citation and the expiration date for submission of taxpayer comments. As it does for final regulations, Mertens prints the preambles to proposed regulations in a separate section of this volume. Proposed regulations are added every three weeks and are indicated in numerical order in the Regulations Status Table. The IRS Semiannual Agenda of Regulations, indicating proposals under study within the Service, also appears in the looseleaf volume.

Because each volume contains only those items amended during the time span it covers, this set cannot be used as a complete text of final regulations.

Rulings. The final set of volumes in this service contains the text of revenue rulings and procedures as well as of less formal IRS pronouncements, such as news releases. Each volume covers a particular time period and includes rulings in numerical order, followed by procedures in numerical order and by other items, which are numbered by Mertens as Miscellaneous Announcements (M.A.). Current items are printed every three weeks.

This set contains several helpful research tools. The looseleaf current volume has a Code-Rulings Table, which provides a chronological listing of every revenue ruling, procedure, and Miscellaneous Announcement involving income tax Code sections or subsections. [See Illustration 159, Section *O*] In addition, there is a Rulings Status Table indicating the number of the most recent ruling or procedure affecting the validity of a previously published item. Mertens indicates the effect on the earlier item (modified, revoked) but provides no *Cumulative Bulletin* citation for either the original or subsequent material.[67] These citations are, of course, unnecessary because full texts of these items are readily accessible in the Rulings volumes.

d. Rabkin & Johnson, *Federal Income, Gift and Estate Taxation* (Matthew Bender)

This service is divided into three segments: treatise; Code and Congressional Reports; and Regulations. Subscribers also receive pamphlets dealing with year-end tax planning.

Treatise. The discussions in Volumes 1–5 are shorter than those in the other services described in this subsection. Citations are incorporated into the body of the text and are harder to skip over than are those in the other services. Textual material, which is divided into sections and arranged by topic, can be located using the subject matter index in Volume 5B as well as through the tables cross referencing Code sections,[68] cases and rulings to textual material. These tables, found in Volume 5A, have main and current sections.

[67] If such citations are needed, they can be located using either the *Cumulative Bulletin* or the *Bulletin Index-Digest System*, both of which are discussed in Section N of this chapter.

[68] References are given for both the 1939 and 1954 Codes.

Volume 5A also includes cross references between the 1939 and 1954 Codes.

Volume 5A contains an alphabetical listing of all cases discussed in this service. Citations for Supreme Court decisions are given to *United States Reports*, to *American Federal Tax Reports (AFTR)*, and to *U. S. Tax Cases (USTC)*. Citations for Court of Appeals and Court of Claims decisions are given to *Federal Reporter*, to *AFTR*, and to *USTC*. Citations for District Court decisions are given to *Federal Supplement*, to *AFTR*, and to *USTC*. Tax Court Rules are printed in this volume.

Code and Congressional Reports. Volumes 6–7B contain the text of the Code in Code section order.[69] A brief legislative history is given for each subsection, including text of selected committee reports and an indication of changes made by various amendments to the Code. The last volume contains a topical index to the Code materials and tables cross referencing the 1939 and 1954 Codes.

Regulations. All currently effective regulations are printed in numerical order in Volumes 8–12. Each regulation is preceded by T.D. numbers and dates for the original version and amendments.[70] Cross references are given to subject matter discussion in the treatise volumes. Selected proposed regulations are printed in numerical order in Volume 12A. The Table of Contents lists these in numerical order. The *Federal Register* date and cross references to treatise discussion precede each proposed regulation.

3. Subject Matter Arrangement—Limited Scope

Various publishers issue textual materials discussing a limited number of Code sections, such as those covering Subchapter S corporations.[71] These texts are extremely useful for research involving very complex areas of tax law. While a comprehensive listing of such publications is beyond the scope of this chapter, the following materials are a representative sample.

a. Anderson, *Tax Factors in Real Estate Operations* (Prentice-Hall).

b. Aronson, *Partnership Income Taxes* (PLI).

c. Bittker & Eustice, *Federal Income Taxation of Corporations and Shareholders* (Warren, Gorham & Lamont).

d. Casey, *Federal Tax Practice* (Callaghan & Co.).

[69] Excise taxes are omitted, however.

[70] However, the text of prior versions cannot be ascertained.

[71] See also Section K, dealing with Form Books, many of which have extensive textual material.

e. Cavitch, *Business Organizations with Tax Planning* (Matthew Bender).

f. Chommie, *Federal Income Taxation* (West).

g. Lowndes, Kramer & McCord, *Federal Estate & Gift Taxes* (West).

h. McKee, Nelson & Whitmire, *Federal Taxation of Partnerships and Partners* (Warren, Gorham & Lamont).

i. Ness & Vogel, *Taxation of the Closely Held Corporation* (Warren, Gorham & Lamont).

j. Peschel & Spurgeon, *Federal Taxation of Trusts, Grantors and Beneficiaries* (Warren, Gorham & Lamont).

k. Weithorn, *Tax Techniques for Foundations and Other Exempt Organizations* (Matthew Bender).

l. Willis, *Partnership Taxation* (Shepard's).

SECTION J. LEGAL PERIODICALS

Commentary on particular tax problems can also be found in various legal periodicals, some of which are concerned exclusively with taxation.[72] While the materials discussed in Section I include selective citations to periodical literature, one can obtain a more extensive list through use of periodical indexes.[73] Many of the indexes discussed in Chapter 17 contain lists of relevant articles,[74] but the following materials will give an even wider selection of readings. Their focus is exclusively on taxation, and they cover periodicals many of the general indexes omit.

1. Indexes to Legal Periodicals

a. *CCH Federal Tax Articles*

This monthly looseleaf reporter contains summaries of articles on federal taxes appearing in legal, accounting, business and related periodicals. Proceedings and papers delivered at major tax institutes are also noted. The contents are arranged in Code section order;

[72] Included in this group are such offerings as *Taxation for Lawyers, Taxes—The Tax Magazine, Tax Law Review,* and *Tax Lawyer.* Also included are annual Institutes on Taxation, such as those given at New York University and the University of Southern California.

[73] There is a description of periodical indexes and their use in Chapter 17, Secs. B and C.

[74] In addition, citations to law review articles can be located using *Shepard's United States Administrative Citations* and *Shepard's Federal Law Citations in Selected Law Reviews.*

each item is given a cross reference number. [See Illustration 160, Section *O*]

There are three separate indexes: Cumulative Code Section Index; Index by Topic; and Index by Author. The latter two indexes have main and current subdivisions, both of which should be checked. Publishers of the articles can be identified in the List of Publications division.

Bound volume 1 covers the years 1954–67; volume 2 covers 1968–72. More recent material is in the looseleaf volume. Because of its format and scope, this will generally be the tax articles index most researchers prefer.

b. *Index to Federal Tax Articles* (Warren, Gorham & Lamont)

Compiled by Professor Gersham Goldstein, this multi-volume, computer-produced work covers the literature on federal income, gift and estate taxation contained in legal, specialized tax, and economic journals, as well as in nonperiodical publications. It has separate subject and author indexes but no Code section index. Within each listing of articles, the most recent entry appears first. This service is updated regularly with supplement volumes.

c. *Tax Planning and Research Indices for Periodicals* (Pro-dex Publishers)

This looseleaf service identifies and chronologically organizes all of the tax articles and other research materials appearing in the major tax-oriented periodicals since 1965.

d. *Shepard's Federal Tax Locator*

This three-volume set started publication in 1974. It is unlike the *Shepard's* publications referred to elsewhere in this chapter in that it is not a citator. Rather, it is an index to current sources of law relating to federal taxation. It brings together in one alphabetical grouping numerous sources of federal tax law. The single grouping contains both subject and author listings. Main entries are listed on the tops of pages, and sub-entries appear in alphabetical order. Each sub-entry cites to the relevant Code provision, Treasury regulations, Tax Court Rules, treaties, Treasury Decisions, and other applicable administrative provisions. Also cited are court decisions, various tax-oriented looseleaf services, and articles from over 120 legal periodicals. Brief descriptions are provided for these items; *Shepard's* is supplemented quarterly.

e. *P–H Federal Taxes*

The Index volume of this looseleaf service contains an Index to Tax Articles, including a supplementary table of new items. Articles are arranged in Code section order, keyed according to paragraph numbers in the *Federal Taxes* compilation volumes.[75] The articles are not described, nor are they indexed by general subject matter or author name. Only articles published within the last few years are listed. Publishers can be identified using the List of Publications in this Index.

2. Digests of Articles

The *Monthly Digest of Tax Articles* (Newkirk Associates) presents significant current tax articles in abridged form. Its descriptions of these articles is far more detailed than are the summaries given in *CCH Federal Tax Articles*; because of this detail, however, fewer articles receive coverage.

SECTION K. FORM BOOKS[76]

There are several form books available to aid lawyers in drafting documents in situations where tax consequences may be determined by the drafter's choice of language. The following list of materials is illustrative of the form books available.

1. Covey, *Marital Deductions and the Use of Formula Provisions*[77] (Michie, Bobbs-Merrill).

2. Nossaman & Wyatt, *Trust Administration and Taxation* (Matthew Bender).

3. *Murphy's Will Forms* (Matthew Bender).

4. Rabkin & Johnson, *Current Legal Forms with Tax Analysis* (Matthew Bender).

5. Bittker, *Federal Income Taxation of Corporations and Shareholders—Forms* (Warren, Gorham & Lamont).

6. McGaffey, *Tax Analysis and Forms* (Callaghan & Co.).

SECTION L. COMPUTERIZED RESEARCH AND MICROFORMS

1. Computerized Research

Researchers with access to one or more computerized data-base systems are able to reduce their search time substantially using the word search technique to locate relevant primary materials.

[75] Use of *Federal Taxes* is described in Section I of this chapter.

[76] Form books are discussed in Chapter 19, Sec. D.

[77] This volume is extremely useful for its textual material.

The *Lexis* Tax Library contains the text of the Code, final and proposed regulations, rulings, procedures and other items appearing in the *Cumulative Bulletins*. *Lexis* also contains letter rulings, court decisions,[78] and committee reports for the 1954 Code.

Westlaw, which added a Tax Data Base in late 1980, includes the above materials with the exception of committee reports. *Westlaw* also contains *Shepard's Citations* within its data base.

2. Microforms

Many of the primary sources are available in microform format as well as in the more familiar book or pamphlet sets. If hard copy is unavailable for a particular item, one should always check to see if its text is in the microform file. Two of the sets most likely to yield this information for tax materials are those produced by Congressional Information Service and by Information Handling Services, both of which are extremely useful for legislative histories.[79] In addition, the *Micro-Mini Prints*, introduced by William S. Hein & Co. in 1981, combine microfiche text with hard-copy tables of contents and are thus quite easy to use.

SECTION M. CITATORS[80]

The three citator services discussed in this section can be used to judge whether or not a particular statute, treaty, regulation, ruling,[81] or judicial decision has been criticized, approved, or otherwise commented upon in a more recent proceeding. Because each citator has a different scope and format, the separate discussions of each will treat each cited primary authority in the same order.

1. Shepard's Citations[82]

Because its coverage is not limited to tax materials, *Shepard's* is probably the best-known citator. It is divided both chronologically and by cited authority into numerous volumes—hardbound, softbound supplements, and advance sheets. While a search using *Shepard's* can thus be extremely tedious in comparison to one using another sys-

78 The data base does not include the earliest decisions at some court levels.

79 CIS produces the *CIS/Microfiche Library*; IHS offers a similar set compiled by law librarians.

80 See Chapter 15 for a general discussion of citators.

81 The *Bulletin Index-Digest System* (N. 1.) and Mertens, *Law of Federal Income Taxation* (I. 2.) can also be used as citators for rulings. Their coverage is more limited than the Commerce Clearing House or Prentice-Hall citators, however.

82 *Shepard's Citations* is discussed in greater detail in Chapter 15.

tem, this service has certain valuable features, such as citations to *A.B.A. Journal* discussions and to *A.L.R.* and *Lawyers' Edition* annotations, which the Prentice-Hall and Commerce Clearing House citators lack.

a. *Statutes and Treaties*

If a statute or treaty has ever been interpreted, or its validity passed upon, by any federal court (including the Tax Court), a citation to the decision will appear in *Shepard's United States Citations—Statutes.* This service will also indicate any subsequent Congressional amendments or repeal of statutory material.

Symbols are used to indicate how the court ruled in each case involving validity. Decisions are grouped by rank of the deciding court in chronological order, but the identity of the deciding circuit or district court is not indicated. *Shepard's Federal Circuit Table* can be used to obtain that information.

Statutes are arranged in Code section order, with tax statutes listed under 26 *U.S.C.* Treaties are ordered according to their volume and page number in *United States Treaties and Other International Agreements*; no indication of country name appears. Case citations are to the volume and page of the reporter where the statute or treaty is first cited, not to the first page of the case.

b. *Regulations*

Issued quarterly, *Shepard's Code of Federal Regulations Citations* indicates action by federal courts other than the Tax Court. In addition to case citations, *Shepard's* provides citations to law review articles discussing the regulations. This citator is arranged in regulations section order; tax regulations are listed as 26 *C.F.R.* Symbols are used to indicate how each court ruled when the regulation's validity was challenged.

c. *Revenue Rulings and Procedures*

There is no *Shepard's* citator for revenue rulings or procedures.

d. *Judicial Decisions*

Case citations are arranged according to the level of court being cited. Tax Court and Board of Tax Appeals decisions are traced through the *United States Administrative Citations* volumes; Court of Appeals, District Court, and Court of Claims decisions are found in two different sets of *Federal Citations*; and Supreme Court decisions are cited in *United States Citations—Cases.*

Each set provides citations for all citing cases other than Tax Court memorandum decisions.[83] Both cited and citing cases are listed by volume and page number, rather than by name. Citations to subsequent decisions indicate the first page where reference to the cited case appears, not the first page of the citing decision.

Standard symbols indicate whether or not later decisions follow the cited decision, and the syllabus or headnote number being discussed is provided. Citing cases are listed by circuit in the *Federal Citations* volumes but not in the other sets;[84] *Shepard's Federal Circuit Table* supplies this information, however.

In addition to the annotations normally appearing in *Shepard's*, the *United States Administrative Citations* volumes also give citations to articles in selected law reviews. Citations to articles discussing other decisions can be obtained from *Shepard's Federal Law Citations in Selected Law Reviews*.

2. P–H Federal Taxes—Citator

Like *Shepard's*, the *P–H Citator* volumes are arranged chronologically and cover all federal taxes in each volume; the volumes are not subdivided by level of court. This service presently consists of several hardbound volumes and a looseleaf volume which is supplemented monthly. Its format requires more time than would a comparable effort using the CCH service described below, but the time will be well spent. For the items it cites, the *P–H Citator* is the most useful of the three citators.

a. *Statutes and Treaties*

This citator does not give citations for materials construing statutes or treaties.

b. *Regulations, Revenue Rulings, and Revenue Procedures*

Each volume has a section for Treasury Decisions and another for revenue rulings and procedures. Cited regulations are listed in T.D. (rather than regulations section) number order; rulings and procedures are listed in numerical order.

83 Although Tax Court memorandum decisions discussing other cases are not indicated, *Shepard's* does indicate cases in which memorandum decisions are discussed.

84 In the other volumes, cases are arranged by level of court, starting with the Supreme Court. Within each grouping, the earliest cases are listed first. Although *Shepard's* indicates syllabus numbers, citing cases are not arranged with regard to these numbers.

Standard symbols are used to indicate whether or not the subsequent material approved, rejected, or otherwise affected the cited regulation, ruling or procedure. Such subsequent material includes all judicial decisions, rulings (including letter rulings), and procedures.

Case citations for citing decisions are given to the P–H case reporter services (*AFTR, P–H Tax Court Reports,* and *P–H Tax Court Memorandum Decisions*) as well as to the official and West publications. With the exception of District Court geographical subdivisions, the jurisdiction of each court hearing a case is indicated.

Citations for rulings and procedures are given to the appropriate volume of the *Cumulative Bulletin* or to *P–H Federal Taxes.* Letter rulings are listed by ruling number followed by a reference to *P–H Federal Taxes.*

c. *Judicial Decisions*

Cited and citing cases are listed by taxpayer name in the Decisions section of each volume. Cited cases are listed alphabetically; citing cases are arranged according to the pertinent syllabus number of the cited case. Within syllabus groupings, cases are listed by rank of the citing court, starting with the Supreme Court. Within each group of courts, the earliest cases appear first. Jurisdiction is indicated for cited and citing decisions. [See Illustration 161, Section *O*].

P–H uses standard symbols to indicate whether or not subsequent decisions follow the cited decision. Citations to subsequent decisions indicate the page where reference to the cited case is made, not to the first page of the citing material. Case citations for all decisions are given to the P–H case reporters as well as to the official and West services.

This citator also includes citations to rulings (including letter rulings) and procedures discussing the cited decision. Acquiescence or nonacquiescence by the IRS in adverse Tax Court decisions is indicated. Citations for revenue rulings and procedures are given to the appropriate volume of the *Cumulative Bulletin* or to *P–H Federal Taxes;* letter rulings are cited by number, followed by a reference to *P–H Federal Taxes.*

3. CCH Standard Federal Tax Reporter [85]

Both the Index and Citator volumes of *SFTR* are used in evaluating the validity of cited items. Unfortunately, this service has only its size to recommend it. While its compactness makes it the easiest system to use, it has the fewest useful features.

[85] The remainder of this looseleaf service is described in Section I of this chapter.

a. *Statutes and Treaties*

No citations are given for materials construing statutes or treaties.

b. *Regulations, Revenue Rulings, and Revenue Procedures*

The Index volume contains Finding Lists for these items. Cited regulations are listed in T.D. (rather than regulations section) number order; rulings and procedures are listed in numerical order. Supplementation is done quarterly.

Case citations for decisions discussing these items are given to the CCH case reporter services (*USTC*, *CCH Tax Court Reporter*, and *CCH Tax Court Memorandum Decisions*) as well as to the official and West publications. No indication is given as to how the citing case dealt with the cited material, a definite disadvantage of this citator service.

Cited rulings and procedures have their location in the *Cumulative Bulletin* indicated. Citing items are listed by number only. Paragraph cross references are given to discussion in the *SFTR* compilation volumes, a feature unique to the CCH citator service.

c. *Judicial Decisions*

The one-volume Citator[86] contains a main case table and quarterly supplements. Although citing cases from all courts are listed, *SFTR* maintains its compact form by limiting itself to items its editors believe are useful in evaluating the cited decisions.

Both cited and citing cases are listed by name. Cited cases are listed alphabetically; citing cases are arranged according to the rank of the citing court, starting with the Supreme Court. Within each group the most recent citing cases are listed first. Jurisdiction is rarely indicated for citing decisions rendered by District Courts.

No indication is made of which syllabus number is involved in the citing case; likewise, no indication is given whether the citing material follows or distinguishes the cited decision. Citations to subsequent decisions indicate the first page of the citing case, not the page where reference is made to the cited material. Case citations for all decisions are given to the CCH case reporters as well as to the official and West services. In addition, Supreme Court decisions also have their *Internal Revenue Bulletin* or *Cumulative Bulletin* location indicated.

This citator also includes citations to rulings (including letter rulings) and procedures discussing the cited decision. Citations for

[86] Although cases involving estate and gift taxes and excise taxes are listed in this volume, citations to them appear only in the Citator sections of *CCH Federal Estate and Gift Tax Reporter* and *CCH Federal Excise Tax Reporter*.

revenue rulings and procedures are given to the appropriate volume of the *Cumulative Bulletin*; letter rulings are cited by number. Acquiescence or nonacquiescence by the IRS in adverse Tax Court decisions is also indicated.

Cross references are made to discussions of cited material in the *SFTR* compilation volumes, a helpful feature of this citator.

Table . Comparison of Selected Citator Features

	Shepard's	P–H	CCH
Cited Material:			
Statutes	x		
Treaties	x		
Regulations	x	x	x
Rulings		x	x
Decisions	x	x	x
Case Citations By:			
Case Name		x	x
Reporter Page	x		
Citing Material:			
Rulings		x	x
Decisions	x	x	x
Syllabus Issue:			
Indicated	x	x	
Grouped Together		x	
Symbols for Result:	x	x	
References to Topical Discussion:	x		x

SECTION N. COLLECTIONS OF PRIMARY SOURCE MATERIALS

The materials which are described below, all of which have been referred to at various points in this chapter, contain the texts of several types of material necessary for tax research. Except as indicated in the following paragraphs, these sets contain no textual discussion of the materials presented.

1. Internal Revenue Bulletin; Cumulative Bulletin; Bulletin Index-Digest System

The three IRS-generated series contain the text of almost every primary authority as well as providing the means to locate included material. As the discussion below indicates, the *Bulletin Index-Digest System* (*Index-Digest*) is invaluable as an aid to using the other two series.

a. *Internal Revenue Bulletin*

The weekly *Internal Revenue Bulletin* is divided into four parts: Part I gives the text of all revenue rulings and final regulations issued during the week; publication is in Code section order. Part II does likewise for treaties, including Treasury Department Technical Explanations (Subpart A), and for tax legislation, including committee reports (Subpart B). Part III contains Revenue Procedures, while Part IV, "Items of General Interest," is varied in content. Its coverage ranges from disbarment notices to announcements of proposed regulations. While *Federal Register* dates and comment deadlines are given for the proposed regulations, their texts are not printed in the *Bulletin*. The weekly *Bulletin* also indicates IRS acquiescence or nonacquiescence in unfavorable Tax Court decisions and prints the text of Supreme Court decisions.

While the *Bulletin* has indexes, they are unwieldy. Every issue contains a cumulative Numerical Finding List for each type of item, listing each in numerical order. There is also a Finding List of Current Action on Previously Published Rulings. The former list lacks any tie-in to Code sections; the latter indicates only IRS, as opposed to judicial, action. The subject matter indexes cover only one month's material.[87] Because of its index format, the *Bulletin* is best used to locate material for which one already has a citation [88] or as a tool for staying abreast of recent developments.

b. *Cumulative Bulletin*

Every six months the material in the *Internal Revenue Bulletin* is republished in a hardbound *Cumulative Bulletin*. The *Cumulative Bulletin* format follows that of the weekly *Bulletin* with three exceptions. First, major tax legislation and committee reports generally appear in a third volume rather than in the two semiannual volumes. Second, only disbarment notices appear from Part IV. Finally, rulings appear in the *Cumulative Bulletin* in semiannual Code section order; this bears no relation to their numerical order. The *Cumulative Bulletin* indexes are as difficult to use as their counterparts in the *Internal Revenue Bulletin*.

c. *Bulletin Index-Digest System*

The *Index-Digest* is issued as four services: Income Tax, Estate and Gift Tax, Employment Tax, and Excise Tax. The Income Tax service, which is the focal point for this discussion, is supplemented quarterly; the other services receive semiannual supplementation.

[87] These indexes, which are subdivided by type of tax, contain separate listings for regulations but not for other primary sources.

[88] Current periodical literature will often be a source of such citations.

The *Index-Digest* can be used to obtain *Internal Revenue Bulletin* or *Cumulative Bulletin* citations for revenue rulings and procedures, Supreme Court and adverse Tax Court decisions, Public Laws, Treasury Decisions, and treaties. In addition, it digests the rulings, procedures, and court decisions.

The following paragraphs explain use of the *Index-Digest* to find citations and digests.

Statutes, Treaties, and Regulations

Specific Code and regulations section additions or amendments can be located using the Topical Index of Public Laws, Treasury Decisions, and Tax Conventions. A *Cumulative Bulletin* citation is given for each item. The Topical Index can also be used to locate treaties, which are listed alphabetically by country under the heading "Tax Conventions."

While the Topical Index is useful when one does not know which Code section is involved, the same information is listed by section in the Finding Lists for Public Laws and Treasury Decisions.

Still another Finding List, "Public Laws Published in the Bulletin," is useful for locating committee report citations and popular names for the various revenue acts.

Rulings and Procedures

The Finding Lists for Revenue Rulings, Revenue Procedures, and Other Items can be used in various ways to locate relevant rulings and procedures. These items are listed in Code and regulations section order in the "Internal Revenue Code of 1954" section, and in ruling and procedure number order in the "Revenue Rulings" and "Revenue Procedures" sections of these Lists. Rulings and procedures involving treaties are listed by country in the "Tax Conventions" section.

None of these Finding Lists provides *Cumulative Bulletin* citations. Instead, citations are given to a digest of each item in the *Index-Digest* itself; the *Cumulative Bulletin* citation follows the digest. Although two steps are required to obtain the citation, the second step frequently saves time. A glance through the digest may indicate the item is not worth reading in full text.[89] [See Illustration 162, Section *O*]

Because the digests are arranged by subject matter, pertinent rulings may be located even though one does not know the particular Code or regulations section involved. In fact, the subject matter di-

[89] Unfortunately, the digest may not include a pertinent holding, in which case exclusive use of the digest would yield inadequate results.

visions are so numerous that the same item will frequently be digested under several different headings.

If one wishes to know if a particular ruling or procedure has been modified or otherwise affected by subsequent IRS action, this information appears in the "Actions on Previously Published Revenue Rulings" section of the Finding Lists. Judicial decisions affecting a ruling are not indicated, however. Whenever a subsequent ruling affects an earlier item, a *Cumulative Bulletin* citation is given for the updating material.[90]

Judicial Decisions

The Finding Lists for Revenue Rulings, Revenue Procedures, and Other Items can be used to locate all Supreme Court decisions and those Tax Court decisions adverse to the government in which the IRS has acquiesced or nonacquiesced.

Supreme Court decisions are listed alphabetically in the "Decisions of the Supreme Court" section of the Finding Lists.[91] They are also listed by the IRS-assigned Court Decision (Ct.D.) number in the "Internal Revenue Code of 1954" materials, arranged according to the applicable Code and regulations sections.

As with rulings and procedures, references to decisions in the Finding Lists give only the digest number. The official and *Cumulative Bulletin* citations follow the digest of the case. Again, because the digests have a subject matter format, decisions can be located directly from the digests without first consulting the Finding Lists.

2. Internal Revenue Acts—Text and Legislative History; U. S. Code Congressional & Administrative News—Internal Revenue Code; U. S. Code Congressional & Administrative News—Federal Tax Regulations

These three West Publishing Co. series can be used in researching the texts and histories of Code and regulations sections.

Internal Revenue Acts, which is issued each year in pamphlet form, contains the full text of currently enacted statutes. The texts of committee reports appear in the second section of each pamphlet. Each pamphlet has indexes for subject matter and for Code sections affected; there are also tables cross referencing public law section numbers to pages in each pamphlet. Acts are listed by name in the Table of Contents. Hardbound volumes, cumulating the material in several years' pamphlets, are issued periodically.

[90] No digests are given for items which have been specifically revoked, superseded, or declared obsolete.

[91] Tax Court decisions are listed alphabetically in another section of the Finding Lists.

The *Internal Revenue Code* volume issued each year contains the text of all existing Code sections. Dates, public law numbers, and *Statutes at Large* citations appear in the brief history of enactment and amendment following each section. Editorial notes indicate effective dates. No indication is given as to how a particular amendment modified an existing section.[92] Each volume contains a subject matter index.

The annual *Federal Tax Regulations* volumes contain the text of all regulations in force on the first day of the year. References are given to the T.D. number, date, and *Federal Register* publication for both original promulgation and all amendments. The final volume for each year contains a subject matter index.

3. U. S. Tax Week (Matthew Bender)

Published weekly, this service prints digests of items its editors deem significant. An annual hardbound volume incorporates the prior year's issues. The items digested are final regulations, revenue rulings and procedures, and judicial decisions. Each issue contains a subject matter index, a numerical listing of T.D.s, rulings and procedures, and an alphabetical case table. Cross references are made to discussions in other textual materials, primarily Rabkin & Johnson, *Federal Income, Gift and Estate Taxation.*

4. Tax Management Primary Sources (Bureau of National Affairs)

Primary Sources is an excellent tool for locating significant proposed legislation and for deriving the legislative history of existing Code sections.

The Current Developments binder of this looseleaf service contains the text of major bills [93] and other related material. Once a bill is printed in this service, its progress through Congress will also be published. One can thus find grouped together the introduced version and all subsequent versions, press releases or *Congressional Record* statements accompanying the introduction, administration testimony at hearings, committee reports, and significant prints. In addition, there is a "Background Materials" section, in which are printed other important materials related to tax legislation. Cross reference to these is provided from each bill to which they relate.

[92] *Primary Sources*, discussed in subsection 4 of this section, provides such information for 1969 and subsequent amendments.

[93] This service selects bills for printing "according to probability of Congressional consideration, overall importance to the business community and relative timeliness of subject." House Bills Section, p. (i).

The "Long Titles" section of the binder prints capsule descriptions of pending tax bills. There is also a "Legislative Calendar," from which one can determine what progress each bill has made in Congress to date. This service is updated as necessitated by new material.

Subscribers can file materials for bills which do not pass in an Unenacted Legislation binder. Materials connected with enacted bills are incorporated into the volumes of *Primary Sources* discussed in the following paragraph.

Extensive legislative histories for selected Code sections comprise the remainder of this service. The sections chosen are traced back to their original 1954 Code versions,[94] and all changes are presented. [See Illustration 163, Section *O*] Among the materials presented for each Code section are presidential messages, committee reports, Treasury Department testimony at hearings, and discussion printed in *Congressional Record.* This service is currently published in three series, each of which covers several years.[95] Within each series, material is presented in Code section order. No coverage is given for Code sections which have not been amended by the Tax Reform Act of 1969 or subsequent legislation.

5. Seidman's Legislative History of Federal Income and Excess Profits Tax Laws [96] (Prentice-Hall)

Pre-1954 Code legislative history can be very relevant in situations where the current law had its origin in the 1939 Code or even earlier.[97] This series follows each such act in reverse chronological order, presenting the text of Code sections, followed by the relevant committee reports and citations to hearings [98] and the *Congressional Record.*[99] Various type styles are used, making it easy to ascertain where in Congress a provision originated or was deleted.

[94] Series I also includes the 1939 Code version for each section covered.

[95] Series I covers the sections affected by the Tax Reform Act of 1969 and all acts through 1975; Series II covers sections affected by the 1976 Tax Reform Act and all acts through 1977; Series III begins with the Revenue Act of 1978.

[96] The two volumes covering 1939 through 1953 include both taxes. Separate volumes for the income tax and the excess profits tax were used for the earlier materials, covering 1861 through 1938 and 1917 through 1947, respectively.

[97] Code § 263, for example, contains language taken almost verbatim from sec. 117 of the 1864 Act. *See* 13 Stat. 282.

[98] Relevant page numbers in the hearings are cited and reference is made to appearances by Treasury representatives.

[99] Citations are made to relevant pages; the text itself is reproduced in some instances.

Seidman's prints proposed sections which failed to be enacted along with relevant history explaining their omission. Such information can be useful in interpreting those provisions which actually were adopted. Although its coverage has great breadth, *Seidman's* does not print every Code section. Omitted are provisions with no legislative history, items without substantial interpretative significance, and provisions the author considered long outmoded.

Seidman's has three indexes. In the Code section index, each section is listed by act and assigned a key number. The same key number is assigned to corresponding sections in each act. The key number index indicates every act, by section number and page in the text, where the item involved appears. There is also a subject index, in which key numbers are listed by topic.

6. The Internal Revenue Acts of the United States: 1909–1950 (William S. Hein & Co., Inc.)

Although covering a shorter time period than *Seidman's* this set's legislative histories are far more comprehensive. In addition to each Congressional version of revenue bills, the 144 volumes contain the full texts of hearings, committee reports, Treasury studies, and regulations. Official pagination is retained for relevant documents. In addition to income and excise taxes, this set includes estate and gift, social security, railroad retirement and unemployment taxes.

The editor, Bernard D. Reams, Jr., has prepared an Index volume to accompany the set. Within this volume are several indexes which can be used in locating relevant materials.

The longest index is chronological. Each Act is listed, followed by all of the items of legislative history. A volume reference is given for each item. Other indexes are provided for Miscellaneous Subjects, such as hearings on items which did not result in legislation; Treasury studies; Joint Committee reports; regulations; Congressional reports; Congressional documents; bill numbers; and hearings. Unfortunately, there is neither a Code section nor a subject matter index.

In this set all hearings are printed together, as are all bills, laws (accompanied by committee reports), studies, and regulations. Thus several volumes will be necessary whenever all materials for a particular law or provision are desired. This is by no means a substantial drawback to using this set; assembling the same materials from elsewhere in the collection (assuming they are all available) would be far more difficult.

7. Daily Tax Report (BNA)

This newsletter, published five times each week, is an invaluable aid in locating current developments in tax law.

Each issue begins with a section describing congressional activity, including bills passed and introduced, committee hearings, and committee reports.

Also printed in the newsletter are texts of Supreme Court decisions and partial texts of decisions rendered by other courts; texts of revenue rulings and procedures and summaries of letter rulings; and texts of statutes, final regulations and proposed regulations. Texts of bills and excerpts from hearings and committee reports also appear when the editors deem the material significant.

The indexes follow a subject matter format, giving a citation to the report number and page where each item appears. There is also a Table of Regulations, which lists rulings and procedures by number and regulations by T.D. number, and a Table of Cases, in which decisions are listed alphabetically. Unfortunately, the indexes never cover more than a two-month period, so several indexes must be used if material involving a particular subject is to be traced for a longer time period.

SECTION O. ILLUSTRATIONS

[Illustration 158]

PAGE FROM CCH STANDARD FEDERAL TAX REPORTER—
NEW MATTERS VOLUME

6 1-22-81

70,251

Latest Additions to Cumulative Index to 1981 Developments for Reports 2-6

See also Cumulative Index at Page 70,301.

From Compilation Paragraph No.			To New Development Paragraph No.
200	.015	Burned out tax shelters will be examined during an audit. *Rewrite*	8291
216B		Proposed amendment of Reg. § 301.6104-3	8987
230A		*Grams*, TCM—Amounts paid from employer's educational fund were includible in gross income of employee	7250
300		Burned out tax shelters will be examined during an audit. *Rewrite*	8291
321	.36	Fees earned by physician paid directly to hospital—IRS Letter Ruling	6950E
	.935	*Taylor*, TCM—Taxpayer liable for amount transferred to trust	7279
322	.115	*Gran*, TCM—Family trust was assignment of income	7286
323	.928	*Antonelli*, TCM—Assignment of income to trust was sham	7269
	.928	*Basham, Jr.*, TCM—Assignment of income to trust was sham	7270
	.928	*Corcoran*, TCM—Assignment of income to trust was sham	7271
324	.75	*Ogiony*—Cert. denied taxpayer 10/14/80.	
	.902	*Ogiony*—Cert. denied taxpayer 10/14/80.	
	.92	Factors listed in determining "true earner" of income *Rewrite*	8289
325	.3495	*Brent*, rev'd and rem'd, CA-5—Wife taxable on half of husband's income	9013.5
372	.4697	Heintz, TCM—Trustee bank accounts revocable	7243
401	.03	*Meyers*, TCM—TAxpayer's constitutional arguments were without merit	7616
	.048	*Lee*, DC—Amish employer not required to pay FICA and FUTA taxes	9012.1
	.09	*Broughton*, aff'd CA-8—Constitutional objections were frivolous	9008.1
	.09	*Davis*, DC—Constitutional allegations dismissed	9019.5
	.09	*Jones*, TCM—Constitutional objections were frivolous	7220
	.09	*Oden*, TCM—Income tax is constitutional	7407
	.214	*Ates*, TCM—Fifth amendment privelege no defense to lack of substantiation	7413
	.22	*Bob Jones University*, rev'd and rem'd, CA-4—IRS properly revoked exempt status of discriminatory religious school	9124
			7238
			7245
			7317
			7421
			9004
			)01.1
			253Q
			9143
			9004
		property	)10.8
	.29	Rev. Rul. 69-228 revoked—Rev. Rul.	6334
537H	.094	*Loewen*, TC—No recapture because transfer of property was merely change in form of ownership	7419
539H		Proposed amendment of Reg. § 1.4803	8976

This cumulative index (and a similar one in the P–H Tax Service) allows a user to find current information on developments happening after the publication of the main volumes.

81(10) CCH—Standard Federal Tax Reports
005—30

¶ 539H

[Illustration 159]

PAGE FROM MERTEN'S LAW OF FEDERAL INCOME TAXATION

1980 TO DATE CODE-RULINGS TABLE

Code Sec.	Rev. Rul., Rev. Proc., or M. A.
61(a)	80–9, 80–14, 80–24 80–99, 80–274
61(a)(1)	80–153
61(a)(4)	M. A. 4834, 5116
62(1)	Rev. Proc. 80–7
62(2)	80–110
62(2)(C)	Rev. Proc. 80–7
72	80–126, 80–258, 80–274 M. A. 5165
77	80–19
79	80–220 Rev. Proc. 80–22
83	80–196, 80–244 Rev. Proc. 80–11 80–22 M. A. 4806, 4868, 5212
83(a)	80–76
83(h)	80–76
85	80–23
103(a)	Rev. Proc. 80–21
103(a)(1)	80–10, 80–11, 80–12 80–13, 80–135, 80–143 80–161 M. A. 4651
103(b)	80–171, 80–251
103(b)(1)	80–10, 80–11, 80–12
103(b)(4)	80–227
103(b)(4)(A)	80–10
103(b)(4)(E)	80–11, 80–197
103(b)(6)(A)	80–100
103(b)(6)(D)	80–12, 80–162
103(b)(6)(E)	80–136
103(c)	80–91, 80–92, 80–193 80–188, 80–204, 80–257 Rev. Proc. 80–1 M. A. 4784, 5096
103(c)(1)	80–13 M. A. 4651

Code Sec.	Rev. Rul., Rev. Proc., or M. A.
162(a)	80–3, 80–119, 80–120 Rev. Proc. 80–7 M. A. 5022
162(a)(2)	80–212
162(c)	80–211
163	80–157 Rev. Proc. 80–22
163(a)	80–248
163(d)	80–54
164(a)	80–94, 80–121
164(a)(3)	80–243
164(a)(4)	80–1
164(b)(5)	80–1
165	80–176 M. A. 5212
165(a)	80–9, 80–17
165(c)	80–9, 80–17
165(c)(2)	80–268
165(c)(3)	80–65
165(h)	M. A. 4692, 4743, 4832 4949, 4950, 5009 5088, 5093, 5159 5184
166	80–24, 80–180 M. A. 4943
166(a)(1)	80–24, 80–56
167	80–174 Rev. Proc. 80–22
167(a)	80–25, 80–93, 80–137
167(d)	Rev. Proc. 80–21
167(h)	80–75
167(k)	80–85
167(m)	80–37, 80–127 Rev. Proc. 80–15 80–33
167(m)(2)	M. A. 4739
170	80–69, 80–77, 80–233 Rev. Proc. 80–7

Mertens, Law of Federal Income Taxation includes volumes containing the text of all revenue rulings. Included in the looseleaf ruling volume is this Table which indicates the various rulings issued under each specific IRS Code Section.

Code Sec.	Rev. Rul., Rev. Proc., or M. A.
	80–173, 80–203 Rev. Proc. 80–22 80–32 M. A. 5212
217	Rev. Proc. 80–7 80–32 M. A. 5022
219	80–268

Code-Rulings Table—Page 90

[Illustration 160]

PAGE FROM CCH FEDERAL TAX ARTICLES

1718 Current Articles (For Reports 212-217) 218 10-80

¶ 8086 Disallowance of certain entertainment, etc., expenses (Code Sec. 274)

"'In-House' Corporate Activity and 'Foreign Convention' Limitations." Barry Leibowicz. 65 American Bar Association Journal, October, 1979, pp. 1569-1571.

Outlines the reporting requirements of Sec. 274 of the Internal Revenue Code with respect to foreign convention expenses, and inquiries into whether in-house activities outside the U.S. may be considered foreign conventions. Reviews the legislative history of Sec. 274, discusses its application, and indicates that it does not appear that Congress intended to bring in-house foreign meetings within the scope of Sec. 274(h). Suggests that clarification is needed in this area to enable companies to conduct world-wide operations by direct contact among its employees and, in some cases, customers.

• '78 ACT

"Travel and Entertainment Expenses, Deferred Compensation and Fringe Benefits Under the Revenue Act of 1978." Gerald I. Lenrow and Ralph Milo. 79 Best's Review, Life/Health Insurance Ed., January, 1979, pp. 64, 66, 68, 69. [Part 1 of a 2-part article.]

This portion of study deals with the modifications that were introduced by the Revenue Act of 1978 on the taxation of travel and entertainment, and examines the new rules relating to facilities, club dues and business meals, sporting and theatrical tickets, investment credit, and disclosure requirements. Further considers the tax rules governing unfunded deferred compensation and self-insured medical expense reimbursement plans.

¶ 8087 Disallowance of Certain Expenses in Connection with Business Use of Home, Rental or Vacation Homes, Etc. (Code Sec. 280A)

"Home Office Expense Deductions: More Trouble Than They Are Worth?" John O. Everett. 58 TAXES,

will the loss of the rollover provisions of Sec. 1034 on the business portion of the residence offset the tax savings generated by

This CCH set is arranged by IRS Code Sections. Under each Section, digests of articles on taxation are given.

Assets of the Distributing Corporation." Everett L. Jassy. 34 Tax Law Review, Summer, 1979, pp. 607-645.

Points out that the taxation of dividend distributions has been the subject of considerable refinement, interpretation and codification, and reviews the cases, rulings and statutory provisions pertaining to the tax treatment of distributions of options to shareholders to acquire assets of the

in *Baumer v. U.S.*, 76-1 USTC ¶ 9329, 580 F.2d 863, and the Tax Court holding in *Gerald v. Redding*, CCH Dec. 35,840, 71 TC 597 (1979), as well as Rev. Rul. 70-521. Suggests that a proper analysis of the cases in the area, consistent with the relevant provisions of the Internal Revenue Code and the treatment of options in other contexts, supports the approach of Rev. Rul. 70-521 and strongly urges that the ghost of

¶ 8086

008 47

[Illustration 161]

PAGE FROM PRENTICE-HALL FEDERAL TAXES CITATOR

12-26-80 **13,001**

COURT AND TC DECISIONS
Treasury Decisions & Rulings start on Page 13,501

—A—

AAGAARD, ROBERT W. & MARGERY B., 56 TC 191, ¶ 56.19 P-H TC
f—Pomeranz, Robert E. & Annie L., 1980 P-H TC Memo 80-190 [See 56 TC 209]
e—Merit Tank & Body Inc., 1980 P-H TC Memo 80-832 [See 56 TC 209]

AARONSON, ALAN, 1970 P-H TC Memo ¶ 70,178
f-2—Knudtson, Kenneth L. & Wadena F., 1980 P-H TC Memo 80-1981

A. & A. TOOL & SUPPLY CO. (DISSOLVED), THE, 1949 P-H TC Memo ¶ 49,117
g—White Tool & Machine Co., 1980 P-H TC Memo 80-1932

A. & A. TOOL & SUPPLY CO. (DISSOLVED), THE v COMM., 182 F2d 300, 39 AFTR 517 (USCA 10)
g-10—White Tool & Machine Co., 1980 P-H TC Memo 80-1932

ABBAS, MIKE; U.S. v, 34 AFTR2d 74-6161, 504 F2d 123 (USCA 9)
e-1—Gardner, John David; U.S. v, 45 AFTR2d 80-1658, 61 F2d 776 (USCA 9)

ABBOTT, GARDNER, 30 BTA 227
g-1—Hamm, Kenneth G. & Bettye W., 1980 P-H TC Memo 80-748

ABBOTT LABORATORIES v I.R.S. 46 AFTR2d 80-5130 (DC DC, 6-12-80)

ABDALLA, JACOB & MARY T., 69 TC 697, ¶ 69.58 P-H TC
e—Johnson, Arthur J., 1980 P-H TC Memo 80-49 [See 69 TC 707]
e-1—Hamrick, J. Nat & Jenice, 1980 P-H TC Memo 80-740

ABEGG v COMM., 26 AFTR2d 70-5154, 429 F2d 1209 (USCA 2)
g-1—Gen. Housewares Corp. v U.S., 45 AFTR 80-1523, 615 F2d 1061 (USCA 5)

ABERCROMBIE, JOHN M. v BREIHAN, DONALD L., 46 AFTR2d 80-5890 (DC SC) (See Abercrombie, John M. v U.S.)

ABERCROMBIE, JOHN M. v U.S., 46 AFTR2d 80-5890 (DC SC, 9-3-80)

ABRAMS, ROBERT, JR. & CLIFFORD, 1974 P-H TC Memo ¶ 74,165
f-1—Olick, Max D. & Hilda, 73 TC 487, 488, 490, 73 P-H TC 272, 273, 274

ABRAMS v U.S., 28 AFTR2d 71-5760 (USCA 2)
f-1—Worley, Carl M. & Constance M., 1980 P-H TC Memo 80-271

ABRAMS v U.S., 28 AFTR2d 71-6120, 333 F Supp 1134 (DC W Va)
f—Gens, Richard H. v U.S., 45 AFTR2d 80-827 (Ct Cl) 615 F2d 1340 [See 28 AFTR2d 71-6129, 333 F Supp 1147]

ABRAMSON; COMM. v, 124 F2d 416, 28 AFTR 779 (USCA 2)
e-2—Freeland, Eugene L. & Mary R., 74 TC (No. 70), 74 P-H TC 529, 530
e-2—Laport, Frank L., 1980 P-H TC Memo 80-1587

ACACIA PARK CEMETERY ASSN., INC., 27 BTA 233
e—Meadowlawn Memorial Gardens, Inc. v. U.S., 46 AFTR2d 80-5561 (Ct Cl) [See 27 BTA 237]
e-1—Meadowlawn Memorial Gardens, Inc. v U.S., 45 AFTR2d 80-1374—80-1375 (Ct Cl Trial Judges Op) [See 27 BTA 237]

ACACIA PARK CEMETERY ASSN., INC. v COMM., 67 F2d 700, 13 AFTR 387 (USCA 7)
e-1—Meadowlawn Memorial Gardens, Inc. v U.S., 45 AFTR2d 80-1370, 80-1371, 80-1374, 80-1375 (Ct Cl Trial Judges Op)
f-4—Meadowlawn Memorial Gardens, Inc. v. U.S., 46 AFTR2d 80-5556, 80-5557, 80-5560, 80-5561 (Ct Cl)

ACER REALTY CO., 45 BTA 333
f—Dunlap, Paul D. & Shirley A., 74 TC (No. 104), 74 P-H TC 774

ACER REALTY CO. v COMM., 132 F2d 512, 30 AFTR 630 (USCA 8)
f-1—Dunlap, Paul D. & Shirley A., 74 TC (No. 104), 74 P-H TC 774

ACF-BRILL MOTORS CO. v COMM., 189 F2d 704, 40 AFTR 764 (USCA 3)
1—Redding, Gerald R. v Comm., 46 AFTR2d 80-5660 (USCA 7)

ACF-BRILL MOTORS CO. (SUCCESSOR), 14 TC 263,

Prentice-Hall publishes a separate citator set for all tax cases. Unlike Shepard's Citations, it is arranged by name of case, rather than by citation.

TC 660

ABRAHAMSON, GUY C. & ELAINE, 1978 P-H TC Memo ¶ 78,026
e-1—Randolph E. & Stella M., 74 TC (No. 21), 74 P-H TC 157
f-1—Clark, James V., 1980 P-H TC Memo 80-1920

ACHONG v COMM., 246 F2d 445, 51 AFTR 899 (USCA 9)
f-1—Curphey, Edwin R., 73 TC 775, 73 P-H TC 42?
f-1—Greenspan, Leon J. & Irene, 1980 P-H TC Memo 80-177

ACHONG, STEPHEN G., 1956 P-H TC Memo ¶ 56,073

Treasury Decisions & Rulings Start on Page 13,501

[Illustration 162]

PAGE FROM IRS BULLETIN—INDEX DIGEST SYSTEM

Digests of Revenue Rulings, Revenue Procedures, and other published items except Public Laws, Treasury Decisions, and Tax Conventions

Abandonment

(See: Losses)

Abatements

(See: Assessments; Refunds and credits)

Account numbers

(See: Identifying numbers)

Accounting methods

(See also specific subject headings)

2.1 Accrual; advance credit for warranty work.

Credits received from a manufacturer for warranty work done by an accrual method dealer pursuant to the manufacturers warranty claim advance program are not includible in the dealer's gross income for a taxable year in which the amount of the credits do not exceed the dealer's unpaid accrued warranty claims. Such amounts represent a reduction of the dealer's accounts receivable due from the manufacturer.§§1.446-1, 1.451-1. (Secs. 446, 451; '54 Code.)

Rev. Rul. 72-595, 1972-2 C.B. 232.

2.2 Accrual; advance payments; dor-

The IRS, as part of its IRS Bulletin Publications, publishes this Digest. It is an excellent tool for locating IRS and certain judicial rulings.

advance payments for services to be performed in the future by accrual basis taxpayers; Rev. Rul. 70-445 superseded.§§1.446-1, 1.451-1. (Secs. 446, 451; '54 Code.)

Rev. Rul. 65-141, 1965-1 C.B. 210;Rev. Rul. 71-299, 1971-2 C.B. 218.

2.3 Accrual; advance payments; future services.

On March 1, 1959, an accrual basis partnership was converted to a subchapter S corporation that, retaining the partnership's accounting system, accrued fees as billed, collected them quarterly in advance, but erroneously deferred the recognition of income until the services were performed. The fiscal year ended January 31, 1960. *Held*, unbilled fees unsupported by January 1960 services and fees billed by and paid to the partnership in 1959 are excludable from corporate income; fees billed by the partnership but collected by the corporation are also excludable. Acquiescence to the first statement; nonacquiesence to the second. (Sec. 451, '54 Code.)

E. Morris Cox, 43 T.C. 448, Acq. & Nonacq., 1965-2 C.B. 4, 7.

2.4 Accrual; advance payments; future services.

Procedures are prescribed under which accrual basis taxpayers will be allowed to defer the inclusion in gross income of payments received, or amounts due and payable, in one taxable year for services to be performed before the end of the next succeeding taxable year. Rev. Proc. 70-21 superseded.§§1.446-1, 1.451-1. (Sec. 601.204, S.P.R.; Secs. 446, 451, '54 Code.)

Rev. Proc. 71-21, 1971-2 C.B. 549.

2.5 Accrual; advance payments; future services.

Advance payments received by a telephone company from subscribers representing a basic monthly charge applicable to the following month's telephone service may be deferred to the extent provided in Rev. Proc. 71-21.§§1.446-1, 1.451-1. (Secs. 446, 451; '54 Code.)

Rev. Rul. 72-49, 1972-1 C.B. 125.

2.6 Accrual; advance payments; service contracts.

Prepaid income from contracts to furnish services and other types of prepaid income, such as prepaid royalties, rent, bonuses, etc., will constitute taxable income in the year of receipt, regardless of whether the period of

An accrual-basis builder of small boats under a Government contract is not required to include in income the 40 percent retainage applicable to each boat until final acceptance of each boat and is not required to include in income the remaining 60 percent of the retainage until final acceptance of all boats specified in the particular contract.§§1.446-1, 1.451-1. (Secs. 446, 451; '54 Code.)

Rev. Rul. 69-314, 1969-1 C.B. 139.

2.8 Accrual; business income.

Under the taxpayer's method of accounting accounts receivable and payable, sales, and purchases were accrued. Inventories were used in computing profit and loss of the proprietorship business. *Held*, the taxpayer was on the accrual method for the purpose of reporting business income and expenses, although salaries were not accrued and no records were kept for nonbusiness income and expenses. (Sec. 41, '39 Code; Sec. 446, '54 Code.)

James J. Standing, 28 T.C. 789, Acq., 1958-2 C.B. 8.

2.9 Accrual; cash; future services; Cropland Adjustment Program.

A lump sum payment received in advance of performance under the "Cropland Adjustment Program" by a taxpayer (producer) who reports income under the cash method is includible in gross income in the taxable year in which the payment is received or made available, whichever is earlier; where the taxpayer (producer) uses the accrual method, the payment is includible in the earlier of the taxable year in which it is received or in which he has a right to receive it. Modified to the extent inconsistent with section 3 of Rev. Proc. 71-21, relating to the permissible methods of treating advance payments for services to be performed in the future by accrual basis taxpayers. Rev. Rul. 70-445 superseded.§§1.446-1, 1.451-1. (Secs. 446, 451; '54 Code.)

Rev. Rul. 68-44, 1968-1 C.B. 191; Rev. Rul. 71-299, 1971-2 C.B. 218.

2.10 Accrual; change in billing procedures.

The change in an accrual method taxpayer's customer contracts and billing system that had the effect of showing a net operating loss in the current year but matching revenues and expenses in future years was not a change in accounting method requiring the Commissioner's permission. (Sec. 446, '54 Code.)

Decision, Inc., 47 T.C. 58, Acq., 1967-2

2.12 Accrual; compensation; mortgage servicing contract.

An accrual method mortgage company agreed with a bank to service mortgages for compensation to be finally determined on the basis of a basic rate but to be paid monthly on a level payment rate. Taxpayer accrued compensation at the basic rate but reported as income only the amounts actually received. *Held*, taxable income included only the amounts actually due under the level payment rate. (Sec. 451, '54 Code.)

Etheridge and Vanneman, Inc., 40 T.C. 461, Acq., 1964-1 (Part 1) C.B. 4.

2.12

[Illustration 163]

PAGE FROM BNA TAX MANAGEMENT—PRIMARY SOURCES

III - 22 §57 [1978] pg. (i)

TAX MANAGEMENT — PRIMARY SOURCES

SEC. 57 — ITEMS OF TAX PREFERENCE

Table of Contents

The BNA Tax Management Series includes volumes entitled Primary Sources. These include the text of federal acts and other documents comprising the legislative history of each act.

11-17-80

PS-23

SECTION P. SUMMARY [100]

A. Research Technique

B. Constitution

C. Statutes

  1. Current Statutes
  2. Codification of Statutes
  3. Citators for Statutes
  4. Pending Legislation

D. Legislative Histories

E. Treaties and Other International Material

  1. Treaties
  2. Citators for Tax Treaties
  3. Other International Material

F. Regulations

  1. Current Final Regulations
  2. Codification of Final Regulations
  3. Citators for Final Regulations
  4. Proposed Regulations
  5. Regulations Under Development

G. Internal Revenue Service Pronouncements

  1. Types of Pronouncements
     a. Rulings
     b. Procedures
     c. Operating Policies
  2. Finding Lists for IRS Pronouncements
  3. Digests of IRS Pronouncements
  4. Texts of Revenue Rulings and Revenue Procedures
  5. Texts of Letter Rulings
  6. Citators for IRS Pronouncements

H. Judicial Reports

  1. Court Organization
  2. Finding Lists for Decisions
  3. Digests of Decisions

[100] This Summary is actually an outline of the topics covered in this chapter and does not include summaries of how to use the various materials.

RESEARCH PROBLEM

Alice Taxpayer sold a tract of vacant land in December 1974. Alice had purchased the land eleven months earlier for $10,000. It turned out to be the last lot needed by a land developer, who offered her $100,000, payable in ten equal annual installments plus 5% interest. Alice received $10,000 as a down payment on December 31, 1974.

The developer experienced financial difficulties in 1975 through 1978. During those years he paid Alice the interest due but made no payments of the principal amount.

On December 31, 1979, the developer paid Alice a $10,000 installment plus interest due for the year.

Alice, who is reporting the transaction as an installment sale, wishes to know:

(1) May she report the $9,000 gain segment of the 1979 installment as long-term capital gain even though she did not hold the land more than one year? Does it matter that she held the developer's note more than one year?

(2) Assume that you answered (1) affirmatively. What is the amount of her § 1202 deduction?

(3) Must Alice recalculate the capital gain component downward because the interest rate is below that required by the § 483 regulations?

(4) If Alice is entitled to report her gain as capital gain, is she subject to the alternative minimum tax on tax preferences, which was added to the Code after she sold her land?

Chapter 25

A GENERAL SUMMARY OF RESEARCH PROCEDURE

SECTION A. RESEARCH PROCEDURE

Legal research is as much an art as it is a science. There are as many approaches to legal research as there are problems to be solved. Each of the various types of research tools available for resolution of legal problems has been discussed in the previous chapters. The final measure is to develop a systematic approach to using the research tools that have been described. It should also be noted that the approach to legal research may be determined by where the research is occurring. Not all law libraries will have all of the sets described, and a detailed knowledge of each research tool will assist in formulating the research problem. Methods of approach will be suggested in this chapter; but, in the end, each researcher must develop a system which best suits his or her needs.

No matter how sophisticated one becomes in any particular field of law, there will always be problems calling for research into areas of the law with which one is utterly unfamiliar. It is at these moments that the basic approach developed as a novice becomes the artful technique of a trained professional.

A worthwhile system of legal research can be broken down into five basic steps. These are:

STEP 1. Identify the legally significant facts.

STEP 2. Frame the legal issues to be researched.

STEP 3. Identify the relevant sources of law.

STEP 4. Research the issues presented.

STEP 5. Communicate the solution of the problem.

The discussion herein will focus on each of these steps individually; however, it is to be remembered that each step is closely interrelated with all the others. In the actual process of executing any one of the steps it may be necessary to simultaneously refine the work done under all of the previous steps.

STEP 1. Identifying Facts of Legal Significance

The first task of a researcher is to isolate the facts surrounding the particular problem to be solved. Some facts have legal significance; others do not. The task of legal research begins with the compiling of a descriptive statement of legally significant facts. As one gains expertise in a particular field of law, one becomes more skilled in the process of isolating facts which have legal significance. It is, however, often difficult for a beginner to identify the significant facts and to discard the insignificant ones. Consequently, when researching a problem in an unfamiliar area of the law, it is usually best to err on the side of over-inclusion rather than on the side of exclusion.

It must also be kept in mind that the words used to describe a particular problem or fact situation may both assist and hinder the research process. Most research tools are indexed by a set of descriptive words. Failure to describe the fact situation in sufficient detail can sometimes cause one to overlook important legal issues because of the failure to find the right words in the index.

STEP 2. Framing the Legal Issues to Be Researched

Writing a clear, concise statement of each legal issue raised by the significant facts is undoubtedly the most important and usually the most difficult task associated with legal research. Failure to frame all of the issues raised by a particular set of facts can and often will lead to an erroneous solution.

It is better, when framing the issues, for a beginner to err on the side of too many issues. Insignificant ones can always be eliminated after they have been thoroughly investigated, and overlapping ones can be consolidated. As a particular issue is researched, it is often discovered that it is overly broad and it becomes evident that the statement of the issue should be narrowed. It may also be necessary at times to split an original issue into two, or to divide it into two sub-issues. Similarly, it may develop that the original issue is too narrow and as a result is not leading to any relevant authority. In such instances, the issue should then be broadened. Many times, during the course of one's research, it becomes apparent that other issues not originally thought of are relevant.

It is for this reason that the task of framing issues may not be completed until the research project is finished.

Once statements of each issue raised by the significant facts have been drafted they should be arranged in a logical pattern which will provide continuity and preserve the integrity of the thought process during the course of the legal research. Logically related issues may be combined as sub-issues under a broader main issue. Issues which depend upon the outcome of more major issues should be arranged accordingly.

When arranging the issues, one should keep in mind that it is usually best to exhaust all relevant legal authority on one issue before going on to research another issue. This technique is more methodical than an approach which exhausts a given legal authority on all the issues raised by the facts before moving on to the next source of law.

The technique of exhausting all relevant authorities on a particular issue before going on to the next issue also serves other practical purposes. It allows one to focus on a fairly narrow area of the law, thus avoiding the temptation to stray into interesting but irrelevant areas. It also allows one to quickly gain some knowledge of the time required to complete the project so that one can accurately schedule each step of the process, ensuring that it will be completed on time.

For these reasons, it is always advisable to frame the issues so that they can be researched independently and to arrange these issues and sub-issues into a logically progressive pattern.

STEP 3. Identifying the Relevant Sources of the Law

Once Steps 1 and 2 have been completed, the next and equally important step is to decide for each issue to be researched which sources to use, which sources not to use, and the order in which these sources should be examined. Failure to give thought to the precise sources to be used before beginning the research on a particular issue may result in omitting a vital source of law. More importantly, it may cause the research to start from the wrong end, unnecessarily increasing the difficulty of the task. For these reasons, the researcher should always prepare a list of sources arranged in the order they will be used for each issue to be researched.

It is convenient to classify general legal problems into four categories: (1) constitutional law, (2) statutory law, (3) case law, and (4) administrative law. Each of these categories is generally divided into federal, state, and local law. In actual practice, most legal problems are interrelated and concern two or more of the above categories, since they may involve both federal and state law. Legal issues cannot really be compartmentalized. This is one reason why it is usually advisable to research each issue separately and completely before turning to the next issue.

Notwithstanding the interrelationship of legal issues, it is still best to list relevant sources of legal authority as separate, independent units. In Section B, a list of sources is suggested, and order of use is given. The sources cover constitutional, statutory, case, and administrative law. It should be kept in mind that if a particular issue overlaps more than one category, one must prepare a list of sources containing authorities drawn from all the applicable categories. In addition, thought must be given as to how to coordinate the use of the relevant sources in obtaining a rapid, accurate solution of the issues being researched. Following the list of sources is a "Chart on Legal Procedure" which summarizes the information previously presented in narrative form.

STEP 4. Researching the Issues Presented

Once the issues have been framed and the sources of legal authority listed in the order in which they are intended to be used, it is time to begin researching the first issue. The first issue should be completed, exhausting all relevant authorities in point, before progressing to the second issue. The first source on the list is entered through its index, using the descriptive words developed by applying the TARP method discussed in Chapter 2. The contents of the first source should be thoroughly exhausted and a list of the statutes, cases, and other relevant authorities should be compiled. If the first source is covered by *Shepard's Citations*, it is *Shepardized*. The first source for all materials in point should be exhausted so that there will be no need to return to this source again during the research of the first issue.

The next step is to read all the authorities cited by the first source. These authorities should be consulted in the following order: (1) constitutions, (2) statutes and local ordinances, (3) cases, (4) administrative materials, and finally (5) secondary authorities. As each of these cited authorities is read, a list of authorities which they cite should be compiled, checking to eliminate duplicates. Each cited source should be *Shepardized* before moving on to the next cited source. The second source on the original list is then consulted and the same process repeated. This pattern continues until all sources on the original list and the authorities they cite are fully researched.

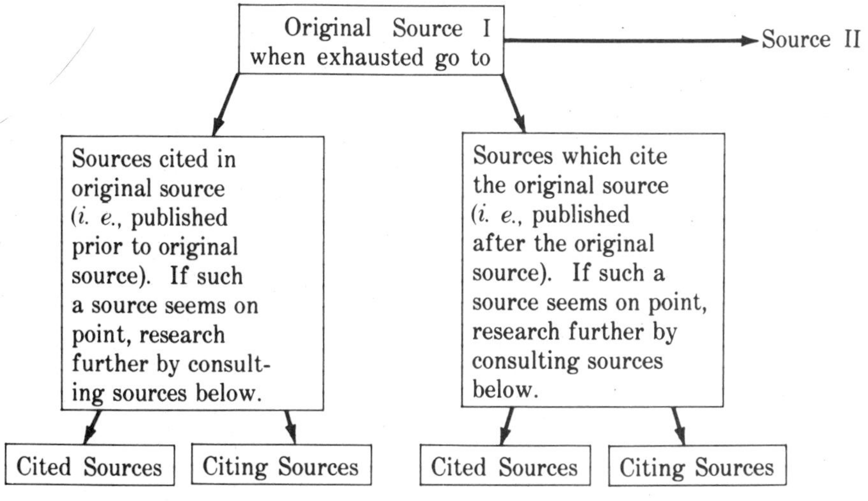

As each new source is evaluated for its relevance, further sources can be developed and pursued in the same two-pronged fashion: consult sources in the text and footnotes for materials the source in hand relied upon, and *Shepardize* for sources which cite to it. For each relevant source located, no matter how far down the chain from the starting point, the same checking should be done. It may be helpful to think of the process as doing further research on a subject on point by consulting both recent and less recent published sources. Beyond simply giving the researcher different sources for points of law, this process should show the development of a legal idea over time and give indications of the trend in the law. But judgment must be exercised at each step of the process or the research will become sidetracked on irrelevant issues. In some instances this "developmental model" of legal research is very obvious. For instance, one may research a constitutional or statutory provision by searching for preceding provisions and legislative history and the most recent judicial interpretations as well as the actual text. All may be useful persuasive authority, but the real value of such a thorough research is the view it affords of the development and trend of the provision in question.

At this point it is worth noting that as one moves down the original list of sources, the frequency of repetitive citations begins to increase rapidly. This means that the available sources in point are beginning to be exhausted. Near the end of the list of sources, it will usually be found that all of the citations are repetitive, indicating that the research is both thorough and complete. Citations should be placed on note cards, organized according to the type of source involved. Failure to maintain an accurate list of citations will result in wasted time and may cause crucial sources of authority to be overlooked.

The following is a quick example of the process just described. Suppose that the problem being researched involves state law. The first source on the list is the local encyclopedia (or a general encyclopedia if a state encyclopedia is not available). The index is checked using the TARP method, the text is read, and a list of citations is developed which, for example, contains citations to the state annotated statutes and to several cases.

Since an encyclopedia cannot be *Shepardized*, the cited authorities, starting with the annotated statutes, are read. The appropriate sections of the annotated statutes are then *Shepardized*.

The next step is to read and *Shepardize* all of the cases cited by the encyclopedia and the citations obtained from the annotated statutes and from *Shepard's Citations*. From this process any additional relevant cases are listed and then *Shepardized*.

Then, go back to the original list of sources and exhaust the second source contained on the list. This will probably be the state annotated statutes. Although this source has already been investigated, this time it is entered through the index using the TARP method. At this point it will usually be discovered that, in exhausting the citations obtained from an encyclopedia, all or most of the statutory provisions located by the use of the index have already been read. One now begins to develop a sense that the statutory authority in point has been exhausted.

The third source on the original list of sources should now be consulted. Suppose that this is the state digest. This is entered through the descriptive word index. Again, it will most likely be discovered that all of the relevant cases in the digest have been previously read, since they were cited by the local encyclopedia. Once any additional cases found in the state digest have been exhausted, the next source on the original list is consulted. This process is continued until the original list of authorities is completed. At this point the research of the first issue is completed, and one can begin the research of the second issue.

As one gains increased expertise in the process of executing legal research, one begins to develop certain shortcuts which increase the researcher's speed without sacrificing accuracy. For example, one may begin to use a host of abbreviations such as those used by *Shepard's Citations.*

Skilled researchers can rapidly evaluate the potential value of a case without reading the entire reported decision. One such technique is as follows: (1) read the headnotes, selecting those which bear on the issue being researched; (2) read that portion of the text relating to the headnotes selected; (3) read the facts of the case and as much of the opinion as is necessary to understand the point of law involved; (4) jot down the headnote numbers for *Shepardizing* if the textual material is in point; (5) jot down every important citation to authority made by the textual material in point; (6) then, read the entire case *only if* it is a vital link in the chain of case law authority in point. Of course, if the skilled researcher discovers at any point in the above process that the case adds nothing to the point of law being researched or that it is of little value for some other reason, the researcher will discard the case and mark it off the list of cases.

Skilled researchers also develop insight into knowing when they can safely terminate their reserach without exhausting every source on their list of authorities. There is no uniform rule which tells one how extensive the research should be in solving a legal problem. The extensiveness of research is often influenced by extraneous factors such as limitations of time, compensation, etc.; the nature of the problems; the legal measures being adopted; and the research habits and attitudes of the researcher.

The preceding discussion in this chapter describes an exhaustive system of legal research; however, such complete procedures are not always necessary. Carrying a problem through all the sources can be needless, unwarranted or repetitious. Common sense and professional insight, therefore, play a significant role in research procedure.

Obviously, there is no pat answer to the question which we, as researchers, ask every time we investigate a legal problem: "Can I safely stop here?"

In the last analysis, the skills of sophisticated researchers are measured as much for the knowledge of what can be omitted as for what and how research materials are used to solve legal problems. In some instances, a skilled researcher merely spot-checks a *single* publication, e. g., a general encyclopedia. A skilled researcher usually does not consult duplicative sources of the same type, i. e., *Am.Jur. 2d* and *C.J.S.* The researcher's stock in trade is *time*; a skilled researcher knows how to wisely use it. On the other hand, the researcher must always solve the problem accurately. For this reason, the novice is cautioned to always err on the side of over-inclusion, duplication, and excessive time, because the work product expected of the novice is no different from that expected of the skilled professional —an accurate solution to the problem.

STEP 5. Communicating the Solution of the Problem

The final step of the research process is somewhat outside the scope of this work, being reserved for individualized instruction at the classroom level. Nevertheless, the true test of the capacity to research legal issues is found in the capacity to communicate the results to other persons.

The notes which were prepared during Step 4, above, should be in a form which can easily be organized and presented orally or in written form. If the research is to be reduced to written form, usually a memorandum of law, there are several techniques which can be used to ensure that the written words accurately convey the results of the research. The most important rule to follow is that the words selected must be objective in nature, avoiding an adversary approach. One must always evaluate the merits of both sides of each legal issue.

The key elements of a well-drafted memorandum of law are: (1) a title identifying the nature of the writing, (2) a statement of the issues presented in the order they are to be discussed, (3) a brief answer for each of the issues presented, (4) a statement of the operative facts, (5) a discussion of each issue presented, and (6) a conclusion (optional). It should be noted that in executing Steps 1 and 2 of the research process, the second and fourth elements of a memorandum of law were completed.

One should begin writing the memorandum by refining the statement of the issues and by reducing the statement of facts to eliminate all irrelevancies. The next step is to outline and then carefully write the discussion section. The brief answer section is then prepared, stating, in as few words as possible, the conclusions drawn in the discussion section of the memorandum. A conclusion section should be used only in complex memoranda when the reader requires a more detailed summary of the problem than is provided by the conclusory statements contained in the brief answer. The entire memorandum should then be given a short, highly descriptive title, and edited for citation errors, literary style, and, most importantly, for brevity.

The discussion section is the heart of the memorandum and deserves a bit more explanation. It should be organized issue by issue. Each issue and sub-issue should be discussed completely before progressing to the next issue. The most widely accepted method of discussing an issue of law employs the following format: (1) state the issue, (2) state the law which applies to the issue, (3) apply the law to the relevant operative facts, and (4) draw a conclusion. This format can be repeated for each issue and sub-issue in the memorandum.

Finally, there are a few common errors which must be avoided if a memorandum is to be a professional document. Backtracking or excessive interplay of issues is to be avoided. Each issue and sub-issue should be distinct and logically complete. Excessive overlapping of thought in the discussion section usually indicates that the issues have not been drafted with sufficient precision.

When an authority is cited it must stand for the proposition asserted. If a citation is to dictum in a case, it must be so identified. One must avoid excessive citation to authority. String citations are rarely appropriate. Try to cite only the leading authority or authorities in point. Do not use quotations as a substitute for analysis and use quotations only where they add to, rather than supplement the body of the memorandum.

Never give the appearance of avoiding resolution of a problem by pleading the need for additional facts. On the other hand, a memorandum should deal with potentially variant outcomes by assuming the existence of any facts which are clearly within the ambit of and which have not been negated by the given fact complex.

The greatest temptation of the novice is to include information which the researcher has spent many hours developing but which were later discovered to be wholly irrelevant to a proper analysis of the issues presented. A novice should expect to investigate a host of irrelevant leads during the research process. Avoid the burning temptation to include this information in the memorandum as it detracts from and often masks the legal analysis which is directly in point.

It must always be remembered that a memorandum is objective in nature. It is not intended to be an adversary document. The presentation of analysis in adversary form casts grave doubt in the mind of the reader as to the objective validity of the memorandum. The task is to explore both the strengths and the weaknesses of each conclusion drawn. The task of the writer is to evaluate, not to persuade.

The first exposure to the mechanics of executing a legal research project from its beginning to its end has now been completed. The system we have discussed is one of the many possible approaches. The ultimate objective of the researcher is to develop the capacity to solve legal problems rapidly and accurately. That capacity can only be developed by constructing a basic, systematic approach to legal research. Therefore, it is now the task of the researcher to synthesize the materials contained in this chapter and to fashion a system of legal research which is commensurate with the researcher's existing professional skills and which assures the researcher of a professional work product each time the system is utilized.

SECTION B. SUGGESTED LIST OF SOURCES[1]

1. Constitutional Law Problem

a. *Federal Constitution*

(1) General Background

For a general discussion of a federal constitutional law question, consult a general legal encyclopedia *(Corpus Juris Secundum* or *American Jurisprudence 2d)*. More critical and detailed studies may be found in the periodical literature by examining the *Current Law Index*, the *Index to Legal Periodicals* or the *Legal Resource Index*. A recent treatise may be consulted to explore the area. Several other interpretative sources are discussed in Chapter 8.

Examine the *American Law Reports* and the *United States Supreme Court Reports* (L.Ed.) for possible annotations.

(2) Text and Interpretation

If the matter is a recognizable federal constitutional problem, consult the following sources:

[1] This section and Section C were authored by Jenni Parrish, Assistant Professor of Law and Law Librarian, University of Pittsburgh.

For the text of the Constitution and its interpretation, *see:*

United States Code Annotated

United States Code Service

Constitution of the United States (Library of Congress ed. 1973; updated by a biennial pocket supplement)

(3) *Shepard's Citations*

Shepardize: (a) several important cases and (b) the applicable provision of the Constitution in *Shepard's United States Citations* and in the appropriate *Shepard's State Citations.* Use *Shepard's Federal Citations* when given an intermediate or lower federal court decision. Numerous case citations under a provision of the Constitution in *Shepard's United States Citations* may make the Constitution section in *Shepard's* unwieldy and unusable.

(4) Additional Cases

Check a United States Supreme Court digest, the *Federal Practice Digest, 2d* (and its earlier editions), or the *American Digest System* for additional judicial interpretations. Not to be overlooked, when available, are the *Lexis* and *Westlaw* data bases as sources of additional cases.

(5) Intent

In the absence of adequate judicial interpretation or to re-examine the meaning given to the Constitution by its framers, the historical source materials cited at footnote 5 in Chapter 8 should be consulted.

b. *State Constitutions*

(1) General Background

For a discussion of a state constitution, consult a local encyclopedia, if one is published for the state, e. g., *Texas Jurisprudence 2d* and *Illinois Law and Practice.*

In the absence of a local encyclopedia, a general encyclopedia *(Corpus Juris Secundum* or *American Jurisprudence 2d)* may provide a helpful general discussion of the question. An *American Law Reports* annotation or a periodical article may also treat the constitutional issue.

(2) Text and Interpretation

The text and case interpretations of a state constitution are included in the appropriate annotated state code. Additional cases may be located through the state digest.

The state Attorney General's opinions should be consulted as a possible source of interpretation of the state constitution. See Chapter 19.

(3) *Shepard's Citations*

Shepardize: (a) several leading cases and (b) the provision of the state constitution in the appropriate *Shepard's State Citations.*

(4) Additional Cases

For cases of other states, consult the *American Digest System.*

The *Index Digest of State Constitutions* (Columbia University, 2d ed. 1959; updated with pocket supplements) cites comparative state constitutions. Through these references, the annotated constitutions of other states may be examined, evaluated and compared. This procedure is useful in citing persuasive decisions from another state whose provision was copied, or where the provision, situation and setting are comparable or where there is a dearth of judicial interpretation of the provision by a particular state court.

Comparative constitutional study may also be pursued by *Shepardizing* cases under their citations in the appropriate *Shepard's Citations.*

(5) Intent

Examine the proceedings, reports and other documents relating to state constitutional conventions for the meaning given the provision by its draftsmen.

2. Statutory Problem

a. *Federal Statute*

(1) General Background

Treatises are available for a number of federal statutory laws, e. g., R. Callman, *Law of Unfair Competition, Trademarks and Monopolies* (3d ed., 1967–, 5 vols.). They provide not only background but also detailed subject information. Thus they are valuable not only for their informational content but also as case finders. Check the subject section of the law library's catalog to locate citation.

Annotations in the *American Law Reports* and the *United States Supreme Court Reports* (L.Ed.) and periodical literature are additional useful secondary aids.

(2) Text and Interpretation

For the text and interpretation of a federal statute which is in force, use the *United States Code Annotated* or the *United States Code Service.* The amendatory history of the act is included in these annotated codes. They will also include annotations of relevant United States Attorney General's opinions.

For the legislative history (intent of the draftsmen) of the act, consult the Congressional bills, reports, hearings and debates. *See* Chapter 10. As explained there, *Congressional Information Service*

(CIS) provides these documents on microfiche for legislation passed in 1970 and thereafter. Prior to 1970, finding the relevant documents is more difficult.

(3) *Shepard's Citations*

Shepardize: (a) the provision *(United States Code* or *Statutes at Large)* for the history and the treatment of the act and (b) several significant cases in *Shepard's United States Citations.* Consult *Shepard's Federal Citations* to *Shepardize* intermediate and lower federal court cases.

State court decisions which cite federal statutes are listed in *Shepard's State Citations* or the regional *Shepard's Citations.*

(4) Additional Cases

Where there are meager case interpretations, examine the United States Supreme Court digests, the *Federal Practice Digest, 2d* or the *American Digest System.*

(5) Other

Where available to the researcher, a *Lexis* or *Westlaw* terminal can retrieve the text of the *United States Code* as well as the texts of federal and state cases in which federal laws have been cited.

b. *State Statute*

(1) General Background

The local encyclopedia is helpful in providing information about and interpretations of a state statute. Local treatises and periodical articles, having more detailed bearing on the act, are equally useful references.

Where there is no local encyclopedia, *American Jurisprudence 2d* and *Corpus Juris Secundum* may give general information on some topics. Annotations in the *American Law Reports* cover statutory law of the several states.

(2) Text and Interpretation

Unannotated state codes provide the texts of the statutes. Annotated state codes give both the texts of the statutes and case interpretations.

The codes provide the amendatory history of the state acts. Legislative histories for state legislation are usually difficult or impossible to compile because of the dearth of published debates, committee reports, hearings, etc. For further comment, see Chapter 11.

Shepard's Law Locators, where available, can also be a helpful interpretative source. See Chapter 15.

If the state's Attorney General has addressed the interpretation of this statute in an opinion, it is certainly worth noting. For a discussion of state Attorneys General opinions, see Chapter 19.

(3) Shepard's Citations

Shepardize: (a) the provision of the state statute and (b) several important cases in the applicable *Shepard's State Citations.*

(4) Additional Cases

For additional cases interpreting the statute, examine the state or regional digest.

If there is a dearth of statutory interpretation in the state, consult the annotated codes of other states for those states' interpretations. Such interpretation can be very persuasive. Some codes list comparative legislation of representative and neighboring states. Consultation of *Uniform Laws Annotated* (discussed in Chapter 18) may also be worthwhile in finding additional cases and commentary.

(5) Other

A number of research guides geared to particular state jurisdictions have appeared in recent years. Where available they should be consulted. See those listed in Appendix B.

c. *Local Ordinances and Codes*

(1) Text and Interpretation

The texts of city ordinances are included in city codes. Generally, city codes are not annotated. Treatises can sometimes be the source of interpretative commentary and case law relevant to municipal legislation. The appropriate state digest is useful in providing interpretations of the city ordinance but the problem must be approached by subject or topic.

In the absence of a current city code, check the ordinances in the office of the city counsel, city clerk, or other local official whose duties include the maintenance of a current file of city laws.

(2) *Shepard's Citations*

Shepardize: (a) the provision of the city code and (b) several significant cases, if existing, in the applicable *Shepard's State Citations.*

(3) Other

Shepard's Ordinance Law Annotations provide annotations on court decisions pertaining to city charters and ordinances.

The *Lexis* and *Westlaw* data bases, where available, should not be overlooked as a source of pertinent case law.

3. Case Law Problem

a. *Federal Cases*

(1) General Background

For background information on federal case law, one of the two standard legal encyclopedias, *Corpus Juris Secundum* or *American Jurisprudence 2d*, should be consulted. For further information, go to a treatise on the particular topic or a relevant law review article. The American Law Institute's *Restatements* can also be valuable aids in finding case law on particular topics (see Chapter 18). The annotations found in *American Law Reports* are good secondary research aids as well.

(2) Texts of Cases

The texts of United States Supreme Court cases may be found in the official *United States Reports,* in *United States Supreme Court Reports* (Lawyers Co-operative Publishing Co.), and in *Supreme Court Reporter* (West Publishing Co.).

Federal circuit courts of appeals decisions are found in *Federal Reporter,* first and second series.

Decisions of federal district courts are selectively reported in *Federal Supplement* and in some subject reporters.

Full discussions of all these reporters are found in Chapter 4.

The *Lexis* and *Westlaw* data bases can also be sources of the text of federal court cases.

(3) *Shepard's Citations*

Shepardize the significant cases in *Shepard's Federal Citations* (*i. e.,* circuit courts of appeals and district court decisions) and *Shepard's United States Citations* (Supreme Court decisions).

(4) Additional Cases

Additional cases may be found in (a) the *U. S. Supreme Court Digest,* (b) *Federal Practice Digest 2d, Modern Federal Practice Digest,* and *Federal Digest,* and (c) looseleaf services on the particular topic.

(5) Other

Records and briefs of federal court cases may be of assistance in interpreting the decisions. Such records and briefs for the United States Supreme Court are commercially published in microform (see Chapter 23). Where such documents are not published, the clerk of the court should be contacted to ascertain the availability of these materials.

b. *State Cases*

(1) General Background

For background information on state case law, the local encyclopedia, if available, may be a good source for a discussion of the topic. In the absence of a local encyclopedia, *American Jurisprudence 2d* or *Corpus Juris Secundum* may be consulted for an exposition of the case law.

American Jurisprudence 2d may give specific references to *American Law Reports* annotations, eliminating the use of A.L.R. indexes or regional digests. In some fields of the law, the researcher might begin with a local treatise or periodical article.

(2) Interpretation

References to state court cases may be found in the appropriate state or regional digest.

(3) *Shepard's Citations*

Shepardize several of the significant cases in *Shepard's State Citations* or in the appropriate regional *Shepard's Citations.*

(4) Additional Cases

Other state digests, the regional digests, and the *American Digest System* provide judicial decisions of other states on the point of law. There may also be a looseleaf service on the topic that will provide abstracts or full text of relevant court decisions, (e. g., CCH's *Labor Law Reporter).*

Shepard's Citations give additional references to cases from other states which have cited an applicable state case.

(5) Other

The *Lexis* and *Westlaw* data bases can provide state court decisions.

4. Administrative Law Problem

a. *Federal Administrative Law*

(1) General Background

Corpus Juris Secundum and *American Jurisprudence 2d* discuss federal administrative law. Pike and Fischer, *Administrative Law,* treatises (e. g., K. Davis, *Administrative Law),* and periodical literature provide more detailed studies of administrative law.

Annotations on the subject are included in the *American Law Reports* and the *United States Supreme Court Reports* (L.Ed.).

(2) Text and Interpretation

The texts of federal administrative regulations are contained in: (a) looseleaf services and (b) the *Code of Federal Regulations* and the *Federal Register.*

The decisions of federal administrative agencies are included in: (a) looseleaf services and (b) agency reports.

Interpretative sources of federal administrative law are: (a) looseleaf services, (b) U.S. Supreme Court digests and (c) *Federal Practice Digest, 2d,* the *Modern Federal Practice Digest* and the *Federal Digest.*

(3) *Shepard's Citations*

Rules and regulations found in the *Code of Federal Regulations* can be *Shepardized* in *Shepard's Code of Federal Regulations Citations.*

Cases of certain agencies (e. g., Federal Trade Commission, Securities and Exchange Commission, *etc.*) may be *Shepardized* in *Shepard's United States Citations* and *Shepard's Federal Citations.*

b. *State Administrative Law*

(1) General Background

Refer to a local encyclopedia for a discussion of state administrative law.

Other secondary aids, such as local treatises, periodical articles and *American Law Reports* annotations are also helpful sources.

(2) Text and Interpretation

If a state has a current administrative code, check it for state regulatory material. In the absence of an administrative code, inquiry should be directed to the appropriate agency for its regulations.

If a looseleaf service covers the state law, it can be consulted for agency rules and decisions (e. g., BNA's *Environmental Reporter).*

Some states publish a work comparable to the *Federal Register* (e. g., *Texas Register, Oklahoma Gazette*), in which recent state agency regulations are discussed. Where available, such a publication should be consulted.

Where the state's Attorney General has analyzed an agency ruling or regulation in an opinion, this should be sought for its interpretative value.

The accessibility of agency decisions should be determined by inquiry at the appropriate state agency.

Interpretative cases are covered by the state or regional digest.

(3) *Shepard's Citations*

Shepardize applicable court cases in *Shepard's State Citations* or the regional *Shepard's Citations*

(4) Additional Cases

Court decisions of other states relating to a comparable administrative law problem may be located in (a) other state digests, (b) regional digests, and (c) the *American Digest System.*

Shepard's Citations also provide citations to cases of other states which cited a state court decision on point.

c. *Local Administrative Law*

(1) Text and Interpretation

If available, city administrative regulations generally are published separately as pamphlets for each body. Information regarding these rules, such as regulatory and licensing provisions, should be obtained directly from the local administrative department.

Cases pertaining to local administrative law are included in the state digest.

(2) *Shepard's Citations*

Shepardize cases on the problem by using *Shepard's State Citations* or a regional *Shepard's Citations.*

SECTION C. CHART ON LEGAL RESEARCH PROCEDURE

CHART ON LEGAL RESEARCH PROCEDURE

RESEARCH PROBLEM	GENERAL BACKGROUND	MORE CRITICAL & DETAILED STUDIES	ANNOTATIONS	TEXT OF LAW	LEGISLATIVE HISTORY	INTERPRETATION	SHEPARDIZING	ADDITIONAL CASES	OTHER
CONSTITUTIONAL LAW									
1. Federal	1. C.J.S. 2. Am. Jur. 2d	1. Treatises 2. *Periodicals:* Index Leg. Per. Legal Resource Index (Current Law Index)	1. A.L.R. Fed. 2. U.S. Sup. Ct. Repts. L. Ed. 3. L.C. Constitution	1. U.S.C. 2. U.S.C.A. 3. U.S.C.S.	1. Citations: U.S.C.A., U.S.C.S., Shep. U.S., U.S.C., Stat. at Large 2. *Intent:* Federalist Papers, etc.	1. U.S.C.A. 2. U.S.C.S. 3. L.C. Constitution 4. U.S. Atty. Gen. ops.	1. *Provisions:* U.S., State 2. *Cases:* Fed. U.S., State	1. U.S. Sup. Ct. Digs. 2. West's Fed. Prac. Dig. 2d, Mod. Fed. Prac. Dig., Fed. Dig. 3. Am. Dig. System	1. LEXIS 2. WESTLAW
2. State	1. Local Ency. 2. C.J.S. or Am. Jur. 2d	1. *Periodicals:* Index Leg. Per. Legal Resource Index (Current Law Index)	A.L.R.	1. State Code 2. State Code Annotated	1. State Const. Convention a. Proceedings b. Reports 2. Locally pub'd Legislative reporters, House and Senate Journals, etc. 3. Local newspapers 4. Local experts	1. State Code Annotated 2. State Dig. 3. State Atty. Gen. ops.	1. *Provisions:* State Cit. 2. *Cases:* State Cit. or Regional Cit.	1. Am. Dig. System 2. Index Digest of State Constitutions, 2d ed.	
STATUTORY LAW									
1. Federal	C.J.S. or Am. Jur. 2d	1. Treatises 2. *Periodicals:* Index Leg. Per. Legal Resource Index (Current Law Index)	1. A.L.R. 2. L. Ed.	1. U.S.C. 2. U.S.C.A.	1. Pre-1970—see Chap. 10 2. Post-1970—C.I.S. 3. Published Legis. Histories	1. U.S.C.A. 2. U.S.C.S. 3. U.S. Atty. Gen. ops.	*Provisions & Cases:* U.S. *Cases:* Fed. *Provisions:* State or Regional Cit.	1. U.S. Sup. Ct. Digs. 2. West's Fed. Prac. Dig. 2d, Mod. Fed. Prac. Dig., Fed. Dig.	LEXIS
2. State	1. Loc. Ency. 2. C.J.S. or Am. Jur. 2d	1. Treatises *Periodicals:* Index Leg. Per. Legal Resource Index (Current Law Index)	A.L.R.	1. State Code 2. State Code Annotated	*Citations:* State Code *Intent:* See Chap. 11	1. State Code Annotated 2. Shepard's Law Locator where available	*Provisions & Cases:* State or Regional Cit.	1. State or Regional Dig. 2. Other States Codes Annot. 3. Uniform Laws Annotated	Legal research guide for the state, where available
3. Local		Treatises		1. Mun. Code 2. Mun. Ordinances 3. Appropriate city official		State Dig.	*Provisions & Cases:* State Citator	Shepard's Ord. Law Annotations	1. LEXIS 2. WESTLAW

CHART ON LEGAL RESEARCH PROCEDURE

RESEARCH PROBLEM	GENERAL BACKGROUND	MORE CRITICAL & DETAILED STUDIES	ANNOTATIONS	TEXT OF LAW OR CASE	LEGISLATIVE HISTORY	INTERPRETATION	SHEPARDIZING	ADDITIONAL CASES	OTHER
CASE LAW 1. Federal	1. C.J.S. 2. Am. Jur. 2d	1. Treatises 2. *Periodicals:* Index Leg. Per. Legal Resource Index (Current Law Index) 3. ALI Restatements	A.L.R.	1. S. CT.: U.S. Reports U.S.S. Ct. Reports (L.Ed.) Supreme Ct. Reporter (West) 2. Fed. Reporter & Federal Reporter, 2d 3. Fed. Supp.			Shepard's U.S. & Fed. Cit.	1. U.S. Sup. Ct. Digs. 2. West's Fed. Prac. Dig. 2d, Mod. Fed. Prac. Dig., Fed.Dig. 3. Looseleaf Services	1. LEXIS 2. WESTLAW 3. Records and Briefs, if available
1. State	1. Local Ency. 2. C.J.S. or Am. Jur. 2d	1. Treatises 2. *Periodicals:* Index Leg. Per. Legal Resource Index (Current Law Index)	A.L.R.	1. National Reporter System 2. State Reports			1. Shepard's State or Regional Cit. 2. National Reporter Blue Book	1. Am. Dig. System 2. Looseleaf Services	1. LEXIS 2. WESTLAW 3. Records and Briefs, if available 4. Restatements of the Law
ADMINISTRATIVE LAW 1. Federal	C.J.S. or Am. Jur. 2d	1. Pike & Fischer 2. Treatises 3. *Periodicals:* Index Leg. Per. Legal Resource Index (Current Law Index)	1. A.L.R. 2. L. Ed.	1. Fed. Reg. & CFR: Rules & Decisions 2. Agency Reps: Decisions 3. Looseleaf Services: Rules & Decisions		1. Looseleaf Services 2. U.S.S. Ct. digs. 3. West's Fed. Prac. Dig. 2d, Mod. Fed. Prac. Dig., Fed. Dig.	1. CFR: Cit. 2. Agency Cases: U.S. Admin. Cit. 3. Ct. Cases: U. S. & Fed. Cits.		
2. State	Local Ency.	1. Local Treatises 2. *Periodicals:* Index Leg. Per. Legal Resource Index (Current Law Index)	A.L.R.	1. Ad. Code, if pub. 2. Register of agency regulations and rulings, if pub. 3. Agency: Rules & Decisions 4. Looseleaf service, if available		1. State or Regional •Dig. 2. State Atty. Gen. ops.	Cases: State Cit. or the regional cit.	1. Other state or regional digs. 2. Am. Dig. System	
3. Local				1. Local Adm. Dept. 2. Pamphlets		State Dig.	Cases: State Cit.	Other state digests	

Appendix A

TABLE OF LEGAL ABBREVIATIONS

Even the legal scholar may occasionally encounter an abbreviation whose complete title is difficult to identify. He or she may have to consult a specialized treatise such as William H. Bryson's *Dictionary of Sigla and Abbreviations to and in Law Books Before 1607* (Charlottesville: University of Virginia, 1975), Doris Bieber's *Dictionary of Legal Abbreviations Used in American Law Books* (Buffalo: William S. Hein, 1979), or Donald Raistrick's *Index to Legal Abbreviations and Citations* (Abingdon: Milton Trading Estate, 1981).

As primary and secondary legal materials continue to proliferate each year, it is virtually impossible to include in one place all their abbreviations and titles. Appendix A is restricted primarily to the English language periodicals, court reports, and looseleaf services which one could expect to find in a large American law school library as of January 1, 1981. In addition, Appendix A includes many esoteric and historical citations. This Appendix is not presumed to be authoritative in any official sense, but to reflect acceptable usage by most members of the legal community. Superseded titles have been retained because they are never out of date as possible citations.

Bibliographic information on legal periodicals may be found in Eugene M. Wypyski's *Legal Periodicals in English* (Dobbs Ferry, N.Y.: Glanville, 1976–79), a looseleaf service.

A

A.	Atlantic Reporter
A.2d	Atlantic Reporter, Second Series
A. & E.	Adolphus & Ellis Queen's Bench (Eng.)
A. & E.Ann. Cas.	American & English Annotated Cases
A. & E.Anno.	Same
A. & E.Cas.	Same
A. & E.Corp. Cas.	American & English Corporation Cases
A. & E.Corp. Cas. (N.S.)	Same, New Series
A. & E.Enc. L. & Pr.	American & English Encyclopedia of Law and Practice
A. & E.Ency.	American & English Encyclopedia of Law
A. & E.Ency. Law	Same
A. & E.P. & P.	American & English Pleading and Practice
A. & E.R.Cas.	American & English Railroad Cases
A. & E.R.Cas. (N.S.)	Same, New Series
A. & E.R.R. Cas.	American & English Railroad Cases
A. & E.R.R. Cas. (N.S.)	Same, New Series
A.B.	Anonymous Reports at end of Benloe, or Bendloe (1661) (Eng.)
A.B.A.J.	American Bar Association Journal
A.B.A.Jour.	Same
A.B.A.Rep.	American Bar Association Reports
A.B.A.Sect. Ins.N. & C.L. Proc.	American Bar Association Section of Insurance, Negligence and Compensation Law Proceedings
A.B.C.Newsl.	International Association of Accident Boards and Commissions Newsletter
A.B.F.Res.J.	American Bar Foundation Research Journal
A.B.F. Research Reptr.	American Bar Foundation Research Reporter
A.C.	Law Reports Appeal Cases (Eng.)
	Law Reports Appeal Cases (Eng.) Third Series
	Appeal Cases (Can.)
	Advance California Reports
A.C.A.	Advance California Appellate Reports
A.C.L.U.Leg. Action Bull.	American Civil Liberties Union Legislative Action Bulletin
A.C.R.	American Criminal Reports
A.D.	American Decisions
A/E Legal Newsl.	A/E Legal Newsletter
AELE Legal Liab. Rep.	AELE Legal Liability Reporter
A.F.L.Rev.	Air Force Law Review
AFTR	American Federal Tax Reports
A.I.D.	Accident/Injury/Damages
A.I.L.C.	American International Law Cases 1783–1968
A.K.Marsh.	A.K. Marshall (Ky.)
A.L.I.	American Law Institute
ALI–ABA CLE Rev.	ALI–ABA CLE Review
A.L.R.	American Law Reports
A.L.R.2d	Same, Second Series
A.L.R.3d	Same, Third Series
A.L.R.Fed.	American Law Reports Federal
A.L.Rec.	American Law Record
A.L.Reg. (N.S.)	American Law Register, New Series
A.L.Reg. (O.S.)	American Law Register, Old Series
A.M. & O.	Armstrong, Macartney & Ogle Nisi Prius (Ir.)
A.M.C.	American Maritime Cases
A.O.C.Newsl.	Administrative Office of the Courts Newsletter
APLA Q.J.	APLA Quarterly Journal
A.P.R.	Atlantic Provinces Reports, 1975–
A.R.	Alberta Reports, 1977–
A.R.C.	American Ruling Cases
A.R.M.	Appeals & Review Memorandum Committee (I.R.Bull.)
A.R.R.	Appeals & Review Recommendation (I.R.Bull.)
A.S.A.Newsl.	Association for the Study of Abortion Newsletter
ASILS Int'l L.J.	ASILS International Law Journal
A.S.R.	American State Reports

A.T.	**Alcohol Tax Unit (I.R.Bull.)**
A.T.L.A.J.	American Trial Lawyers Association Journal
ATLA L.J.	Journal of the Association of Trial Lawyers of America
Ab.N.	**Abstracts, Treasury Decisions, New Series**
Abb.	**Abbott (U.S.)**
Abb.Adm.	Abbott's Admiralty (U.S.)
Abb.App.Dec.	Abbott's Appeal Decisions (N.Y.)
Abb.Dec.	Abbott's Decisions (N.Y.)
Abb.Dict.	Abbott's Dictionary
Abb.N.Cas.	**Abbott's New Cases (N.Y.)**
Abb.Prac.	**Abbott's Practice** (N.Y.)
Abb.Prac.N.S.	**Same, New Series**
Abb.R.P.S.	**Abbott's Real Property Statutes (Wn.)**
A'Beck.Res. Judgm.	**A'Beckett's** Reserved **Judgments** (Victoria)
Abogada Int'l	Abogada Internacional
Abs.	Abstracts, Treasury Decisions Ohio Law Abstract
Abstr.Crim & Pen.	Abstracts on Criminology and Penology
Acad.Pol. Sci.Proc.	Academy of Political Science Proceedings
Act.	Acton Prize Cases Privy Council (Eng.)
Acta Cancel-ariae	**English Chancery Reports**
Acta Crim.	Acta Criminologica
Acta Jur.	Acta Juridica
Acton	**Acton Prize Cases Privy Council (Eng.)**
Ad. & El.	Adolphus & Ellis Queen's Bench (Eng.)
Ad. & El. (N.S.)	Same, New Series
Ad.Ct.Dig.	Administrative Court Digest
Ad.L.	Administrative Law
Ad.L.2d	Same, Second Series
Ad.L.Bull.	Administrative Law Bulletin
Ad.L.News	Administrative Law News
Ad.L.Newsl.	Administrative Law Newsletter
Ad.L.Rev.	Administrative Law Review
Adams	Adams (Me.) Adams (N.H.)
Add.	Addison (Pa.)
Add.Eccl.Rep.	Addams' Ecclesiastical Reports (Eng.)
Add.Penn.	Addison (Pa.)
Add.Rep.	Same
Adel.L.Rev.	Adelaide Law Review
Adm. & Ecc.	Admiralty & Ecclesiastical (Eng.)
Advocate	The Advocate
Advocates' Q.	Advocates' Quarterly
Afr.L.Dig.	African Law Digest
Afr.L.R.	African Law Reports
Afr.L.R., Mal.Ser.	African Law Reports, Malawi Series
Afr.L.R., Sierre L.Ser.	African Law Reports, Sierre Leone Series
Afr.L.Stud.	African Law Studies
Agr.L.J.	Agriculture Law Journal
Agri.Dec.	Agriculture Decisions
Aik.	Aikens (Vt.)
Air L.	Air Law
Air L.Rev.	Air Law Review
Akron L.Rev.	Akron Law Review
Ala.	Alabama
Ala.App.	Alabama Court of Appeals
Ala.L.J.	Alabama Law Journal
Ala.L.Rev.	Alabama Law Review
Ala.Law.	The Alabama Lawyer
Ala.Sel.Cas.	Alabama Select Cases
Ala.St.B. Found.Bull.	Alabama State Bar Foundation Bulletin
Alaska	Alaska Reports
Alaska B.Brief	Alaska Bar Brief
Alaska B.J.	Alaska Bar Journal
Alaska L.J.	Alaska Law Journal
Alb.L.J.	Albany Law Journal
Alb.L.Q.	Alberta Law Quarterly
Alb.L.R.	Alberta Law Reports
Alb.L.Rev.	Albany Law Review
Albany L.Rev.	Same
Albuquerque B.J.	Albuquerque Bar Journal
Alc. & N.	Alcock & Napier King's Bench (Ir.)
Alc.Reg.Cas.	Alcock Registry Cases (Ir.)
Ald.	Alden's Condensed Reports (Pa.)
Aleyn	Aleyn, King's Bench (Eng.)
Alison Pr.	Alison Practice (Sc.)
All E.R.	All England Law Reports
All India Crim.Dec.	All India Criminal Decisions
All India Rptr.	All India Reporter
All N.L.R.	All Nigeria Law Reports
All Pak. Leg.Dec.	All Pakistan Legal Decisions
Allen	Allen (Mass.)
Allen N.B.	Allen, New Brunswick
Allinson	Allinson, Pa.Superior District Courts

Alta.	Alberta Law Reports
Alta.L.	Alberta Law
Alta.L.Q.	Alberta Law Quarterly
Alta.L.Rev.	Alberta Law Review
Alternatives	Alternatives
Am. & E.Corp. Cas.	American & English Corporation Cases
Am. & E.Corp. Cas. (N.S.)	Same, New Series
Am. & E.R. Cas.	American & English Railroad Cases
Am. & E.R. Cas. (N.S.)	Same, New Series
Am. & Eng. Ann.Cas.	American & English Annotated Cases
Am. & Eng. Eq.D.	American & English Decisions in Equity
Am. & Eng. Pat.Cas.	American & English Patent Cases
Am.Acad. Matri.Law. J.	American Academy of Matrimonial Lawyers Journal
Am.B.News	American Bar News
Am.B.R. (N.S.)	American Bankruptcy Reports, New Series
Am.Bankr.L.J.	American Bankruptcy Law Journal
Am.Bankr. Reg.	American Bankruptcy Register (U.S.)
Am.Bankr. Rep.	American Bankruptcy Reports
Am.Bankr. Rev.	American Bankruptcy Review
Am.Bus.L.J.	American Business Law Journal
Am.Corp.Cas.	American Corporation Cases
Am.Cr.	American Criminal Reports
Am.Crim.L.Q.	American Criminal Law Quarterly
Am.Crim. L.Rev.	American Criminal Law Review
Am.Dec.	American Decisions
Am.Elect.Cas.	American Electrical Cases
Am.Fed. Tax R.	American Federal Tax Reports
Am.Fed. Tax R.2d	Same, Second Series
Am.For.L. Ass'n Newsl.	American Foreign Law Association Newsletter
Am.Hist.Rev.	American Historical Review
Am.Ind.J.	American Indian Journal
Am.Ind.L. Newsl.	American Indian Law Newsletter
Am.Ind.L.Rev.	American Indian Law Review
Am.Insolv. Rep.	American Insolvency Reports
Am.J.Comp.L.	American Journal of Comparative Law
Am.J.Crim.L.	American Journal of Criminal Law
Am.J.For. Psych.	American Journal of Forensic Psychiatry
Am.J.Int.L.	American Journal of International Law
Am.J.Juris.	American Journal of Jurisprudence
Am.J.L. & Med.	American Journal of Law and Medicine
Am.J.Legal Hist.	American Journal of Legal History
Am.J.Police Sci.	American Journal of Police Science
Am.J.Trial Advocacy	American Journal of Trial Advocacy
Am.Jur.	American Jurisprudence American Jurist
Am.Jur.2d	American Jurisprudence, Second Series
Am.L.Ins.	American Law Institute
Am.L.J.	American Law Journal (Pa.)
Am.L.J. (N.S.)	Same, New Series
Am.L.Mag.	American Law Magazine
Am.L.Rec.	American Law Record (Ohio)
Am.L.Reg.	American Law Register
Am.L.Reg. (N.S.)	Same, New Series
Am.L.Reg. (O.S.)	Same, Old Series
Am.L.Rev.	American Law Review
Am.L.Sch. Rev.	American Law School Review
Am.L.T. Bankr.	American Law Times Bankruptcy Reports
Am.Lab.Leg. Rev.	American Labor Legislation Review
Am.Law.	American Lawyer
Am.Law Rec.	American Law Record
Am.Law Reg.	American Law Register
Am.Negl.Cas.	American Negligence Cases
Am.Negl.Rep.	American Negligence Reports
Am.Notary	American Notary
Am.Pol.Sci. Rev.	American Political Science Review
Am.Pr.Rep.	American Practice Reports (D.C.)
Am.Prob.	American Probate Reports
Am.Prob. (N.S.)	Same, New Series
Am.R.	American Reports
Am.R. & Corp.	American Railroad Corporation
Am.R.Rep.	American Railway Reports

Am.Railw.Cas.	American Railway Cases (Smith & Bates)
Am.Rep.	American Reports
Am.Ry.Rep.	American Railway Reports
Am.Soc'y Int'l L.Proc.	American Society of International Law Proceedings
Am.St.R.	American State Reports
Am.St.R.D.	American Street Railway Decisions
Am.St.Rep.	American State Reports
Am.Tr.M.Cas.	American Trademark Cases (Cox)
Am.Trial Law.J.	American Trial Lawyers Journal
Am.Trial Law.L.J.	American Trial Lawyers Law Journal
Am.U.Intra.L. Rev.	American University Intramural Law Review
Am.U.L. Rev.	American University Law Review
Amb.	Ambler, Chancery (Eng.)
Ames	Ames (R.I.) Ames (Minn.)
Ames K. & B.	Ames, Knowles & Bradley (R.I.)
Amicus	Amicus (South Bend, Ind.) Amicus (Thousand Oaks, CA)
An.B.	Anonymous Reports at end of Benloe, or Bendloe (1661) (Eng.)
And.	Anderson Common Pleas (Eng.)
Andr.	Andrews King's Bench (Eng.)
Ang.	Angell (R.I.)
Ang. & Dur.	Angell & Durfee (R.I.)
Anglo-Am. L.Rev.	Anglo-American Law Review
Animal Rights L.Rep.	Animal Rights Law Reporter
Ann.	Annaly's Hardwicke King's Bench (Eng.)
Ann.Cas.	American Annotated Cases
Ann.Dig.	Annual Digest and Reports of International Law Cases
Ann.Indus. Prop.L.	Annual of Industrial Property Law
Ann.L.Reg. U.S.	Annual Law Register of the United States
Ann.Leg. Forms Mag.	Annotated Legal Forms Magazine
Ann.Rev. Int'l Aff.	Annual Review of International Affairs
Ann.Survey Afr.L.	Annual Survey of African Law
Ann.Survey Am.L.	Annual Survey of American Law
Ann.Survey Commonw. L.	Annual Survey of Commonwealth Law
Ann.Survey Ind.L.	Annual Survey of Indian Law
Ann.Survey S.Afr.L.	Annual Survey of South African Law
Ann.Tax Cas.	Annotated Tax Cases
Annals	Annals of the American Academy of Political and Social Science
Annals Air & Space	Annals of Air and Space Law
Annaly	Annaly's Hardwicke King's Bench (Eng.)
Anst.	Ansthruther, Exchequer (Eng.)
Anth.N.P.	Anthon's Nisi Prius (N.Y.)
Antitrust Bull.	Antitrust Bulletin
Antitrust L. & Econ. Rev.	Antitrust Law and Economics Review
Antitrust L.J.	Antitrust Law Journal
Antitrust L.Sym.	Antitrust Law Symposium
App.	Appleton (Me.)
App.Cas.	Law Reports Appeal Cases (Eng.)
App.Cas.2d	Same, Second Series
App.Court Ad. Rev.	Appellate Court Administration Review
App.D.C.	Appeal Cases (D.C.)
App.Div.	Appellate Division (N.Y.)
App.Div.2d	Same, Second Series
App.N.Z.	Appeal Reports (New Zealand)
App.R.N.Z.	Same, Second Series
App.Rep.Ont.	Ontario Appeal Reports
Arb.J.	Arbitration Journal
Arb.J. (N.S.)	Same, New Series
Arb.J. (O.S.)	Same, Old Series
Arb.L.Dig.	Arbitration Law: A Digest of Court Decisions
Archer	Archer (Fla.)
Archer & H.	Archer & Hogue (Fla.)
Argus L.R.	Argus Law Reports (Aust.)
Ariz.	Arizona
Ariz.App.	Arizona Appeals Reports
Ariz.B.J.	Arizona Bar Journal
Ariz.L.Rev.	Arizona Law Review
Ariz.St.L.J.	Arizona State Law Journal
Ark.	Arkansas
Ark.Just.	Arkley's Justiciary (Sc.)
Ark.L.J.	Arkansas Law Journal
Ark.L.Rev.	Arkansas Law Review

Ark.Law.	The Arkansas Lawyer
Ark.Law.Q.	Arkansas Lawyer Quarterly
Armour	Queen's Bench, Manitoba Temp. Wood, by Armour
Arms.Con. Elec.	Armstrong's Contested Elections (N.Y.)
Army Law.	Army Lawyer
Arn.	Arnold Common Pleas (Eng.)
Arn. & H.	Arnold & Hodges Queen's Bench (Eng.)
Arnold	Arnold Common Pleas (Eng.)
Art & L.	Art and the Law
Ashm.	Ashmead (Pa.)
Asian Comp. L.Rev.	Asian Comparative Law Review
Aspin.	Aspinall's Maritime Cases (Eng.)
Ass'n Trial Law.Am. Newsl.	Association of Trial Lawyers of American Newsletter
Ateneo L.J.	Ateneo Law Journal
Atk.	Atkyns Chancery (Eng.)
Atl.	Atlantic Reporter
Atomic Energy L.J.	Atomic Energy Law Journal
Att'y Gen.	Attorney General
Att'y Gen.L.J.	Attorney General's Law Journal
Att'y Gen.Rep.	United States Attorneys General's Reports
Atty.Gen.	Attorney General
Atwater	Atwater (Minn.)
Auck.U.L.Rev.	Auckland University Law Review
Aust.Jur.	Australian Jurist
Aust.L.T.	Australian Law Times
Austl. & N.Z. J.Crim.	Australian and New Zealand Journal of Criminology
Austl.Argus L.R.	Australian Argus Law Reports
Austl.Bankr. Cas.	Australian Bankruptcy Cases
Austl.Bus. L.Rev.	Australian Business Law Review
Austl.Com.J.	Australian Commercial Journal
Austl.Convey. & Sol.J.	Australian Conveyancer and Solicitors Journal
Austl.Current L.Rev.	Australian Current Law Review
Austl.J. For.Sci.	Australian Journal of Forensic Sciences
Austl.Jur.	Australian Jurist
Austl.L.J.	Australian Law Journal
Austl.L.J. Rep.	Australian Law Journal Reports
Austl.L.Times	Australian Law Times
Austl.Law.	Australian Lawyer
Austl.Tax	Australian Tax Decisions
Austl.Tax Rev.	Australian Tax Review
Austl.Y.B. Int'l L.	Australian Yearbook of International Law
Austr.C.L.R.	Commonwealth Law Reports, Australia
Auto.Cas.	Automobile Cases
Auto. Cas.2d	Same, Second Series
Auto.L.Rep.	Automobile Law Reporter (CCH)
Av.Cas.	Aviation Cases
Av.L.Rep.	Aviation Law Reporter (CCH)

B

B.	Weekly Law Bulletin
B. & A.	Barnewall & Alderson, King's Bench (Eng.)
B. & Ad.	Barnewall & Adolphus King's Bench (Eng.)
B. & Ald.	Barnewall & Alderson, King's Bench (Eng.)
B. & Arn.	Barron & Arnold Election Cases (Eng.)
B. & Aust.	Barron & Austin Election Cases (Eng.)
B. & B.	Ball & Beatty's Chancery (Ir.) Broderip & Bingham Common Pleas (Eng.)
B. & C.	Barnewall & Cresswell's King's Bench (Eng.)
B. & C.R.	Reports of Bankruptcy & Companies Winding up Cases (Eng.)
B. & D.	Benloe & Dalison Common Pleas (Eng.)
B. & F.	Broderip & Freemantle's Ecclesiastical (Eng.)
B. & H.Cr. Cas.	Bennet & Heard's Criminal Cases (Eng.)
B. & H.Crim. Cas.	Same
B. & Macn.	Brown & Macnamara Railway Cases (Eng.)
B. & P.	Bosanquet & Puller, Common Pleas (Eng.)
B. & P.N.R.	Bosanquet & Puller's New Reports (Eng.)
B. & S.	Best & Smith, Queen's Bench (Eng.)

B.Bull.	Bar Bulletin
B.C.	British Columbia
B.C.Branch Lec.	Canadian Bar Association, British Columbia Branch Meeting Program Reports
B.C.C.	Bail Court Cases (Eng.)
B.C.Envt'l Aff.L.Rev.	Boston College Environmental Affairs Law Review
B.C.Ind. & Com.L.Rev.	Boston College Industrial and Commercial Law Review
B.C.Int'l & Comp.J.L.	Boston College International and Comparative Law Journal
B.C.L.Notes	British Columbia Law Notes
B.C.L.Rev.	Boston College Law Review
B.D. & O.	Blackham, Dundas & Osborne, Nisi Prius (Ir.)
B.Exam.	Bar Examiner
B.Exam.J.	Bar Examination Journal
B.I.C.I.L. Newsl.	British Institute of International and Comparative Law Newsletter
B.I.L.C.	British International Law Cases
B.Leader	Bar Leader
B.Mon.	B. Monroe (Ky.)
BNA	Bureau of National Affairs
BNA Sec.Reg.	Securities Regulation & Law Report
B.R. (Army)	Board of Review (Army)
B.R.C.	British Ruling Cases
B.R.–J.C. (Army)	Board of Review and Judicial Council of the Army
B.T.A.	Board of Tax Appeals Reports
B.U.L.Rev.	Boston University Law Review
B.W.C.C.	Butterworth's Workmen's Compensation Cases (Eng.)
B.Y.U.L.Rev.	Brigham Young University Law Review
Bac.Abr.	Bacon's Abridgment (Eng.)
Bag. & Har.	Bagley & Harman (Cal.)
Bagl.	Bagley (Cal.)
Bagl. & H.	Bagley & Harman (Cal.)
Bail Ct.Cas.	Bail Court Cases (Lowndes & Maxwell) (Eng.)
Bail.Eq.	Bailey's Equity (S.C.)
Baild.	Baildon's Select Cases in Chancery (Eng.)
Bailey	Bailey's Law (S.C.)
Bal.Ann. Codes	Ballinger's Annotated Codes & Statutes (Wash.)

Bal.Pay't Rep.	Balance of Payments Reports (CCH)
Baldw.	Baldwin (U.S.)
Balf.Pr.	Balfour's Practice (Sc.)
Ball & B.	Ball & Beatty Chancery (Ir.)
Balt.L.T.	Baltimore Law Transcript
Ban. & A.	Banning & Arden Patent Cases (U.S.)
Bank. & Ins.R.	Bankruptcy & Insolvency Reports (Eng.)
Bank.Cas.	Banking Cases
Bank.Ct.Rep.	Bankrupt Court Reports
Bank.L.J.	Banking Law Journal
Banking L.J.	Same
Bankr.B. Bull.	Bankruptcy Bar Bulletin
Bankr.L.Rep.	Bankruptcy Law Reporter (CCH)
Bankr.Reg.	National Bankruptcy Register (N.Y.)
Banks	Banks (Kan.)
Bann.	Bannister's Common Pleas (Eng.)
Bann. & A.	Banning & Arden, Patent Cases (U.S.)
Bann. & Ard.	Same
Bar. & Arn.	Barron & Arnold, Election Cases (Eng.)
Bar. & Aust.	Barron & Austin, Election Cases (Eng.)
Barb.	Barber (Ark.) Barbour (N.Y.)
Barb.Ch.	Barbour's Chancery (N.Y.)
Barber	Barber (N.Y.)
Barn.	Barnardiston, King's Bench (Eng.)
Barn. & Ad.	Barnewall & Adolphus, King's Bench (Eng.)
Barn. & Ald.	Barnewall & Alderson, King's Bench (Eng.)
Barn. & C.	Barnewall & Cresswell, King's Bench (Eng.)
Barn. & Cress.	Same
Barn.Ch.	Barnardiston Chancery (Eng.)
Barnes	Barnes Practice Cases (Eng.)
Barnes' Notes	Barnes' Notes (Eng.)
Barnet	Barnet's Reports, Common Pleas (Eng.)
Barr	Barr (Pa.)
Barr.Ch.Pr.	Barroll Chancery Practice (Md.)
Barr.MSS.	Barradall Manuscript Reports (Va.)
Barrister	Barrister (Chicago)

Barrister	Barrister (Coral Gables, Fla.)
Barrister	Barrister (Davis, Cal.)
Barrister	Barrister (Toronto)
Bart.Elec. Cas.	Bartlett's Election Cases
Bates Ch.	Bates Chancery (Del.)
Batty	Batty, King's Bench (Ir.)
Baxt.	Baxter (Tenn.)
Bay	Bay (Mo.) Bay (S.C.)
Baylor L. Rev.	Baylor Law Review
Beasl.	Beasley (N.J.)
Beav.	Beavan Rolls Court (Eng.)
Beav. & W. Ry.Cas.	Beavan & Walford's Railway & Canal Cases (Eng.)
Beav.R. & C. Cas.	Beavan, Railway & Canal Cases (Eng.)
Beaw.Lex Mer.	Beawes Lex Mercatoria (Eng.)
Bee	Bee's Admiralty U.S. District Court (S.C.)
Bee Adm.	Bee's (U.S.)
Bee C.C.R.	Bee's Crown Cases Reserved (Eng.)
Belg.Rev. Int'l L.	Belgian Review of International Law
Bell.	Bellewe, King's Bench (Eng.)
Bell App.Cas.	Bell's Appeal Cases, House of Lords (Sc.)
Bell C.C.	Bell's Crown Cases Reserved (Eng.)
Bell Cas.	Bell's Cases (Sc.)
Bell.Cas.t.H. VIII	Bellewe, King's Bench, temp. Henry VIII (Eng.)
Bell.Cas.t.R.II	Same, temp. Richard II (Eng.)
Bell Comm.	Bell's Commentaries (Eng.)
Bell Cr.C.	Bell's Crown Cases Reserved (Eng.)
Bell H.L.	Bell's Appeal Cases, House of Lords (Sc.)
Bell P.C.	Bell's Parliament Cases (Sc.)
Bell Sc.Cas.	Bell's Scotch Court of Sessions Cases
Bell Ses.Cas.	Same
Bellewe	Bellewe, King's Bench (Eng.)
Ben.	Benedict (U.S. District Court)
Ben. & H.L.C.	Bennett & Heard Leading Criminal Cases (Eng.)
Bendl.	Bendloe's English Common Pleas
Bened.	Benedict (U.S. District Court)
Benl.	Benloe's Common Pleas (Eng.) Benloe's King's Bench (Eng.)
Benl. & D.	Benloe & Dalison Common Pleas (Eng.)
Benl. & Dal.	Benloe & Dalison Common Pleas (Eng.)
Benl.K.B.	Benloe's King's Bench (Eng.)
Benl.Old	Benloe Old English Common Pleas
Benn.	Bennett (Cal.) Bennett (Dakota) Bennett (Mo.)
Bent.	Bentley's Chancery (Ir.)
Berry	Berry (Mo.)
Bibb	Bibb (Ky.)
Bibl.Cott.	Cotton MSS.
Bick.	Bicknell (Nev.)
Bick. & H.	Bickness & Hawley (Nev.)
Big.Ov.Cas.	Bigelow's Overruled Cases
Bill Rights J.	Bill of Rights Journal
Bill Rights Rev.	Bill of Rights Review
Bing.	Bingham New Cases Common Pleas (Eng.)
Binn.	Binney (Pa.)
Biss.	Bissell (U.S.)
Bitt.Rep. in Ch.	Bittleson's Reports, Queen's Bench (Eng.)
Bitt.W. & P.	Bittleson, Wise & Parnell Practice Cases (Eng.)
Bk.	Black (U.S.)
Bl.	William Blackstone's King's Bench (Eng.)
Bl.H.	Henry Blackstone's Common Pleas (Eng.)
Bl.W.	William Blackstone's King's Bench (Eng.)
Bla.	Same
Bla.H.	Henry Blackstone's Common Pleas (Eng.)

Bla.W.	William Blackstone's King's Bench (Eng.)
Black	Black (Ind.)
	Black (U.S.)
Black L.J.	Black Law Journal
Black.	William Blackstone's King's Bench (Eng.)
Black.Cond.	Blackwell's Condensed Reports (Ill.)
Black.Cond. Rep.	Same
Black.D. & O.	Blackham, Dundas & Osborne Nisi Prius (Ir.)
Black.H.	Henry Blackstone's Common Pleas (Eng.)
Black.Jus.	Blackerby's Justices' Cases (Eng.)
Blackf.	Blackford (Ind.)
Blackst.R.	William Blackstone's King's Bench (Eng.)
Blackw.Cond.	Blackwell's Condensed Reports (Ill.)
Blair Co.	Blair County (Pa).
Blake	Blake (Mont.)
Blake & H.	Blake & Hedge (Mont.)
Bland	Bland's Chancery (Md.)
Blatchf.	Blatchford (U.S.)
Blatchf. & H.	Blatchford & Howland (U.S. District Court)
Blatchf.Prize Cas.	Blatchford's Prize Cases (U.S.)
Bleckley	Bleckley (Ga.)
Bli.	Bligh House of Lords (Eng.)
Bli. (N.S.)	Same, New Series
Bligh	Same
Bligh (N.S.)	Same, New Series
Bliss	Bliss Delaware County (Pa.)
Blue Sky L.Rep.	Blue Sky Law Reporter (CCH)
Bluett	Bluett's Isle of Man Cases
Bombay L.J.	Bombay Law Journal
Bond	Bond (U.S.)
Book of Judg.	Book of Judgments (Eng.)
Boor.	Booraem (Calif.)
Bos.	Bosworth, Superior Court (N.Y.)
Bos. & P.	Bosanquet & Puller, Common Pleas (Eng.)
Bos. & P.N.R.	Bosanquet & Puller's New Reports Common Pleas (Eng.)
Bos. & Pul.	Bosanquet & Puller, Common Pleas (Eng.)
Bos.Pol.Rep.	Boston Police Reports
Bost.L.R.	Boston Law Reporter
Boston B.J.	Boston Bar Journal
Bosw.	Bosworth, Superior Court (N.Y.)
	Boswell (Sc.)
Bott Poor Law Cas.	Bott's Poor Laws Settlement Cases (Eng.)
Bott's Set. Cas.	Same
Bould.	Bouldin (Ala.)
Bouv.	Bouvier Law Dictionary
Bov.Pat.Cas.	Bovill's Patent Cases
Boyce	Boyce (Del.)
Br. & B.	Broderip & Bingham, Common Pleas (Eng.)
Br. & Col.	British & Colonial Prize Cases
Br. & F.Ecc.	Broderick & Freemantle's Ecclesiastical Cases (Eng.)
Br. & Gold.	Brownlow & Goldesborough's Common Pleas (Eng.)
Br. & L.	Brownlow & Lushington's Admiralty Cases (Eng.)
Br. & Lush.	Same
Br.N.C.	Brooks New Cases, King's Bench (Eng.)
Br.N.Cas.	Same
Bract.	Bracton De Legibus et consuetudinibus Angliae (Eng.)
Bradf.	Bradford (Iowa)
Bradf.Surr.	Bradford's Surrogate Court (N.Y.)
Bradl.	Bradley (R.I.)
Bradw.	Bradwell (Ill.)
Brame	Brame (Miss.)
Branch	Branch (Fla.)
Brantly	Brantly (Md.)
Brayt.	Brayton (Vt.)
Breese	Breese (Ill.)
Brev.	Brevard (S.C.)
Brew.	Brewer (Md.)
	Brewster (Pa.)
Brews.	Brewster (Pa.)
Bridg.	J. Bridgmore, Common Pleas (Eng.)
Bridg.J.	Sir J. Bridgman, Common Pleas (Eng.)
Bridg.O.	Sir Orlando Bridgman, Common Pleas (Eng.)
Brief	The Brief
Briefcase	Briefcase
Brightly	Brightly (Pa.)
Brightly El. Cas.	Brightly's Leading Election Cases (Pa.)
Brisb.	Brisbin (Minn.)

Brit.J. Criminol.	British Journal of Criminology
Brit.Cr.Cas.	British Crown Cases
Brit.J.Ad.L.	British Journal of Administrative Law
Brit.J.Law & Soc'y	British Journal of Law and Society
Brit.Prac. Int'l L.	British Practice in International Law
Brit.Ship.L.	British Shipping Laws (Stevens)
Brit.Tax Rev.	British Tax Review
Brit.Y.B. Int'l L.	British Year Book of International Law
Bro. & F.	Broderick & Freemantle's Ecclesiastical (Eng.)
Bro. & Fr.	Same
Bro. & Lush.	Browning & Lushington's Admiralty (Eng.)
Br.Eccl.	Brown's Ecclesiastical (Eng.)
Bro.Just.	Brown's Justiciary (Sc.)
Brock.	Brockenbrough (U.S.)
Brock. & Hol. Cas.	Brockenbrough & Holmes Cases (Va.)
Brock.Cas.	Brockenbrough's Cases (Va.)
Brod. & F.Ecc. Cas.	Broderick & Freemantle's Ecclesiastical Cases (Eng.)
Brod. & Fr. Ecc.Cas.	Same
Brodix Am. & El.Pat.Cas.	Brodix American & English Patent Cases
Brook Abr.	Brook's Abridgment (Eng.)
Brooklyn Barrister	Brooklyn Barrister
Brooklyn J. Int'l L.	Brooklyn Journal of International Law
Brooklyn L.Rev.	Brooklyn Law Review
Brook N.Cas.	Brook's New Cases, King's Bench (Eng.)
Brooks	Brooks (Mich.)
Brown	Brown (Miss.)
	Brown (Mo.)
	Brown (Neb.)
Brown & MacN.	Brown & MacNamara, Railway Cases (Eng.)
Brown & R.	Brown & Rader (Mo.)
Brown A. & R.	Brown's United States District Court Admiralty & Revenue Cases
Brown Adm.	Brown's Admiralty (U.S.)
Brown Ch.	Brown's Chancery (Eng.)
Brown Dict.	Brown's Law Dictionary
Brown Ecc.	Brown's Ecclesiastical (Eng.)
Brown N.P.	Brown's Nisi Prius (Mich.)
Brown Parl. Cas.	Brown's House of Lords Cases (Eng.)
Brown P.C.	Same
Brown. & L.	Browning & Lushington, Admiralty (Eng.)
Browne	Browne (Mass.)
	Browne Common Pleas (Pa.)
Browne & G.	Browne & Gray (Mass.)
Browne & H.	Browne & Hemingway (Miss.)
Browne Bank Cas.	Browne's National Bank Cases
Brownl. & G.	Brownlow & Goldesborough, Common Pleas (Eng.)
Bruce	Bruce (Sc.)
Brunn.Coll. Cas.	Brunner's Collected Cases (U.S.)
Bt.	Benedicts (U.S.)
Buck	Buck Bankrupt Cases (Eng.)
	Buck (Mont.)
Buck.	Bucknill's Cooke's Cases of Practice Common Pleas (Eng.)
Buck.Dec.	Buckner's Decisions (Freeman's Chancery) (Miss.)
Buffalo L.Rev.	Buffalo Law Review
Bull.	Weekly Law Bulletin
Bull.Am.Acad. Psych. & L.	Bulletin of the American Academy of Psychiatry and the Law
Bull.Can.Welfare L.	Bulletin of Canadian Welfare Law
Bull. Copyright Soc'y	Bulletin of the Copyright Society of the U.S.A.
Bull.Czech.L.	Bulletin of Czechoslovak Law
Bull.Int'l Fiscal Doc.	Bulletin for International Fiscal Documentation
Bull.L.Science & Tech.	Bulletin of Law, Science and Technology
Bull.Legal Devel.	Bulletin of Legal Developments
Bull.Waseda U. Inst.Comp.L.	Bulletin, Waseda University Institute of Comparative Law
Buller N.P.	Buller's Nisi Prius (Eng.)
Bulstr.	Bulstrode (London) King's Bench (Eng.)
Bunb.	Bunbury Exchequer (Eng.)
Burf.	Burford (Okla.)
Burgess	Burgess (Ohio)
Burk	Burk (Va.)

Burlesque Rep.	Skillman's New York Police Reports
Burnett	Burnett (Ore.) Burnett (Wis.)
Burr.	Burrow, King's Bench (Eng.)
Burr.S.Cases	Burrow's Settlement Cases (Eng.)
Burr.t.M.	Burrow's Reports, temp. Mansfield (Eng.)
Bus. & L.	Business and Law
Bus.L.Rev.	Business Law Review (England)
Bus.L.Rev.	Business Law Review (United States)
Bus.Law	The Business Lawyer
Bus.Reg.L. Rep.	Business Regulation Law Report
Busb.Eq.	Busby Equity (N.C.)
Busb.L.	Busbee Law (N.C.)
Bush	Bush (Ky.)
Buxton	Buxton (N.C.)

C

C.	Cowen (N.Y.)
C. & A.	Cooke & Alcock King's Bench and Exchequer (Ir.)
C. & C.	Case and Comment Colemand & Caines Cases (N.Y.)
C. & D.	Corbett & Daniel's Election Cases (Eng.) Crawford & Dix's Abridged Cases (Ir.)
C. & D.A.C.	Crawford & Dix's Abridged Cases (Ir.)
C. & D.C.C.	Crawford & Dix's Circuit Cases (Ir.) Crawford & Dix's Criminal Cases (Ir.)
C. & E.	Cababe & Ellis Queen's Bench (Eng.)
C. & F.	Clark & Finnelly House of Lords (Eng.)
C. & J.	Crompton & Jervis Exchequer (Eng.)
C. & K.	Carrington & Kirwan Nisi Prius (Eng.)
C. & L.	Connor & Lawson's Chancery (Ir.)
C. & L.C.C.	Caines & Leigh Crown Cases (Eng.)
C. & M.	Carrington & Marshman's Nisi Prius (Eng.) Crompton & Meeson's Exchequer (Eng.)
C. & Marsh.	Carrington & Marshman's Nisi Prius (Eng.)
C. & N.	Cameron & Norwood's North Carolina Conference
C. & P.	Carrington & Payne's Nisi Prius (Eng.) Craig & Phillips Chancery (Eng.)
C. & R.	Cockburn & Rowe's Election Cases
C. & S.	Clarke & Scully's Drainage Cases (Ont.)
[ ] C.A.	Recueils de Jurisprudence du Quebec, Cour d'appel, 1970–
C.A.A.	Civil Aeronautics Authority Reports
C.A.B.	Civil Aeronautics Board Reports
C.A.D.	Customs Appeals Decisions
C.B.	Cumulative Bulletin (Internal Revenue) Common Bench (Manning, Granger & Scott) (Eng.)
C.B. (N.S.)	Common Bench (Manning, Granger & Scott), New Series (Eng.)
C.B.C.	Colliers Bankruptcy Cases
C.B.R.	Canadian Bankruptcy Reports
C.C.	Ohio Circuit Court Reports
C.C. (N.S.)	Ohio Circuit Court Reports, New Series
C.C.A.	Circuit Court of Appeals (U.S.)
C.C.C.	Canadian Criminal Cases, 1893–1962
[ ] C.C.C.	Canadian Criminal Cases, 1963–
CCF	Federal Contract Cases, CCH
CCH	Commerce Clearing House
CCH Atom. En.L.Rep.	Atomic Energy Law Reporter (CCH)
CCH Comm. Mkt.Rep.	Common Market Reporter (CCH)

CCH Fed. Banking L. Rep.	Federal Banking Law Reporter (CCH)
CCH Fed.Sec. L.Rep.	Federal Securities Law Reporter (CCH)
CCH Inh.Est. & Gift Tax Rep.	Inheritance, Estate, and Gift Tax Reporter (CCH)
CCH Lab.Arb. Awards	Labor Arbitration Awards (CCH)
CCH Lab.Cas.	Labor Cases (CCH)
CCH Lab.L. Rep.	Labor Law Reporter (CCH)
CCH Stand. Fed.Tax Rep.	Standard Federal Tax Reporter (CCH)
CCH State Tax Cas. Rep.	State Tax Cases Reporter (CCH)
CCH State Tax Rev.	State Tax Review (CCH)
CCH Tax Ct.Mem.	Tax Court Memorandum Decisions (CCH)
CCH Tax Ct.Rep.	Tax Court Reporter (CCH)
C.C.L.T.	Canadian Cases on the Law of Torts, 1976–
C.C.P.A.	Court of Customs & Patent Appeals (U.S.)
	Court of Customs & Patent Appeals Reports
C.C.Supp.	City Court Reports Supplement (N.Y.)
C.D.	U. S. Customs Court Decisions
	Commissioner of Patents
	Ohio Circuit Decisions
C.E.Gr.	C. E. Greene's Equity (N.J.)
C.E.Greene	Same
C.F.R.	Code of Federal Regulations
C.I.L.C.	Commonwealth International Law Cases
C.I.L.J.S.A.	Comparative and International Law Journal of Southern Africa
C.J.	Corpus Juris
C.J.Ann.	Corpus Juris Annotations
C.J.S.	Corpus Juris Secundum
C.L.A.I.T.	Constitutions and Laws of the American Indian Tribes (Scholarly Resources)
C.L.A.S.	Criminal Law Audio Series
C.L.Chambers	Chambers' Common Law (Upper Can.)
C.L.L.C.	Canadian Labour Law Cases
C.L.L.R.	Canadian Labor Law Reports (CCH)
C.L.R.	Common Law Reports (Eng.)
	Common Law Reports (Aust.)
	Cyprus Law Reports
C.L.Rec.	Cleveland Law Record
C.L.Reg.	Cleveland Law Register
C.L.Rep.	Cleveland Law Reporter
C.L.S.R.	Computer Law Service Reporter
CLU J.	CLU Journal
C.L.W.	Commercial Laws of the World (Oceana)
C.M. & R.	Crompton, Meeson & Roscoe Exchequer (Eng.)
C.M.A.R.	Canadian Court Martial Appeal Reports, 1957–
C.M.R.	Court-Martial Reports
C.M.R. (Air Force)	Court-Martial Reports of the Judge Advocate General of the Air Force
C.P.C.	Carswell's Practice Cases, 1976–
C.P.Coop.	C. P. Cooper Chancery (Eng.)
C.P.D.	Law Reports Common Pleas Division (Eng.) (1865–1880)
C.P.R.	Canadian Patent Reporter
C.P.Rep.	Common Pleas Reporter (Pa.)
C.R.	Criminal Reports (Canada)
C.R.A.C.	Canadian Reports, Appeal Cases
C.R.C.	Canadian Railway Cases
C.R.T.C.	Canadian Railway & Transport Cases
C.Rob.	Christopher Robinson's Admiralty (Eng.)
C.S.C.R.	Cincinnati Superior Court Reporter
C.S.T.	Capital Stock Tax Division (I.R.Bull.)
C.T.	Carriers Taxing Ruling (I.R.Bull.)
[ ] C.T.C.	Canada Tax Cases
C.T.L.J.	California Trial Lawyers Journal
C.T.S.	Consolidated Treaty Series
C.W.Dud.	C. W. Dudley's Law or Equity (S.C.)
C.W.Dudl.Eq.	C. W. Dudley's Equity (S.C.)
Cab. & E.	Cababe & Ellis Queen's Bench (Eng.)
Cahiers	Les Cahiers de Droit
Cai.	Caines (N.Y.)
Cai.Cas.	Caines' Cases
Cai.R.	Caines' Reports
Cal.	California

Cal.2d	California, Second Series
Cal.3d	California Reports, Third Series
Cal.App.	California Appellate
Cal.App.2d	California Appellate, Second Series
Cal.App.3d	California Appellate Reports, Third Series
Cal.App.Dec.	California Appellate Decisions
Cal.Dec.	California Decisions
Cal.Ind.Acci. Dec.	California Industrial Accidents Decision
Cal.Jur.	California Jurisprudence
Cal.Jur.2d	California Jurisprudence, Second Edition
Cal.L.Rev.	California Law Review
Cal.Leg.Rec.	California Legal Record
Cal.Prac.	California Practice
Cal.Rptr.	California Reporter (West)
Cal.S.B.J.	California State Bar Journal
Cal.St.B.J.	California State Bar Journal
Cal.Unrep. Cas.	California Unreported Cases
Cal.W.Int'l L.J.	California Western International Law Journal
Cal.W.L.Rev.	California Western Law Review
Calcutta W.N.	Calcutta Weekly Notes
Cald.	Caldecott's Magistrate's and Settlement Cases (Eng.)
	Caldwell (W.Va.)
Cald.J.P.	Caldecott's Magistrate's and Settlement Cases (Eng.)
Cald.M.Cas.	Same
Cald.Mag.Cas.	Same
Cald.S.C.	Same
Cald.Sett.Cas.	Same
Call	Call (Va.)
Calthr.	Calthrop (Eng.)
Cam.	Cameron's Privy Council Decisions
Cam. & N.	Cameron & Norwood's Conference (N.C.)
Cam.Cas.	Cameron's Cases (Can.)
Cambrian L. Rev.	Cambrian Law Review
Cambridge L.J.	Cambridge Law Journal
Cameron	Cameron's Supreme Court Cases
Cameron Pr.	Cameron's Practice (Can.)
Camp	Camp (N.D.)
Campaign L. Rep.	Campaign Law Reporter
Campb.	Campbell (Neb.)
	Campbell's Nisi Prius (Eng.)
Campb.L.G.	Campbell's Legal Gazette (Pa.)
Campbell L. Rev.	Campbell Law Review
Can.App.Cas.	Canadian Appeal Cases
Can.B.A.J.	Canadian Bar Association Journal
Can.B.Ass'n Y.B.	Canadian Bar Association: Year Book
Can.B.J.	Canadian Bar Journal
Can.B.R.	Canadian Bar Review
Can.B.Rev.	Same
Can.Bankr. Ann.	Canadian Bankruptcy Reports Annotated
Can.Bankr. Ann. (N.S.)	Same, New Series
Can.Bus.L.J.	Canadian Business Law Journal
Can.Com.L. Rev.	Canadian Communications Law Review
Can.Com.R.	Canadian Commercial Law Reports
Can.Community L.J.	Canadian Community Law Journal
Can.Cr.Cas.	Canadian Criminal Cases
Can.Crim.	Criminal Reports (Can.)
Can.Crim. Cas. (N.S.)	Canadian Criminal Cases, New Series
Can.Crim. Cas.Ann.	Canadian Crimnial Cases Annotated
Can.Env.L. News	Canadian Environmental Law News
Can.Exch.	Canadian Exchequer
Can.Green Bag	Canadian Green Bag
Can.Human Rights Rep.	Canadian Human Rights Reporter
Can.J.Correction	Canadian Journal of Correction
Can.J. Crim & Corr.	Canadian Journal of Criminology and Corrections
Can.J.Fam.L.	Canadian Journal of Family Law
Can.L.J.	Canada Law Journal
Can.L.J. (N.S.)	Same, New Series
Can.L.R.B.R.	Canadian Labour Relations Board Reports, 1974–
Can.L.Rev.	Canadian Law Review
Can.L.T. Occ.N.	Canadian Law Times Occasional Notes
Can.L.Times	Canadian Law Times
Can.Lab.	Canadian Labour
Can.Law.	Canadian Lawyer
Can.Legal Stud.	Canadian Legal Studies
Can.Mun.J.	Canadian Municipal Journal

Can.Native L. Rep.	Canadian Native Law Reporter
Can.Oil & Gas	Canadian Oil and Gas (Butterworths)
Can.Pub.Ad.	Canadian Public Administration
Can.R.Cas.	Canadian Railway Cases
Can.Ry.Cas.	Same
Can.S.C.	Canada Supreme Court
Can.S.Ct.	Canada Supreme Court Reports
Can.Tax App.Bd.	Canada Tax Appeal Board Cases
Cas.Tax Cas.Ann.	Canada Tax Cases Annotated
Can.Tax Found.Rep. Proc.Tax Conf.	Canadian Tax Foundation Report of Proceedings of the Tax Conference
Can.Tax.J.	Canadian Tax Journal
Can.Tax News	Canadian Tax News
Can.–U.S.L.J.	Canada–United States Law Journal
Can.Wel.	Canadian Welfare
Can.Y.B.Int'l L.	Canadian Yearbook of International Law
Cane & L.	Cane & Leigh's Crown Cases Reserved (Eng.)
Cap.U.L.Rev.	Capital University Law Review
Car. & K.	Carrington & Kirwan, Nisi Prius (Eng.)
Car. & P.	Carrington & Payne, Nisi Prius (Eng.)
Car.H. & A.	Carrow, Hamerton & Allen (Eng.)
Carolina L.J.	Carolina Law Journal
Carolina L. Repos.	Carolina Law Repository
Carp.	Carpenter (Cal.)
Carp.P.C.	Carpmael Patent Cases (Eng.)
Carribean L.J.	Carribean Law Journal
Cart.B.N.A.	Cartwright's Constitutional Cases (Can.)
Carter	Carter (Ind.)
	Carter Common Pleas (Eng.)
Carth.	Carthew King's Bench (Eng.)
Cartwr.Cas.	Cartwright's Cases (Can.)
Cary	Cary Chancery (Eng.)
Cas.C.L.	Cases in Crown Law (Eng.)
Cas.t.Hardw.	Cases temp. Hardwicke King's Bench (Eng.)
Cas.t.Holt	Cases temp. Holt, King's Bench (Eng.)
Cas.t.King	Cases temp. King, Chancery (Eng.)
Cas.t.Northington	Cases temp. Northington, Chancery Reports (Eng.)
Cas.t.Talb.	Cases temp. Talbot, Chancery (Eng.)
Cas.t.Wm. III	Cases temp. William III (Eng.)
Cas.Tak. & Adj.	Cases Taken and Adjudged (Reports in Chancery, First Edition) (Eng.)
Case & Com.	Case & Comment
Case W.Res.J. Int'l L.	Case Western Reserve Journal of International Law
Case W.Res. L.Rev.	Case Western Reserve Law Review
Casey	Casey (Pa.)
Cass.Prac. Cas.	Cassels' Practice Cases (Can.)
Cass.S.C.	Cassels' Supreme Court Decisions
Cates	Cates (Tenn.)
Cath.Law.	The Catholic Lawyer
Cath.U.L.Rev.	Catholic University of America Law Review
Censorship Today	Censorship Today
Cent.Dig.	Century Digest
Centr.L.J.	Central Law Journal
Ceylon L.Rev.	Ceylon Law Review
Ch.	Law Reports, Chancery (Eng.)
	Law Reports Chancery Division, Third Series
Ch.Cal.	Calendar of Proceedings in Chancery (Eng.)
Ch.Cas.	Cases in Chancery (Eng.)
Ch.Chamb.	Chancery Chambers (Upper Can.)
Ch.Col.Op.	Chalmer's Colonial Opinions
Ch.D.	Law Reports, Chancery Division (Eng.)
Ch.D.2d	Same, Second Series
Ch.Prec.	Precedents in Chancery
Ch.R.	Upper Canada Chambers Reports
Ch.R.M.	R. M. Charlton (Ga.)
Ch.Rep.	Chancery Reports (Eng.)
	Chancery Reports (Ir.)
Ch.Sent.	Chancery Sentinel (N.Y.)
Ch.T.U.P.	T.U.P. Charlton (Ga.)
Cha.App.	Chancery Appeal Cases English Law Reports
Chamb.Rep.	Chancery Chambers (Ont.)
Chandl.	Chandler (N.H.)
	Chandler (Wis.)
Chaney	Chaney (Mich.)
Charley Pr. Cas.	Charley's Practice Cases (Eng.)

Charlt.	Charlton, R.M. (Ga.)
	Charlton, T.U.P. (Ga.)
Chase	Chase (U.S.)
Chest.Co.	Chester County (Pa.)
Chev.Ch.	Cheve's Chancery (S.C.)
Chev.Eq.	Same
Cheves	Cheves Law (S.C.)
Chi.B. Record	Chicago Bar Record
Chi.-Kent L.Rev.	Chicago-Kent Law Review
Chi.Leg.N.	Chicago Legal News (Ill.)
Chic.L.T.	Chicago Law Times
Chicago L.B.	Chicago Law Bulletin
Chicago L.J.	Chicago Law Journal
Chicago L.Rec.	Chicago Law Record
Chicano L.Rev.	Chicano Law Review
Chin.L. & Gov't	Chinese Law and Government
China L.Rev.	China Law Review
Chip.	Chipman (N.Bruns.)
	Chipman (Vt.)
Chit.	Chitty's Bail Court (Eng.)
Chit.B.C.	Same
Chitt.	Same
Chitty's L.J.	Chitty's Law Journal
Choyce Cas.Ch.	Choyce's Cases in Chancery (Eng.)
Chr.Rep.	Chamber Reports (Upper Can.)
Chr.Rob.	Christopher Robinson's Admiralty (Eng.)
Chy.Chrs.	Upper Canada Chancery Chambers Reports
Cin.B. Ass'n J.	Cincinnati Bar Association Journal
Cin.L.Rev.	Cincinnati Law Review
Cin.Law Bull.	Weekly Law Bulletin (Ohio)
Cin.Mun.Dec.	Cincinnati Municipal Decisions
Cin.R.	Cincinnati Superior Court Reporter
Cin.S.C.R.	Same
Cin.S.C.Rep.	Same
Cinc.L.Bul.	Same
Cinc.Sup.Ct. Rep.	Same
Cincinnati Law Bull.	Weekly Law Bulletin (Ohio)
Cir.Ct.Dec.	Ohio Circuit Court Decisions
City Ct.R.	City Court Reports (N.Y.)
City Ct.R. Supp.	City Court Reports Supplements (N.Y.)
City Hall Rec.	City Hall Recorder (N.Y.)
City Hall Rep.	City Hall Reporter, Lomas (N.Y.)
Civ. & Mil. L.J.	Civil and Military Law Journal
Civ.Lib.	Civil Liberty
Civ.Lib.Dock.	Civil Liberties Docket
Civ.Lib.Rev.	Civil Liberties Review
Civ.Lib.Rptr.	Civil Liberties Reporter
Civ.Litigation Rep.	Civil Litigation Reporter (CEB)
Civ.Proc.R.	Civil Procedure Reports (N.Y.)
Civ.Rights Dig.	Civil Rights Digest
Cl. & F.	Clark & Finnelly, House of Lords (Eng.)
Clark	Clark (Ala.)
	Clark (Pa.)
Clark & F.	Clark & Finnelly, House of Lords (Eng.)
Clark & F. (N.S.)	Same, New Series
Clark App.	Clark Appeal Cases House of Lords (Eng.)
Clark Col.Law	Clark Colonial Law
Clarke	Clarke (Iowa)
	Clarke (Mich.)
Clarke & S. Dr.Cas.	Clarke & Scully's Drainage Cases (Ont.)
Clarke Ch.	Clarke Chancery (N.Y.)
Class Act.Rep.	Class Action Reports
Clayt.	Clayton's Reports York Assizes (Eng.)
Clearinghouse Rev.	Clearinghouse Review
Clemens	Clemens (Kan.)
Clev.Bar Ass'n J.	Cleveland Bar Association Journal
Clev.St. L.Rev.	Cleveland State Law Review
Cleve.L.Rec.	Cleveland Law Record (Ohio)
Cleve.L.Reg.	Cleveland Law Register (Ohio)
Cleve.L.Rep.	Cleveland Law Reporter (Ohio)
Cleve.Law R.	Cleveland Law Reporter (Ohio)
Cleve.Law Rec.	Cleveland Law Record (Ohio)
Cleve.Law Reg.	Cleveland Law Register (Ohio)
Clev.-Mar.L. Rev.	Cleveland-Marshall Law Review
Cliff.	Clifford (U.S.)
Clif.South.El. Cas.	Clifford, Southwick Election Cases
Clk's Mag.	Clerk's Magazine (London)
	Clerk's Magazine (R.I.)
	Clerk's Magazine (Upper Can.)

Co.Ct.Cas.	County Court Cases (Eng.)
Co.Ct.Ch.	County Court Chronicle (Eng.)
Co.Ct.Rep.	Pennsylvania County Court Reports
Co.Inst.	Coke's Institutes (Eng.)
Co.Litt.	Coke on Littleton (Eng.)
Co.Mass.Pr.	Colby Mass. Practice
Co.P.C.	Coke Pleas of the Crown (Eng.)
Cobb	Cobb (Ala.)
	Cobb (Ga.)
Cochr.	Cochran (Nova Scotia)
	Cochrane (N.D.)
Cockb. & R.	Cockburn & Rowe's Election Cases (Eng.)
Cocke	Cocke (Ala.)
	Cocke (Fla.)
Code Rep.	Code Reporter (N.Y.)
Code Rep. (N.S.)	Code Reporter, New Series (N.Y.)
Coff.Prob.	Coffey's Probate (Cal.)
Coke	Coke King's Bench (Eng.)
Col.	Coleman (Ala.)
Col. & C.Cas.	Coleman & Caine's Cases (N.Y.)
Col.Cas.	Coleman's Cases (N.Y.)
Col.Int'l Dr. Comp.	Colloque International de Droit Comparé
Col.L.Rev.	Columbia Law Review
Cold.	Coldwell
Coldw.	Coldwell (Tenn.)
Cole	Cole (Ala.)
	Cole (Iowa)
Cole. & Cai. Cas.	Coleman & Caines' Cases
Cole.Cas.	Coleman's Cases
Coll.	Collyer's Chancery (Eng.)
Coll. & E. Bank.	Collier's & Eaton's American Bankruptcy Reports
Coll.L.Bull.	College Law Bulletin
Coll.L.Dig.	College Law Digest
Colles	Colles Cases in Parliament (Eng.)
Colo.	Colorado
Colo.App.	Colorado Appeals
Colo.Law Rep.	Colorado Law Reporter
Colo.Law.	Colorado Lawyer
Colombo L.Rev.	Colombo Law Review (Ceylon)
Coltm.	Coltman Registration Appeal Cases (Eng.)
Colq.	Colquit (Modern) (Eng.)
Colum. Human Rights L.Rev.	Columbia Human Rights Law Review
Colum.J. Envt'l L.	Columbia Journal of Environmental Law
Colum.J.Int'l Aff.	Columbia Journal of International Affairs
Colum.J.L. & Soc.Prob.	Columbia Journal of Law and Social Problems
Colum.J. Transnat'l L.	Columbia Journal of Transnational Law
Colum.L.Rev.	Columbia Law Review
Colum.Soc'y Int'l L.Bull.	Columbia Society of International Law Bulletin
Colum. Survey Human Rights L.	Columbia Survey of Human Rights Law
Com. & L.	Communications and the Law
Com. & Mun. L.Rep.	Commercial & Municipal Law Reporter
Com.B.	Common Bench (Manning, Granger & Scott) (Eng.)
Com.Cas.	Commercial Cases Since 1895 (Eng.)
Com.Dec.	Commissioners' Decisions (Patent)
Com.L.	Commercial Law (Can.)
Com.L.J.	Commercial Law Journal
Com.P.Reptr.	Common Pleas Reporter (Scranton)
Comb.	Comberbach, King's Bench (Eng.)
Comb.B. (N.S.)	Common Bench (Manning, Granger & Scott) (Eng.)
Comm.Cause	Common Cause
Comm.Mkt. L.R.	Common Market Law Reports
Comm.Mkt. L.Rev.	Common Market Law Review
Commodity Futures L.Rep.	Commodity Futures Law Reporter (CCH)
Community Prop.J.	Community Property Journal
Commw.Arb.	Commonwealth Arbitration Reports
Commw.L.R.	Commonwealth Law Reports
Comp.Dec.	U. S. Comptroller of Treasury Decisions
Comp.Gen.	U. S. Comptroller General Decisions
Comp. Jurid.Rev.	Comparative Juridical Review
Comp.L.J.	Company Law Journal
Comparisons in L. & Monet.Com.	Comparisons in Law and Monetary Comments
Comptr.Treas. Dec.	U. S. Comptroller of Treasury Decisions
Computer L. & Tax	Computer Law and Tax Report

Computer L.J.	Computer Law Journal
Computers & L.	Computers and Law
Comst.	Comstock Appeals (N.Y.)
Comyns	Comyns King's Bench and Common Pleas (Eng.)
Comyns Dig.	Comyns Digest (Eng.)
Con.B.J.	Connecticut Bar Journal
Condit. Sale-Chat. Mort.Rep.	Conditional Sale-Chattel Mortgage (CCH)
Conf.	Conference Reports (N.C.)
Conf.Teach. Int'l L.	Conference of Teachers of International Law
Cong.Dig.	Congressional Digest
Cong.Rec.	Congressional Record (U.S.)
Conn.	Connecticut
Conn.B.J.	Connecticut Bar Journal
Conn.Cir.Ct.	Connecticut Circuit Court Reports
Conn.L.Rev.	Connecticut Law Review
Conn.Supp.	Connecticut Supplement
Conn.Surr.	Connolly's Surrogate (N.Y.)
Conov.	Conover (Wis.)
Const.	Constitution
Const.Afr. States	Constitutions of African States (Oceana)
Const.Dep. & Sp.Sov.	Constitutions of Dependencies and Special Sovereignties
Const.Nations	Constitutions of Nations (Nijhoff)
Const.Rep.	Constitutional Reports (S.C.)
Const.Rev.	Constitutional Review
Const.World	Constitutions of the Countries of the World (Oceana)
Consumer Prod.Saf'y Guide	Consumer Product Safety Guide (CCH)
Contemp. Drug Prob.	Contemporary Drug Problems
Convey.	Conveyancer
Convey. (N.S.)	Conveyancer & Property Lawyer, New Series
Cook Vice-Adm.	Cook's Vice-Admiralty (Lower Can.)
Cooke	Cooke Cases of Practice, Common Pleas (Eng.)
	Cooke (Tenn.)
Cooke & A.	Cooke & Alcock King's Bench (Ir.)
Cooley	Cooley (Mich.)
Coop.	Cooper (Fla.)
	Cooper's Chancery (Eng.)
	Cooper's Chancery (Tenn.)
Coop.C. & P. R.	Cooper's Chancery Practice Reporter (U.S.)
Coop.Pr.Cas.	Cooper's Practice Cases (Eng.)
Coop.t.Brough.	Cooper's Cases temp. Brougham Chancery (Eng.)
Coop.t.Cott.	Cooper's Cases temp. Cottenham Chancery (Eng.)
Coop.t.Eldon	Cooper's Reports temp. Eldon Chancery (Eng.)
Cope	Cope (Cal.)
Copp Min.Dec.	Copp's Mining Decisions (U.S.)
Copp's Land Owner	Copp's Land Owner
Copy.	Copyright
Copy.Bull.	Copyright Bulletin
Copyright L. Sym.	Copyright Law Symposium (ASCAP)
Corb. & D.	Corbett & Daniels Election Cases (Eng.)
Cornell Int'l L.J.	Cornell International Law Journal
Cornell L.F.	Cornell Law Forum
Cornell L.J.	Cornell Law Journal
Cornell L.Q.	Cornell Law Quarterly
Cornell L.Rev.	Cornell Law Review
Corp.Counsel Rev.	Corporate Counsel Review
Corp.J.	Corporation Journal
Corp.L.Rev.	Corporation Law Review
Corp.Pract. Comment.	Corporate Practice Commentator
Corp.Pract. Rev.	Corporate Practice Review
Corp.Reorg.	Corporate Reorganizations
Corp.Reorg. & Am.Bank. Rev.	Corporate Reorganization & American Bankruptcy Review
Coup.	Couper's Justiciary (Sc.)
Court. & MacL.	Courtenay & MacLean (Sc.)
Coutlea	Coutlea's Supreme Court Cases
Cow.	Cowen (N.Y.)
Cow.Cr.	Cowen's Criminal (N.Y.)
Cowp.	Cowper King's Bench (Eng.)
Cowp.Cas.	Cowper's Cases (Chancery) (Eng.)
Cox	Cox (Ark.)
Cox & Atk.	Cox & Atkinson Registration Appeals (Eng.)
Cox Am.T. Cas.	Cox's American Trademark Cases

Cox C.C.	Cox's Criminal Cases (Eng.)
Cox Ch.	Cox's Chancery (Eng.)
Cox Crim.Cas.	Cox's Criminal Cases
Cox Eq.	Cox's Equity
Cox J.S.Cas.	Cox's Joint Stock Cases (Eng.)
Coxe	Coxe (N.J.)
Cr. & M.	Crompton & Meeson, Exchequer (Eng.)
Cr. & Ph.	Craig & Phillips Chancery (Eng.)
Cr.App.	Criminal Appeals (Eng.)
Cr.App.R.(S.)	The Criminal Appeal Reports (Sentencing)
Cr.Cas.Res.	Crown Cases Reserved, Law Reports (Eng.)
Crabbe	Crabbe (U.S.)
Craig & Ph.	Craig & Phillips Chancery (Eng.)
Cranch	Cranch (U.S.)
Cranch C.C.	Cranch's Circuit Court (U.S.)
Cranch Pat. Dec.	Cranch's Patent Decisions (U.S.)
Crane	Crane (Mont.)
Craw.	Crawford (Ark.)
Crawf. & D. Abr.Cas.	Crawford & Dix's Abridged Cases (Ir.)
Crawf. & Dix	Crawford & Dix Circuit Cases (Ir.)
	Crawford & Dix Criminal Cases (Ir.)
Creighton L.Rev.	Creighton Law Review
Crim.	Criminologie
Crim. & Soc. Just.	Crime and Social Justice
Crim.App.	Criminal Appeal Reports
Crim.App. Rep.	Cohen's Criminal Appeals Reports (Eng.)
Crim.Case & Com.	Criminal Case and Comment
Crim.Def.	Criminal Defense
Crim.Just.	Criminal Justice
Crim.Just. & Behav.	Criminal Justice and Behavior
Crim.Just. Newsl.	Criminal Justice Newsletter
Crim.Just.Q.	Criminal Justice Quarterly
Crim.Just.Rev.	Criminal Justice Review
Crim.L.Bull.	Criminal Law Bulletin
Crim.L.J.	Criminal Law Journal
Crim.L.Mag.	Criminal Law Magazine (N.J.)
Crim.L.Mag. & Rep.	Criminal Law Magazine and Reporter
Crim.L.Q.	Criminal Law Quarterly
Crim.L.Rec.	Criminal Law Recorder
Crim.L.Rep.	Criminal Law Reporter
Crim.L.Rev.	Criminal Law Review (Manhattan)
Crim.L.Rev. (Eng.)	Criminal Law Review (Eng.)
Crim.L.Rptr.	Criminal Law Reporter
Crim.Rep. (N.S.)	Criminal Reports, New Series
Crime & Delin'cy	Crime & Delinquency
Crime & Delin'cy Abst.	Crime and Delinquency Abstracts
Crime & Delin'cy Lit.	Crime and Delinquency Literature
Criminologica	Criminologica
Criminologist	Criminologist
Criminology	Criminology
	Croke's King's Bench
Cripp Ch.Cas.	Cripp's Church & Clergy Cases
Critch.	Critchfield (Ohio St.)
Cro.	Croke's King's Bench (Eng.)
Cro.Car.	Croke temp. Charles I (Eng.)
Cro.Eliz.	Croke temp. Elizabeth (Eng.)
Cro.Jac.	Croke temp. James I King's Bench (Eng.)
Cromp.	Star Chamber Cases (Eng.)
Cromp. & J.	Crompton & Jervis Exchequer (Eng.)
Cromp. & M.	Crompton & Meeson Exchequer (Eng.)
Cromp.M. & R.	Crompton, Meeson & Roscoe, Exchequer (Eng.)
Crosw.Pat. Cas.	Croswell's Collection of Patent Cases (U.S.)
Crounse	Crounse (Neb.)
Crumrine	Crumrine (Pa.)
Ct.Cl.	Court of Claims (U.S.)
Ct.Cust. & Pat.App.	Court of Customs & Patent Appeals
Ct.Cust.App.	Court of Customs Appeals (U.S.)
Ct.Rev.	Court Review
Cum.Bull.	Cumulative Bulletin
Cum.L.Rev.	Cumberland Law Review
Cum.-San. L.Rev.	Cumberland-Sanford Law Review
Cumb.L.Rev.	Cumberland Law Review
Cummins	Cummins (Idaho)
Cunn.	Cunningham King's Bench (Eng.)
Cur.Leg. Thought	Current Legal Thought

Current Com. & Leg.Mis.	Current Comment and Legal Miscellany
Current L.	Current Law
Current L. & Soc.Prob.	Current Law and Social Problems
Current L.Y.B.	Current Law Yearbook
Current Legal Prob.	Current Legal Problems
Current Legal Thought	Current Legal Thought
Current Med.	Current Medicine for Attorneys
Curry	Curry (La.)
Curt.	Curtis Circuit Court (U.S.)
Curt.Eccl.	Curtis Ecclesiastical (Eng.)
Cush.	Cushing (Mass.)
Cust.App.	United States Customs Appeals
Cust.Ct.	Custom Court Reports (U.S.)
Cyc.	Cyclopedia of Law & Procedure
Czech.J. Int'l L.	Czechoslovak Journal of International Law
Czech.Y.B. Int'l L.	Czechoslovak Yearbook of International Law

D

D.	Disney (Ohio)
	Ohio Decisions
D. & B.	Dearsley & Bell's Crown Cases (Eng.)
D. & B.C.C.	Same
D. & C.	Dow & Clark's Parliamentary Cases (Eng.)
	Deacon & Chitty's Bankruptcy Cases (Eng.)
D. & Ch.	Same
D. & Chit.	Same
D. & E.	Dwinford & East's King's Bench Term Reports (Eng.)
D. & J.	De Gex & Jones' Chancery (Eng.)
D. & J.B.	De Gex & Jones Bankruptcy (Eng.)
D. & L.	Dowling & Lowndes Bail Court (Eng.)
D. & M.	Davison & Merivale's Queen's Bench (Eng.)
D. & P.	Denison & Pearce's Crown Cases (Eng.)
D. & R.	Dowling & Ryland's King's Bench (Eng.)
D. & R.M.C.	Dowling & Ryland's Magistrates' Cases (Eng.)
D. & R.Mag. Cas.	Same
D. & R.N.P.	Dowling & Ryland's Nisi Prius Cases (Eng.)
D. & R.N.P.C.	Same
D. & S.	Drewry & Smale's Chancery (Eng.)
	Deane & Swabey's Ecclesiastical (Eng.)
D. & Sm.	Drewry & Smale's Chancery (Eng.)
D. & Sw.	Deane & Swabey Ecclesiastical (Eng.)
D. & W.	Drewry & Walsh's Chancery (Ir.)
	Drewry & Warren's Chancery (Ir.)
D. & War.	Drewry & Warren's Chancery (Ir.)
D.B.	Domesday Book
D.B. & M.	Dunlop, Bell & Murray (Sc.)
D.C.	Treasury Department Circular (I.R.Bull.)
	District of Columbia
D.C.A.	Dorion's Queen's Bench (Can.)
D.C.App.	District of Columbia Appeals
D.C.B.J.	District of Columbia Bar Journal
D.C.Cir.	District of Columbia Court of Appeals Cases
D.Chip.	D. Chipman (Vt.)
D.Chipm.	Same
D.D.C.	District Court, District of Columbia
D.Dec.	Dix's School Decisions (N.Y.)
D.I.L. (Hack.)	Digest of International Law (Hackworth)
D.I.L. (Moore)	Digest of International Law (Moore)
D.I.L. (White.)	Digest of International Law (Whiteman)
D.L.R.	Dominion Law Reports (Can.) 1912–1922
[ ] D.L.R.	Same, 1923–1955
D.L.R.2d	Same, Second Series
D.L.R.3d	Same, Third Series, 1969–present
D.P.R.	Decisiones de Puerto Rico
D.Rep.	Ohio Decisions Reprint

D.Repr.	Same
D.T.C.	Dominion Tax Cases
Dak.	Dakota
Dak.L.Rev.	Dakota Law Review
Dal.C.P.	Dalison's Common Pleas (Eng.)
Dale	Dale (Okla.)
Dale Ecc.	Dale's Ecclesiastical (Eng.)
Dale Eccl.	Same
Dale Leg.Rit.	Dale's Legal Ritual (Eng.)
Dalhousie L.J.	Dalhousie Law Journal
Dall.	Dallam's Decisions
	Dallas (Pa.)
	Dallas (U.S.)
Dall. in Keil.	Dallison in Keilway's King's Bench (Eng.)
Dalr.	Dalrymple's Decisions (Sc.)
Daly	Daly (N.Y.)
Dan.	Daniell's Exchequer & Equity (Eng.)
Dana	Dana (Ky.)
Dane Abr.	Dane's Abridgment (Eng.)
Dann	Dann (Ariz.)
	Dann (Cal.)
Dann.	Danner (Ala.)
Dans. & L.	Danson & Lloyd's Mercantile Cases (Eng.)
Dans. & Lld.	Same
D'Anv.Abr.	D'Anver's Abridgment (Eng.)
Dass.Ed.	Dassler's Edition, Kansas Reports
Dauph.Co.	Dauphin County (Pa.)
Dav. & M.	Davison & Merivale Queen's Bench (Eng.)
Dav. & Mer.	Same
Daveis	Daveis (Ware) (U.S.)
Davies or Davis	Davis King's Bench (Ir.)
Davis	Daveis (Ware) (U.S.)
	Davis (Hawaii)
	Davis King's Bench (Ir.)
Davys	Davys King's Bench
Day	Day (Conn.)
Dayton	3 Ohio Miscellaneous Decisions
Dayton T.R.	Same
Dayton Term Rep.	Iddings' Term Reports (Ohio)
Dea.	Deady, U. S. Circuit & District Courts (Cal. & Ore.)
Dea. & Chit.	Same
Dea. & Sw.	Deane & Swabey's Ecclesiastical (Eng.)
	Deane & Swabey's Probate & Divorce (Eng.)

Deac.	Deacon, Bankruptcy (Eng.)
Deac. & C.	Deacon & Chitty, Bankruptcy (Eng.)
Deac. & Chit.	Same
Deacon & C.	Same
Deacon, Bankr.Cas.	Deacon, Bankruptcy (Eng.)
Deady	Deady, U. S. Circuit and District Courts (Cal. & Ore.)
Deane	Deane (Vt.)
	Deane (& Swabey's) Probate & Divorce (Eng.)
Deane & S. Eccl.Rep.	Deane & Swabey's Ecclesiastical (Eng.)
Deane & Sw.	Same
Deane Ecc.	Same
Deane Ecc. Rep.	Same
Dears.	Dearsley & Bell Crown Cases (Eng.)
Dears. & B.	Same
Dears. & B. C.C.	Same
Dears.C.C.	Same
Deas & A.	Deas & Anderson (Sc.)
Deas & And.	Same
Dec.Com.Pat.	Decisions of Commissioner of Patents
Dec.Dig.	Decennial Digest
Dec.Rep.	Ohio Decisions Reprint
Dec.U.S. Compt.Gen.	Decisions of U. S. Comptroller General
Decalogue	Decalogue Journal
Def.L.J.	Defense Law Journal
De G. & J.	De Gex & Jones, Chancery (Eng.)
De G. & Sm.	De Gex & Smale, Chancery (Eng.)
De G.F. & J.	De Gex, Fisher & Jones, Chancery (Eng.)
De G.J. & S.	De Gex, Jones & Smith, Chancery (Eng.)
De G.M. & G.	De Gex, Macnaughten & Gordon, Chancery (Eng.)
De Gex	De Gex Bankruptcy (Eng.)
Del.	Delaware
Del.Ch.	Delaware Chancery
Del.Co.	Delaware County (Pa.)
Del.County	Delaware County Reports
Del.Cr.Cas.	Delaware Criminal Cases
Del.J.Corp.L.	Delaware Journal of Corporate Law
Dem.	Demarest's Surrogate (N. Y.)
Dem.Surr.	Same

Den.	Denio (N.Y.) Denis (La.)
Den. & P.	Denison & Pearce's Crown Cases (Eng.)
Den. & P.C.C.	Same
Den.C.C.	Denison's Crown Cases (Eng.)
Den.L.J.	Denver Law Journal
Den.L.N.	Denver Legal News
Denio	Denio (N.Y.)
Denis	Denis (La.)
Den.J. Int'l L. & Policy	Denver Journal of International Law and Policy
De Paul L. Rev.	De Paul Law Review
Dept.State Bull.	Department of State Bulletin, United States
Des.	Dessaussure's Equity (S. C.)
Desaus.Eq.	Same
Dess.	Same
Dessaus.	Same
Det.Coll.L. Rev.	Detroit College of Law Review
Det.L.J.	Detroit Law Journal
Det.L.Rev.	Detroit Law Review
Det.Leg.N.	Detroit Legal News
Detroit L.Rev.	Detroit Law Review
Dev.	Devereux's Equity (N.C.) Devereux's Law (N.C.) Devereux's U. S. Court of Claims
Dev. & B.	Devereux & Battle's Equity (N.C.) Devereux & Battle's Law (N.C.)
Dev.Ct.Cl.	Devereux's Court of Claims (U.S.)
Dew.	Dewey (Kan.)
De Witt	De Witt (Ohio)
Di.	Dyer's King's Bench (Eng.)
Dice	Dice (Ind.)
Dick.	Dickens' Chancery (Eng.) Dickinson's Equity (N.J.)
Dick.L.Rev.	Dickinson Law Review
Dicta	Dicta of Denver Bar Association
Dig.C.L.W.	Digest of Commercial Laws of the World (Oceana)
Dill.	Dillon, Circuit Court (U.S.)
Dine Israel	Dine Israel
Dirl.Dec.	Direlton's Decisions (Sc.)
Disn.	Disney (Ohio)
Disney	Same
Docket	Docket (Lebanon, Pa.) Docket (St. Paul, Minn.)
Docket Call	Docket Call
Dod.	Dodson's Admiralty (Eng.)
Dod.Adm.	Same
Dods.	Same
Dom.L.R.	Dominion Law Reports (Can.)
Donaker	Donaker (Ind.)
Donn.	Donnelly's Chancery (Eng.) Donnelly's Irish Land Cases
Donnelly	Same
Dorion	Dorion (Lower Can.)
Doshisha L. Rev.	Doshisha Law Review
Doug.	Douglas (Mich.) Douglas' King's Bench (Eng.)
Dougl.	Douglas (Mich.)
Dougl.El.Cas.	Douglas Election Cases (Eng.)
Dougl.K.B.	Douglas' King's Bench (Eng.)
Dow	Dow's House of Lords (Parliamentary) Cases (Eng.)
Dow.	Dowling's Practice Cases (Eng.)
Dow & Cl.	Dow & Clark's House of Lords Cases (Eng.)
Dow. & L.	Dowling & Lowndes' Bail Court (Eng.)
Dowl. & Lownd.	Dowling & Lowndes' Practice Cases (Eng.)
Dowl. & R.	Dowling & Ryland's King's Bench (Eng.) Dowling & Ryland's Queen's Bench & Magistrates' Cases (Eng.)
Dowl.P.C. (N.S.)	Dowling Practice Cases, New Series (Eng.)
Dowl.Pr.Cas.	Dowling Practice Cases (Eng.)
Down. & Lud.	Downton & Luder's Election Cases (Eng.)
Drake L.Rev.	Drake Law Review
Draper	Draper (Upper Can.)
Drew	Drew (Fla.)
Drew.	Drewry's Chancery (Eng.)
Drew. & S.	Drewry & Smale's Chancery (Eng.)
Drinkw.	Drinkwater Common Pleas (Eng.)
Drug Abuse L.Rev.	Drug Abuse Law Review
Drug L.J.	Drug Law Journal

Drury	Drury's Chancery (Ir.)
Dublin U.L. Rev.	Dublin University Law Review
Dudl.	Dudley (Ga.)
	Dudley's Equity (S.C.)
	Dudley's Law (S.C.)
Duer	Duer's Superior Court (N. Y.)
Duke B. Ass'n J.	Duke Bar Association Journal
Duke L.J.	Duke Law Journal
Duke's Charitable Uses	Duke's Charitable Uses (Eng.)
Dunc.Ent.Cas.	Duncan Entail Cases (Sc.)
Dunc.N.P.	Duncombe Nisi Prius
Dunl.	Dunlop, Bell & Murray (Sc.)
Dunl.B. & M.	Same
Dunlop	Dunlop (Sc.)
Dunn.	Dunning's King's Bench (Eng.)
Duq.L.Rev.	Duquesne Law Review
Duq.U.L.Rev.	Duquesne University Law Review
Durf.	Durfee (R.I.)
Durfee	Same
Durie	Durie (Sc.)
Durn. & E.	Durnford & East's King's Bench (Term Reports) (Eng.)
Dutch.	Dutcher's Law (N.J.)
Duv.	Duval's Supreme Court (Can.)
	Duval's Reports (Can.)
Dy.	Dyer's King's Bench (Eng.)
Dyer	Same

E

E.	East's King's Bench (Eng.)
E. & A.	Spink's Ecclesiastical & Admiralty (Eng.)
	Upper Canada Error & Appeal Reports, Grant
E. & B.	Ellis & Blackburn's Queen's Bench (Eng.)
E. & E.	Ellis & Ellis' Queen's Bench (Eng.)
E. & I.	English & Irish Appeals, House of Lords (Eng.)
E.A.S.	Executive Agreement Series, United States
E.Afr.L.J.	East African Law Journal
E.Afr.L.R.	East Africa Law Reports
E.Afr.L.Rev.	Eastern Africa Law Review
E.B. & E.	Ellis, Blackburn & Ellis' Queen's Bench (Eng.)
E.B. & S.	Ellis, Best & Smith's Queen's Bench (Eng.)
E.C.	English Chancery
E.C.L.	English Common Law
ECLR	European Competition Law Review
E.C.R.	Reports of Cases before the Court of Justice of the European Communities
E.D.S.	E. D. Smith (N.Y.)
E.D.Smith	Same
E.E.	English Exchequer
E.E.C.J.O.	Official Journal of the European Communities
E.E.C.L.	Encyclopedia of European Community Law (Bender)
E.E.O.C.Compliance Manual	Equal Employment Opportunity Commission Compliance Manual (CCH)
E.E.R.	English Ecclesiastical Reports
E.G.L.	Encyclopedia of Georgia Law
E.L. & Eq.	English Law & Equity Reports
E.L.R.	Eastern Law Reporter (Can.)
E.P.D.	Employment Practices Decisions (CCH)
E.R.	East's King's Bench (Eng.)
E.R.C.	English Ruling Cases
	Environmental Reporter Cases
E.School L.Rev.	Eastern School Law Review
E.T.	Estate Tax Division (I.R. Bull.)
E.T.R.	Estates & Trusts Reports, 1977–
Ea.	East's King's Bench (Eng.)
Eag. & Y.	Eagle & Young's Tithe Cases (Eng.)
Eag.T.	Eagle's Commutation of Tithes (Eng.)
Earth L.J.	Earth Law Journal
East	East's King's Bench (Eng.)
	Eastern Reporter (U.S.)
East P.C.	East's Pleas of the Crown (Eng.)
East.J.Int'l L.	Eastern Journal of International Law
East.L.R.	Eastern Law Reporter (Can.)
East.Rep.	Eastern Reporter (U.S.)

East.T.	Eastern Term (Eng.)
East.U.S.Bus. L.Rev.	Eastern United States Business Law Review
Ebersole	Ebersole (Iowa)
Eccl. & Adm.	Spink's Ecclesiastical & Admiralty (Upper Can.)
Eccl.R.	Ecclesiastical Reports (Eng.)
Eccl.Rep.	Same
Ecology L.Q.	Ecology Law Quarterly
Ed.	Eden's Chancery (Eng.)
Ed.Ch.	Edward's Chancery (N.Y.)
Eden	Eden's Chancery (Eng.)
Edg.	Edgar (Sc.)
Edinb.L.J.	Edinburgh Law Journal
Edm.Sel.Cas.	Edmond's Select Cases (N. Y.)
Edw.	Edwards (Mo.)
	Edward's Chancery (N.Y.)
Edw.Abr.	Edward's Abridgment Privy Council
	Edward's Abridgment Prerogative Court Cases
Edw.Adm.	Edward's Admiralty (Eng.)
Edw.Ch.	Edward's Chancery (N.Y.)
Edw.Lead.Dec.	Edward's Leading Decisions in Admiralty
Edw.Pr.Cas.	Edward's Prize Cases (Eng.Admiralty)
Edw.Pr.Ct. Cas.	Edward's Prerogative Court Cases
Efird	Efird (S.C.)
El.	Elchie's Decisions (Sc.)
El. & B.	Ellis & Blackburn's Queen's Bench (Eng.)
El. & Bl.	Same
El. & El.	Ellis & Ellis, Queen's Bench (Eng.)
El.B. & E.	Ellis, Blackburn & Ellis' Queen's Bench (Eng.)
El.B. & El.	Same
El.B. & S.	Ellis, Best & Smith's Queen's Bench (Eng.)
El.Bl. & El.	Ellis, Blackburn & Ellis' Queen's Bench (Eng.)
El.Cas.	Election Cases
El Paso Trial Law.Rev.	El Paso Trial Lawyers Reviews
Elchies'	Elchies' Decisions (Sc.)
Elect.Cas. (N.Y.)	Election Cases, Armstrong, New York
Elect.Rep.	Election Reports, Ontario
Ell. & Bl.	Ellis & Blackburn's Queen's Bench (Eng.)
Ell.Bl. & Ell.	Ellis, Blackburn & Ellis' Queen's Bench (Eng.)
Els.W.Bl.	Elsley's Edition of Wm. Blackstone's King's Bench (Eng.)
Em.App.	Emergency Court of Appeals (U.S.)
Emory L.J.	Emory Law Journal
Empl.Rel.L.J.	Employee Relations Law Journal
Empl.Saf'y & Health Guide	Employment Safety and Health Guide (CCH)
Enc.Pl. & Pr.	Encyclopedia of Pleading & Practice
Enc.U.S.Sup. Ct.Rep.	Encyclopedia of United States Supreme Court Reports
Energy Controls	Energy Controls (P–H)
Energy L.J.	Energy Law Journal
Energy Users Rep.	Energy Users Report (BNA)
Eng.	English (Ark.)
Eng.Adm.	English Admiralty
Eng.Adm.R.	Same
Eng.C.C.	English Crown Cases
Eng.C.L.	English Common-Law Reports
Eng.Ch.	English Chancery Condensed English Chancery
Eng.Com.L.R.	English Common-Law Reports
Eng.Cr.Cas.	English Crown Cases
Eng.Ecc.R.	English Ecclesiastical Reports
Eng.Eccl.	Same
Eng.Exch.	English Exchequer
Eng.Hist.Rev.	English Historical Review
Eng.Ir.App.	Law Reports English & Irish Appeals
Eng.Judg.	English Judges (Sc.)
Eng.L. & Eq.	English Law & Equity Reports
Eng.L. & Eq.R.	Same
Eng.Rep.	English Reports, Full Reprint
Eng.Rep.R.	Same
Eng.Ry. & C. Cas.	English Railway and Canal Cases
Eng.Sc.Ecc.	English & Scotch Ecclesiastical Reports
Env.Affairs	Environmental Affairs
Env.L.	Environmental Law
Env.L.Rev.	Environmental Law Review
Env.L.Rptr.	Environmental Law Reporter
Env.Pol'y & L.	Environmental Policy and Law
Env.Rptr.	Environment Reporter (B.N.A.)
Envt'l L.J.	Environmental Law Journal

Eq.Cas.Abr.	Equity Cases Abridged (Eng.)
Eq.Rep.	Harper's Equity (S.C.)
Equity Rep.	Equity Reports (Gilbert) (Eng.) Harper's Equity (S.C.) English Chancery Appeals
Err. & App.	Error & Appeals (Upper Can.)
Ersk.	Erskine (U.S.C.C. in 35 Ga.)
Esp.	Espinasse's Nisi Prius (Eng.)
Esp.N.P.	Same
Est. & Tr.Q.	Estates and Trusts Quarterly
Est.Plan.	Estate Planning
Est.Plan.Rev.	Estate Planning Review (CCH)
Euer	Euer Doctrina Placitandi (Eng.)
Eur.Consult. Ass.Deb.	Council of Europe Consultative Assembly, Official Report of Debates
Eur.L.Dig.	European Law Digest
Eur.L.Newsl.	European Law Newsletter
Eur.L.Rev.	European Law Review
Eur.Parl.Deb.	Debates of the European Parliament
Eur.Parl.Docs.	European Parliament Working Documents
Eur.Tax.	European Taxation
Eur.Trans.L.	European Transport Law
Eur.Y.B.	European Yearbook
Eurolaw Com. Intel.	Eurolaw Commercial Intelligence
Europ.T.S.	European Treaty Series
Evans	Evans, Washington Territory Reports
Ex.	Exchequer Reports (Eng.)
Ex.C.R.	Exchequer Court Reports (Can.) (1923–present)
Ex.D.	Law Reports Exchequer Division (Eng.) (To 1880)
Ex.Div.	Same
Examiner	Examiner (New York) Examiner (Quebec)
Excerpta Crim.	Excerpta Criminologica
Exch.	Exchequer (Welsby, Hurlstone & Gordon) (Eng.) Exchequer (Sc.)
Exch.Can.	Exchequer Reports (Can.)
Exch.Cas.	Exchequer Cases (Sc.)
Exch.Rep.	Exchequer Reports
Exec.Order	Executive Order
Eyre	Eyre's King's Bench (Eng.)

F

F.	Federal Reporter (U.S.)
F.2d	Same, Second Series
F. & F.	Foster & Finlanson Nisi Prius (Eng.)
F.A.D.	Federal Anti-Trust Decisions
F.B.C.	Fonblanque's Bankruptcy Cases (Eng.)
FBILEB	F.B.I. Law Enforcement Bull.
F.C.	Faculty Collection of Decisions (Sc.)
[ ] F.C.	Canada Federal Court Reports, 1971–
F.C.A.	Federal Code Annotated
F.C.C.	Federal Communication Commission Reports
F.Carr.Cas.	Federal Carriers Cases (CCH)
F. (Ct.Sess.)	Fraser's Court of Sessions Cases (Sc.)
F.D.Cosm.L. Rep.	Food, Drug, Cosmetic Law Reporter (CCH)
F.E.P.Cas.	Fair Employment Practice Cases
F.H.L.	Fraser, House of Lords (Sc.)
F.L.J.	Forum Law Journal (U. of Baltimore)
F.L.P.	Florida Law and Practice
F.M.C.	Federal Maritime Commission Reports
F.O.I.Dig.	F.O.I. Digest
F.O.I.C.R.	Freedom of Information Center Reports
F.P.C.	Federal Power Commission Decisions
FR	Federal Register
F.R.D.	Federal Rules Decisions
F.Supp.	Federal Supplement
F.T.C.	Federal Trade Commission Decisions
Fac.L.Rev.	Faculty of Law Review (Toronto)
Fairf.	Fairfield (Me.)
Falc.	Falconer's Court of Sessions Cases (Sc.)
Falc. & F.	Falconer & Fitzherbert's Election Cases (Eng.)

Fam.L. Commtr.	Family Law Commentator
Fam.L.Newsl.	Family Law Newsletter
Fam.L.Q.	Family Law Quarterly
Fam.L.Rep.	Family Law Reporter (BNA)
Fam.L.Rev.	Family Law Review
Far.	Farresley's King's Bench (Eng.)
Far East. L.Rev.	Far Eastern Law Review
Fed.	Federal Reporter (U.S.)
Fed.B.A.J.	Federal Bar Association Journal
Fed.B.J.	Federal Bar Journal
Fed.B.News	Federal Bar News
Fed.Carr.Rep.	Federal Carriers Reporter (CCH)
Fed.Cas.	Federal Cases (U.S.)
Fed.Com.B.J.	Federal Communications Bar Journal
Fed.Com.L.J.	Federal Communications Law Journal
Fed.Est. & Gift Tax Rep.	Federal Estate and Gift Tax Reporter (CCH)
Fed.Juror	Federal Juror
Fed.L.Rep.	Federal Law Reports
Fed.L.Rev.	Federal Law Review
Fed.Prob.	Federal Probation
Fed.Reg.	Federal Register
Fed.Rules Serv.	Federal Rules Service
Fed.Rules Serv.2d	Same, Second Series
Fed'n Ins. Counsel Q.	Federation of Insurance Counsel Quarterly
Ferg.Cons.	Fergusson's Consistory (Divorce) (Sc.)
Fergusson	Fergusson (of Kilkeran) (Sc.)
Fin.Tax. & Comp.L.	Finance Taxation and Company Law (Pakistan)
Finch	Finch's Chancery (Eng.)
Fire & Casualty Cas.	Fire and Casualty Cases (CCH)
Fish.Pat.Cas.	Fisher's Patent Cases (U.S.)
Fish.Pat.R.	Fisher's Patent Reports (U.S.)
Fish.Prize Cas.	Fisher's Prize Cases (U.S.)
Fitzh.	Fitzherbert's Abridgment (Eng.)
Fitzh.N.Br.	Fitzherbert's Natura Brevium (Eng.)
Fla.	Florida
Fla. & K.	Flanagan & Kelly, Rolls (Ir.)
Fla.B.J.	Florida Bar Journal
Fla.Jur.	Florida Jurisprudence
Fla.L.J.	Florida Law Journal
Fla.St.U.L. Rev.	Florida State University Law Review
Fla.Supp.	Florida Supplement
Flan. & Kel.	Flanagan & Kelly, Rolls (Ir.)
Flipp.	Flippin (U.S.)
Fogg	Fogg (N.H.)
Fonbl.	Fonblanque's Bankruptcy (Eng.)
Food Drug Cosm.L.J.	Food, Drug, Cosmetic Law Journal
For.Sci.	Forensic Science
For.Tax Bull.	Foreign Tax Law Bi-Weekly Bulletin
Ford.L.Rev.	Fordham Law Review
Ford.Urban L.J.	Fordham Urban Law Journal
Fordham Int'l L.F.	Fordham International Law Forum
Fordham L.Rev.	Fordham Law Review
Fordham Urb. L.J.	Fordham Urban Law Journal
Form.	Forman (Ill.)
Forr.	Forrest's Exchequer (Eng.)
Forrester	Forrester's Chancery Cases temp. Talbot (Eng.)
Fort.L.J.	Fortnightly Law Journal
Fortesc.	Fortescue's King's Bench (Eng.)
Forum	The Forum
Fost.	Foster's Crown Cases (Eng.) Foster (Hawaii) Foster's Legal Chronicle Reports (Pa.) Foster (N.H.)
Found.L.Rev.	Foundation Law Review
Fount.Dec.	Fountainhall's Decisions (Sc.)
Fox	Fox's Registration Cases (Eng.) Fox's Decisions (Me.)
Fox & S.	Fox & Smith's King's Bench (Ir.)
Fox Pat.C.	Fox's Patent, Trade Mark, Design and Copyright Cases
Fran.Coll.L.J.	Franciso College Law Journal
France	France (Colo.)

Fraser	Fraser, Court of Session Cases (Sc.)
Freem.	Freeman (Ill.)
Freem.Ch.	Freeman's Chancery (Miss.)
Freem.K.B.	Freeman's King's Bench (Eng.)
French	French (N.H.)
Fuller	Fuller (Mich.)

G

G. & D.	Gale & Davison's Queen's Bench (Eng.)
G. & G.	Goldsmith & Guthrie (Mo.)
G. & J.	Gill & Johnson (Md.)
	Glyn & Jameson's Bankruptcy (Eng.)
G. & R.	Geldert & Russell (N.S.)
GA	Decisions of General Appraisers (U.S.)
G.C.M.	General Counsel's Memorandum (I.R.Bull.)
G.Coop.	G. Cooper's Chancery (Eng.)
G.S.R.	Gongwer's State Reports (Ohio)
Ga.	Georgia
Ga.App.	Georgia Appeals
Ga.B.J.	Georgia Bar Journal
Ga.Bus.Law.	Georgia Business Lawyer
Ga.Dec.	Georgia Decisions
Ga.J.Int'l & Comp.L.	Georgia Journal of International & Comparative Law
Ga.L.J.	Georgia Law Journal
Ga.L.Rep.	Georgia Law Reports
Ga.L.Rev.	Georgia Law Review
Ga.St.B.J.	Georgia State Bar Journal
Ga.Supp.	Georgia Supplement (Lester)
Galb.	Galbraith (Fla.)
Galb. & M.	Galbraith & Meek (Fla.)
Gale	Gale's Exchequer (Eng.)
Gale & D.	Gale & Davison's Queen's Bench (Eng.)
Gale & Dav.	Same
Gall.	Gallison (U.S. Circuit Court)
Gard.N.Y. Reptr.	Gardenier's New York Reporter
Garden.	Gardenhire (Mo.)
Gaz.	Weekly Law Gazette (U.S.)
	Gazette
Gaz.Bankr.	Gazette of Bankruptcy
Gaz.L.R.	Gazette Law Reports
Geld. & M.	Geldart & Maddock's Chancery (Eng.)
Geld. & O.	Geldert & Oxley (N.S.)
Geo.L.J.	Georgetown Law Journal
Geo.Wash.L. Rev.	George Washington Law Review
George	George (Miss.)
Gibb.Surr.	Gibbon's Surrogate (N.Y.)
Gibbs	Gibbs (Mich.)
Giff.	Giffard's Chancery (Eng.)
Giff. & H.	Giffard & Hemming's Chancery (Eng.)
Gil.	Gilman (Ill.)
Gilb.	Gilbert's Chancery (Eng.)
Gilb.C.P.	Gilbert's Common Pleas (Eng.)
Gilb.Cas.	Gilbert's Cases, Law & Equity (Eng.)
Gilb.Exch.	Gilbert's Exchequer (Eng.)
Gildr.	Gildersleeve (N.Mex.)
Gilf.	Gilfillan (Minn.)
Gill	Gill (Md.)
Gill & J.	Gill & Johnson (Md.)
Gill & Johns.	Same
Gilm.	Gilmer (Va.)
Gilm. & Falc.	Gilmour & Falconer (Sc.)
Gilp.	Gilpin (U.S.)
Gl. & J.	Glyn & Jameson's Bankruptcy Cases (Eng.)
Glanv.	Glanville De Legibus et Consuetudinibus Angliae (Eng.)
Glanv.El.Cas.	Glanville's Election Cases (Eng.)
Glasc.	Glascock (Ir.)
Glendale L. Rev.	Glendale Law Review
Glenn	Glenn (Louisiana Annual)
Glyn & J.	Glyn & Jameson's Bankruptcy Cases (Eng.)
Glyn & Jam.	Same
Godb.	Godbolt's King's Bench (Eng.)
Godson	Godson, Mining Commissioner's Cases, 1911–1917.

Goebel	Goebel's Probate (Ohio)
Gold. & G.	Goldsmith & Guthrie (Mo.)
Golden Gate L.Rev.	Golden Gate Law Review
Golden Gate U.L.Rev.	Golden Gate University Law Review
Gonz.L.Rev.	Gonzaga Law Review
Gonz.Pub.Lab. L.Rep.	Gonzaga Special Report: Public Sector Labor Law
Gottschall	Gottschall (Ohio)
Gouldsb.	Gouldsborough's King's Bench (Eng.)
Gov't Cont. Rep.	Government Contracts Reporter (CCH)
Gow	Gow's Nisi Prius (Eng.)
Gr.	Grant, Upper Canada Chancery Reports
Granger	Granger (Ohio)
Grant	Grant's Cases (Pa.)
Grant Err. & App.	Grant's Error & Appeal (Upper Can.)
Gratt.	Grattan (Va.)
Gray	Gray (Mass.)
	Gray (N.C.)
Graya	Graya
Green	Green Equity (N.J.)
	Green Law (N.J.)
	Green (Okla.)
	Green (R.I.)
Green Bag	Green Bag
Green Cr.	Green's Criminal Law (Eng.)
Greene	Greene (Iowa)
	Greene's Annotated Cases (N.Y.)
Greenl.	Greenleaf (Me.)
Greenl.Ov.Cas.	Greenleaf's Overruled Cases
Grein.Pr.	Greiner Louisiana Practice
Griffith	Griffith (Ind.)
Gris.	Griswold (Ohio)
Griswold	Same
Group Legal Rev.	Group Legal Review
Guild Notes	Guild Notes
Guild Prac.	Guild Practitioner
Guthrie	Guthrie (Mo.)
Gwill.T.Cas.	Gwillim's Tithe Cases (Eng.)

H

H.	Handy (Ohio)
H. & B.	Hudson & Brooke's King's Bench (Ir.)
H. & C.	Hurlstone & Coltman's Exchequer (Eng.)
H. & D.	Hill & Denio, Lalor's Supplement (N.Y.)
H. & G.	Harris & Gill (Md.)
	Hurlstone & Gordon's Exchequer (Eng.)
H. & H.	Harrison & Hodgin's Municipal Reports (Upper Can.)
	Horn & Hurlstone's Exchequer (Eng.)
H. & J.	Harris & Johnson (Md.)
	Hayes & Jones' Exchequer (Ir.)
H. & J.Ir.	Same
H. & M.	Hening & Munford (Va.)
	Hemming & Miller's Vice-Chancery (Eng.)
H. & M.Ch.	Hemming & Miller's Vice-Chancery (Eng.)
H. & McH.	Harris & McHenry (Md.)
H. & N.	Hurlstone & Norman's Exchequer (Eng.)
H. & R.	Harrison & Rutherford's Common Pleas (Eng.)
H. & S.	Harris & Simrall (Miss.)
H. & T.	Hall & Twell's Chancery (Eng.)
H. & W.	Harrison & Wollaston's King's Bench (Eng.)
	Hurlstone & Walmsley's Exchequer (Eng.)
H.Bl.	Henry Blackstone's Common Pleas (Eng.)
H.C.L.M.	Health Care Labor Manual
H.L.Cas.	House of Lords Cases (Eng.)
H.L.N.R.	Health Lawyers News Report
H.W.Gr.	H. W. Green's Equity (N.J.)
Ha.	Hare's Vice-Chancery (Eng.)
Ha. & Tw.	Hall & Twell's Chancery (Eng.)
Had.	Hadley (N.H.)
Hadd.	Haddington MSS Reports (Sc.)
Hadl.	Hadley (N.H.)
Hagan	Hagan (Utah)
Hagans	Hagans (W.Va.)
Hagg.Adm.	Haggard's Admiralty (Eng.)
Hagn. & M.	Hagner & Miller (Md.)
Hailes Dec.	Haile's Decisions (Sc.)

Hale	Hale (Cal.)
	Hale's Common Law (Eng.)
Hale P.C.	Hale's Pleas of the Crown (Eng.)
Hall	Hall (N.H.)
	Hall's Superior Court (N.Y.)
Hal & Tw.	Hall & Twell's Chancery (Eng.)
Hall.	Hallett (Colo.)
Halst.	Halsted's Equity (N.J.)
	Halsted's Law (N.J.)
Ham.	Hammond (Ga.)
	Hammond (Ohio)
Ham. & J.	Hammond & Jackson (Ga.)
Ham.A. & O.	Hamerton, Allen & Otter, New Session Cases (Eng.)
Hamlin	Hamlin (Me.)
Hamline L.Rev.	Hamline Law Review
Hammond	Hammond (Ohio)
Han.	Handy (Ohio)
Han.N.B.	Hannay's Reports (New Brunswick)
Hand	Hand (N.Y.)
Handy	Handy (Ohio)
Hans.	Hansbrough (Va.)
Har.	Harrington (Del.)
	Harrington's Chancery (Mich.)
	Harrison (La.)
	Harrison's Chancery (Mich.)
Harc.	Harcarse, Decisions (Sc.)
Hard.	Hardesty Term Reports (Del.)
Hardes.	Same
Hardin	Hardin (Ky.)
Hardres	Hardres' Exchequer (Eng.)
Hare	Hare's Vice-Chancery (Eng.)
Hare & W.	American Leading Cases, Hare & Wallace
Harg.	Hargrove (N.C.)
Harp.	Harper's Equity (S.C.)
	Harper's Law (S.C.)
Harper	Harper's Conspiracy Cases (Md.)
Harr.	Harrington
Harr.	Harrison (Ind.)
	Harrison (N.J.)
Harr. & H.	Harrison & Hodgins' Municipal Reports (Upper Can.)
Harr. & Hodg.	Same
Harr. & J.	Harris & Johnson (Md.)
Harr. & M.	Harris & McHenry (Md.)
Harr. & R.	Harrison & Rutherford's Common Pleas (Eng.)
Harr. & W.	Harrison & Wollaston's King's Bench (Eng.)
Harr.Ch.	Harrison's Chancery (Eng.)
Harris	Harris (Pa.)
Harris & G.	Harris & Gill (Md.)
Harris & S.	Harris & Simrall (Miss.)
Hart.	Hartley (Tex.)
Hart. & H.	Hartley & Hartley (Tex.)
Harv.Bus.Rev.	Harvard Business Review
Harv.C.R.—C.L.L.Rev.	Harvard Civil Rights–Civil Liberties Law Review
Harv.Envt'l L. Rev.	Harvard Environmental Law Review
Harv.Int'l L.J.	Harvard International Law Journal
Harv.J.L. & Pub.Pol'y	Harvard Journal of Law and Public Policy
Harv.J.Legis.	Harvard Journal on Legislation
Harv.L.Rev.	Harvard Law Review
Harv.L.S.Bull.	Harvard Law School Bulletin
Harv.W.Tax Ser.	Harvard World Tax Series (CCH)
Harv.Women L.J.	Harvard's Women's Law Journal
Hasb.	Hasbrouck (Idaho)
Hask.	Haskell (U.S. Mine) (Fox's Decisions)
Hast.	Hastings (Me.)
Hastings Const.L.Q.	Hastings Constitutional Law Quarterly
Hastings Int'l & Comp.L. Rev.	Hastings International and Comparative Law Review
Hastings L.J.	Hastings Law Journal
Havil.	Haviland (Prince Edward Island)
Hawaii	Hawaii Reports
Hawaii B.J.	Hawaii Bar Journal
Hawk.	Hawkins' Louisiana Annual
Hawk.P.C.	Hawkins' Pleas of the Crown
Hawks	Hawks (N.C.)
Hawl.	Hawley (Nev.)
Hay & H.	Hay & Hazelton (U.S.)
Hay & M.	Hay & Marriott's Admiralty (Eng.)
Hay.	Haywood
Hayes	Hayes' Exchequer (Ir.)
	Hayes (Sc.)
Hayes & J.	Hayes & Jones' Exchequer (Ir.)

Hayw.	Haywood (N.C.)
	Haywood (Tenn.)
Haz.Reg.	Hazard's Register (Pa.)
Head	Head (Tenn.)
Heath	Heath (Me.)
Hedges	Hedges (Mont.)
Heisk.	Heiskell (Tenn.)
Helm	Helm (Nev.)
Hem. & M.	Heming & Miller's Vice-Chancery (Eng.)
Heming.	Hemingway (Miss.)
Hemp.	Hempstead's Circuit Court Reports
Hempst.	Hempstead (U.S.)
Hen. & M.	Hening & Munford (Va.)
Henn.Law.	Hennepin Lawyer
Henning CLE Rep.	Henning CLE Reporter
Hepb.	Hepburn (Colo.)
Het.	Hetley's Common Pleas (Eng.)
Hibb.	Hibbard (N.H.)
Hight	Hight (Iowa)
Hil.T.	Hilary Term (Eng.)
Hill	Hill (Ill.)
	Hill (N.Y.)
	Hill's Equity (S.C.)
	Hill's Law (S.C.)
Hill & D.	Hill & Denio (N.Y.)
Hillyer	Hillyer (Cal.)
Hilt.	Hilton (N.Y.)
Hines	Hines (Ky.)
Hitotsubashi J.L. & Pol.	Hitotsubashi Journal of Law and Politics
Hob.	Hobart's Common Pleas & Chancery (Eng.)
Hobart	Hobart's King's Bench (Eng.)
Hod.	Hodges' Common Pleas (Eng.)
Hodg.El.	Hodgin's Election (Upper Can.)
Hodges	Hodges' Common Pleas (Eng.)
Hoffm.	Hoffman's Chancery (N.Y.)
	Hoffman's Land Cases (U.S.)
Hofstra L. Rev.	Hofstra Law Review
Hog.	Hogan's Rolls Court (Ir.)
Hogue	Hogue (Fla.)
Holl.	Hollingshead (Minn.)
Holmes	Holmes (Ore.)
	Holmes (U.S.)
Holt Adm.	Holt's Admiralty Cases (Eng.)
Holt Eq.	Holt's Equity Vice-Chancery (Eng.)
Holt K.B.	Holt's King's Bench (Eng.)
Holt N.P.	Holt's Nisi Prius (Eng.)
Home	Home MSS. Decisions, Court of Sessions (Sc.)
Hong Kong L.J.	Hong Kong Law Journal
Hook.	Hooker (Conn.)
Hope Dec.	Hope's Decisions (Sc.)
Hopk.	Hopkins' Chancery (N.Y.)
Hopk.Dec.	Hopkinson's Admiralty Decisions (Pa.)
Hopw. & C.	Hopwood & Coltman's Registration Appeal Cases (Eng.)
Hopw. & P.	Hopwood & Philbrick's Registration Appeal Cases (Eng.)
Horner	Horner (S.D.)
Horw.Y.B.	(Horwood) Year Book of Edward I
Hosea	Hosea (Ohio)
Hoskins	Hoskins (N.D.)
Houghton	Houghton (Ala.)
Hous.J.Int'l L.	Houston Journal of International Law
Hous.L.Rev.	Houston Law Review
Hous.Law.	Houston Lawyer
Housing & Devel.Rep.	Housing and Development Reporter (BNA)
Houst.	Houston (Del.)
Houst.Cr.	Houston Criminal Cases (Del.)
Houst.L.Rev.	Houston Law Review
Houston Law.	Houston Lawyer
Hov.	Hovenden's Supplement, Vesey's Chancery (Eng.)
How.	Howard (Miss.)
	Howard (U.S. Supreme Court)
	Howell (Nev.)
How. & Beat.	Howell & Beatty (Nev.)
How. & N.	Howell & Norcross (Nev.)
How.A.Cas.	Howard's Appeal Cases (N.Y.)
How.Ch.	Howard's Chancery (Ir.)
How.L.J.	Howard Law Journal
How.N.P.	Howell's Nisi Prius (Mich.)
How.Pr.	Howard's Practice (N.Y.)
How.Pr. (N.S.)	Same, New Series
How.St.Tr.	Howell's State Trials (Eng.)
Howard L.J.	Howard Law Journal
Hubb.	Hubbard (Me.)
Hud. & B.	Hudson & Brooke's King's Bench (Ir.)

Hughes	Hughes (Ky.)
	Hughes (U.S.)
Human Rights	Human Rights
Human Rights J.	Human Rights Journal
Human Rights Rev.	Human Rights Review
Human Rights U.S.S.R.	Human Rights in U.S.S.R.
Hume	Hume's Decisions (Sc.)
Humph.	Humphrey
Humphr.	Humphrey's (Tenn.)
Hun	Hun (N.Y.)
Hung.L.Rev.	Hungarian Law Review
Hunt.Torrens	Hunter's Torrens Cases
Hurl. & G.	Hurlstone & Gordon's Exchequer (Eng.)
Hurl. & W.	Hurlstone & Walmsley's Exchequer (Eng.)
Hutch.	Hutcheson (Ala.)
Hutt.	Hutton's Common Pleas (Eng.)

I

I. & N.Dec.	Immigration and Nationality Decisions
[ ] I.A.C.	Immigration Appeal Cases 1970–
ICC	Interstate Commerce Commission
I.C.C.Pract.J.	Interstate Commerce Commission Practitioners' Journal
I.C.J.	International Court of Justice Reports
I.C.J.Y.B.	Yearbook of the International Court of Justice
I.D.	Interior Department Decisions, Public Land (Since v. 53)
IIC	International Review of Industrial Property and Copyright Law
I.L.C.Newsl.	International Legal Center Newsletter
I.L.E.	Indiana Law Encyclopedia
I.L.P.	Illinois Law and Practice
I.L.R.	Insurance Law Reporter (Can.)
	International Law Reports
I.L.W.	Investment Laws of the World (Oceana)
I.O.C.C.Bull.	Interstate Oil Compact Commission Bulletin
I.R.	Internal Revenue Decisions
I.R.B.	Internal Revenue Bulletin
I.R.C.	Internal Revenue Code
I.R.R.Newsl.	Individual Rights and Responsibilities Newsletter
ISL L.Rev.	ISL Law Review
IT	Internal Revenue Bulletin
I.T.R.	Irish Term Reports (Ridgeway)
Idaho	Idaho Reports
Idaho L.J.	Idaho Law Journal
Idaho L.Rev.	Idaho Law Review
Idd.T.R.	Idding's Term Reports (Dayton, Ohio)
Idding	Same
Iddings T.R.D.	Same
Idea	Idea
Ill.	Illinois Reports
Ill.2d	Same, Second Series
Ill.App.	Illinois Appellate Court
Ill.App.2d	Same, Second Series
Ill.App.3d	Same, Third Series
Ill.B.J.	Illinois Bar Journal
Ill.Cir.	Illinois Circuit Court
Ill.Cont.L.Ed.	Illinois Continuing Legal Education
Ill.Cont. Legal Ed.	Same
Ill.Ct.Cl.	Illinois Court of Claims Reports
Ill.L.B.	Illinois Law Bulletin
Ill.L.Q.	Illinois Law Quarterly
Ill.L.Rev.	Illinois Law Review
Immig.B.Bull.	Immigration Bar Bulletin
Immig.Newsl.	Immigration Newsletter
Ind.	Indiana
Ind. & Intell. Prop.Austl.	Industrial and Intellectual Property in Australia
Ind. & Lab. Rel.Rev.	Industrial and Labor Relations Review
Ind.Advocate	Indian Advocate
Ind.App.	Indiana Appellate Court Reports
Ind.Cl.Comm.	Indian Claims Commission Decisions
Ind.J. Int'l L.	Indian Journal of International Law
Ind.L.J.	Indiana Law Journal
Ind.L.Q.Rev.	Indian Law Quarterly Review
Ind.L.Rev.	Indiana Law Review
	Indian Law Review
Ind.L.Stud.	Indiana Law Student
Ind.Legal F.	Indiana Legal Forum
Ind.Prop.	Industrial Property
Ind.Prop.Q.	Industrial Property Quarterly
Ind.Rel.J. Econ. & Soc.	Industrial Relations: Journal of Economy and Society
Ind.S.C.	Indiana Superior Court

Ind.Y.B.Int'l Aff.	Indian Yearbook of International Affairs
India Crim. L.J.R.	India Criminal Law Journal Reports
India S.Ct.	India Supreme Court Reports
Indian Cas.	Indian Cases
Indian Jurist	Indian Jurist
Indian L.J.	Indian Law Journal
Indian L.R. [e.g.] Allahabad Ser.	Indian Law Reports [e.g.] Allahabad Series
Indian Rul.	Indian Rulings
Indian Terr.	Indian Territory Reports
Indus.L.J.	Industrial Law Journal
Indus.L.Rev.	Industrial Law Review
Indus.Rel.L.J.	Industrial Relations Law Journal
Inequal.Ed.	Inequality in Education
Ins.Counsel J.	Insurance Counsel Journal
Ins.Liability Rep.	Insurance Liability Reporter
Ins.L.J.	Insurance Law Journal (Pa.)
Ins.L.Rep.	Insurance Law Reporter (CCH)
Inst.Ad.Legal Stud.Ann.	Institute of Advanced Legal Studies Annual
Inst.Est.Plan.	Institute on Estate Planning (U. of Miami)
Inst.Lab.Rel. Bull.	Institute for Labor Relations Bulletin
Inst.Min.L.	Institute on Mineral Law (La.S.U.)
Inst.Plan. & Zoning	Institute on Planning and Zoning
Inst.Plan., Zoning & E.D.	Institute on Planning, Zoning and Eminent Domain
Inst.Sec.Reg.	Institute on Securities Regulation (PLI)
Int.Arb.J.	International Arbitration Journal
Int.Jurid. Assn.Bull.	International Juridical Association Bulletin
Int.Rev.Bull.	Internal Revenue Bulletin
Int.Rev. Code	Internal Revenue Code
Int.Rev.Code of 1954	Internal Revenue Code of 1954
Int.Rev.Rec.	Internal Revenue Record
Intell.Prop.L. Rev.	Intellectual Property Law Review
Inter Alia	Inter Alia
Inter-Am.L. Rev.	Inter-American Law Review
Interior Dec.	United States Interior Department Decisions
Int'l & Comp. L.Bull.	International and Comparative Law Bulletin
Int'l & Comp. L.Q.	International and Comparative Law Quarterly
Int'l Aff.	International Affairs
Int'l Arb. Awards	Reports of International Arbitral Awards
Int'l Arb.J.	International Arbitration Journal
Int'l B.J.	International Bar Journal
Int'l Bus. Lawyer	International Business Lawyer
Int'l Bus.Ser.	International Business Series (Ernst & Ernst)
Int'l Concil.	International Conciliation
Int'l Crim. Pol.Rev.	International Criminal Police Review
Int'l Dig. Health Leg.	International Digest of Health Legislation
Int'l Encycl. Comp.L.	International Encyclopedia of Comparative Law
Int'l J.	International Journal
Int'l J.Crim. & Pen.	International Journal of Criminology and Penology
Int'l J.L. & Psych.	International Journal of Law and Psychiatry
Int'l J.L.Lib.	International Journal of Law Libraries
Int'l J.Legal Res.	International Journal of Legal Research
Int'l J.Off. Ther. & Comp.Crim.	International Journal of Offender Therapy and Comparative Criminology
Int'l J.Pol.	International Journal of Politics
Int'l J.Soc.L.	International Journal of the Sociology of the Law
Int'l Jurid. Ass'n Bull.	International Juridical Association Monthly Bulletin
Int'l L.Doc.	International Law Documents
Int'l L.News	International Law News
Int'l L.Persp.	International Law Perspective
Int'l L.Q.	International Law Quarterly
Int'l L.Stud.	International Law Studies
Int'l Lab.Rev.	International Labour Review
Int'l Law.	The International Lawyer
Int'l Legal Ed.Newsl.	International Legal Education Newsletter
Int'l Legal Materials	International Legal Materials
Int'l Rev.Ad. Sci.	International Review of Administrative Sciences
Int'l Rev.Crim. Policy	International Review of Criminal Policy
Int'l Soc'y of Barr.Q.	International Society of Barristers Quarterly
Int'l Survey L.D.L.L.	International Survey of Legal Decisions on Labour Laws
Int'l Sym. Comp.L.	International Symposium on Comparative Law
Int'l Tax J.	International Tax Journal
Int'l Trade L.J.	International Trade Law Journal
Int'l Woman Law.	International Woman Lawyer
Intramural L.J.	Intramural Law Journal

Intramural L.Rev.	Intramural Law Review
Iowa	Iowa Reports
Iowa L.B.	Iowa Law Bulletin
Iowa L.Rev.	Iowa Law Review
Ir.	Law Reports (Ir.)
Ir.C.L.	Irish Common Law
Ir.Ch.	Irish Chancery
Ir.Cir.	Irish Circuit Reports
Ir.Eccl.	Irish Ecclesiastical Reports
Ir.Eq.	Irish Equity
Ir.Jur.	Irish Jurist
Ir.L. & Eq.	Irish Law & Equity
Ir.L.T.R.	Irish Law Times Reports
Ir.R.	Irish Reports
Ir.R.C.L.	Irish Reports Common Law
Ir.R.Eq.	Irish Reports Equity
Ired.	Iredell's Law (N.C.)
Ired.Eq.	Iredell's Equity (N.C.)
Irv.Just.	Irvine's Justiciary (Sc.)
Israel L.Rev.	Israel Law Review
Israel Y.B. Human Rights	Israel Yearbook on Human Rights
Issues Crim.	Issues in Criminology
Iustitia	Iustitia

J

J. & C.	Jones & Cary's Exchequer (Ir.)
J. & H.	Johnson & Hemming's Chancery (Eng.)
J. & L.	Jones & La Touche's Chancery (Ir.)
J. & La T.	Same
J. & S.	Jones & Spencer's Superior Court (N.Y.)
J. & W.	Jacob & Walker's Chancery (Eng.)
JAG Bull.	JAG Bulletin (USAF)
JAG J.	JAG Journal
JAG L.Rev.	United States Air Force JAG Law Review
J.A.M.A.	Journal of the American Medical Association
J.Accountancy	Journal of Accountancy
J.Afr.L.	Journal of African Law
J.Air L. & Com.	Journal of Air Law and Commerce
J.Am.Jud. Soc'y	Journal of the American Judicature Society
J.Am.Soc'y C.L.U.	Journal of the American Society of Chartered Life Underwriters
J.Ass'n L. Teachers	Journal of the Association of Law Teachers
J.B.Ass'n D.C.	Journal Bar Association of the District of Columbia
J.B.Ass'n St.Kan.	Journal of the Bar Association of the State of Kansas
J.B.Moore	J. B. Moore's Common Pleas (Eng.)
J.Beverly Hills B.Ass'n	Journal of the Beverly Hills Bar Association
J.Bridg.	Sir John Bridgman's Common Pleas (Eng.)
J.Bridgm.	Same
J.Bus.L.	Journal of Business Law
J.C.	Johnson's Cases (N.Y.)
J.C. & U.L.	The Journal of College & University Law
J.C.N.P.S.	Journal of Collective Negotiations in the Public Sector
J.C.R.	Johnson's Chancery (N.Y.)
J.Can.B.Ass'n	Journal of the Canadian Bar Association
	Johnson's Chancery (N.Y.)
J.Ceylon L.	Journal of Ceylon Law
J.Ch.	Johnson's Chancery (N.Y.)
J.Church & St.	Journal of Church and State
J.Coll. & U.L.	Journal of College and University Law
J.Comm.Mkt. Stud.	Journal of Common Market Studies
J.Comp.Leg. & Int'l L.3d	Journal of Comparative Legislation and International Law, Third Series
J.Confl.Res.	Journal of Conflict Resolution
J.Cons.Affairs	Journal of Consumer Affairs
J.Const. & Parl.Stud.	Journal of Constitutional and Parliamentary Studies
J.Contemp.L.	Journal of Contemporary Law
J.Contemp. R.D.L.	Journal of Contemporary Roman-Dutch Law
J.Corp.L.	Journal of Corporation Law
J.Corp.Tax.	Journal of Corporate Taxation
J.Crim.Just.	Journal of Criminal Justice
J.Crim.L. (Eng.)	Journal of Criminal Law (Eng.)
J.Crim.L. (U.S.)	Journal of Criminal Law and Criminology (U.S.)
J.Crim.L. & Criminology	Journal of Criminal Law and Criminology

J.Crim.L., C. & P.S.	Journal of Criminal Law, Criminology and Police Science
J.Crim.Sci.	Journal of Criminal Science
J.D.	Juris Doctor
J.Denning L.Soc'y	Journal of the Denning Law Society
J.Energy & Devel.	Journal of Energy and Development
J.Eth.L.	Journal of Ethiopian Law
J.Fam.L.	Journal of Family Law
J.For.Med.	Journal of Forensic Medicine
J.For.Med. Soc'y	Journal of the Forensic Medicine Society
J.For.Sci.	Journal of Forensic Sciences
J.For.Sci. Soc'y	Journal of the Forensic Science Society
J.Health Pol. Pol'y & L.	Journal of Health, Politics, Policy & Law
J.Ind.L.Inst.	Journal of the Indian Law Institute
J.Int'l Aff.	Journal of International Affairs
J.Int'l Comm.Jur.	Journal of the International Commission of Jurists
J.Int'l L. & Dipl.	Journal of International Law and Diplomacy
J.Int'l L. & Econ.	Journal of International Law and Economics
J.Int'l L. & Pol.	Journal of International Law and Politics
J.Islam. & Comp.L.	Journal of Islamic and Comparative Law
J.J.Mar.	J. J. Marshall (Ky.)
J.J.Marsh. (Ky.)	Same
J.Juris.	Journal of Jurisprudence
J.Juv.L.	Journal of Juvenile Law
J.Kan.B.Ass'n	Journal of the Kansas Bar Association
J.L.	Journal of Law
J.L. & Econ.	Journal of Law & Economics
J.L. & Educ.	Journal of Law and Education
J.L. & Pol.	Journal of Law and Politics
J.L.Soc'y	Journal of the Law Society of Scotland
J.Land & P.U.Econ.	Journal of Land and Public Utility Economics
J.Law & Econ.	Journal of Law and Economics
J.Law & Econ.Dev.	Journal of Law and Economic Development
J.Law Reform	Journal of Law Reform
J.Legal Ed.	Journal of Legal Education
J.Legal Educ.	Journal of Legal Education
J.Legal Med.	Journal of Legal Medicine
J.Legal Prof.	Journal of the Legal Profession
J.Legal Stud.	Journal of Legal Studies
J.Legis.	Journal of Legislation
J.Mar.J.Prac. & Proc.	John Marshall Journal of Practice and Procedure
J.Mar.L.J.	John Marshall Law Journal
J.Mar.L.Q.	John Marshall Law Quarterly
J.Mar.Law & Com.	Journal of Maritime Law and Commerce
J.Mo.Bar	Journal of the Missouri Bar
J.P.	Justice of the Peace (Eng.)
J.P.Sm.	J. P. Smith's King's Bench (Eng.)
J.Pat.Off. Soc'y	Journal of the Patent Office Society
J.Pension Plan. & Compliance	Journal of Pension Planning & Compliance
J.Plan. & Env.L.	Journal of Planning and Environment Law
J.Pol.Sci. & Admin.	Journal of Police Science and Administration
J.Prod.Liability	Journal of Products Liability
J.Psych. & L.	Journal of Psychiatry and Law
J.Pub.L.	Journal of Public Law
J.R.	Johnson (N.Y.)
J.Radio L.	Journal of Radio Law
J.Real Est. Tax.	Journal of Real Estate Taxation
J.Reprints Antitrust L. & Econ.	Journal of Reprints for Antitrust Law and Economics
J.S.Gr.(N.J.)	J. S. Green (N.J.)
J.Soc.Welfare L.	Journal of Social Welfare Law
J.Soc'y Comp. Leg.	Journal of the Society of Comparative Legislation
J.Soc'y Pub. Tchrs. L.	Journal of the Society of Public Teachers of Law
J.Space L.	Journal of Space Law
J.World Trade L.	Journal of World Trade Law
Jac.	Jacob's Chancery (Eng.)
Jac. & W.	Jacob & Walker's Chancery (Eng.)
Jac. & Walk.	Same
Jac.L.Dict.	Jacob's Law Dictionary
Jack.	Jackson (Ga.)
Jack. & L.	Jackson & Lumpkin (Ga.)
Jack.Tex.App.	Jackson's Texas Appeals
James	James' Reports (Nova Scotia)

James. & Mont.	Jameson & Montagu's Bankruptcy (Eng.)
Jap.Ann.Int'l L.	Japanese Annual of International Law
Japan Ann.L. & Pol.	Japan Annual of Law and Politics
Jebb	Jebb's Crown Cases (Ir.)
Jebb & B.	Jebb & Bourke's Queen's Bench (Ir.)
Jebb & S.	Jebb & Symes' Queen's Bench (Ir.)
Jebb & Sym.	Same
Jebb C.C.	Jebb's Crown Cases (Ir.)
Jeff.	Jefferson (Va.)
Jenk.	Jenkins' Exchequer (Eng.)
Jenk.Cent.	Same
Jenks	Jenks' (N.H.)
Jenn.	Jennison (Mich.)
Jew.Y.B. Int'l L.	Jewish Yearbook of International Law
Jo. & La T.	Jones & La Touche's Chancery (Ir.)
John.	Johnson (N.Y.)
	Johnson's Vice-Chancery (Eng.)
John Mar.J. Prac. & Proc.	John Marshall Journal of Practice and Procedure
John Marsh. L.J.	John Marshall Law Journal
John Marsh. L.Q.	John Marshall Law Quarterly
Johns.	Johnson (N.Y.)
	Johnson's Vice-Chancery (Eng.)
Johns. & H.	Johnson & Hemming's Chancery (Eng.)
Johns. & Hem.	Same
Johns.Cas.	Johnson's Cases (N.Y.)
Johns.Ch.	Johnson's Chancery Decisions (Md.)
	Johnson's Chancery (N.Y.)
Johns.Ct.Err.	Johnson's Court of Errors (N.Y.)
Johns.Dec.	Johnson's Chancery Decisions (Md.)
Johns.N.Z.	Johnson's New Zealand Reports
Johns.U.S.	Johnson's U. S. Circuit Court Decisions
Jon. & L.	Jones & La Touche's Chancery (Ir.)
Jon. & La T.	Same
Jones	Jones (Ala.) (Mo.) (Pa.)
	Jones' Exchequer (Ir.)
	Jones' Law or Equity
	Jones, T., King's Bench (Eng.)
	Jones' Reports (Upper Can.)
	Jones, W., King's Bench (Eng.)
Jones & C.	Jones & Cary's Exchequer (Ir.)
Jones & L.	Jones & La Touche's Chancery (Ir.)
Jones & La T.	Same
Jones & McM. (Pa.)	Jones & McMurtrie (Pa.)
Jones & S.	Jones & Spencer's Superior Court (N.Y.)
Jones & Spen.	Same
Jones, B. & W. (Mo.)	Jones, Barclay & Whittelsey (Mo.)
Josephs	Josephs (Mo.)
Jud.Rep.	Judicial Repository (N.Y.)
Jud.Conduct Rep.	Judicial Conduct Reporter
Jud.Repos.	Same
Judd	Judd (Hawaii)
Judge Advoc. J.	The Judge Advocate Journal
Judges' J.	Judges' Journal
Judge's J.	Judge's Journal
Judicature	Journal of the American Judicature Society
	Judicature
Jur.	Jurist (Eng.)
Jur. (N.S.)	Jurist, New Series
Jurid.Rev.	Juridical Review
Jurimetrics J.	Jurimetrics Journal
Juris.	Jurisprudence
Jurist	Jurist (Wash., D. C.)
Just.Cas.	Justiciary Cases
Just.L.R.	Justice's Law Reporter (Pa.)
Just.P.	Justice of the Peace and Local Government Review
Just.Syst.J.	Justice System Journal
Justinian	Justinian
Juv. & Fam. Courts J.	Juvenile and Family Courts Journal
Juv.Ct.J.	Juvenile Court Journal
Juv.Ct. Judges J.	Juvenile Court Judges Journal
Juv.Just.	Juvenile Justice

K

K. & G.	Keane & Grant's Registration Appeal Cases (Eng.)
K. & Gr.	Same
K. & G.R.C.	Same
K.B.	Law Reports King's Bench (Eng.)
K.Counsel	King's Counsel

K.L.R.	Kenya Law Reports
Kames Dec.	Kames' Decisions (Sc.)
Kames Elucid.	Kames' Elucidation (Sc.)
Kames Rem. Dec.	Kames' Remarkable Decisions (Sc.)
Kames Sel. Dec.	Kames' Select Decisions (Sc.)
Kan.	Kansas
Kan.App.	Kansas Appeals
Kan.B.Ass'n J.	Kansas Bar Association Journal
Kan.C.L.Rep.	Kansas City Law Reporter
Kan.City L.Rev.	Kansas City Law Review
Kan.L.J.	Kansas Law Journal
Kan.L.Rev.	University of Kansas Law Review
Kan.St.L.J.	Kansas State Law Journal
Karachi L.J.	Karachi Law Journal (Pakistan)
Kay	Kay's Vice-Chancery (Eng.)
Kay & J.	Kay & Johnson's Chancery (Eng.)
Ke.	Keen's Rolls Court (Eng.)
Keane & G. R.C.	Keane & Grant's Registration Appeal Cases (Eng.)
Keane & Gr.	Same
Keb.	Keble's King's Bench (Eng.)
Keen	Keen's Rolls Court (Eng.)
Keil.	Keilway's King's Bench (Eng.)
Kel.C.C.	Kelyng's Crown Cases (Eng.)
Kel.W.	Kelyng's Chancery (Eng.)
Kellen	Kellen (Mass.)
Kelly	Kelly (Ga.)
Kelly & C.	Kelly & Cobb (Ga.)
Kenan	Kenan (N.C.)
Keny.	Kenyon (Lord) King's Bench (Eng.)
	Kenyon, Notes (Hammer)
Keny.Ch.	Kenyon's Chancery (Eng.)
Kenya L.R.	Kenya Law Reports
Kerala L.J.	Kerala Law Journal
Kern	Kern (Md.)
Kern.	Kernan (N.Y.)
Kerr	Kerr (Ind.)
	Kerr (N.B.)
	Kerr's Civil Procedure (N.Y.)
Keyes	Keyes (N.Y.)
Kilk.	Kilkerran's Decisions (Sc.)
Kilkerran	Same
King	King's Civil Practice Cases (Colo.)
	King's Louisiana Annual
Kingston L.Rev.	Kingston Law Review
Kirby	Kirby (Conn.)
Kn.P.C.	Knapp's Privy Council (Eng.)
Knapp	Knapp's Privy Council (Eng.)
Knapp & O.	Knapp & Ombler's Election Cases (Eng.)
Knight's Ind.	Knight's Industrial Reports
Knowles	Knowles (R.I.)
Knox	Knox (N.S.W.)
Knox & F.	Knox & Fitzhardinge (N.S.W.)
Kobe U.L.Rev.	Kobe University Law Review
Korea L.Rev.	Korea Law Review
Korean J. Comp.L.	Korean Journal of Comparative Law
Korean J. Int'l L.	Korean Journal of International Law
Korean L.	Korean Law
Kreider	Kreider (Wash.)
Kress	Kress (Pa.)
Kulp	Kulp (Pa.)
Kwansei Gak. L.Rev.	Kwansei Gaknin Law Review
Ky.Bench & B.	Ky Bench and Bar
Ky.	Kentucky
Ky.Comment'r	Kentucky Commentator
Ky.Dec.	Kentucky Decisions
Ky.L.J.	Kentucky Law Journal
Ky.L.R.	Kentucky Law Reporter
Ky.L.Rptr.	Same
Ky.Op.	Kentucky Opinions
Ky.St.B.J.	Kentucky State Bar Journal
Kyoto L.Rev.	Kyoto Law Review

L

L. & B.Bull.	Weekly Law and Bank Bulletin (Ohio)
L. & C.	Leigh & Cave's Crown Cases Reserved (Eng.)
L. & C.	Lefroy and Cassels' Practice Cases (Ont.)
L. & Computer Tech.	Law and Computer Technology
L. & E.	English Law & Equity Reports (Boston)
L. & E.Rep.	Law & Equity Reporter (N.Y.)
L. & Just.	Law and Justice
L. & Leg. GDR	Law and Legislation in the German Democratic Republic
L. & Lib.	Law and Liberty

L. & M.	Lowndes & Maxwell, Bail Cases (Eng.)
L. & Order	Law and Order
L. & Psych. Rev.	Law and Psychology Review
L.A.B.J.	Los Angeles Bar Journal
L.A.C.	Labour Arbitration Cases
L.A.G.Bull.	L.A.G. Bulletin
L.A.J.P.E.L.	Latin American Journal of Politics, Economics and Law
L.Advertiser	Law Advertiser
L.Am.Soc'y	Law in American Society
L.Book Adviser	Law Book Adviser
L.C.	Lower Canada
L.C.D.	Ohio Decisions (Ohio Lower Decisions)
L.C.Jur.	Lower Canada Jurist
L.C.L.J.	Lower Canada Law Journal
L.C.R.	Land Compensation Reports 1971–
L.C.Rep.S.Qu.	Lower Canada Reports Seignorial Questions
L.Chron.	Law Chronicle
L.Chron. & L. Stud.Mag.	Law Chronicle and Law Students' Magazine
L.Chron. & L. Stud.Mag., (N.S.)	Law Chronicle and Law Students' Magazine, New Series
L.Coach	Law Coach
L.Comment'y	Law Commentary
L.D.	Land Office Decisions (U.S.)
L.D.L.R.	Land Development Law Reporter
L.East.Eur.	Law in Eastern Europe
L.Ed.	Lawyers' Edition, U. S. Supreme Court Reports
L.Ed.2d	Same, Second Series
L.G.	Law Glossary
L.Gaz.	Law Gazette
L.Guard.	Law Guardian
L. in Soc'y	Law in Society
L. in Trans.Q.	Law in Transition Quarterly
L.Inst.J.	Law Institute Journal
L.Inst.J. Vict.	Law Institute Journal of Victoria
L.J.Adm.	Law Journal Admiralty (Eng.)
L.J.Bankr.	Law Journal Bankruptcy (Eng.)
L.J.C.P.	Law Journal Common Pleas, Old Series (Eng.)
L.J.C.P. (O.S.)	Law Journal Common Pleas Old Series (Eng.)
L.J.Ch.	Law Journal Chancery, New Series (Eng.)
L.J.Ch. (O.S.)	Law Journal Chancery, Old Series (Eng.)
L.J.Eccl.	Law Journal Ecclesiastical (Eng.)
L.J.Exch.	Law Journal Exchequer, New Series (Eng.)
L.J.Exch. (O.S.)	Law Journal Exchequer, Old Series (Eng.)
L.J.H.L.	Law Journal House of Lords, New Series
L.J.K.B.	Law Journal King's Bench, New Series (Eng.)
L.J.K.B. (O.S.)	Law Journal King's Bench, Old Series (Eng.)
L.J.M.C.	Law Journal Magistrate Cases, New Series (Eng.)
L.J.M.C. (O.S.)	Law Journal Magistrate Cases, Old Series (Eng.)
L.J.Mag.	Law Journal New Series Common Law, Magistrates Cases (discontinued)
L.J.N.C.	Law Journal Notes of Cases (Eng.)
L.J.O.S.	Law Journal, Old Series (1822–1830)
L.J.P. & M.	Law Journal Probate & Matrimonial (Eng.)
L.J.P.C.	Law Journal Privy Council (Eng.)
L.J.P.C. (N.S.)	Same, New Series
L.J.P.D. & Adm.	Law Journal Probate, Divorce & Admiralty (Eng.)
L.J.Q.B.	Law Journal Queen's Bench, New Series (Eng.)
L.Japan	Law in Japan
L.L.J.	Law Library Journal
L.Lib.	Law Librarian
L.Lib.J.	Law Library Journal
L.M. & P.	Lowndes, Maxwell & Pollock's Bail Cases (Eng.)
L.M.C.L.Q.	Lloyd's Maritime and Commercial Law Quarterly
L.Mag. & Rev.	Law Magazine and Review
L.N.T.S.	League of Nations Treaty Series
L.Notes Gen. Pract.	Law Notes for the General Practitioner
L.Off.Econ. & Mgt.	Law Office Economics and Management
L.Q.	Law Quarterly
L.Q.Rev.	Law Quarterly Review
L.R.	Law Recorder (Ir.)
	Law Reports (Eng.)
	Ohio Law Reporter
L.R.A.	Lawyers' Reports Annotated (U.S.)
L.R.A. & E.	Law Reports Admiralty & Ecclesiastical (Eng.)

L.R.A. (N.S.)	Lawyers' Reports Annotated, New Series
L.R.App.Cas.	Law Reports House of Lords Appeal Cases (Eng.)
L.R.C.C.	Law Reports Crown Cases (Eng.)
L.R.C.C.R.	Law Reports Crown Cases Reserved (Eng.)
L.R.C.P.	Law Reports Common Pleas Cases (Eng.)
L.R.C.P.D.	Law Reports Common Pleas Division (Eng.)
L.R.Ch.	Law Reports Chancery Appeal Cases (Eng.)
L.R.Ch.D.	Law Reports Chancery Division (Eng.)
L.R.Eq.	Law Reports Equity Cases (Eng.)
L.R.Exch.	Law Reports Exchequer Cases (Eng.)
L.R.Exch.D.	Law Reports Exchequer Division (Eng.)
L.R.H.L.	Law Reports House of Lords (English & Irish Appeal Cases)
L.R.H.L.Sc.	Law Reports, House of Lords (Scotch Appeal Cases)
L.R.Indian App.	Law Reports. Indian Appeals (Eng.)
L.R.Ir.	Law Reports (Ir.)
L.R. (N.S.)	Irish Law Recorder, New Series
L.R.N.S.W.	Law Reports New South Wales
L.R.P.C.	Law Reports Privy Council (Eng.)
L.R.P. & D.	Law Reports Probate & Divorce (Eng.)
L.R.Q.B.	Law Reports, Queen's Bench (Eng.)
L.R.Q.B.Div.	Law Reports, Queen's Bench Division (Eng.)
L.R.R.	Labor Relations Reporter
L.R.R.M.	Labor Relations Reference Manual (BNA)
L.R.S.A.	Law Reports, South Australia
L.Record.	Law Recorder
L.Rev.Dig.	Law Review Digest
L.S.G.	Law Society Gazette (Eng.)
L.Stud.Helper	Law Student's Helper
L.Stud.J.	Law Students' Journal
L.T.	Law Times (Pa.)
L.T. (N.S.)	Law Times, New Series (Eng.)
L.T. (O.S.)	Law Times, Old Series (Eng.)
L.T.G.F. Newsl.	Lawyers' Title Guaranty Funds Newsletter
L.T.R. (N.S.)	Law Times Reports, New Series (Eng.)
L.T.Rep.N.S.	Law Times, Reports, New Series (Eng.)
L.Teacher	Law Teacher
L.Trans.Q.	Law in Transition Quarterly
La.	Louisiana
La.Ann.	Louisiana Annual
La.App.	Louisiana Appeals
La.App. (Orleans)	Court of Appeal, Parish of Orleans
La.B.J.	Louisiana Bar Journal
La.L.J.	Louisiana Law Journal
La.L.Rev.	Louisiana Law Review
La.T.R.	Martin's Louisiana Term Reports
Lab.	Labatt's District Court (Cal.)
Lab. & Auto. Bull.	Labor and Automation Bulletin
Lab.Arb.	Labor Arbitration Reports (BNA)
Lab.L.J.	Labor Law Journal
Lab.Rel.L. Letter	Labor Relations Law Letter
Lab.Rel.Rep.	Labor Relations Reporter
Lack.Jur.	Lackawanna Jurist (Pa.)
Lack.Leg.N.	Lackawanna Legal News (Pa.)
Lack.Leg.Rec.	Lackawanna Legal Record (Pa.)
Lackawanna B.	Lackawanna Bar
Ladd	Ladd (N.H.)
Lalor	Lalor's Supplement to Hill & Denio (N.Y.)
Lamar	Lamar (Fla.)
Lamb	Lamb (Wis.)
Lanc.Bar	Lancaster Bar (Pa.)
Lanc.L.Rev.	Lancaster Law Review (Pa.)
Land & Water L. Rev.	Land and Water Law Review
Land Dec.	Land Decisions (U.S.)
Land Use & Env.L.Rev.	Land Use and Environment Law Review
Lane	Lane's Exchequer (Eng.)
Lans.	Lansing (Mich.)
Latch	Latch's King's Bench (Eng.)
Lath.	Lathrop (Mass.)
Law	Law
Law & Bk. Bull.	Weekly Law and Bank Bulletin (Ohio)
Law & Computer Tech.	Law and Computer Technology
Law & Contemp.Prob.	Law and Contemporary Problems

Law & Housing J.	Law and Housing Journal
Law & Human Behavior	Law and Human Behavior
Law & Pol'y Int'l Bus.	Law and Policy in International Business
Law & Pol'y Q.	Law and Policy Quarterly
Law & Psych. Rev.	Law and Psychology Review
Law & Soc. Ord.	Law and the Social Order Arizona State Law Journal
Law & Soc'y Rev.	Law and Society Review
Law Cases	Law Cases, Wm. I to Rich. I (Eng.) (Placita Anglo-Normannica)
Law.Committee News	Lawyers Committee News
Law Inst.J.	Law Institute Journal
Law Lib.J.	Law Library Journal
Law.Med.J.	Lawyers Medical Journal
Law Notes	Law Notes
Law Q.Rev.	Law Quarterly Review
Law Rep.	Law Reports (Eng.) (1865–1875)
	Law Reporter (Mass.)
Law Rep. (N.S.)	Law Reports, New Series (N.Y.)
Law Rev.J.	Law Review Journal
Law Soc'y Gaz.	Law Society's Gazette (London)
	Law Society Gazette (Toronto)
Law Soc'y J.	Law Society Journal (Boston)
	Law Society Journal (New South Wales)
Law.	Lawyer
Law. & Magis. Mag.	Lawyer's and Magistrate's Magazine
Law.Am.	Lawyer of the Americas
Lawasia	Lawasia
Lawr.	Lawrence (Ohio)
Lawrence	Same
Lawyer & Banker	Lawyer and Banker and Central Law Journal
Lawyer's Med.J	Lawyers' Medical Journal
Ld.Raym.	Lord Raymond's King's Bench (Eng).
Lea	Lea (Tenn.)
Leach C.C.	Leach's Crown Cases, King's Bench (Eng.)
League of Nations Off.J.	League of Nations Official Journal
Learn. & L.	Learning and the Law
Lect.L.S.U.C.	Special Lectures of the Law Society of Upper Canada
Lee	Lee (Calif.)
Lee Eccl.	Lee's Ecclesiastical (Eng.)
Lee t.Hardw.	Lee temp. Hardwicke, King's Bench (Eng.)
Leese	Leese (Neb.)
Leg. & Ins.R.	Legal & Insurance Reporter (Pa.)
Leg.Chron.	Legal Chronicle (Pa.)
Leg.Gaz.	Legal Gazette Reports (Pa.)
Leg.Int.	Legal Intelligencer (Pa.)
Leg.Op.	Legal Opinions (Pa.)
Leg.Rec.	Legal Record (Pa.)
Leg.Rep.	Legal Reporter (Tenn.)
Leg.Rev.	Legal Review (Eng.)
Legal Aspects Med.Prac.	Legal Aspects of Medical Practice
Legal Med.Ann.	Legal Medicine Annual
Legal Med.Q.	Legal Medical Quarterly
Legal Obser.	Legal Observer
Legal Res.J.	Legal Research Journal
Legal Resp. Child Adv. Protection	Legal Response: Child Advocacy and Protection
Lehigh Co. L.J.	Lehigh County Law Journal (Pa.)
Lehigh Val. L.R.	Lehigh Valley Law Reporter (Pa.)
Leigh	Leigh (Pa.)
Leigh & C.	Leigh & Cave's Crown Cases (Eng.)
Leigh & C. C.C.	Same
Leo.	Leonard, King's Bench, Common Pleas, Exchequer (Eng.)
Leon.	Same
Lester	Lester (Ga.)
Lester & B.	Lester & Butler's Supplement (Ga.)
Lev.	Leving, King's Bench, Common Pleas (Eng.)
Lew.C.C.	Lewin's Crown Cases (Eng.)
Lewis	Lewis (Mo.) (Nev.)
	Lewis' Kentucky Law Reporter
Lex & Sci.	Lex et Scientia
Ley	Ley King's Bench, Common Pleas, Exchequer, Court of Wards and Court of Star Chamber (Eng.)
Liaison	Liaison
Liberian L.J.	Liberian Law Journal

Life Cas.	Life (Health & Accident) Cases (CCH)
Life Cas.2d	Same, Second Series
Lincoln L.Rev.	Lincoln Law Review
Litigation	Litigation
Livingston's M.L.Mag.	Livingston's Monthly Law Magazine
Ll. & G.t.Pl.	Lloyd & Goold temp. Plunkett, Chancery (Ir.)
Ll. & G.t.S.	Lloyd & Goold temp. Sugden, Chancery (Ir.)
Ll. & W.	Lloyd & Welsby Mercantile Cases (Eng.)
Ll.L.Rep.	Lloyd's List Reports (Eng.)
Lloyd's L.Rep.	Lloyds Law Reports
Lloyds Mar. & Com.L.Q.	Lloyds Maritime and Commercial Law Quarterly
Lloyd's Rep.	Lloyd's List Law Reports Admiralty
Local Ct. & Mun.Gaz.	Local Courts and Municipal Gazette
Local Gov't	Local Government and Magisterial Reports
Local Gov't R.Austl.	Local Government Reports of Australia
Lock.Rev.Cas.	Lockwood's Reversed Cases (N.Y.)
Lofft	Lofft's King's Bench (Eng.)
Lois Rec.	Lois Recentes du Canada
London L.Rev.	City of London Law Review
Long & R.	Long & Russell's Election Cases (Mass.)
Long Beach B.Bull.	Long Beach Bar Bulletin
Longf. & T.	Longfield & Townsend's Exchequer (Ir.)
Louisville Law.	Louisville Lawyer
Low.Can. Jurist	Lower Canada Jurist
Low.Can.L.J.	Lower Canada Law Journal
Low.Can.R.	Lower Canadian Reports
Lowell	Lowell (U.S.)
Lower Ct.Dec.	Lower Court Decisions (Ohio)
Loy.L.A.Int'l & Comp.L. Ann.	Loyola of Los Angeles Int'l & Comparative Law Annual
Loy.U.Chi. L.J.	Loyola University of Chicago Law Journal
Loyola Cons. Prot.J.	Loyola Consumer Protection Journal (Los Angeles)
Loyola Dig.	Loyola Digest
Loyola L.A.L.Rev.	Loyola of Los Angeles Law Review
Loyola L.Rev.	Loyola Law Review (New Orleans)
Loyola Law.	Loyola Lawyer
Loyola U.L.J.	Loyola University Law Journal (Chicago)
Ludd.	Ludden (Me.)
Lump.	Lumpkin (Ga.)
Lush.	Lushington's Admiralty (Eng.)
Lutw.	Lutwyche's Common Pleas (Eng.)
Lutw.Reg.Cas.	Lutwyche's Registration Cases (Eng.)
Luz.L.J.	Luzerne Law Journal (Pa.)
Luz.L.T.	Luzerne Law Times (Pa.)
Luz.Leg.Obs.	Luzerne Legal Observer (Pa.)
Luz.Leg.Reg.	Luzerne Legal Register (Pa.)
Lynd.	Lyndwoode, Provinciale (Eng.)
Lyne	Lyne's Chancery (Ir.)

M

M. & A.	Montague & Ayrton's Bankruptcy (Eng.)
M. & Ayr.	Same
M. & B.	Montague & Bligh's Bankruptcy (Eng.)
M. & C.	Montague & Chitty's Bankruptcy (Eng.)
	Mylne & Craig's Chancery (Eng.)
M. & Cht. Bankr.	Montague & Chitty's Bankruptcy (Eng.)
M. & G.	Maddock & Geldhart's Chancery (Eng.)
	Manning & Granger's Common Pleas (Eng.)
M. & Gel.	Maddock & Geldhart's Chancery (Eng.)
M. & Gord.	Macnaghten & Gordon's Chancery (Eng.)
M. & H.	Murphy & Hurlstone's Exchequer (Eng.)
M. & K.	Mylne & Keen's Chancery (Eng.)
M. & M.	Moody & Malkin's Nisi Prius (Eng.)
M. & McA.	Montague & McArthur's Bankruptcy (Eng.)
M. & P.	Moore & Payne's Common Pleas & Exchequer (Eng.)

M. & R.	Maclean & Robinson's Appeal Cases (Sc.)
	Manning & Ryland's King's Bench (Eng.)
	Moody & Robinson's Nisi Prius (Eng.)
M. & R.M.C.	Manning & Ryland's Magistrates' Cases, King's Bench (Eng.)
M. & Rob.	Moody & Robinson's Nisi Prius (Eng.)
M. & S.	Manning & Scott's Common Pleas (Eng.)
	Maule & Selwyn's King's Bench (Eng.)
	Moore & Scott's Common Pleas (Eng.)
M. & Scott	Same
M. & W.	Meeson & Welsby's Exchequer (Eng.)
M. & W.Cas.	Mining & Water Cases (Annotated)
M. & Y.	Martin & Yerger (Tenn.)
M.A.L.C.M.	Mercantile Adjuster and the Lawyer and Credit Man
M.C.C.	Mixed Claims Commission
	Motor Carriers' Cases (I.C.C.)
M.C.J.	Michigan Civil Jurisprudence
M.C.R.	Montreal Condensed Reports, 1854 & 1884
M.D.	Master's Decisions (Patents)
M.F.P.D.	Modern Federal Practice Digest
M.L.Dig. & R.	Monthly Digest & Reporter (Que.) 1892–1893
M.L.E.	Maryland Law Encyclopedia
M.L.P.	Michigan Law and Practice
M.L.R.	Military Law Reporter
M.L.R. (Q.B.)	Montreal Law Reports (Queen's Bench)
M.L.R. (S.C.)	Montreal Law Reports (Superior Court)
M.P.L.R.	Municipal and Planning Law Reports. 1976–
M.P.R.	Maritime Province Reports
M.P.T.M.H.	Major Peace Treaties of Modern History 1648–1967
M.V.R.	Motor Vehicle Reports, 1978–

Mac.	Macnaghten's Chancery (Eng.)
Mac. & G.	Macnaghten & Gordon's Chancery (Eng.)
Mac. & Rob.	Maclean & Robinson's Appeals, House of Lords (Sc.)
McAll.	MacAllister (U.S.)
MacAr.	McArthur's District of Columbia
	MacArthur's Patent Cases
MacAr. & M.	MacArthur & Mackey's District of Columbia Supreme Court
MacAr. & Mackey	Same
MacAr.Pat. Cas.	MacArthur's Patent Cases (D.C.)
MacArth.	MacArthur (D.C.)
	MacArthur's Patent Cases (D.C.)
MacArth. & M.	MacArthur & Mackey (D.C.)
McBride	McBride (Mo.)
McC.	McCahon (Kan.)
McCah.	Same
McCarter	McCarter's Chancery (N.J.)
McCartney	McCartney's Civil Procedure (N.Y.)
McClell.	McClelland's Exchequer (Eng.)
McClell. & Y.	McClelland & Younge's Exchequer (Eng.)
McCook	McCook (Ohio)
McCord	McCord's Chancery (S.C.)
McCork.	McCorkle (N.C.)
McCrary	McCrary (U.S.)
MacFarl.	MacFarlane, Jury Court (Sc.)
McG.	McGloin (La.)
McGill L.J.	McGill Law Journal
Mackey	Mackey
MacL.	MacLean, U. S. Circuit Court
MacL. & R.	Maclean & Robinson's House of Lords (Eng.)
McLean	McLean (U.S.)
McMul.	McMullan's Chancery (S.C.)
	McMullan's Law (S.C.)
Macn. & G.	Macnaghten & Gordon's Chancery (Eng.)
Macph.	Macpherson, Court of Sessions (Sc.)
Macph.L. & B.	Macpherson, Lee & Bell (Sc.)
Macph.S. & L.	Macpherson, Shireff & Lee (Sc.)

Macq.	Macqueen's Scotch Appeal Cases
Macr.	Macrory's Patent Cases (Eng.)
McWillie	McWillie (Miss.)
Madd.	Maddock (Mont.)
	Maddock's Chancery (Eng.)
Madd. & B.	Maddock & Back (Mont.)
Madd.Ch.Pr.	Maddock's Chancery Practice (Eng.)
Madras L.J.	Madras Law Journal
Madras L.J. Crim.	Madras Law Journal Criminal
Mag.	Magruder (Md.)
Mag. & Const.	Magistrate and Constable
Mag.Cas.	Magisterial Cases
Mag.Mun. Par.Law.	Magistrate and Municipal and Parochial Lawyer
Maine L.Rev.	Maine Law Review
Mal.L.J.	Malayan Law Journal
Mal.L.Rev.	Malaya Law Review
Malloy	Malloy's Chancery (Ir.)
Malone	Malone's Heiskell (Tenn.)
Man.	Manitoba Law
	Manning (Mich.)
Man. & G.	Manning & Granger's Common Pleas (Eng.)
Man. & Ry. Mag.	Manning & Ryland's Magistrates' Cases (Eng.)
Man. & S.	Manning & Scott's Common Bench (Old Series) (Eng.)
Man.B.News	Manitoba Bar News
Man.G. & S.	Manning, Granger & Scott's Common Bench (Eng.)
Man.Gr. & S.	Same
Man.L.J.	Manitoba Law Journal
Man.t.Wood	Manitoba temp. Wood
Man.Unrep. Cas.	Manning's Unreported Cases (La.)
Mann.	Manning (Mich.)
Mann. & G.	Manning & Granger's Common Pleas (Eng.)
Mansf.	Mansfield (Ark.)
Manson	Manson's Bankruptcy (Eng.)
Mar.L.Cas. (N.S.)	Maritime Law Cases, New Series
Mar.Law.	Maritime Lawyer
Mar.N. & Q.	Maritime Notes and Queries
Mar.Prov.	Maritime Provinces Reports
March	March's King's Bench (Eng.)
Marijuana Rev.	The Marijuana Review
Mark's & Sayre's	Mark's & Sayre's (Ala.)
Marq.L.Rev.	Marquette Law Review
Mars.Adm.	Marsden's Admiralty (Eng.)
Marsh.	Marshall, A. K. (Ky.)
	Marshall, J. J. (Ky.)
	Marshall (U.S.)
	Marshall (Utah)
	Marshall's Common Pleas (Eng.)
Mart. & Y.	Martin & Yerger (Tenn.)
Martin	Martin (Ga.) (Ind.) (La.) (U.S.)
	Martin's Decisions (Law) (N.C.)
Martin Mining	Martin Mining Cases
	Martin's New Series (La.)
Marv.	Marvel (Del.)
Mason	Mason (U.S.)
Mass.	Massachusetts
Mass.App.Dec.	Massachusetts Appellate Decisions
Mass.App.Div.	Massachusetts Appellate Division Reports
Mass.App.Rep.	Massachusetts Appeals Court Reports
Mass.L.Q.	Massachusetts Law Quarterly
Mass.L.Rev.	Massachusetts Law Review
Mathews	Mathews (W.Va.)
Matson	Matson (Conn.)
Md.	Maryland
Md.App.	Maryland Appellate Reports
Md.B.J.	Maryland Bar Journal
Md.Ch.	Maryland Chancery
Md.L.F.	Maryland Law Forum
Md.L.Rec.	Maryland Law Record
Md.L.Rep.	Maryland Law Reporter
Md.L.Rev.	Maryland Law Review
Me.	Maine
Me.L.Rev.	Maine Law Review
Means	Means (Kan.)
Med.L. & Pub. Pol.	Medicine, Law and Public Policy
Med.-Legal Crim.Rev.	Medico-Legal and Criminological Review
Med.-Legal J.	Medico-Legal Journal
Med.-Legal Soc'y Trans.	Medico-Legal Society Transactions
Med.Sci. & L.	Medicine, Science and the Law
Med.Trial Tech.Q.	Medical Trial Technique Quarterly
Medd.	Meddaugh (Mich.)
Media L.Notes	Media Law Notes
Medico-Legal J.	Medico-Legal Journal

Meg.	Megone Company Cases (Eng.)
Meigs	Meigs (Tenn.)
Melanesian L.J.	Melanesian Law Journal (Papua and New Guinea)
Melb.U.L. Rev.	Melbourne University Law Review
Memp.L.J.	Memphis Law Journal (Tenn.)
Mem.St. U.L.Rev.	Memphis State University Law Review
Menken	Menken's Civil Procedure (N.Y.)
Mercer Beasley L.Rev.	Mercer Beasley Law Review
Mercer L.Rev.	Mercer Law Review
Meredith Lect.	W. C. J. Meredith Memorial Lectures
Meriv.	Merivale's Chancery (Eng.)
Met.	Metcalf
Metc.	Metcalf (Mass.) (R.I.) (Ky.)
Miami L.Q.	Miami Law Quarterly
Mich.	Michigan
Mich.App.	Michigan Court of Appeals Reports
Mich.L.Rev.	Michigan Law Review
Mich.N.P.	Michigan Nisi Prius
Mich.St.B.J.	Michigan State Bar Journal
Mich.T.	Michaelmas Term (Eng.)
Michie's Jur.	Michie's Jurisprudence of Va. and W.Va.
Mid.East L. Rev.	Middle East Law Review
Mil.L.Rev.	Military Law Review
Miles	Miles (Pa.)
	Miles' Philadelphia District Court
Mill.	Miller (Law) (Md.)
Mill Const.	Mill's Constitutional Reports (S.C.)
Mill.Dec.	Miller's Decisions (U.S.)
Mills	Mills (N.Y. Surrogate)
Milw.	Milward's Ecclesiastical (Ir.)
Min.	Minor (Ala.)
Minn.	Minnesota
Minn.Cont. L.Ed.	Minnesota Continuing Legal Education
Minn.Cont. Legal Ed.	Same
Minn.L.Rev.	Minnesota Law Review
Misc.	Miscellaneous (N.Y.)
Misc.Dec.	3 Ohio Miscellaneous Decisions
Miss.	Mississippi
Miss.C.L.Rev.	Mississippi College Law Review
Miss.Dec.	Mississippi Decisions (Jackson)
Miss.L.J.	Mississippi Law Journal
Miss.St.Cas.	Mississippi State Cases
Mister	Mister (Mo.)
Mitchell's Mar.Reg.	Mitchell's Maritime Register
Mo.	Missouri
Mo.A.R.	Missouri Appellate Reporter
Mo.App.	Missouri Appeals
Mo.B.J.	Missouri Bar Journal
Mo.Dec.	Missouri Decisions
Mo.L.Rev.	Missouri Law Review
Moak	Moak (Eng.)
Mod.	Modern (Eng.)
Mod.L. & Soc'y	Modern Law and Society
Mod.L.Rev.	Modern Law Review
Mod.Pract. Comm.	Modern Practice Commentator
Moll.	Molloy's Chancery (Ir.)
Mon.	Monroe, B. or T. B. (Ky.)
Monash U.L. Rev.	Monash University Law Review
Mont.	Montana Reports
Mont. & Ayr.	Montagu & Ayrton's Bankruptcy (Eng.)
Mont. & M.	Montagu & McArthur's Bankruptcy (Eng.)
Mont.L.Rev.	Montana Law Review
Mont.Super.	Montreal Law Reports (Superior Court)
Month.Dig. Tax Articles	Monthly Digest of Tax Articles
Month.L.J.	Monthly Journal of Law (Wash.)
Month.L.Mag.	Monthly Law Magazine (London)
Month.L.Rep.	Monthly Law Reporter (Boston)
	Monthly Law Reports (Can.)
Month.L.Rev.	Monthly Law Review
Month.Leg. Exam.	Monthly Legal Examiner (N.Y.)
Month.West. Jur.	Monthly Western Journal (Bloomington)
Montr.Cond. Rep.	Montreal Condensed Reports
Montr.Leg.N.	Montreal Legal News
Montr.Q.B.	Montreal Law Reports Queen's Bench
Moo.C.C.	Moody's Crown Cases Reserved (Eng.)
Moo.P.C.	Moore, Privy Council
Moo.P.C. (N.S.)	Moore, New Series, Privy Council
Mood. & Mack.	Moody & Mackin's Nisi Prius (Eng.)

Mood. & Malk.	Moody & Malkin's Nisi Prius (Eng.)
Mood. & Rob.	Moody & Robinson's Nisi Prius (Eng.)
Moody Cr.C.	Moody's Crown Cases Reserved (Eng.)
Moon	Moon (Ind.)
Moore	Moore (Ala.) (Ark.) (Tex.)
Moore & S.	Moore & Scott's Common Pleas (Eng.)
Moore & W.	Moore & Walker (Tex.)
Moore C.P.	Moore's Common Pleas (Eng.)
Moore Indian App.	Moore's Indian Appeals (Eng.)
Moore K.B.	Moore's King's Bench (Eng.)
Moore P.C.C.	Moore's Privy Council Cases (Eng.)
Morg.	Morgan's Chancery Acts & Orders (Eng.)
Morr.	Morrill's Bankruptcy Cases (Eng.)
	Morris (Cal.) (Iowa) (Miss.)
Morr.St.Cas.	Morris State Cases (Miss.)
Morr.Trans.	Morrison's Transcript U. S. Supreme Court Decisions
Morris.	Morrissett's (Ala.)
Morrow	Morrow (Ore.)
Morse Exch. Rep.	Morse's Exchequer Reports (Can.)
Mosely	Mosely's Chancery (Eng.)
Moult.Ch.	Moulton's Chancery Practice (N.Y.)
Mun.	Munford (Va.)
Mun.Att'y	Municipal Attorney
Mun.Corp.Cas.	Municipal Corporation Cases
Mun.L.Ct.Dec.	Municipal Law Court Decisions
Mun.L.J.	Municipal Law Journal
Mun.Ord.Rev.	Municipal Ordinance Review
Mun.Rep.	Municipal Reports, Canada
Munf.	Munford (Va.)
Munic. & P.L.	Municipal & Parish Law Cases (Eng.)
Mur.	Murray's New South Wales Reports
	Murray's Scotch Jury Court Reports
Mur. & H.	Murphy & Hurlstone's Exchequer (Eng.)
Mur. & Hurl.	Same
Murph.	Murphy (N.C.)
Murph. & H.	Murphy & Hurlstone's Exchequer (Eng.)
Murr.	Murray's Scotch Jury Court Reports
Murr.Over. Cas.	Murray's Overruled Cases
Myer Fed.Dec.	Myer's Federal Decisions
Myl. & C.	Mylne & Craig's Chancery (Eng.)
Myl. & Cr.	Same
Myl. & K.	Mylne & Keen's Chancery (Eng.)
Mylne & K.	Same
Myr.	Myrick's Probate (Cal.)
Myr.Prob.	Same
Myrick (Cal.)	Same
Mysore L.J.	Mysore Law Journal

N

NACCA L.J.	NACCA Law Journal
NLADA Brief.	NLADA Briefcase
NOLPE Notes	NOLPE Notes
NOLPE School L.J.	NOLPE School Law Journal
NOLPE School L.Rep.	NOLPE School Law Reporter
N. & H.	Nott & Huntington's U. S. Court of Claims
N. & M.	Neville & Manning's King's Bench (Eng.)
N. & Mc.	Nott & McCord (S.C.)
N. & McC.	Same
N. & Macn.	Nevile & Macnamara Railway & Canal Cases (Eng.)
N. & P.	Nevile & Perry's King's Bench (Eng.)
N.Atlantic Reg.Bus. L.Rev.	North Atlantic Regional Business Law Review
N.B.	New Brunswick
N.B.Eq.	New Brunswick Equity
N.B.Rep.	New Brunswick Reports
N.Benl.	New Benloe, King's Bench (Eng.)
N.C.	North Carolina
N.C.App.	North Carolina Court of Appeals Reports
N.C.C.	New Chancery Cases (Eng.)
N.C.C.A.	Negligence & Compensation Cases Annotated

N.C.Cent. L.J.	North Carolina Central Law Journal
N.C.Conf.	North Carolina Conference Reports
N.C.J.Int'l L. & Com.Reg.	North Carolina Journal of International Law and Commercial Regulation
N.C.L.Rev.	North Carolina Law Review
N.C.T.Rep.	North Carolina Term Reports
N.Cent. School L.Rev.	North Central School Law Review
N.Chipm.	North Chipman (Vt.)
N.D.	North Dakota
N.D.J.Legis.	N.D. Journal of Legislation
N.D.L.Rev.	North Dakota Law Review
N.E.	Northeastern Reporter
N.E.2d	Northeastern Reporter, Second Series
N.Eng.J. Prison L.	New England Journal on Prison Law
N.Eng.L.Rev.	New England Law Review
N.H.	New Hampshire
N.H.B.J.	New Hampshire Bar Journal
N.I.M.L.O. Mun.L.Rev.	N.I.M.L.O. Municipal Law Review
N.Ir.L.Q.	Northern Ireland Legal Quarterly
N.Ir.L.R.	Northern Ireland Law Reports
N.J.	New Jersey
	New Jersey Reports
N.J.Eq.	New Jersey Equity
N.J.L.	New Jersey Law
N.J.L.J.	New Jersey Law Journal
N.J.L.Rev.	New Jersey Law Review
N.J.Law	New Jersey Law Reports
N.J.Misc.	New Jersey Miscellaneous Reports
N.J.St.B.J.	New Jersey State Bar Journal
N.J.Super.	New Jersey Superior Court and County Court Reports
N.Ky.L.Rev.	Northern Kentucky Law Review
N.Ky.St.L.F.	Northern Kentucky State Law Forum
N.L.R.B.	National Labor Relations Board Reports
N.M.	New Mexico
N.M.L.R.	Nigerian Monthly Law Reports
N.M.L.Rev.	New Mexico Law Review
NOLPE Sch. L.J.	NOLPE School Law Journal
N.M.L.Rev.	New Mexico Law Review
N.P.	Ohio Nisi Prius Reports
N.P. (N.S.)	Ohio Nisi Prius Reports, New Series
N.P. & G.T. Rep.	Nisi Prius & General Term Reports (Ohio)
N.R.A.B. (4th Div.)	National Railroad Adjustment Board Awards
N.R.	National Reporter, 1974–
N.S.	Nova Scotia
N.S.Dec.	Nova Scotia Decisions
N.S.R.	Nova Scotia Reports
N.S.W.	New South Wales State Reports
N.S.W.St.R.	New South Wales State Reports
N.S.Wales	New South Wales
N.S.Wales L.	New South Wales Law
N.S.Wales L.R.Eq.	New South Wales Law Reports Equity
N.W.	Northwestern Reporter
N.W.2d	Same, Second Series
N.W.T.L.R.	North West Territories Law Reports
N.W.Terr.	Northwest Territories Supreme Court Reports
N.Y.	New York
N.Y.2d	New York Court of Appeals Reports, Second Series
N.Y.Anno.Cas.	New York Annotated Cases
N.Y.Anno.Dig.	New York Annotated Digest
N.Y.App.Div.	New York Supreme Court Appellate Division Reports
N.Y.Cas.Err.	New York Cases in Error (Claim Cases)
N.Y.Ch.Sent.	Chancery Sentinel (N.Y.)
N.Y.City Ct.	New York City Court
N.Y.City Ct. Supp.	New York City Court Supplement
N.Y.City H. Rec.	New York City Hall Recorder
N.Y.Civ.Pro.	New York Civil Procedure
N.Y.Civ.Pro. R. (N.S.)	Same, New Series
N.Y.Civ.Proc.	New York Civil Procedure
N.Y.Civ.Proc. (N.S.)	Same, New Series
N.Y. Code Rep.	New York Code Reporter
N.Y.Code Rep. (N.S.)	New York Code Reports, New Series
N.Y.Cond.	New York Condensed Reports
N.Y.Cont. L.Ed.	New York Continuing Legal Education

N.Y.Cont. Legal Ed.	Same
N.Y.County Law.Ass'n B.Bull.	New York County Lawyers Association Bar Bulletin
N.Y.Cr.	New York Criminal
N.Y.Crim.	New York Criminal Reports
N.Y.Daily L.Gaz.	New York Daily Law Gazette
N.Y.Daily L.Reg.	New York Daily Law Register
N.Y.Dep't R.	New York Department Reports
N.Y.Elec.Cas.	New York Election Cases
N.Y.Jud. Repos.	New York Judicial Repository
N.Y.Jur.	New York Jurisprudence New York Jurist
N.Y.L.Cas.	New York Leading Cases
N.Y.L.F.	New York Law Forum
N.Y.L.J.	New York Law Journal
N.Y.L.Rec.	New York Law Record
N.Y.L.Rev.	New York Law Review
N.Y.L.Sch.Int'l L.Soc'y J.	New York Law School International Law Society Journal
N.Y.L.Sch.L. Rev.	New York Law School Law Review
N.Y.Leg.N.	New York Legal News
N.L.Leg. Obs.	New York Legal Observer
N.Y.Misc.	New York Miscellaneous Reports
N.Y.Misc.2d	Same, Second Series
N.Y.Month.L. Bull.	New York Monthly Law Bulletin
N.Y.Month.L. Rep.	New York Monthly Law Reports
N.Y.Mun.Gaz.	New York Municipal Gazette
N.Y.P.R.	New York Practice Reports
N.Y.Pr.Rep.	Same
N.Y.Rec.	New York Record
N.Y.S.	New York Supplement
N.Y.S.2d	Same, Second Series
N.Y.Sea Grant L. & Pol'y J.	New York Sea Grant Law and Policy Journal
N.Y.St.	New York State Reporter
N.Y.St.B.J.	New York State Bar Journal
N.Y.Super.	New York Superior Court
N.Y.Supp.	New York Supplement
N.Y.U.Conf. Charitable	New York University Conference on Charitable Foundations Proceedings
N.Y.U.Conf. Lab.	New York University Conference on Labor
[e.g.] N.Y.U. Inst.on Fed.Tax.	New York University Institute on Federal Taxation
N.Y.U.Intra.L. Rev.	New York Intramural Law Review
N.Y.U.J.Int'l L. & Pol.	New York University Journal of International Law and Politics
N.Y.U.L. Center Bull.	New York University Law Center Bulletin
N.Y.U.L.Q. Rev.	New York University Law Quarterly Review
N.Y.U.L.Rev.	New York University Law Review
N.Y.U.Rev. L. & Soc. Change	New York University Review of Law and Social Change
N.Y.Wkly.Dig.	New York Weekly Digest
N.Z.L.J.	New Zealand Law Journal
N.Z.L.R.	New Zealand Law Reports
N.Z.U.L.Rev.	New Zealand Universities Law Review
Napt.	Napton (Mo.)
Napton	Same
Narcotics Control Dig.	Narcotics Control Digest
Narcotics L.Bull.	Narcotics Law Bulletin
Nat.Bankr. Reg.	National Bankruptcy Register (U.S.)
Nat.Corp.Rep.	National Corporation Reporter
Nat.L.Rep.	National Law Reporter
Nat.Munic. Rev.	National Municipal Review
Nat.Reg.	National Register (By Mead)
Nat'l Civic Rev.	National Civic Review
Nat'l Income Tax Mag.	National Income Tax Magazine
Nat'l J.Crim. Def.	National Journal of Criminal Defense
Nat'l Legal Mag.	National Legal Magazine
Nat'l Mun.Rev.	National Municipal Review
Nat'l School L.Rptr.	National School Law Reporter
Nat'l Taiwan U.L.Rev.	National Taiwan University Law Journal
Nat'l Tax J.	National Tax Journal
Nat'l L.F.	Natural Law Forum
Nat.Resources J.	Natural Resources Journal
Nat.Resources L.Newsl.	Natural Resources Law Newsletter
Nat.Resources Law.	Natural Resources Lawyer
Neb.	Nebraska

Neb. (Unoff.)	Nebraska Unofficial Reports
Neb.L.Bul.	Nebraska Law Bulletin
Neb.L.Rev.	Nebraska Law Review
Neb.St.B.J.	Nebraska State Bar Journal
Negl. & Comp.Cas. Ann.	Negligence & Compensation Cases Annotated
Negl. & Comp.Cas. Ann. (N.S.)	Same, New Series
Negl. & Comp.Cas. Ann.3d	Same, Third Series
Negl.Cas.	Negligence Cases (CCH)
Negl.Cas.2d	Same, Second Series
Negro.Cas.	Bloomfield's Manumission (N.J.)
Nels.	Nelson's Chancery (Eng.)
Nels.Abr.	Nelson's Abridgment (Eng.)
Neth.Int'l L.Rev.	Netherlands International Law Review
Neth.Y.B. Int'l Law	Netherlands Yearbook of International Law
Nev.	Nevada
Nev. & P.	Neville & Perry's King's Bench (Eng.)
Nev.St.Bar J.	Nevada State Bar Journal
New Eng.L. Rev.	New England Law Review
New Eng.J. Prison L.	New England Journal of Prison Law
New L.J.	New Law Journal
New Rep.	New Reports in All Courts (Eng.)
New Sess.Cas.	New Session Cases (Eng.)
New Yugo.L.	New Yugoslav Law
New Zeal.L.	New Zealand Law
New.	Newell (Ill.)
Newb.Adm.	Newberry's Admiralty (U.S.)
Newf.S.Ct.	Newfoundland Supreme Court Decisions
Newfoundl.	Newfoundland
Nfld. & P.E. I.R.	Newfoundland and Prince Edward Reports, 1971–
Nfld.R.	Newfoundland Reports
Nfld.Sel.Cas.	Tucker's Select Cases (Nfld.) 1817–1828
Nigeria L.R.	Nigeria Law Reports
Nigerian Ann. Int'l L.	Nigerian Annual of International Law
Nigerian L.J.	Nigerian Law Journal
Noise Reg.Rep.	Noise Regulation Reporter (BNA)
Nolan	Nolan, Magistrates' Cases (Eng.)
Norc.	Norcross (Nev.)
Norris	Norris (Pa.)
North	North (Ill.)
North & G.	North & Guthrie (Mo.)
North.	Northington's Chancery (Eng.)
North.Co.	Northampton County Legal News (Pa.)
Northrop U.L. J.Aerospace Energy & Env.	Northrop University Law Journal of Aerospace, Energy and the Environment
Northumb.Co. Leg.News	Northumberland County Legal News (Pa.)
Northumb. Legal J.	Northumberland Legal Journal
Notes of Cas.	Notes of Cases (Eng.)
Notre Dame Law.	Notre Dame Lawyer
Nova L.J.	Nova Law Journal
Noy	Noy, King's Bench (Eng.)
Nuclear L.Bull.	Nuclear Law Bulletin
Nuclear Reg. Rep.	Nuclear Regulation Reporter (CCH)
Nw.J.Int'l L. & Bus.	Northwestern Journal of International Law & Business
Nw.U.L.Rev.	Northwestern University Law Review

O

O.	Ohio, Oklahoma, Oregon
O.A.	Ohio Appellate
O.A.R.	Same Ontario Appeal Reports
O.App.	Ohio Appellate
O.B. & F.N.Z.	Olliver, Bell & Fitzgerald's New Zealand Reports
O.Ben.	Old Benloe, Common Pleas (Eng.)
O.Benl.	Same
O.Bridgm.	Orlando Bridgman, Common Pleas (Eng.)
O.C.A.	Ohio Courts of Appeals Reports
O.C.C.	Ohio Circuit Court Decisions Ohio Circuit Court Reports
O.C.C. (N.S.)	Ohio Circuit Court Reports, New Series
O.C.D.	Ohio Circuit Decisions

O.C.S.	Office of Contract Settlement Decisions
O.D.	Office Decisions (I.R. Bull.)
	Ohio Decisions
O.D.C.C.	Ohio Circuit Decisions
O.D.N.P.	Ohio Decisions
O.Dec.Rep.	Ohio Decisions Reprint
O.E.M.	Office of Emergency Management
O.F.D.	Ohio Federal Decisions
O.G.	Official Gazette (U.S.) Patent Office
O.G.Pat.Off.	Same
O.L.A.	Ohio Law Abstract
O.L.B.	Weekly Law Bulletin (Ohio)
O.L.D.	Ohio (Lower) Decisions
O.L.J.	Ohio Law Journal
O.L.Jour.	Same
O.L.N.	Ohio Legal News
O.L.R.	Ohio Law Reporter
	Ontario Law Reports, 1901–1930
O.L.R.B.	Ontario Labour Relations Board Monthly Report
O.L.Rep.	Ohio Law Reporter
O.Legal News	Ohio Legal News
O.Lower D.	Ohio (Lower) Decisions
O.M.B.R.	Ontario Municipal Board Reports, 1973–
O.N.P.	Ohio Nisi Prius
O.N.P. (N.S.)	Same, New Series
O.O.	Ohio Opinions
O.R.	Ontario Reports, 1882–1900
[ ] O.R.	Same, 1931 to present
O.S.	Ohio State Reports
O.S.C.D.	Ohio Supreme Court Decisions (Unreported Cases)
O.S.H.Dec.	Occupational, Safety, and Health Decisions (CCH)
O.S.H.Rep.	Occupational, Safety, and Health Reporter (BNA)
O.S.L.J.	Ohio State Law Journal
O.S.U.	Ohio Supreme Court Decisions (Unreported Cases)
O.St.	Ohio State Reports
O.Su.	Ohio Supplement
O.W.N.	Ontario Weekly Notes, 1909–1932
[ ] O.W.N.	Same, 1933–1962
O.W.R.	Ontario Weekly Reporter
Obiter Dictum	Obiter Dictum
Ōcean Dev. & Int'l L.J.	Ōcean Development and International Law Journal
Odeneal	Odeneal (Ore.)
Off.Brev.	Officina Brevium
Off.Gaz.	Official Gazette (U.S.) Patent Office
Official Rep.Ill. Courts Commission	Official Reports: Illinois Courts Commission
Officer	Officer (Minn.)
Ogd.	Ogden (La.)
Oh.	Ohio Reports (1821–1852)
Oh.A.	Ohio Court of Appeals
Oh.Cir.Ct.	Ohio Circuit Court
Oh.Cir.Ct. (N.S.)	Same, New Series
Oh.Cir.Dec.	Ohio Circuit Decisions
Oh.Dec.	Ohio Decisions
Oh.Dec. (Reprint)	Ohio Decisions (Reprint)
Oh.F.Dec.	Ohio Federal Decisions
Oh.Jur.	Ohio Jurisprudence
Oh.L.Bull.	Ohio Law Bulletin
Oh.L.Ct.D.	Ohio Lower Court Decisions
Oh.L.J.	Ohio Law Journal
Oh.L.Rep.	Ohio Law Reporter
Oh.Leg.N.	Ohio Legal News
Oh.N.P.	Ohio Nisi Prius
Oh.N.P. (N.S.)	Same, New Series
Oh.Prob.	Ohio Probate
Oh.S. & C.P.	Ohio Superior & Common Pleas Decisions
Oh.S.C.D.	Ohio Supreme Court Decisions (Unreported Cases)
Oh.St.	Ohio State Reports
Ohio	Ohio Reports (1821–1852)
Ohio App.	Ohio Appellate Reports
Ohio App.2d	Same, Second Series
Ohio Bar	Ohio State Bar Association Reports
Ohio C.A.	Ohio Courts of Appeals Reports
Ohio C.C.	Ohio Circuit Court Reports
Ohio C.C.R.	Same
Ohio C.C.R. (N.S.)	Same, New Series
Ohio C.Dec.	Ohio Circuit Decisions
Ohio Cir.Ct.	Ohio Circuit Court Decisions
Ohio Cir.Ct. (N.S.)	Ohio Circuit Court Reports, New Series
Ohio Cir.Ct.R.	Ohio Circuit Court Reports
Ohio Cir.Ct.R. (N.S.)	Same, New Series
Ohio Ct.App.	Ohio Courts of Appeals Reports

Ohio Dec.	Ohio Decisions
Ohio Dec. Repr.	Ohio Decisions Reprint
Ohio F.Dec.	Ohio Federal Decisions
Ohio Fed.Dec.	Same
Ohio Jur.	Ohio Jurisprudence
Ohio Jur.2d	Same, Second Edition
Ohio L.Abs.	Ohio Law Abstract
Ohio L.B.	Weekly Law Bulletin (Ohio)
Ohio L.J.	Ohio Law Journal
Ohio L.R.	Ohio Law Reporter
Ohio Law Abst.	Ohio Law Abstract
Ohio Law Bull.	Weekly Law Bulletin (Ohio)
Ohio Law J.	Ohio Law Journal
Ohio Law R.	Ohio Law Reporter
Ohio Leg.N.	Ohio Legal News
Ohio Legal N.	Same
Ohio Lower Dec.	Ohio (Lower) Decisions
Ohio Misc.	Ohio Miscellaneous Reports
Ohio Misc.Dec.	3 Ohio Miscellaneous Decisions
Ohio N.P.	Ohio Nisi Prius Reports
Ohio N.P. (N.S.)	Same, New Series
Ohio (N.S.)	Ohio Reports, Annotated
Ohio N. U.L.Rev.	Ohio Northern University Law Review
Ohio Op.	Ohio Opinions
Ohio Op.2d	Same, Second Series
Ohio Prob.	Goebel's Ohio Probate Reports
Ohio R.Cond.	Ohio Reports Condensed
Ohio S. & C.P. Dec.	Ohio Decisions
Ohio S.U.	Ohio Supreme Court Decisions (Unreported Cases)
Ohio St.	Ohio State Reports
Ohio St.2d	Same, Second Series
Ohio St.L.J.	Ohio State Law Journal
Ohio St. (N.S.)	Ohio State Reports, Annotated
Ohio Sup. & C.P.Dec.	Ohio Decisions
Ohio Supp.	Ohio Supplement
Ohio Unrep. Jud.Dec.	Pollack's Ohio Unreported Judicial Decisions Prior to 1823
Ohio Unrept. Cas.	Ohio Supreme Court Decisions (Unreported Cases)
Oil & Gas Compact Bull.	Oil and Gas Compact Bulletin
Oil & Gas Inst.	Oil and Gas Institute
Oil & Gas J.	Oil and Gas Journal
Oil & Gas L. & Tax.Inst. (Sw.Legal Fdn.)	Oil & Gas Law & Taxation Institute (Southwestern Legal Foundation)
Oil & Gas Rptr.	Oil and Gas Reporter
Oil & Gas Tax Q.	Oil and Gas Tax Quarterly
Okla.	Oklahoma
Okla.B. Ass'n J.	Oklahoma Bar Association Journal
Okla.City U.L. Rev.	Oklahoma City University Law Review
Okla.Cr.	Oklahoma Criminal
Okla.Crim.	Oklahoma Criminal Reports
Okla.L.J.	Oklahoma Law Journal
Okla.L.Rev.	Oklahoma Law Review
Okla.S.B.J.	Oklahoma State Bar Journal
Olcott	Olcott (U.S.)
Oliv.B. & L.	Oliver, Beavan & Lefroy (Eng. Ry. & Canal Cases)
Olliv.B. & F.	Olliver, Bell & Fitzgerald (New Zealand)
O'M. & H.El. Cas.	O'Malley & Hardcastle, Election Cases (Eng.)
Ont.	Ontario Reports
Ont.A.	Ontario Appeals
Ont.El.Cas.	Ontario Election Cases
Ont.Elec.	Same
Ont.L.	Ontario Law
Ont.L.J.	Ontario Law Journal
Ont.L.J. (N.S.)	Same, New Series
Ont.L.R.	Ontario Law Reports
Ont.Pr.	Ontario Practice
Ont.W.N.	Ontario Weekly Notes
Ont.W.R.	Ontario Weekly Reporter
Op.	Opinions of Attorneys General (U.S.)
Op.Att'y Gen.	Opinions of the Attorney General, United States
Op.Sol.Dept.	Opinions of the Solicitor, U. S. Department of Labor
Ops.Atty.Gen.	Opinions of Attorneys General (U.S.)
Or.	Oregon
Or.L.Rev.	Oregon Law Review
Orange County B.J.	Orange County Bar Journal
Ore.	Oregon Reports
Ore.App.	Oregon Court of Appeals Reports
Ore.L.Rev.	Oregon Law Review
Ore.St.B.Bull.	Oregon State Bar Bulletin
Ore.Tax Ct.	Oregon Tax Court Reports

Orleans' App.	Orleans' Appeals (La.)
Orleans Tr.	Orleans Term Reports (La.)
Ormond	Ormond (Ala.)
Osaka Pref. Bull.	University of Osaka Prefecture Bulletin
Osaka U.L. Rev.	Osaka University Law Review
Osgoode Hall L.J.	Osgoode Hall Law Journal
Otago L.Rev.	Otago Law Review
Ottawa L.Rev.	Ottawa Law Review
Otto	Otto (U.S.)
Out.	Outerbridge (Pa.)
Outerbridge	Same
Over.	Overton (Tenn.)
Overt.	Same
Overton	Same
Ow.	Owen's King's Bench & Common Pleas (Eng.)
Owen	Same
Oxford Law.	Oxford Lawyer
Oxley	Young's Vice Admiralty Decisions (Nova Scotia) (By Oxley)

P

P.	Pacific Reporter
	Pickering (Mass.)
	Probate
	Law Reports Probate, Divorce & Admiralty Division, Third Series
P.2d	Pacific Reporter, Second Series
P. & B.	Pugsley & Burbridge's Reports, New Brunswick
P. & C.	Prideaux & Cole's New Sessions Cases (Eng.)
P. & D.	Perry & Davison's Queen's Bench (Eng.)
P. & F. Radio Reg.	Radio Regulation Reporter
P. & H.	Patton & Heath (Va.)
P. & K.	Perry & Knapp Election Cases (Eng.)
P. & W.	Penrose & Watts (Pa.)
P.C.	Price Control Cases (CCH)
P.C.I.J.	Permanent Court of International Justice Advisory Opinions, Cases, Judgments, Pronouncements
P.C.I.J.Ann.R.	Permanent Court of International Justice Annual Reports
P.Coast L.J.	Pacific Coast Law Journal
P.D.	Law Reports Probate, Divorce & Admiralty Division, Second Series Division
	Pension and Bounty (U.S. Dept. of Interior)
P.Div.	Law Reports, Probate Division (Eng.)
PEAL	Publishing, Entertainment, Advertising and Allied Fields Law Quarterly
P.E.I.	Haszard & Warburton's Reports (P.E.I.)
P.F.Smith	P. F. Smith (Pa.)
P–H	Prentice-Hall
P–H Am.Lab. Arb.Awards	American Labor Arbitration Awards (P–H)
P–H Am.Lab. Cas.	American Labor Cases (P–H)
P–H Corp.	Corporation (P–H)
P–H Est.Plan.	Estate Planning (P–H)
P–H Fed. Taxes	Federal Taxes (P–H)
P–H Fed.Wage & Hour	Federal Wage and Hour (P–H)
P–H Ind.Rel., Lab.Arb.	Industrial Relations, American Labor Arbitration (P–H)
P–H Ind.Rel., Union Conts.	Industrial Relations, Union Contracts and Collective Bargaining (P–H)
P–H Soc.Sec. Taxes	Social Security Taxes (P–H)
P–H State & Local Taxes	State and Local Taxes (P–H)
P–H Tax Ct.Mem.	Tax Court Memorandum Decisions (P–H)
P–H Tax Ct.Rep. & Mem.Dec.	Tax Court Reported and Memorandum Decisions (P–H)
P.L.Mag.	Pacific Law Magazine
P.L.E.	Pennsylvania Law Encyclopedia
P.L.Rep.	Pacific Law Reporter
P.Jr. & H.	Patton, Jr., & Heath (Va.)
P.R.	Parliamentary Reports
	Probate Reports
	Practice Reports (Ont.)
	Puerto Rico Supreme Court Reports
P.R. & D.El. Cas.	Power, Rodwell & Dew's Election Cases (Eng.)
P.R.F.	Puerto Rico Federal Reports
P.R.R.	Puerto Rico Reports
P.T.	Processing Tax Division (I.R.Bull.)

P.U.Fort.	Public Utilities Fortnightly
P.U.R.	Public Utilities Reports
P.U.R. (N.S.)	Same, New Series
P.U.R.3d	Same, Third Series
P.Wms.	Peere-Williams Chancery (Eng.)
Pa.	Pennsylvania
Pa.B.A.Q.	Pennsylvania Bar Association Quarterly
Pa.B.Brief	Pennsylvania Bar Brief
Pa.C.P.	Common Pleas Reporter
Pa.C.Pl.	Penn. Common Pleas
Pa.Cas.	Penn. Supreme Court Cases (Sadler)
Pa.Co.Ct.	Penn. County Court
Pa.D. & C.	Penn. District & County Reporter
Pa.D. & C.2d	Same, Second Series
Pa.Dist.	Penn. District Reporter
Pa.Fid.	Pennsylvania Fiduciary Reporter
Pa.L.J.	Pennsylvania Law Journal
Pa.L.J.R.	Clark's Penn. Law Journal Reports
Pa.L.Rec.	Pennsylvania Law Record
Pa.Misc.	Pennsylvania Miscellaneous Reports
Pa.State	Penn. State Reports
Pa.Super.	Penn. Superior Court Reporter
Pac.	Pacific Reporter
Pac.L.J.	Pacific Law Journal
Paige	Paige's Chancery (N.Y.)
Paine	Paine (U.S.)
Pak.Crim.L.J.	Pakistan Criminal Law Journal
[e.g.] Pak.L.R.Lahore Ser.	Pakistan Law Reports, [e.g.] Lahore Series
Palm.	Palmer (N.H.) (Vt.)
	Palmer, King's Bench & Common Pleas (Eng.)
Pan-Am.T.S.	Pan-American Treaty Series
Papua & N.G.	Papua and New Guinea Law Reports
Papy	Papy (Fla.)
Park.	Parker's Exchequer (Eng.)
Park.Cr.	Parker's Criminal Reports (N.Y.)
Park.Cr.Cas.	Same
Park.Ins.	Parker's Insurance
Parker	Parker (N.H.)
Parker Cr. Cas.	Parker's Criminal Reports (N.Y.)
Pars.Dec.	Parson's Decisions (Mass.)
Pars.Eq.Cas.	Parsons' Select Equity Cases (Pa.)
Pasch.	Paschal (Tex.)
Pat. & T.M. Rev.	Patent & Trade Mark Review
Pat. & Tr.Mk. Rev.	Same
Pat.Cas.	Reports of Patent, Design and Trade Mark Cases
Pat.L.Rev.	Patent Law Review
Pat.Off.Rep.	Patent Office Reports
Pat.T.M. & Copy.J.	Patent, Trademark & Copyright Journal
Pater.Ap.Cas.	Paterson's Appeal Cases (Sc.)
Paton App. Cas.	Paton's Appeal Cases (Can.)
Patr.Elec.Cas.	Patrick, Contested Elections (Ont.) 1824–1849
Patt. & H.	Patton & Heath (Va.)
Peab.L.Rev.	Peabody Law Review
Peake N.P.	Peake's Nisi Prius (Eng.)
Peake N.P. Add.Cas.	Peake, Additional Cases Nisi Prius (Eng.)
Pearce C.C.	Pearce's (Dearsley's) Crown Cases (Eng.)
Pearson	Pearson, Common Pleas (Pa.)
Peck	Peck (Ill.)
	Peck (Tenn.)
Peck.El.Cas.	Peckwell's Election Cases (Eng.)
Peeples	Peeples (Ga.)
Peeples & Stevens	Peeples & Stevens (Ga.)
Peere Williams	Peere Williams' Chancery (Eng.)
Peere Wms.	Same
Pen.	Pennington's Law (N.J.)
Pen. & W.	Penrose and Watts
Penn.B.A.Q.	Penn.Bar Association (Quarterly)
Penn.Del.	Pennewill (Del.)
Pennyp.	Pennypacker (Pa.)
Pennyp.Col. Cas.	Pennypacker's Colonial Cases
Penr. & W.	Penrose & Watts (Pa.)
Pension Rep.	Pension Reporter (BNA)
Pepperdine L.Rev.	Pepperdine Law Review
Perry & K.	Perry & Knapp's Election Cases (Eng.)
Pers.Finance L.Q.	Personal Finance Law Quarterly Report
Pers.Inj. Comment'r	Personal Injury Commentator
Pet.	Peters
Pet.Ab.	Petersdorf's Abridgment
Pet.Adm.	Peters' Admiralty (U.S.)

Pet.Br.	Petit (Or Little) Brook (Brooke) New Cases King's Bench (Eng.)
Pet.C.C.	Peters' Circuit Court (U.S.)
Peters	Peters (U.S.)
Pheney Rep.	Pheney's New Term Reports. See Harrison & Wollaston (Eng.)
Phil.	Phillips' (Ill.)
	Phillips' Chancery (Eng.)
	Phillips' Equity (N.C.)
	Phillips' Law (N.C.)
Phil.El.Cas.	Phillips Election Cases (Eng.)
Phil.Int'l L.J.	Philippine International Law Journal
Phil.L.J.	Philippine Law Journal
Phila.	Philadelphia (Pa.)
Philanthrop.	Philanthropist
Phillim.	Phillimore Ecclesiastical (Eng.)
Pick.	Pickering (Mass.)
Pickle	Pickle (Tenn.)
Pig. & R.	Pigott & Rodwell's Registration Cases (Eng.)
Pike	Pike (Ark.)
Pin.	Pinney (Wis.)
Pinn.	Pinney (Wis.)
Pipe Roll Soc'y	Publications of the Pipe Roll Society
Pipe Roll Soc'y (N.S.)	Publications of the Pipe Roll Society, New Series
Pitblado Lect.	Isaac Pitblado Lectures on Continuing Legal Education
Pitts.L.J.	Pittsburgh Legal Journal
Pitts.Leg.J. (N.S.)	Pittsburgh Legal Journal, New Series (Pa.)
Pitts.Rep.	Pittsburgh Reports (Pa.)
Pittsb.	Pittsburgh (Pa.)
Pittsb.Leg.J.	Pittsburgh Legal Journal (Pa.)
Pittsb.R. (Pa.)	Pittsburgh Reporter (Pa.)
Pl.Ang.-Norm.	Placita Anglo-Normannica Cases (Bigelow)
Plan. & Comp.	Planning and Compensation Reports
Plan., Zoning & E.D.Inst.	Planning, Zoning & Eminent Domain Institute
Plowd.	Plowden, King's Bench (Eng.)
Pol.	Pollack's Ohio Unreported Judicial Decisions Prior to 1823
	Pollexfen, King's Bench (Eng.)
Pollexf.	Same
Pol.Sci.Q.	Political Science Quarterly
Pol.Y.B. Int'l L.	Polish Yearbook of International Law
Police J.	Police Journal
Police L.Q.	Police Law Quarterly
Poll.Contr. Guide	Pollution Control Guide (CCH)
Pollution Abs.	Pollution Abstracts
Poly L.Rev.	Poly Law Review
Pomeroy	Pomeroy (Cal.)
Poor L. & Local Gov't Mag.	Poor Law and Local Government Magazine
Poph.	Popham, King's Bench & Common Pleas & Chancery (Eng.)
Port.	Porter (Ala.) (Ind.)
Portia L.J.	Portia Law Journal
Portland U.L. Rev.	Portland University Law Review
Porto Rico Fed.	Porto Rico Federal
Posey	Posey (Tex.)
Posey Unrep. Cas.	Posey's Unreported Commissioner Cases (Texas)
Post	Post (Mich.) (Mo.)
Potomac L.Rev.	Potomac Law Review
Potter	Potter (Wyo.)
Pow.Surr.	Power's Surrogate (N.Y.)
Pr.	Price (Exchequer) (Eng.)
Pr.Edw.Isl.	Prince Edward Island
Pr.Reg.B.C.	Practical Register, Bail Court (Eng.)
Pr.Reg.C.P.	Practical Register Common Pleas (Eng.)
Pr.Reg.Ch.	Practical Register Chancery (Eng.)
Pr.Rep.	Practice Reports (Eng.)
	Practice Reports (Upper Can.)
Prac.Law.	Practical Lawyer
Prec.Ch.	Precedents in Chancery (Eng.)
Preview	Preview of United States Supreme Court Cases
Price	Price (Exchequer) (Eng.)
	Price's Mining Commissioner's Cases (Ont.)
Price Pr.Cas.	Price's Notes of Practice Cases (Eng.)
Prick.	Prickett (Idaho)
Prin.Dec.	Printed Decisions (Sneed's) (Ky.)
Prison L. Rptr.	Prison Law Reporter
Probation & Parole L.Rep.	Probation and Parole Law Reports
Probation & Parole L.Sum.	Probation and Parole Law Summaries

Prob. & Prop.	Probate and Property
Prob.Law.	Probate Lawyer
Prob.Rep.	Probate Reports (Ohio)
Prod.Liab.Int'l	Product Liability International
Prod.Safety & Liab.Rep.	Product Safety and Liability Reporter (BNA)
Prop. & Comp.	Property and Compensation Reports
Prop.Law.	Property Lawyer
Prosecutor	Prosecutor
Prouty	Prouty (Vt.)
Pub.Ad.Rev.	Public Administration Review
Pub.Cont.L.J.	Public Contract Law Journal
Pub.Cont. Newsl.	Public Contract Newsletter
Pub.Employee Rel.Rep.	Public Employee Relations Reports
Pub.Int'l L.	Public International Law
Pub.L.	Public Law
Pub.Land & Res.L.Dig.	Public Land and Resources Law Digest
Pub.Util.Fort.	Public Utilities Fortnightly
Pugs.	Pugsley (New Brunswick)
Pugs. & B.	Pugsley & Burbridge (New Brunswick)
Pugs. & T.	Pugsley & Trueman (New Brunswick)
Puls.	Pulsifer (Me.)
Pulsifer	Same
Pyke	Pyke (Lower Can.)
	Pyke's Reports, King's Bench (Que.)

Q

Q.B.	Law Reports, Queen's Bench, Third Series
Q.B.D.	Law Reports, Queen's Bench Division, Second Series
Q.B.L.C.	Queen's Bench (Lower Canada)
Q.B.U.C.	Queen's Bench (Upper Canada)
Q.Intramural L.J.	Queen's Intramural Law Journal
Q.L.	Quebec Law
Q.L.J.	Queen's Law Journal
Q.L.R.	Quebec Law Reports
Q.L.Rev.	Quarterly Law Review
Q.Newsl.-Spec. Comm.Env.L.	Quarterly Newsletter-Special Committee on Environmental Law
Que.B.R.; Que.C.S.	Quebec Rapports Judicaires Officiels (Banc de la Reine; Cour supérieure)
[ ] Que.C.A.	Quebec Official Reports (Court of Appeal) 1970–
[ ] Que.K.B. or [ ] Que. Q.B.	Quebec Official Reports (King's Bench or Queen's Bench) 1941 to present
Que.L.	Quebec Law
Que.L.R.	Quebec Law Reports
Que.Pr.	Quebec Practice
Que.Prac.	Quebec Practice Reports
Que.Q.B. or Que.K.B.	Quebec Official Reports (Queen's Bench or King's Bench) 1892–1941
Que.Rev.Jud.	Quebec Revised Judicial
Que.S.C.	Quebec Official Reports (Superior Court) 1892–1941
[ ] Que.S.C.	Same, 1942 to present
Que.Super.	Quebec Reports Superior Court
Queens B.Bull.	Queens Bar Bulletin
Queensl.	Queensland Reports
Queensl.J.P.	Queensland Justice of the Peace
Queensl.J.P. Rep.	Queensland Justice of the Peace Reports
Queensl.L.	Queensland Law
Queensl.L.J.	Queensland Law Journal
Queensl.L. Soc'y J.	Queensland Law Society Journal
Queensl.Law.	Queensland Lawyer
Queensl.S.C.R.	Queensland Supreme Court Reports
Queensl.St. Rep.	Queensland State Reports
Queensl.W.N.	Queensland Weekly Notes
Quincy	Quincy (Mass.)
Quis Cust.	Quis Custodiet?

R

R.	Rawle (Pa.)
	The Reports, Coke's King's Bench (Eng.)
R. & C.	Russell & Chesley (Nova Scotia)
R. & Can.Cas.	Railway & Canal Cases (Eng.)
R. & Can.Tr. Cas.	Railway & Canal Traffic Cases (Eng.)
R. & M.	Russell & Mylne's Chancery (Eng.)

R. & M.C.C.	Ryan & Moody's Crown Cases (Eng.)
R. & N.L.R.	Rhodesia and Nyasaland Law Reports
R. & R.	Russell & Ryan Crown Cases (Eng.)
R. 1 Cro.	Croke, Elizabeth
R. 2 Cro.	Croke, James I.
R. 3 Cro.	Croke, Charles I.
R.A.C.	Ramsay's Appeal Cases (Que.)
R.C.L.	Ruling Case Law
[ ] R.D.F.Q.	Recueil de droit fiscal Quebecois, 1977–
[ ] R.D.T.	Revue de Droit du Travail, 1963–
R. de D. McGill	Revue de Droit De McGill
R.E.D.	Russell's Equity Decisions (Nova Scotia)
R.I.	Rhode Island
R.I.B.J.	Rhode Island Bar Journal
R.J.R.Q.	Quebec Revised Reports
R.L. & S.	Ridgeway, Lapp & Schoales, King's Bench (Ir.)
R.L. & W.	Robert, Leaming & Wallis County Court (Eng.)
R.L.B.	U. S. Railroad Labor Board Decisions
R.M.C.C.	Ryan & Moody's Crown Cases (Eng.)
R.M.C.C.R.	Same
R.M.Charlt.	R. M. Charlton (Ga.)
R.P.	Rapports de Pratique de Quebec/Quebec Practice Reports, 1898–
R.P.C.	Reports of Patent Cases
R.P. & W.	(Rawle) Penrose & Watt (Pa.)
R.P.R.	Real Property Reports, 1977–
R.P.W.	Same as R.P. & W.
R.R.	Pike & Fischer Radio Regulation Revised Reports (Eng.)
R.R.2d	Pike & Fischer Radio Regulation, Second Series
Race	Race
Race Rel.L. Rep.	Race Relations Law Reporter
Race Rel.L. Survey	Race Relations Law Survey
Rader	Rader (Mo.)
Rand	Rand (Ohio)
Rand.	Randolph (Kan.) (Va.) Randall (Ohio)
Rand.Ann.	Randolph Annual (La.)
Raney	Raney (Fla.)
Rawle	Rawle (Pa.)
Raym.	Raymond (Iowa)
Real Est.L.J.	Real Estate Law Journal
Real Est. L.Rep.	Real Estate Law Report
Real Est.Rev.	Real Estate Review
Real Prop. Prob. & Tr.J.	Real Property, Probate and Trust Journal
Reap.Dec.	U. S. Customs Court Reappraisement Dec. (From Treas. Dec. & C.D.)
Rec.L.	Recent Law
Rec.Laws	Recent Laws in Canada
Record of N.Y.C.B.A.	Record of the Association of the Bar of the City of New York
Recueil des Cours	Recueil des Cours
Redf. & B.	Redfield & Bigelow's Leading Cases (Eng.)
Redf.Surr.	Redfield's Surrogate (N.Y.)
Reding.	Redington (Me.)
Reese	Reese, Heiskell's (Tenn.)
Reeve Eng.L.	Reeve's English Law
Ref.J.	Referees' Journal (Journal of National Association of Referees in Bankruptcy)
Rel. & Pub. Order	Religion and the Public Order
Remy	Remy (Ind.)
Rep.Atty.Gen.	Attorneys General's Reports (U.S.)
Rep.Pat.Cas.	Reports of Patent Cases (Eng.)
Rep.Pat.Des. & Tr.Cas.	Reports of Patents Designs & Trademark Cases
Reports	Reports Coke's King's Bench (Eng.)
Reprint	English Reports, Full Reprint
Rept.t.Finch	Cases temp. Finch (Chancery) (Eng.)
Rept.t.Holt	Cases temp. Holt (King's Bench) (Eng.)
Res Ipsa	Res Ipsa Loquitur
Res Judic.	Res Judicatae
Res. & Eq. Judgm.	Reserved & Equity Judgments (N.S.Wales)
Res.L. & Econ.	Research in Law and Economics
Res.L. & Soc.	Research in Law and Sociology
Restric. Prac.	Reports of Restrictive Practices Cases
Rettie	Rettie, Crawford & Melville's Session Cases (Sc.)
Rev.Bar.	Revue du Barreau

Rev.Barreau Que.	Revue de Barreau de Quebec
Rev.C.Abo.Pr.	Revista de Derecho del Colegio de Abogados de Puerto Rico
Rev.Con-temp.L.	Review of Contemporary Law
Rev.Crit.	Revue Critique (Can.)
Rev.D.P.R.	Revista de Derecho Puertorriqueno
Rev.D.U.S.	Revue de Droit Université de Sherbrooke
Rev. de Legis.	Revue de Legislation (Can.)
Rev.Gen.D.	Revue Générale de Droit
Rev.Ghana L.	Review of Ghana Law
Rev.Int'l Comm.Jur.	Review of the International Commission of Jurists
Rev., Jud., & Police J.	Revenue, Judicial, and Police Journal
Rev.Jur.U. Inter.P.R.	Revista Juridica de law Universidad Interamericana de Puerto Rico
Rev.Jur. U.P.R.	Revista Juridica de la Universidad de Puerto Rico
Rev.L. & Soc. Change	Review of Law and Social Change
Rev.Leg.	Revue Legale (Can.)
Rev.Leg. (N.S.)	Same, New Series
Rev.Leg. (O.S.)	Same, Old Series
Rev.Legale	Revue Legale
Rev.Litigation	Review of Litigation
Rev.Not.	Revue de Notariat Revue du Notariat
Rev.P.R.	Revista de Derecho Puertorriqueno
Rev.Pol.L.	Review of Polish Law
Rev.R.	Revised Reports (Eng.)
Rev.Rep.	Revised Reports (Eng.)
Rev.Sec.Reg.	Review of Securities Regulation
Rev.Sel. Code Leg.	Review of Selected Code Legislation
Rev.Soc.L.	Review of Socialist Law
Rev.Stat.	Revised Statutes
Revised Rep.	Revised Reports (Eng.)
Reyn.	Reynolds (Miss.)
Rhodesian L.J.	Rhodesian Law Journal
Rice	Rice's Equity (S.C.) Rice's Law (S.C.)
Rich.	Richardson (N.H.) Richardson's Equity (S.C.) Richardson's Law (S.C.)
Rich. & H.	Richardson & Hook's Street Railway Decisions
Rich. & W.	Richardson & Woodbury (N.H.)
Rich.C.P.	Richardson's Practice, Common Pleas (Eng.)
Rich.Ct.Cl.	Richardson's Court of Claims
Ridg.Ap.	Ridgeway's Appeals Parliament Cases (Ir.)
Ridg.App.	Same
Ridg.L. & S.	Ridgeway, Lapp & Schoales' King's Bench (Ir.)
Ridg.P.C.	Ridgeway's Parliamentary Cases (Ir.)
Ridg.t.Hardw.	Ridgeway temp. Hardwicke, Chancery, King's Bench
Ried.	Riedell (N.H.)
Rights	Rights
Riley	Riley (W.Va.) Riley's Equity (S.C.) Riley's Law (S.C.)
Ritchie	Ritchie's Equity (Can.)
Rob.	Robard (Mo.) Robard Conscript Cases (Tex.) Robert's Louisiana Annual Robertson (Hawaii) Robertson's Marine Court (N.Y.) Robertson's Superior Court (N.Y.) Robinson (Calif.) (Colo.) (La.) (Nev.) (Upper Can.) (Va.) Robinson's (La.) Annual
Rob. & J.	Robard & Jackson (Tex.) Robertson & Jacob's Marine Court (N.Y.)
Rob.Adm.	Robinson, Admiralty (Eng.)
Rob.Eccl.	Robertson's Ecclesiastical (Eng.)
Rob.L. & W.	Robert, Leaming & Wallis' County Court (Eng.)
Robb Pat.Cas.	Robb's Patent Cases (U.S.)
Robert.App. Cas.	Robertson's Appeal Cases (Sc.)
Robin.App.Cas.	Robinson's Appeal Cases (House of Lords) (Sc.)
Rocky Mt.L. Rev.	Rocky Mountain Law Review
Rocky Mt.Min. L.Inst.	Rocky Mountain Mineral Law Institute
Rocky Mt.Min. L.Newsl.	Rocky Mountain Mineral Law Newsletter
Rocky Mt. Miner.L.Rev.	Rocky Mountain Mineral Law Review
Rodm.	Rodman (Ky.)
Rogers	Rogers (La.) Annual

Roll.	Rolle (King's Bench) (Eng.)
Rolle	Same
Rolle Abr.	Rolle's Abridgment (Eng.)
Rom.Cas.	Romilly's Notes of Cases (Eng.)
Root	Root (Conn.)
Rose	Rose Bankruptcy (Eng.)
Rose's Notes (U.S.)	Rose's Notes on U. S. Reports
Ross Lead.Cas.	Ross Leading Cases (Eng.)
Rot.Chart.	Rotulus Chartarum (The Charter Roll)
Rot.Claus.	Rotuli Clause (The Close Roll)
Rot.Parl.	Rotulae Parliamentarum
Rot.Pat.	Rotuli Patenes
Rot.Plac.	Rotuli Placitorum
Rotuli Curiae Reg.	Rotuli Curiae Regis (Eng.)
Rowe	Rowe, Parliament & Military Cases (Eng.)
Rowell	Rowell (Vt.)
Rowell El.Cas.	Rowell Election Cases (U.S.)
Rucker	Rucker (W.Va.)
Ruff. & H.	Ruffin & Hawks (N.C.)
Runn.	Runnell (Iowa)
Rus.	Russell's Election Cases (Nova Scotia)
Rus. & C.Eq. Cas.	Russell & Chesley's Equity Cases (N.S.)
Russ. & Geld.	Russell & Geldert (N.S.)
Russ. & M.	Russell & Mylne Chancery (Eng.)
Russ. & Ry.	Russell & Ryan Crown Cases (Eng.)
Russ.El.Cas.	Russell's Election Reports (Can.)
	Russell's Election Cases (Mass.)
Russ.Eq.Cas.	Russell's Equity Cases (N.S.)
Russ.t.Eld.	Russell's Chancery temp. Eldon (Eng.)
Russell	Russell's Chancery (Eng.)
Rutgers J. Computers Tech. & L.	Rutgers Journal of Computers, Technology and the Law
Rutgers J. Computers & Law	Rutgers Journal of Computers and the Law
Rutgers L.Rev.	Rutgers Law Review
Rutgers U.L. Rev.	Rutgers University Law Review
Rut.-Cam.L.J.	Rutgers-Camden Law Journal
Ry. & M.	Ryan & Moody's Nisi Prius (Eng.)
Ry.M.C.C.	Ryan & Moody Crown Cases (Eng.)
Ryan & M.	Ryan & Moody's Nisi Prius (Eng.)
Ryde	Ryde's Rating Appeals (Eng.)

S

S.	Shaw, Dunlop & Bell (Sc.)
	Shaw's Appeal Cases, House of Lords (Sc.)
	Southern Reporter
S.A.G.	Sentencis arbitrales de griefs (Quebec) 1970–
SALT News	SALT News
S. & B.	Smith & Batty's King's Bench (Ir.)
S. & C.	Saunders & Cole's Bail Court (Eng.)
S. & C.P.Dec.	Ohio Decisions
S. & D.	Shaw, Dunlop & Bell's 1st Series (Sc.)
S. & L.	Schoales & Lefroy's Chancery (Ir.)
S. & M.	Smedes & Maclean's Appeal Cases, House of Lords (Sc.)
	Smedes & Marshall (Miss.)
S. & M.Ch.	Smedes & Marshall's Chancery (Miss.)
S. & Mar.	Smedes & Marshall (Miss.)
S. & Mar.Ch.	Smedes & Marshall's Chancery (Miss.)
S. & R.	Sergeant & Rawle (Pa.)
S. & S.	Sausse & Scully's Rolls Court (Ir.)
	Simons & Stuart's Vice-Chancery (Eng.)
S. & Sc.	Sausse & Scully's Rolls Court (Ir.)
S. & Sm.	Searle & Smith's Probate & Divorce Cases (Eng.)
S. & T.	Swabey & Tristram's Probate & Divorce Cases (Eng.)
S.Afr.L.J.	South African Law Journal
S.Afr.L.R.	South African Law Reports

S.Afr.L.R. App.	South African Law Reports Appellate
S.Afr.L.Rev.	South African Law Review
S.Afr.L.T.	South African Law Times
S.Afr.Tax Cas.	South African Tax Cases
S.Aust.L.	South Australian Law
S.Austl.	South Australia State Reports
S.Austl.L.R.	South Australian Law Reports
S.B.J.	State Bar Journal (Cal.)
S.C.	Court of Session Cases (Sc.) South Carolina
S.C.Cas.	Supreme Court Cases (Cameron's) (Can.)
S.C.Eq.	South Carolina Equity
S.C.L.Q.	South Carolina Law Quarterly
S.C.L.Rev.	South Carolina Law Review
S.C.R.	Supreme Court Reports (Canada) 1876–1922
[ ]S.C.R.	Same, 1923 to present
S.Cal.L.Rev.	Southern California Law Review
S.Calif.Law Rev.	Southern California Law Review
S.Ct.	Supreme Court Reporter (U.S.)
S.Ct.Rev.	Supreme Court Review
S.D.	South Dakota
S.D.L.Rev.	South Dakota Law Review
S.D.St.B.J.	South Dakota State Bar Journal
S.E.	South Eastern Reporter
S.E.2d	Same, Second Series
S.E.C.	U. S. Security and Exchange Commission Decisions
S.F.L.J	San Francisco Law Journal
S.Ill.U.L.J.	Southern Illinois University Law Journal
S.L.C.	Stuart's Appeal Cases (Lower Can.)
S.L.J.R.	Sudan Law Journal and Reports
S.M.	Solicitor's Memorandum (Treasury) (I.R.Bull.)
S.Pac.L.Rev.	South Pacific Law Review
S.R.	Solicitor's Recommendation (I.R.Bull.)
S.R. & O. and S.I.Rev.	Statutory Rules & Orders and Statutory Instruments Revised
S.S.L.R.	Selective Service Law Reporter
S.S.T.	Social Security Tax Ruling (I.R.Bull.)
S.T.	Sales Tax Division (I.R. Bull.)
S.Tex.L.J.	South Texas Law Journal
S.U.L.Rev.	Southern University Law Review
S.W.	South Western Reporter
S.W.2d	Same, Second Series
S.W.L.J.	South Western Law Journal (Nashville)
Sadler	Sadler's Cases (Pa.)
St. John's L.Rev.	St. John's Law Review
St. Louis L.Rev.	St. Louis Law Review
St. Louis U.L.J.	St. Louis University Law Journal
St. Mary's L.J.	St. Mary's Law Journal
Sal.	Salinger (Iowa)
Salk.	Salkeld King's Bench Common Pleas & Exchequer (Eng.)
Samoan P.L.J.	Samoan Pacific Law Journal
San Diego L. Rev.	San Diego Law Review
San Fern.V.L. Rev.	San Fernando Valley Law Review
San Fran.L.J.	San Francisco Law Journal
Sand.I.Rep.	Sandwich Islands Reports (See Robertson's Reports) (Hawaii)
Sandf.	Sandford's Superior Court (N.Y.)
Sandf.Ch.	Sandford Chancery (N.Y.)
Sanf.	Sanford (Ala.)
Santa Clara L. Rev.	Santa Clara Law Review
Santa Clara Law.	Santa Clara Lawyer
Santo Tomas L.Rev.	University of Santo Tomas Law Review
Sar.Ch.Sen.	Saratoga Chancery Sentinel
Sask.	Saskatchewan Law Reports
Sask.B.Rev.	Saskatchewan Bar Review
Sask.L.	Saskatchewan Law
Sask.L.Rev.	Saskatchewan Law Review
Sau. & Sc.	Sausee & Scully, Rolls Court (Ir.)
Sauls.	Saulsbury (Del.)
Saund.	Saunders King's Bench (Eng.)
Saund. & Cole	Saunders & Cole, Bail Court (Eng.)
Sav.	Savile, Common Pleas & Exchequer (Eng.)
Sawy.	Sawyer Circuit Court (U.S.)
Sax.	Saxton's Chancery (N.J.)

Say.	Sayer, King's Bench (Eng.)
Sc.Sess.Cas.	Scotch Court of Sessions Cases
Sc.St.Crim.	Scandinavian Studies in Criminology
Sc.St.L.	Scandinavian Studies in Law
Scam.	Scammon (Ill.)
Sch. & Lef.	Schoales & Lefroy, Equity (Ir.)
Scher.	Scherer's Miscellaneous Reports (N.Y.)
Schm.L.J.	Schmidt's Law Journal (New Orleans)
Schuyl.L.Rec.	Schuylkill Legal Record (Pa.)
Scot.Jur.	Scottish Jurist
Scot.L.J.	Scottish Law Journal and Sheriff Court Record
Scot.L.Mag.	Scottish Law Magazine and Sheriff Court Reporter
Scot.L.Rep.	Scottish Law Reporter
Scot.L.Rev.	Scottish Law Review and Sheriff Court Reports
Scot.L.T.	Scottish Law Times
Scots L.T.R.	Scots Law Times Reports
Scott	Scott Common Pleas (Eng.)
Scott N.R.	Scott's New Reports, Common Pleas (Eng.)
Scr.L.T.	Scranton Law Times (Pa.)
Scrivener	Scrivener
Sea Grant L. & Pol'y J.	Sea Grant Law and Policy Journal
Sea Grant L.J.	Sea Grant Law Journal
Search and Seizure	Search and Seizure Bulletin
Sec.L.Rev.	Securities Law Review
Sec.Reg. & Trans.	Securities Regulation and Transfer Report
Sec.Reg.L.J.	Securities Regulation Law Journal
Sel.Cas.	Yates' Select Cases (N.Y.)
Sel.Cas.Ch.	Select Cases in Chancery (Eng.)
Sel.Serv.L. Rptr.	Selective Service Law Reporter
Seld.	Selden's Notes (N.Y.)
Selden	Selden's N. Y. Court of Appeals
Selw.N.P.	Selwyn's Nisi Prius (Eng.)
Seoul L.J.	Seoul Law Journal
Serg. & R.	Sergeant & Rawle (Pa.)
Sess.Ca.	Sessions Cases King's Bench (Eng.)
Sess.Cas.	Court of Sessions Cases (Sc.)
	Sessions Cases King's Bench (Eng.)
Sess.Laws	Session Laws

Seton Hall L. Rev.	Seton Hall Law Review
Seton Hall Leg.J.	Seton Hall Legislative Journal
Sex.L.Rep.	Sexual Law Reporter
Sex Prob.Ct. Dig.	Sex Problems Court Digest
Shad.	Shadford's Victoria Reports
Shan.	Shannon (Tenn.)
Shand	Shand (S.C.)
Shand Pr.	Shand, Practice, Court of Sessions (Sc.)
Shaw	Shaw (Vt.)
	Shaw Appeal Cases, English House of Lords From Scotland
	Shaw, Scotch Justiciary Cases
	Shaw, Scotch Teind Reports, Court of Sessions
Shaw & D.	Shaw & Dunlop (Sc.)
Shaw & Dunl.	Same
Shaw & M.	Shaw & McLean Appeals, House of Lords (Sc.)
Shaw & Macl.	Same
Shaw App.	Shaw Appeal Cases (Sc.)
Shaw Crim. Cas.	Shaw's Criminal Cases, Justiciary Court (Sc.)
Singapore L. Rev.	Singapore Law Review
Shaw, D. & B.	Shaw, Dunlop & Bell's Court of Sessions (1st Series) (Sc.)
	Shaw, Dunlop & Bell's Session Cases (Sc.)
Shaw, D. & B. Supp.	Shaw, Dunlop, & Bell's Supplement, House of Lords Decisions (Sc.)
Shaw Dec.	Shaw's Decisions in Scotch Court of Sessions (1st Series)
Shaw, Dunl. & B.	Shaw, Dunlop & Bell's Sessions Cases (Sc.)
Shaw, W. & C.	Shaw, Wilson & Courtnay, House of Lords
Shep.	Shepherd (Ala.)
	Shepley (Me.)
Shep.Abr.	Sheppard's Abridgment
Shep.Sel.Cas.	Shepherd's Select Cases (Ala.)
Sher.Ct.Rep.	Sheriff Court Reports (Sc.)
Shingle	Shingle
Shipp	Shipp (N.C.)
Shirl.	Shirley (N.H.)
Shirl.L.C.	Shirley's Leading Crown Cases (Eng.)
Show.	Shower King's Bench (Eng.)

Show.P.C.	Shower's Parliamentary Cases (Eng.)
Sick.	Sickel's Court of Appeals (Eng.)
Sid.	Siderfin King's Bench (Eng.)
Sil.	Silver Tax Division (I.R. Bull.)
Silv.A.	Silvernail's Appeals (N.Y.)
Silv.Sup.	Silvernail's Supreme Court (N.Y.)
Silv.Unrep.	Silvernail's Unreported Cases (N.Y.)
Sim.	Simmon's (Wis.)
	Simon's Vice-Chancery (Eng.)
Sim. (N.S.)	Simon's Vice-Chancery, New Series (Eng.)
Sim. & C.	Simmons & Conover (Wis.)
Sim. & St.	Simons & Stuart's Vice-Chancery (Eng.)
Skill.Pol.Rep.	Skillman's N. Y. Police Reports
Skin.	Skinner (King's Bench) (Eng.)
Skink.	Skinker (Mo.)
Sm. & M.	Smedes & Marshall (Miss.)
Sm. & M.Ch.	Smedes & Marshall, Chancery (Miss.)
Sm. & S.	Smith & Sager's Drainage Cases (Ont.), 1904–1917
Smale & G.	Smale & Gifford's Vice-Chancery (Eng.)
Smith	Smith (Calif.) (Dak.) (Eng.) (Ind.) (Me.) (Mo.) (N.H.) (Wis.)
	Smith, E. B. (Ill.)
	Smith, E. D. Common Pleas (N.Y.)
	Smith, E. H. Court of Appeals (N.Y.)
	Smith, E. P. Court of Appeals (N.Y.)
	Smith, P. F. (Pa.)
Smith & B.	Smith & Batty, King's Bench (Ir.)
Smith & B.R.C.	Smith & Bates, American Railway Cases
Smith & G.	Smith & Guthrie (Mo.)
Smith & H.	Smith & Heiskell (Tenn.)
Smith C.C.M.	Smith Circuit Courts-Martial (Me.)
Smith Cond.	Smith's Condensed Alabama Reports
Smith K.B.	Smith's King's Bench (Eng.)
Smith L.J.	Smith's Law Journal
Smith Lead. Cas.	Smith's Leading Cases (Eng.)

Smith Reg. Cas.	Smith's Registration Cases (Eng.)
Smy.	Smythe Common Pleas (Ir.)
Smythe	Same
Sneed	Sneed (Tenn.)
	Sneed's Decisions (Ky.)
Sneed Dec.	Sneed's Kentucky Decisions
Sneedy Ky.	Same
Snow	Snow (Utah)
So.	Southern Reporter
So.2d	Same, Second Series
So.Calif.L. Rev.	Southern California Law Review
So.Car.Const.	South Carolina Constitutional Reports
So.Car.L.J.	South Carolina Law Journal
So.L.J.	Southern Law Journal (Nashville)
So.L.Q.	Southern Law Quarterly
So.L.Rev.	Southern Law Review (Nashville)
	Southern Law Review (St. Louis)
So.L.Rev. (N.S.)	Southern Law Review, New Series (St. Louis)
So.Law T.	Southern Law Times
So.Tex.L.J.	South Texas Law Journal
So.U.L.Rev.	Southern University Law Review
Soc. & Lab. Bull.	Social and Labour Bulletin
Soc.Action & L.	Social Action and the Law
Soc.Sec.Bull.	Social Security Bulletin
Sol.	Solicitor
Sol.J.	Solicitor's Journal (Eng.)
Sol.Op.	Solicitor's Opinions (I.R. Bull.)
Sol.Q.	Solicitor Quarterly
Solar L.Rep.	Solar Law Reporter
Somerset L.J.	Somerset Legal Journal
Southard	Southard (N.J.)
Southwestern L.J.	Southwestern Law Journal
Soviet Jewry L.Rev.	Soviet Jewry Law Review
Soviet L. & Gov't	Soviet Law and Government
Soviet Stat. & Dec.	Soviet Statutes and Decisions
Soviet Y.B. Int'l L.	Soviet Year-Book of International Law
Spaulding	Spaulding (Me.)
Spear	Spear's Law (S.C.)
Spear Ch.	Spear's (or Speer) Chancery (S.C.)
Spear Eq.	Spear's Equity (S.C.)
Speer	See Spear

Spenc.	Spencer (Minn.)
	Spencer Law (N.J.)
Spencer	Spencer Law (N.J.)
Spinks	Spinks Ecclesiastical and Admiralty (Eng.)
Spinks Eccl. & Adm.	Same
Spoon.	Spooner (Wis.)
Spooner	Same
Spott.	Spottiswoode (Sc.)
Spott.C.L. Rep.	Spottiswoode's Common Law
Spottis.	Spottiswoode (Sc.)
Spottis.C.L. & Eq.Rep.	Common Law & Equity Reports published by Spottiswoode
Spottis.Eq.	Spottiswoode's Equity (Sc.)
Sprague	Sprague (U. S. District Court Admiralty)
St.Rep.	State Reporter
St.Rep.N.S.W.	State Reports (New South Wales)
Stafford	Stafford (Vt.)
Stair	Stair (Sc.)
Stan.Envt'l L.Ann.	Stanford Environmental Law Annual
Stan.J.Int'l Stud.	Stanford Journal of International Studies
Stan.L.Rev.	Stanford Law Review
Stan.Pa.Prac.	Standard Pennsylvania Practice
Stant.	Stanton (Ohio)
Stanton	Same
Star Ch.Cas.	Star Chamber Cases (Eng.)
Stark.	Starkie's Nisi Prius (Eng.)
Stat.	Statutes at Large (U.S.)
Stat. at L.	Same
State Court J.	State Court Journal
State Gov't	State Government
State Tr.	State Trials (Eng.)
Stath.Abr.	Statham's Abridgment
Stetson L.Rev.	Stetson Law Review
Stev. & G.	Stevens & Graham (Ga.)
Stew.	Stewart (Ala.) (S.D.)
	Stewart's Reports (N.S.)
Stew. & P.	Stewart & Porter (Ala.)
Stew.Admr.	Stewart's Admiralty (N.S.)
Stew.Eq.	Stewart's Equity (N.J.)
Stewart	Stewart's Vice-Admiralty Reports (N.S.)
Stiles	Stiles (Iowa)
Still.Eccl.Cas.	Stillingfleet's Ecclesiastical Cases (Eng.)
Stiness	Stiness (R.I.)
Stockett	Stockett (Md.)
Stockt.	Stockton's Equity (N.J.)
Stockt.Vice-Adm.	Stockton's Vice-Admiralty (N.B.)
Stockton	Same
Storey	Storey
Story	Story (U.S.)
Story Eq.Jur.	Story on Equity Jurisprudence
Str.	Strange's King's Bench (Eng.)
Stra.	Same
Strahan	Strahan (Ore.)
Straits L.J. & Rep.	Straits Law Journal and Reporter
Stratton	Stratton (Ore.)
Stringf.	Stringfellow (Mo.)
Strob.	Strobhart's Law (S.C.)
Strob.Eq.	Strobhart's Equity (S.C.)
Stu.M. & P.	Stuart, Milne & Peddie (Sc.)
Stu.Mil. & Ped.	Same
Stuart	Stuart's King's Bench (Lower Can.)
Stuart Vice-Adm.	Stuart's Vice-Admiralty (Lower Can.)
Stud.Int'l Fiscal L.	Studies on International Fiscal Law
Stud.L. & Econ.Dev.	Studies in Law and Economic Development
Student Law.	Student Lawyer
Student Law. J.	Student Lawyer Journal
Studia Canonica	Studia Canonica
Style	Style, King's Bench, Rolle & Glyn's Decisions (Eng.)
Suffolk Transnat'l L.J.	Suffolk Transnational Law Journal
Suffolk U.L. Rev.	Suffolk University Law Review
Summerfield	Summerfield (Nev.)
Sumn.	Sumner Circuit Court (U.S.)
Sup. & C.P. Dec.	Ohio Decisions
Sup.Ct.	Superior Court (Pa.)
Sup.Ct.Hist. Soc'y Y.B.	Supreme Court Historical Society Yearbook
Sup.Ct.Hist. Soc'y Q.	Supreme Court Historical Society Quarterly
Sup.Ct.Rep.	Supreme Court Reporter (U.S.)
Sup.Ct.Rev.	Supreme Court Review
Susq.Leg. Chron.	Susquehanna Legal Chronical (Pa.)
Sw.L.J.	Southwestern Law Journal
Sw.U.L.Rev.	Southwestern University Law Review
Swab.	Swabey's Admiralty (Eng.)

Swab. & Tr.	Swabey & Tristram, Probate & Divorce (Eng.)
Swan	Swan (Tenn.)
Swanst.	Swanston Chancery (Eng.)
Sween.	Sweeney's Superior Court (N.Y.)
Swin.	Swinton's Registration Appeal Cases (Sc.)
Sydney L. Rev.	Sydney Law Review
Syme	Syme's Justiciary Cases (Sc.)
Symposium Jun.B.	Symposium l'Association de jeune Barreau de Montreal
Syn.Ser.	Synopsis Series of Treasury Decisions (U.S.)
Syracuse J. Int'l L. & Com.	Syracuse Journal of International Law and Commerce
Syracuse L. Rev.	Syracuse Law Review

T

T.	Tappan's Reports (Ohio)
	Tobacco Division (I.R.Bull.)
T. & C.	Thompson & Cook N. Y. Supreme Court Reports
T. & G.	Tyrwhitt & Granger's Exchequer (Eng.)
T. & M.	Temple & Mew's Crown Cases (Eng.)
T. & P.	Turner & Phillips' Chancery (Eng.)
T. & R.	Turner & Russell's Chancery (Eng.)
T.B. & M.	Tracewell, Bowers & Mitchell, Comptroller's Decisions (U.S.)
T.B.M.	Tax Board Memorandum (I.R.Bull.)
T.B.Mon.	T. B. Monroe (Ky.)
T.B.R.	Advisory Tax Board Recommendation (I.R.Bull.)
T.B.R.	Tariff Board Reports, 1937–1962
T.C.	Tax Court of the United States Reports
TCR	Tribal Court Reporter
T.D.	Treasury Decisions
t.Holt	Same as Modern Cases (Eng.)
T.I.A.S.	Treaties and Other International Acts Series (U.S.)
T.I.Agree.	Treaties and Other International Agreements of the United States of America 1776–1949
T.I.F.	Treaties in Force
T.Jones	Thomas Jones, King's Bench and Common Pleas (Eng.)
T.L.R.	Times Law Reports (Eng.)
T.M.Bull.	Trade Mark Bulletin (U.S.)
T.M.Bull. (N.S.)	Same, New Series
T.M.M.	Tax Management Memorandum (BNA)
T.M.Rep.	Trade Mark Reporter
T.N.E.C.	Temporary National Economic Committee
T.R.	Term Reports, King's Bench (Durnford & East) (Eng.)
T.Raym.	Thomas Raymond, King's Bench (Eng.)
T.S.	Treaty Series (U.S.)
T.T.	Jurisprudence de droit de travail, 1970–
T.U.P.Charlt.	T. U. P. Charlton (Ga.)
Tait	Tait's Manuscript Decisions (Sc.)
Tal.	Cases temp. Talbot, Chancery (Eng.)
Talb.	Same
Tam.	Tamlyn (Rolls Court) (Eng.)
Taml.	Same
Tamlyn	Tamlyn's Chancery (Eng.)
Tamlyn Ch.	Same
Taney	Taney, Circuit Court (U.S.)
Tann.	Tanner (Ind.)
Tanner	Same
Tapp.	Tappan's Reports (Ohio)
Tappan	Same
Tasm.	Tasmanian State Reports
Tasm.L.R.	Tasmania Law Reports
Tasm.U.L. Rev.	Tasmania University Law Review
Taun.	Taunton, Common Pleas (Eng.)
Taunt.	Same

Tax A.B.C.	Canada Tax Appeal Board Cases
Tax Adm'rs News	Tax Administrators News
Tax Advisor	The Tax Advisor
Tax Cas.	Tax Cases (Eng.)
Tax Counselor's Q.	Tax Counselor's Quarterly
Tax L.Rep.	Tax Law Reporter
Tax L.Rev.	Tax Law Review
Tax Law.	The Tax Lawyer
Tax Mag.	Tax Magazine
Tax Pract. Forum	Tax Practitioners Forum
Tax. for Law.	Taxation for Lawyers
Tax.R.	Taxation Reports
Taxes	Taxes, The Tax Magazine
Tay.	Taylor's Carolina Reports (N.C.)
	Taylor's King's Bench (Can.)
	Taylor's Term Reports (N.C.)
Taylor	Same
Taylor, U.C.	Taylor, King's Bench (Ont.)
Tel-Aviv U. Stud.L.	Tel-Aviv University Studies in Law
Temp. & M.	Temple & Mew Crown Cases (Eng.)
Temp.Geo.II	Cases in Chancery temp. Geo. II. (Eng.)
Temp.L.Q.	Temple Law Quarterly
Temp.Wood	Manitoba Reports temp. Wood (Can.)
Temple & M.	Temple & Mew Crown Cases (Eng.)
Temple L.Q.	Temple Law Quarterly
Tenn.	Tennessee
Tenn.App.	Tennessee Appeals
Tenn.App. Bull.	Tennessee Appellate Bulletin
Tenn.B.J.	Tennessee Bar Journal
Tenn.C.C.A.	Tennessee Court of Civil Appeals
Tenn.Cas.	Shannon's Tennessee Cases
Tenn.Ch.	Tennessee Chancery, Cooper
Tenn.Ch.App.	Tennessee Chancery Appeals
Tenn.Civ.App.	Tennessee Court of Civil Appeals
Tenn.Crim. App.	Tennessee Criminal Appeals Reports
Tenn.L.Rev.	Tennessee Law Review
Tenn.Leg.Rep.	Tennessee Legal Reporter
Term	Term Reports, King's Bench (See Durnford & East) (Eng.)
Term N.C.	Term Reports, North Carolina (Taylor)
Term R.	Term Reports, King's Bench (See Durnford and East) (Eng.)
Term Rep.	Same
Terr.	Terrell (Tex.)
Terr. & Wal.	Terrell & Walker (Tex.)
Terr.L.R.	Territories' Law Reports N. W.
Terry	Terry
Tex.	Texas
Tex.A.Civ. Cas.	White & Wilson's Civil Cases (Tex.)
Tex.A.Civ. Cas. (Wilson)	Texas Court of Appeal Civil Cases
Tex.App.	Texas Civil Appeals Cases
	Texas Court of Appeals Cases
Tex.B.J.	Texas Bar Journal
Tex.Civ.App.	Texas Civil Appeals
Tex.Civ.Rep.	Same
Tex.Com.App.	Texas Commission Appeals
Tex.Cr.App.	Texas Criminal Appeals
Tex.Cr.R.	Same
Tex.Crim.	Texas Criminal Reports
Tex.Ct.App. R.	Texas Court of Appeals Reports
Tex.Dec.	Texas Decisions
Tex.Int.L. Forum	Texas International Law Forum
Tex.Int'l L.F.	Same
Tex.Int'l L.J.	Texas International Law Journal
Tex.Jur.	Texas Jurisprudence
Tex.Jur.2d	Same, Second Series
Tex.L.J.	Texas Law Journal
Tex.L.Rev.	Texas Law Review
Tex.Law.	Texas Lawman
Tex.S.Ct.	Texas Supreme Court Reporter
Tex.So.U.L. Rev.	Texas Southern University Law Review
Tex.Supp.	Texas Supplement
Tex.Tech L. Rev.	Texas Tech Law Review
Tex.Unrep. Cas.	(Posey's) Unreported Cases (Tex.)
Texas L.Rev.	Texas Law Review
Th. & C.	Thompson & Cook's N. Y. Supreme Court
Thatcher Cr.	Thatcher's Criminal Cases (Mass.)
Thayer	Thayer (Ore.)
Themis	La Revue Juridique Themis
Thom.	Thomson's Reports (Nova Scotia)

Thomas & Fr.	Thomas & Franklin Chancery (Md.)
Thomp.	Thompson (Cal.)
Thomp.Tenn. Cas.	Thompson's Unreported Tennessee Cases
Thompson & C.	Thompson & Cook New York Supreme Court
Thomson	Thomson's Reports (Nova Scotia)
Thor.	Thorington (Ala.)
Thorpe	Thorpe's Louisiana Annual
Thur.Marsh. L.J.	Thurgood Marshall Law Journal
Tiff.	Tiffany Court Appeals (N.Y.)
Tiffany	Same
Till.	Tillman (Ala.)
Tillman	Same
Timber Tax J.	Timber Tax Journal
Tinw.	Tinwald (Sc.)
Title News	Title News
Tobey	Tobey (R.I.)
Toth.	Tothill's Chancery (Eng.)
Tr. & Est.	Trusts & Estates
Tr. & H.Pr.	Troubat & Haly's Practice (Pa.)
Trace. & M.	Tracefell & Mitchell (Comptroller's Decisions) (U.S.)
Trade Cas.	Trade Cases (CCH)
Trade Reg. Rep.	Trade Regulation Reporter (CCH)
Trade Reg. Rev.	Trade Regulation Review
Trademark Bull.	Trade-Mark Bulletin
Trademark Bull. (N.S.)	Same, New Series
Trademark Rep.	Trade-Mark Reporter
Trans. & Wit.	Transvaal & Witswatersrand Reports
Transc.A.	Transcript Appeals (N.Y.)
Transit L.Rev.	Transit Law Review
Transp.L.J.	Transportation Law Journal
Trauma	Trauma
Tread.Const.	Treadway's Constitutional Rep. (S.C.)
Treas.Dec.	Treasury Decisions (U.S.)
Trem.P.C.	Tremaine, Pleas of Crown

Trent L.J.	Trent Law Journal
Trial	Trial
Trial Law. Forum	Trial Lawyers Forum
Trial Law. Guide	Trial Lawyer's Guide
Trial Law.Q.	Trial Lawyers' Quarterly
Trin.T.	Trinity Term (Eng.)
Tripp	Tripp (Dak.Terr.)
Tru.	Trueman's Equity Cases (N.B.)
Tru.Railw. Rep.	Truman, American Railway Reports
Truem.Eq. Cas.	Trueman's Equity Cases (N.B.)
Trust Bull.	Trust Bulletin
Trust Terr.	Trust Territory Reports
Tuck.	Tucker (Mass.)
Tuck. & C.	Tucker & Clephane (D.C.)
Tuck.Dist. of Col.	Tucker's Appeals (D.C.)
Tuck.Sel.Cas.	Tucker's Select Cases (Newf.)
Tuck.Surr.	Tucker's Surrog[illegible] (N.Y.)
Tul.L.Rev.	Tulane Law Review
Tul.Tax Inst.	Tulane Tax Institute
Tulane L.Rev.	Tulane Law Review
Tulsa L.J.	Tulsa Law Journal
Tupp.App.	Tupper's Appeal Reports (Ont.)
Turn.	Turner (Ark.)
	Turner (Ky.)
	Turner & Russell's Chancery (Eng.)
Turn. & P.	Turner & Phillips' Chancery (Eng.)
Turn. & Ph.	Same
Turn. & R.	Turner & Russell's Chancery (Eng.)
Turn. & Rus.	Same
Turn. & Russ.	Same
Tutt.	Tuttle (Cal.)
Tutt. & C.	Tuttle & Carpenter (Cal.)
Tutt. & Carp.	Same
Tyler	Tyler (Vt.)
Tyng	Tyng (Mass.)
Tyrw.	Tyrwhitt Exchequer (Eng.)
Tyrw. & G.	Tyrwhitt & Granger Exchequer (Eng.)

U

U.Ark.Little Rock L.J.	University of Arkansas at Little Rock Law Journal
U.B.C.L.Rev.	University of British Columbia Law Review
U.B.C.Notes	University of British Columbia Legal Notes
U.Balt.L.Rev.	University of Baltimore Law Review

U.Bridgeport L.Rev.	University of Bridgeport Law Review
U.C.	Upper Canada
U.C. (O.S.)	Upper Canada Queen's Bench Reports, Old Series
U.C.App.	Upper Canada Appeal Reports
U.C.App. Rep.	Same
U.C.C.L.J.	Uniform Commercial Code Law Journal
U.C.C.Law Letter	Uniform Commercial Code Law Letter
U.C.C.P.	Upper Canada Common Pleas Reports
U.C.C.P.D.	Upper Canada Common Pleas Division Reports (Ont.)
U.C.C.Rep. Serv.	Uniform Commercial Code Reporting Service
U.C.Ch.	Upper Canada Chancery Reports
U.C.Ch. Rep.	Same
U.C.Cham.	Upper Canada Chamber Reports
U.C.Chamb. Rep.	Same
U.C.Chan.	Upper Canada Chancery Reports
U.C.D.L.Rev.	University of California at Davis Law Review
U.C.E. & A.	Upper Canada Error & Appeals Reports
U.C.Err. & App.	Same
U.C.I.S.	Benefit Series, Unemployment Compensation Interpretation Service
	Federal Series, Unemployment Compensation Interpretation Service
	State Series, Unemployment Compensation Interpretation Service
U.C.Jur.	Upper Canada Jurist
U.C.K.B.	Upper Canada King's Bench Reports, Old Series
U.C.L.A. Intra.L.Rev.	U.C.L.A. Intramural Law Review
U.C.L.A. L.Rev.	U.C.L.A. Law Review
U.C.L.A.—Alaska L. Rev.	U.C.L.A.—Alaska Law Review
U.C.L.J.	Upper Canada Law Journal
U.C.L.J. (N.S.)	Same, New Series
U.C.P.R.	Upper Canada Practice Reports
U.C.Pr.	Same
U.C.Q.B.	Upper Canada Queen's Bench Reports
U.C.Q.B. (O.S.)	Same, Old Series
U.C.R.	Upper Canada Queen's Bench Reports
U.C.Rep.	Upper Canada Reports
U.Chi.L.Rec.	University of Chicago Law School Record
U.Chi.L.Rev.	University of Chicago Law Review
U.Cin.L.Rev.	University of Cincinnati Law Review
U.Colo.L. Rev.	University of Colorado Law Review
U.Dayton L. Rev.	University of Dayton Law Review
U.Det.J.Urb.L.	University of Detroit Journal of Urban Law
U.Det.L.J.	University of Detroit Law Journal
U.East. L.J.	University of the East Law Journal
U.Fla.L.Rev.	University of Florida Law Review
U.Ghana L.J.	University of Ghana Law Journal
U.Hawaii L.Rev.	University of Hawaii Law Review
U.I.L.R.	University of IFE Law Reports (Nigeria)
U.Ill.L.F.	University of Illinois Law Forum
U.Ill.L.Forum	University of Illinois Law Forum
U.Kan.City L.Rev.	University of Kansas City Law Review
U.Kan.L.Rev.	University of Kansas Law Review
UMKC L.Rev.	UMKC Law Review
U.Miami L. Rev.	University of Miami Law Review
U.Mich.J.L. Ref.	University of Michigan Journal of Law Reform
U.Mo.Bull.L. Ser.	University of Missouri Bulletin Law Series
U.Mo.K.C. L.Rev.	University of Missouri at Kansas City Law Review
U.N.	United Nations Law Reports
U.N.B.L.J.	University of New Brunswick Law Journal
U.N.Comm. Int'l Trade L.Y.B.	United Nations Commission on International Trade Law Yearbook

U.N.Doc.	United Nations Documents
U.N. ECOSOC	United Nations Economic and Social Council Records
U.N. GAOR	United Nations General Assembly Official Records
U.N.Jur.Y.B.	United Nations Juridical Yearbook
U.N.M.T.	United Nations Multilateral Treaties
U.N.R.I.A.A.	United Nations Reports of International Arbitral Awards
U.N.Res., Ser. I	United Nations Resolutions, Series I
U.N. SCOR	United Nations Security Council Official Records
U.N.T.S.	United Nations Treaty Series
U.New S. Wales L.J.	University of New South Wales Law Journal
U.Newark L.Rev.	University of Newark Law Review
U.Pa.L.Rev.	University of Pennsylvania Law Review
U.Pitt.L.Rev.	University of Pittsburgh Law Review
U.Puget Sound L.Rev.	University of Puget Sound Law Review
U.Queensl.L.J.	University of Queensland Law Journal
U.Rich.L.Rev.	University of Richmond Law Review
U.S.	United States Reports
U.S. & Can. Av.	United States and Canadian Aviation Reports
U.S.App.	United States Appeals
U.S.Av.R.	Aviation Reports (U.S.)
U.S.Aviation	Same
U.S.C.	United States Code
U.S.C. (Supp.)	United States Code, Supplement
U.S.C.A.	U. S. Code Annotated
U.S.C.Govt'l Rev.	University of South Carolina Governmental Review
U.S.C.M.A.	United States Court of Military Appeals
U.S.C.S.	United States Code Service
U.S.Code Cong. & Ad.News	United States Code Congressional & Administrative News
U.S.Ct.Cl.	United States Court of Claims Reports
U.S.D.C.	United States District Court
U.S.I.C.C.V.R.	U. S. Interstate Commerce Commission Valuation Reports
U.S.Jur.	United States Jurist (D.C.)
U.S.L.Ed.	United States Supreme Court Reports, Lawyers' Edition
U.S.L.J.	United States Law Journal
U.S.L.Mag.	United States Law Magazine
U.S.L.Rev.	United States Law Review
U.S.L.Week	United States Law Week
U.S.Law.Ed.	United States Supreme Court Reports, Lawyers' Edition
U.S.M.C.	U. S. Maritime Commission
U.S.M.L.Mag.	United States Monthly Law Magazine
U.S.P.Q.	United States Patent Quarterly
U.S.S.B.	U. S. Shipping Board
U.S.S.C.Rep.	United States Supreme Court Reports
U.S.Sup.Ct. Rep.	United States Supreme Court Reporter (West)
U.S.T.	United States Treaties and Other International Agreements
U.S.T.D.	United States Treaty Development
U.S.Tax Cas.	United States Tax Cases (CCH)
U.S.V.A.A.D.	U. S. Veterans Administration Administrator's Decisions
U.S.V.B.D.D.	U. S. Veterans Bureau Directors Decisions
U.San.Fernando V.L.Rev.	University of San Fernando Valley Law Review
U.S.F.L.Rev.	University of San Francisco Law Review
[e.g.] U.So.Cal. 1955 Tax Inst.	University of Southern California Tax Institute
U.Tasm.L. Rev.	University of Tasmania Law Review (or Tasmania University Law Review)
U.Tol.L.Rev.	University of Toledo Law Review
U.Tor.Fac.L. Rev.	University of Toronto Faculty of Law Review
U.Tor.L.Rev.	University of Toronto School of Law Review
U.Toronto Fac. L.Rev.	University of Toronto Faculty of Law Review
U.Toronto L.J.	University of Toronto Law Journal
U.Toronto Sch. L.Rev.	University of Toronto School of Law Review

U.W.Austl.L. Rev.	University of Western Australia Law Review
U.W.L.A.L. Rev.	University of West Los Angeles Law Review
U.Wash.L. Rev.	University of Washington Law Review
U.Windsor L.Rev.	University of Windsor Law Review
Udal	Fiji Law Reports (Fiji)
Uganda L.Foc.	Uganda Law Focus
Un.Prac.News	Unauthorized Practice News
Unempl.Ins. Rep.	Unemployment Insurance Reporter (CCH)
Unif.L.Conf. Can.	Uniform Law Conference of Canada
Unific.L.Y.B.	Unification of Law Yearbook
Uniform L.Rev.	Uniform Law Review
Unof.	Unofficial Reports
Up.Can.L.J.	Upper Canada Law Journal
Urb.L. & Pol'y	Urban Law and Policy
Urb.L.Ann.	Urban Law Annual
Urb.Law.	Urban Lawyer
Urban Affairs Rep.	Urban Affairs Reporter (CCH)
Urban L.Rev.	Urban Law Review
Utah	Utah
Utah 2d	Same, Second Series
Utah L.Rev.	Utah Law Review
Util.L.Rep.	Utilities Law Reporter (CCH)
Util.Sect. Newsl.	Utility Section Newsletter

V

V.C.Rep.	Vice Chancellor's Reports (Eng.)
V.I.	Virgin Islands Reports
V.I.B.J.	Virgin Islands Bar Journal
VJNRL	Virginia Journal of Natural Resources Law
V.R.	Valuation Reports, Interstate Commerce Commission
Va.	Virginia
Va.Bar News	Virginia Bar News
Va.Cas.	Virginia Cases
Va.Ch.Dec.	Chancery Decisions (Va.)
Va.Dec.	Virginia Decisions
Va.J.Int'l L.	Virginia Journal of International Law
Va.J.Nat. Resources L.	Virginia Journal of Natural Resources Law
Va.L.J.	Virginia Law Journal
Va.L.Reg.	Virginia Law Register
Va.L.Reg. (N.S.)	Same, New Series
Va.L.Rev.	Virginia Law Review
Va.R.	Virginia Reports (Gilmer)
Val.R. (I.C.C.)	Interstate Commerce Commission Valuation Reports
Val.U.L.Rev.	Valparaiso University Law Review
Van K.	Van Koughnett's Common Pleas (Upper Can.)
Van Ness Prize Cas.	Van Ness Prize Cases (U.S.)
Vand.J. Transnat'l L.	Vanderbilt Journal of Transnational Law
Vand.L.Rev.	Vanderbilt Law Review
Vaug.	Vaughan Common Pleas (Eng.)
Vaugh.	Same
Vaughan	Same
Vaux	Vaux Decisions (Pa.)
	Vaux Recorder's Decisions (Pa.)
Ve.	Vesey Chancery Reports (Eng.)
	Vesey, Senior, Chancery (Eng.)
Ve. & B.	Vesey & Beames Chancery (Eng.)
Veaz.	Veazey (Vt.)
Veazey	Same
Vent.	Ventris King's Bench (Eng.)
	Ventris Common Pleas (Eng.)
Ventr.	Ventris King's Bench (Eng.)
Ver.	Vermont
Vern.	Vernon's Cases (Eng.)
Vern. & S.	Vernor & Scriven, King's Bench (Ir.)
Vern. & Sc.	Same
Vern. & Scr.	Same
Vern. & Scriv.	Same
Vern.Ch.	Vernon's Chancery (Eng.)
Ves.	Vesey Chancery Reports (Eng.)
	Vesey, Senior, Chancery (Eng.)
Ves. & B.	Vesey & Beames' (Eng.)
Ves. & Bea.	Same
Ves. & Beam.	Same
Ves.Jr.	Vesey, Junior, Chancery (Eng.)

Ves.Jun.	Same
Ves.Jun.Supp.	Vesey, Junior, Supplement, Chancery (Eng.)
Ves.Sen.	Vesey, Senior, Chancery (Eng.)
Ves.Sr.	Same
Ves.Supp.	Vesey, Senior, Supplement, Chancery (Eng.)
Vez.	Vezey, Same as Vesey
Vict.	Victoria
Vict.Admr.	Victorian Admiralty
Vict.Eq.	Victorian Equity
Vict.L.	Victorian Law
Vict.L.R.	Victorian Law Reports
Vict.L.R.Min.	Victorian Law Mining Reports
Vict.L.T.	Victorian Law Times
Vict.Rev.	Victorian Review
Vict.St.Tr.	Victorian State Trials
Vict.U.L.Rev.	Victoria University Law Review
Vict.U.Well. L.Rev.	Victoria University of Wellington Law Review
Vil. & Br.	Vilas & Bryant's Ed. Reports (Wis.)
Vilas	Vilas' N. Y. Criminal Reports
Vill.L.Rev.	Villanova Law Review
Vin.Abr.	Viner's Abridgment (Eng.)
Vin.Supp.	Viner's Abridgment Supplement (Eng.)
Vir.	Virgin (Me.)
Virgin	Same
Virgin Is.	Virgin Islands
Vr.	Vroom's Law Reports (N.J.)
Vroom	Same
Vroom (G.D.W.)	Vroom, G. D. W. (N.J.)
Vroom (P.D.)	Vroom, P. D. (N.J.)
Vt.	Vermont
Vt.L.Rev.	Vermont Law Review

W

W.	Watts (Pa.)
	Wandell (N.Y.)
	Wheaton's Supreme Court (U.S.)
	Wright (Ohio)
W.A'B. & W.	Webb, A'Beckett & Williams (Victoria)
W.A.C.A.	Selected Judgments of the West African Court of Appeals
W. & C.	Wilson & Courtenay's Appeal Cases
W. & M.	Woodbury & Minot Circuit Court (U.S.)
W. & S.	Watts & Sergeant (Pa.)
	Wilson & Shaw's Appeal Cases (Sc.)
W. & W.	White & Webb's Victorian Reports
W. & W.Vict.	Wyatt & Webb's Victorian Reports
W.Afr.App.	West African Court of Appeal Reports
W.Austl.Ind. Gaz.	Western Australia Industrial Gazette
W.Austl.J.P.	Western Australia Justice of the Peace
W.Austl.L.R.	Western Australia Law Reports
W.Bl.	Sir William Blackstone's King's Bench & Common Pleas (Eng.)
W.Bla.	Same
W.C.C.	Washington's Circuit Court (U.S.)
	Workmen's Compensation Cases
W.C.Ins.Rep.	Workmen's Compensation & Insurance Reports
W.C.Rep.	Workmen's Compensation Reports
W.Coast Rep.	West Coast Reporter
W.F.P.D.2d	West's Federal Practice Digest, Second Series
W.H. & G.	Welsby, Hurlstone & Gordon's Exchequer (Eng.)
W.H.Cases	Wage & Hour Cases
W.H.Man.	Wages & Hours Manual
W.H.R.	Wage & Hour Reporter
W.Jo.	William Jones King's Bench, Common Pleas, House of Lords and Exchequer (Eng.)
W.Jones	Same
W.Kel.	William Kellynge, King's Bench & Chancery (Eng.)
W.L.A.C.	Western Labour Arbitration Cases, 1966–
W.L.Bull.	Weekly Law Bulletin
W.L.G.	Weekly Law Gazette (Ohio)
W.L.Gaz.	Same
W.L.J.	Western Law Journal

W.L.Jour.	Weekly Law Journal
W.L.M.	Western Law Monthly (Ohio)
W.L.R.	Weekly Law Reports (Eng.) Western Law Reporter Women Law Reporter
W.L.T.	Western Law Times and Reports
W.N.	Weekly Notes (Eng.)
W.New Eng.L. Rev.	Western New England Law Review
W.Ont.L.Rev.	Western Ontario Law Review
W.R.	Weekly Reports
W.Res.L. Rev.	Western Reserve Law Review
W.Rob.	William Robinson's Admiralty (Eng.)
W.St.U.L.Rev.	Western State University Law Review
W.Va.	West Virginia
W.Va.Crim. Just.Rev.	West Virginia Criminal Justice Review
W.Va.L.Q.	West Virginia Law Quarterly
W.Va.L.Rev.	West Virginia Law Review
W.W. & D.	Willmore, Wollaston & Davison, Queen's Bench (Eng.)
W.W. & H.	Willmore, Wollaston & Hodges' Queen's Bench (Eng.)
W.W.D.	Western Weekly Digests, 1975–
W.W.Harr.	W. W. Harrington (Del.)
W.W.R.	Western Weekly Report (Can.)
W.W.R. (N.S.)	Same, New Series, 1951–1955
Wa.	Watts (Pa.) Wage and Hour Reporter
Wage & Hour Cas.	Wage and Hour Cases (BNA)
Wage & Hour Rep.	Wage & Hour Reporter
Wage-Price L. & Econ. Rev.	Wage-Price Law and Economics Review
Wake For. L.Rev.	Wake Forest Law Review
Wake Forest Intra.L.Rev.	Wake Forest Intramural Law Review
Wake Forest L.Rev.	Wake Forest Law Review
Wal.By L.	Wallis, Irish Chancery (By Lyne)
Wal.Jr.	Wallace Junior (U.S.)
Walk.	Walker (Ala.) (Miss.) (Pa.) (Tex.)
Walk.Ch.	Walker's Chancery (Mich.)
Walk.Ch.Cas.	Same
Wall.	Wallace (U.S.) (Philadelphia)
Wall.C.C.	Wallace Circuit Court (U.S.)
Wall.Jr.	Wallace Junior (U.S.)
Wall.Rep.	Wallace's Supreme Court Reports (U.S.) Wallace, The Reporters
Wall.Sr.	Wallace Senior (U.S.)
Wallis	Wallis' Chancery (Ir.)
Wallis by L.	Wallis, Irish Chancery (By Lyne)
Walsh	Walsh's Registry Cases (Ir.)
Ward.	Warden (Ohio)
Ward. & Sm.	Warden & Smith (Ohio)
Warden's Law & Bk.Bull.	Weekly Law & Bank Bulletin (Ohio)
Ware	Ware, District Court (U.S.)
Wash.	Washington Washington Reports (Va.)
Wash.2d	Washington Reports, Second Series
Wash.App.	Washington Appellate Reports
Wash. & Haz. P.E.I.	Washburton & Hazard's Reports (Prince Edward Island)
Wash. & Lee L.Rev.	Washington & Lee Law Review
Wash.C.C.	Washington Circuit Court (U.S.)
Wash.L.Rep.	Washington Law Reporter (D.C.)
Wash.L.Rev.	Washington Law Review
Wash.Terr.	Washington Territory
Wash.Terr. (N.S.)	Same, New Series
Wash.Ty.	Washington Territory
Wash.U.L.Q.	Washington University Law Quarterly
Washb.	Washburn (Vt.)
Washburn L.J.	Washburn Law Journal
Watts	Watts (Pa.) (W.Va.)
Watts & S.	Watts & Sergeant (Pa.)
Watts & Ser.	Same
Watts & Serg.	Same
Wayne L.Rev.	Wayne Law Review
Webb	Webb (Kans.) (Tex.) Webb's Civil Appeals (Tex.)
Webb & D.	Webb & Duval (Tex.)

Webb & Duval	Same
Webb, A'B. & W.	Webb, A'Beckett & Williams Reports (Aust.)
Webs.Pat.Cas.	Webster's Patent Cases (Eng.)
Week.Cin.L.B.	Weekly Law Bulletin (Ohio)
Week.Dig.	Weekly Digest (N.Y.)
Week.Jur.	Weekly Jurist (Ill.)
Week.L.Gaz.	Weekly Law Gazette (Ohio)
Week.L.Rec.	Weekly Law Record
Week.Law Bull.	Weekly Law Bulletin (Ohio)
Week.Law Gaz.	Weekly Law Gazette (Ohio)
Week.Notes Cas.	Weekly Notes of Cases (London)
	Weekly Notes of Cases (Pa.)
Week.Rep.	Weekly Reporter (Eng.)
Week.Trans. Rep.	Weekly Transcript Reports (N.Y.)
Weekly L.R.	Weekly Law Reports (Eng.)
Welfare L. Bull.	Welfare Law Bulletin
Welfare L. News	Welfare Law News
Welsb.H. & G.	Welsby, Hurlstone & Gordon's Exchequer (Eng.)
Welsby H. & G.	Same
Welsh	Welsh's Registry Cases (Ir.)
Wend.	Wendell (N.Y.)
Wenz.	Wenzell (Minn.)
Wes.C.L.J.	Westmoreland County Law Journal
West	West's Chancery (Eng.)
West Ch.	West's Chancery (Eng.)
West Va.	West Virginia
West.	Weston (Vt.)
West.Austl.	Western Australian Reports
West.Jur.	Western Jurist (Des Moines)
West.L.Gaz.	Western Law Gazette (Ohio)
West.L.J.	Western Law Journal
West.L.M.	Western Law Monthly (Ohio)
West.L.Mo.	Same
West.L.Month.	Same
West.L.R.	Western Law Reporter (Can.)
West.L.Rev.	Western Law Review
West.Law J.	Western Law Journal
West.Law M.	Western Law Monthly (Ohio)
West.Legal Obser.	Western Legal Observer
West.R.	Western Reporter
West.School L.Rev.	Western School Law Review
West.St.U.L. Rev.	Western State University Law Review
West t.Hardw.	West temp. Hardwicke, Chancery (Eng.)
West.Week. Rep.	Western Weekly Reports (Can.)
West.Wkly.	Western Weekly (Can.)
Western Res. L.Rev.	Western Reserve Law Review
Westm.	Statute of Westminster (Eng.)
Westm.L.J.	Westmoreland Law Journal (Pa.)
Wethey	Wethey's Queen's Bench (Upper Can.)
Whart.	Wharton (Pa.)
Whart.Law Dict.	Wharton's Law Lexicon
Whart.St.Tr.	Wharton's State Trials (U.S.)
Wheat.	Wheaton (U.S.)
Wheel.	Wheeler's Criminal Cases (N.Y.)
	Wheelock (Tex.)
Wheeler Abr.	Wheeler's Abridgment
Wheeler C.C.	Wheeler's Criminal Cases (N.Y.)
Whit.Pat.Cas.	Whitman's Patent Cases (U.S.)
White	White (W.Va.) (Tex.)
	White's Justiciary Cases (Sc.)
White & T. Lead. Cas.Eq.	White & Tudor's Leading Cases in Equity (Eng.)
White & W.	White & Wilson (Tex.)
Whitm.Lib. Cas.	Whitman's Libel Cases (Mass.)
Whitt.	Whittlesey (Mo.)
Whitt.L.Rev.	Whittier Law Review
Wight	Wight's Election Cases (Sc.)
Wight.	Wightwick, Exchequer (Eng.)
Wightw.	Wightwick, Exchequer (Eng.)
Wilc.	Wilcox (Ohio)
Wilc.Cond.	Wilcox Condensed Ohio Reports
Wilcox	Wilcox (Ohio)
	Wilcox (Pa.)
Wilcox Cond.	Wilcox Condensed Ohio Reports

Wilk.	Wilkinson (Aust.)
	Wilkinson Court of Appeals and Civil Appeals (Tex.)
Will.	Williams (Mass.)
	Willson (Tex.)
Will.L.J.	Willamette Law Journal
Will. Woll. & Dav.	Willmore, Wollaston & Davison Queen's Bench (Eng.)
Will.Woll. & H.	Willmore, Wollaston & Hodges' Queen's Bench (Eng.)
Will.Woll. & Hodg.	Same
Willamette L.J.	Willamette Law Journal
Willes	Willes, King's Bench & Common Pleas (Eng.)
Williams	Williams (Mass.) (Utah) (Vt.)
	Peere-Williams' English Chancery Reports
Williams & Bruce Ad.Pr.	Williams & Bruce's Admiralty Practice
Williams P.	Peere-Williams' English Chancery Reports
Williams-Peere	Same
Willm.W. & D.	Willmore, Wollaston & Davison's Queen's Bench (Eng.)
Willm.W. & H.	Willmore, Wollaston & Hodges' Queen's Bench (Eng.)
Willson	Willson Civil Cases (Tex.)
Willson, Civ. Cas.Ct.App.	Same
Wilm.	Wilmot's Notes (Eng.)
Wils.	Wilson (Cal.) (Minn.) (Ore.)
	Wilson (Superior Court) (Ind.)
	Wilson's King's Bench & Common Pleas (Eng.)
Wils. & S.	Wilson & Shaw (House of Lords) (Sc.)
Wils.Ch.	Wilson's Chancery (Eng.)
Wils.C.P.	Wilson's Common Pleas (Eng.)
Wils.Exch.	Wilson's Exchequer (Eng.)
Wils.K.B.	Wilson's King's Bench (Eng.)
Wils.P.C.	Wilson's Privy Council (Eng.)
Winch	Winch, Common Pleas (Eng.)
Winst.	Winston (N.C.)
Wis.	Wisconsin
Wis.2d	Wisconsin Reports, Second Series
Wis.B.Bull.	Wisconsin Bar Bulletin
Wis.B.T.A.	Wisconsin Board of Tax Appeals Reports
Wis.L.N.	Wisconsin Legal News
Wis.L.Rev.	Wisconsin Law Review
Wisc.Stud. B.J.	Wisconsin Student Bar Journal
Wis.Tax. App.C.	Wisconsin Tax Appeals Commission Reports
Withrow	Withrow (Iowa)
Wkly.Dig.	Weekly Digest (N.Y.)
Wkly.L.Bul.	Weekly Law Bulletin (Ohio)
Wkly.L.Gaz.	Weekly Law Gazette (Ohio)
Wkly.Law Bull.	Weekly Law Bulletin (Ohio)
Wkly.N.C.	Weekly Notes of Cases (Pa.)
Wkly.Rep.	Weekly Reporter (Eng.)
Wm. & Mary L.Rev.	William & Mary Law Review
Wm. & Mary Rev.Va.L.	William and Mary Review of Virginia Law
Wm.Mitchell L.Rev.	William Mitchell Law Review
Wol.	Wolcott's Chancery (Del.)
	Wollaston's English Bail Court Reports (Eng.)
Wolf. & B.	Wolferstan & Bristow's Election Cases (Eng.)
Wolf. & D.	Wolferstan & Dew's Election Cases (Eng.)
Woll.	Wollaston's English Bail Court Reports
Woll.P.C.	Same
Woman Offend.Rep.	Woman Offender Report
Women & L.	Women and Law
Women Law. J.	Women Lawyer's Journal
Women's Rights L. Rptr.	Women's Rights Law Reporter
Wood.	Woodbury & Minot, Circuit Court (U.S.)

Wood. & M.	Same
Woodb. & M.	Same
Woods	Woods Circuit Court (U.S.)
Woodw.	Woodward's Decisions (Pa.)
Woolw.	Woolworth (Neb.)
	Woolworth Circuit Court (U.S.)
Workmen's Comp.L.Rev.	Workmen's Compensation Law Review
World Jurist	World Jurist
World Pol.	World Polity
Wright	Wright (Ohio) (Pa.)
Wy. & W.	Wyatt & Webb (Vict.)
Wy.. W. & A'Beck.	Wyatt, Webb & A'Beckett (Vict.)
Wyo.	Wyoming
Wyo.L.J.	Wyoming Law Journal
Wythe	Wythe's Chancery (Va.)

Y

Y.	Yeates' (Pa.)
Y. & C.	Younge & Collyer's Chancery (Eng.)
Y. & C.C.C.	Same
Y. & J.	Younge & Jervis' Exchequer (Eng.)
Y.A.D.	Young's Admiralty Decisions (Nova Scotia)
Y.B.	Year Book, King's Bench, etc. (Eng.)
Y.B. (Rolls Series)	Year Books Rolls Series (Eng.)
Y.B. (Sel. Soc.)	Year Books (Selden Society) (Eng.)
Y.B.A.A.A.	Yearbook of the Association of Attenders and Alumni of the Hague Academy of International Law
Y.B.A.S.L.	Yearbook of Air and Space Law
Y.B.Ed. I	Year Books, Edward I
Y.B.Eur. Conv. on Human Rights	Yearbook of the Europeon Convention on Human Rights
Y.B.Human Rights	Yearbook on Human Rights
Y.B.Int'l Org.	Yearbook of International Organizations
Y.B.Int'l L. Comm'n	Yearbook of the International Law Commission
Y.B.League	Yearbook of the League of Nations
Y.B.P. 1, Edw. II	Year Books, Part 1, Edward II
Y.B.S.C.	Year Books, Selected Cases
Y.B.U.N.	Yearbook of the United Nations
Y.B.World Pol.	Yearbook of World Polity
Yale L.J.	Yale Law Journal
Yale Rev.Law & Soc.Act'n	Yale Review of Law and Social Action
Yale Stud. World Pub. Ord.	Yale Studies in World Public Order
Yates Sel.Cas.	Yates' Select Cases (N.Y.)
Yea.	Yeates (Pa.)
Yearb.	Year Book, King's Bench (Eng.)
Yearb.P.7, Hen.VI	Year Books, Part 7, Henry VI
Yeates	Yeates (Pa.)
Yel.	Yelverton, King's Bench (Eng.)
Yelv.	Same
Yerg.	Yerger (Tenn.)
York Leg.Rec.	York Legal Record (Pa.)
Yorke Ass.	Yorke Assizes (Clayton)
You.	Younge's Exchequer (Eng.)
You. & Coll. Ch.	Younge & Collyer's Exchequer (Eng.)
You. & Coll. Ex.	Same
You. & Jerv.	Younge & Jervis Exchequer (Eng.)
Young	Young (Minn.)
Young Adm.	Young Admiralty (N.S.)
Young Adm. Dec.	Same
Young Naut. Dict.	Young's Nautical Dictionary
Younge	Younge's Exchequer (Eng.)
Younge & C.Ch. Cas.	Younge & Collyer's Chancery or Exchequer Equity (Eng.)
Younge & C. Exch.	Younge & Collyer's Exchequer Equity (Eng.)
Younge & Coll. Ex.	Same
Younge & J.	Younge & Jervis Exchequer (Eng.)
Younge & Je.	Same
Younge Exch.	Younge Exchequer (Eng.)
Younge M.L. Cas.	Younge Maritime Law Cases (Eng.)
Yugo.L.	Yugoslav Law

Z

Zab.	Zabriskie (N.J.)
Zambia L.J.	Zambia Law Journal
Zane	Zane (Utah)

Appendix B

STATE GUIDES TO LEGAL RESEARCH

As discussed in Chapter 1, the United States consists of 51 major legal systems, one for each state and the federal government. While the state systems have much in common, each is the product of a unique history and legal background. Methods of legislating, codifying, and court reporting vary from state to state. Where possible, a researcher should take the time to learn the unusual aspects of legal research in each state's materials in which extended research is conducted.

In many states law librarians who are familiar with legal research have published guides detailing the legal history and organization of their states. The list below is a compilation of such guides. A researcher contemplating or beginning anything more involved than preliminary research in one of the states listed below would be well advised to consult the guides first. Such a first step could save much time and effort in the endeavor.

California	D. Henke, *California Law Guide* (2d ed. 1976).
Colorado	Weinstein, Colorado Legal Source Materials, 7 COLO. LAW 2084. (1978).
Florida	R. Brown, *Guide to Florida Legal Research* (1980). H. French, *Research in Florida Law* (2d ed. 1965). B. Girtman, *Courts, Reports, and Digests: Girtman's Compendium of Federal and Florida Case Law, Where to Find It and How to Cite It* (1979).
Georgia	L. Chanin, *Reference Guide to Georgia Legal History* (1980).
Illinois	R. Jacobs et al., *Illinois Legal Research Sourcebook* (1977).
Indiana	S. Taylor and K. Welker, *1978 Model Bibliography of Indiana Legal Materials.*
Louisiana	K. Wallach, *Louisiana Legal Research Manual* (1972).
Michigan	R. Beer, *An Annotated Guide to the Legal Literature of Michigan* (1973).
New Jersey	N.J. Law and Legislative Reference Bureau, *Legal Research Guide for the New Jersey State Library* (1957).
New Mexico	A. Poldervaart, *Manual for Effective New Mexico Legal Research* (1955).
New York	Brown, *An Annotated Bibliography of Current New York State Practice Materials,* 73 LAW LIB.J. 28 (1980).

North Carolina	I. Kavass & B. Christensen, *Guide to North Carolina Legal Research* (1973).
Pennsylvania	E. Surrency, *Research in Pennsylvania Law* (2d ed. 1965).
South Carolina	R. Mills & J. Schultz, *South Carolina Legal Research Handbook* (1976).
Tennessee	L. Laska, *Tennessee Legal Research Handbook* (1977).
Texas	M. Boner, *A Reference Guide to Texas Law and Legal History* (1976).
Washington	Washington Law Library, *Legal Research Guide* (1978).
Wisconsin	D. Danner, *Legal Research in Wisconsin* (1980).
	W. Knudson, *Wisconsin Legal Research Guide* (2d ed. 1972).

Appendix C

LEGAL RESEARCH IN TERRITORIES OF THE UNITED STATES

The United States has never possessed a large colonial empire and has lost most of the territory it controlled at its territorial peak immediately following World War II. The United States has lost former territories either by absorption (Alaska, Hawaii), the granting of complete independence (Philippines), or by ceding its rights to other nations (The Panama Canal Zone, Okinawa). Areas remaining under United States sovereignty are small in size, and with the exception of Puerto Rico, in population as well.

Basic documents and constitutions of American dependencies may be found in:

Constitutions of the United States National and State (2d ed.) Vol. VI. Published for the Legislative Drafting Research Fund of Columbia University by Oceana Publications, Inc., Dobbs Ferry, N.Y., 1978, edited by Alexander Platt.

Constitutions of Dependencies and Special Sovereignties, Vol. I (loose-leaf). Oceana Publications, Inc., Dobbs Ferry, edited by A. & P. Blaustein.

Background information, in the form of annual reports of governors, is published by the State Department (for the Trust Territories of the Pacific Islands) and the Department of the Interior.

The publications listed by territory below are usually issued under the authority of the local governments and constitute the main body of primary legal research material.

AMERICAN SAMOA

American Samoa was annexed by the United States pursuant to a treaty with Britain and Germany in 1899. Executive power is vested in a governor who was not popularly elected until 1977. The governor also has veto power over a bicameral legislature. As with other U. S. Pacific territories, American Samoa is administered under the U. S. Department of the Interior.

Statutes:

American Samoa Code, Government Secretary of American Samoa for the Territory of American Samoa, Equity Publishing Corp., Orford, N.H., 1973.

The code is annotated and updated annually by pocket parts. Included in the main code are a main index and separate indexes for the Samoan and United States Constitutions, tables showing the distribution, in this code, of the sections of the 1949 and 1961 codes and the acts of the legislature.

Court Reports:

American Samoa Reports, the Government of American Samoa, Equity Publishing Corp., Orford, N.H., 1977– .

Covers the period from 1900 to the present. The opinions of the District Courts of American Samoa, the Trial Division of the High Court of American Samoa, and the Appellate Division of the High Court of American Samoa are included. Each volume contains a table of cases reported, a table of lands considered, a table of Matai titles considered, and tables of statutes and regulations cited or construed in the opinions. Each case has headnotes which are used also to make up the digest located at the end of each volume.

Law Reviews:

The Samoan Pacific Law Journal, American Samoa Bar Association, Pago Pago, American Samoa. 1971– . Triannual.

In addition to the normal law review articles, the review contains case summaries and headnotes of cases for the year in the last issue for that year, and the first issue in the following year contains a digest of all decisions for the previous year.

Legislative Materials:

Fono Journal, American Samoa Legislature, Pago Pago, American Samoa, 1948–1952 (?). Includes regular and special sessions.

The Annual Fono was a predecessor of the Legislature of American Samoa. It began as an advisory body made up of selected Samoa title holders who met once a year to discuss questions placed on an annual agenda by the government.

House Journal, American Samoa Legislature, 3d – . 1953– .

Sessions of the first and second Legislatures were held jointly with the Senate.

Senate Journal, American Samoa Legislature, 3d – . 1953– .

GUAM

Guam, like Puerto Rico, was ceded by Spain in the 1898 Treaty of Paris. It elected its first civilian governor in 1970 and has a 21-member unicameral legislature. Guam has less autonomy than Puerto Rico and is under the jurisdiction of the U.S. Department of the Interior.

Statutes:

The Civil Code of the Territory of Guam, 1970. Prepared under the direction of the Tenth Guam Legislature by John A. Bohn, Walnut Creek, California, 1970, 2 vols.

The Code of Civil Procedure and the Probate Code of the Territory of Guam, 1970. Prepared under the direction of the Tenth Guam Legislature by John A. Bohn, Walnut Creek, CA, 1970, 2 vols.

The Government Code of the Territory of Guam, 1970. Prepared under the direction of the Tenth Guam Legislature by John A. Bohn, Walnut Creek, CA, 1970, 3 vols.

The Penal Code of the Territory of Guam, 1970. Prepared under the direction of the Tenth Guam Legislature by John A. Bohn, Walnut Creek, CA, 1970, 1 vol.

Guam has its own legislature. Its relations with the United States federal government are under the general administrative supervision of the Secretary of the Interior (48 U.S.C.A. § 1421a). The legislative power of Guam extends to all subjects of legislation of local application not inconsistent with the laws of the United States applicable to Guam (48 U.S.C.A. § 1423a).

Court Reports:

Guam Reports, Equity Publishing Corp., Orford, N.H., 1979.

This is a current looseleaf service which includes all cases from January, 1955 to the present. It contains all the written opinions of the Appellate Division of the District Court of Guam. It is expected that bound volumes of the reports will follow, but as yet there are none.

The District Court of Guam has, in all cases arising under the laws of the United States, the jurisdiction of a district court of the U.S. and has original jurisdiction in all other causes in Guam (48 U.S.C.A. § 1424).

Administrative Rules and Regulations:

Administrative Rules and Regulations of the Government of Guam, Secretary of the Legislature, Agana, Guam.

This is a three-volume looseleaf set which is annually supplemented. An Office of Compiler of Laws has been established in Guam in conjunction with the Guam Law Revision Commission. Specific inquiries about the availability of the regulatory code and its supplementation should be directed to the Executive Secretary of the Guam Law Revision Commission Compiler of Laws.

Legislative Materials:

Guam Legislative Session Laws, Guam Law Revision Commission, Agana.

One or two volumes are published for each session of the legislature.

PUERTO RICO

Puerto Rico was ceded by Spain to the United States under the 1898 Treaty of Paris. Since 1917 its citizens have been citizens of the United

States, and since 1952 it has had approximately the same control over its internal affairs as do states of the United States. Puerto Rico currently has "commonwealth status" with only non-voting representation in the U.S. Congress.

Statutes:

Laws of Puerto Rico Annotated, Equity Publishing Corp., Orford, N.H., 1965, 12 vols.

Updated annually by pocket parts which are quite slow (they are usually at least a year behind). The annotations include not only court cases but also cross references to *Rules and Regulations of Puerto Rico.* There are historical notes to trace the development of various sections. *Laws of Puerto Rico Annotated* is published in separate English and Spanish editions, as both languages are official. The basic source of statutory law in Puerto Rico is the legislature, which consists of two houses, the Senate and the House of Representatives. It is vested with all local legislative powers except as otherwise provided in Chapter 4 of Title 48 of the U.S.C. (48 U.S.C.A. § 811).

Session Laws:

Laws of Puerto Rico, 1900– , Equity Publishing Corp., Orford, N.H.

The session laws are published in bound volumes, approximately two years after the close of a session.

Court Reports:

Puerto Rico Reports, Equity Publishing Corp., Orford, N.H., Vols. 1–100. (English version suspended with vol. 100).

This includes all cases adjudged in the Supreme Court of Puerto Rico from 1900–1972.

Decisions de Puerto Rico, Equity Publishing Corp., Orford, N.H., vols. 1– .

The Spanish version of the reports of the Supreme Court of Puerto Rico continues to be published, but there is approximately a two-year delay before a volume of decisions is published. There is a U.S. District Court of Puerto Rico which is part of the First Circuit. Puerto Rico's Supreme Court is its highest court and its decisions can be reviewed by the Supreme Court of the United States (28 U.S.C. §§ 1252, 1254, 1258).

Administrative Rules and Regulations:

Rules and Regulations of Puerto Rico, Commonwealth of Puerto Rico. Department of State, San Juan, Puerto Rico, 1957–1972.

A looseleaf service containing the codification of all regulations adopted by the Executive Branch of Puerto Rico.

Puerto Rico Register, Commonwealth of Puerto Rico, Department of State, San Juan, Puerto Rico, 1957– .

This looseleaf service is published periodically (about seven times a year), and contains new regulations and amendments to existing regulations, thus keeping the *Rules and Regulations of Puerto Rico* up to date.

In 1975 Escrutinio Legislative, Inc. entered the field of Puerto Rico's regulations and began publishing a weekly description of those promulgated during the previous seven days, including register number, date of issuance, promulgating agency and a brief description.

The publisher has also added executive orders to the weekly listing. The service is called *Escrutinio Ejecutivo* and is available in both English and Spanish, with a quarterly cumulative index, arranged alphabetically by agency name. This service is unique to Puerto Rico.

On February 28, 1979, Escrutinio published a *Catalog of Regulations.* This reference manual includes a description of every regulation promulgated since January, 1972 (the last update of *Rules and Regulations*) and is cross indexed by promulgating agency and law(s) under which promulgated. It is updated annually, and is designed as an interim measure until *Rules and Regulations* can be brought up to date. The weekly regulations service is designed to keep the subscriber up to date between recompilations of the *Catalog.*

Law Reviews:

Revista De Derecho Puertorriqueño. Quarterly publication of the Universidad Catolica de Puerto Rico, School of Law, Ponce, PR, 1961– .

Revista del Colegio de Abogados de Puerto Rico. Quarterly publication of the Colegio de Abogados de Puerto Rico, San Juan, PR, 1939– .

Revista Juridica de la Universidad de Puerto Rico. Quarterly publication of the Escuela de Derecho de la Universidad de Puerto Rico, Rio Piedras, PR, 1932– .

Revista Juridica de la Universidad Interamericana de Puerto Rico. A triannual publication of the Universidad Interamericana de Puerto Rico, Santure, PR, 1964– .

Revista Puertrriqueña sobre los Derechos Humanos. A bilingual quarterly publication of the Puerto Rico Legal Project, New York, NY, 1977– .

Administrative Rules and Regulations:

Shepard's Puerto Rico Citations, Shepard's/McGraw-Hill, Colorado Springs, Colorado, 1968– .

This is a complete citation system showing all citations by the Puerto Rico and federal courts to the Puerto Rico cases reported in the various series of Puerto Rico reports and all citations by the Puerto Rico and federal courts to the Constitution of the Commonwealth of Puerto Rico, the Organic Acts, and codes and laws, acts, ordinances, and court rules. All citations by the Puerto Rico Courts to the United States Constitution and federal statutes are also shown.

Informes del Secretario, Puerto Rico Department of Justice, San Juan, Puerto Rico, 1903– .

The *Informes* come out irregularly but are kept up to date.

TRUST TERRITORY OF THE PACIFIC ISLANDS

The legal status of the Trust Territory is changing and uncertain. Administered by the United States under a trust relationship for the United Nations, the islands were scheduled to become independent in 1981. The nature of this independence and the resulting entities are unclear. It appears that the resulting territories will continue to have a close, dependent relationship with the United States. It also appears that what was formerly a single United States territory will now become four territories, each autonomous, but relying upon the common body of law developed when the entire area was the Trust Territory of the Pacific Islands. The four new territories are (1) the Commonwealth of the Northern Mariana Islands (self-governing since 1978), (2) the Federated States of Micronesia, (3) the Marshall Islands, and (4) the Palau Islands. All four have drafted and approved constitutions.

Statutes:

Code of the Trust Territory of the Pacific Islands, edited by John Richard Steincipher, Book Publishing Co., Seattle, WA 1970, with 1975 cumulative supplement.

Court Reports:

Reports of the Trust Territory of the Pacific Islands, edited by Sharon N. Ruzumna, Thomas L. Whittington, and Donald T. Bliss, Equity Publishing Corp., Orford, NH, 1969– .

This publication contains the opinions of the High Court of the Trust Territory of the Pacific Islands, Appellate and Trial Divisions. Six volumes have been published covering the period from 1951–1974.

Administrative Rules and Regulations:

Territorial Register, Bureau of Public Affairs, Saipan, Mariana Is., 2 vols., published bi-monthly.

VIRGIN ISLANDS

Formerly the Danish West Indies, the Virgin Islands of the United States were purchased by the United States in 1917. A local government consisting of a governor and a 15-member Senate has existed since 1954. The territory sends a non-voting delegate to the United States House of Representatives. Past efforts to draft a formal constitution securing a greater measure of self-government have been unsuccessful.

Statutes:

Session Laws of the Virgin Islands, Office of the Government Secretary, Charlotte Amalie, Saint Thomas, Virgin Islands, Equity Publishing Corp., Orford, N.H., 1955– .

Published annually, this publication contains the complete text of all laws and resolutions enacted by the legislature and approved by the governor. It also contains a résumé of legislative activities which gives a short summary of action taken on every bill introduced in the legislature for that year. The messages of the governor (mainly veto messages) can be found in the appendix of each volume. Each volume contains a table showing bill numbers of acts and resolutions, a table showing the corresponding sections of the *Virgin Islands Code* to the new acts, and a topical index.

Virgin Islands Code Annotated, Office of the Government Secretary, Charlotte Amalie, Saint Thomas, Virgin Islands, Equity Publishing Corp., Orford, N.H., (2d ed.), 1967– .

Annotated and updated annually with pocket parts, it contains the complete text of documents and acts having historical and current significance to the Virgin Islands (i. e., the Danish Colonial Law of 1906; the 1916 Convention between the United States and Denmark providing for the cession of the Danish West Indies; and the Organic Acts). There are distribution tables showing where provisions of prior laws were carried into the *Code.* An index is also included.

Administrative Rules and Regulations:

Virgin Islands Rules and Regulations, Government Secretary for the Government of the Virgin Islands, Equity Publishing Corp., Orford, N.H., 1959– .

Contained in three looseleaf binders for easy updating, this provides an official record of all departmental regulations filed with the Government Secretary. The regulations have been classified by subject matter and arranged and numbered to correspond with the pertinent titles and chapters of the *Virgin Island Code.* A source note under the first section of each regulation or group of regulations shows the officer or agency which issued it, and the approval and effective dates. The set contains a topical index and a table of agencies showing the regulations adopted by each agency or department. The *Virgin Islands Rules and Regulations* is kept up to date by means of the *Virgin Islands Register.*

Virgin Islands Register, Government Secretary for the Government of the Virgin Islands, Equity Publishing Corp., Orford, N.H., 1960– .

Each issue of the *Register* is published in two parts. Part 1 (called *Temporary and Special Materials*) contains gubernatorial proclamations, executive orders and reorganization plans, documents or classes of documents as the governor shall determine from time to time to have general applicability and legal effect, and such documents and classes of documents as may be required to be published by the legislature. Part 2 (called *Amendments and Additions to Rules and Regulations*) contains supplementary looseleaf pages. Volumes for 1960–70 were issued by the Government Secretary for the Government of the Virgin Islands; 1971– , by the Lieutenant Governor for the Government of the Virgin Islands.

Court Reports:

Virgin Islands Reports, the Government of the Virgin Islands, Equity Publishing Corp., Orford, N.H., 1959– .

Beginning in 1917, the *Reports* contain opinions of the District Court of the Virgin Islands, and with respect to cases originating in the Virgin Islands, of the United States Court of Appeals for the Third Circuit and the Supreme Court of the United States. Also included are opinions of the District Court Commissioners (if not reversed), opinions of the police (now municipal) courts if they discuss questions of the law, opinions of the Tax Court of the United States in Virgin Islands cases, and opinions of the Attorney General of the United States with respect to matters concerning the Virgin Islands. Each opinion has headnotes, and each volume has a table of cases reported and tables of statutes, treaties, executive orders, court procedural rules, etc., cited or construed, and a topical digest of the cases found in that volume.

The *Reports* are kept up to date by a looseleaf service containing current cases, but the update service is more than a year behind.

Attorney General Opinions:

Opinions of the Attorney General of the Virgin Islands, the Lieutenant Governor for the Government of the Virgin Islands, Equity Publishing Corp., Orford, N.H., 1965– .

This service contains all important opinions of general significance rendered from 1935 by the chief legal officer of the Government of the Virgin Islands, variously designated as Government Attorney, the District Attorney, the United States Attorney, and the Attorney General of the Virgin Islands. Each volume contains numbered headnotes at the beginning of the opinions (summarizing the legal points therein) and a digest of legal points at the end of the volume. Also included are tables listing federal and local laws; federal state and local judicial opinions; and regulations and executive orders cited throughout the opinions.

Journals:

Virgin Islands Bar Journal. Virgin Islands Bar Association, Christiansted, St. Croix, Virgin Islands, January 1967– . An annual publication which ceased publication in 1969.

OTHER UNITED STATES TERRITORIES

The United States is in the process of divesting itself of the remainder of its overseas territories with the exception of uninhabited islands or island military outposts. The most publicized recent example has been the Panama Canal Zone. At the time of treaty ratification, the Canal Zone had its own American court system and legal code. It will continue in force in those areas remaining under American control to the end of the transition period (through 1982), but eventually the entire area will be under complete Panamanian sovereignty. The United States similarly ceded Okinawa to Japan after lengthy negotiations in 1972.

In 1980, the United States renounced its claims to several small Pacific Islands which are now the independent nations of Kiribati and Tuvalu, as well as ceding several others to New Zealand.

The only other territory under a claim of United States sovereignty with a civilian population is the Corn Islands, whose small population has been administered by Nicaragua with United States acquiescence since 1971.

INDEX

References are to Pages

Italic type indicates Titles of Publications

†